THIRTEEN
QUESTIONS
IN ETHICS

THIRTEEN QUESTIONS IN ETHICS

G. Lee Bowie
Mount Holyoke College

Meredith W. Michaels
Hampshire College

Kathleen Higgins
University of Texas, Austin

Under the general editorship of

Robert J. Foglein
Dartmouth College

Harcourt Brace Jovanovich College Publishers

Fort Worth   Philadelphia   San Diego   New York   Orlando   Austin   San Antonio
Toronto   Montreal   London   Sydney   Tokyo

Acquisitions Editor: Bill McLane
Manuscript Editor: Karl Yambert
Production Editor: Leslie Leland
Designer: Diana Jean Parks
Production Manager: Mandy Van Dusen

Cover painting: © 1991 Anthony Grant

ISBN: 0-15-591744-7

Library of Congress Catalog Number: 19-77856

Printed in the United States of America

Copyrights and acknowledgments appear on pages 645–48,
which constitute a continuation of the copyright page.

Preface

This book originated as a companion to *Twenty Questions: An Introduction to Philosophy* (Bowie, Michaels, and Solomon). An underlying assumption of that book, and of this one, is that philosophy, though a discipline in its own right, can nevertheless be located in and generated by a variety of different and disparate intellectual endeavors. Our experience as teachers has persuaded us that, far from disturbing the disciplinary sanctity of philosophy, the incorporation of a wide array of readings from a wide array of sources actually promotes the virtues of philosophical critique and reflection. *Thirteen Questions in Ethics* attempts to create a generous and imaginative context within which students can struggle with and come to understand some of the central problems in ethics. We have deliberately made flexible the boundaries between ethics and other regions of philosophy — political and social philosophy, metaphysics, and epistemology — in order that students come to appreciate the conceptual complexity of ethical deliberation.

We have also been careful, both in the questions that we chose to address and in the particular selections we adopted, to include issues and points of view that are too often missing from textbooks in ethics. Thus, we have included not only a chapter on racism, but have also incorporated questions about race into other chapters. Similarly, we have endeavored to represent feminist perspectives throughout the text. Our assumption is that the inclusion of particular, socially located perspectives reinforces the view that ethics itself is morally responsive.

Many different courses can be constructed from the readings in this book. Some instructors will want to include a theory section in their course. We have organized the readings to accommodate this. Although any such boundaries are bound to be somewhat artificial, we have supposed that Part I could be approached pretheoretically, as a way of getting a "hook" into moral issues to which students will have an immediate connection. Instructors can easily insert a section on ethical theory after this part and then take up topics in Parts II and III (Questions in Individual Ethics and Questions in Social Ethics). Alternatively, a course in Applied Ethics can move smoothly from Part I directly into Parts II and III. It is also easy to imagine courses that focus on feminist approaches to ethics or on classical approaches.

We hope that there are many ways that this book can be used that we have not been able to anticipate. We encourage the instructor, and the student, to play with the readings to create yet more ways of involving students in their development of some perspective on the problems of ethics. One great hope of a book that achieves the sort of diversity that we have sought here is that students will be inspired to browse beyond the range of the approach adopted by their particular instructor. The wise instructor will encourage students to range freely through these selections in the expectation that they will discover material that will lead them further, possibly in unforeseen directions. We have tried, throughout, to foster a view of the nature of ethical inquiry that encourages such exploration.

The efforts involved in the development of this text have been nearly as diverse as the materials included. Bob Solomon was deeply involved in the development of the underlying concept, and also in its articulation. We are enormously indebted to him for this help. Bill McLane of Harcourt Brace Jovanovich fostered our initial ideas, and has been instrumental in bringing them to fruition. We would also like to thank the rest of the book team at Harcourt Brace Jovanovich: Karl Yambert, Manuscript Editor; Leslie Leland, Production Editor; Diana Jean Parks, Designer; and Mandy Van Dusen, Production Manager. Sevilla Claydon, Rachel Tan, and later Nancy Doby, were instrumental in unearthing sometimes obscure, occasionally bizarre, materials for inclusion. Apart from the material included here, another even more eccentric text could have been developed from work that they located but that we have not included. Sonja Al-Sofi, Anna May Dion, Hina Shamsi, and Abigail Severance have worked well beyond the call of duty on the details of bringing such a collection together. Ruth Hammen and Leni Bowen maintained calm in the face of chaos. In addition, Marlene Fried, Jay Garfield, Julie Inness, David Tebaldi, Jenene Allison, Baruch Brody, Douglas Buhrer, Elizabeth During, Betty Sue Flowers, Dale Flowers, Janice Frey, Paula Fulks, Robert Gooding-Williams, Cynthia Gordon, Robert Kane, Sam Keen, Allesandra Lippucci, Sandra Lynch, Steve Moninger, Linda E. Patrik, Jorge Valadez, and Laura Syron have made valuable contributions. We are grateful to all of them.

Contents

3

How Can I Make Sense of Sex? / 93

PART
TWO

Individual Ethics

4

What Is Reproductive Freedom? / 153

5

Is It Ever Right to Lie? / 207

6

How Should I Make Money? / 239

7

What Are My Rights? / 273

PART
THREE

Social Ethics

8

How Does Racism Affect My Life? / 325

9

Can There Be Equality Between Men and Women? / 373

10

Can We Control Violence? / 419

11

What Should We Sacrifice for Animals and the Environment? / 463

12

How Should I Respond to Poverty? / 527

13

What Are the Proper Ends of Medicine? / 581

PART ONE

Preliminary
Questions

1

What
Kind
of Person
Do I
Want to
Be?

Throughout your childhood, you were probably asked on a regular basis, "What do you want to be when you grow up?" If you were like most children, you had different answers at different times. Perhaps one year you wanted to be a firefighter and the next a professional dancer. Maybe every now and then a new experience motivated you to contemplate a life that you never considered before. After your first science class, for instance, you may have imagined what it would be like to work in a laboratory, perhaps discovering a new element or a cure for cancer. Television probably had an impact on your thinking as well. Maybe televised accounts of various space missions made you fantasize about being an astronaut. And some of you are probably continuing to reconsider your plans as a consequence of your experiences during college.

You may have had less concrete aspirations as well. Maybe you wanted to be "just like" an admired aunt or uncle. You probably had heroes, both among the people you knew personally and among the fictitious or actual characters that you encountered through movies, television, books, and magazines. While your childhood choice of heroes and your style of expressing enthusiasm for them may seem an embarrassment to you now, you may still find that your experiences have left you with some strong ideas about what you do and do not admire in a person.

One basic concern of ethics has to do with how to conduct your life. Are some ways of arranging one's life better than others? On what basis can one determine this?

Philosophers have often discussed these concerns by appealing to the notion of **virtue**. A virtue is a trait that is desirable for a person to possess. Some philosophers (called **teleologists**) argue that particular traits are desirable because they lead to particular results. Others (called **deontologists**) contend that certain types of behavior are desirable whether or not they are rewarded with desirable consequences — they are simply the "right" way to live.

A number of contemporary American philosophers have endorsed Aristotle's emphasis on virtue as central to good living. Among these is Laurence Thomas. In "Justice, Happiness and Self-Knowledge," Thomas defends an argument advanced by Plato, Aristotle's teacher, regarding the virtue of justice. Plato, in his dialogue, *The Republic*, argued (through his character Socrates) that unjust people are necessarily unhappy. Thomas focuses on a particular kind of unjust person, specifically, the unjust person who pretends to be caring. The habit of disguising her real attitude renders such a person vulnerable to self-deception, argues Thomas.

Lynne McFall considers another long-heralded virtue, integrity, to be important for the modern individual. Observing that integrity involves being "undivided; an integral whole," she considers what such a state of being involves. To have integrity, she concludes, you need coherence among your principles, motivations, and actions; a commitment to values that are genuinely important; and an unconditional commitment to certain of your values. This last requirement has a surprising consequence. Although moral principles are frequently thought to demand impartiality toward everyone, personal integrity may require unconditional commitment to family and friends, which amounts to a very partial attitude. Thus, certain conceptions of morality may be in tension with the kind of personal integrity that McFall defends. But she concludes that personal integrity is nonetheless basic to a fulfilled sense of individual identity; it is essential to having values in any fundamental sense.

Some traits considered virtuous by one society are deplored by another. Ambition, for example, has been differently valued even within the Western tradition. The ancient Athenians believed in aspiration, but considered "ambition," as we know it, a fault. Medieval Christian writers tended to treat "ambition" as akin to pride and thus as a sin. Contemporary America most often treats ambition as fundamental to success in one's career and other aspects of life. J. Krishnamurti, writing from the perspective of another tradition, considers ambition to be akin to greed. Not only does he consider it to be a non-virtue, Krishnamurti believes that ambition leads its possessor away from happiness, not toward it.

Besides reflections on particular ideal traits one would like to have, the question, "What kind of person do I want to be?" is likely to stimulate fantasies of particular styles of living. "A life of adventure," "the good life," "living dangerously" — such expressions conjure images of a whole orientation to life itself. Simone Weil cautions that the life that sounds good in literature (or, we might add, that looks good in the movies) is not likely to be satisfying in fact. A genuinely good life might sound dull in description but nevertheless result in happiness. What, we might ask ourselves in response, is a good balance between excitement and routine?

Søren Kierkegaard, in "The Rotation Method," depicts what he sees as the folly of structuring one's life with an eye to avoiding boredom. His satirical recipe for keeping pleasures fresh is extreme: always break off any particular enjoyment while it is at its peak and return to it after a period of abstinence. The argument advanced by Kierkegaard's narrator is scarcely persuasive, but it is worth considering why such a "principled" life sounds so unattractive.

In contrast to constructing one's life around principles, Friedrich Nietzsche opts for virtues. But in opposition to other philosophers who emphasize virtue, Nietzsche insists that virtues are radically individual. Moreover, he contends that the best way to organize one's life is through "style," not through "moral" practices at all. The person who causes harm to others, Nietzsche contends, is the person who is dissatisfied with himself; such dissatisfaction stems from lack of style.

By comparison with most other readings in this chapter, Bertrand Russell offers advice that seems, on first glance, to be remarkably banal. He advises us to take up "impersonal interests." He argues that hobbies and other interests that do not pertain to your practical affairs are valuable aids to happiness, for they help you to overcome pettiness and replenish yourself after being worn from the efforts and cares that fill adult life. Being open to ideas and pursuits that we value for their own sake is, in Russell's view, an indication of greatness of soul. Even when things go wrong, Russell argues, an interest in things outside the scope of one's practical concerns is a source of consolation. Such interests help us to see things in proportion.

In our century, some disasters have seemed catastrophic beyond proportion. In the face of them, the question of what traits one wants to have may seem dwarfed. Etty Hillesum, a young Jewish woman who died in Auschwitz, confronted her era with the conviction that only personal virtue—courage, faith, and particularly love—could challenge the evil she saw around her. This chapter closes with some selections from her diaries, in which she discusses her endeavors to respond to her experiences by becoming more, not less, humane.

LAURENCE THOMAS

Justice, Happiness, and Self-Knowledge

LAURENCE THOMAS *teaches philosophy at Syracuse University and writes in the areas of social philosophy and moral psychology. He is the author of* Living Morally *(1989).*

No man can, for any considerable time, wear one face to himself and another to the multitude without finally getting bewildered as to which is the true one.

— NATHANIEL HAWTHORNE

THE Platonic view that every just person is, in virtue of being such, happier than any unjust person, since all among the latter are unhappy, strikes a most responsive chord in the hearts of a great many persons. But it would seem that this idea has less of a foothold in reality than it does in our hearts. It is far too difficult to deny that there are unjust persons who are happy. Indeed, some even seem to be happier than many a just person.

So I shall lower my sights. Rather than attempting to defend as sound the Platonic view, I shall argue that the just person is favored to be happier than a certain kind of unjust person whom I shall simply call a masquerader — this is, an individual who is frequently concerned to masquerade as a deeply caring person. To this end, I shall defend two theses. One is the Justice/Self-Knowledge (JSK) thesis: when it comes to interpersonal relationships the just person has more self-knowledge than a masquerader. The other is the Happiness/Self-Knowledge (HSK) thesis: other things equal, a person's happiness is more secure if it stems from the self-knowledge which he possesses with respect to the realization of his endeavors. Though obviously weaker than what Plato was after,

I take it that the view which I am concerned to defend is very much in keeping with the spirit of his thought. . . .

Unjust treatment being what it is, willing targets of injustice are hard to come by. Thus, an unjust person can carry out his unjust exploits only if he is sufficiently powerful that he can simply beat into submission all who stands in his way or he is fairly good at catching people off guard. Given the latter, it in no way follows that every or any unjust person must be what I have called a masquerader. For we can imagine an exceedingly clever and crafty unjust person who always manages to catch his targets of injustice unaware and then to escape without detection. Presumably, anyone who possessed Gyges' ring could do these things. We can even imagine that this person is widely known to be unjust, but nonetheless successfully thwarts all attempts to apprehend him. Again, a person with Gyges' ring could presumably pull this off. So, we can imagine a viciously unjust person who never has to give the impression that he will act unjustly.

But so much for what we can imagine. In the actual world, no unjust person possesses anything remotely resembling a Gyges' ring. Accordingly, an unjust person could not be within striking range of some of his targets of injustice but for the fact that he gives them every reason to believe that he will not treat them unjustly. That is, in general an unjust person cannot carry out his unjust exploits without, upon occasion, having to deceive some others into thinking that he will not treat them unjustly. Again, from none of this does it follow that every or any unjust person must be a masquerader. However, once it is seen that deceiving people can very much facilitate leading an unjust life, it becomes obvious that it will suit the purposes of some unjust persons to be masqueraders, since a person can have no better reason to think that she will not be treated unjustly by another than that she has reason to believe that the person cares deeply about her. But one pays an enormous price for being a masquerade.

For, if we believe that we genuinely care deeply about a person, then we do not want it to turn out, at least not too often, that the primary explanation for our displaying caring behavior toward him is other than that we genuinely care about him. And as we shall see, if an unjust person is a masquerader, then on that account alone, he cannot help but be less certain than the just person as to why he is moved to display caring behavior toward his friends and loved ones. . . .

There are two reasons cum explanations why the masquerader will be moved to display caring behavior toward someone: (a) an intrinsic one, that is, he cares deeply about the person or (b) an extrinsic one, that is, he stands to gain some benefit which is not simply that of taking delight in displaying caring behavior toward the person in question. More precisely, in the latter case the behavior is not motivated by love or concern for the person in question. Respectively, we have genuine and simulated caring behavior. It goes without saying that these two explanations are not

mutually exclusive. Quite the contrary, because having close ties with some person or the other is essential to our psychological well-being and displays of caring behavior serve to maintain such ties, then it is clearly to a person's advantage to display such behavior from time to time towards those with whom he has close ties. In other words, a person always has an extrinsic reason for displaying caring behavior towards those with whom he has close ties. . . . [I]f we take ourselves to care deeply about a person, then we want the fact that we care deeply about him to be the primary explanation, if not the only explanation, for our displaying caring behavior toward him. We do not want the explanation to be that we will benefit in return, even if we know this to be so, as in the maintenance of close ties. We want the reason for our displaying caring behavior to be an intrinsic one rather than an extrinsic one.

Now, in view of the fact that it is a characteristic feature of the unjust person who is a masquerader that, except when it comes to those about whom he cares deeply, he is moved to display caring behavior toward others precisely because it is to his extrinsic advantage to do so, the obvious question is this: How can he be sure that this is not also the explanation for why he is moved to display caring behavior toward his friends and loves ones? How can he be sure that his caring behavior toward them is genuine rather than simulated? Or, to put the question in terms of intrinsic and extrinsic reasons: How can he be sure that it is for intrinsic rather than extrinsic reasons that he displays caring behavior towards his friends and loves ones? At first blush, it might seem natural to suppose that the masquerader can simply rely upon the difference in the way he would feel when, on the one hand, displaying caring behavior toward those whom he cares deeply about and, on the other, displaying caring behavior toward his targets of injustice. But can he? I think not.

Obviously enough, the best substitute for something is one that is all but indistinguishable from the genuine article. Now, the fact of the matter is that in general human beings are fairly good monitors of human behavior. Over time, especially, we become quite good at sizing up the depth of a person's sincerity. And the key element in our assessment is a person's non-verbal behavior, which refers to all bodily behavior including how a person says what he says. So, by verbal behavior alone what is meant is simply the words which a person utters. Given that utterances of the appropriate sort can be produced at will, it should come as no surprise that non-verbal behavior plays a fundamentally important role in our assessment. Moreover, among friends and loved ones, especially, much of the non-verbal behavior is spontaneous and affective. If Jones and Smith are close friends and Jones tells Smith that she, Jones, has just won a Nobel Prize or has just lost her son, then Smith should respond with joy in the first case, sadness in the second, and spontaneously in either case. That he should so respond is not really a matter open for discussion. Smith's attitude toward Jones should be such that the appropriate feelings (emotions) are automatically engaged, as it were, depending on the news conveyed to him. He does not need to deliberate about whether to have them. Hence, the feelings he displays are, and come across as being, a natural outcome of what he actually feels. Putting the point this way allows for the fact that we do not always deem it appropriate to display our feelings, though presumably the story I have just told is not one where this holds.

As the preceding remarks should make clear, a person is best able to simulate deeply caring behavior, and will be most successful at passing himself off as a close friend or loved one if, simply upon cue, he is actually able to bring himself to experience the feelings that are appropriate for the occasion. For only then will his simulated caring behavior have the spontaneity and naturalness to it that is characteristic of behavior among those who are close to one another when one party informs the other of either his good fortune or his misfortune.

Now, to be sure, on the view which I have presented if a person is simulating deeply caring behavior, then his experiencing the appropriate feelings constitutes an act on his part, since he brings it about that he experiences them, whereas this is not the case for the person who experiences feelings on account of actually caring deeply about a person. Here, only an event occurs; for the person's attitude toward the individual in question is such that the appropriate feelings automatically come about upon learning what has happened to that individual. So it might be thought that a person who is adept at simulating deeply caring behavior should have no difficulty in distinguishing such behavior from that which is genuine. But . . . this surmise is mistaken. . . .

After all, our automatically experiencing the appropriate sorts of feelings towards a person is what serves as the bedrock of our belief that we care deeply about him. We cannot become adept at simulating deeply caring behavior without causing a severe fault to run through this bedrock. For precisely what this adeptness comes to is our being able to bring it about that we will automatically experience the appropriate feelings though we do not, in fact, care deeply about the person. We cannot have it both ways. We cannot be adept at experiencing the feelings we want to experience toward others and not have an erosion in our confidence to judge correctly whether our deeply caring behavior is simulated or genuine. And the feelings which we automatically experience cannot serve as the bedrock of our belief that we care deeply about a person if we are not confident that we would not experience them but for the fact that we have the appropriate attitude toward that person.

The masquerader has no immunity in this regard. An inevitable consequence of his adeptness at simulating deeply caring behavior is that he will find eroded his confidence in his judgment that his displays of caring behavior toward those whom he takes himself to care about are indeed genuine rather than simulated.

We can make the argument tighter. What is characteristic of the masquerader is that extrinsic reasons for displaying caring behavior can cause him to experience spontaneously, in the appropriate circumstances, the very feelings that intrinsic reasons of this sort can cause him to experience spontaneously. He has come to be this way on account of his concern to be able to pass himself off as a deeply caring person from time to time. But it will be remembered that there is always an extrinsic reason why a person should display caring behavior toward those with whom he has close ties. The problem for the masquerader, then, is this: Since (1) there is always an extrinsic reason for him to display caring behavior toward those with whom he has close ties, (2) he can easily enough be moved to display such behavior for extrinsic reasons, since he is a basically unjust person, and (3) extrinsic reasons for displaying caring behavior can result in his experiencing spontaneously, the appropriate circumstances, the very same feelings that intrinsic reasons of this sort can cause him to experience spontaneously, then it follows that (4) the masquerader cannot simply rely

upon his feelings as evidence that his displays of caring behavior toward those with whom he has close ties is genuine. Now, if (5) the just person can rely upon such feelings whereas the masquerader cannot or, at any rate, the former can do so to a significantly greater extent than the latter, then it follows that the masquerader cannot be as confident as the just person as to why he (the masquerader) is moved to display caring behavior toward his friends and loved ones. It is not a characteristic feature of the just person that, because he desires to treat others justly, he will be moved to pass himself off as one who cares deeply about others when actually he does not. The just life does not require that one be adept at simulating deeply caring behavior; nor, a fortiori, does it require that one be adept at simulating just behavior.

Hence, leading a just life does not require a skill the very having of which casts an enormous shadow of doubt upon why one is moved to display caring behavior toward a person. It can even be allowed that the just person masks his feelings upon occasion. Parents who have just been dismissed from their jobs might manage to hide, at least for the moment, their situation from their daughter, who has received word that she has won a Rhodes Scholarship, since they do not wish to detract from her moment of glory. Notice, however, that this masking on their part cannot in any way be considered a constitutive part of leading a just life; whereas for the masquerader, simulating caring feelings is a constitutive part of his leading an unjust life. If these remarks are sound, then the JSK thesis holds. . . .

Let us turn now to the Happiness/Self-Knowledge thesis: other things equal, a person's happiness is more secure if it stems from the self-knowledge which he possesses with respect to the realization of his endeavors. The truth of this thesis can be easily made out.

Occasional luck can truly be a wonderful thing; too much of it, though, will destroy our self-confidence. For the more it turns out that the explanation for our successes is luck the less our successes reflect positively upon us, since the more it turns out that luck is the explanation for our successes the less they can be credited to our own abilities, skills, and ingenuity. So, for the overwhelming majority of cases, we want the explanation of our successes to be none other than that we have properly and skillfully employed our natural assets. We want to be the author of our successes, let us say. These remarks are not meant to be an aside. On the contrary, they make it abundantly clear that we do not wish to be plagued with self-doubt as to whether or not we are the author of our successes. This is significant for the simple reason that, other things equal, the less a person is plagued with self-doubt in this regard, the happier he is. Needless to say, it matters not whether the endeavors are constitutive of our interpersonal relationships. These remarks should suffice to show that the Happiness/Self-Knowledge thesis is sound.

It should be obvious how the HSK thesis bears on the unjust person who is a masquerader. As I have said, whether we are basically just or unjust, we want our displays of caring behavior toward those whom we deeply care about to be genuine. The problem for the masquerader is just that in this regard he is plagued with significantly more self-doubt than the (basically) just person. In this very important respect, then, the masquerader is favored to be less happy than the (basically) just person.

LYNNE McFALL

Integrity

LYNNE McFALL *teaches philosophy at Syracuse University. She publishes fiction as well as philosophy. Her books include* The One True Story of the World *and* Happiness.

> *Olaf (upon what were once knees)*
> *does almost ceaselessly repeat*
> *'there is some shit I will not eat'*
>
> e. e. cummings

Coherence

Integrity is the state of being "undivided; an integral whole." What sort of coherence is at issue here? I think there are several.

One kind of coherence is simple consistency: consistency within one's set of principles or commitments. One cannot maintain one's integrity if one has unconditional commitments that conflict, for example, justice and personal happiness, or conditional commitments that cannot be ranked, for example, truth telling and kindness.

Another kind of coherence is coherence between principle and action. Integrity requires "sticking to one's principles," moral or otherwise, in the face of temptation, including the temptation to redescription.

Take the case of a woman with a commitment to marital fidelity. She is attracted to a man who is not her husband, and she is tempted. Suppose, for the purity of the example, that he wants her too but will do nothing to further the affair; the choice is hers. Now imagine your own favorite scene of seduction.

After the fact, she has two options. (There are always these two options, which makes the distinction between changing one's mind and weakness of the will problematic, but assume that this is a clear case.) She can (1) admit to having lost the courage of her convictions (retaining the courage of her mistakes) or (2) rewrite her principles in various ways (e.g., by making fidelity a general principle, with exceptions, or by retroactively canceling her "subscription"). Suppose she chooses the latter. Whatever she may have gained, she has lost some integrity. Weakness of the will is one contrary of integrity. Self-deception is another. A person who admits to having succumbed to temptation has more integrity than the person who sells out, then fixes the books, but both suffer its loss.

A different sort of incoherence is exhibited in the case where someone does the right thing for (what he takes to be) the wrong reason. For example, in Dostoevsky's *The Devils*, Stepan Verkhovensky says, "All my life I've been lying. Even when I spoke the truth. I never spoke for the sake of the truth, but for my own sake." Coherence between principle and action is necessary but not sufficient. One's action might *correspond* with one's principle, at some general level of description, but be inconsistent with that principle more fully specified. If one values not just honesty but honesty for its own sake, then honesty motivated by self-interest is not enough for integrity.

So the requirement of coherence is fairly complicated. In addition to simple consistency, it puts constraints on the way in which one's principles may be held (the "first-person" requirement), on how one may act given one's principles (coherence between principle and action), and on how one may be motivated in acting on them (coherence between principle and motivation). Call this *internal coherence.* . . .

To summarize the argument so far: personal integrity requires that an agent (1) subscribe to some consistent set of principles or commitments and (2), in the face of temptation or challenge, (3) uphold these principles or commitments, (4) for what the agent takes to be the right reasons.

These conditions are rather formal. Are there no constraints on the *content* of the principles or commitments a person of integrity may hold?

Integrity and Importance

Consider the following statements.

Sally is a person of principle: pleasure.

Harold demonstrates great integrity in his single-minded pursuit of approval.

John was a man of uncommon integrity. He let nothing — not friendship, not justice, not truth — stand in the way of his amassment of wealth.

That none of these claims can be made with a straight face suggests that integrity is inconsistent with such principles.

A person of integrity is willing to bear the consequences of her convictions, even when this is difficult, that is, when the consequences are unpleasant. A person whose only principle is "Seek my own pleasure" is not a candidate for integrity because there is no possibility of conflict — between pleasure and principle — in

which integrity could be lost. Where there is no possibility of its loss, integrity cannot exist.

Similarly in the case of the approval seeker. The single-minded pursuit of approval is inconsistent with integrity. Someone who is describable as an egg sucker, brownnose, fawning flatterer cannot have integrity, whatever he may think of the merits of such behavior. A commitment to spinelessness does not vitiate its spinelessness — another of integrity's contraries.

The same may be said for the ruthless seeker of wealth. A person whose only aim is to increase his bank balance is a person for whom nothing is ruled out: duplicity, theft, murder. Expedience is *contrasted* to a life of principle, so an ascription of integrity is out of place. Like the pleasure seeker and the approval seeker, he lacks a "core," the kind of commitments that give a person character and that makes a loss of integrity possible. In order to sell one's soul, one must have something to sell. . . .

Most of us, when tempted to "sell out," are tempted by pleasure, approval, money, status, or personal gain of some other sort. The political prisoner under the thumbscrew wants relief, however committed he may be to the revolution. Less dramatically, most of us want the good opinion of others and a decent standard of living. Self-interest in these forms is a legitimate aim against which we weigh our other concerns. But most of us have other "higher," commitments, and so those who honor most what we would resist are especially liable to scorn.

This tendency to objectify our own values in the name of personal integrity can best been seen, I think, in a more neutral case. Consider the following claim:

The connoisseur showed real integrity in preferring the Montrachet to the Mountain Dew.

Even if he was sorely tempted to guzzle the Mountain Dew and forbore only with the greatest difficulty, the connoisseur, we would say, did not show integrity in preferring the better wine. Why? Resisting temptation is not the only test of integrity; the challenge must be to something *important*. . . .

One may die for beauty, truth, justice, the objection might continue, but not for Montrachet. Wine is not that important. . . .

When we grant integrity to a person, we need not *approve* of his or her principles or commitments, but we must at least recognize them as ones a reasonable person might take to be of great importance and ones that a reasonable person might be tempted to sacrifice to some lesser yet still recognizable goods. It may not be possible to spell·out these conditions without circularity, but that this is what underlies our judgments of integrity seems clear enough. Integrity is a personal virtue granted with social strings attached. By definition, it precludes "expediency, artificiality, or shallowness of any kind." The pleasure seeker is guilty of shallowness, the approval seeker of artificiality, and the profit seeker of expedience of the worst sort. . . .

Integrity, Friendship, and the Olaf Principle

An attitude essential to the notion of integrity is that there are some things that one is not prepared to do, or some things one *must* do. I shall call this the "Olaf Principle," in honor of e. e. cummings's poem about Olaf, the "conscientious object-or." This principle requires that some of one's commitments be unconditional.

In what sense?

There are, in ordinary moral thought, expressions of the necessity or impossibility of certain actions or types of actions

that do not neatly correspond to the notions of necessity and impossibility most often catalogued by moral theorists. "I *must* stand by my friend" (or "I *cannot* let him down") may have no claim to logical, psychological, rational, or moral necessity in any familiar sense. There is nothing logically inconsistent in the betrayal of friendship, or one could never be guilty of it. It is not psychologically impossible, since many have in fact done it and survived to do it again. Rationality does not require unconditional allegiance, without some additional assumptions, for one may have better reason to do a conflicting action, for example, where the choice is between betraying a friend and betraying one's country (although I am sympathetic to E. M. Forster's famous statement to the contrary). Nor is the necessity expressed one that has a claim to universality, for different persons may have different unconditional commitments. Impartiality and absoluteness are not what is at stake, for the choice may be between a friend and ten innocent strangers, and one person may have different unconditional commitments at different times. It is not clear, then, what sense of *unconditional commitment* is at issue.

Unless corrupted by philosophy, we all have things we think we would never do, under any imaginable circumstances, whatever we may give to survival or pleasure, power and the approval of strangers; some part of ourselves beyond which we will not retreat, some weakness however prevalent in others that we will not tolerate in ourselves. And if we do that thing, betray that weakness, we are not the persons we thought; there is nothing left that we may even in spite refer to as *I*.

I think it is in this sense that some commitments must be unconditional: they are conditions of continuing as ourselves.

Suppose, for example, that I take both friendship and professional advancement to be great goods, and my best friend and I are candidates for a promotion. Suppose, too, that I know the person who has the final decision has an unreasoned hatred of people who drink more than is socially required, as my friend does. I let this be known, not directly of course, with the predictable result that I am given the promotion.

Now in one sense I have not done anything dishonest. My friend may be the first to admit the pleasure he takes in alcohol. It may even be one of the reasons I value his friendship. (Loyal drinking companions are not easy to come by.) But this is clearly a betrayal of friendship. Is it so obviously a failure of integrity?

In *any* conflict between two great goods, I may argue, one must be "betrayed." And between you and me, I choose me.

What is wrong with this defense?

To beat someone out of a job by spreading vicious truths is proof that I am no friend. It is in the nature of friendship that one cannot intentionally hurt a friend in order to further one's own interests. So if I claim to be this person's friend, then I am guilty of incoherence, and therefore lack integrity.

Why does incoherence seem the wrong charge to make? The answer, I think, is that it is much too weak.

Some of our principles or commitments are more important to us than others. Those that can be sacrificed without remorse may be called *defeasible* commitments. For many of us, professional success is an important but defeasible commitment. I would like to be a successful philosopher, esteemed by my colleagues and widely published, but neither success nor failure will change my sense of personal worth.

Contrasted to defeasible commitments are *identity-conferring* commitments: they reflect what we take to be most important and so determine, to large extent, our (moral) identities. . . .

For many of us, friendship is an identity-conferring commitment. If we betrayed a friend in order to advance our careers, we could not "live with" ourselves; we would not be the persons we thought we were. This is what it means to have a "core": a set of principles or commitments that makes us who we are. Such principles cannot be justified by reference to other values, because they are the most fundamental commitments we have; they determine what, for us, is to *count* as a reason. . . .

Moral Integrity

If integrity is a moral virtue, then it is a special sort of virtue. One cannot be solely concerned with one's own integrity, or there would be no object for one's concern. Thus integrity seems to be a higher-order virtue. To have moral integrity, then, it is natural to suppose that one must have some lower-order moral commitments; that moral integrity adds a moral requirement to personal integrity. . . .

What makes something a moral principle?

One commonly accepted view is that moral principles are characterized by impartiality and universality. Assuming this is true, it follows that moral integrity will require that these conditions be met.

Is this plausible?

Let us return to the principled adulterer and look at it from the husband's point of view. At first he feels betrayed and is hurt. Then he stops to consider what impartiality requires. Perhaps my wife's new lover makes her happier than I can, he reasons, and the affair will certainly make her lover happier, so there is all that happiness to be weighed against my pain. The children are grown, so it is not hurting them. Impartiality seems to require that I grant her this freedom, even encourage it.

Second example. Suppose you are having a bad day. The car breaks down on the way to teach a class in which three students fall asleep and the rest are bored or belligerent. Your latest philosophical masterpiece has come back in the mail with a note from the editor saying that the referees' comments were too abusive to decently pass on to you. During office hours your best student wonders aloud what moral theory has to do with anything that genuinely worries anyone. You have been worrying about that yourself. You wait an hour for a friend who was supposed to meet you at noon but who seems to have forgotten. On the way back from drinking your lunch, just as despair is about to take over for self-pity, you run into K. He sees by your wild eyes that you are in a bad way. He is just going to lunch, he says, and invites you along. You agree, having had nothing to eat since the English muffin your toaster burned for breakfast. While waiting to order, he listens sympathetically to your litany of unrelieved bad luck and real failure. He tries to cheer you up. Feeling better, you express your appreciation, tell him that he is a good friend. He says he is only doing his moral duty. You smile, thinking this philosophical irony. His blank expression suggests you are wrong. Over Caesar salad he tells you about his dear wife, whom he married because no one was more in need of love, nor so unlikely to find it. Somewhere between the main course and the coffee you realize he was not kidding. He is only doing for you what he would do for anyone in your sorry state — his duty.

The fairly simple point of these examples is that impartiality is incompatible with friendship and love, and so incompat-ible with personal integrity where friendship and love are identity-conferring commitments.

What does moral integrity require?

Any identity-conferring commitment *except* to impartiality will be inconsistent with impartiality. If moral integrity presupposes personal integrity, and personal integrity requires identity-conferring commitments, then moral integrity is, generally, inconsistent with impartiality. . . .

Conclusion

Moral integrity is as much a threat to social morality as personal integrity. The difference is that the attack comes from *within* the moral point of view, and its target is impartiality. Perhaps, then, integrity should be given up, as having a moral cost that is too great.

I think this would be a mistake. The reason is made graphically clear in a story by the science fiction writer Theodore Sturgeon, called "The Dark Room." In this story the narrator, Conway, has a friend named Beck who regularly gives cocktail parties at which everyone who attends is eventually humiliated. A sweet old woman, the author of children's books, tells an obscene story. A man who prides himself on his dignity and decorum urinates on the living room floor. An undercover agent walks up to a CIA man and spills his guts. And at the most recent party, Conway's loyal wife ends up in bed with one of the other guests. This gets his attention; on reflection he sees the pattern of humiliation and resolves to find out what's going on. Breaking into Beck's house while he's out of town Conway comes upon an alien being who has the ability to take on any form, to be whatever people want to see. The alien confesses that he feeds on the humiliation of humans. Without it he will die. He finances the parties for Beck in order to get new victims, whose humiliation he causes. This explanation satisfies Conway except for one thing: why, having attended every party, has *he* never been humiliated? The alien explains that Conway is an "immune": a creature who cannot be humiliated because there is nothing he would not do.

Without integrity, and the identity-conferring commitments it assumes, there would be nothing to fear the loss of, not because we are safe but because we have nothing to lose.

J. KRISHNAMURTI
Ambition

J. KRISHNAMURTI (1895–1986) *was a spiritual teacher and social critic who lived in California and traveled to Europe and his native India to teach. Works by Krishnamurti include* From Darkness to Light *(1980),* Commentaries on Living *(1973), and* At the Feet of the Master.

YOU know I have been talking about fear; and it is very important for us to be conscious and aware of fear. Do you know how it comes into being? Throughout the world we can see that people are perverted by fear, twisted in their ideas, in their feelings, in their activities. So we ought to go into the problem of fear from every possible angle, not only from the moral and economic viewpoint of society, but also from the point of view of our inward, psychological struggles.

As I have said, fear for outward and inward security twists the mind and distorts our thinking. I hope you have thought a little about this, because the more clearly you consider this and see the truth of it, the freer you will be from all dependence. The older people have not brought about a marvellous society; the parents, the ministers, the teachers, the rulers, the priests have not created a beautiful world. On the contrary, they have created a frightful, brutal world in which everybody is fighting somebody; in which one group is against another, one class against another, one nation against another, one ideology or set of beliefs against another. The world in which you are growing up is an ugly world, a sorrowful world, where the older people try to smother you with their ideas, their beliefs, their ugliness; and if you are merely going to follow the ugly pattern of the older people who have brought about this monstrous society, what is the point of being educated, what is the point of living at all?

If you look around you will see that throughout the world there is appalling destruction and human misery. You may read about wars in history, but you do not know the actuality of it, how cities are completely destroyed, how the hydrogen bomb, when dropped on an island, causes the whole island to disappear. Ships are bombed and they go up into thin air.

There is appalling destruction due to this so-called advancement, and it is in such a world you are growing up. You may have a good time while you are young, a happy time; but when you grow older, unless you are very alert, watchful of your thoughts, of your feelings, you will perpetuate this world of battles, of ruthless ambitions, a world where each one is competing with another, where there is misery, starvation, over-population and disease.

So, while you are young, is it not very important for you to be helped by the right kind of teacher to think about all these things, and not just be taught to pass some dull examinations? Life is sorrow, death, love, hate, cruelty, disease, starvation, and you have to begin to consider all these things. That is why I feel it is good that you I should go into these problems together, so that your intelligence is awakened and you begin to have some real feeling about all these things. Then you will not grow up just to be married off and become a thoughtless clerk or a breeding machine, losing yourself in this ugly pattern of life like waters in the sands.

One of the causes of fear is ambition, is it not? And are you all not ambitious? What is your ambition? To pass some examination? To become a governor? Or, if you are very young, perhaps you just want to become an engine-driver, to drive engines across a bridge. But why are you ambitious? What does it mean? Have you ever thought about it? Have you noticed older people, how ambitious they are? In your own family, have you not heard your father or your uncle talk about getting more salary, or occupying some prominent position? In our society — and I have explained what our society is — everybody is doing that, trying to be on top. They all want to become somebody, do they not? The clerk wants to become the manager, the manager wants to become something bigger, and so on and so on —

the continual struggle to become. If I am a teacher, I want to become the principal; if I am the principal, I want to become the manager. If you are ugly, you want to be beautiful. Or you want to have more money, more *saris*, more clothes, more furniture, houses, property — more and more and more. Not only outwardly, but also inwardly, in the so-called spiritual sense, you want to become somebody, though you cover that ambition by a lot of words. Have you not noticed this? And you think it is perfectly all right, don't you? You think it is perfectly normal, justifiable, right.

Now, what has ambition done in the world? So few of us have ever thought about it. When you see a man struggling to gain, to achieve, to get ahead of somebody else, have you ever asked yourself what is in his heart? If you will look into your own heart when you are ambitious, when you are struggling to become somebody, spiritually or in the wordly sense, you will find there the worm of fear. The ambitious man is the most frightened of men, because he is afraid to be what he is. He says, "If I remain what I am, I shall be nobody, therefore I must be somebody, I must become a magistrate, a judge, a minister". If you examine this process very closely, if you go behind the screen of words and ideas, beyond the wall of status and success, you will find there is fear; because the ambitious man is afraid to be what he is. He thinks that what he is in himself is insignificant, poor, ugly; he feels lonely, utterly empty, therefore he says, "I must go and achieve something". So either he goes after what he calls God, which is just another form of ambition, or he tries to become somebody in the world. In this way his loneliness, his sense of inward emptiness — of which he is really frightened — is covered up. He runs away from it, and ambition becomes the means through which he can escape.

So, what is happening in the world? Everybody is fighting somebody. One man feels less than another and struggles to get to the top. There is no love, there is no consideration, there is no deep thought. Our society is a constant battle of man against man. This struggle is born of the ambition to become somebody, and the older people encourage you to be ambitious. They want you to amount to something, to marry a rich man or a rich woman, to have influential friends. Being frightened, ugly in their hearts, they try to make you like themselves; and you in turn *want* to be like them, because you see the glamour of it all. When the governor comes, everybody bows down to the earth to receive him, they give him garlands, make speeches. He loves it, and you love it too. You feel honored if you know his uncle or his clerk, and you bask in the sunshine of his ambition, his achievements. So you are easily caught in the ugly web of the older generation, in the pattern of this monstrous society. Only if you are very alert, constantly watchful, only if you are not afraid and do not accept, but question all the time — only then will you not be caught, but go beyond and create a different world.

That is why it is very important for you to find your true vocation. Do you know what 'vocation' means? Something which you love to do, which is natural to you. After all, that is the function of education — to help you grow independently so that you are free of ambition and can find your true vocation. The ambitious man has never found his true vocation; if he had, he would not be ambitious.

So, it is the responsibility of the teachers, of the principal, to help you to be intelligent, unafraid, so that you can find your true vocation, your own way of life, the way you really want to live and earn your livelihood. This implies a revolution in thinking; because, in our present society, the man who can talk, the man who can write, the man who can rule, the man who has a big car, is thought to be in a marvellous position; and the man who digs in the garden, who cooks, who builds a house, is despised.

Are you aware of your own feelings when you look at a mason, at the man who mends the road, or drives a taxi, or pulls a cart? Have you noticed how you regard him with absolute contempt? To you he hardly even exists. You disregard him; but when a man has a title of some kind, or is a banker, a merchant, a *guru*, or a minister, you immediately respect him. But if you really find your true vocation, you will help to break down this rotten system completely; because then, whether you are a gardener, or a painter, or an engineer, you will be doing something which you love with your whole being; and that is not ambition. To do something marvellously well, to do it completely, truly, according to what you deeply think and feel — that is not ambition and in that there is no fear.

To help you to discover your true vocation is very difficult, because it means that the teacher has to pay a great deal of attention to each student to find out what he is capable of. He has to help him not to be afraid, but to question, to investigate. You may be a potential writer, or a poet, or a painter. Whatever it is, if you really love to do it, you are not ambitious; because in love there is no ambition.

So, is it not very important while you are young that you should be helped to awaken your own intelligence and thereby find your true vocation? Then you will love what you do, right through life, which means there will be no ambition, no competition, no fighting another for position, for prestige; and then perhaps you will be able to create a new world. In that new world all the ugly things of the older generation will cease to exist — their wars, their mischief, their separative gods, their rituals which mean absolutely nothing, their sovereign governments, their violence. That is why the responsibility of the teachers, and of the students, is very great.

SIMONE WEIL

Evil

SIMONE WEIL (1909–1943) *was born into a wealthy Jewish family in France, and eventually became a devoted Catholic. She left her job as a teacher to work in factories, and then went on to fight in the Spanish Civil War as well as for the Free French. Her works include* Gravity and Grace *(1942) and* The Need for Roots *(1943).*

MONOTONY of evil: never anything new, everything about it is *equivalent*. Never anything real, everything about it is imaginary.

It is because of this monotony that quantity plays so great a part. A host of women (Don Juan) or of men (Célimène), etc. One is condemned to false infinity. That is hell itself.

Evil is licence and that is why it is monotonous: everything has to be drawn from ourselves. But it is not given to man to create, so it is a bad attempt to imitate God.

Not to recognize and accept this impossibility of creating is the source of many an error. We are obliged to imitate the act of creation, and there are two possible imitations—the one real and the other apparent—preserving and destroying.

There is no trace of 'I' in the act of preserving. There is in that of destroying. The 'I' leaves it mark on the world as it destroys.

Literature and morality. Imaginary evil is romantic and varied; real evil is gloomy, monotonous, barren, boring. Imaginary good is boring; real good is always new, marvellous, intoxicating. Therefore 'imaginative literature' is either boring or immoral (or a mixture of both). It only escapes from this alternative if in some way it passes over to the side of reality through the power of art—and only genius can do that.

SØREN KIERKEGAARD

The Rotation Method

SØREN KIERKEGAARD (1813–1855) *was a Danish philosopher and theologian. Generally recognized as the father of existentialism and religious irrationalism, he believed that each individual must choose his own way of life. Christianity is one such choice.*

SHOULD one wish to attain the maximum momentum, even to the point of almost endangering the driving power, one need only say to oneself: Boredom is the root of all evil. Strange that boredom, in itself so staid and stolid, should have such power to set in motion. The influence it exerts is altogether magical, except that it is not the influence of attraction, but of repulsion.

In the case of children, the ruinous character of boredom is universally acknowledged. Children are always well-behaved as long as they are enjoying themselves. This is true in the strictest sense; for if they sometimes become unruly in their play, it is because they are already beginning to be bored — boredom is already approaching, though from a different direction. In choosing a governess one, therefore, takes into account not only her sobriety, her faithfulness, and her competence, but also her aesthetic qualifications for amusing the children; and there would be no hesitancy in dismissing a governess who was lacking in this respect, even if she had all the other desirable virtues. Here, then, the principle is clearly acknowledged; but so strange is the way of the world, so pervasive the influence of habit and boredom, that this is practically the only case in which the science of aesthetics receives its just dues. If one were to ask for a divorce because his wife was tiresome, or demand the abdication of a king because he was boring to look at, or the banishment of a preacher because he was tiresome to listen to, or the dismissal of a prime minister, or the execution of a journalist, because he was terribly tiresome, one would find it impossible to force it through. What wonder, then, that the world goes from bad to worse, and that its evils increase more and more, as boredom increases, and boredom is the root of all evil.

The history of this can be traced from the very beginning of the world. The gods were bored, and so they created man. Adam was bored because he was alone, and so Eve was created. Thus boredom entered the world, and increased in proportion to the increase of population. Adam was bored alone; then Adam and Eve were bored together; then Adam and Eve and Cain and Abel were bored *en famille*; then the population of the world increased, and the peoples were bored *en masse*. To divert themselves they conceived the idea of constructing a tower high enough to reach the heavens. This idea is itself as boring as the tower was high, and constitutes a terrible proof of how boredom gained the upper hand. The nations were scattered over the earth, just as people now travel abroad, but they continued to be bored. Consider the consequences of this boredom. Humanity fell from its lofty height, first because of Eve, and then from the Tower of Babel. What was it, on the other hand, that delayed the fall of Rome, was it not *panis* and *circenses*? And is anything being done now? Is anyone concerned about planning some means of diversion? Quite the contrary, the impending ruin is being accelerated. It is proposed to call a constitutional assembly. Can anything more tiresome be imagined, both for the participants themselves, and for those who have to hear and read about it? It is proposed to improve the financial condition of the state by practicing economy. What could be more tiresome? . . .

All men are bores. The word itself suggests the possibility of a subdivision. It may just as well indicate a man who bores others as one who bores himself. Those who bore others are the mob, the crowd, the infinite multitude of men in general. Those who bore themselves are the elect, the aristocracy; and it is a curious fact that those who do not bore themselves usually bore others, while those who bore themselves entertain others. Those who do not bore themselves are generally people who, in one way or another, keep themselves extremely busy; these people are precisely on this account the most tiresome, the most utterly unendurable. This species of animal life is surely not the fruit of man's desire and woman's lust. Like all lower forms of life, it is marked by a high degree of fertility, and multiplies endlessly. It is inconceivable that nature should require nine months to produce such beings; they ought rather to be turned out by the score. The second class, the aristocrats, are those who bore themselves. As noted above, they generally entertain others — in a certain external sense sometimes the mob, in a deeper sense only their fellow initiates. The more profoundly they bore themselves, the more powerfully do they serve to divert these latter, even when their boredom reaches its zenith, as when they either die of boredom (the passive form) or shoot themselves out of curiosity (the active form). . . .

Now since boredom as shown above is the root of all evil, what can be more natural than the effort to overcome it? Here, as everywhere, however, it is necessary to give the problem calm consideration; otherwise one may find oneself driven by the daemonic spirit of boredom deeper and deeper into the mire in the very effort to escape. Everyone who feels bored cries out for change. With this demand I am in complete sympathy, but it is necessary to act in accordance with some settled principle. . . .

My method does not consist in change of field, but resembles the true rotation method in changing the crop and the mode of cultivation. Here we have at once the principle of limitation, the only saving principle in the world. The more you limit yourself, the more fertile you become in invention. A prisoner in solitary confinement for life becomes very inventive, and a spider may furnish him with much entertainment. One need only hark back to one's schooldays. We were at an age when aesthetic considerations were ignored in the choice of one's instructors, most of whom were for that reason very tiresome; how fertile in invention one then proved to be! How entertaining to catch a fly and hold it imprisoned under a nut shell and to watch how it pushed the shell around; what pleasure from cutting a hole in the desk, putting a fly in it, and then peeping down at it through a piece of paper! How entertaining sometimes to listen to the monotonous drip of water from the roof! How close an observer one becomes under such circumstances, when not the least noise nor movement escapes one's attention! Here we have the extreme application of the method which seeks to achieve results intensively, not extensively.

The more resourceful in changing the mode of cultivation one can be, the better;

but every particular change will always come under the general categories of *remembering* and *forgetting*. Life in its entirety moves in these two currents, and hence it is essential to have them under control. . . .

To forget — all men wish to forget, and when something unpleasant happens, they always say: Oh, that one might forget! But forgetting is an art that must be practiced beforehand. The ability to forget is conditioned upon the method of remembering, but this again depends upon the mode of experiencing reality. Whoever plunges into his experiences with the momentum of hope will remember in such wise that he is unable to forget. *Nil admirari* is therefore the real philosophy. No moment must be permitted so great a significance that it cannot be forgotten when convenient; each moment ought, however, to have so much significance that it can be recollected at will. Childhood, which is the age which remembers best, is at the same time most forgetful. The more poetically one remembers, the more easily one forgets; for remembering poetically is really only another expression for forgetting. In a poetic memory the experience has undergone a transformation, by which it has lost all its painful aspects. To remember in this manner, one must be careful how one lives, how one enjoys. Enjoying an experience to its full intensity to the last minute will make it impossible either to remember or to forget. For there is then nothing to remember except a certain satiety, which one desires to forget, but which now comes back to plague the mind with an involuntary remembrance. Hence, when you begin to notice that a certain pleasure or experience is acquiring too strong a hold upon the mind, you stop a moment for the purpose of remembering. No other method can better create a distaste for continuing the experience too

long. From the beginning one should keep the enjoyment under control, never spreading every sail to the wind in any resolve; one ought to devote oneself to pleasure with a certain suspicion, a certain wariness, if one desires to give the lie to the proverb which says that no one can have his cake and eat it too. . . .

One must guard against *friendship*. How is a friend defined? He is not what philosophy calls the necessary other, but the superfluous third. . . . What are the infallible marks of friendship? Mutual assistance in word and deed. Two friends form a close association in order to be everything to one another, and that although it is impossible for one human being to be anything to another human being except to be in his way. To be sure one may help him with money, assist him in and out of his coat, be his humble servant, and tender him congratulations on New Year's Day, on the day of his wedding, on the birth of a child, on the occasion of a funeral.

But because you abstain from friendship it does not follow that you abstain from social contacts. On the contrary, these social relationships may at times be permitted to take on a deeper character, provided you always have so much more momentum in yourself that you can sheer off at will, in spite of sharing for a time in the momentum of the common movement. . . .

The essential thing is never to stick fast, and for this it is necessary to have oblivion back of one. The experienced farmer lets his land lie fallow now and then, and the theory of social prudence recommends the same. Everything will doubtless return, though in a different form; that which has once been present in the rotation will remain in it, but the mode of cultivation will be varied. You therefore quite consistently hope to meet your friends and acquaintances in a better world, but you do not share the fear of the crowd that they will be altered so that you cannot recognize them; your fear is rather lest they be wholly unaltered. It is remarkable how much significance even the most insignificant person can gain from a rational mode of cultivation.

One must never enter into the relation of *marriage*. Husband and wife promise to love one another for eternity. This is all very fine, but it does not mean very much; for if their love comes to an end in time, it will surely be ended in eternity. If, instead of promising forever, the parties would say: until Easter, or until May-day comes, there might be some meaning in what they say; for then they would have said something definite, and also something that they might be able to keep. And how does a marriage usually work out? In a little while one party begins to perceive that there is something wrong, then the other party complains, and cries to heaven: faithless! faithless! A little later the second party reaches the same standpoint, and a neutrality is established in which the mutual faithlessness is mutually canceled, to the satisfaction and contentment of both parties. But it is now too late, for there are great difficulties connected with divorce. . . . One must always take care not to enter into any relationship in which there is a possibility of many members. . . .

If you have a wife it is difficult; if you have a wife and perhaps a child, it is troublesome; if you have a wife and children, it is impossible. . . .

But because a man does not marry, it does not follow that his life need be wholly deprived of the erotic element. And the erotic ought also to have infinitude; but poetic infinitude, which can just as well be limited to an hour as to a month. When two beings fall in love with one another and begin to suspect that they

were made for each other, it is time to have the courage to break it off; for by going on they have everything to lose and nothing to gain. . . .

One should never accept appointment to an official position. If you do, you will become a mere Richard Roe, a tiny little cog in the machinery of the body politic; you even cease to be master of your own conduct, and in that case your theories are of little help. You receive a title, and this brings in its train every sin and evil. The law under which you have become a slave is equally tiresome, whether your advancement is fast or slow. A title can never be got rid of except by the commission of some crime which draws down on you a public whipping; even then you are not certain, for you may have it restored to you by royal pardon. . . .

If one now, according to the theory of social jurisprudence, varies the soil — for if he had contact with one person only, the rotation method would fail as badly as if a farmer had only one acre of land, which would make it impossible for him to fallow, something which is of extreme importance — then one must also constantly vary himself, and this is the essential secret. For this purpose one must necessarily have control over one's moods. To control them in the sense of producing them at will is impossible, but prudence teaches how to utilize the moment. As an experienced sailor always looks out over the water and sees a squall coming from far away, so one ought always to see the mood a little in advance. One should know how the mood affects one's own mind and the mind of others, before putting it on. You first strike a note or two to evoke pure tones, and see what there is in a man; the intermediate tones follow later. The more experience you have, the more readily you will be convinced that there is often much in a man which is not suspected. When sentimental people, who as such are extremely tiresome, become angry, they are often very entertaining. Badgering a man is a particularly effective method of exploration.

The whole secret lies in arbitrariness. People usually think it easy to be arbitrary, but it requires much study to succeed in being arbitrary so as not to lose oneself in it, but so as to derive satisfaction from it. One does not enjoy the immediate but something quite different which he arbitrarily imports into it. You go to see the middle of a play, you read the third part of a book. By this means you insure yourself a very different kind of enjoyment from that which the author has been so kind as to plan for you. You enjoy something entirely accidental; you consider the whole of existence from this standpoint; let its reality be stranded thereon. I will cite an example. There was a man whose chatter certain circumstances made it necessary for me to listen to. At every opportunity he was ready with a little philosophical lecture, a very tire-

some harangue. Almost in despair, I suddenly discovered that he perspired copiously when talking. I saw the pearls of sweat gather on his brow, unite to form a stream, glide down his nose, and hang at the extreme point of his nose in a drop-shaped body. From the moment of making this discovery, all was changed. I even took pleasure in inciting him to begin his philosophical instruction, merely to observe the perspiration on his brow and at the end of his nose. . . .

The so-called social pleasures for which we prepare a week or two in advance amount to so little; on the other hand, even the most insignificant thing may accidentally offer rich material for amusement. It is impossible here to go into detail, for no theory can adequately embrace the concrete. Even the most completely developed theory is poverty-stricken compared with the fullness which the man of genius easily discovers in his ubiquity.

FRIEDRICH NIETZSCHE

Giving Style to One's Character

FRIEDRICH NIETZSCHE (1844–1900) *was a German philosopher who spent much of his life traveling in northern Italy and Switzerland. He was a harsh critic of Christianity and Judeo-Christian morality who argued that both religion and morality are products of the resentment of the weak and rejections of the ancient virtue of nobility.*

TO "give style" to one's character—that is a grand and a rare art! He who surveys all that his nature presents in its strength and in its weakness, and then fashions it into an ingenious plan, until everything appears artistic and rational, and even the weaknesses enchant the eye—exercises that admirable art. Here there has been a great amount of second nature added, there a portion of first nature has been taken away:—in both cases with long exercise and daily labour at the task. Here the ugly, which does not permit of being taken away, has been concealed, there it has been re-interpreted into the sublime. Much of the vague, which refuses to take form, has been reserved and utilised for the perspectives: — it is meant to give a hint of the remote and immeasurable. In the end, when the work has been completed, it is revealed how it was the constraint of the same taste that organised and fashioned it in whole and in part: whether the taste was good or bad is of less importance than one thinks, — it is sufficient that it was *a taste*! — It will be the strong imperious natures which experience their most refined joy in such constraint, in such confinement and perfection under their own law; the passion of their violent volition lessens at the sight of all disciplined nature, all conquered and ministering nature: even when they have palaces to build and gardens to lay out, it is not to their taste to allow nature to be free. — It is the reverse with weak characters who have not power over themselves, and *hate* the restriction of style: they feel that if this repugnant constraint were laid upon them, they would necessarily become *vulgarised* under it: they become slaves as soon as they serve, they hate service. Such intellects — they may be intellects of the first rank — are always concerned with fashioning and interpreting themselves and their surroundings as *free* nature — wild, arbitrary, fantastic, confused and surprising: and it is well for them to do so, because only in this manner can they please themselves! For one thing is needful: namely, that man should *attain to* satisfaction with himself — be it but through this or that fable and artifice: it is only then that man's aspect is at all endurable! He who is dissatisfied with himself is ever ready to avenge himself on that account: we others will be his victims, if only in having always to endure his ugly aspect. For the aspect of the ugly makes one mean and sad.

BERTRAND RUSSELL

Impersonal Interests

BERTRAND RUSSELL (1872–1970) *was one of the greatest philosophers of this century. He wrote an enormous number of books and articles, from* Principia Mathematica *(1910–1913, with Alfred North Whitehead) to some notorious poems in favor of "free love" and atheism. He was too controversial for most universities, and a famous court case prevented him from teaching at City College of New York. He did, however, win the Nobel Prize for Literature in 1950. At the age of 89, he was jailed for protesting against nuclear arms.*

I WISH to consider not those major interests about which a man's life is built, but those minor interests which fill his leisure and afford relaxation from the tenseness of his more serious preoccupations. In the life of the average man his wife and children, his work and his financial position occupy the main part of his anxious and serious thought. Even if he has extra-matrimonial love affairs, they probably do not concern him as profoundly in themselves as in their possible effects upon his home life. The interests which are bound up with his work I am not for the present regarding as impersonal interests. A man of science, for example, must keep abreast of research in his own line. Towards such research his feelings have the warmth and vividness belonging to something intimately concerned with his career, but if he reads about research in some quite other science with which he is not professionally concerned he reads in quite a different spirit, not professionally, less critically, more disinterestedly. Even if he has to use his mind in order to follow what is said, his reading is nevertheless a relaxation, because it is not connected with his responsibilities. If the book interests him, his interest is impersonal in a sense which cannot be applied to the books upon his own subject. It is such interests lying outside the main activities of a man's life that I wish to speak about in the present chapter.

One of the sources of unhappiness, fatigue and nervous strain is inability to be interested in anything that is not of practical importance in one's own life. The result of this is that the conscious mind gets no rest from a certain small number of matters, each of which probably involves some anxiety and some element of worry. Except in sleep the conscious mind is never allowed to lie fallow while subconscious thought matures its gradual wisdom. The result is excitability, lack of sagacity, irritability, and a loss of sense of proportion. All these are both causes and effects of fatigue. As a man gets more tired, his external interests fade, and as they fade he loses the relief which they afford him and becomes still more tired. This vicious circle is only too apt to end in a breakdown. What is restful about external interests is the fact that they do not call for any action. Making decisions and exercising volition are very fatiguing, especially if they have to be done hurriedly and without the help of the subconscious. Men who feel that they must "sleep on it" before coming to an important decision are profoundly right. But it is not only in sleep that the subconscious mental processes can work. They can work also while a man's conscious mind is occupied elsewhere. The man who can forget his work when it is over and not remember it until it begins again next day is likely to do his work far better than the man who worries about it throughout the intervening hours. And it is very much easier to forget work at the times when it ought to be forgotten if a man has many interests other than his work than it is if he has not. It is, however, essential that these interests should not exercise those very faculties which have been exhausted by his day's work. They should not involve will and quick decision, they should not, like gambling, involve any financial element, and they should as a rule not be so exciting as to produce emotional fatigue and preoccupy the subconscious as well as the conscious mind.

A great many amusements fulfill all these conditions. Watching games, going to the theater, playing golf, are all irreproachable from this point of view. For a man of a bookish turn of mind reading unconnected with his professional activities is very satisfactory. However important a worry may be, it should not be thought about throughout the whole of the waking hours.

In this respect there is a great difference between men and women. Men on the whole find it very much easier to forget their work than women do. In the case of women whose work is in the home this is natural, since they do not have the change of place that a man has when he leaves the office to help them to acquire a new mood. But if I am not mistaken, women whose work is outside the home differ from men in this respect almost as much as those who work at home. They find it, that is to say, very difficult to be interested in anything that has for them no practical importance. Their purposes govern their thoughts and their activities, and they seldom become absorbed in some wholly irresponsible interest. I do not of course deny that exceptions exist, but I am speaking of what seems to me to be the usual rule. In a women's college, for example, the women teachers, if no man is present, talk shop in the evening, while in a man's college the men do not. This characteristic appears to women as a higher degree of conscientiousness than that of men, but I do not think that in the long run it improves the quality of their work. And it tends to produce a certain narrowness of outlook leading not infrequently to a kind of fanaticism.

All impersonal interests, apart from their importance as relaxation, have various other uses. To begin with, they help a man to retain his sense of proportion. It is very easy to become so absorbed in our own pursuits, our own circle, our own type of work, that we forget how small a part this is of the total of human activity and how many things in the world are entirely unaffected by what we do. Why should one remember this? you may ask. There are several answers. In the first place, it is good to have as true a picture of the world as is compatible with necessary activities. Each of us is in the world for no very long time, and within the few years of his life has to acquire whatever he is to know of this strange planet and its place in the universe. To ignore our opportunities for knowledge, imperfect as they are, is like going to the theater and

not listening to the play. The world is full of things that are tragic or comic, heroic or bizarre or surprising, and those who fail to be interested in the spectacle that it offers are forgoing one of the privileges that life has to offer.

Then again a sense of proportion is very valuable and at times very consoling. We are all inclined to get unduly excited, unduly strained, unduly impressed with the importance of the little corner of the world in which we live, and of the little moment of time comprised between our birth and death. In this excitement and overestimation of our own importance there is nothing desirable. True, it may make us work harder, but it will not make us work better. A little work directed to a good end is better than a great deal of work directed to a bad end, though the apostles of the strenuous life seem to think otherwise. Those who care much for their work are always in danger of falling into fanaticism, which consists essentially in remembering one or two desirable things while forgetting all the rest, and in supposing that in the pursuit of these one or two any incidental harm of other sorts is of little account. Against this fanatical temper there is no better prophylactic than a large conception of the life of man and his place in the universe. This may seem a very big thing to invoke in such a connection, but apart from this particular use, it is in itself a thing of great value.

It is one of the defects of modern higher education that it has become too much a training in the acquisition of certain kinds of skill, and too little an enlargement of the mind and heart by an impartial survey of the world. You become absorbed, let us say, in a political contest, and work hard for the victory of your own party. So far, so good. But it may happen in the course of the contest that some opportunity of victory presents itself which involves the use of methods calculated to increase hatred, violence and suspicion in the world. For example, you may find that the best road to victory is to insult some foreign nation. If your mental purview is limited to the present, or if you have imbibed the doctrine that what is called efficiency is the only thing that matters, you will adopt such dubious means. Through them you will be victorious in your immediate purpose, while the more distant consequences may be disastrous. If, on the other hand, you have as part of the habitual furniture of your mind the past ages of man, his slow and partial emergence out of barbarism, and the brevity of his total existence in comparison with astronomical epochs — if, I say, such thoughts have molded your habitual feelings, you will realize that the momentary battle upon which you are engaged cannot be of such importance as to risk a backward step towards the darkness out of which we have been slowly emerging. Nay, more, if you suffer defeat in your immediate objective, you will be sustained by the same sense of its momentariness that made you unwilling to adopt degrading weapons. You will have, beyond your immediate activities, purposes that are distant and slowly unfolding, in which you are not an isolated individual but one of the great army of those who have led mankind towards a civilized existence. If you have attained to this outlook, a certain deep happiness will never leave you, whatever your personal fate may be. Life will become a communion with the great of all ages, and personal death no more than a negligible incident.

If I had the power to organize higher education as I should wish it to be, I should seek to substitute for the old orthodox religions — which appeal to few among the young, and those as a rule the least intelligent and the most obscuran-

tist — something which is perhaps hardly to be called religion, since it is merely a focusing of attention upon well-ascertained facts. I should seek to make young people vividly aware of the past, vividly realizing that the future of man will in all likelihood be immeasurably longer than his past, profoundly conscious of the minuteness of the planet upon which we live and of the fact that life on this planet is only a temporary incident; and at the same time with these facts which tend to emphasize the insignificance of the individual, I should present quite another set of facts designed to impress upon the mind of the young the greatness of which the individual is capable, and the knowledge that throughout all the depths of stellar space nothing of equal value is known to us. Spinoza long ago wrote of human bondage and human freedom; his form and his language make his thought difficult of access to all students of philosophy, but the essence of what I wish to convey differs little from what he has said.

A man who has once perceived, however temporarily and however briefly, what makes greatness of soul, can no longer be happy if he allows himself to be petty, self-seeking, troubled by trivial misfortunes, dreading what fate may have in store for him. The man capable of greatness of soul will open wide the windows of his mind, letting the winds blow freely upon it from every portion of the universe. He will see himself and life and the world as truly as our human limitations will permit; realizing the brevity and minuteness of human life, he will realize also that in individual minds is concentrated whatever of value the known universe contains. And he will see that the man whose mind mirrors the world becomes in a sense as great as the world. In emancipation from the fears that beset the slave of circumstance he will experience a profound joy, and through all the vicissitudes of his outward life he will remain in the depths of his being a happy man.

Leaving these large speculations and returning to our more immediate subject, namely the value of impersonal interests, there is another consideration which makes them a great help towards happiness. Even in the most fortunate lives there are times when things go wrong. Few men except bachelors have never quarreled with their wives; few parents have not endured grave anxiety owing to the illnesses of their children; few business men have avoided times of financial stress; few professional men have not known periods when failure stared them in the face. At such times a capacity to become interested in something outside the cause of anxiety is an immense boon. At such times when in spite of anxiety there is nothing to be done at the moment, one man will play chess, another will read detective stories, a third will become absorbed in popular astronomy, a fourth will console himself by reading about the excavations at Ur of the Chaldees. Any one of these four is acting wisely, whereas the man who does nothing to distract his mind and allows his trouble to acquire a complete empire over him is acting unwisely and making himself less fit to cope with his troubles when the moment for action arrives. Very similar considerations apply to irreparable sorrows such as the death of some person deeply loved. No good is done to any one by allowing oneself to become sunk in grief on such an occasion. Grief is unavoidable and must be expected, but everything that can be done should be done to minimize it. It is mere sentimentality to aim, as some do, at extracting the very uttermost drop of misery from misfortune. I do not of course deny that a man may be broken by sorrow, but I do say that every man should do his utmost to escape this fate, and should seek any distraction, however trivial, provided it is not in itself harmful or degrading. Among those I regard as harmful and degrading I include such things as drunkenness and drugs, of which the purpose is to destroy thought, at least for the time being. The proper course is not to destroy thought but to turn it into new channels, or at any rate into channels remote from the present misfortune. It is difficult to do this if life has hitherto been concentrated upon a very few interests and those few have now become suffused with sorrow. To bear misfortune well when it comes, it is wise to have cultivated in happier times a certain width of interests, so that the mind may find prepared for it some undisturbed place suggesting other associations and other emotions than those which are making the present difficult to bear.

A man of adequate vitality and zest will surmount all misfortunes by the emergence after each blow of an interest in life and the world which cannot be narrowed down so much as to make one loss fatal. To be defeated by one loss or even by several is not something to be admired as a proof of sensibility, but something to be deplored as a failure in vitality. All our affections are at the mercy of death, which may strike down those whom we love at any moment. It is therefore necessary that our lives should not have that narrow intensity which puts the whole meaning and purpose of our life at the mercy of accident.

For all these reasons the man who pursues happiness wisely will aim at the possession of a number of subsidiary interests in addition to those central ones upon which his life is built.

ETTY HILLESUM
A Precious Slice of Life

ETTY HILLESUM *was a Dutch Jew living in Amsterdam during the Holocaust. In September 1943 she was deported to Auschwitz, and died soon after at the age of 29.*

27 February, Friday Morning, 10 O'clock

. . . How rash to assert that man shapes his own destiny. All he can do is determine his inner responses. You cannot know another's inner life from his circumstances. To know that you must know his dreams, his relationships, his moods, his disappointments, his sickness and his death. . . .

Very early on Wednesday morning a large group of us were crowded into the Gestapo hall, and at that moment the circumstances of all our lives were the same. All of us occupied the same space, the men behind the desk no less than those about to be questioned. What distinguished each one of us was only our inner attitudes. I noticed a young man with a sullen expression, who paced up and down looking driven and harassed and making no attempt to hide his irritation. He kept looking for pretexts to shout at the helpless Jews: 'Take your hands out of your pockets . . .' and so on. I thought him more pitiable than those he shouted at, and those he shouted at I thought pitiable for being afraid of him. When it was my turn to stand in front of his desk, he bawled at me, 'what the hell's so funny?' I wanted to say, 'Nothing's funny here except you,' but refrained. 'You're still smirking,' he bawled again. And I, in all innocence, 'I didn't mean to, it's my usual expression.' And he, 'Don't give me that, get the hell out of here,' his face saying,

'I'll deal with you later.' And that was presumably meant to scare me to death, but the device was too transparent.

I am not easily frightened. Not because I am brave but because I know that I am dealing with human beings and that I must try as hard as I can to understand everything that anyone ever does. And that was the real import of this morning: not that a disgruntled young Gestapo officer yelled at me, but that I felt no indignation, rather a real compassion, and would have liked to ask, 'Did you have a very unhappy childhood, has your girlfriend let you down?' Yes, he looked harassed and driven, sullen and weak. I should have liked to start treating him there and then, for I know that pitiful young men like that are dangerous as soon as they are let loose on mankind. But all the blame must be put on the system that uses such people. What needs eradicating is the evil in man, not man himself.

Something else about this morning: the perception, very strongly borne in, that despite all the suffering and injustice I cannot hate others. All the appalling things that happen are no mysterious threats from afar, but arise from fellow beings very close to us. That makes these happenings more familiar, then, and not so frightening. The terrifying thing is that systems grow too big for men and hold them in a satanic grip, the builders no less than the victims of the system, much as large edifices and spires, created by men's hands, tower high above us, dominate us, yet may collapse over our heads and bury us.

12 March 1942,
Thursday Evening, 11.30

How indescribably beautiful it all was, Max, our cup of coffee, the cheap cigarette and that walk through the darkened city, arm in arm, and the fact that we two were together. Anyone who knew about our past would have found it strange and quite incredible, this meeting out of the blue—just because Max intends to get married and wants me of all people to give him advice. But that's what was so beautiful—to be able to come back to a friend of one's youth and see oneself reflected in the light of his own greater maturity. At the start of the evening he said, 'I don't know what it is, but something in you has changed. I think you have turned into a real woman.' And at the end, 'The change is not for the worse, believe me, your features, your gestures, they're as lively and expressive as ever, but now there's so much more wisdom behind them, it's so nice to be with you,' and he shone his flashlight briefly in my face, nodded in recognition and said decidedly, 'It's you all right.' And then, half clumsily and half familiarly, our cheeks brushed and we moved on and drew apart. It really was beautiful. And paradoxical though it must sound: perhaps it was our first real meeting. As we walked on he said suddenly, 'I think that perhaps over the years we can grow into real friends.' And so nothing is ever lost. People do return to you, you live with them inside you until a few years later they are back with you again.

On 8 March I had written to S., 'My passion used to be nothing but a desperate clinging to—to what, exactly? To something one cannot cling to with the body.'

And it was the body of this man, who now walked beside me like a brother, to which I had once clung in terrible despair. That, somehow, was the most gladdening thing: something had survived, the pleasing and familiar exchange of ideas, the sharing of each other's presence, the revival of memories that no longer haunted us, who once had lived so destructively off each other. Although by the end, of course, we were both emotionally exhausted.

Still, it was the old Max who suddenly asked, 'Have you had an affair with anyone else since then?' I held up two fingers. Later when I said I might marry a refugee so that I could be with him when they sent him to a camp, he pulled a face. As we took our leave, he said, 'You won't do anything foolish, will you? I'm so afraid you'll come to grief.' And I, 'I won't come to grief, don't worry.' And I wanted to add something, but by then we had moved too far away from each other. If you have a rich inner life, I would have said, there probably isn't all that much difference between the inside and outside of a camp. Would I myself be able to live up to such sentiments? There are few illusions left to us. Life is going to be very hard. We shall be torn apart, all who are dear to one another. I don't think the time is very far off now. We shall have to steel ourselves inwardly more and more.

I would love to read the letters I wrote to him when I was eighteen. He said, 'I always had such ambitions for you, I expected great works from you.' I said, 'Max, they'll come. There's no hurry. Can't we be patient?' 'Yes, I know you can write. Now and then I read over the letters you wrote to me; you can write.'

Still, it's a comforting thought that things like that can still happen in this riven world of ours. Many more things perhaps than we are prepared to admit to ourselves. A youthful love suddenly rediscovering itself, smiling back at its own past. And reconciled to it. That's what had happened to me. I set the tone that evening and Max went along with it, and that said a good deal.

So, everything is no longer pure chance, a bit of a game now and then, an exciting adventure. Instead I have the feeling that I have a destiny, in which the events are strung significantly together. When I think how we talked together through the dark city, older now, softened by the past, feeling that we still had so much to tell each other but vague about when we should meet again, I am filled with a profound and solemn gratitude that this could happen in my life. It is now close on midnight and I'm going to bed. It's been a good day. At the end of each day I feel the need to say: life is very good after all. I have my own philosophy now, one I'm prepared to speak up for, which is saying a lot for the self-conscious girl I've always been. . . .

Saturday Morning, 10 O'clock

. . . That was my day, then, a long day. And the most important thing about it all? That the branches of the tree outside my window have been lopped off.

The night before the stars had still hung like glistening fruit in the heavy branches, and now they climbed, unsure of themselves, up the bare, ravaged trunk. Oh, yes, the stars: for a few nights, some of them, lost, deserted, grazed over the wide, forsaken, heavenly plain.

For a moment, when the branches were being cut, I became sentimental. And for that moment I was deeply sad. Then I suddenly knew: I should love the new landscape, too, love it in my own way. Now the two trees rise up outside my window like imposing, emaciated ascetes, thrusting into the bright sky like two daggers.

And on Thursday evening the war raged once again outside my window and I lay there watching it all from my bed. Bernard was playing a Bach record next door. It had sounded so powerful and glowing, but then, suddenly, there were planes, ack-ack fire, shooting, bombs — much noisier than they have been for a long time. It seemed to go on right beside the house. And it suddenly came to me again: there must be so many houses all over the world which are collapsing each day under just such bombs as these.

And Bach went gallantly on, now faint and small. And I lay there in my bed in a very strange mood. Filaments of light along the menacing bare trunk outside my window. A constant pounding. And I thought to myself: any minute now a piece of shrapnel could come through that window. It's quite possible. And it's equally possible that there would be a lot of pain. And yet I felt so deeply peaceful and grateful, there in my bed, and meekly resigned to all the disasters and pains that might be in store for me.

All disasters stem from us. Why is there a war? Perhaps because now and then I might be inclined to snap at my neighbour. Because I and my neighbour and everyone else do not have enough love. Yet we could fight war and all its excrescences by releasing, each day, the love which is shackled inside us, and giving it a chance to live. And I believe that I will never be able to hate any human being for his so-called 'wickedness', that I shall only hate the evil that is within me, though hate is perhaps putting it too strongly even then. In any case, we cannot be lax enough in what we demand of others and strict enough in what we demand of ourselves.

Yes, the trees, sometimes at night their branches would bow down under the weight of the fruit of the stars, and now they are menacing daggers piercing the bright spring air. Yet even in their new shape and setting they are unspeakably beautiful. I remember a walk along an Amsterdam canal, one dreamlike summer night, long, long ago. I had visions then of ruined cities. I saw old cities vanish and new cities arise and I thought to myself, even if the whole of this world is bombed to bits, we shall build a new world, and that one too will pass, and still life will be beautiful, always beautiful.

Even ill-fated Rotterdam. What a bizarre new landscape, so full of eerie fascination, yet one we might also come to love again. We human beings cause monstrous conditions, but precisely because we cause them we soon learn to adapt ourselves to them. Only if we become such that we can no longer adapt ourselves, only if, deep inside, we rebel against every kind of evil, will we be able to put a stop to it. Aeroplanes, streaking down in flames, still have a weird fascination for us—even aesthetically—though we know, deep down, that human beings are being burnt alive. As long as that happens, while everything within us does not yet scream out in protest, so long will we find ways of adapting ourselves, and the horrors will continue.

Does that mean I am never sad, that I never rebel, always acquiesce, and love life no matter what the circumstances? No, far from it. I believe that I know and share the many sorrows and sad circumstances that a human being can experience, but I do not cling to them, I do not prolong such moments of agony. They pass through me, like life itself, as a broad, eternal stream, they become part of that stream, and life continues. And as a result all my strength is preserved, does not become tagged on to futile sorrow or rebelliousness.

And finally: ought we not, from time to time, open ourselves up to cosmic sadness? One day I shall surely be able to say to Ilse Blumenthal, 'Yes, life is beautiful, and I value it anew at the end of every day, even though I know that the sons of mothers, and you are one such mother, are being murdered in concentration camps. And you must be able to bear your sorrow; even if it seems to crush you, you will be able to stand up again, for human beings are so strong, and your sorrow must become an integral part of yourself, part of your body and your soul, you mustn't run away from it, but bear it like an adult. Do not relieve your feelings through hatred, do not seek to be avenged on all German mothers, for they, too, sorrow at this very moment for their slain and murdered sons. Give your sorrow all the space and shelter in yourself that is its due, for if everyone bears his grief honestly and courageously, the sorrow that now fills the world will abate. But if you do not clear a decent shelter for your sorrow, and instead reserve most of the space inside you for hatred and thoughts of revenge—from which new sorrows will be born for others—then sorrow will never cease in this world and will multiply. And if you have given sorrow the space its gentle origins demand, then you may truly say: life is beautiful and so rich. So beautiful and so rich that it makes you want to believe in God.' . . .

And the people, the friends, my many friends! Nowadays there are hardly any accidental relationships left; you have a deep if subtly different relationship with each person, and must not be disloyal to one for the sake of the other. There are no wasted and boring minutes any longer, one has to keep learning how to take one's rest between two deep breaths or in a five-minute chat. . . .

21 July,
Tuesday Evening, 7 O'clock

. . . I feel as if I were the guardian of a precious slice of life, with all the responsibility that entails. . . .

29 September

Let me just note down one more thing for myself: Matthew 6:34: Take therefore no thought for the morrow: for the morrow shall take thought for the things of itself. Sufficient unto the day is the evil thereof.

We have to fight them daily, like fleas, those many small worries about the morrow, for they sap our energies. We make mental provision for the days to come and everything turns out differently, quite differently. Sufficient unto the day. The things that have to be done must be done, and for the rest we must not allow ourselves to become infested with thousands of petty fears and worries, so many motions of no confidence in God. Everything will turn out all right with my residence permit and with my ration book; right now there's no point in brooding about it, and I would do much better to write a Russian essay. Ultimately, we have just one moral duty: to reclaim large areas of peace in ourselves, more and more peace and to reflect it towards others. And the more peace there is in us, the more peace there will also be in our troubled world.

Just had a short telephone conversation with Toos. Jopie writes, 'Don't send any more parcels. Everything is in turmoil.' Haanen sent a letter to his wife: too short to make sense but long enough to make everyone nervous. Nasty. And it set off a bad reaction in me as well. We have to fight that. Must turn our backs on all these pointless rumours, which spread like an infectious disease. Now and then I get an inkling of what goes on in all these unhappy people. Their lives are so impoverished and so empty. And then they say what I have heard from so many of them, 'I can't read any books these days, I just can't concentrate any longer. In the past my house was always full of flowers, but now, well, I no longer care for that sort of thing.' Impoverished, empty lives. Can they be taught to 'work' on themselves, to find peace in themselves? To live a productive and confident life despite all these fears and rumours? To know that one can fling oneself down on one's knees in the farthest and quietest corner of one's inner life and stay there kneeling until the sky above looks sunny and clear again? I felt it once more in the flesh, last night, what human beings have to suffer these days. It is good to be reminded of that from time to time, if only to learn how to fight it. And then to continue undisturbed through the wide and open landscape that is one's own heart. But I haven't reached that point yet. First to the dentist, and this afternoon to my appointment at the Jewish Council in Keizersgracht.

30 September

To be true to one's own spontaneity, to what one set out to do in an all too spontaneous moment.

To be true to every feeling and thought that has started to germinate.

To be true in the fullest sense of the word, to be true to God, to one's own best moments.

If I have one duty in these times, it is to bear witness. I think I have learned to take it all in, to read life in one long stretch. And in my youthful arrogance I am often sure that I can remember every least thing I see and that I shall be able to relate it all one day. Still, I must try to put it down now.

I seem able to see ever more clearly the gaping chasms which swallow up man's creative powers and *joie de vivre*. They are holes in our own mind. Sufficient unto the day is the evil thereof. And: man suffers most through his fears of suffering. The body keeps leading the spirit, when it should be the other way round. 'You live too cerebral a life.' And why now? Because I would not surrender my body to your greedy hands? How strange men are! How much I want to write. Somewhere deep inside me is a workshop in which Titans are forging a new world. I once wrote in despair: 'it is inside my little skull that this world must be rethought, that it must be given fresh clarity.' I still occasionally think so, with the same, almost diabolical, presumption. I know how to free my creative powers more and more from the snares of material concerns, from the idea of hunger and cold and danger. They are, after all, imaginary phantoms, not the reality. Reality is something one shoulders together with all the suffering that goes with it, and with all the difficulties. And as one shoulders them so one's resilience grows

stronger. But the *idea* of suffering (which is not the reality, for real suffering is always fruitful and can turn life into a precious thing) must be destroyed. And if you destroy the ideas behind which life lies imprisoned as behind bars, then you liberate your true life, its real mainsprings, and then you will also have the strength to bear real suffering, your own and the world's. . . .

Later

I have the feeling that my life is not yet finished, that it is not yet a rounded whole. A book, and what a book, in which I have got stuck half-way. I would so much like to read on. There have been moments when I have felt as if my whole life had been one great preparation for community living, when in fact I have always led a very private life. . . .

9 October

. . . Paradoxical though it may sound: whenever one tries too desperately to be physically close to some beloved person, whenever one throws all one has into one's longing for that person, one is really giving him short change. For one has no reserves left then for a true encounter. . . .

2

How Should I Treat My Family and Friends?

Your best friend has started dating someone, so you are pleased when you are to meet this important new person and your friend for dinner. You arrive at the chosen restaurant at the appointed time, only to discover that the date is someone that you know and had hoped to start dating yourself. The slogan "all's fair in love and war" crosses your mind. But you feel that it would be wrong to interfere. You might be able to attract your friend's date, but that would be the wrong way to treat your friend.

Certain interpersonal relationships — friendship, marriage, dating relationships, and close ties of kinship — carry with them particular ethical obligations. Our obligations to family members and friends are what Kant terms **meritorious duties**. Unlike duties that can be fulfilled by performing (or refraining from) a particular act (**necessary duties**, in Kant's terminology), meritorious duties are on-going moral demands that will never be satisfied once and for all. One cannot, for instance, discharge the obligation to care for one's elderly parents simply by writing a large check. Part of the reason that a check is a deficient response to the obligation involved is that family and friends are typically thought to be objects of particular care and concern. Our relationships to our families and our friends are not just one more source of obligations among many — for most of us, they are central priorities in our lives.

However, the ethical issues that pertain to interpersonal relationships do not generally stem from disagreement regarding whether or not special relationships obligate us in special ways. Instead, moral debate usually centers on the tensions between our obligations to those close to us and our other moral obligations. Sophocles' concern in *Antigone*, written in the fifth century B.C., shows that the problem of conflicting loyalties has been a disturbing moral problem for generations. Antigone is the sister of Polyneices, who has been killed in a dispute for the kingship of Thebes. The new king, Creon, has ordered that Polyneices' body be left unburied. But this creates a dilemma for Antigone. Should she obey the law, as pronounced by the king? Or should she fulfill her familial obligation to her brother by burying him? She decides to bury Polyneices. Creon responds by ordering her walled up in a tomb, ignoring the protestations of his son Haemon, who is engaged to Antigone. The excerpt included in this chapter includes Antigone's confrontation with Creon as well as Haemon's attempt to change his father's mind. (Things do not go well in the rest of the play. While in the tomb, Antigone hangs herself. Haemon breaks into the tomb, discovers that Antigone is dead, and kills himself. Creon's wife, Eurydice, hearing the news, also commits suicide.)

Daniel Callahan considers what specific moral and legal obligations grown children have to their elderly parents in contemporary America. Many elderly parents, lacking support from any other source, need the support of their children. Although this does not establish that children have a moral obligation, it does suggest the importance of the parent–child bond in the lives of many Americans. The fact that some children do not act on such a moral obligation, if in fact they perceive one, has led some states to pass laws mandating that children contribute to their elderly parents' support. But Callahan concludes that such laws may be extremely destructive. They may, he argues, undercut the nurturing ties of affection and loyalty, substituting mere monetary support for a richer kind of support that elderly people really need. Callahan observes that typical moral language seems ill-suited for the parent–child bond. Children's obligations to parents are not special cases of obligations to friends, as some have argued — children might have obligations to their parents whether or not their parents have been their "friends" over the course of their lives. Nor are parents contractual parties to whom children "owe" specific kinds of support.

Lin Yutang presents a very different perspective on the relationship of parents and children. Deploring the attitude toward aging that he observes in the West, he defends the Chinese ideal of filial obligation. The traditional Chinese view is that children owe their aged parents a home and constant personal attention as a debt of gratitude. By contrast, the West places a high value on a youth-oriented individualism that, in Lin's view, foolishly pretends that the individual is literally independent of the family. How much better, Lin suggests, to embrace both the fact of aging and the relationships of family in order to grow old gracefully and happily.

The moral dilemma presented in the excerpt from Mark Twain's *Huckleberry Finn* is startling. It portrays Huck Finn's moral quandary about whether his loyalty to his friend Jim, an escaped slave, outweighs his responsibility to Jim's owner to restore her property. Loyalty wins out, in what we might see as a clear victory of right thinking over racism. But from Huck's perspective, given his conditioning, he follows his emotions rather than his reason, which makes him feel that "reason is wrong." This portrait of Huck raises the question of which is a firmer guide in matters of interpersonal relationships: reason or emotion, principle or a sense of caring?

Stuart Miller and Janice Raymond both emphasize the importance of same-sex friendships for personal fulfillment in our modern world — but both also emphasize the difficulties involved in developing friendships. Miller observes that modern mobility, the way in which most marriages are constructed, and the ideology of personal growth and independence have conspired to discourage contemporary American men from looking for significant friendships with men. Raymond similarly believes that women's friendships suffer from the conditions of modern life, and that women have been too brainwashed by a male-dominated ideology to hold their female friendships in high esteem. Miller and Raymond address their audiences of men and women, respectively, and urge them to make their same-sex friendships major priorities in their lives. Both are convinced that placing greater emphasis on friendship would provide what is missing in the lives of so many Americans, who do not find their adult lives fully satisfying.

Lillian B. Rubin addresses the differences between men and women that often interfere with friendships between the sexes. Rubin suggests that many basic differences in typical male and female perspectives stem from the fact that both boys and girls are usually mothered by women. In the traditional division of responsibilities between the spouses, the original provider of all good things is, for the girl infant, a member of the same sex, but, for the boy infant, a member of the opposite sex. Because mothers do not always provide everything the infant wants when the child wants it, the mother is also the original object of anger. Female mothering, as a result, makes it likely that the boy child, when later differentiating himself from the mother, will project his feelings about her onto women in general, and in consequence will feel tremendous ambivalence toward them. The girl child, who will continue to identify with the mother throughout her life, will have more difficulty developing a strong sense of self than will the boy. Rubin suggests that many problems between men and women in later life can be illuminated by a consideration of the basic difference in perspective that results from the fact that women are the primary caretakers of infants.

SOPHOCLES
Antigone

SOPHOCLES *was an Athenian tragedian and statesman of the fifth century* B.C. *His best-known works are the Theban Plays:* Oedipus the King, Oedipus at Colonus, *and* Antigone.

CHORUS

What strange vision meets my eyes,
Fills me with a wild surprise?
Sure I know her, sure 'tis she,
The maid Antigone.
Hapless child of hapless sire,
Didst thou recklessly conspire,
Madly brave the King's decree?
Therefore are they haling thee?

[ENTER GUARD BRINGING ANTIGONE]

GUARD

Here is the culprit taken in the act
Of giving burial. But where's the King?

CHORUS

There from the palace he returns in time.

[ENTER CREON]

CREON

Why is my presence timely? What has chanced?

GUARD

No man, my lord, should make a vow, for if
He ever swears he will not do a thing,
His afterthoughts belie his first resolve.
When from the hail-storm of thy threats I fled
I sware thou wouldst not see me here again;
But the wild rapture of a glad surprise
Intoxicates, and so I'm here forsworn.
And here's my prisoner, caught in the very act,
Decking the grave. No lottery this time;
This prize is mine by right of treasure-trove.

So take her, judge her, rack her, if thou wilt.
She's thine, my liege; but I may rightly claim
Hence to depart well quit of all these ills.

CREON

Say, how didst thou arrest the maid, and where?

GUARD

Burying the man. There's nothing more to tell.

CREON

Hast thou thy wits? Or know'st thou what thou say'st?

GUARD

I saw this woman burying the corpse
Against thy orders. Is that clear and plain?

CREON

But how was she surprised and caught in the act?

GUARD

It happened thus. No sooner had we come,
Driven from thy presence by those awful threats,
Than straight we swept away all trace of dust,
And bared the clammy body. Then we sat
High on the ridge to windward of the stench,
While each man kept his fellow alert and rated
Roundly the sluggard if he chanced to nap.
So all night long we watched, until the sun
Stood high in heaven, and his blazing beams
Smote us. A sudden whirlwind then upraised
A cloud of dust that blotted out the sky,
And swept the plain, and stripped the woodlands bare,
And shook the firmament. We closed our eyes
And waited till the heaven-sent plague should pass.
At last it ceased, and lo! there stood this maid.
A piercing cry she uttered, sad and shrill,
As when the mother bird beholds her nest
Robbed of its nestlings; even so the maid
Wailed as she saw the body stripped and bare,
And cursed the ruffians who had done this deed.
Anon she gathered handfuls of dry dust,
Then, holding high a well-wrought brazen urn,

Thrice on the dead she poured a lustral stream.
We at the sight swooped down on her and seized
Our quarry. Undismayed she stood, and when
We taxed her with the former crime and this,
She disowned nothing. I was glad — and grieved;
For 'tis most sweet to 'scape oneself scot-free,
And yet to bring disaster to a friend
Is grievous. Take it all in all, I deem
A man's first duty is to serve himself.

CREON

Speak, girl, with head bent low and downcast eyes,
Dost thou plead guilty or deny the deed?

ANTIGONE

Guilty. I did it, I deny it not.

CREON

[TO GUARD]
Sirrah, begone whither thou wilt, and thank
Thy luck that thou hast 'scaped a heavy charge.

[TO ANTIGONE]
Now answer this plain question, yes or no,
Wast thou acquainted with the interdict?

ANTIGONE

I knew, all knew; how should I fail to know?

CREON

And yet wert bold enough to break the law?

ANTIGONE

Yea, for these laws were not ordained of Zeus,
And she who sits enthroned with gods below,
Justice, enacted not these human laws.
Nor did I deem that thou, a mortal man,
Could'st by a breath annul and override
The immutable unwritten laws of Heaven.
They were not born to-day nor yesterday;
They die not; and none knoweth whence they sprang.
I was not like, who feared no mortal's frown,
To disobey these laws and so provoke

The wrath of Heaven. I know that I must die,
E'en hadst thou not proclaimed it; and if death
Is thereby hastened, I shall count it gain.
For death is gain to him whose life, like mine,
Is full of misery. Thus my lot appears
Not sad, but blissful; for had I endured
To leave my mother's son unburied there,
I should have grieved with reason, but not now.
And if in this thou judgest me a fool,
Methinks the judge of folly's not acquit.

CHORUS

A stubborn daughter of a stubborn sire,
This ill-starred maiden kicks against the pricks.

CREON

Well, let her know the stubbornest of wills
Are soonest bended, as the hardest iron,
O'er-heated in the fire to brittleness,
Flies soonest into fragments, shivered through.
A snaffle curbs the fieriest steed, and he
Who in subjection lives must needs be meek.
But this proud girl, in insolence well-schooled,
First overstepped the established law, and then —
A second and worse act of insolence —
She boasts and glories in her wickedness.
Now if she thus can flout authority
Unpunished, I am woman, she the man.
But though she be my sister's child or nearer
Of kin than all who worship at my hearth,
Nor she nor yet her sister shall escape
The utmost penalty, for both I hold,
As arch-conspirators, of equal guilt.
Bring forth the other; even now I saw her
Within the palace, frenzied and distraught.
The workings of the mind discover oft
Dark deeds in darkness schemed, before the act.
More hateful still the miscreant who seeks
When caught, to make a virtue of a crime.

ANTIGONE

Would'st thou do more than slay thy prisoner?

CREON

Not I, thy life is mine, and that's enough.

ANTIGONE

Why dally then? To me no word of thine
Is pleasant: God forbid it e'er should please;
Nor am I more acceptable to thee.
And yet how otherwise had I achieved
A name so glorious as by burying
A brother? so my townsmen all would say,
Were they not gagged by terror. Manifold
A king's prerogatives, and not the least
That all his acts and all his words are law.

CREON

Of all these Thebans none so deems but thou.

ANTIGONE

These think as I, but bate their breath to thee.

CREON

Hast thou no shame to differ from all these?

ANTIGONE

To reverence kith and kin can bring no shame.

CREON

Was his dead foeman not thy kinsman too?

ANTIGONE

One mother bare them and the self-same sire.

CREON

Why cast a slur on one by honouring one?

ANTIGONE

The dead man will not bear thee out in this.

CREON

Surely, if good and evil fare alike.

ANTIGONE

The slain man was no villain but a brother.

CREON

The patriot perished by the outlaw's brand.

ANTIGONE

Nathless the realms below these rites require.

CREON

Not that the base should fare as do the brave.

ANTIGONE

Who knows if this world's crimes are virtues there?

CREON

Not even death can make a foe a friend.

ANTIGONE

My nature is for mutual love, not hate.

CREON

Die then, and love the dead if love thou must,
No woman shall be master while I live. . . .

CHORUS

Thy might, O Zeus, what mortal power can quell?
Not sleep that lays all else beneath its spell,
Nor moons that never tire: untouched by Time,
    Throned in the dazzling light
    That crowns Olympus' height,
Thou reignest King, omnipotent, sublime.

    Past, present, and to be,
    All bow to thy decree,
    All that exceeds the mean by Fate
    Is punished, Love or Hate.

Hope flits about on never-wearying wings;
Profit to some, to some light loves she brings,
But no man knoweth how her gifts may turn,
Till 'neath his feet the treacherous ashes burn.
Sure 'twas a sage inspired that spake this word;
    If evil good appear
    To any, Fate is near;
And brief the respite from her flaming sword.

Hither comes in angry mood
Haemon, latest of thy brood;
Is it for his bride he's grieved,
Of her marriage-bed deceived,
Doth he make his mourn for thee,
Maid forlorn, Antigone?

[ENTER HAEMON]

CREON

Soon shall we know, better than seer can tell.
Learning my fixed decree anent thy bride,
Thou mean'st not, son, to rave against thy sire?
Know'st not whate'er we do is done in love?

HAEMON

O father, I am thine, and I will take
Thy wisdom as the helm to steer withal.
Therefore no wedlock shall by me be held
More precious than thy loving governance.

CREON

Well spoken: so right-minded sons should feel,
In all deferring to a father's will.
For 'tis the hope of parents they may rear
A brood of sons submissive, keen to avenge
Their father's wrongs, and count his friends their own.
But who begets unprofitable sons,
He verily breeds trouble for himself,
And for his foes much laughter. Son, be warned
And let no woman fool away thy wits.
Ill fares the husband mated with a shrew,
And her embraces very soon wax cold.
For what can wound so surely to the quick
As a false friend? So spue and cast her off,
Bid her go find a husband with the dead.
For since I caught her openly rebelling,
Of all my subjects the one malcontent,
I will not prove a traitor to the State.
She surely dies. Go, let her, if she will,
Appeal to Zeus the God of Kindred, for
If thus I nurse rebellion in my house,
Shall not I foster mutiny without?
For whoso rules his household worthily,
Will prove in civic matters no less wise.

But he who overbears the laws, or thinks
To overrule his rulers, such an one
I never will allow. Whome'er the State
Appoints, must be obeyed in everything,
Both small and great, just and unjust alike.
I warrant such an one in either case
Would shine, as King or subject; such a man
Would in the storm of battle stand his ground,
A comrade leal and true; but Anarchy —
What evils are not wrought by Anarchy!
She ruins States, and overthrows the home,
She dissipates and routs the embattled host;
While discipline preserves the ordered ranks.
Therefore we must maintain authority
And yield no tittle to a woman's will.
Better, if needs be, men should cast us out
Than hear it said, a woman proved his match.

CHORUS

To me, unless old age have dulled my wits,
Thy words appear both reasonable and wise.

HAEMON

Father, the gods implant in mortal men
Reason, the choicest gift bestowed by heaven.
'Tis not for me to say thou errest, nor
Would I arraign thy wisdom, if I could;
And yet wise thoughts may come to other men
And, as thy son, it falls to me to mark
The acts, the words, the comments of the crowd.
The commons stand in terror of thy frown,
And dare not utter aught that might offend,
But I can overhear their muttered plaints,
Know how the people mourn this maiden doomed
For noblest deeds to die the worst of deaths.
When her own brother slain in battle lay
Unsepulchred, she suffered not his corse
To lie for carrion birds and dogs to maul:
Should not her name (they cry) be writ in gold?
Such the low murmurings that reach my ear.
O father, nothing is by me more prized
Than thy well-being, for what higher good
Can children covet than their sire's fair fame,
As fathers too take pride in glorious sons?
Therefore, my father, cling not to one mood,

And deem not thou art right, all others wrong.
For whoso thinks that wisdom dwells with him,
That he alone can speak or think aright,
Such oracles are empty breath when tried.
The wisest man will let himself be swayed
By others' wisdom and relax in time.
See how the trees beside a stream in flood
Save, if they yield to force, each spray unharmed,
But by resisting perish root and branch.
The mariner who keeps his mainsheet taut,
And will not slacken in the gale, is like
To sail with thwarts reversed, keel uppermost.
Relent then and repent thee of thy wrath;
For, if one young in years may claim some sense,
I'll say 'tis best of all to be endowed
With absolute wisdom; but, if that's denied,
(And nature takes not readily that ply)
Next wise is he who lists to sage advice.

CHORUS

If he says aught in season, heed him, King.

[TO HAEMON]
Heed thou thy sire too; both have spoken well.

CREON

What, would you have us at our age be schooled,
Lessoned in prudence by a beardless boy?

HAEMON

I plead for justice, father, nothing more.
Weigh me upon my merit, not my years.

CREON

Strange merit this to sanction lawlessness!

HAEMON

For evil-doers I would urge no plea.

CREON

Is not this maid an arrant law-breaker?

HAEMON

The Theban commons with one voice say, No.

CREON

What, shall the mob dictate my policy?

HAEMON

'Tis thou, methinks, who speakest like a boy.

CREON

Am I to rule for others, or myself?

HAEMON

A State for one man is no State at all.

CREON

The State is his who rules it, so 'tis held.

HAEMON

As monarch of a desert thou wouldst shine.

CREON

This boy, methinks, maintains the woman's cause.

HAEMON

If thou be'st woman, yes. My thought's for thee.

CREON

O reprobate, would'st wrangle with thy sire?

HAEMON

Because I see thee wrongfully perverse.

CREON

And am I wrong, if I maintain my rights?

HAEMON

Talk not of rights; thou spurn'st the due of Heaven.

CREON

O heart corrupt, a woman's minion thou!

HAEMON

Slave to dishonour thou wilt never find me.

CREON

Thy speech at least was all a plea for her.

HAEMON

And thee and me, and for the gods below.

CREON

Living the maid shall never be thy bride.

HAEMON

So she shall die, but one will die with her.

CREON

Hast come to such a pass as threaten me?

HAEMON

What threat is this, vain counsels to reprove?

CREON

Vain fool to instruct thy betters; thou shalt rue it.

HAEMON

Wert not my father, I had said thou err'st.

CREON

Play not the spaniel, thou a woman's slave.

HAEMON

When thou dost speak, must no man make reply?

CREON

This passes bounds. By heaven, thou shalt not rate
And jeer and flout me with impunity.

Off with the hateful thing that she may die
At once, beside her bridegroom, in his sight.

HAEMON

Think not that in my sight the maid shall die,
Or by my side; never shalt thou again
Behold my face hereafter. Go, consort
With friends who like a madman for their mate.

[EXIT HAEMON]

•   •   •

CHORUS

Love resistless in fight, all yield at a glance of thine eye,
Love who pillowed all night on a maiden's cheek dost lie,
Over the upland folds thou roam'st, and the trackless sea.
Love the gods captive holds. Shall mortals not yield to thee?

Mad are thy subjects all, and even the wisest heart
Straight to folly will fall, at a touch of thy poisoned dart.
Thou didst kindle the strife, this feud of kinsman with kin,
By the eyes of a winsome wife, and the yearning her heart to win.
For as her consort still, enthroned with Justice above,
Thou bendest man to thy will, O all invincible Love.

Lo I myself am borne aside,
From Justice, as I view this bride.
(O sight an eye in tears to drown)
Antigone, so young, so fair,
Thus hurried down
Death's bower with the dead to share.

ANTIGONE

Friends, countrymen, my last farewell I make;
My journey's done.
One last fond, lingering, longing look I take
At the bright sun.
For Death who puts to sleep both young and old
Hales my young life,
And beckons me to Acheron's dark fold,
An unwed wife.

No youths have sung the marriage song for me,
   My bridal bed
No maids have strewn with flowers from the lea,
   'Tis Death I wed.

CHORUS

But bethink thee, thou art sped,
Great and glorious, to the dead.
Thou the sword's edge hast not tasted,
No disease thy frame hath wasted.
Freely thou alone shalt go
Living to the dead below.

ANTIGONE

Nay, but the piteous tale I've heard men tell
   Of Tantalus' doomed child,
Chained upon Sipylus' high rocky fell,
   That clung like ivy wild,
Drenched by the pelting rain and whirling snow,
   Left there to pine,
While on her frozen breast the tears aye flow —
   Her fate is mine.

CHORUS

She was sprung of gods, divine,
Mortals we of mortal line.
Like renown with gods to gain
Recompenses all thy pain.
Take this solace to thy tomb
Hers in life and death thy doom.

ANTIGONE

Alack, alack! Ye mock me. Is it meet
   Thus to insult me living, to my face?
Cease, by our country's altars I entreat,
   Ye lordly rulers of a lordly race.
O fount of Dirce, wood-embowered plain
   Where Theban chariots to victory speed,
Mark ye the cruel laws that now have wrought my bane
   The friends who show no pity in my need!
Was ever fate like mine? O monstrous doom,
   Within a rock-built prison sepulchred,

To fade and wither in a living tomb,
   An alien midst the living and the dead.

CHORUS

In thy boldness over-rash
Madly thou thy foot didst dash
'Gainst high Justice' altar stair.
Thou a father's guilt dost bear.

ANTIGONE

At this thou touchest my most poignant pain,
   My ill-starred father's piteous disgrace,
The taint of blood, the hereditary stain,
   That clings to all of Labdacus' famed race.
Woe worth the monstrous marriage-bed where lay
   A mother with the son her womb had borne;
Therein I was conceived, woe worth the day,
   Fruit of incestuous sheets, a maid forlorn,
And now I pass, accursèd and unwed,
   To meet them as an alien there below;
And thee, O brother, in marriage ill-bestead,
   'Twas thy dead hand that dealt me this deathblow.

CHORUS

Religion has her claims, 'tis true,
Let rites be paid when rites are due.
Yet is it ill to disobey
The powers who hold by might the sway.
Thou hast withstood authority,
A self-willed rebel, thou must die.

ANTIGONE

Unwept, unwed, unfriended, hence I go,
   No longer may I see the day's bright eye;
Not one friend left to share my bitter woe,
   And o'er my ashes heave one passing sigh.

CREON

If wail and lamentation aught availed
To stave off death, I trow they'd never end.
Away with her, and having walled her up
In a rock-vaulted tomb, as I ordained,

Leave her alone at liberty to die,
Or, if she choose, to live in solitude,
The tomb her dwelling. We in either case
Are guiltless as concerns this maiden's blood.
Only on earth no lodging shall she find.

ANTIGONE

O grave, O bridal bower, O prison house
Hewn from the rock, my everlasting home,
Whither I go to join the mighty host
Of kinsfolk, Persephassa's guests long dead,
The last of all, of all most miserable,
I pass, my destined span of years cut short.
And yet good hope is mine that I shall find
A welcome from my sire, a welcome too,
From thee, my mother, and my brother dear;
For with these hands, I laved and decked your limbs
In death, and poured libations on your grave.
And last, my Polyneices, unto thee
I paid due rites, and this my recompense!
Yet am I justified in wisdom's eyes.
For even had it been some child of mine,
Or husband mouldering in death's decay,
I had not wrought this deed despite the State.
What is the law I call in aid? 'Tis thus
I argue. Had it been a husband dead
I might have wed another, and have borne
Another child, to take the dead child's place.
But, now my sire and mother both are dead,
No second brother can be born for me.
Thus by the law of conscience I was led
To honour thee, dear brother, and was judged
By Creon guilty of a heinous crime.
And now he drags me like a criminal,
A bride unwed, amerced of marriage-song
And marriage-bed and joys of motherhood,
By friends deserted to a living grave.
What ordinance of heaven have I transgressed?
Hereafter can I look to any god
For succour, call on any man for help?
Alas, my piety is impious deemed.
Well, if such justice is approved of heaven,
I shall be taught by suffering my sin;
But if the sin is theirs, O may they suffer
No worse ills than the wrongs they do to me!

CHORUS

The same ungovernable will
Drives like a gale the maiden still.

CREON

Therefore, my guards who let her stay
Shall smart full sore for their delay.

ANTIGONE

Ah, woe is me! This word I hear
Brings death most near.

CHORUS

I have no comfort. What he saith,
Portends no other thing than death.

ANTIGONE

My fatherland, city of Thebes divine,
Ye gods of Thebes whence sprang my line,
Look, puissant lords of Thebes, on me;
The last of all your royal house ye see.
Martyred by men of sin, undone.
Such meed my piety hath won.

[EXIT ANTIGONE]

DANIEL CALLAHAN
What Do Children Owe Elderly Parents?

DANIEL CALLAHAN *is Director of The Hastings Center for Biomedical Ethics. A philosopher by training, he received his Ph.D. from Harvard. He has written extensively on medical ethics and abortion.*

IN the spring of 1983 the Reagan administration announced that states may under Medicaid legally require children to contribute to the support of their elderly parents. At the time a number of states were considering or enacting just such laws. The administration, one spokesman said, was not proposing anything inherently new. It was simply responding to a state request for clarification of the existing Medicaid law, and wanted only to say that state statutes enforcing family responsibility laws were not in conflict with federal policy.

As it turned out, the administration's initiative was a policy shift whose time had not come. While a number of states flirted for a time with new family responsibility policies, only a few (Virginia, Idaho, and Mississippi, for example) actually adopted them, and even fewer seem to be enforcing them. As pressing as the state Medicaid nursing home burden is, it rapidly became clear that there is little general sentiment to force children to provide financially for their elderly parents.

Nonetheless, Reagan's initiative was an important social and policy event and raises significant moral issues. In one form or another, the idea is likely to arise again. Anything that can be done to raise revenue to reduce the Medicaid burden probably will be done. Three questions are thus worth considering. What kind of a moral obligation do children have toward the welfare of their elderly parents? Can it be said that the changed health, longevity, and social circumstances of the elderly justify a shift in traditional moral obligations? Even if children do have some significant duties to parents, is it still legitimate to ask the state to take over much of the direct burden of care?

The first question is of course an old one. Each generation has had to make its own sense of the biblical injunction that we should honor our fathers and mothers. It neither tells us in what "honor" consists nor how far filial obligation should be carried. As a piece of practical advice, however, it once made considerable sense. In most traditional and agricultural societies,

parents had considerable power over the lives of their offspring. Children who did not honor their parents risked not only immediate privation, but also the loss of the one inheritance that would enable them to raise and support their own families — land they could call their own.

The advent of industrialization brought about a radical change. It reduced the direct coercive power of parents over their children, setting into motion a trend toward the independence of both parents and children that has been a mark of contemporary society. Though the affective bond between parents and children has so far endured in the face of industrialization and modernity, the combination of actual attachment and potential independence frames the question of the obligation of children toward their elderly parents.

The moral ideal of the parent–child relationship is that of love, nurture, and the mutual seeking for the good of the other. While the weight of the relationship will ordinarily shift according to the age of children and their parents, mutual respect and reciprocity have been a central part of the moral standard. Yet the reality of human lives can stand in the way of the realization of moral ideals. Just as not all children are lovable, neither do all parents give the welfare of their children their serious attention and highest priority. Many children do not find their parents lovable and feel no special sense of duty toward them. Many parents are not happy with the way their children turn out, or with the kind of lives they live, and do not seek to remain intertwined with them.

To what extent, and under what circumstances, flaws and faults of that kind can be said to alter the mutual obligations is obviously an important question. Yet even when the affectional bonds between parent and child are strong, it is still by no means clear what each morally owes to the other. If parents ought to help their children to grow up and flourish, should they go so far as to seriously jeopardize their own future welfare in doing so? If children should honor their elderly parents, how great a sacrifice ought that to entail?

The Changing Status of the Elderly

The present relationship between children and their elderly parents is shaped in part by the changing status of the elderly in society. A rising number and increasing proportion of our population are elderly. The "young old" (65–75) appear to be in better health than ever, but as people live longer, there is also an increasing number of the "old old" (75 +) who are frail and dependent. Despite a variety of public programs and considerable improvement in recent decades, a significant proportion of the elderly (about 25 percent in 1980) still live in poverty or near-poverty. A large proportion do not have immediate family or relatives to whom they can turn for either financial or emotional assistance, and many — particularly women — live alone or in institutions. Even so, as Victor Fuchs notes in summarizing available data, rising income has "made it possible for an ever higher percentage [of the elderly] to maintain their own households, health permitting."

Independence, however, need not mean an absence of family ties. Gerontologists take great pleasure in demolishing what they tell us are two prevalent myths, that the caring family has disappeared, and that the elderly are isolated from their children. There has indeed been a decline in the number of elderly who live with their children or other relatives, from three-fifths in 1960 to one-third in 1980, and an equally sharp drop — down to 1

percent — in the number of elderly who depend upon their children for financial support. Yet it still seems to be true, as Ethel Shanas has noted, that "most old people live close to at least one of their children and see at least one child often. Most old people see their siblings and relatives often, and old people, whether bedfast or housebound because of ill health, are twice as likely to be living at home as to be residents in an institution. . . ." In addition, it is estimated that 60–80 percent of all disabled or impaired persons receive significant family help.

One important change involves the proportion of young and old who believe that children should be financially responsible for their elderly parents. This has shifted downward (from about 50 percent in the mid-fifties to 10 percent in the mid-seventies), and a simultaneous reduction in financial assistance has occurred. However, this need not be taken as an indication of a diminished sense of filial responsibility. The advent of Social Security, and the increasing financial strength of the elderly for other reasons, all indicate important social variables that have reduced financial pressure on children to support parents.

Other social changes could eventually alter that situation. The increasing number of divorced families, of small families, and of families where both spouses work, have created the possibility of a reduced sense of obligation in the future, though that has yet clearly to materialize. In his 1981 book *New Rules*, the pollster Daniel Yankelovich wrote that "one of the most far-reaching changes in [moral] norms relates to what parents believe they owe their children and what their children owe them. Nowhere are the changes in the unwritten social contract more significant or agonizing. The overall pattern is clear: today's parents expect to make fewer sacrifices for their children than in the past, but they also demand less from their offspring in the form of future obligations than their parents demanded of them. . . . Sixty-seven percent [of Americans surveyed] believe that 'children do not have an obligation to their parents regardless of what their parents have done for them.'". . .

What the Law Says

Some twenty-six states at present have statutes that can require children to provide financial support for needy parents. Though erratically administered, difficult to implement, and of doubtful financial value, they remain as testimony to an effort dating back to the early seventeenth century to shift from the public to the private sphere the care of poverty-stricken elderly. While such laws had no precedent in either common law or medieval law, they came into being in England with the Elizabethan Poor Law of 1601, representing a culmination of at least three centuries of efforts to cope with the problem of the poor in general. The Poor Law did not concentrate on the children of the elderly, but extended the network of potential support to include the fathers and mothers, and the grandfathers and grandmothers, of the poor. The family, as a unit, was to be responsible for poverty-stricken kinfolk.

When these laws passed over into the American scene, during the seventeenth and eighteenth centuries, the focus was on the responsibility of children toward their elderly parents, though a few states have retained the wider scope. Blackstone's famous *Commentaries* succinctly state the moral basis of such a responsibility: "The duties of children to their parents arise from a principle of natural justice and retribution. For to those who gave us existence we naturally owe subjection and obedience during our minority, and honor and reverence ever after; they who protected the weakness of our infancy are entitled to our protection in the infirmity of their age; they who by sustenance and education have enabled their offspring to prosper ought in return to be supported by that offspring in case they stand in need of assistance."

The American state laws were little invoked during the eighteenth and nineteenth centuries, but they were increasingly turned to during the twentieth century, particularly in the aftermath of the depression and World War II. While there is broad historical agreement that the primary purpose of the laws was to protect the public from the burden of caring for the poor, including the elderly, the laws were buttressed by a variety of moral assumptions.

Martin R. Levy and Sara W. Gross have identified three moral premises that underlie the American laws and developed some cogent criticisms of them. First, "the duty of a child to support his parents is a mirror-image of the parents' responsibility to support a child." They point out the doubtful logic of that position. In procreation parents not only bring a child into the world, but by the same action undertake the moral obligation of sustaining that child, whose existence is entirely dependent upon the parents. As Levy and Gross put it, "In the converse situation of the duty of a child to support a parent, there is no proximate cause, no volitional act, and no rational basis for the demand of support. The child has not acted to bring about the life of the parent. While the father assumes the voluntary status of fatherhood, the child assumes no duty by having been born. His birth is the result of the act of the father and mother, and such a result cannot logically or physically be turned into a proximate cause."

While they do not deny that there can be a moral bond of love and affection, "moral duty and gratitude, or lofty ideals, cannot be used as a justification for the taking of property." By focusing on "the taking of property," the authors focus on a relatively narrow point.

The second general moral premise turns on what they call "the relational interest of family status." They mean that the simple fact of a family relationship—creating a special tie between parent and child, both biological and social—may itself engender the basis for a demand made upon children to support their elderly parents. Yet they point out that the relational interests are both too broad and too narrow to serve as a reasonable criterion for determining the duty to provide support. "It is too broad in . . . that not all children love and revere their parents. The status of a child confers no special emotional tie in and of itself." It is too narrow in that, if emotional commitment is the standard, then a child would logically be bound to support everyone to whom he or she is tied by emotional commitment, whether family member or not.

The analogy of a contract provides the third moral premise. Since the child was at one time supported by the parent, does not that create an implicit contract requiring that the child in turn support the parent when that becomes necessary? Levy and Gross point out that no direct contract is negotiated between parent and child when the child is procreated, and that any analogy must thus be based on an implied or quasi-contract. But the analogy of an implied contract does not work: the two parties necessary to the making of a contract did not exist simultaneously. A common standard in the law, moreover, is that neither the carrying out of a duty, nor the promise of rendering a performance already required by duty, is a sufficient condition of a return promise—an obligation to do likewise.

Parents as "Friends"

Although Levy and Gross effectively dispatch the argument that the benefits bestowed by parents upon children automatically entail a duty of the children in return to aid parents, there is considerably more that needs to be said. Are we to hold that the obligation flows in one direction only, that because children were given no choice about being born, they owe nothing whatever to their parents? That seems too extreme. At the least, it fails to explain why in fact many children feel an obligation toward their parents, nor does it sufficiently plumb the moral depths of the family relationship.

The late Jane English also argued that the language of "owing" is mistakenly applied in the circumstances. Children "owe" parents nothing at all—which is not to say that there are not many things that children ought to do for their parents. Instead, she held that "the duties of grown children are those of friends and result from love between them and their parents, rather than being things owed in repayment for the parents' earlier sacrifices." In situations where one person does a favor for another, there may be an obligation to reciprocate, but parents do not do favors for their children in the same sense that strangers or acquaintances may do them for each other. The bond that should unite parents and children is that of friendship, and "friendship ought to be characterized by *mutuality* rather than reciprocity: friends offer what they can give and accept what they need without regard for the total amount of benefits exchanged. And friends are motivated by love rather than by the prospect of repayment. Hence, talk of 'owing' is singularly out of place in friendship." Thus children ought to do things for their parents, but the "ought" is that which follows from friendship; it resists both quantitative measurement and the stricter language of owing something in return for earlier benefits.

While English's argument has some plausibility, it is ultimately unsatisfying. Friendship can certainly exist between parent and child, but it often does not. Quite apart from those circumstances where parents have neglected their children or otherwise alienated their affection, they may have little in common other than their biological origins. Moreover, the nature of the friendship that exists between parent and child can and usually will be different from the kind that exists between and among those who are unrelated. A child might plausibly say that, while he is not a friend of his parents, he nonetheless feels toward them respect and love. To push the same point further, many children actively dislike their parents, find no pleasure in their company, and yet feel they ought to do things for them despite those feelings. In distinguishing between favors and friendship, English says that "another difference between favors and friendships is that after a friendship ends, the duties of friendship end." That may be true enough in the case of nonfamily relationships, but it then raises all the more forcefully the question of whether friendship, however much it may mark a relationship between parent and child, can catch the fullness of the moral bond.

The origin and nature of the parent–child bond—or whatever other relationship may exist—is unique. By the procreation of children parents create a social unit that otherwise would not and could not exist. If children do not select their parents, neither do parents select their individual children (they choose to have *a* child, not *this* child). Even so, the family relationship is not something one can simply take or leave. It is a fundamental and unavoidable part of our social nature as human beings. That psychotherapists can spend a good deal of time untangling problems between parents and children provides at least a clue to the emotional depth of the biological relationship, whether marked by unhappiness or happiness. We can and do drift away from ordinary friendships, but parents stay in our memory and exert their influence even in the face of distance or active hostility. Whether we like it or not, we are in some sense always one with our parents, both because of the unique circumstances by which we came to know them and because of the long period of nurture when we were utterly dependent upon them. The mutual interaction of parents and children, even when friendships exist, cannot then entirely be reduced to the category of friendship. The emotional and biological bond between parent and child gives the relationship a permanent and central place in our lives, quite apart from whether that relationship turns out well or poorly. That cannot be said of friendship in the usual sense of the term.

Capturing Intimacy in Moral Language

Ferdinand Schoeman catches some of this flavor when he argues that the traditional language of morality, that of rights and obligations, does not seem to fit well in describing the bond among family members: "We *share ourselves* with those with whom we are intimate and are aware that they do the same with us. Traditional moral boundaries, which give rigid shape to the self, are transparent to this kind of sharing. This makes for nonabstract moral relationships in which talk about rights of others, respect for others, and even welfare of others is to a certain extent irrelevant." Perhaps Schoeman takes things a bit far, but he tries to make clear that the intimacy of family relationships forces us into revealing and sharing a self that may not be revealed to others on the public stage. While it is often the case that parents do not really know their own child, just as often they do, even when their perceptions differ from those of the child. Whether they understand their child or not, the fact that they shared considerable intimacy when the child was young gives them access to a self that others may never see. For their part, children have unique access to parents, seeing a side of them that may never be revealed to others.

Another powerful candidate for the source of obligation is that of gratitude on the part of children toward their parents. Gratitude would be due, not simply because parents discharged their obligations toward the children, but because in their manner of doing so they went beyond the demands of mere duty, giving voluntarily of themselves in a way neither required nor ordinarily expected of them. As Jeffrey Blustein notes, "Duties of gratitude are owed only to those who have helped or benefited us freely, without thought of personal gain, simply out of a desire to protect or promote our well-being. The givers may hope for some return, but they do not give in expectation of it." A consequence of this line of reasoning, however, is that only those parents who did more than was morally required could be said to have a right to the gratitude of their children. And it is by no means obvious that a "debt of gratitude" carries with it a strict obligation to provide like goods or services, that is, to go beyond what is otherwise required.

I am searching here with some difficulty for a way to characterize the ethical nature of the parent–child relationship, a relationship that appears almost but not quite self-evident in its reciprocal moral claims and yet oddly elusive also. We seem to say too much if we try to reduce the relationship to mutual moral duties, rights and obligations. That implies a rigor and formalism which distorts the moral bond. We say too little if we try to make it a matter of voluntary affection only. Yet we cannot, I suspect, totally dismiss the language of obligation nor would we want to give up the ideal of mutual affection either. If the procreation and physical rearing of a child does not automatically entail reciprocal duties toward the parents when they are needy and dependent, it is certainly possible to imagine a sense of obligation arising when parents have done far more for children than would morally be required of them. My own parents, for example, did not throw me out on my own when I reached eighteen. They sacrificed a good deal to provide me with a higher education, and in fact provided financial support for my graduate education until I was thirty, topping that off by giving my wife and me a down-payment on our first house. They did it out of affection, rather than duty, but I certainly felt I owed them something in return in their old age. There need not be, then, any necessary incompatibility between feeling both affection and a sense of duty. But we lack a moral phrase that catches both notions in one concept; and neither taken separately is quite right.

The Power of Dependence

Another aspect of the relationship between children and their elderly parents bears reflection. Much as young children will have a special dependence upon parents, as those human beings above all others who have a fateful power over their destinies, so many elderly parents can come in dire circumstances similarly to depend upon their children. In a world of strangers or fleeting casual acquaintances, of distant government agencies and a society beyond their control, elderly parents can see in their children their only hope for someone who ought to care for them. Neither parent nor child may want this kind of emotional dependence, and each might wish that there were an alternative. Nonetheless, parents may be forced to throw themselves upon their children simply because there is no other alternative. Who else is likely to care?

Can that sense of utter need, if not for money then only for affection and caring, in and of itself create a moral obligation? It is surely a difficult question whether, as a general matter, a moral obligation is incurred when one human being is rendered by circumstance wholly dependent upon another — whether, that is, the dependency itself creates the obligation, quite apart from any other features of the relationship. A moral claim of that kind will inevitably be controversial, if only because it is (regretfully) common to rest claims of obligation upon implicit or explicit contracts of one kind or another; or upon features of the relationship that can be subjected to a utilitarian calculation. It is difficult in this case plausibly to invoke such norms. Still, the power of sheer dependence — whether of newborn child upon parent or elderly, dependent parent upon child — can be potent in its experienced moral demands. The fate of one or more persons rests in the hands of another. The issue, as it presents itself, may be less one of trying to discover the grounds of obligation that would require

a response than one of trying to find grounds for ignoring a demand that so patently assaults the sensibilities. It is not so much "must I?" as it is "how can I not?"

Joel Feinberg, commenting on the moral place of gratitude, moves in a similar direction when he writes, "My benefactor once freely offered me his services when I needed them. . . . But now circumstances have arisen in which he needs help, and I am in a position to help him. Surely, I owe him my services now, and he would be entitled to resent my failure to come through." A qualification is in order here: gratitude is ordinarily thought due only when, as noted above, a benefactor has gone beyond ordinary duties. In some cases, parents may have only done their duty, and in such a minimal way that no gratitude seems due them. We are then brought back to the starkest moral situation — in which the dependency only seeks to establish a claim on us.

In trying to unravel the nature of the possible moral obligations, it may be helpful to speak of some specific claims or demands that might be made. Money is by no means the only, or necessarily the most important, benefit that parents can ask of their children. Children can also contribute their time and physical energy, and provide affection and psychological support. On a scale of moral priorities, it would be difficult to persuasively argue that parents have an obligation to deprive their own dependent children of necessary financial support in order to support their elderly parents. By virtue of procreating those children, the latter have a claim upon them that their parents cannot equal. Of course, where a surplus exists after their own children have been taken care of, the financial support of needy parents might become obligatory, particularly if there were no other available sources of support. Ordinarily, however, their principal economic duties will be toward their own children.

The same cannot necessarily be said of providing either physical help or affection to their parents. While the giving of physical help or affection could readily be merged, I think it is useful to distinguish between them. Physical help — such as assistance in moving, cleaning, shopping, and trips to visit friends or doctors — is a somewhat different contribution to the welfare of the elderly than simply talking with them. Parents of young children may not readily be able to adapt their schedules to such demands upon their time or energy. Yet they may be able to provide affection, either by visits at times they find convenient, or through letters and telephone calls. An inability to provide some kinds of care does not exempt children from providing other forms. In fact, the available evidence suggests that affection is most wanted, and it is not difficult to understand why. The uncertainties of old age, the recognition of growing weakness and helplessness, can above all generate the desire to believe that at least some people in the world care about one's fate, and are willing to empathetically share that burden which few of us would care to bear alone — a recognition that life is gradually coming to an end and that nature is depriving us of our body, our individuality, and our future.

In terms of financial obligations, there is considerable evidence from human experience in general, and from state efforts to impose financial burdens upon children in particular, that enforced legal obligations of children toward parents are mutually destructive. If only from the viewpoint of promoting family unity and affection, the provision of economic and medical care for the elderly by the gov-

ernment makes considerable sense. Ben Wattenberg quotes someone who nicely catches an important point: "We [older folks] don't like to take money from our kids. We don't want to be a burden. They don't like giving us money, either. We all get angry at each other if we do it that way. So we all sign a political contract to deal with what anthropologists would call the 'intergenerational transfer of wealth.' The young people *give* money to the government. I *get* money from the government. That way we can both get mad at the government and keep on loving each other."

If the burden of economic care of the elderly can be difficult even for the affluent, it can be impossible for the poor. Moreover, adults with elderly parents ought not to be put in the position of trying to balance the moral claims of their own children against those of their parents, or jeopardizing their own old age in order to sustain their parents in their old age. Though such conflicts may at times be inescapable, society ought to be structured in a way that minimizes them. The great increase in life expectancy provides a solid reason, if one was ever needed, for arguing that all of us collectively through the state — rather than the children of the elderly — should supply their basic economic support. Both parents and children legitimately want an appropriate independence, not the kind that sunders their relationship altogether or makes it merely contingent upon active affection. A balance is sought between that independence which enables people to have a sense of controlling their own destinies, and those ties of obligation and affection that render each an indispensable source of solace in the face of a world that has no special reason to care for them.

A minimal duty of any government should be to do nothing to hinder, and if possible do something to protect, the natural moral and filial ties that give families their power to nurture and sustain. To exploit that bond by coercively taxing families is, I believe, to threaten them with great harm. It is an action that presupposes a narrower form of moral obligation of children to parents than can rationally be defended. At the same time it promises to rupture those more delicate moral bonds, as powerful as they are conceptually elusive, that sustain parents and children in their lives together. Such bonds do not necessarily rule out financial incentives for children to care for their aged parents, as some recent legislative proposals suggest. But if such incentives are to receive support, in that case considerable care would be needed to guard against an exploitation of parents by avaricious children. There are, I ruefully note, as many ways to corrupt the parent–child relationship as ways to sustain it.

LIN YUTANG

On Growing Old Gracefully

LIN YUTANG (1895–1976) *was a novelist and a philosopher. Among his many books are* The Importance of Living *(1937) and* The Wisdom of China and India *(1955).*

IN my efforts to compare and contrast Eastern and Western life, I have found no differences that are absolute except in this matter of the attitude towards age, which is sharp and clearcut and permits of no intermediate positions. The differences in our attitude towards sex, toward women, and toward work, play and achievement are all relative. The relationship between husband and wife in China is not essentially different from that in the West, nor even the relationship between parent and child. Not even the ideas of individual liberty and democracy and the relationship between the people and their ruler are, after all, so very different. But in the matter of our attitude toward age, the difference is absolute, and the East and the West take exactly opposite points of view. This is clearest in the matter of asking about a person's age or telling one's own. In China, the first question a person asks the other on an official call, after asking about his name and surname is, "What is your glorious age?" If the person replies apologetically that he is twenty-three or twenty-eight, the other party generally comforts him by saying that he has still a glorious future, and that one day he may become old. But if the person replies that he is thirty-five or thirty-eight, the other party immediately exclaims with deep respect, "Good luck!"; enthusiasm grows in proportion as the gentleman is able to report a higher and higher age, and if the person is anywhere over fifty, the inquirer immediately drops his voice in humility and respect. That is why all old people, if they can, should go and live in China, where even a beggar with a white beard is treated with extra kindness. People in middle age actually look forward to the time when they can celebrate their fifty-first birthday, and in the case of successful merchants or officials, they would celebrate even their forty-first birthday with great pomp and glory. But the fifty-first birthday, or the half-century mark, is an occasion of rejoicing for people of all classes. The sixty-first is a happier and grander occasion than the fifty-first and the seventy-first is still happier and grander, while a man able to celebrate his eighty-first birthday is actually looked upon as one specially favored by heaven. The wearing of a beard becomes the special prerogative of those who have become grandparents, and a man doing so without the necessary qualifications, either of being a grandfather or being on the other side of fifty, stands in danger of being sneered at behind his back. The result is that young men try to pass themselves off as older than they are by imitating the pose and dignity and point of view of the old people, and I have known young Chinese writers graduated from the middle schools, anywhere between twenty-one and twenty-five, writing articles in the magazines to advise what "the young men ought and ought not to read," and discussing the pitfalls of youth with a fatherly condescension.

This desire to grow old and in any case to appear old is understandable when one understands the premium generally placed upon old age in China. In the first place, it is a privilege of the old people to talk, while the young must listen and hold their tongue. "A young man is supposed to have ears and no mouth," as a Chinese saying goes. Men of twenty are supposed to listen when people of thirty are talking, and these in turn are supposed to listen when men of forty are talking. As the desire to talk and to be listened to is almost universal, it is evident that the further along one gets in years, the better chance he has to talk and to be listened to when he goes about in society. It is a game of life in which no one is favored, for everyone has a chance of becoming old in his time. Thus a father lecturing his son is obliged to stop suddenly and change his demeanor the moment the grandmother opens her mouth. Of course he wishes to be in the grandmother's place. And it is quite fair, for what right have the young to open their mouth when the old men can say, "I have crossed more bridges than you have crossed streets!" What right have the young got to talk?

In spite of my acquaintance with Western life and the Western attitude toward age, I am still continually shocked by certain expressions for which I am totally unprepared. Fresh illustrations of this attitude come up on every side. I have heard an old lady remarking that she has had several grandchildren, but, "It was the first one that *hurt*." With the full knowledge that American people hate to be thought of as old, one still doesn't quite expect to have it put that way. I have made allowance for people in middle age this side of fifty, who, I can understand, wish to leave the impression that they are still active and vigorous, but I am not quite prepared to meet an old lady with gray hair facetiously switching the topic of conversation to the weather, when the conversation without any fault of mine naturally drifted toward her age. One continually forgets it when allowing an old man to enter an elevator or a car first; the habitual expression "after age" comes up to my lips, then I restrain myself and am at a loss for what to say in its place. One day, being forgetful, I blurted out the usual phrase in deference to an extremely dignified and charming old man, and the old man seated in the car turned to his wife and remarked jokingly to her, "This young man has the cheek to think that he is younger than myself!"

The whole thing is as senseless as can be. . . . I see no way out of it until the American people begin somewhat to despise work and efficiency and achievement. I suspect when an American father looks upon the home and not the office as his ideal place in life, and can openly tell people, as Chinese parents do, with absolute equanimity that now he has a good son taking his place and is honored to be fed by him, he will be anxiously looking forward to that happy time, and will count the years impatiently before he reaches fifty.

It seems a linguistic misfortune that hale and hearty old men in America tell people that they are "young," or are told that they are "young" when really what is meant is that they are healthy. To enjoy health in old age, or to be "old and healthy," is the greatest of human luck, but to call it "healthy and young" is but to detract from that glamour and impute imperfection to what is really perfect. After all, there is nothing more beautiful in this world than a healthy wise old man, with "ruddy checks and white hair," talking in a soothing voice about life as one who knows it. The Chinese realize this, and have always pictured an old man with "ruddy cheeks and white hair" as *the symbol of ultimate earthly happiness.* . . .

I have no doubt that the fact that the old men of America still insist on being so busy and active can be directly traced to individualism carried to a foolish extent. It is their pride and their love of independence and their shame of being dependent upon their children. But among the many human rights the American people have provided for in their Constitution, they have strangely forgotten about the right to be fed by their children, for it is a right and an obligation growing out of service. How can any one deny that parents who have toiled for their children in their youth, have lost many a good night's sleep when they were ill, have washed their diapers long before they could talk and have spent about a quarter of a century bringing them up and fitting them for life, have the right to be fed by them and loved and respected when they are old? Can one not forget the individual and his pride of self in a general scheme of home life in which men are justly taken care of by their parents and, having in turn taken care of their children, are also justly taken care of by the latter? The Chinese have not got the sense of individual independence because the whole conception of life is based upon mutual help within the home; hence there is no shame attached to the circumstance of one's being served by his children in the sunset of one's life. Rather it is considered good luck to have children who can take care of one. One lives for nothing else in China.

In the West, the old people efface themselves and prefer to live alone in some hotel with a restaurant on the ground floor, out of consideration for their children and an entirely unselfish desire not to interfere in their home life. But the old people *have* the right to interfere, and if interference is unpleasant, it is nevertheless natural for all life, particularly the domestic life, is a lesson in restraint. . . .

The Chinese idea supporting this personal service to old parents is expressly defended on the sole ground of gratitude. The debts to one's friends may be numbered, but the debts to one's parents are beyond number. Again and again, Chinese essays on filial piety mention the fact of washing diapers, which takes on significance when one becomes a parent himself. In return, therefore, is it not right that in their old age, the parents should be served with the best food and have their favorite dishes placed before them? The duties of a son serving his parents are pretty hard, but it is sacrilege to make a comparison between nursing one's own parents and nursing a stranger in a hospital. For instance, the following are some of the duties of the junior at home, as prescribed by T'u Hsishih and incorporated in a book of moral instruction very popular as a text in the old schools:

> In the summer months, one should, while attending to his parents, stand by their side and fan them, to drive away the heat and the flies and mosquitoes. In winter, he should see that the bed quilts are warm enough and the stove fire is hot enough, and see that it is just right by attending to it constantly. He should also see if there are holes or crevices in the doors and windows, that there may be no draft, to the end that his parents are comfortable and happy.

> A child above ten should get up before his parents in the morning, and after the toilet go to their bed and ask if they have had a good night. If his parents have already gotten up, he should first curtsy to them before inquiring after their health, and should retire with another curtsy after the question. Before going to bed at night, he should prepare the bed, when the parents are going to sleep, and stand by until he sees that they have fallen off to sleep and then pull down the bed curtain and retire himself.

Who, therefore, wouldn't want to be an old man or an old father or grandfather in China?

This sort of thing is being very much laughed at by the proletarian writers of China as "feudalistic," but there is a charm to it which makes any old gentleman inland cling to it and think that modern China is going to the dogs. The important point is that *every man grows old in time* if he lives long enough, as he certainly desires to. If one forgets this foolish individualism which seems to assume that an individual can exist in the abstract and be literally independent, one must admit that we must so plan our pattern of life that the golden period lies ahead in old age and not behind us in youth and innocence. For if we take the reverse attitude, we are committed without our knowing to a race with the merciless course of time, forever afraid of what lies ahead of us—a race, it is hardly necessary to point out, which is quite hopeless and in which we are eventually all defeated. No one can really stop growing old; he can only cheat himself by not admitting that he is growing old. And since there is no use fighting against nature, one might just as well grow old gracefully. The symphony of life should end with a grand finale of peace and serenity and material comfort and spiritual contentment, and not with the crash of a broken drum or cracked cymbals.

MARK TWAIN
You Can't Pray a Lie

MARK TWAIN (BORN SAMUEL LANGHORNE CLEMENS; 1835–1910) *was a noted humorist and novelist. He is especially known for his highly autobiographical stories of boyhood on the Mississippi:* The Adventures of Tom Sawyer *(1876) and* The Adventures of Huckleberry Finn *(1884). Twain's writing is regarded as some of the most representative of nineteenth-century American life.*

WE went drifting down into a big bend, and the night clouded up and got hot. The river was very wide, and was walled with solid timber on both sides; you couldn't see a break in it hardly ever, or a light. We talked about Cairo, and wondered whether we would know it when we got to it. I said likely we wouldn't because I had heard say there warn't but about a dozen houses there, and if they didn't happen to have them lit up, how was we going to know we was passing a town? Jim said if the two big rivers joined together there, that would show. But I said maybe we might think we was passing the foot of an island and coming into the same old river again. That disturbed Jim — and me too. So the question was, what to do? I said, paddle ashore the first time a light showed, and tell them pap was behind, coming along with a trading scow, and was a green hand at the business, and wanted to know how far it was to Cairo. Jim thought it was a good idea, so we took a smoke on it and waited.

There warn't nothing to do now but to look out sharp for the town, and not pass it without seeing it. He said he'd be mighty sure to see it, because he'd be a free man the minute he seen it, but if he missed it he'd be in a slave country again and no more show for freedom. Every little while he jumps up and says:

"Dah she is!"

But it warn't. It was Jack-o'-lanterns, or lightning-bugs; so he set down again, and went to watching, same as before. Jim said it made him all over trembly and feverish to be so close to freedom. Well, I can tell you it made me all over trembly and feverish, too, to hear him, because I began to get it through my head that he *was* most free — and who was to blame for it? Why, *me*. I couldn't get that out of my conscience, no how nor no way. It got to troubling me so I couldn't rest; I couldn't stay still in one place. It hadn't ever come home to me before, what this thing was that I was doing. But now it did; and it stayed with me, and scorched me more and more. I tried to make out to myself that *I* warn't to blame, because *I* didn't run Jim off from his rightful owner; but it warn't no use, conscience up and says, every time, "But you knowed he was running for his freedom, and you could 'a' paddled ashore and told somebody." That was so — I couldn't get around that no way. That was where it pinched. Conscience says to me, "What had poor Miss Watson done to you that you could see her nigger go off right under your eyes and never say one single word? What did that poor old woman do to you that you could treat her so mean? Why, she tried to learn you your book, she tried to learn you your manners, she tried to be good to you every way she knowed how. *That's* what she done."

I got to feeling so mean and miserable I most wished I was dead. I fidgeted up and down the raft, abusing myself to myself, and Jim was fidgeting up and down past me. We neither of us could keep still. Every time he danced around and says, "Dah's Cairo!" it went through me like a shot, and I thought if it *was* Cairo I reckoned I would die of miserableness.

Jim talked out loud all the time while I was talking to myself. He was saying how the first thing he would do when he got to a free state he would go to saving up money and never spend a single cent, and when he got enough he would buy his wife, which was owned on a farm close to where Miss Watson lived; and then they would both work to buy the two children, and if their master wouldn't sell them, they'd get an Ab'litionist to go and steal them.

It most froze me to hear such talk. He wouldn't ever dared to talk such talk in his life before. Just see what a difference it made in him the minute he judged he was about free. It was according to the old saying "Give a nigger an inch and he'll take an ell." Thinks I, this is what comes of my not thinking. Here was this nigger, which I had as good as helped to run away, coming right out flat-footed and saying he would steal his children — children that belonged to a man I didn't even know; a man that hadn't ever done me no harm.

I was sorry to hear Jim say that, it was such a lowering of him. My conscience got to stirring me up hotter than ever, until at last I says to it, "Let up on me — it ain't too late yet — I'll paddle ashore at the first light and tell." I felt easy and happy and light as a feather right off. All my troubles was gone. I went to looking out sharp for a light, and sort of singing to myself. By and by one showed. Jim sings out:

"We's safe, Huck, we's safe! Jump up and crack yo' heels! Dat's de good ole Cairo at las', I jis knows it!"

I says:

"I'll take the canoe and go and see, Jim. It mightn't be, you know."

He jumped and got the canoe ready, and put his old coat in the bottom for me to set on, and give me the paddle; and as I shoved off, he says:

"Pooty soon I'll be a-shout'n for joy, en I'll say, it's all on accounts o' Huck; I's a free man, en I couldn't ever ben free ef it hadn' ben for Huck; Huck done it. Jim won't ever forgit you, Huck; you's de bes' fren' Jim's ever had; en you's de *only* fren' ole Jim's got now."

I was paddling off, all in a sweat to tell on him; but when he says this, it seems to kind of take the tuck all out of me. I went along slow then, and I warn't right down certain whether I was glad I started or whether I warn't. When I was fifty yards off, Jim says:

"Dah you goes, de ole true Huck; de on'y white genlman dat ever kep' his promise to old Jim."

Well, I just felt sick. But I says, I *got* to do it — I can't get *out* of it. Right then along comes a skiff with two men in it with guns, and they stopped and I stopped. One of them says:

"What's that yonder?"

"A piece of a raft," I says.

"Do you belong on it?"

"Yes, sir."

"Any men on it?"

"Only one, sir."

"Well, there's five niggers run off tonight up yonder, above the head of the bend. Is your man white or black?"

I didn't answer up prompt. I tried to, but the words wouldn't come. I tried for a second or two to brace up and out with it but I warn't man enough — hadn't the spunk of a rabbit. I see I was weakening; so I just give up trying and up and says:

"He's white."

"I reckon we'll go and see for ourselves."

"I wish you would," says I, "because it's pap that's there, and maybe you'd help me tow the raft ashore where the light is. He's sick — and so is mam and Mary Ann."

"Oh, the devil! we're in a hurry, boy. But I s'pose we've got to. Come, buckle to your paddle, and let's get along."

I buckled to my paddle and they laid to their oars. When we had made a stroke or two I says:

"Pap'll be mighty much obleeged to you, I can tell you. Everybody goes away when I want them to help me tow the raft ashore, and I can't do it by myself."

"Well, that's infernal mean. Odd, too. Say, boy, what's the matter with your father?"

"It's the — a — the — well, it ain't anything much."

They stopped pulling. It warn't but a mighty little ways to the raft now. One says:

"Boy, that's a lie. What *is* the matter with your pap? Answer up square now, and it'll be the better for you."

"I will, sir, I will, honest — but don't leave us, please. It's the — the — Gentlemen, if you'll only pull ahead, and let me heave you the headline, you won't have to come a-near the raft — please do."

"Set her back. John, set her back!" says one. They backed water. "Keep away, boy — keep to looard. Confound it, I just expect the wind has blowed it to us. Your's pap's got the smallpox, and you know it precious well. Why didn't you come out and say so? Do you want to spread it all over!"

"Well," says I, a-blubbering, "I've told everybody before, and they just went away and left us."

"Poor devil, there's something in that. We are right down sorry for you, but we — well, hang it, we don't want the smallpox, you see. Look here, I'll tell you what to do. Don't you try to land by yourself, or you'll smash everything to pieces. You float along down about twenty miles, and you'll come to a town on the left-hand side of the river. It will be long after sunup then, and when you ask for help you tell them your folks are all down with chills and fever. Don't be a fool again, and let people guess what is the matter. Now we're trying to do you a kindness; so you just put twenty miles between us, that's a good boy. It wouldn't do any good to land yonder where the light is — it's only a woodyard. Say, I reckon your father's poor, and I'm bound to say he's in pretty hard luck. Here, I'll put a twenty-dollar gold piece on this board, and you get it when it floats by. I feel mighty mean to leave you; but my kingdom! it won't do to fool with smallpox, don't you see?"

"Hold on, Parker," says the man, "here's twenty to put on the board for me. Good-by, boy; you do as Mr. Parker told you, and you'll be all right."

"That's so, my boy — good-by, good-by. If you see any runaway niggers you get help and nab them, and you can make some money by it."

"Good-by, sir," says I; "I won't let no runaway niggers get by me if I can help it."

They went off and I got aboard the raft, feeling bad and low, because I knowed very well I had done wrong, and I see it warn't no use for me to try to learn to do right; a body that don't get *started* right when he's little ain't got no show — when the pinch comes there ain't nothing to back him up and keep him to his work, and so he gets beat. Then I thought a minute, and says to myself, hold on; s'pose you'd 'a' done right and give Jim up would you felt better than what you do now? No, says I, I'd feel bad — I'd feel just the same way I do now. Well, then, says I, what's the use you learning to do right when it's troublesome to do right and ain't no trouble to do wrong, and the wages is just the same? I was stuck. I couldn't answer that. So I reckoned I wouldn't bother no more about it, but after this always do whichever come handiest at the time. . . .

I went to the raft, and set down in the wigwam to think. But I couldn't come to nothing. I thought till I wore my head sore, but I couldn't see no way out of the trouble. After all this long journey, and after all we'd done for them scoundrels, here it was all come to nothing, everything all busted up and ruined, because they could have the heart to serve Jim such a trick as that, and make him a slave again all his life, and amongst strangers, too, for forty dirty dollars.

Once I said to myself it would be a thousand times better for Jim to be a slave at home where his family was, as long as he'd *got* to be a slave, and so I'd better write a letter to Tom Sawyer and tell him to tell Miss Watson where he was. But I soon give up that notion for two things: she'd be mad and disgusted at his rascality and ungratefulness for leaving her, and so she'd sell him straight down the river again; and if she didn't, everybody naturally despises an ungrateful nigger, and they'd make Jim feel it all the time, and so he'd feel ornery and disgraced. And then think of *me*! It would get all around that Huck Finn helped a nigger to get his freedom; and if I was ever to see anybody from that town again I'd be ready to get down and lick his boots for shame. That's just the way: a person does a low-down

thing, and then he don't want to take no consequences of it. Thinks as long as he can hide, it ain't no disgrace. That was my fix exactly. The more I studied about this the more my conscience went to grinding me, and the more wicked and low-down and ornery I got to feeling. And at last, when it hit me all of a sudden that here was the plain hand of Providence slapping me in the face and letting me know my wickedness was being watched all the time from up there in heaven, whilst I was stealing a poor old woman's nigger that hadn't ever done me no harm, and now was showing me there's One that's always on the lookout, and ain't a-going to allow no such miserable doings to go only just so fur and no further, I most dropped in my tracks I was so scared. Well, I tried the best I could to kinder soften it up somehow for myself by saying I was brung up wicked, and so I warn't so much to blame; but something inside of me kept saying, "There was the Sunday school, you could 'a' gone to it; and if you'd 'a' done it they'd 'a' learnt you there that people that acts as I'd been acting about that nigger goes to everlasting fire."

It made me shiver. And I about made up my mind to pray, and see if I couldn't try to quit being the kind of a boy I was and be better. So I kneeled down. But the words wouldn't come. Why wouldn't they? It warn't no use to try and hide it from Him. Nor from *me*, neither. I knowed very well why they wouldn't come. It was because my heart warn't right; it was because I warn't square; it was because I was playing double. I was letting *on* to give up sin, but away inside of me I was holding on to the biggest one of all. I was trying to make my mouth *say* I would do the right thing and the clean thing, and go and write to that nigger's owner and tell where he was; but deep down in me I knowed it was a lie, and He knowed it. You can't pray a lie—I found that out.

So I was full of trouble, full as I could be; and didn't know what to do. At last I had an idea; and I says, I'll go and write the letter—and *then* see if I can pray. Why, it was astonishing, the way I felt as light as a feather right straight off, and my troubles all gone. So I got a piece of paper and a pencil, all glad and excited, and set down and wrote:

Miss Watson, your runaway nigger Jim is down here two mile below Pikesville, and Mr. Phelps has got him and he will give him up for the reward if you send.

HUCK FINN

I felt good and all washed clean of sin for the first time I had ever felt so in my life, and I knowed I could pray now. But I didn't do it straight off, but laid the paper down and set there thinking—thinking how good it was all this happened so, and how near I come to being lost and going to hell. And went on thinking. And got to thinking over our trip down the river; and I see Jim before me all the time: in the day and in the nighttime, sometimes moonlight, sometimes storms, and we a-floating along, talking and singing and laughing. But somehow I couldn't seem to strike no places to harden me against him, but only the other kind. I'd see him standing my watch on top of his'n, 'stead of calling me, so I could go on sleeping; and see him how glad he was when I come back out of the fog; and when I come to him again in the swamp, up there where the feud was; and such-like times; and would always call me honey, and pet me, and do everything he could think of for me, and how good he always was; and at last I struck the time I saved him by telling the men we had smallpox aboard, and he was so grateful, and said I was the best friend old Jim ever had in the world, and the *only* one he's got now; and then I happened to look around and see that paper.

It was a close place. I took it up, and held it in my hand. I was a-trembling, because I'd got to decide, forever, betwixt two things, and I knowed it. I studied a minute, sort of holding my breath, and then says to myself:

"All right, then, I'll *go* to hell"—and tore it up.

STUART MILLER
Men and Friendship

STUART MILLER *has served as the Director of Development at Esalen Institute in San Francisco and Big Sur, California. He has written several books, including* Hot Springs: The True Adventures of the First New York Jewish Literary Intellectual in the Human Potential Movement *(1971) and* Men and Friendship *(1983).*

IN the face of such social forces as rationalism, professionalism, economic and physical mobility, and individualism—all tending to destroy intimacy—modern people have attempted to substitute for the old tight fabric of relationships one relationship alone. Over the last two centuries, romantic love has come to be as seen as something to which everybody, not just the rich person, is entitled. Moreover, romantic love, as the social historian Carl Degler has traced its evolution, has come to be seen as something one combines with marriage.

Most people's imaginations have come to be dominated by the idea of a lifelong, exciting intimacy with one person of the opposite sex. That this expectation is not universally realized does not stop people from trying. Despite the high divorce rate, a far greater percentage of the American population marries now than ever before.

In a world that tends to denature the emotional being, the modern man or woman clings to a spouse. It is not surprising, then, that most Americans will tell you their spouses are their best friends, although many more men will so declare than women. As a result, fear and guilt are attached to relationships outside marriage. When a man, for example, wants to go out at night with the boys, he doesn't just go; he tells them that first he must ask his wife whether their social schedule will allow it. There is no implied free social time for him other than that negotiated and granted by his wife.

A similar compact binds the woman, of course, although the women's movement has given women more liberty for outside relationships with their own sex than men now have. In essence, the man has become totally emotionally dependent on his wife. And because of changes in women's legal status and their increasing opportunities for professional work, a husband fears making a mistake. A wife can now afford to walk out on him, after all, and even take the children.

Increasingly, vital masculine energy that might be used to bond with another man is drained away. He may want the particularly adventurous flavor of male companionship, even deep friendship, but he is cautious about asking for it. The problem then arises that, as rich as his relationship with his wife may be, he eventually suffers from claustrophobia, from a sense of being suffocated in the arms of the Great Mother, an archetype he gradually projects on his spouse as his relationships with men become less vital.

Many women are aware of this pattern and occasionally encourage their husbands to seek male friends. But the social forces we have discussed stand in his way. The result, ironically, is that the wife finds her husband less interesting and adventurous than she wants and the husband experiences himself as a male failure, not sufficiently strong or adept enough even to implement his wife's simple, good advice. We are back, then, to the Great Mother and the kind of resentments that turn marital relationships sour.

All this tends directly to undermine the sexual life of the couple. Sexual attraction and excitation depend in part on perceived differences between partners, which are then bridged by the spark of sexual expression. When the sense of male and female difference becomes too diluted, as in many rather close and boring marriages, people get less sexy. The sexologist C. A. Tripp notes that "many women intuitively understand this refueling operation, and although they may miss their men who 'are off with the boys,' they use the time themselves to recuperate, correctly sensing that they are ultimate benefactors of men's diversion from them. Their hunch is right, as is the hunch of other women who feel a pensive disquietude with men who have no close male ties." In sum, if men had deep relationships with other men, their married sex lives would be better.

• • •

Part of the reason contemporary men attempt to put all their emotional and personal needs into the nest of romantic marriage comes from their deep feelings of hurt, shame, and guilt attendant upon the transitoriness and the failure of their earlier close male friendships. Because of all the historical forces we have noted, impermanence is typical of male friendships, as of all other relationships in our time. Some recent scholars of friendship, like the American psychologists John Reisman and Joel Block, urge us to accept such changes as a simple fact of modern life. They profess to be puzzled that the

ancient ideal of "lifelong loyalty" in friendship be so much admired by people when, in fact, most friendships do not last a lifetime. They urge that people become more realistic, acknowledge that different friends serve different needs at different periods of life, and that this procession of more or less temporary relationships is a normal part of personal growth.

Valuing personal growth more than consistency in human relations is, of course, a strikingly modern stance. As an idea, it arises from the whole trend toward individualism and self-expression that marks the modern person, particularly the American. Unfortunately, the ideology of growth further helps to corrode human relationships; by putting individual growth over mutual association it helps to destroy the very idea of serious male friendship. . . .

Our modern mobility, which separates men from one another in the most cruel ways, combines with our individualistic ideology of personal growth to litter our past with dead friendships. We rush to fill a puzzling emptiness with the love of women and with notions of our growth into rational adults.

All men know that these tactics don't entirely work. This changing and tearing up, particularly of masculine relationships, that were supposed to have an enduring strength about them, are corrosive to men's souls. So we come to doubt others and to hate ourselves. We come to doubt life itself. We can try to be "mature." . . . Or we can try to be the way many psychologists say we should be, telling ourselves that life is simply that way and that friends serve different functions at different times. So many tools for our living. But that is not at all, not at all what we had in mind for our male friendships. . . .

I declare that true male friendship, the

kind that very, very few adult men in America and Europe have with one another, requires intimacy, complicity, engagement, and commitment. It is a relationship profoundly personal.

Intimacy, being at ease, being understood and understanding, one can find more frequently in modern life than friendship, now that a growing informality of manners and an acceptance of a certain emotional expressiveness have definitely signaled our difference from the more repressive aspects of nineteenth-century social life. Indeed, a dozen modern interests contribute toward moments of intimacy — from psychology, psychotherapy, and encounter groups through nostalgia for the proletarian and the natural or rural, through the cultivated casualness of the modern workplace, to experimentation with drugs and involvement in political and religious movements. The same tendencies promote the increasing occurrence of moments, however fleeting, of complicity, a feeling of secret understanding and even of revolt or secession from society and from wearing our normal social personae.

Friendship between men may be on its way back. Indeed, from younger men one sometimes gets the impression that they are determined to maintain male friendship in their lives. The recent proliferation of popular books on the subject of friendship in general, despite their oversimplifications and lack of feeling, give further evidence that a renewal of male friendship may be preparing itself somewhere in the collective unconscious.

Intimacy and complicity, however, do not by themselves make friendship. Even familiarity — cosiness and trust and occasional supportiveness — can be mistaken for friendship. True friendship must also be true engagement with the friend — a very frequent mutual holding in the mind and heart. Though the centrifugal pressures of modern life limit the frequency of the physical presence of friends, engagement makes physical proximity less of a problem. Male friendship can thus be thought of as a place in a man's inner being, a space in his life, that is daily occupied by another man, a place that is regularly charged with love, concern, thoughtfulness — and, sometimes, resentment, anger, even deep hurt. *Engagement* means emotional involvement.

True friendship implies commitment, the understanding that a friend will be there, will not let go, that a friend will maintain the engagement in the face of obstacles, misunderstandings, and temptations, that a friend is prepared to undertake inconveniences, even sacrifices.

A true male friendship is personal. The relationship is its own context. Friendship may arise from another relationship — work, for example — but it is not dependent upon it. Male friendship is just one man and another. That so many friendships break up or attenuate into nothing when common place, interest, or work are no longer shared means that men have not had the essential friendship.

If a man changes religion or political belief, that does not change an essential friendship. The friends have been truly involved with each other, not just with parties, organizations, or even, extreme as it may seem, with mutual ideas or interests. All these other elements have their own value and importance, but from the point of view of male friendship, they are merely the furnishings, at most a supporting context, tools for the friendship.

A man's high-voltage engagement with another man, each of whom has a daily place in the other's inner being — from such inwardness, all necessary, dignified, and pleasant actions can grow. That's male friendship.

And, yes, it is rare.

I say to others, "If you can stand the quest for a true male friend, it is worthwhile." Each man will find his own way, but I have some brief advice.

In our times, we must first truly accept the necessity for an art of male friendship. Though Willie Morris makes his point about friendship being a grace that one receives, it is not generally sufficient to await the coming of such a gift. Why even those who most strictly speaking seek grace are always busy trying to get what they know can only be given by God. As talented artists who are busy working away at practice and execution, so must friends be diligent. Without deliberately focusing on my need for male friendship, I would have continued to miss Larry — both who he is and his availability for friendship. I have met many people who claim that friendship must be "wholly natural," that it must "just happen to you," and that "it can't be meditated or forced — that's too cold-blooded!" Believe me, there is nothing cold-blooded in thinking about love, about those we love, and in giving and seeking love.

This is especially true in our own cool and changing world. While a whole gamut of human relationships were "natural" in some older societies, they are no longer so in modern urban life. No type of human relationship is a given anymore, is seemingly "natural." Morris and others who plead for simple naturalness in relationships are not new voices. But just as couples these days must work at — indeed, continually reinvent — marriage and child-rearing, men must, if they are to have it, work at male friendship.

What makes a deliberate approach to friendship so necessary now is that everything in our culture is against it. Paradoxically, to keep up one's attention and effort, one must remain continually conscious of the formidable obstacles to committed, intimate, engaged, and personal relations. Ferruccio discussed some of the opposing forces: the calls of work and family life, the squeeze of time, the cynicism that comes with aging. There are, as we saw earlier, many others. The list is endless and every person should add to it. It is good to look your enemy in the eye.

Bold acts of consciousness are, I think, the true basis for an art of friendship these days. No gimmicks will work. The arts of friendship we need are inner acts, acts of the depth of the heart, of self-searching, and of decision.

Inwardly accepting the necessity to give friendship one's closest attention and recalling the social obstacles to friendship are the two basic inner acts.

Others are:

Being willing to acknowledge the hurt of your own loneliness. We live in a lonely time when no one is alone. Our mobile conditions give most of us an enormous but shifting and, therefore, superficial acquaintance. Let the reality of your loneliness be a spur to your own authentic quest.

Being shameless in thinking, then talking, about male friendship because it is important. Make room for friendship in your life. Make a federal case out of it.

Being willing to be hurt, repeatedly, by people you befriend.

Being persistent. People will back away from you, frightened because they have been hypnotized by society into believing they haven't the time, the energy, the interest, to be friends. They are simply not used to friendship anymore. Bizarre as it may seem, deep friendship strikes them as bizarre. Keep coming.

Committing time to friendship: time for writing letters, for thinking about friends, for telephoning friends, for disappointments, for generous acts.

Acting forthrightly with your friend and with the courage of your own delicate needs and desires by living the openness, generosity, and commitment you want from him. You thus help create an example, a magnetic field, in which (with luck) a man may respond. Friendship may arise.

A cunning hint: be willing to ask your friend for favors, to take, to sacrifice a part of your independence.

One hope: the art gets easier. Gradually, you give up the shame and embarrassment while still retaining an essential vulnerability.

After all such art, pray for grace.

•   •   •

Personal initiatives, however, will not be wholly sufficient. The fact that male friendship is as dead as it is requires collective action. So often in the personal quest for friendship, thinking a lack of a true male friend is a problem to solve alone, a man finds himself feeling crazy. Jung puts it well:

> A collective problem, if not recognized as such, always appears as a personal problem, and in individual cases may give the impression that something is out of order in the realm of the personal psyche. The personal sphere is indeed disturbed, but such disturbances need not be primary; they may well be secondary; the consequences of an insupportable change in the social atmosphere.

The current social atmosphere renders true friendship between men very difficult. When you decide to take male friendship seriously, to make it a real presence in your own life, then you and I both have a better chance of succeeding at our friendships. Our behavior seems, again,

more natural, and we take courage from one another.

Let courage then be the word to close upon. A Frenchman, about sixty years old, gray-haired, wiry, and distinguished, one who had ridden his cavalry mount to the front to face the Nazi tanks invading France only to be compelled to retreat in shame, tried to put the whole matter of friendship in brief perspective: "Of course friendship is dead now. There was a time, and I remember my father talking about it, when men had other images in their minds about how to behave. Men were supposed to be steady, to adhere to heroic codes, to keep their word, and to be willing to sacrifice. One learned it by example in many families. My father taught me that one should behave in life with 'honor and elegance.' That was almost all the advice he had to give me. But such talk seems absurd now, doesn't it, because we have become a people of sellers and buyers. Our attitudes toward human relationships are those of supermarket shoppers: we want what is cheap and quick and easy; we want variety; and we want novelty. But friendship requires a whole other set of mind, doesn't it? Commitment, courage. . ."

Recently, as I have become convinced that Larry Alexander is really available for friendship with me, that he is capable of or, at least, that he may be willing to commit himself to our friendship, I have felt a paradoxical emotion. I have been seeking a true male friend for so long and, at last, here is a possibility. Yet something in me draws away from Larry.

Puzzled, I attend to this feeling. To my dishonor, I hear within me a seductive whispering, a little inner beast posing the questions that dissolve all manliness: "Are you sure you want to get this involved? Do you think you can afford to take on another person? What if he makes demands of you: he gets sick, he loses his money?"

This reflexive cringing from all true engagement is a curious emotion. Probably it is part of human nature, the instinct of self-preservation asserting itself, a deep suspicion of involvement with others, of involvement with anyone outside myself.

A reaction known even to our most ancient poets.

To meet such fears, only courage will do.

Oh Gods! Let me have the strength and the courage to love my friends!

—PINDAR'S PRAYER

JANICE RAYMOND
The Conditions of Female Friendship

JANICE RAYMOND *teaches women's studies at the University of Massachusetts at Amherst. She writes extensively about issues in feminist ethics. Her books include* A Passion for Friends *(1986) and (edited with Dorchen Leidholdt)* The Sexual Liberals and the Attack on Feminism *(1990).*

Thoughtfulness

Thinking is a necessary condition of female friendship. The thinking I advocate is better described by the word *thoughtfulness*. In my use of it, *thoughtfulness* is characterized on the one hand by ability to reason and on the other by considerateness and caring. It is this kind of thoughtfulness that is necessary for Gyn/affection.

The commonly accepted definition of *thoughtfulness* is concern for others, attentiveness to others' needs, and considerateness for others. However, the word in its primary sense means literally "full of thought." Other meanings are "absorbed in thought," "meditative," or "characterized by careful reasoned thinking." Thus the word thoughtfulness contains a dual meaning and poses another tension. I contend that these two meanings must come together and be expressed in Gyn/affection.

Thoughtfulness has contributed much to the divisions and dissensions among women. . . .

Many women have expressed disappointment and frustration at the lack of thoughtfulness that pervades many women's groups and that women seem to accept as a matter of course in feminist relationships and gatherings.

On the other hand, many women have been socialized to react almost instinctually to other people's needs, mostly those of men and children. Women have been drained by a kind of thoughtfulness that is really lacking in thought to the extent that it is indiscriminately given, without thinking about the conditions under which it is extended and the fact that it is left to women in any context to be thoughtful. Here the thinking is missing from thoughtfulness so that women give and give, extend themselves constantly, and deal and deal with the needs of others in what has at times almost amounted to a feminine compulsion. The thoughtfulness that most women are trained to extend in a hetero-relational context is not born out of Self-directed thinking. Many women "go into robot" performing "emotional labor" to fulfill all sorts of others' needs. For women, the cost of this kind of thoughtfulness has been the obliteration of thinking.

A vision of female friendship restores the thinking to thoughtfulness. At the same time, it restores a thoughtfulness to thinking, that is a respect and considerateness for another's needs. Only thoughtfulness, in its more expanded meaning, can sustain female friendship and give it daily life. A thinking friendship must become a thoughtful friendship in the full sense of the word *thoughtfulness*. Many women may be brilliant thinkers, but that thinking has to be accompanied by a genuine attentiveness and respect for other women if female friendship is to flourish. On the other hand, many women may be caring and considerate of others, but if this thoughtfulness lacks a Self-directed thinking that "prepares us ever anew to meet whatever we must meet in our daily lives," it reinforces socialized femininity rather than female friendship. The word *thoughtfulness* conveys the meaning of a thinking considerateness and a considerate thinking. It is not accidental that it has such a dual meaning. A woman who truly thinks is, more expansively, full of thought in many realms. . . .

"Intercourse with oneself" is crucial to both the idea of thinking and that of friendship, for it is where both come together. Thinking is where I keep myself company, where I find my original friend, if you will. It is the solitude, as opposed

to loneliness, where I am alone with, but not lonely in, the companionship of myself. Thinking is where I am at home with myself when, for all sorts of reasons, I withdraw from the world. "The partner who comes to life when you are alert and alone is the only one from whom you can never get away — except by ceasing to think." This is one of the major reasons why women have lost their Selves — because they have stopped thinking. By not thinking, an individual loses her original friendship with her Self. Through thinking, a person discovers that she can be her real Self. In discovering this, she also realizes that the conversation that took place in the duality of thinking activity — that is, the duality of "myself with myself," the "two-in-one," or "the one who asks and the one who answers" — enables conversation with others. When I discover, through thinking, that I can converse with my real Self, I have to realize that such a conversation is possible with others. This is the awakening of female friendship in which the search for others like my Self begins. . . .

A woman must be at the same time a friend to her original Self and to others. Which comes first is hard to determine. What is clear is that thinking and friendship go hand in hand. . . .

Passion

As female friendship is characterized by thoughtfulness, it is also marked by passion. Friendship is a passion but, in my vision, it is a thoughtful passion. It manifests a thinking heart.

The tension between thinking and feeling, as signified in the phrase "thoughtful passion," is evident in the etymology of the word *passion*. *Passion* derives from Old French and Latin roots meaning "suffering, pain or some disorder of body or spirit." It also means being "affected by external agency." However, etymologies are often multidimensional, and so we find another meaning of *passion* defined as "any kind of feeling by which the mind is powerfully affected or moved . . . an eager outreaching of the mind toward something" (*Oxford English Dictionary*).

A passionate friendship upholds the integrity between thought and passion. In passionate friendship, there is no separation between the two. It is not so much that they merge, but that they have not been fractured to begin with. . . .

A thoughtfully passionate friendship is passion at its most active. It keeps passion active and does not allow it to degenerate into its more passive modes. More concretely, it helps two women to become their own person. There is a dynamic integrity of existence in a thoughtful passion that is missing in more sentimental friendship. Friendship that is characterized by thoughtful passion ensures that a friend does not lose her Self in the heightened awareness of and attachment to another woman.

The loss of Self has happened most frequently in lover relationships. And, in fact, passion is generally associated with lovers, not with friends, or not with friends who aren't lovers. There has been much discussion of passion within the lover relationship, but not much talk of friendship within love. It is my opinion that when a lover finds that she is losing her Self in the heightened awareness of and attachment to another woman in a sexually passionate relationship, the friendship is problematic. Either the friendship wasn't strong initially or it got swallowed up in the sexual passion of the lover relationship. Thus passion deteriorates into its more passive mode, engulfing a necessary friendship and eclipsing its ability to generate a needed thoughtfulness about the

friendship that is required for passion to survive and thrive.

In any kind of lover relationship that is committed, one's lover should be one's best friend. And if one's best friend is one's lover, she should also be the primary passion of her lover's life. A truly passionate love life, above all, must be pervaded by a thoughtful passion. . . .

When a woman lives as a woman, among women, among men, she at the same time questions the man-made world but does not dissociate from it, assimilate to it, or allow it to define her as a victim in it. She demands her place in it as a woman whose affinities are with women. She takes on the existence of what Mary Daly might refer to as "defiant deviant." Hannah Arendt might have named her a "conscious pariah," and Virginia Woolf would have probably welcomed her into the "Society of Outsiders." I prefer the term *inside outsider* because it helps to make clear the dual tension of women who see the man-made world for what it is and exist in it with worldly integrity, while at the same time seeing beyond it to something different. The term also highlights the reality of women who know that they can never really be insiders yet who recognize the liabilities of the dissociated outsider.

The inside outsider lives in the world with worldly integrity, weaving the strands of feminist wisdom into the texture of the world and paving the way for the entrance of women as women, that is, women on our own terms, into the world. As an inside outsider, a woman's work is characterized by the dual tension between her feminism and her worldliness. Her worldliness is dependent on her feminist vision, yet her feminist vision is actualized in her worldly location. . . .

The practical question, however, is How and where do women participate in the world? The worldliness I am advocating is not necessarily that of joining the antinuclear movement, the state legislature, or any other such worldly activities on their own terms. The terms of such endeavors are rarely woman-defined or woman-oriented. If participation in such worldly activities, or in others, is to be engaged in with worldly integrity, this participation must be on our terms, not in an absolute sense but in a way that enables woman-identified women to work within these worlds with integrity and with the ability to effect change — in other words, to work as inside outsiders.

If integrity means "that from which nothing can be taken," women must learn a few lessons from the feminist political past. Historically, women have been the mainstays of the abolitionist movements, peace movements, and other movements for human rights and social justice worldwide. In all of these movements, the feminist question was rarely highlighted. As a result, women did not participate in such movements on our own terms, and a worldly integrity was lacking. There are, of course, exceptions to this, but I am speaking in general.

On a more particular level, it might be helpful to give some concrete examples of how a woman functions as an inside outsider. Or, in other words, how does a woman live and act with worldly integrity? There are individual women and women's groups explicitly dedicated to women's causes. They may work in organizations specifically devoted to battered women, to the feminist campaign against pornography, or in various service organizations that meet women's needs. Or, as individuals, they may defend women in court, institute legislation against rape or for equal pay, or dismantle discriminatory and oppressive structures in which many women live their domestic and work lives.

They may edit feminist journals, provide women-centered health care, and/or teach Women's Studies. All these types of feminist work have made a profound impact on the man-made world, changing, for example, the face of patriarchal legislation, health care, and learning, as well as creating more woman-centered and institutional structures. . . .

In the final analysis, worldliness is a materializing of dual vision, of two sights-seeing. Liberation, if it requires "seeing with more than ordinary sight," also requires "seeing with ordinary sight." As vision radically upheaves the existent man-made world, it must at some point give rise to coherent groups, lasting structures, and patterns of worldly activity. As vision disturbs, it must also stabilize. The structures of women living in the world must also be built.

> It is a fact of social/political movements that radicalism does not sustain a movement. For a movement to endure, its broad base and widespread influence must be assured. But radicalism is *essential* for the life of a movement, as it will bring to it the most uncompromising critique of the abusive, exploitative power that the movement seeks to undermine and overcome. It is the presence of radical critique which assures us that the movement will not devolve to simple reform — that is, patchwork on an exploitative, corrupt, and ruthless power structure.

Women must use this radicalism to re-fashion women's existence in the real world. However, without structure and stability, radicalism will be frantic, bursting with energy, but short-lived. In this process, we must keep the tension between movement and stasis. Feminist far-sighted vision is meaningless unless it is accompanied by near-sighted realism which gives it shape and staying power. It is also meaningless unless such dual vision can translate into happiness — a happiness in this world.

Happiness

There has not been much talk or writing about happiness in the women's movement. It is almost as if feminists expected that happiness could come about only in some future life, after the struggle is won and the revolution over. Malraux once noted that in the twentieth century, the so-called intellectuals found in revolution what many others formerly sought in eternal life; that is, the revolution "saves those that make it."

Many women have defined feminism only in political terms, accentuating struggle against male tyranny. They have failed to see that just as feminism is a politics of risk and resistance, it must hold out to women some promise of happiness now. Organized sisterhood against the conditions of female oppression and the feminist fight against all states of atrocities against women serve as a powerful bulwark against the forces and structures of patriarchy. However, a purely political feminism, emphasizing only conflict and resistance, bears too strong a resemblance to religious eschatologies (theologies of the future) that would have women believe that the true happiness is achievable only in some life to come.

What is happiness? We use the term today more in a psychological sense, that is, as a disposition, feeling, or state of being that a person experiences. Originally, however, the term had an ethical meaning. In its earliest philosophical usage, happiness was connected with moral purpose, with teleology. Happiness was found in the fulfillment of some activity, end, or goal of life. Aristotle reminds us

that happiness is an activity of the mind, of contemplation. Combining these meanings, happiness has also been defined as the feeling that accompanies the activity of the whole self, or the feeling of self-realization. Along with this, happiness means the harmonious life itself.

My own definition of happiness is an amalgam and rephrasing of these meanings. On the one hand happiness, as I am describing it, is striving for the full use of one's powers. It is attained in fulfilling certain ends or purposes. On the other hand, one must experience happiness. Therefore, it is a state of existence which I think can best be summarized in Nadezhda Mandelstam's translation of the Russian word *zhizneradostny* as "life-glad." Literally, she means to be glad in/about/with life. To be "life-glad" adds a certain depth and substance to the word *happiness*. In short, then, happiness is striving for the full use of one's powers that make one "life-glad."

I do not mean to speak about happiness as if it is an all-or-nothing existence. For example, a woman can be happy in her work but unhappy at home. Happiness implies, however, that one is constantly seeking for the integrity of the Self and that it is a process. It is, as I said, a striving. But the more that endeavor is transformed into existence, the more one is "life-glad." It should not be, as Charlotte Brontë noted, a task. "No mockery in this world ever sounds to me so hollow as that of being told to cultivate happiness. What does such advice mean? Happiness is not a potato, to be planted in mould, and tilled with manure."

Female friendship gives women the context in which to be "life-glad." It creates a private and public sphere where happiness can become a reality. It provides encouragement and environment for the full use of one's powers. And since the profession of friendship means that the one who befriends has a greater interest in her friend's happiness than in that of others in general, female friendship strives for the full use of the friend's powers.

———————◆·◆·◆———————

LILLIAN B. RUBIN
The Child Within

LILLIAN B. RUBIN *is a writer whose works include* Quiet Rage *(1986) and* Intimate Strangers: Men and Women Together *(1983).*

IF we want to know what contributes to the unique personality traits a person displays, it's to the particular events of life that we would look. "What place did he hold in the family constellation?" we would ask. "What kind of relationships existed between the parents? Between parents and child? What did it mean to be the oldest child in the family? The one in the middle? What was the child's experience when he had to have surgery at eight? When he was caught masturbating at twelve? How did he experience the family's poverty? Their wealth? What was the effect of a divorce? Of a death in the family?" And so on. But, when we want to understand something about men and women at the more general level, something that will teach us why women so uniformly behave one way about certain things, men another, then it's to their shared experience that we look — to their culture, to their biology, to the social institutions within which they live, grow, and work, and to the fact that it is women who mother. . . .

To understand how and why it works that way, we must take a short journey into psychological theory. It isn't an easy one — partly because the road is paved with psychological concepts whose meaning is not always patently clear or immediately apparent. But they're essential if we're to go beyond what we already know about the differences between women and men and into a realm of understanding we have not reached before.

The journey starts with Freud. Whatever one may think of psychoanalytic theory, with its development Freud gave us the first clear expression of the fact that adult personality rests on early childhood experience. We may quarrel about some or all of the elements of the theory today, but hardly a murmur is heard to contest the underlying premise on which it is based: We must look to childhood if we are to understand certain central elements of adulthood.

As critics and followers developed and expanded the original Freudian theory, new understandings emerged about the psychology of infancy. First Melanie Klein, later the theorists of what has come to be known as the British object relations school showed quite convincingly that crucial experiences in the development of a child come much earlier and from a different source than Freud had articulated. Instead of satisfactory development resting on the successful resolution of the oedipal conflict, as early psychoanalytic theory held, these later theorists came to understand the importance of the pre-oedipal period — the years between birth and five — in the developmental scheme. And, instead of a bundle of instincts and impulses which had to be tamed by parents as the agents of society, they came to see the inner life of a small child as a world made up of what they called "objects." It's an ugly word to use when referring to people and relationships. But they chose it in an attempt to make clear that each of these "objects" is not, in fact, a person or even a thing, but an internal *representation* of it as filtered through the child's unique inner experience and consciousness. In ordinary language, then, such "objects" are essentially the mental images we carry inside us — internalizations of people and things that we come to know and identify with.

But what does it mean to internalize something? How can we even know that internalization exists? Can we see it, feel it? The answer is yes. But the experience of it requires us to take a step inside ourselves — to move from the objects of the external world to their representations in our internal one.

At the simplest level, for example, if I say the word "chair," what happens? Immediately we form a mental image of a chair. The *kind* of chair we each see may be different, but the *idea* of "chair" brings to mind the imagery of something to sit on. That's internalization — the mental representation of "chair" we carry inside us.

When we move from things to people, it gets somewhat more complicated because, with a person, there's a relationship involved — a continuing and dynamic interaction in which things both change and remain the same. Consequently, both conscious and unconscious processes are more at issue, and the *meanings* we give to our internal images are at least as important as whatever the external reality might be.

When I say the word "mother," therefore, it calls up a complex response. We may think first of a woman because that's how we have internalized the *idea* of mother, that's how the idea has become symbolized inside us. But there's also a real person who has been mother to each of us. Therefore, we carry inside a representation of her as well — a representation, it must be emphasized, that's not necessarily an accurate rendering of the real person but one we have invested with motives and meanings that may have little to do with reality.

The baby who cries in terror when mother leaves, for example, does so because she or he doesn't yet have the internal development to believe in the existence of what's not immediately present. Therefore, every departure feels like an abandonment — an abandonment that, for a small child, is also a threat to life itself. Mother, of course, returns; for her that was never in doubt. But until the child develops the capacity to carry mother's image inside, there's no certainty for him or her. With that development, separation becomes tolerable. But the fears generated in those early months of life — the sense of mother as powerful, as arbitrary, as wholly in control — do not go away completely. A constant and loving mother may reassure the child and palliate the fears, but the *experience* of the child in those terror-stricken moments leaves its residue in the internalized image of mother.

It's a complicated image, however — formed differently at different stages of development. But each successive formation doesn't obliterate the last one; rather, each is layered over the one before it, the earliest ones living at deeper levels of the unconscious than the later ones. So the mother we experienced in infancy is there beneath the mother of later childhood who lies beneath the one we internalized in adolescence—each of them filtered through the experiences of the developing child in a continuing and complex interaction between the child, the mother, and the needs of both as they were expressed at different developmental points.

This is how it happens that we can catch a glimpse of the real mother at some unexpected moment and find ourselves thinking in surprise, "Why, I never realized she's so small." The experience of her as large and powerful is the internalization of the child; the realization of her actual size comes from the adult who is brought up short by the contradiction between the reality and the unconscious imagery that's thrust into consciousness in an unexpected moment.

This, also, is why, when we think or talk about our own mother, we often surprise ourselves by the contradictory things we say and feel. At one time, she may have been experienced as an all-nurturing mother; at another, as an angry withholding one. We have, therefore, internalized both images and, depending on the circumstances in our adult life, will sometimes experience one as the reality, sometimes the other. But it's the internalized mother of our infancy that will concern us throughout the pages of this book—the image of the one who dominated the years of our childhood from our first days on earth, the years when we were beginning to know and experience the world, to internalize it, if you will.

And how does all this help us to understand our troubled relations with each other? How does it explain the fact that we so often feel like strangers even while living together in close and intimate relationships?

It took the work of Nancy Chodorow, a sociologist, and Dorothy Dinnerstein, a psychologist, to give us the clues. Standing squarely on the shoulders of the traditions I have sketched so briefly here, and buttressed by the ferment of modern feminist thinking, these writers began to wonder about these "objects" we internalize in infancy, about these mental representations that become a part of our internal psychic life. And they dared to ask questions never before seriously addressed, the crucial one being: What is the effect on human development of the fact that only women mother? Until they questioned the unquestionable, psychological theory had taken for granted that mother was, and ought to be, the primary parent—that it was the natural destiny of a woman and, if not the only, surely the best road to well-being for a child. . . .

From the beginning, life is a process of forming attachments, internalizing representations from the external world, and making identifications with significant people from that world. Since it is mother who is the primary caregiver—who feeds us, shelters us, comforts us, holds us in her arms to allay our fears—it is she with whom we make our first attachment, she with whom we form a symbiotic bond within which we do not yet know self from other. For each of us, then, whether a girl or a boy, it is a woman who is in this primary position in our inner life—a woman who is the object of our most profound attachment, a woman who becomes our first loved other.

As the first weeks and months of life pass, this infantile attachment becomes less global, more differentiated. This is the time when we see in the child the first glimmering of the ability to distinguish self from other — and with it, the earliest development of the capacity for identification, for the internalization of another into our inner psychic life.

Identification, in this case, is simply another step in the process of internalization — an extension of it, we might say. In the infant, it signals the beginning of a separate sense of self while, at the same time, forging a new kind of link with mother. It's the first inchoate ability to identify with another as one *like* self. And because a woman has been the primary person in the life of the child until this time, it is with her that this first identification is made. Hers is the imagery that is internalized — the representation that lives inside the small child, the one that the nascent self is measured against. . . .

Infancy passes; the child leaves the mother's arms, crawls to the floor, eventually stands straight and walks away. The period of separation and individuation, until now just budding, comes into flower. This is the time when "I" and "you" become more clearly distinguishable to the child, when self and other take on a compelling reality. Thus, it's also the period when the issues of separation and unity come clamorously to the fore — when the child lives in ambivalent oscillation between the desire first for one, then for the other.

It's at once an exciting time for a child and a frightening one, both to be seen quite clearly in any toddler — the triumph as the little one runs off followed by the sudden anxious return. The scene is a familiar one. A small child at play abruptly leaves the toy that a moment earlier had held such fascination, rushes back to mother, climbs onto her lap, holds her tightly, almost urgently. Mother prepares to comfort the little one for a while, only to find herself just as suddenly holding a small mass of wriggling humanity struggling to get away. Reassured of her presence, the child can return to play.

Separation and unity — these are the themes that dominate this period of life. For the child who has had what British psychoanalyst D. W. Winnicott calls "good enough" mothering, the fear that separation means abandonment, the anxiety that outside her presence mother and/or self may cease to exist, will be less acute; for the less fortunate one, more so.

But there is no perfect parenting, no possibility of meeting and assuaging every anxiety a small child experiences. It's simply not in the nature of life, may not even be desirable. Indeed, the parent who seeks to shield a child from the anguish of separation does him or her as much harm as the parent who thrusts the child into separating prematurely. Such misguided attempts at protection may offer some momentary comfort, but they also deprive the child of the joy to be experienced in the developing independence, of the sense of safety that comes with knowing a self exists and can be relied on, of the pleasure of becoming acquainted with that emerging self.

Separation and unity — the excitement and fear, the triumph and anxiety they generate — will remain continuing themes in adult life. How these needs were dealt with when we were small children makes a difference, of course. Depending on our past, they may be more or less powerful, more or less determinate of the kinds of relationships we have with others in our present. But the most we can expect is that they will be less rather than more. And long after the conflict between our need for separation and our desire for unity has left center stage, these issues will live inside us to influence the next act.

Thus, in adulthood, when we find ourselves in an intimate relationship, we each experience again, even if only in highly attenuated form, those early struggles around separation and unity — the conflict between wanting to be one with another and the desire for an independent, autonomous self. For each woman and man who comes into a marriage stirs the yearnings from an unremembered but still powerfully felt past; each brings with her or him two people — the adult who says, "I do," and the child within who once knew both the agony and the ecstasy of a symbiotic union. Ecstasy, because in the mother's arms the infant could experience the bliss of unity and the security that accompanies it. Agony, because from birth onward life seems a series of separations — each one an insistent reminder of those past and those yet to come, each one experienced as a threat to survival itself.

Of course, as adults we know there's no return to the old symbiotic union; of course, survival is no longer at stake in separation. But the child within feels as if this were still the reality. And the adult responds to the archaic memory of those early feelings even though they're very far from consciousness. Thus, we don't usually know what buffets us about — what makes us eager to plunge into a relationship one moment and frightens us into anxious withdrawal the next. We know only that we long for closeness and connection with another, and that we feel unaccountably uncomfortable when we get it — that, without warning, we begin to feel anxious in some ill-defined and indefinable way. A thirty-nine-year-old man I spoke with gave voice to just such feelings.

Judy and I are close in a way that I'm not close with anyone else. She even knows what I'm thinking a lot of the time. But that's not all a piece of cake.

I mean, sometimes I like it that she knows me so well; it's soothing and feels safe. But then there's times when, all of a sudden, I feel like: Christ, I need to get away from her before she eats me up or something. I know it sounds crazy, but it's what it feels like. I don't know why, but when I'm feeling like that, I actually feel like a scared kid. But what am I scared of? Damned if I know!

. . . The process by which a child separates is a complicated one, including within it several major developmental tasks. Paramount among them is the need to develop an independent, coherent, and continuing sense of self — a self that's unique and separate from any other, one we can recognize as our own, one that can function effectively in the world to get some primary needs met, one that knows an "I" exists irrespective of what happens in a relationship, whether with the mother of infancy or the lover of adult life. This psychological self is the internal analog of our physical self — not visible in the same way, but equally important to our sense of who and what we are.

In this process, two things are central: the crystallization of a gender identity and the maintenance of what psychologists call "ego boundaries" — those personal psychological boundaries of the self that serve to set us off from the rest of the world. This, in large part, is what a child's separation struggle is all about — a struggle that's different for boys and for girls just because it's a woman who has mothered them both.

It's not that the lot of one is easier than the other; growing up is hard for children of either gender. But the problems they encounter with each developmental task are different and, depending upon the issue in process at any given time, are sometimes harder for girls, sometimes for boys. Thus, when the task is to establish the boundaries of self, the identity between mother and daughter make that more complicated for a girl than for a boy. Just because they are the same gender, it's more difficult for a girl to separate, harder for her or her mother to know where one ends and the other begins. On the other hand, when we look at another central issue in this developing selfhood — the establishment of a gender identity, which means the internalization and consolidation of the knowledge that says, "I am a girl"; "I am a boy" — the identity between mother and daughter is a help not a hindrance, while the difference between mother and son makes it a much more difficult and complicated issue for a boy. . . .

Normally the process of gender differentiation starts at birth and continues through the first few years of a child's life. Differences in gender are, of course, biological. But gender *identity* and the *behavior* that flows from it are another matter, as much of the research on the establishment of gender identity shows. Give a child the wrong gender label for the first years of life and — regardless of what later genital development shows, regardless of serious attempts to correct the error — gender confusion will persist, most likely for life.

When a boy who has been raised by a woman confronts the need to establish his gender identity, it means a profound upheaval in his internal world. Despite the fact that other connections are made during the early months of life — with father, with siblings, with grandparents, even with babysitters — if mother has been the main caregiver, the attachment and the identification with her remain the primary ones. Now, in order to identify with his maleness, he must renounce this connection with the first person outside self to be internalized into his inner psychic world — the one who has been so deeply embedded in his psychic life as to seem a part of himself — and seek instead a deeper attachment and identification with father. But this father with whom he is expected to identify has, until this time, been a secondary character in his internal life, often little more than a sometimes pleasurable, sometimes troublesome shadow on the consciousness of the developing child.

It's a demanding, complicated, and painful process that takes its toll on a boy who must grow into a man. Although they happen at different times in the life of the infant and are two separate psychological processes, identification and attachment are so closely linked that the child can't give up one without an assault on the other. With the repression of the identification with mother, therefore, the attachment to her becomes ambivalent. He still needs her, but he can't be certain anymore that she will be there, that she can be trusted.

To protect against the pain wrought by this radical shift in his internal world, he builds a set of defenses that, in many important ways, will serve him, for good or ill, for the rest of his life. This is the beginning of the development of ego boundaries that are fixed and firm — barriers that rigidly separate self from other, that circumscribe not only his relationships with others but his connection to his inner emotional life as well.

The deprivation he experiences in having to relinquish this early connection may explain some part of the aggressiveness that's said to be so natural in men. When directed against women, it can be understood as a response to that early loss, and to the sense of betrayal that went with it. For, as a child, his inner experience is not that he did something but that something was done to him — that this mother who had, until then, been the loved adult on whom he could count, with whom he could identify, abandoned him to the shadowy and alien world of men. How, then, could she — or any woman — ever be wholly trusted again?

Whether true in the literal sense or not is irrelevant; it's the way the experience is internalized and understood by the child that counts. In this sense, the need for such repression engenders feelings of abandonment that are, in themselves, enough to stimulate plenty of rage. But it seems to me that we are witness also to a case of aggression turned outward in an attempt to compensate for the original aggression that was turned inward when, as a small child, he had to sunder his inner life so ruthlessly.

Parenthetically, it's in this developmental sequence that we can make sense of the contempt for women we see so often among men. If we consider the dilemma of the small boy and the internal rupture this separation requires, we can understand that the contempt is born of fear, not arrogance — the fear of a child who finds himself pressed to reject so powerful an inner presence as mother has been in his early life. It's a fear so great that he can live with it only by disempowering her — by convincing himself that she's a weak and puny creature whose lack of maleness must doom her forever to a subordinate and contemptible place in the world.

Difficult though the development of a separate and independent self may be for a boy, there are differences between himself and his mother that help the boundaries to become sharp and clear. He is, after all, anatomically male; she, female. In fact, it seems reasonable to speculate that men's self-conscious concern with their penis as an organ of identity origi-

nates in these early years. It makes sense, doesn't it? When, as a small child, the time comes for a boy to separate himself from mother in favor of an identification with a man, what else can he do to give some reality to the task ahead; how else can he make reasonable this demand that feels so *un*reasonable?

For girls, the process of developing an independent sense of self presents a wholly different set of obstacles. It's another of those contradictions that makes this developmental tale so elusive and so provocative. Just as the fact that there are no obvious differences between a girl and her mother makes the process of establishing a gender identity easier for girls than for boys, the problem of separating — of defining and experiencing self as an autonomous, bounded individual — is harder.

In the normal developmental course, the formation of a gender identity in a girl requires no wrenching breaks with the past. She's a girl, mother's a woman; the one, she understands intuitively, leads quite naturally to the other. Since she need not displace the internalized representation of the loved mother, there's no need to build defenses against feeling and attachment, therefore, no need for the kind of rigid boundaries a man develops as a means of protecting and maintaining those defenses. This means that, as a woman, she'll develop ego boundaries that are more permeable than a man's — a fact of paramount importance in the management of both her internal life and her external one.

It is in this part of the developmental scenario that we see the birth of the empathic capacities for which women are so justly known. The context within which separation takes place and identity is forged means that a girl never has to separate herself as completely and irrevocably as a boy must. Her sense of herself, therefore, is never as separate as his; she experiences herself always as more continuous with another; and the maintenance of close personal connections will continue to be one of life's essential themes for her. As a result, she will preserve the capacity, born in the early symbiotic union, for participating in another's inner life, for sensing another's emotional states almost as if they were her own — the capacity that, in an adult, we call empathy.

For the same reasons, a girl develops a more complex internal life than a boy. As she grows toward maturity, she not only retains her identification with mother as a vital part of her inner life, she internalizes father as a loved other as well. This process takes place much later, long after gender identity has been consolidated. But it is, nevertheless, central to an understanding of the differences in the internal life of a woman and a man. For, when a boy internalizes father and banishes mother, he is left with only one significant other who is actively experienced in his inner psychic life, only one with whom he must negotiate. For a girl, there are two. It may not seem like much, but the difference in psychic structure, therefore in personality development, is enormous. For it means that a woman's inner relational negotiations become triangular while a man's remain dyadic. . . .

Repression can drive the banished wishes and needs into his unconscious, but they live there to demand a hearing another day. Thus, the yearning for the repressed part will continue to make itself felt, pushing him to recreate the archaic infantile situation in adulthood in the hope that, this time, the outcome will be a different one. This means that he'll probably spend the rest of his life trying to re-establish that first exclusive relationship with another while also struggling with his ambivalence about the attachment — swinging between his wariness of emotional connection and his wish to find again that early ecstatic experience with a woman.

When he marries, he takes comfort in having found again the union with a woman he had to renounce so long ago. When the first child arrives, however, all he has longed for and finally acquired is threatened once more — the exclusive relationship lost, the dream disrupted. So he retreats — angry at his wife, demanding, competitive, jealous of his own child, while also ashamed of these feelings inside him that he doesn't understand, certainly doesn't welcome. Recalling just such an unhappy set of circumstances, a thirty-year-old father said:

> I had been lonely for a long time — a long time. Then when Ellen and I got married, it changed. I finally had someone in my life who was really there for me. I was a little intimidated about the idea of marriage before we did it — you know, I was worried about my independence and things like that. But, once we decided, I can't explain what happened to me; it was like coming home again.
>
> Those first two years were almost perfect. Even her pregnancy was great. But when the kid was born everything changed; it sort of all fell apart. It seemed like she was busy with him all the time. And I felt like I didn't count anymore. It was like the bottom fell out of everything, and I got resentful of Danny, then I felt terrible. What kind of father am I to feel angry at a little kid like that? But I couldn't help how I felt. I hated it; I hated the whole damned thing, but I couldn't help it. It was too late. He was here and it felt like things would never be the same again for me and Ellen. There'd never be just the two of us again.

"It was like coming home again," he says. And as in that other life, that other home, an exclusive relationship with a woman is gone — the pain of that old loss making even more intensely poignant the experience of this new one. . . .

A woman has difficulty understanding her husband's possessiveness and need for exclusivity precisely because of the triangular configuration of her inmost psychic life. It's here that we can see the source of a woman's relative ease with both new baby and husband. This is the internal constellation that equips women for the kind of complex negotiation of relationships in the external world for which they are known. We see it all the time: women whose exquisitely tuned ability to find their way around the world of human relationships enables them to navigate the emotional demands of a variety of relationships with considerably more comfort and ease than is possible for men. Thus, they become the emotional managers in the family — interpreting fathers and children to each other, siblings to one another, keeping extended family relationships in good order, maintaining the family friendships as well as their own.

For a woman, then, the sameness with mother, and the continuity of identification it permits, enables the development of these capacities. For a man, difference and discontinuity dominate the early developmental period and, therefore, disable the growth of these same qualities. It's true that many men consider themselves too busy or too important to attend to such mundane matters. But alongside that truth lies another one that has been less apparent to most of us. For, in reality, most men are not very good at interpersonal negotiations that are laden with emotional content because their inner relational life was left relatively impoverished by the need to repress their early primary identification with mother. Therefore, they turn their attention to those matters they can do well — managing those aspects of life such as work and finances that seem to be more subject to rational control — and call those important to cover their incapacity in those things their wives do so well. But it isn't, as lore would have it, that women are "doing what comes naturally." Rather, their acuity in these matters is a product of the process I've been talking about, which itself is the result of the fact that it's only women who mother.

These are the parameters within which we struggle to relate to each other. For women, the issue of maintaining separation dominates; for men, it's sustaining unity that's so difficult — problems that make themselves felt around every important issue in a marriage, from the conflicts we experience around intimacy and dependency to the way we parent our children.

3

How Can I Make Sense of Sex?

During the past several years a conservative political movement has advocated the boycott of Barbie dolls. According to that movement's spokespeople, Barbie dolls, with their voluptuous figures and suggestive clothing, encourage children to think about sex and so contribute to a social climate that condones early sexual activity, teenage pregnancy, and the deterioration of family values. Simultaneously, and with less concentrated efforts, feminist organizations have also urged parents to avoid purchasing Barbie and her pals. On their line of reasoning, Barbie is to be shunned because she and Ken represent the sort of gender stereotyping that contributes to gender inequality. In addition, Barbie represents female sexuality in its most oppressive form. Barbie exists principally as an object of male desire. Her exaggerated proportions remind us that women are valued only in so far as they meet the demands of male sexual fantasy.

These Barbie Doll Wars provide us with a sense of the complexities of sexual morality. It may seem odd that conservatives and feminists should line up together against Barbie dolls, given that they have entirely different evaluations of prevailing sexual ethics and behavior. After all, conservatives tend to worry about preserving the traditional family, while feminists generally regard the traditional family as a principal site of the oppression of women. What is clear from this odd coincidence of views regarding Barbie dolls is that any particular sexual morality must be understood not simply through those things it encourages and prohibits but also through the motivations behind it.

As Robert Solomon notes in his essay, sex and sexuality pervade our lives. Though sex may have a clearly defined biological purpose, its biological purpose is only rarely why one worries or fantasizes about it, or engages in it. Human sexuality intersects with other human characteristics and capacities in complex ways; it cannot be reduced to a purely biological phenomenon. Accordingly, this chapter provides a wide-ranging introduction to various issues of sexual ethics, beginning with contraception and ending with pornography, after considering adultery and homosexuality.

Solomon's arguments regarding the nature and purpose of sex remind us that sexuality is not a simple function of individual choice and desire. What we desire and what we choose are constructed within particular social settings. According to the prevailing moral canon, to desire someone else's spouse, and then to act on that desire, is to betray the sanctity of marriage. Richard Wasserstrom explores the presuppositions behind this view of adultery and wonders whether it promotes an excessively restrictive concept of intimate, interpersonal relationships. Richard D. Mohr raises similar questions about homosexuality in his essay. Both Wasserstrom and Mohr make it clear that monogamous heterosexuality is far from the being the norm in actual practice. We must then examine critically the reasons for and consequences of the general societal proscription against sexual behavior that falls outside the bounds of what we might expect Ozzie and Harriet to do in their bedroom. Audre Lorde's essay, focusing on the struggles of black women, and black lesbians in particular, emphasizes the importance of looking at the relationship between sexuality and political power in our effort to understand sexual morality.

The issue of pornography occupies the last section of the chapter. In the classical debate over pornography, those who opposed it on the grounds that it contributed to the degradation of traditional values were pitted against those who endorsed a more liberal sexuality morality coupled with a general belief in freedom from censorship. The selections here provide some more recent debates over pornography, including feminist arguments that pornography contributes to the exploitation and oppression of women. While G. L. Simon provides a standard liberal defense of pornography, Catharine MacKinnon places pornography in the context of violence against women and hence challenges the terms of that liberal defense. The importance of MacKinnon's account for contemporary discussions of pornography is immense. Ellen Willis, while concurring with significant elements of MacKinnon's analysis, nevertheless worries about the negative consequences of a feminist campaign against sexuality.

ROBERT C. SOLOMON

Sex, Contraception, and Conceptions of Sex

ROBERT C. SOLOMON *teaches philosophy and business at the University of Texas at Austin. His books include* In the Spirit of Hegel, From Hegel to Existentialism, About Love, It's Good Business, *and* A Passion for Justice.

. . . males and females united without any premeditated design, as chance, occasion, or desire brought them together, nor had they any great occasion for language to make known what they had to say to each other. They parted with the same ease.

JEAN-JACQUES ROUSSEAU

THERE is the myth: 'free sex', as told by a philosophical libertine who practiced it freely. It is a distinctively male fantasy, of course; one might say, a paradigm of irresponsibility. But suppose the problem of unwanted pregnancy — and to see it as a problem at all is already an enormous philosophical and political leap — could be solved. Could sex not then become as Jean-Jacques fantasized it, 'free' and divorced from morals and even manners? 'Liberated from our biology' as Shulamith Firestone once put it: how different would our sexual world be?

Does effective contraceptive technology alter our conception of sex? Does it 'free' sex from extraneous fears and moral concerns? When I started my research into the topic, I thought I knew; what had had a more direct and dramatic effect on sexual conduct than the availability of the pill in the 1960s, and what could be more obvious than the 'sexual revolution' then set in motion? But on further investigation and reflection, I began to realize that our modern medical miracles had ancient, however less effective counterparts, and that sexual revolutions, looking at the whole of history, have been a dime-a-dozen. With that in mind, and without lacking gratitude for the advances of modern medicine, I want to answer the question with a qualified 'No.' Our new contraceptive technology has not altered our conceptions of sex in anything like the radical 'revolutionary' ways we sometimes imagine.

Sexual intercourse began
In nineteen sixty-three
(Which was rather late for me) —
Between the end of the
CHATTERLEY ban
And the Beatles' first LP.

PHILIP LARKIN
High Windows

I would like to throw open to question the concept taken most for granted in contemporary discussions of contraception — sex. For a philosopher to even ask 'what, really, is sex?' is to open him or herself up to ridicule. (Who else would ask such a question?) 'What is the problem?' it is replied curtly, with a smirk, occasionally coupled with an offer of an ostensive definition. 'Sex is, — well, sex is — just what it is'. It is straightforward biology, which happens (usually) to involve two people, and more importantly, which happens to be fun. Unfortunately, fun has its price, for nature's purpose is not the same as our purposes. But, fortunately, in sex as in so much of modern life, human technology has taken control of nature. Sex is one thing; reproduction is something else. A thousand generations have enjoyed one only along with the other. We, finally, have separated them.

Reproduction, because it involves the lives of other human beings in the most dramatic way imaginable, their very creation, is at the center of our moral concerns; indeed, until recently, the very concept of a person's 'morals' was far more concerned with his or her sexual behavior than with any other virtues or vices. But now, severing sex and reproduction, also threatens to divorce sex and morals, according to the fears of many contemporary moralists. In fact, this has not happened. What current technology, coupled with the current sexual counter revolution, shows us is that sexuality is still at the heart of morality, and though there are the most serious questions of life and death involved in questions of reproduction there remain equally ethical — if not so mortal — questions of morals in our non-reproductive conception of sex. Sex, in other words, is not as 'free' as the sexual revolutionaries once thought.

What is sex? It is, in some sense, the coupling of bodies in certain, not so strictly circumscribed ways. There is a central paradigm, which provides the continuity with most of the animal kingdom and even a small minority of plants — heterosexual intercourse. Indeed, given the flat and untitillating use of the word 'sex' in biology textbooks to describe the behavior of scorpions and fish, not to mention pine trees, one gets the idea that sex

for us is much the same physical process, except that we alone in the kingdoms of life have chosen to make a moral issue of it. But this is wholly misleading, if it is not actually fraudulent. In fact, most human sex has about as much continuity with arachnids and dicotyledons as eating the Sunday wafer and sipping the Passover wine have to do with nutrition.

Sex is ideas. Sex is not about conception — at least, not usually; our conceptions about sex are far more tied to our morals than our gonads, though, to be sure, one can easily and amusingly imagine how different our sexual fantasies might be if our organs were differently constituted, say, on the bottom of one foot or — reminiscent of a once popular but physiologically dubious movie — inside of the mouth or the throat. This essay, accordingly, is about our sexual conceptions, not about conception or contraception as such. Indeed, what continues to strike me as remarkable is that, despite the dramatic developments two decades ago, changes in contraceptive technology are not the major determinants of our conceptions of sex. My historical thesis in a nutshell: attitudes about sex determine the acceptability of contraception, at least as much as the availability of effective contraception determines attitudes about sex.

The Teleology of Sex: The Purpose of Sex

Sex is not just 'matter in motion' (we may refrain from mentioning the many more imaginative metaphors), plus the pleasurable sensations thereby promoted and produced. Sex, like virtually all human activities and like most biological phenomena, has a purpose, or purposes. In the perspective of biology, of course, that purpose is clear enough: the perpetuation of the species. Pleasure, the expression or the stimulation of romantic love, getting even with the husband or getting a good grade the hard way are at most epiphenomena, perhaps effective motivation, but probably of no real relevance at all. Yet only rarely, if ever, does one 'have sex' within the biological perspective. The purpose of sex is therefore only rarely, if ever, the same as 'nature's purpose' — the perpetuation of the species. There is also OUR purpose or purposes, what we desire over and above — or instead of — fulfilling our biological roles as self-perpetuating links in a chain that extends from Adam and Eve or perhaps rather Lucy to Nietzsche's *übermensch* or 'the last man.'

Philosophers — following the ancient Greeks — like to refer to the purpose of a phenomenon as its 'telos'; thus we can speak of the 'teleology of sex' — its ultimate purpose. But our teleology immediately splits at least in two, for there is what we have called, with evolutionary naivete, 'nature's purpose,' and then there are our various purposes, which are not the same thing. Indeed, once we introduce that distinction, we immediately begin to wonder how the two have ever been connected, except for the contingencies of biology — in the same way that one might wonder how it is that the miracle that we call 'language' has such an intimate connection with the organ of ingestion (Jacques Derrida aside, I should add).

'Nature's Purpose'

To talk of 'nature's purpose' is, of course, naive. We no longer talk so easily of the teleology of the world — as Aristotle did so long ago and as Hegel and his henchmen did with less ease a century and a half ago. We prefer causal models, efficient rather than final causes, physio-chemical processes rather than instincts

and collectively unconscious cunning. Nevertheless, we can say, controversially but a bit oddly, that sex does serve a purpose — whether or not we want to say that sex has a purpose. Sex provides — for the moment — the only means of reproduction of human beings, though whether this is a good thing in the eyes of some larger telos is an awesome question I would not want to broach here. And sometimes, about 2.3 periods per lifetime for most Americans, considerably less for many couples in other cultures whose birth rate is inversely higher, nature's purpose does indeed coincide with at least one of the purposes of the heterosexual couple having intercourse. (It is logically possible, of course, that a homosexual couple might also adopt this telos, but this possibility is not a fruitful topic of discussion.) This happy harmony is not our concern here, however; it is the divorce rather than the marriage of sex and conception that interests us. Let us turn, therefore, to persons' purposes, leaving nature to fend for herself.

Persons' Purposes

It is with persons' purposes that the teleology of sex becomes complicated. I have not mentioned some parallel complications in nature, for example, male dogs or chimps mounting other males, not in procreative confusion but as an unchallengable gesture of dominance. I do want to consider such behavior, however, in the context of human sexuality. To take a more common example, it is often said, in many languages, that to have intercourse with a woman is to 'possess' her. I do not take such talk lightly, and the fact that the woman in question may or may not conceive as the result of the possessive act does not seem to be relevant to the matter. I choose this somewhat feudal example to underscore the sometimes less-than-romantic theme of the theory that I will be presenting here; sex is not, in addition to its biological functions, just a matter of pleasure or the expression of love. The human purposes of sex are spread across an enormous range of symbolic and practical concerns, from love and intentional debasement to a mere sleep aid. To talk about 'the purpose' of sex, even confining ourselves to 'our purposes' is a serious mistake. It does not follow, however, that this diversity makes impossible a unified theory of sexuality. Indeed, it is the diversity itself that has to be explained.

By 'persons' purposes,' I do not mean conscious purposes, nor, of course, do I refer only to explicit and mutually agreed upon purposes. The cooperative telos of the transparently self-reflective and psychologically explicit sado-masochist couple is one thing; the fumbling, confused clash of desires, fantasies, habits, expectations and aims that most of us take to bed with us is quite different as well as more common. Indeed, it is part of the ethics of sex (as opposed to the ethics of reproduction) that most of our purposes remain unspoken; it is a matter of curiosity as well as 'liberation' that we have recently been encouraged to make explicit our fantasies and desires. Not surprisingly, most of these tend to be rather mechanical ('touch me here') rather than the more significant messages and meanings that such behavior expresses, knowingly or not.

I do not want to attack the profound question of 'the unconscious,' much less the even more problematic Jungian notion of a 'collective' unconscious. There is no doubt that such a thing, consisting at least of those most basic biological impulses and residual instincts, which Kraft-Ebbing misleadingly calls 'the 6th, genital sense.'

But whether there is an extinct-laden unconscious is quite another matter, and at least one proto-Jungian philosopher, Nietzsche, vehemently denied the collectivity of our impulses, turning the tables to insist that our 'herd-consciousness' is to be found in consciousness, our individuality in our instincts. Our own view of sexuality, as opposed to some of our theories about it, seems to side with Nietzsche. Each of us appears to belabor the illusion—against all evidence—that each of us is sexually unique. But—back to the point—many of our purposes, individual or collective, instinctual or learned, are not conscious. When told about them—if we have not already been too jaded by 80 years of Freud—we would probably deny them, or, at least, dismiss them as minor aberrations, and 'out of character.'

What Do I Want
When I Want You?

Any discussion of human sexuality involves more than a catalog of organs, feelings, physiological and behavioral responses; sex is first of all desire, both temporally and, less obviously, phenomenologically. Indeed, one might make a case that sex without desire is not sexuality at all, though one hesitates to suggest or imagine what it might be. But what is it that one desires?

The glib answers are soon forthcoming, along with that familiar smirk and a number of rude responses. Such responses, however, are largely limited to adolescents and academic seminars. A novice may think that the 'end' (telos as well as terminus) of sex is successful intercourse (though even the notion of 'success' should be carefully scrutinized here). But clearly despite certain philosophical protests, sex is not one of those activities that is 'desired for its own sake' (if anything is so desired). It is not just that sex sometimes serves a telos, but that it always does. If there is anything like a purely sexual impulse (and they are very rare if they exist in us at all), we still have to say something such as 'it is the satisfaction of the impulse' that is in question, not sex for sex's sake. Indeed, we should want to know more about this alleged 'impulse' (which was 'discovered' or 'postulated', in fact fabricated — at the end of the 19th century). Some animals perhaps may experience something like 'pure sexual desire,' but this is noteworthy only insofar as it is also isolated and empty, virtually unrelated to any other activities and something of a mystery to the animal itself. Dennett, in an unusual bit of anthropomorphizing, imagines a bird in the midst of its instinctual behavior, musing to itself, 'Why am I doing this?' Clearly few mammals enjoy such an impulse; sex becomes a matter of status as well as species-preservation, and, watching my male dog's behavior around a female in heat, it is clear that sexual desire supplies only a small if not minimal motive, and is interwoven inseparably with a half dozen other concerns. When we return to human sexuality, we might be far closer to the mark by beginning, not with the obvious but with the obscure, not with the simple-minded aim of wanting intercourse but with the 'infinite yearning' of *eros* suggested by Aristophanes in Plato's *Symposium*. In philosophy, it is always better to err towards the infinite than to get trapped in the picayune.

So, what is sexual desire? Indeed, is it possible (as Michel Foucault hints) that we ought to give up such talk as quite misleading and mythological, as if sex were indeed a distinct and isolated impulse with only the most peculiar and often antagonistic connections with our other motives and desires? Without going

quite so far, we can begin to appreciate the complexity of what we call 'sexual desire' and its intricate connections with other desires and motives. Sex is not a distinct activity, except according to certain customs and rituals which make it so. Accordingly, sexual desire is not an easily distinguished mode of desire — which is how it is possible to produce those yearly disclosures that football, Pac-Man, quoits, metaphysics, process philosophy and eating artichokes are sexual. Who can say where one desire starts and another ends? How is it that Eric Rohmer's obsessive desire to touch Claire's Knee is highly sexual while the practiced intercourse of a jaded Don Juan may be just about as sexual as his desire to get it over with and go home to watch the Tonight Show? When we begin to analyse sexual desire, therefore, we should not be surprised that there is much more to it than sex. Indeed, sometimes sex might not even be part of it at all.

How could this be? And what does it have to do with the topic of contraception and conceptions of sex. First of all, the example of Claire's Knee — and if that sounds too fantastic consider your day-to-day furtive glance around the office — shows, if not yet convincingly, that the end of sex and sexual desire need not be sexual intercourse. Indeed, one might be obsessed with sex but find the very idea of intercourse unthinkable. One should therefore not leap to the now nearly automatic conclusion that such a desire must be 'repressed' or 'suppressed' or any other 'pressed' including 'un-ex-pressed.' If sexual desire is not necessarily aimed at intercourse — heterosexual intercourse in particular — then the supposed essential tie between sex and sexual desire and those rather constricted activities in which pregnancy is possible is dramatically weakened. This is not to deny that most heterosexual couplings do end (terminus if not telos) in intercourse of the most often-prescribed variety. It is only to say that sexual desire is not so firmly connected to intercourse as is often supposed. Our sexual conceptions are far more independent of considerations concerning the consequences of intercourse than the linkage between contraceptive technology and sexual freedom suggests.

Functionalism

In a society schooled in efficiency, in which ethics and utility are often thought to be the same, in which even physical exercise is supposed to serve a purpose, we should not be surprised that our conceptions of sex tend to turn to questions of function — to the uses of sex. My discussion of the teleology of sex might be viewed as part and parcel of this pragmatist orientation, and desirable as it might seem 'for its own sake,' sex in America is almost always defended in terms of some further goal — good health, happiness and interpersonal satisfaction. The idea of chastity horrifies us, and medical science has not been slow to catalog through the ages the various malfunctions that cruelly follow this unnatural abstinence.

Yet, the pragmatic notion of 'having a function,' like the more classical notion of teleology, is not a singular notion. It admits a variety of interpretations, from the traditional biological accounts of 'instinct' and 'species preservation' (that is, 'nature's purpose' — serving that natural function), to the Freudian account of pleasure as the purpose, however construed, in terms of the hydraulics of the 'psychic apparatus,' not the phenomenal sensations of 'fun.' But of particular interest to us here is the first of these interpretations, sex's natural function, reproduction. (Note that 'procreation,' even in the word itself, takes us at least one infinite step beyond nature.) What are we to make of the inescapably close connection — some philosophers even suggest entailment — between sexual desire and heterosexual intercourse?

The standard view, I take it, is this: sexuality changes with changes in its circumstances, the technology of contraception in particular. Taken as a hypothesis, the view suggests the following reading of history: in epochs where contraception is effective and available, sex is plentiful, relatively unrepressed and 'free.' Where contraception is not effective or available, sex tends to be prohibited, timid and fearful. But even a casual reading of the literature shows that not only is this hypothesis wrong, but its very foundation is upsidedown. (I refer here to the study of John Reed[s] who demonstrates this hypothesis with intriguing detail). The correlation between contraceptive efficiency and sexual attitudes is most unclear; indeed there are cultures with no 'protection' against pregnancy that are highly promiscuous, and just as many cultures with relatively effective contraception that are, in our terms, 'Victorian.' (Oddly enough, many of the actual Victorians fall into the first class, rather than the second.) Thus the whole notion that contraceptive apparatus determines the nature of sexuality is inverted; it is rather attitudes toward sexuality — and, of course, attitudes towards population growth and the practicalities of having children — that determine the interest in, the effectiveness of, and the availability of contraception. Of course, there are societies in which readily available contraception is withheld from the public precisely in order to counteract a casual or promiscuous attitude towards sexuality. Witness the Reagan Administration's abortive and stupidly misconceived 'Squeal Rule,' according to which the parents of a young girl must be notified if she is to receive birth control information. Conservatives quickly respond, though for the wrong reasons, that information about birth control has not proven to lower the bastard birth rate, and some come to the correct conclusion — though with the wrong motives — that attitudes toward sex are not determined and are not therefore alterable through technological know-how alone. But these are standard twists and turns in the history of sexuality, not its primary path. It is the utter failure of the 'Squeal Rule,' not its paternalistic intentions, that has made us aware that sexual attitudes do not depend on technological availability; technological availability pivots on sexual attitudes, in this case, an atavistic nostalgia for the days of virginity, when sex was more feared than desired.

Functionalism, crudely conceived, is the view that sex serves the conveniences of life; it is desired when it is convenient, not desired when inconvenient, with contraception high on the list of conveniences. This is, however, a crude view of sex, and a crude view of life as well. Again let's remember Aristophanes' reference to eros and an 'infinite yearning.' We will not understand that yearning unless we give up the functional, as well as the biological, view of sex.

What is "Sex"?

The genealogy of 'sex' begins, no doubt, with the birds and the bees. But it is a thin 'natural' history of love that does not soon see that the very word "natural" — in a cultural context — is a *moral* term. 'Nature' might aim at propagation of the genotype, but cultures are concerned with group solidarity, rank and status, rules, respect and, for the sake of authority as well as order, prohibitions. To

think that all of this is functional in the crude sense, aimed at population control or convenience, is nonsense. Indeed, much of the history of the availability of contraception is the history of power politics: the priests against the witches, the Republicans against the remnants of the counter-culture. What is 'natural' depends not on biology but on ideology.

Our concept of 'nature' is inherited from Aristotle, the Greeks, the church, the Enlightenment. In all of its forms, it displays one of the more glamorous sophistries in Western thinking: the appeal to a silent and therefore incontrovertible Nature in the defense of particularly provincial practices. Indeed, it is rarely biological nature that is in question: it is more usually 'natural reason,' which is, as often suggested, most unnatural, even 'a bit of the divine.' When philosophers sought a 'natural religion,' for example, they were not after nature worship or what Santayana called 'animal faith': they were after rational arguments. And when there are demands for 'natural sex,' it is not bestiality or rear-entry intercourse that is preferred; the call is rather to 'rational sex,' which means, that for which there are accepted standards and arguments (most notably what I have elsewhere called 'the two-minute emissionary-missionary male-superior ejaculation service,' with some credit to John Barth). Whether or not sex is the danger to civilization that Freud thought it was, the traditional emphasis has been on quick and efficient sex, just enough to satisfy what D. H. Lawrence called 'evacuation lust' and, in the larger scheme of things, to ensure an adequate supply of progeny to maintain the status quo. Indeed, in our genealogy of sex and 'sex,' we should look to the social politics of classes and inheritance rights before the technological availability of contraception.

What then is sex? Like most loaded terms in our vocabulary, 'sex' defies definition. It is rather a political term, to be used in ways more defined by power than by established semantics. Like most loaded philosophical terms, it shifts, suspiciously, between an indisputable paradigm and abstract arguments of the sort we have gotten used to since Kraft-Ebbing and Freud. The paradigm is heterosexual intercourse, embellished with perhaps minimal preparatory passion ('foreplay') and typically succeeded by sleep or television rather than pregnancy. One might say, following some Oxford philosophers, that 'if that isn't sex, nothing is.' Perhaps, but the difficult task, hidden in this paradigm case argument, is to specify the feature of that paradigm. Is it the presence of male and female, or just the presence of two people? Is orgasm necessary to the paradigm? For both or only for the male? Is ejaculation of the male sufficient? (Ejaculation being the physical event of which orgasm is the more holistic phenomenon). Must two people go 'all the way' or is it sufficient just that they want to? Indeed, is it even necessary for the paradigm that the genitals are the focus of attention, though, as a matter of contingency, we might quickly note that there are certain non-logical advantages to their inclusion.

'Sex' is a plastic, political term: the presence of an indisputable paradigm does not lessen its flexibility or its controversiality. The test case, perhaps, will always be homosexuality. Is it included in the paradigm? Does it count in a culture as 'natural sex'? In our own society, there are clearly no agreed upon answers to these questions. But before we try to tighten the link between ideological questions about sexual conceptions and technological questions about contraception, we should focus our attention on homosexuality. Here is, to say the obvious, a mode of sexuality in which pregnancy and contraception are not issues. But what we find is that homosexuality displays a history that is parallel to and usually a part of the history of heterosexuality. Its values are typically the same. Even its gestures and gender (not sex) identities are the same. To say that this is because it models itself after heterosexuality is to betray both a bias and a woeful historical blindness. Indeed, the most celebrated example of a homosexual culture — the ancient Greeks — despised women and heterosexuality, so much so that, in Plato's symposium virtually all of the speakers take pains to point out the inferiority of that merely functional domestic *eros* in contrast to the divine status of that 'higher' *eros* between men (more properly, between youths and men). What do we find when we look at Greek homosexuality — a licentious free-for-all with no restrictions, given the irrelevance of conception? Not at all. Indeed, the best books on the subject as well as the ancient texts themselves show us quite clearly that the sexual ethic among the Greeks was, if anything, more precise and much less hypocritical than the sexual mores of modern heterosexual cultures. Again, sex is determined by ethics, not biology (though once again I hasten to add that the contingencies of our bodies surely provide the material for that ethics; as the Marquis de Sade once commented, against the popular 'argument from design' that was circulating in natural theology: if God had not intended the anus to be used for sex he would not have shaped and positioned it so conveniently).

Sexual Paradigms

I have by now, I hope, conveyed some sense of my thesis that our sexual conceptions are not wholly determined by the more mechanical contingencies of medical research. There is a logical and, more importantly, a cultural gap between functions and ideas, and it is more often the ideas that influence the functions rather than the other way around. (Even Marx and Engels would agree with this version of idealism, given that I have included most of the political and economic influences on the side of the 'ideas.') Our conception of sex is to a certain extent centered on a paradigm, the two minute emissionary-missionary male-superior ejaculation service.

The Paradigm need not be an ideal; indeed most paradigms tend to be boring examples, even in discussions of sex. But this paradigm has many facets, and so too draws upon many perspectives. In fact, heterosexual intercourse is not itself a paradigm so much as it is the convergence of many paradigms, and the job of a philosopher in addition to enjoying the practice, is to develop a theory in which these various paradigms are distinguished and played off against one another. There are four basic paradigms:

> (1) the reproductive or procreative paradigm; (2) the pleasure or 'recreational' paradigm; (3) the metaphysical or 'Platonic' paradigm; and (4) the intersubjective communication paradigm.

The Reproductive Paradigm

The reproductive model has perhaps always been overemphasized, but, in the religious dress of 'procreation,' it has been especially well-nourished under the auspices of the Christian church. It is a paradigm which distills off the pleasures and Romantic overtones of sex and reduces it to a matter of dutiful service to the species — or to God. The paradigm is typically embellished and not left in its

cold biological state, but even so it is distinctively unconcerned with questions of mutual expression and tenderness. (The union of souls as well as bodies is a secondary development.) The paradigm of reproductive sexuality is the effective and efficient ejaculation of the male into the female. His orgasm is a bonus; hers is of no importance whatever. Indeed, excess enjoyment, wasting time and — most essentially — 'wasting seed,' is perversion. Indeed, although the concept of 'perversion' did not really enter into sexual ethics and medicine until the 19th century, the prohibitions against masturbation, sodomy, and all other manners of 'wasting seed' are found clearly even in the Old Testament. Needless to say, the sole paradigm here is heterosexual intercourse. Homosexuality has no place whatever, and even love and pleasure are at most of secondary importance as enticements, not telos.

Though nourished by religion, the reproductive model does not depend on religion for its persistence. Kant once argued that our sexual appetites are justified only insofar as they serve Nature's End, not our own. So too partisan politics or simple excessive biological conscientiousness can promote the reproductive paradigm. A Darwinian might see sex this way; a couple desperate to have children may temporarily conceive of their sexuality in this way, a sexual moralist might literally refer to 'natural sex' — in an argument against homosexuality for example — without invoking religion at any point. Indeed, this is often the more powerful and harder to refute version of moral arguments concerning sexuality, that our 'natural' desires are aimed at reproduction, whether consciously or not. 'Natural sex' is therefore sex aimed at reproduction, whether or not *we* aim at reproduction — or even thwart it — in our sexual activities. One might suggest, for instance, that such sex in general is 'practice' for the real thing, an odd suggestion which has, nevertheless, a considerable history behind it.

A paradigm is not necessarily an exclusive perspective, a set of blinders which permit only a single telos or conception. It is rather a matter of focus, a way of picking out certain features as essential and pushing others into the background. The reproductive paradigm highlights the biological consequences and minimizes the recreational and expressive features of sex. The procreational version of the paradigm adds to this the theology of divine design. Neither version need eliminate or ignore the other aspects of sexuality, but their emphasis already establishes an ethical framework. It is this framework within which the morals of contraception become heated issues, and it is within this framework that the technology of contraception has the greatest effect on our sexual conceptions. But there are other paradigms, and with them, other ethics and other concerns.

The Pleasure Paradigm

The pleasure paradigm might be called 'liberal' as a reaction against the more conservative reproductive/procreative paradigm. It is, for the most part, the paradigm that provided the ideology of the sexual revolution of the 1960's and it is no coincidence that the most effective means of birth control ever invented coincided with this new ideology. But 'most effective' does not mean new or novel, and effectiveness is only one factor in the determination of sexual attitudes. Morals are often more effective than technological effectiveness or, in the case of the sexual revolution, some say the 'lack of morals.' Which is cause, which is effect? But here

again we run up against that too simple-minded deterministic thesis. It is absurd to say that 'the pill' had nothing to do with the new attitude of freedom that defined the so-called 'revolution,' but it is equally nonsense to insist that it is by itself the cause of that cultural explosion. Contrary to traditional Freudian imagery, the 1960's were not the time of '*eros* unchained' (one popular phrase of the period). There was not a massive libido suddenly released. Rather, there was a shift in paradigms, a swing of the *Zeitgeist* which included, not coincidentally, a new technology.

The real father of the sexual revolution is not Doctor Rock or Doctor Hertig but that ideologist of the libido, Sigmund Freud. It is Freud, for all of his personal sexual conservativism, who most soundly attacks the traditional reproductive procreational paradigm and puts in its place a model of sex with pleasure as its telos and its defining characteristic. Sex, for Freud, is not Nature's purpose, but rather the primary drive of the 'psychic apparatus' to discharge itself. The pleasure paradigm, like the reproductive paradigm, rests on a biological foundation. It is the nervous system that is the locus of Freud's theory, and its physiological basis that determines the telos of sex. The goal of the nervous system, and of the organism, is Catharsis, Freud tells us. Its principle is homeostasis, or 'the constancy principle.' Its ultimate aim is emptiness and relaxation (a formulation that later led Freud into his flirtation with 'the Nirvana principle' and 'the death instinct'). The release of built-up tension is pleasure; the retention of tension is pain. The release or 'catharsis' of tension in sexuality produces the orgasm, and it is the pleasure of the orgasm — that is, the pleasure of release — that is the end of sexuality, not the procreative consequences of ejaculation.

Thus it is important to note how central Freud's distinction between physical and psychic satisfaction becomes; it is the latter that is essential to successful sex, not the former. This simple picture is complicated by the fact that in addition to this 'primary process' there is a complex system of ego-needs, which involves identification with certain sexual 'objects.' Accordingly, sex becomes concerned with the satisfaction of these secondary drives as well, and the simple pleasure of sex is complicated if not thwarted by the need for acceptance, security, and love. One might note the echo of Jean-Jacques Rousseau here, for Freud was also a 'romantic' of sorts, but a pessimist à la Schopenhauer rather than a hopeful visionary like Rousseau. It is worth taking full note of the fact that, as release of tension, masturbation plays a central role in Freud's notion of sex, while in the reproductive paradigm this is at best a perversion, if not irrelevant to sex altogether.

The notion of 'discharge' or 'catharsis' in Freud's paradigm is obviously based on a male-oriented perspective. In this as well as in its biological foundation, it is not entirely distinct from the reproductive model. Understanding Freud, however, is not primarily a matter of the history of medicine so much as it is a socio-cultural concern; and his rebellion against the reproductive model is part and parcel of a far more general rebellion against a certain kind of society. So too, the pleasure model in its more modern version, whether the American Civil Liberties Union version which allows any sexual activity between 'mutually consenting adults,' or the more vulgar version that simply insists, 'if it feels good, do it,' consists in part of a rebellion against restrictions no longer acceptable, paradigms no longer unchallengable. As a 'liberating' paradigm, the pleasure model needs

no defense. A more difficult question is whether it is the best paradigm, a question that has become increasingly urgent in the counter-revolutionary years of the last decade.

What ails the pleasure paradigm? Fifteen years ago Rollo May wrote in a best-selling book, *Love and Will*, that the sexual revolution has wrought its own forms of repression and unhappiness. His argument turns too much — in accord with that psychiatric genre — on the pathological, on the failures and victims of the revolution rather than its beneficiaries. Nevertheless, as both Freud and May warn us, with some justification, the plight of the neurotic may be a mirror — if a distorting mirror — of the pathology of everyday life. If the reproductive model makes sex too restrictive, the pleasure model makes it too conceptually permissive. Furthermore, any model of sexuality which makes masturbation as central or more central than intercourse, any model that refers to the other person in sexual desire as an 'object,' is an unlikely candidate for an adequate model of most of our sexual lives. Again, the paradigm may be liberating, but that does not mean that it is wholly adequate in itself.

Three main points of contention against the pleasure paradigm are the following:

(a) Aristotle argued 2500 years ago that pleasure is never the end of any of our activities, including sex. It is rather the accompaniment of good activity, the enjoyment that comes from being virtuous and fulfilling one's telos. Thus the question becomes; What is the telos of sex that it gives us so much pleasure? What is it that we satisfy? What do we want? To say that pleasure is the *telos* of sex is to confuse the play with its musical accompaniment. (In that context, a consideration of the very different moods of making love, and the music that one might play along with them, is revealing.)

(b) Sex is mutual activity; masturbation, no matter how satisfying, is not our paradigm. At least part of the answer to the questions in (a) above is that there is satisfaction in being with or 'having' another person, not as a 'secondary' concern, as Freud has it, but as a primary concern. The promiscuity and lack of discrimination of aroused males aside, it is not an 'object' of sex we seek, but a partner.

(c) Moreover, because sex depends on concepts and paradigms as well as basic biology, our sexual behavior is never 'without meaning.' Some meanings, however, are demeaning, and every sexual act has its significance. To think that one can indulge in the traditionally most powerful symbolic activity in almost every culture without its meaning anything is an extravagant self-deception, which, nonetheless, does not prevent its wide-spread appearance in libertines and rakes of all ages.

The Metaphysical Paradigm

The metaphysical paradigm is by far the most poetic of the four. We demand "meaningful" relationships; this paradigm provides meaning. The metaphysical paradigm is Romantic love or eros; its classic text is Plato's *Symposium* (thus I would also call it 'the Platonic paradigm,' which is not to be conflated with the asexual notion of 'Platonic love' that emerged 15 centuries later). In simpleminded parlance, it is the vision that two people are 'made for each other.' Protestant Christianity often supplements or even replaces the procreative paradigm with this metaphysical paradigm, thus shifting the religious as well as the sexual emphasis to love (*agape* not *eros*). The best picture of the metaphysical para-

digm, however, is Aristophanes' wonderful tale in the *Symposium*, of a double creature cleft in two ('like an apple') by Zeus and ever since trying to find its 'other half.' And indeed sex does sometimes seem like that, an experience so overwhelming and filled with significance that questions about the technology of contraception are not even plausible candidates for the defining features of our sexual conceptions.

The Intersubjective Paradigm

The intersubjective or communication paradigm is the paradigm I would most like to defend, but I will not try to do so here. What I will do here is offer it through an example, and then use it to conclude why it is that, in the course of my research. I have decided to minimize the seemingly obvious influence of sexual technology on sexual attitudes and concepts. The example comes from Jean-Paul Sartre. For Sartre, unlike Freud, sex is essentially interpersonal. He does not deny that masturbation is sexual; there just is not anything very interesting to say about it. It is not just the consequences of sex that count; it is its meaning. But where the metaphysical paradigm tends to take a rather rosy view of meaning, Sartre sees quite clearly that meanings can be different. His dark vision is summarized in his famous play, *Huis Clos* (*No Exit*): 'Hell is other people.' Sex, accordingly, is essentially conflict, or, rather, it is the central battleground of our interpersonal wars. Sex is intersubjective: it is primarily concerned not with pregnancy or pleasure nor even togetherness, but rather with effecting as definitively as possible the other person's constitution of both him or herself, and oneself as well. It is a battle of domination and freedom, Sartre tells us. Sex focuses the most inert parts of the body — breasts and buttocks — not for pleasure and not for the sake of reproduction but, symbolically, Sartre says, 'to turn the other into an object,' to reduce him or her to a mere body in one's control. Every caress is manipulation; pleasure is an instrument, and one's own pleasure — far from being the goal of sex — may easily be a distraction and a defeat.

I do not endorse this gloomy view which, if taken whole, would put most of us in the land of the voluntary chaste. But its structure I consider nothing less than revolutionary — more revolutionary than even Freud's pleasure paradigm and the much touted sexual revolutions of the past. What Sartre does for us is to shift the paradigm once again, to sex as expression. It is not one's own pleasure that counts primarily (though one need not be indifferent to it) nor is it even the pleasure one produces in one's partner. Mutual pleasure production is not the telos of sex, even when, as so often, it is the most explicit focus of sex. (Kant, who died a virgin, once described sex as 'mutual masturbation.' One can correct Sartre's

pessimistic picture by noting that love, too, is expressed through sex, but it is essential not to leap too quickly to the naive romanticism that says that only love is, or ought to be, expressed by sex. Sex is like a language, and there is no clear limit to the interpersonal feelings that it can express, given an adequate vocabulary and what we might call sexual literacy.

Conclusion: Conceptions and Conception

My purpose here has been to demonstrate the conceptual complexity of a phenomenon too often viewed as primitive and uncomplicated, as if only the consequences are complications, not sex itself. I have shown that there is much more to sexuality than an enjoyable and occasionally productive biological process, and that the technology of sexual consequences — if I may call it that — is only part of, not the essential determinant of, the nature of our sexual lives.

RICHARD WASSERSTROM

Is Adultery Immoral?

RICHARD WASSERSTROM *teaches philosophy at the University of California, Los Angeles. He has published widely in ethics and legal philosophy.*

MANY discussions of the enforcement of morality by the law take as illustrative of the problem under consideration the regulation of various types of sexual behavior by the criminal law. It was, for example,

the Wolfenden Report's recommendations concerning homosexuality and prostitution that led Lord Devlin to compose his now famous lecture, "The Enforcement of Morals." And that lecture in turn provoked important philosophical responses

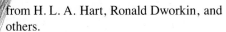

from H. L. A. Hart, Ronald Dworkin, and others.

Much, if not all, of the recent philosophical literature on the enforcement of morals appears to take for granted the immorality of the sexual behavior in question. The focus of discussion, at least, is whether such things as homosexuality, prostitution, and adultery ought to be made illegal even if they are immoral, and not whether they are immoral.

I propose in this paper to think about the latter, more neglected topic, that of sexual morality, and to do so in the following fashion. I shall consider just one kind of behavior that is often taken to be a case of sexual immorality — adultery. I am interested in pursuing at least two questions. First, I want to explore the question of in what respects adulterous behavior falls within the domain of morality at all. For this surely is one of the puzzles one encounters when considering the topic of sexual morality. It is often hard to see on what grounds much of the behavior is deemed to be either moral or immoral, for example, private homosexual behavior between consenting adults. I have purposely selected adultery because it seems a more plausible candidate for moral assessment than many other kinds of sexual behavior.

The second question I want to examine is that of what is to be said about adultery, without being especially concerned to stay within the area of morality. I shall endeavor, in other words, to identify and to assess a number of the major arguments that might be advanced against adultery. I believe that they are the chief arguments that would be given in support of the view that adultery is immoral, but I think they are worth considering even if some of them turn out to be nonmoral arguments and considerations.

A number of the issues involved seem to me to be complicated and difficult. In a number of places I have at best indicated where further philosophical exploration is required without having successfully conducted the exploration myself. The paper may very well be more useful as an illustration of how one might begin to think about the subject of sexual morality than as an elucidation of important truths about the topic.

Before I turn to the arguments themselves there are two preliminary points that require some clarification. Throughout the paper I shall refer to the immorality of such things as breaking a promise, deceiving someone, etc. In a very rough way, I mean by this that there is something morally wrong that is done in doing the action in question. I mean that the action is, in a strong sense of "*prima facie*," *prima facie* wrong or unjustified. I do not mean that it may never be right or justifiable to do the action; just that the fact that it is an action of this description always does count against the rightness of the action. I leave entirely open the question of what it is that makes actions of this kind immoral in this sense of "immoral."

The second preliminary point concerns what is meant or implied by the concept of adultery. I mean by "adultery" any case of extramarital sex, and I want to explore the arguments for and against extramarital sex, undertaken in a variety of morally relevant situations. Someone might claim that the concept of adultery is conceptually connected with the concept of immorality, and that to characterize behavior as adulterous is already to characterize it as immoral or unjustified in the sense described above. There may be something to this. Hence the importance of making it clear that I want to talk about extramarital sexual relations. If they are always immoral, this is something that must be shown by argument. If the concept of adultery does in some sense entail or imply immorality, I want to ask whether that connection is a rationally based one. If not all cases of extramarital sex are immoral (again, in the sense described above), then the concept of adultery should either be weakened accordingly or restricted to those classes of extramarital sex for which the predication of immorality is warranted.

One argument for the immorality of adultery might go something like this: what makes adultery immoral is that it involves the breaking of a promise, and what makes adultery seriously wrong is that it involves the breaking of an important promise. For, so the argument might continue, one of the things the two parties promise each other when they get married is that they will abstain from sexual relationships with third persons. Because of this promise both spouses quite reasonably entertain the expectation that the other will behave in conformity with it. Hence, when one of the parties has sexual intercourse with a third person he or she breaks that promise about sexual relationships which was made when the marriage was entered into, and defeats the reasonable expectations of exclusivity entertained by the spouse.

In many cases the immorality involved in breaching the promise relating to extramarital sex may be a good deal more serious than that involved in the breach of other promises. This is so because adherence to this promise may be of much greater importance to the parties than is adherence to many of the other promises given or received by them in their lifetime. The breaking of this promise may be much more hurtful and painful than is typically the case.

Why is this so? To begin with, it may have been difficult for the nonadulterous spouse to have kept the promise. Hence that spouse may feel the unfairness of having restrained himself or herself in the absence of reciprocal restraint having

been exercised by the adulterous spouse. In addition, the spouse may perceive the breaking of the promise as an indication of a kind of indifference on the part of the adulterous spouse. If you really cared about me and my feelings — the spouse might say — you would not have done this to me. And third, and related to the above, the spouse may see the act of sexual intercourse with another as a sign of affection for the other person and as an additional rejection of the nonadulterous spouse as the one who is loved by the adulterous spouse. It is not just that the adulterous spouse does not take the feelings of the spouse sufficiently into account, the adulterous spouse also indicates through the act of adultery affection for someone other than the spouse. I will return to these points later. For the present, it is sufficient to note that a set of arguments can be developed in support of the proposition that certain kinds of adultery are wrong just because they involve the breach of a serious promise which, among other things, leads to the intentional infliction of substantial pain by one spouse upon the other.

Another argument for the immorality of adultery focuses not on the existence of a promise of sexual exclusivity but on the connection between adultery and deception. According to this argument, adultery involves deception. And because deception is wrong, so is adultery.

Although it is certainly not obviously so, I shall simply assume in this paper that deception is always immoral. Thus the crucial issue for my purposes is the asserted connection between extramarital sex and deception. Is it plausible to maintain, as this argument does, that adultery always does involve deception and is on that basis to be condemned?

The most obvious person on whom deceptions might be practiced is the nonparticipating spouse; and the most obvious thing about which the nonparticipating spouse can be deceived is the existence of the adulterous act. One clear case of deception is that of lying. Instead of saying that the afternoon was spent in bed with A, the adulterous spouse asserts that it was spent in the library with B, or on the golf course with C.

There can also be deception even when no lies are told. Suppose, for instance, that a person has sexual intercourse with someone other than his or her spouse and just does not tell the spouse about it. Is that deception? It may not be a case of lying if, for example, the spouse is never asked by the other about the situation. Still, we might way, it is surely deceptive because of the promises that were exchanged at marriage. As we saw earlier, these promises provide a foundation for the reasonable belief that neither spouse will engage in sexual relationships with any other persons. Hence the failure to bring the fact of extramarital sex to the attention of the other spouse deceives that spouse about the present state of the marital relationship.

Adultery, in other words, can involve both active and passive deception. An adulterous spouse may just keep silent or, as is often the fact, the spouse may engage in an increasingly complex way of life devoted to the concealment of the facts from the nonparticipating spouse. Lies, half-truths, clandestine meetings, and the like may become a central feature of the adulterous spouse's existence. These are things that can and do happen, and when they do they make the case against adultery an easy one. Still, neither active nor passive deception is inevitably a feature of an extramarital relationship.

It is possible, though, that a more subtle but pervasive kind of deceptiveness is a feature of adultery. It comes about because of the connection in our culture between sexual intimacy and certain feelings of love and affection. The point can be made indirectly at first by seeing that one way in which we can, in our culture, mark off our close friends from our mere acquaintances is through the kinds of intimacies that we are prepared to share with them. I may, for instance, be willing to reveal my very private thoughts and emotions to my closest friends or to my wife, but to no one else. My sharing of these intimate facts about myself is from one perspective a way of making a gift to those who mean the most to me. Revealing these things and sharing them with those who mean the most to me is one means by which I create, maintain, and confirm those interpersonal relationships that are of most importance to me.

Now in our culture, it might be claimed, sexual intimacy is one of the chief currencies through which gifts of this sort are exchanged. One way to tell someone — particularly someone of the opposite sex — that you have feelings of affection and love for them is by allowing to them or sharing with them sexual behaviors that one doesn't share with the rest of the world. This way of measuring affection was certainly very much a part of the culture in which I matured. It worked something like this. If you were a girl, you showed how much you liked someone by the degree of sexual intimacy you would allow. If you liked a boy only a little, you never did more than kiss — and even the kiss was not very passionate. If you liked the boy a lot and if your feeling was reciprocated, necking, and possibly petting, was permissible. If the attachment was still stronger and you thought it might even become a permanent relationship, the sexual activity was correspondingly more intense and more intimate, although whether it would ever lead to sexual intercourse depended on whether the parties (and particularly the girl) accepted fully the prohibition on nonmarital sex. The situation for the boy was related, but not exactly the same. The assumption was that males did not naturally link sex with affection in the way in which females did. However, since women did, males had to take this into account. That is to say, because a woman would permit sexual intimacies only if she had feelings of affection for the male and only if those feelings were reciprocated, the male had to have and express those feelings, too, before sexual intimacies of any sort would occur.

The result was that the importance of a correlation between sexual intimacy and feelings of love and affection was taught by the culture and assimilated by those growing up in the culture. The scale of possible positive feelings toward persons of the other sex ran from casual liking at the one end to the love that was deemed essential to and characteristic of marriage at the other. The scale of possible sexual behavior ran from brief, passionless kissing or hand-holding at the one end to sexual intercourse at the other. And the correlation between the two scales was quite precise. As a result, any act of sexual intimacy carried substantial meaning with it, and no act of sexual intimacy was simply a pleasurable set of bodily sensations. Many such acts were, of course, more pleasurable to the participants because they were a way of saying what the participants feelings were. And sometimes they were less pleasurable for the same reason. The point is, however, that in any event sexual activity was much more than mere bodily enjoyment. It was not like eating a good meal, listening to good music, lying in the sun, or getting a pleasant back rub. It was behavior that meant a great deal concerning one's feelings for persons of the opposite sex in whom one was most interested and with whom one was most involved. It was

among the most authoritative ways in which one could communicate to another the nature and degree of one's affection.

If this sketch is even roughly right, then several things become somewhat clearer. To begin with, a possible rationale for many of the rules of conventional sexual morality can be developed. If, for example, sexual intercourse is associated with the kind of affection and commitment to another that is regarded as characteristic of the marriage relationship, then it is natural that sexual intercourse should be thought properly to take place between persons who are married to each other. And if it is thought that this kind of affection and commitment is only to be found within the marriage relationship, then it is not surprising that sexual intercourse should only be thought to be proper within marriage.

Related to what has just been said is the idea that sexual intercourse ought to be restricted to those who are married to each other as a means by which to confirm the very special feelings that spouses have for each other. Because the culture teaches that sexual intercourse means that the strongest of all feelings for each other are shared by the lovers, it is natural that persons who are married to each other should be able to say this to each other in this way. Revealing and confirming verbally that these feelings are present is one thing that helps to sustain the relationship; engaging in sexual intercourse is another.

In addition, this account would help to provide a framework within which to make sense of the notion that some sex is better than other sex. As I indicated earlier, the fact that sexual intimacy can be meaningful in the sense described tends to make it also the case that sexual intercourse can sometimes be more enjoyable than at other times. On this view, sexual intercourse will typically be more enjoyable where the strong feelings of affection are present than it will be where it is merely "mechanical." This is so in part because people enjoy being loved, especially by those whom they love. Just as we like to hear words of affection, so we like to receive affectionate behavior. And the meaning enhances the independently pleasurable behavior.

More to the point, moreover, an additional rationale for the prohibition on extramarital sex can now be developed. For given this way of viewing the sexual world, extramarital sex will almost always involve deception of a deeper sort. If the adulterous spouse does not in fact have the appropriate feelings of affection for the extramarital partner, then the adulterous spouse is deceiving that person about the presence of such feelings. If, on the other hand, the adulterous spouse does have the corresponding feelings for the extramarital partner but not toward the nonparticipating spouse, the adulterous spouse is very probably deceiving the nonparticipating spouse about the presence of such feelings toward that spouse. Indeed, it might be argued, whenever there is no longer love between the two persons who are married to each other, there is deception just because being married implies both to the participants and to the world that such a bond exists. Deception is inevitable, the argument might conclude, because the feelings of affection that ought to accompany any act of sexual intercourse can only be held toward one other person at any given time in one's life. And if this is so, then the adulterous spouse always deceives either the partner in adultery or the nonparticipating spouse about the existence of such feelings. Thus extramarital sex involves deception of this sort and is for this reason immoral even if no deception vis-à-vis the occurrence of the act of adultery takes place.

What might be said in response to the foregoing arguments? The first thing that might be said is that the account of the connection between sexual intimacy and feelings of affection is inaccurate. Not inaccurate in the sense that no one thinks of things that way, but in the sense that there is substantially more divergence of opinion than that account suggests. For example, the view I have delineated may describe reasonably accurately the concepts of the sexual world in which I grew up, but it does not capture the sexual *weltanschauung* of today's youth at all. Thus, whether or not adultery implies deception in respect to feelings depends very much on the persons who are involved and the way they look at the "meaning" of sexual intimacy.

Second, the argument leaves to be answered the question of whether it is desirable for sexual intimacy to carry the sorts of messages described above. For those persons for whom sex does have these implications, there are special feelings and sensibilities that must be taken into account. But it is another question entirely whether any valuable end — moral or otherwise — is served by investing sexual behavior with such significance. That is something that must be shown and not just assumed. It might, for instance, be the case that substantially more good than harm would come from a kind of demystification of sexual behavior: one that would encourage the enjoyment of sex more for its own sake and one that would reject the centrality both of the association of sex with love and of love with only one other person.

I regard these as two of the more difficult, unresolved issues that our culture faces today in respect to thinking sensibly about the attitudes toward sex and love that we should try to develop in ourselves and in our children. Much of the contemporary literature that advocates sexual liberation of one sort or another embraces one or the other of two different views about the relationship between sex and love.

One view holds that sex should be separated from love and affection. To be sure sex is probably better when the partners genuinely like and enjoy each other. But sex is basically an intensive, exciting sensuous activity that can be enjoyed in a variety of suitable settings with a variety of suitable partners. The situation in respect to sexual pleasure is no different from that of the person who knows and appreciates fine food and who can have a very satisfying meal in any number of good restaurants with any number of congenial companions. One question that must be settled here is whether sex can be so demystified; another, more important question is whether it would be desirable to do so. What would we gain and what might we lose if we all lived in a world in which an act of sexual intercourse was no more or less significant or enjoyable than having a delicious meal in a nice setting with a good friend? The answer to this question lies beyond the scope of this paper.

The second view seeks to drive the wedge in a different place. It is not the link between sex and love that needs to be broken; rather, on this view, it is the connection between love and exclusivity that ought to be severed. For a number of the reasons already given, it is desirable, so this argument goes, that sexual intimacy continue to be reserved to and shared with only those for whom one has very great affection. The mistake lies in thinking that any "normal" adult will only have those feelings toward one other adult during his or her lifetime — or even at any time in his or her life. It is the concept of adult love, not ideas about sex, that, on this view, needs demystification. What are

thought to be both unrealistic and unfortunate are the notions of exclusivity and possessiveness that attach to the dominant conception of love between adults in our and other cultures. Parents of four, five, six, or even ten children can certainly claim and sometimes claim correctly that they love all of their children, that they love them all equally, and that it is simply untrue to their feelings to insist that the numbers involved diminish either the quantity or the quality of their love. If this is an idea that is readily understandable in the case of parents and children, there is no necessary reason why it is an impossible or undesirable ideal in the case of adults. To be sure, there is probably a limit to the number of intimate, "primary" relationships that any person can maintain at any given time without the quality of the relationship being affected. But one adult ought surely be able to love two, three, or even six other adults at any one time without that love being different in kind or degree from that of the traditional, monogamous, lifetime marriage. And as between the individuals in these relationships, whether within a marriage or without, sexual intimacy is fitting and good.

The issues raised by a position such as this one are also surely worth exploring in detail and with care. Is there something to be called "sexual love" which is different from parental love or the nonsexual love of close friends? Is there something about love in general that links it naturally and appropriately with feelings of exclusivity and possession? Or is there something about sexual love, whatever that may be, that makes these feelings especially fitting here? Once again the issues are conceptual, empirical, and normative all at once: What is love? How could it be different? Would it be a good thing or a bad thing if it were different?

Suppose, though, that having delineated these problems we were now to pass them by. Suppose, moreover, we were to be persuaded of the possibility and the desirability of weakening substantially either the links between sex and love or the links between sexual love and exclusivity. Would it not then be the case that adultery could be free from all of the morally objectionable features described so far? To be more specific, let us imagine that a husband and wife have what is today sometimes characterized as an "open marriage." Suppose, that is, that they have agreed in advance that extramarital sex is — under certain circumstances — acceptable behavior for each to engage in. Suppose, that as a result there is no impulse to deceive each other about the occurrence or nature of any such relationships, and that no deception in fact occurs. Suppose, too, that there is no deception in respect to the feelings involved between the adulterous spouse and the extramarital partner. And suppose, finally, that one or the other or both of the spouses then has sexual intercourse in circumstances consistent with these understandings. Under this description, so the agreement might conclude, adultery is simply not immoral. At a minimum, adultery cannot very plausibly be condemned either on the ground that it involves deception or on the ground that it requires the breaking of a promise.

At least two responses are worth considering. One calls attention to the connection between marriage and adultery; the other looks to more instrumental arguments for the immorality of adultery. Both issues deserve further exploration.

One way to deal with the case of the "open marriage" is to question whether the two persons involved are still properly to be described as being married to each other. Part of the meaning of what it is for two persons to be married to each other, so this argument would go, is to have committed oneself to have sexual relationships only with one's spouse. Of course, it would be added, we know that that commitment is not always honored. We know that persons who are married to each other often do commit adultery. But there is a difference between being willing to make a commitment to marital fidelity, even though one may fail to honor that commitment, and not making the commitment at all. Whatever the relationship may be between the two individuals in the case described above, the absence of any commitment to sexual exclusivity requires the conclusion that their relationship is not a marital one. For a commitment to sexual exclusivity is a necessary although not a sufficient condition for the existence of a marriage.

Although there may be something to this suggestion, as it is stated it is too strong to be acceptable. To begin with, I think it is very doubtful that there are many, if any, *necessary* conditions for marriage; but even if there are, a commitment to sexual exclusivity is not such a condition.

To see that this is so, consider what might be taken to be some of the essential characteristics of a marriage. We might be tempted to propose that the concept of marriage requires the following: a formal ceremony of some sort in which mutual obligations are undertaken between two persons of the opposite sex; the capacity on the part of the persons involved to have sexual intercourse with each other; the willingness to have sexual intercourse only with each other; and feelings of love and affection between the two persons. The problem is that we can imagine relationships that are clearly marital and yet lack one or more of these features. For example, in our own society, it is possible for two persons to be married without going through a formal ceremony, as in the common-law marriages recognized in some jurisdictions. It is also possible for two persons to get married even though one or both lacks the capacity to engage in sexual intercourse. Thus, two very elderly persons who have neither the desire nor the ability to have intercourse can, nonetheless, get married, as can persons whose sexual organs have been injured so that intercourse is not possible. And we certainly know of marriages in which love was not present at the time of the marriage, as, for instance, in marriages of state and marriages of convenience.

Counterexamples not satisfying the condition relating to the abstention from extramarital sex are even more easily produced. We certainly know of societies and cultures in which polygamy and polyandry are practiced, and we have no difficulty in recognizing these relationships as cases of marriages. It might be objected, though, that these are not counterexamples because they are plural marriages rather than marriages in which sex is permitted with someone other than with one of the persons to whom one is married. But we also know of societies in which it permissible for married persons to have sexual relationships with persons to whom they were not married, for example, temple prostitutes, concubines, and homosexual lovers. And even if we knew of no such societies, the conceptual claim would still, I submit, not be well taken. For suppose all of the other indicia of marriage were present: suppose the two persons were of the opposite sex. Suppose they had the capacity and desire to have intercourse with each other, suppose they participated in a formal ceremony in which they understood themselves voluntarily to be entering into a relationship with each other in which substantial mu-

tual commitments were assumed. If all these conditions were satisfied, we would not be in any doubt about whether or not the two persons were married even though they had not taken on a commitment of sexual exclusivity and even though they had expressly agreed that extramarital sexual intercourse was a permissible behavior for each to engage in.

A commitment to sexual exclusivity is neither a necessary nor a sufficient condition for the existence of a marriage. It does, nonetheless, have this much to do with the nature of marriage: like the other indicia enumerated above, its presence tends to establish the existence of a marriage. Thus, in the absence of a formal ceremony of any sort, an explicit commitment to sexual exclusivity would count in favor of regarding the two persons as married. The conceptual role of the commitment to sexual exclusivity can, perhaps, be brought out through the following example. Suppose we found a tribe which had a practice in which all the other indicia of marriage were present but in which the two parties were *prohibited* ever from having sexual intercourse with each other. Moreover, suppose that sexual intercourse with others was clearly permitted. In such a case we would, I think, reject the idea that the two were married to each other and we would describe their relationship in other terms, for example, as some kind of formalized, special friendship relation — a kind of heterosexual "blood-brother" bond.

Compare that case with the following. Suppose again that the tribe had a practice in which all of the other indicia of marriage were present, but instead of a prohibition on sexual intercourse between the persons in the relationship there was no rule at all. Sexual intercourse was permissible with the person with whom one had this ceremonial relationship, but it was no more or less permissible than with a number of other persons to whom one was not so related (for instance, all consenting adults of the opposite sex). Although we might be in doubt as to whether we ought to describe the persons as married to each other, we would probably conclude that they were married and that they simply were members of a tribe whose views about sex were quite different from our own.

What all of this shows is that *a prohibition* on sexual intercourse between the two persons involved in a relationship is conceptually incompatible with the claim that the two of them are married. The *permissibility* of intramarital sex is a necessary part of the idea of marriage. But no such incompatibility follows simply from the added permissibility of extramarital sex.

These arguments do not, of course, exhaust the arguments for the prohibition on extramarital sexual relations. The remaining argument that I wish to consider — as I indicated earlier — is a more instrumental one. It seeks to justify the prohibition by virtue of the role that it plays in the development and maintenance of nuclear families. The argument, or set of arguments, might, I believe, go something like this.

Consider first a farfetched nonsexual example. Suppose a society were organized so that after some suitable age — say, 18, 19, or 20 — persons were forbidden to eat anything but bread and water with anyone but their spouse. Persons might still choose in such a society not to get married. Good food just might not be very important to them because they have underdeveloped taste buds. Or good food might be bad for them because there is something wrong with their digestive system. Or good food might be important to them, but they might decide that the enjoyment of good food would get in the

way of the attainment of other things that were more important. But most persons would, I think, be led to favor marriage in part because they preferred a richer, more varied, diet to one of bread and water. And they might remain married because the family was the only legitimate setting within which good food was obtainable. If it is important to have society organized so that persons will both get married and stay married, such an arrangement would be well suited to the preservation of the family, and the prohibitions relating to food consumption could be understood as fulfilling that function.

It is obvious that one of the more powerful human desires is the desire for sexual gratification. The desire is a natural one, like hunger and thirst, in the sense that it need not be learned in order to be present within us and operative upon us. But there is in addition much that we do learn about what the act of sexual intercourse is like. Once we experience sexual intercourse ourselves — and in particular once we experience orgasm — we discover that it is among the most intensive, short-term pleasures of the body.

Because this is so, it is easy to see how the prohibition upon extramarital sex helps to hold marriage together. At least during that period of life when the enjoyment of sexual intercourse is one of the desirable bodily pleasures, persons will wish to enjoy those pleasures. If one consequence of being married is that one is prohibited from having sexual intercourse with anyone but one's spouse, then the spouses in a marriage are in a position to provide an important source of pleasure for each other that is unavailable to them elsewhere in the society.

The point emerges still more clearly if this rule of sexual morality is seen as of a piece with the other rules of sexual morality. When this prohibition is coupled, for example, with the prohibition on non-marital sexual intercourse, we are presented with the inducement both to get married and to stay married. For if sexual intercourse is only legitimate within marriage, then persons seeking that gratification which is a feature of sexual intercourse are furnished explicit social directions for its attainment; namely marriage.

Nor, to continue the argument, is it necessary to focus exclusively on the bodily enjoyment that is involved. Orgasm may be a significant part of what there is to sexual intercourse, but it is not the whole of it. We need only recall the earlier discussion of the meaning that sexual intimacy has in our own culture to begin to see some of the more intricate ways in which sexual exclusivity may be connected with the establishment and maintenance of marriage as the primary heterosexual, love relationship. Adultery is wrong, in other words, because a prohibition on extramarital sex is a way to help maintain the institutions of marriage and the nuclear family.

Now I am frankly not sure what we are to say about an argument such as this one. What I am convinced of is that, like the arguments discussed earlier, this one also reveals something of the difficulty and complexity of the issues that are involved. So, what I want now to do — in the brief and final portion of this paper — is to try to delineate with reasonable precision what I take several of the fundamental, unresolved issues to be.

The first is whether this last argument is an argument for the *immorality* of extramarital sexual intercourse. What does seem clear is that there are differences between this argument and the ones considered earlier. The earlier arguments condemned adulterous behavior because it was behavior that involved breaking of a promise, taking unfair advantage, or deceiving another. To the degree to which the prohibition on extramarital sex can be supported by arguments which invoke considerations such as these, there is little question but that violations of the prohibition are properly regarded as immoral. And such a claim could be defended on one or both of two distinct grounds. The first is that things like promise-breaking and deception are just wrong. The second is that adultery involving promise-breaking or deception is wrong because it involves the straightforward infliction of harm on another human being — typically the nonadulterous spouse — who has a strong claim not to have that harm so inflicted.

The argument that connects the prohibition on extramarital sex with the maintenance and preservation of the institution of marriage is an argument for the instrumental value of the prohibition. To some degree this counts, I think, against regarding all violations of the prohibition as obvious cases of immorality. This is so partly because hypothetical imperatives are less clearly within the domain of morality than are categorical ones, and even more because instrumental prohibitions are within the domain of morality only if the end they serve or the way they serve it is itself within the domain of morality.

What this should help us see, I think, is the fact that the argument that connects the prohibition on adultery with the preservation of marriage is at best seriously incomplete. Before we ought to be convinced by it, we ought to have reasons for believing that marriage is a morally desirable and just social institution. And this is not quite as easy or obvious a task as it may seem to be. For the concept of marriage is, as we have seen, both a loosely structured and complicated one. There may be all sorts of intimate, interpersonal relationships which will resemble but not be identical with the typical marriage relationship presupposed by the traditional sexual morality. There may be a number of distinguishable sexual and loving arrangements which can all legitimately claim to be called *marriages*. The prohibitions of the traditional sexual morality may be effective ways to maintain some marriages and ineffective ways to promote and preserve others. The prohibitions of the traditional sexual morality may make good psychological sense if certain psychological theories are true, and they may be purveyors of immense psychological mischief if other psychological theories are true. The prohibitions of the traditional sexual morality may seem obviously correct if sexual intimacy carries the meaning that the dominant culture has often ascribed to it, and they may seem equally bizarre when sex is viewed through the perspective of the counterculture. Irrespective of whether instrumental arguments of this sort are properly deemed moral arguments, they ought not to fully convince anyone until questions like these are answered.

RICHARD D. MOHR

Gay Basics
Some Questions, Facts, and Values

RICHARD D. MOHR, *who teaches philosophy at the University of Illinois, is a scholar specializing in ancient Greek thought. His most recent book is* Gays/Justice: A Study of Ethics, Society and Law *(1988).*

Who Are Gays Anyway?

A recent Gallup poll found that only one in five Americans reports having a gay or lesbian acquaintance. This finding is extraordinary given the number of practicing homosexuals in America. Alfred Kinsey's 1948 study of the sex lives of 12,000 white males shocked the nation: 37 percent had at least one homosexual experience to orgasm in their adult lives; an additional 13 percent had homosexual fantasies to orgasm; 4 percent were exclusively homosexual in their practices; another 5 percent had virtually no heterosexual experience; and nearly 20 percent had at least as many homosexual as heterosexual experiences.

Two out of five men one passes on the street have had orgasmic sex with men. Every second family in the country has a member who is essentially homosexual and many more people regularly have homosexual experiences. Who are homosexuals? They are your friends, your minister, your teacher, your bank teller, your doctor, your mail carrier, your officemate, your roommate, your congressional representative, your sibling, parent, and spouse. They are everywhere, virtually all ordinary, virtually all unknown.

Several important consequences follow. First, the country is profoundly ignorant of the actual experience of gay people. Second, social attitudes and practices that are harmful to gays have a much greater overall harmful impact on society than is usually realized. Third, most gay people live in hiding — in the closet — making the "coming out" experience the central fixture of gay consciousness and invisibility the chief characteristic of the gay community.

Ignorance, Stereotype, and Morality

Ignorance about gays, however, has not stopped people from having strong opinions about them. The void which ignorance leaves has been filled with stereotypes. Society holds chiefly two groups of anti-gay stereotypes; the two are an oddly contradictory lot. One set of stereotypes revolves around alleged mistakes in an individual's gender identity: lesbians are women that want to be, or at least look and act like, men — bull dykes, diesel dykes; while gay men are those who want to be, or at least look and act like, women — queens, fairies, limp-wrists, nellies. These stereotypes of mismatched genders provide the materials through which gays and lesbians become the butts of ethniclike jokes. These stereotypes and jokes, though derisive, basically view gays and lesbians as ridiculous.

Another set of stereotypes revolves around gays as a pervasive, sinister, conspiratorial threat. The core stereotype here is the gay person as child molester, and more generally as sex-crazed maniac. These stereotypes carry with them fears of the very destruction of family and civilization itself. Now, that which is essentially ridiculous can hardly have such a staggering effect. Something must be afoot in this incoherent amalgam.

Sense can be made of this incoherence if the nature of stereotypes is clarified. Stereotypes are not *simply* false generalizations from a skewed sample of cases examined. Admittedly, false generalizing plays some part in the stereotypes a society holds. If, for instance, one takes as one's sample homosexuals who are in psychiatric hospitals or prisons, as was done in nearly all early investigations, not surprisingly one will probably find homosexuals to be of a crazed and criminal cast. Such false generalizations, though, simply confirm beliefs already held on independent grounds, ones that likely led the investigator to the prison and psychiatric ward to begin with. Evelyn Hooker, who in the late fifties carried out the first rigorous studies to use nonclinical gays, found that psychiatrists, when presented with case files including all the standard diagnostic psychological profiles — but omitting indications of sexual orientation — were unable to distinguish files of gays from those of straights, even though they believed gays to be crazy and supposed themselves to be experts in detecting craziness. These studies proved a profound embarrassment to the psychiatric establishment, the financial well-being of which has been substantially enhanced by "curing" allegedly insane gays. The studies led the way to the American Psychiatric Association finally in 1973 dropping homosexuality from its registry of mental illnesses. Nevertheless, the stereotype of gays as sick continues apace in the mind of America.

False generalizations *help maintain* stereotypes; they do not *form* them. As the history of Hooker's discoveries shows, stereotypes have a life beyond facts; their origin lies in a culture's ideology — the general system of beliefs by which it lives — and they are sustained across generations by diverse cultural transmissions, hardly any of which, including slang and jokes, even purport to have a scientific basis. Stereotypes, then, are not the products of bad science but are social constructions that perform central functions in maintaining society's conception of itself.

On this understanding, it is easy to see that the anti-gay stereotypes surrounding gender identification are chiefly means of reinforcing still powerful gender roles in society. If, as this stereotype presumes and condemns, one is free to choose one's social roles independently of gender, many guiding social divisions, both domestic and commercial, might be threatened. The socially gender-linked distinctions between breadwinner and homemaker, boss and secretary, doctor and nurse, protector and protected would blur. The accusations "dyke" and "fag" exist in significant part to keep women in their place and to prevent men from breaking ranks and ceding away theirs.

The stereotypes of gays as child molesters, sex-crazed maniacs, and civilization destroyers function to displace (socially irresolvable) problems from their actual source to a foreign (and so, is it thought, manageable) one. Thus the stereotype of child molester functions to give the family unit a false sheen of absolute innocence. It keeps the unit from being examined too closely for incest, child abuse, wife-battering, and the terrorism of constant threats. The stereotype teaches that the problems of the family are not internal to it, but external.

One can see these cultural forces at work in society's and the media's treatment of current reports of violence, especially domestic violence. When a mother kills her child or a father rapes his daughter—regular Section B fare even in major urban papers—this is never taken by reporters, columnists, or pundits as evidence that there is something wrong with heterosexuality or with traditional families. These issues are not even raised. But when a homosexual child molestation is reported it is taken as confirming evidence of the way homosexuals are. One never hears of heterosexual murders, but one regularly hears of "homosexual" ones. Compare the social treatment of Richard Speck's sexually motivated mass murder of Chicago nurses with that of John Wayne Gacy's murders of Chicago youths. Gacy was in the culture's mind taken as symbolic of gay men in general. To prevent the possibility that The Family was viewed as anything but an innocent victim in this affair, the mainstream press knowingly failed to mention that most of Gacy's adolescent victims were homeless hustlers. That knowledge would be too much for the six o'clock news and for cherished beliefs.

Because "the facts" largely don't matter when it comes to the generation and maintenance of stereotypes, the effects of scientific and academic research and of enlightenment generally will be, at best, slight and gradual in the changing fortunes of lesbians and gay men. If this account of stereotypes holds, society has been profoundly immoral. For its treatment of gays is a grand scale rationalization, a moral sleight-of-hand. The problem is not that society's usual standards of evidence and procedure in coming to judgments of social policy have been misapplied to gays; rather when it comes to gays, the standards themselves have simply been ruled out of court and disregarded in favor of mechanisms that encourage unexamined fear and hatred.

Are Gays Discriminated Against? Does It Matter?

Partly because lots of people suppose they don't know any gay people and partly through willful ignorance of its own workings, society at large is unaware of the many ways in which gays are subject to discrimination in consequence of widespread fear and hatred. Contributing to this social ignorance of discrimination is the difficulty for gay people, as an invisible minority, even to complain of discrimination. For if one is gay, to register a complaint would suddenly target one as a stigmatized person, and so in the absence of any protections against discrimination, would simply invite additional discrimination. Further, many people, especially those who are persistently downtrodden and so lack a firm sense of self to begin with, tend either to blame themselves for their troubles or to view injustice as a matter of bad luck rather than as indicating something wrong with society. The latter recognition would require doing something to rectify wrong and most people, especially the already beleaguered, simply aren't up to that. So for a number of reasons discrimination against gays, like rape, goes seriously underreported.

First, gays are subject to violence and harassment based simply on their perceived status rather than because of any actions they have performed. A recent extensive study by the National Gay Task Force found that over 90 percent of gays and lesbians had been victimized in some form on the basis of their sexual orientation. Greater than one in five gay men and nearly one in ten lesbians had been punched, hit, or kicked; a quarter of all gays had had objects thrown at them; a third had been chased; a third had been sexually harassed; and 14 percent had been spit on — all just for being perceived as gay.

The most extreme form of anti-gay violence is "queerbashing" — where groups of young men target a person who they suppose is a gay man and beat and kick him unconscious and sometimes to death amid a torrent of taunts and slurs.

Such seemingly random but in reality socially encouraged violence has the same social origin and function as lynchings of blacks — to keep a whole stigmatized group in line. As with lynchings of the recent past, the police and courts have routinely averted their eyes, giving their implicit approval to the practice.

Few such cases with gay victims reach the courts. Those that do are marked by inequitable procedures and results. Frequently judges will describe "queerbashers" as "just all-American boys." Recently a District of Columbia judge handed suspended sentences to queerbashers whose victim had been stalked, beaten, stripped at knife point, slashed, kicked, threatened with castration, and pissed on, because the judge thought the bashers were good boys at heart — after all, they went to a religious prep school.

Police and juries will simply discount testimony from gays; they typically construe assaults on and murders of gays as "justified" self-defense — the killer need only claim his act was a panicked response to a sexual overture. Alternatively, when guilt seems patent, juries will accept highly implausible "diminished capacity" defenses, as in the case of Dan White's 1978 assassination of openly gay San Francisco city councilman Harvey Milk: Hostess Twinkies made him do it.

These inequitable procedures and results collectively show that the life and liberty of gays, like those of blacks, simply count for less than the life and liberty of members of the dominant culture.

The equitable rule of law is the heart of an orderly society. The collapse of the rule of law for gays shows that society is willing to perpetrate the worst possible injustices against them. Conceptually there is only a difference in degree between the collapse of the rule of law and systematic extermination of members of a population simply for having some group status independent of any act an individual has performed. In the Nazi concentration camps, gays were forced to wear pink triangles as identifying badges, just as Jews were forced to wear yellow stars. In remembrance of that collapse of the rule of law, the pink triangle has become the chief symbol of the gay rights movement.

Gays are subject to widespread discrimination in employment — the very means by which one puts bread on one's table and one of the chief means by which individuals identify themselves to themselves and achieve personal dignity. Governments are leading offenders here. They do a lot of discriminating themselves, require that others do it (e.g., government contractors), and set precedents favoring discrimination in the private sector. The federal government explicitly discriminates against gays in the armed forces, the CIA, FBI, National Security Agency, and the state department. The federal government refuses to give security clearances to gays and so forces the country's considerable private sector military and aerospace contractors to fire known gay employees. State and local governments regularly fire gay teachers, policemen, firemen, social workers, and anyone who has contact with the public. Further, through licensing laws states officially bar gays from a vast array of occupations and professions — everything from doctors, lawyers, accountants, and nurses to hairdressers, morticians, and used car dealers. The American Civil Liberties Union's handbook *The Rights of Gay People* lists 307 such prohibited occupations.

Gays are subject to discrimination in a wide variety of other ways, including private-sector employment, public accommodations, housing, immigration and naturalization, insurance of all types, custody and adoption, and zoning regula-tions that bar "singles" or "nonrelated" couples. All of these discriminations affect central components of a meaningful life; some even reach to the means by which life itself is sustained. In half the states, where gay sex is illegal, the central role of sex to meaningful life is officially denied to gays.

All these sorts of discriminations also affect the ability of people to have significant intimate relations. It is difficult for people to live together as couples without having their sexual orientation perceived in the public realm and so becoming targets for discrimination. Illegality, discrimination, and the absorption by gays of society's hatred of them all interact to impede or block altogether the ability of gays and lesbians to create and maintain significant personal relations with loved ones. So every facet of life is affected by discrimination. Only the most compelling reasons could justify it.

But Aren't They Immoral?

Many people think society's treatment of gays is justified because they think gays are extremely immoral. To evaluate this claim, different senses of "moral" must be distinguished. Sometimes by "morality" is meant the overall beliefs affecting behavior in a society — it's mores, norms, and customs. On this understanding, gays certainly are not moral: lots of people hate them and social customs are designed to register widespread disapproval of gays. The problem here is that this sense of mo-rality is merely a *descriptive* one. On this understanding *every* society has a morality — even Nazi society, which had racism and mob rule as central features of its "morality," understood in this sense. What is needed in order to use the notion of morality to praise or condemn behavior is a sense of morality that is *prescriptive* or *normative* — a sense of morality whereby, for instance, the descriptive morality of the Nazis is found wanting.

As the Nazi example makes clear, that something is descriptively moral is nowhere near enough to make it normatively moral. A lot of people in a society saying something is good, even over eons, does not make it so. Our rejection of the long history of socially approved and state-enforced slavery is another good example of this principle at work. Slavery would be wrong even if nearly everyone liked it. So consistency and fairness require that we abandon the belief that gays are immoral simply because most people dislike or disapprove of gays or gay acts, or even because gay sex acts are illegal.

Furthermore, recent historical and anthropological research has shown that opinion about gays has been by no means universally negative. Historically, it has varied widely even within the larger part of the Christian era and even within the church itself. There are even societies — current ones — where homosexuality is not only tolerated but a universal compulsory part of social maturation. Within the last thirty years, American society has undergone a grand turnabout from deeply ingrained, near total condemnation to near total acceptance on two emotionally charged "moral" or "family" issues: contraception and divorce. Society holds its current descriptive morality of gays not because it has to, but because it chooses to.

If popular opinion and custom are not enough to ground moral condemnation of homosexuality, perhaps religion can. Such argument proceeds along two lines. One claims that the condemnation is a direct revelation of God, usually though the Bible; the other claims to be able to detect condemnation in God's plan as manifested in nature.

One of the more remarkable discoveries of recent gay research is that the Bible may not be as univocal in its condemnation of homosexuality as has been usually believed. Christ never mentions homosexuality. Recent interpreters of the Old Testament have pointed out that the story of Lot at Sodom is probably intended to condemn inhospitality rather than homosexuality. Further, some of the Old Testament condemnations of homosexuality seem simply to be ways of tarring those of the Israelites' opponents who happened to accept homosexual practices when the Israelites themselves did not. If so, the condemnation is merely a quirk of history and rhetoric rather than a moral precept.

What does seem clear is that those who regularly cite the Bible to condemn an activity like homosexuality do so by reading it selectively. Do ministers who cite what they take to be condemnations of homosexuality in Leviticus maintain in their lives all the hygienic and dietary laws of Leviticus? If they cite the story of Lot at Sodom to condemn homosexuality, do they also cite the story of Lot in the cave to praise incestuous rape? It seems then not that the Bible is being used to ground condemnations of homosexuality as much as society's dislike of homosexuality is being used to interpret the Bible.

Even if a consistent portrait of condemnation could be gleaned from the Bible, what social significance should it be given? One of the guiding principles of society, enshrined in the Constitution as a check against the government, is that decisions affecting social policy are not made on religious grounds. If the real ground of the alleged immorality invoked by governments to discriminate against gays is religious (as it has explicitly been even in some recent court cases involving teachers and guardians), then one of the major commitments of our nation is violated.

But Aren't They Unnatural?

The most noteworthy feature of the accusation of something being unnatural (where a moral rather than an advertising point is being made) is that the plaint is so infrequently made. One used to hear the charge leveled against abortion, but that has pretty much faded as anti-abortionists have come to lay all their chips on the hope that people will come to view abortion as murder. Incest used to be considered unnatural but discourse now usually assimilates it to the moral machinery of rape and violated trust. The charge comes up now in ordinary discourse only against homosexuality. This suggests that the charge is highly idiosyncratic and has little, if any, explanatory force. It fails to put homosexuality in a class with anything else so that one can learn by comparison with clear cases of the class just exactly what it is that is allegedly wrong with it.

Though the accusation of unnaturalness looks whimsical, in actual ordinary discourse when applied to homosexuality, it is usually delivered with venom aforethought. It carries a high emotional charge, usually expressing disgust and evincing queasiness. Probably it is nothing but an emotional charge. For people get equally disgusted and queasy at all sorts of things that are perfectly natural — to be expected in nature apart from artifice — and that could hardly be fit subjects for moral condemnation. Two typical examples in current American culture are some people's responses to mothers' suckling in public and to women who do not shave body hair. When people have strong emotional reactions, as they do in these cases, without being able to give good reasons for them, we think of them not as operating morally, but rather as being obsessed and manic. So the feelings of disgust that some people have to gays will hardly ground a charge of immorality. People fling the term "unnatural" against gays in the same breath and with the same force as they call gays "sick" and "gross." When they do this, they give every appearance of being neurotically fearful and incapable of reasoned discourse.

When "nature" is taken in *technical* rather than ordinary usages, it looks like the notion also will not ground a charge of homosexual immorality. When unnatural means "by artifice" or "made by humans," it need only be pointed out that virtually everything that is good about life is unnatural in this sense, that the chief feature that distinguishes people from other animals is their very ability to make over the world to meet their needs and desires, and that their well-being depends upon these departures from nature. On this understanding of human nature and the natural, homosexuality is perfectly unobjectionable.

Another technical sense of natural is that something is natural and so, good, if it fulfills some function in nature. Homosexuality on this view is unnatural because it allegedly violates the function of genitals, which is to produce babies. One problem with this view is that lots of bodily parts have lots of functions and just because some one activity can be fulfilled by only one organ (say, the mouth for eating) this activity does not condemn other functions of the organ to immorality (say, the mouth for talking, licking stamps, blowing bubbles, or having sex). So the possible use of the genitals to produce children does not, without more, condemn the use of the genitals for other purposes, say, achieving ecstasy and intimacy.

The functional view of nature will only provide a morally condemnatory sense to the unnatural if a thing which might have many uses has but one proper function to the exclusion of other possible functions. But whether this is so cannot be established simply by looking at the thing. For what is seen is all its possible functions. The notion of function seemed like it might ground moral authority, but instead it turns out that moral authority is needed to define proper function. Some people try to fill in this moral authority by appeal to the "design" or "order" of an organ, saying, for instance, that the genitals are designed for the purpose of procreation. But these people cheat intellectually if they do not make explicit *who* the designer and orderer is. If it is God, we are back to square one—holding others accountable for religious beliefs.

Further, ordinary moral attitudes about childbearing will not provide the needed supplement which in conjunction with the natural function view of bodily parts would produce a positive obligation to use the genitals for procreation. Society's attitude toward a childless couple is that of pity not censure—even if the couple could have children. The pity may be an unsympathetic one, that is, not registering a course one would choose *for oneself*, but this does not make it a course one would *require* of others. The couple who discovers they cannot have children are viewed not as having thereby had a debt canceled, but rather as having to forgo some of the richness of life, just as a quadriplegic is viewed not as absolved from some moral obligation to hop, skip, and jump, but as missing some of the richness of life. Consistency requires then that, at most, gays who do not or cannot have children are to

be pitied rather than condemned. What *is* immoral is the willful preventing of people from achieving the richness of life. Immorality in this regard lies with those social customs, regulations, and statutes that prevent lesbians and gay men from establishing blood or adoptive families, not with gays themselves.

Sometimes people attempt to establish authority for a moral obligation to use bodily parts in a certain fashion simply by claiming that moral laws are natural laws and vice versa. On this account, inanimate objects and plants are good in that they follow natural laws by necessity, animals by instinct, and persons by a rational will. People are special in that they must first discover the laws that govern them. Now, even if one believes the view—dubious in the post-Newtonian, post-Darwinian world—that natural laws in the usual sense ($E = mc^2$, for instance) have some moral content, it is not at all clear how one is to discover the laws in nature that apply to people.

On the one hand, if one looks to people themselves for a model—and looks hard enough—one finds amazing variety, including homosexuality as a social ideal (upper-class fifty-century Athens) and even as socially mandatory (Melanesia today). When one looks to people, one is simply unable to strip away the layers of social custom, history, and taboo in order to see what's really there to any degree more specific than that people are the creatures that make over their world and are capable of abstract thought. That this is so should raise doubts that neutral principles are to be found in human nature that will condemn homosexuality.

On the other hand, if one looks to nature apart from people for models, the possibilities are staggering. There are fish that change gender over their lifetimes: should we "follow nature" and be operative transsexuals? Orangutans, genetically our next of kin, live completely solitary lives without social organization of any kind: ought we to "follow nature" and be hermits? There are many species where only two members per generation reproduce: should we be bees? The search in nature for people's purpose, far from finding sure models for action, is likely to leave one morally rudderless.

But Aren't Gays Willfully the Way They Are?

It is generally conceded that if sexual orientation is something over which an individual — for whatever reason — has virtually no control, then discrimination against gays is especially deplorable, as it is against racial and ethnic classes, because it holds people accountable without regard for anything they themselves have done. And to hold a person accountable for that over which the person has no control is a central form of prejudice.

Attempts to answer the question whether or not sexual orientation is something that is reasonably thought to be within one's own control usually appeal simply to various claims of the biological or "mental" sciences. But the ensuing debate over genes, hormones, twins, early childhood development, and the like, is as unnecessary as it is currently inconclusive. All that is needed to answer the question is to look at the actual experience of gays in current society and it becomes fairly clear that sexual orientation is not likely a matter of choice. For coming to have a homosexual identity simply does not have the same sort of structure that decision making has.

On the one hand, the "choice" of the gender of a sexual partner does not seem to express a trivial desire that might be as easily well fulfilled by a simple substitu-

tion of the desired object. Picking the gender of a sex partner is decidedly dissimilar, that is, to such activities as picking a flavor of ice cream. If an ice-cream parlor is out of one's flavor, one simply picks another. And if people were persecuted, threatened with jail terms, shattered careers, loss of family and housing, and the like, for eating, say, rocky road ice cream, no one would ever eat it; everyone would pick another easily available flavor. That gay people abide in being gay even in the face of persecution shows that being gay is not a matter of easy choice.

On the other hand, even if establishing a sexual orientation is not like making a relatively trivial choice, perhaps it is nevertheless relevantly like making the central and serious life choices by which individuals try to establish themselves as being of some type. Again, if one examines gay experience, this seems not to be the case. For one never sees anyone setting out to become a homosexual, in the way one does see people setting out to become doctors, lawyers, and bricklayers. One does not find "gays-to-be" picking some end — "At some point in the future, I want to become a homosexual" — and then setting about planning and acquiring the ways and means to that end, in the way one does see people deciding that they want to become lawyers, and then sees them plan what courses to take and what sort of temperaments, habits, and skills to develop in order to become lawyers. Typically gays-to-be simply find themselves having homosexual encounters and yet at least initially resisting quite strongly the identification of being homosexual. Such a person even very likely resists have such encounters, but ends up having them anyway. Only with time, luck, and great personal effort, but sometimes never, does the person gradually come to accept her or his orientation, to view it as a given material condition of life, coming as materials do with certain capacities and limitations. The person begins to act in accordance with his or her orientation and its capacities, seeing its actualization as a requisite for an integrated personality and as a central component of personal well-being. As a result, the experience of coming out to oneself has for gays the basic structure of a discovery, not the structure of a choice. And far from signaling immorality, coming out to others affords one of the few remaining opportunities in ever more bureaucratic, mechanistic, and socialistic societies to manifest courage.

How Would Society at Large Be Changed If Gays Were Socially Accepted?

Suggestions to change social policy with regard to gays are invariably met with claims that to do so would invite the destruction of civilization itself: after all, isn't that what did Rome in? Actually Rome's decay paralleled not the flourishing of homosexuality but its repression under the later Christianized emperors. Predictions of American civilization's imminent demise have been as premature as they have been frequent. Civilization has shown itself rather resilient here, in large part because of the country's traditional commitments to a respect for privacy, to individual liberties, and especially to people minding their own business. These all give society an open texture and the flexibility to try out things to see what works. And because of this one now need not speculate about what changes reforms in gay social policy might bring to society at large. For many reforms have already been tried.

Half the states have decriminalized homosexual acts. Can you guess which of the following states still have sodomy

laws: Wisconsin, Minnesota; New Mexico, Arizona; Vermont, New Hampshire; Nebraska, Kansas. One from each pair does and one does not have sodomy laws. And yet one would be hard pressed to point out any substantial difference between the members of each pair. (If you're interested, it is the second of each pair with them.) Empirical studies have shown that there is no increase in other crimes in states that have decriminalized. Further, sodomy laws are virtually never enforced. They remain on the books not to "protect society" but to insult gays, and for that reason need to be removed.

Neither has the passage of legislation barring discrimination against gays ushered in the end of civilization. Some 50 counties and municipalities, including some of the country's largest cities (like Los Angeles and Boston), have passed such statutes and among the states and colonies Wisconsin and the District of Columbia have model protective codes. Again, no more brimstone has fallen in these places than elsewhere. Staunchly anti-gay cities, like Miami and Houston, have not been spared the AIDS crisis.

Berkeley, California, has even passed domestic partner legislation giving gay couples the same rights to city benefits as married couples, and yet Berkeley has not become more weird then it already was.

Seemingly hysterical predictions that the American family would collapse if such reforms would pass proved false, just as the same dire predictions that the availability of divorce would lessen the ideal and desirability of marriage proved completely unfounded. Indeed if current discriminations, which drive gays into hiding and into anonymous relations, were lifted, far from seeing gays raze American families, one would see gays forming them.

Virtually all gays express a desire to have a permanent lover. Many would like to raise or foster children—perhaps those alarming numbers of gay kids who have been beaten up and thrown out of their "families" for being gay. But currently society makes gay coupling very difficult. A life of hiding is a pressure-cooker existence not easily shared with another. Members of non-gay couples are here asked to imagine what it would take to erase every trace of their own sexual orientation for even just a week.

Even against oppressive odds, gays have shown an amazing tendency to nest. And those gay couples who have survived the odds show that the structure of more usual couplings is not a matter of destiny but of personal responsibility. The so-called basic unit of society turns out not to be a unique immutable atom, but can adopt different parts, be adapted to different needs, and even be improved. Gays might even have a thing or two to teach others about division of labor, the relation of sensuality and intimacy, and stages of development in such relations.

If discrimination ceased, gay men and lesbians would enter the mainstream of the human community openly and with self-respect. The energies that the typical gay person wastes in the anxiety of leading a day-to-day existence of systematic disguise would be released for use in personal flourishing. From this release would be generated the many spinoff benefits that accrue to a society when its individual members thrive.

Society would be richer for acknowledging another aspect of human richness and diversity. Families with gay members would develop relations based on truth and trust rather than lies and fear. And the heterosexual majority would be better off for knowing that they are no longer trampling their gay friends and neighbors.

Finally and perhaps paradoxically, in extending to gays the rights and benefits it has reserved for its dominant culture, America would confirm its deeply held vision of itself as a morally progressing nation, a nation itself advancing and serving as a beacon for others—especially with regard to human rights. The words with which our national pledge ends—"with liberty and justice for all"—are not a description of the present but a call for the future. Ours is a nation given to a prophetic political rhetoric which acknowledges that morality is not arbitrary and that justice is not merely the expression of the current collective will. It is this vision that led the black civil rights movement to its successes. Those congressmen who opposed that movement and its centerpiece, the 1964 Civil Rights Act, on obscurantist grounds, but who lived long enough and were noble enough, came in time to express their heartfelt regret and shame at what they had done. It is to be hoped and someday to be expected that those who now grasp at anything to oppose the extension of that which is best about America to gays will one day feel the same.

AUDRE LORDE

Scratching the Surface
Some Notes on Barriers to Women and Loving

AUDRE LORDE *A black lesbian feminist poet, has written extensively in prose and poetry on feminism, heterosexism, racism, and the interrelation of oppressions.*

Racism: *The belief in the inherent superiority of one race over all others and thereby the right to dominance.*

Sexism: *The belief in the inherent superiority of one sex and thereby the right to dominance.*

Heterosexism: *The belief in the inherent superiority of one pattern of loving and thereby its right to dominance.*

Homophobia: *The fear of feelings of love for members of one's own sex and therefore hatred of those feelings in others.*

THE above forms of human blindness stem from the same root — the inability to recognize or tolerate the notion of difference as a beneficial and dynamic human force, and one which is enriching rather than threatening to the defined self.

To a large degree, at least verbally, the black community has moved beyond the "two steps behind her man" mode of sexual relations sometimes mouthed as desirable during the sixties. This was a time when the myth of the black matriarchy as a social disease was being presented by racist forces for an excuse or diversion, to redirect our attentions away from the real sources of black oppression.

For black women as well as black men, it is axiomatic that if we do not define ourselves for ourselves, we will be defined by others — for their use and to our detriment. The development of self-defined black women, ready to explore and pursue our power and interests within our communities, is a vital component in the war for black liberation. The image of the Angolan woman with a baby on one arm and a gun in the other is neither romantic nor fanciful. Black women in this country coming together to examine our sources of strength and support, and to recognize our common social, cultural, emotional, and political interests, is a development which can only contribute to the power of the black community as a whole. For it is only through the coming together of self-actualized individuals, female and male, that any real advances can be made. The old sexual power-relationships based on a dominant/subordinate model between unequals have not served us as a people, nor as individuals.

Black women who define ourselves and our goals beyond the sphere of a sexual relationship can bring to any endeavor the realized focus of a completed and therefore empowered individual. Black women and black men who recognize that the development of their particular strengths and interests does not diminish the other, do not diffuse their energies fighting for control over each other. We focus our attentions against the real economic, political and social forces at the heart of this society which are ripping ourselves and our children and our worlds apart.

Increasingly, despite opposition, black women are coming together to explore and to alter those manifestations of our society which oppress us in ways different from the oppression of black men. This is no threat to black men, and is only seen as one by those black men who choose to embody within themselves those same manifestations of female oppression. For instance, enforced sterilization and unavailable abortions are tools of oppression against black women, as is rape. Only to those black men who are unclear as to the paths of their own self-definition can the self-actualization and self-protective bonding of black women be seen as a threatening development.

Today, the red herring of homophobia and lesbian-baiting is being used in the black community to obscure the true double face of racism/sexism. Black women sharing close ties with each other, politically or emotionally, are not the enemies of black men. Too frequently, however, an attempt to rule by fear tactics is practiced by some black men against those black women who are more ally than enemy. These tactics are sometimes expressed as threats of emotional rejection: "Their poetry wasn't too bad but I couldn't take all those lezzies (lesbians)." The man who says this is warning every black woman present who is interested in a relationship with men — and most black women are — that (1) if she wishes to have her work considered she must eschew any other allegiance except to him and (2) any woman who wishes his friendship and/or support had better not be "tainted" by woman-identified interests.

If such threats of labelling, vilification and/or emotional isolation are not enough to bring black women docilely into camp as followers, or persuade them to avoid each other as political or emotional support for each other, then the rule by terror can be expressed physically, as on the campus of a New York college recently, where black women sought to come together around feminist concerns. Violently threatening phone calls were made to those black women who dared to explore the possibilities of a feminist connection with non-black women. Some of these women, intimidated by these threats and the withdrawal of male approval, did turn against their sisters. When threats did not prevent the attempted coalition of black feminists, the resulting hysteria left some black women beaten and raped. Whether the threats by black men actually led to these assaults, or merely encouraged the climate of hostility within which they could occur, the results upon the women attacked were the same.

Wars and jails have decimated the ranks of black males of marriageable age. The fury of many black heterosexual women against white women who date black men is rooted in this unequal sexual equation, since whatever threatens to widen that equation is deeply and articulately resented. But this is essentially unconstructive resentment because it extends sideways, and can never result in true progress on the issue, because it does not question the vertical lines of power or authority, nor the sexist assumptions which dictate the terms of the competition. And the racism of white women can be better addressed where it is less complicated by their own sexual oppression. In this situation it is not the non-black woman who calls the tune, but rather the black man who turns away from himself in his sisters, or who, through a fear borrowed from white men, reads her strength not as a resource but as challenge.

All too often the message comes loud and clear to black women from black men: "I am the prize and there are not too many of me and remember I can always go elsewhere. So if you want me you'd better stay in your place which is away from each other, or I will call you lesbian and wipe you away." Black women are programmed to define themselves within this male attention and to compete with each other for it, rather than to recognize their common interests.

The tactic of encouraging horizontal or lateral hostility to becloud the real and more pressing issues of oppression is by no means new, nor limited to relations between women. The same tactic is used to continue or exacerbate the separation between black women and black men. In discussions around the hiring and firing of black faculty at universities, the charge is frequently heard that black women are more easily hired than are black men. For this reason, black women's problems of promotion and tenure are not to be considered as important, since they are only "taking jobs away from black men." Here again, energy is being wasted on battles which extend horizontally, over the pitifully few crumbs allowed us, rather than being used in a joining of forces to fight for a more realistic representation of black faculty. This would be a vertical battle against the racist policies of the academic structure itself, one which could result in real power and change. And of course, it is the structure at the top which desires changelessness, and so profits from these apparently endless kitchen wars.

Instead of keeping our attentions focused upon the real enemies, enormous energy is being wasted in the black community today by both black men and het-

erosexual black women, in anti-lesbian hysteria. Yet women-identified women — those who sought their own destinies and attempted to execute them in the absence of male support — have been around in all of our communities for a long time. As Yvonne Flowers of York College pointed out in a recent discussion, the unmarried aunt, childless or otherwise, whose home and resources were often a welcome haven for different members of the family, was a familiar figure in many of our childhoods. And within the homes of our black communities today, it is not the black lesbian who is battering and raping our under-age girl-children, out of displaced and sickening frustration.

The black lesbian has come under increasing attack from both black men and heterosexual black women. In the same way that the existence of the self-defined black woman is no threat to the self-defined black man, the black lesbian is an emotional threat only to those black women who are unsure of, or unable to, express their feelings of kinship and love for other black women, in any meaningful way. For so long, we have been encouraged to view each other with suspicion, as eternal competitors, or as the visible face of our own self-rejection.

But traditionally, black women have always bonded together in support of each other, however uneasily and in the face of whatever other allegiances which militated against that bonding. We have banded together with each other for wisdom and strength and support, even when it was only a relationship to one man. We need only look at the close — although highly complex and involved — relationship between African co-wives; or at the Amazon warriors of ancient Dahomey, who fought together as the Kings' main and most ferocious bodyguard. We need only look at the more promising power wielded by the West African Market Women Associations of today, and those governments which have risen and fallen at their pleasure.

In a verbatim retelling of her life, a 92-year-old Efik-Ibibio woman of Nigeria recalls her love for another woman:

> I had a woman friend to whom I revealed my secrets. She was very fond of keeping secrets to herself. We acted as husband and wife. We always moved hand in glove and my husband and hers knew about our relationship. The villagers nicknamed us twin sisters. When I was out of gear with my husband, she would be the one to restore peace. I often sent my children to go and work for her in return for her kindnesses to me. My husband being more fortunate to get more pieces of land than her husband, allowed some to her, even though she was not my co-wife.

The Fon of Dahomey still have 12 different kinds of marriage, one of which is known as "giving the goat to the buck," where a woman of independent means marries another woman who then may or may not bear children, all of whom will belong to the blood line of the other woman. Some marriages of this kind are arranged to provide heirs for women of means who wish to remain "free," and some are homosexual relationships. Marriages of this kind occur throughout Africa, in several different places among different peoples.

In all of these cases, the women involved are recognized parts of their communities, evaluated not by their sexuality but by their respective places within the community.

While a piece of each black woman remembers the old ways of another place and time, when we enjoyed each other in a sisterhood of work and play and power, other pieces of us, less functional, eye each other with suspicion as we have been programmed to do. In the interests of separation, and to keep us out of touch with our own power, black women have been taught to view each other as always suspect, heartless competitors for the scarce male, the all-important prize that will legitimize our existence. This becomes an ultimate and dehumanizing denial of self, no less lethal than that dehumanization of racism which is so closely allied to it.

If the recent hysterical rejection of lesbians in the black community is based solely upon an aversion to the idea of sexual contact between members of the same sex (a contact existing for ages in most of the female compounds across the African continent, from reports) why then is the idea of sexual contact between black men so much more easily accepted, or unremarked? Is the reality of the imagined threat the existence of a self-motivated, self-defined black woman who will not fear nor suffer some terrible retribution from the gods because she does not necessarily seek her face in a man's eyes, even if he has fathered her children? Female-headed households in the black community are not always situations by default.

The distortion of relationship which says "I disagree with you, or I do not share your lifestyle, so I must destroy you" leaves black people with basically uncreative victories, defeated in any common struggle. That is jugular vein psychology, based on a fallacy which holds that your assertion or affirmation of your self must mean an attack upon my self—or that my defining myself will somehow prevent or retard your self-definition. The supposition that one sex needs the other's acquiescence in order to exist prevents both from moving together as self-defined persons toward a common goal.

This is a prevalent mistake among oppressed peoples, and is based upon the false notion that there is only a limited and particular amount of freedom that must be divided up between us, with the largest and juiciest pieces going as spoils to the victor or the stronger. So instead of joining together to fight for more, we quarrel between ourselves for a larger slice of the one pie. Black women fight between ourselves over men instead of pursuing and using who we are and our strengths; black women and men fight between ourselves over who has more of a right to freedom, instead of seeing each other's struggles as part of our own; black and white women fight between ourselves over who is the more oppressed, instead of seeing those areas in which our causes are the same. (Of course, this last separation is worsened by the intransigent racism that white women too often fail to, or cannot, address in themselves.)

As black women we have the right and responsibility to define ourselves, and to seek our allies in common cause with black men against racism, and with white women against sexism. But most of all as black women we have a right to recognize each other without fear and to love where we choose, for both homosexual and heterosexual black women today share a history of bonding and strength that our particular sexual preferences should not blind us to.

G. L. SIMONS

Is Pornography Beneficial?

G. L. SIMONS *is an English author whose many works include the book,* A Place for Pleasure: A History of the Brothel, *published in 1975.*

THE heresy (to some ears) that pornography is harmless is compounded by the even greater impiety that it may be beneficial. Some of us are managing to adjust to the notion that pornography is unlikely to bring down the world in moral ruin, but the idea that it may actually do good is altogether another thing. When we read of Professor Emeritus E. T. Rasmussen, a pioneer of psychological studies in Denmark, and a government adviser, saying that there is a possibility 'that pornography can be beneficial', many of us are likely to have *mixed* reactions, to say the least. In fact this thesis can be argued in a number of ways.

The simplest approach is to remark that people enjoy it. This can be seen to be true whether we rely on personal testimony or the most respectable index of all in capitalist society — 'preparedness to pay'. The appeal that pornography has for many people is hardly in dispute, and in a more sober social climate that would be justification enough. Today we are not quite puritan enough to deny that *pleasure* has a worthwhile place in human life: not many of us object to our food being tasty or our clothes being attractive. It was not always like this. In sterner times it was *de regueur* to prepare food without spices and to wear the plainest clothes. The cult of puritanism reached its apotheosis in the most fanatical asceticism, where it was fashionable for holy men to wander off into a convenient desert and neglect the body to the point of cultivating its lice as 'pearls of God'. In such a bizarre philosophy pleasure was not only condemned in its sexual manifestations but in all areas where the body could conceivably take satisfaction. These days we are able to countenance pleasure in most fields but in many instances still the case for *sexual* pleasure has to be argued.

Pleasure is not of course its own justification. If it clearly leads to serious malaise, early death, or the *dis*pleasure of others, then there is something to be said against it. But the serious consequences have to be demonstrated: it is not enough to condemn certain forms of pleasurable experience on the grounds of *possible* ill effect. With such an approach *any* human activity could be censured and freedom would have no place. In short, if something is pleasurable and its bad effects are small or nonexistent then it is to be encouraged: opposition to such a creed should be recognized as an unwholesome antipathy to human potential. Pleasure is a good except where it is harmful (and where the harmfulness is *significant*). . . .

That pornography is enjoyable to many people is the first of the arguments in its favour. In any other field this would be argument enough. It is certainly sufficient to justify many activities that have — unlike a taste for pornography — demonstrably harmful consequences. Only in a sexually neurotic society could a tool for heightening sexual enjoyment be regarded as reprehensible and such as to warrant suppression by law. The position is well summarized in the *first* of the Arts Council's twelve reasons for advocating the repeal of the Obscenity Publications Acts:

> It is not for the State to prohibit private citizens from choosing what they may or may not enjoy in literature or art unless there were incontrovertible evidence that the result would be injurious to society. There is no such evidence.

A further point is that availability of pornography may *aid*, rather than frustrate normal sexual development. Thus in 1966, for example, the New Jersey Committee for the Right to Read presented the findings of a survey conducted among nearly a thousand psychiatrists and psychologists of that state. Amongst the various personal statements included was the view that 'sexually stimulating materials' might help particular people develop a normal sex drive. In similar spirit, Dr. John Money writes that pornography 'may encourage normal sexual development and broadmindedness', a view that may not sound well to the anti-pornographers. And even in circumstances where possible dangers of pornography are pointed out conceivable good effects are sometimes acknowledged. In a paper issued by The Danish Forensic Medicine Council it is pointed out that neurotic and sexually shy people may, by reading pornographic descriptions of normal sexual activity, be freed from some of their apprehension regarding sex and may thereby attain a freer and less frustrated attitude to the sexual side of life.

There is related evidence to show that suppression of sexual interest in the home is connected with distorted sexual development leading to perverted or criminal activity. In a household hostile to pornography one would expect to find a degree of sexual tension not conducive to the wholesome sexual growth of young people. The Kinsey *Sex Offenders* report, already mentioned, shows that offenders have, on average, less contact with explicitly sexual material than do other members of the community. And in the Hughes study (1970), quoted by the U.S. Commission, we find that conversation with sexual neurotics almost invariably reveals 'that in their childhood any mention of sexual subjects was tabooed in their homes', and the impression is created that they have been told 'too little about sex life and that *they have read too little rather than too much erotic literature*' (my italics). . . .

It can also be argued, as part of the view that pornography *aids* normal sexual development, that availability of explicit erotica *protects* young people — a point somewhat contrary to the expectations of the traditional anti-pornographers. Apart from the possibility that potential sex criminals may have their unwholesome drives neutralized by pornography — a possibility considered later — it is also likely that availability of sexual material prevents the growth in young people of distorted and obsessive attitudes. The Danish Jergen Langkilde, a former Crown prosecuting council and now a Chief Constable of a large provincial district and a leading Conservative Member of Parliament, has stated that censorship has been lifted in Denmark to protect young people: in former times the illegality of pornography gave it a morbid fascination — 'and young people were among those buying it'. The Danish Pornography Committee, of which Langkilde was a member, took expert advice to the effect that 'once the adult sector of society could declare that pornography was unimportant if left to a free choice, the young would lose interest'. 'That is exactly what has happened with both young and old.' This was the impression of Roy Perrot, writing in

The Observer. He noted that it was *very rare* to see anyone under the early twenties in the Danish porno shops and cinemas, the 'regulars' being a small group of men in late middle age.

Rektor Ole Barfoed, headmaster of one of Copenhagen's biggest mixed grammar schools, is reported as having views broadly representative of those of other teachers in the city. He said that pornography has never posed any problem in the school though there is a porno shop 'just around the corner'. Since the relaxation of the law the pupils' interest in pornographic material has dropped to nil. If therefore it is argued that pornography has detrimental effects on the development of children and we wish therefore to reduce the quantity consumed we would be well advised to make it legal. Nor is this to say that the small amount of pornography that would then be consumed would be *harmful*, though in small amount: it would mean rather that erotic literature and art would begin to take its place as one area of human experience. If we banned motorcars we would almost certainly create a morbid fascination for them. It is certainly possible to argue that a *measured* interest in various things is a healthy way of responding to modern society: but we do not create a balanced world-outlook by lending certain phenomena the aura of tantalizing illegality.

One argument in favour of pornography is that it can serve as a substitute for actual sexual activity involving another person or other people. This argument has two parts, relating as it does to (1) people who fantasize over *socially acceptable* modes of sexual involvement, and (2) people who fantasize over types of sexual activity that would be regarded as illegal or at least immoral. The first type relates to lonely and deprived people who for one reason or another have been unable to form 'normal' sexual contacts with other people; the second type are instances of the much quoted *catharsis* argument. . . .

Pornography can serve as a substitute for both the knowledge of which some people have been deprived and the pleasure in sexual experience which they have not enjoyed. One can well imagine men or women too inhibited to secure sexual satisfaction with other adults and where explicit sexual material can alleviate some of their misery. It is facile to remark that such people should seek psychiatric assistance or even 'make an effort': the factors that prevent the forming of effective sexual liaisons are just as likely to inhibit any efforts to seek medical or other assistance. Pornography provides sex *by proxy*, and in such usage it can have a clear justification.

It is also possible to imagine circumstances in which men or women — for reasons of illness, travel or bereavement — are unable to seek sexual satisfaction with spouse or other loved one. Pornography can help here too. Again it is easy to suggest that a person abstain from sexual experience, or, if having *permanently* lost a spouse, seek out another partner. Needless to say such advice is often quite impractical — and the alternative to pornography may be prostitution or adultery. Montagu notes that pornography can serve the same purpose as 'dirty jokes', allowing a person to discharge harmlessly repressed and unsatisfied sexual desires.

In this spirit, Mercier (1970) is quoted by the U.S. Commission:

> it is in periods of sexual deprivation — to which the young and the old are far more subject than those in their prime — that males, at any rate, are likely to reap psychological benefit from pornography.

And also Kenneth Tynan (1970):

> For men on long journeys, geographically cut off from wives and mistresses, pornography can act as a portable memory, a welcome shortcut to remembered bliss, relieving tension without involving disloyalty.

It is difficult to see how anyone could object to the use of pornography in such circumstances, other than on the grounds of a morbid anti-sexuality.

The *catharsis argument* has long been put forward to suggest that availability of pornography will neutralize 'aberrant' sexual tendencies and so reduce the incidence of sex crime or clearly immoral behaviour in related fields. (Before evidence is put forward for this thesis it is worth remarking that it should not be necessary to demonstrate a *reduction* in sex crime to justify repeal of the Obscenity Laws. It should be quite sufficient to show that an *increase* in crime will not ensue following repeal. We may even argue that a small increase may be tolerable if other benefits from easy access to pornography could be shown: but it is no part of the present argument to put this latter contention.)

Many psychiatrists and psychologists have favoured the catharsis argument. Chesser, for instance, sees pornography as a form of voyeurism in which — as with sado-masochistic material — the desire to hurt is satisfied passively. If this is so and the analogy can be extended we have only to look at the character of the voyeur — generally furtive and clandestine — to realize that we have little to fear from the pornography addict. Where consumers are preoccupied with fantasy there is little danger to the rest of us. Karpman (1959), quoted by the U.S. Commission, notes that people reading 'salacious literature' are less likely to become sexual offenders than those who do not since the reading often neutralizes 'aberrant sexual interests'.

Similarly the Kronhausens have argued that 'these "unholy" instruments' may be a safety-valve for the sexual deviate and potential sex offender. And Cairns, Paul and Wishner (1962) have remarked that *obscene materials* provide a way of releasing strong sexual urges without doing harm to others.

It is easy to see the plausibility of this argument. The popularity of all forms of sexual literature — from the superficial, *sexless*, sentimentality of the popular women's magazine to the clearest 'hard-core' porn — has demonstrated over the ages the perennial appetite that people have for fantasy. To an extent, a great extent with many single people and frustrated married ones, the fantasy constitutes an important part of the sex-life. The experience may be vicarious and sterile but it self-evidently fills a need for many individuals. If literature, as a *symbol* of reality, can so involve human sensitivities it is highly likely that when the sensitivities are *distorted* for one reason or another the same sublimatory function can occur: the 'perverted' or potentially criminal mentality can gain satisfaction, as does the lonely unfortunate, in sex *by proxy*. If we wanted to force the potential sex criminal on to the streets in search of a human victim perhaps we would do well to deny him his sublimatory substitutes: deny him fantasy and he will be forced to go after the real thing. . . .

The most frequently quoted research study into the connections between the drop in the Danish sex crime rate and the repeal of obscenity legislation is that by Bert Kutschinsky. . . . In the section of his report termed 'Towards an Explanation of the Decrease in Registered Sex Crimes in Copenhagen' . . . Kutschinsky describes the way in which the study was conducted, i.e. largely in the form of a detailed questionnaire and interviews with around 400 representative citizens of Copenhagen. Specific attention was given to such factors as possible changing attitudes to sex crime and circumstances in which a report to the police would be undertaken. Explanations of the sex crime drop on the ground of changing attitudes of victims or other such arguments are tentatively ruled out, and the conclusion was stated that 'the abundant availability of hard-core pornography in Denmark may have been the direct cause of a veritable decrease in the actual amount of sex crime committed' in the areas of *peeping* and (*physical*) *indecency towards girls*. Quite rightly, the report ends with an appeal for more research but clearly there are strong circumstantial grounds for thinking that availability of pornographic material does satisfy a number of potential sex criminals to the point where deliberate interference with innocent victims is significantly less likely.

The importance of this possibility should be fully faced. If a causal connection *does* exist between availability of pornographic material and a *reduction* in the amount of sex crime — and the evidence is wholly consistent with this possibility rather than its converse — then people who deliberately restrict pornography by supporting repressive legislation are prime architects of sexual offences against the individual. The anti-pornographers would do well to note that their anxieties may be driving them into a position the exact opposite of the one they explicitly maintain — their commitment to reduce the amount of sexual delinquency in society.

The most that the anti-pornographers can argue is that at present the evidence is inconclusive — a point that would be taken by Kutschinsky *et al.* But if the inconclusive character of the data is once admitted then the case for repressive legislation falls at once. For in a *free* society, or one supposedly aiming after freedom, social phenomena are, like individuals, innocent until proven guilty — and an activity will be permitted unless there is clear evidence of its harmful consequences. This point was well put — in the specific connection with pornography — by Bertrand Russell, talking when he was well over 90 to Rupert Crawshay-Williams.

After noting how people beg the question of causation in instances such as the Moors murders (where the murders and the reading of de Sade *may* have a common cause), Russell ('Bertie') said that on the whole he disapproved of sadistic pornography being available. But when Crawshay-Williams put the catharsis view, that such material might provide a harmless release for individuals who otherwise may be dangerous, Russell said at once — 'Oh well, if that's true, then I don't see that there is anything against sadistic pornography. In fact it should be encouraged. . . .' When it was stressed that there was no preponderating evidence either way Russell argued that we should fall back on an overriding principle — 'in this case the principle of free speech'.

Thus in the absence of evidence of harm we should be permissive. Any other view is totalitarian. . . .

Pornography can also serve as an aid to education, particularly in the present circumstances of sexual repression and official hypocrisy. Pornography, in fact, is pretty well the only place where 'deviant' sexual behaviour is dealt with in a candid evocative fashion divorced from sterile moralizing or clear dishonesty. In a social climate antipathetic to the simple dissemination of basic information about sexual practice pornography can perform a useful function. This point is stressed by the Kronhausens — '*erotic realism in literature can serve a most useful function* in sex education. In fact, we believe that there can hardly be any argument on this point among sensible people.' (Italics in original.)

Explicit sexual material can also give us insight into the mentality of minority groups, into their sexual behaviour and aesthetic preferences. The anti-pornographers want to erect a wall around what they fondly imagine to be sexual *normality* and to prohibit intercourse, sexual or other, with persons on the other side. This is a recipe for persecution and intolerance; and it should have no place in liberal society.

There is widespread agreement — even among many repressive elements — that much trouble can be caused for the individual if his sexual impulses are crushed under excessive puritanism. Many of the opponents of pornography are still prepared to argue for effective sex education to allow growth to sexual maturity without the distorting influence of prejudice and falsehood. But pornography, reviled and feared, is still one of the most effective tools for breaking down the bogus sensitivities that masquerade in ethical garb. The concern of the anti-pornographer is often a pseudo-morality: he professes ideals in which we would all happily concur, and then makes their realization less likely by advocating social policies of suppression, book-burning and the like. The clear anti-sexuality that underlies and fuels most of the effort of the anti-pornographers must be faced; and we must try to help our children to grow up without fear of sex and the tools that encourage its expression. . . .

The benefits of pornography have clearly been established — by personal testimony and academic research (albeit limited), by the undenied gratification brought to lonely and other people. We should not worry too much about fantasy in human reflections, nor should we think that fantasy — especially sexual fantasy — will lead us to seek an *actual* realization. Sexual appetite *can* be satiated *by proxy*, as it were — and there are obvious circumstances in which such satiation should be positively encouraged. In orgasmic release the pressures for sexual initiative evaporate on the wind, and the prospect of excited men roaming the streets in search of victims is unreal. That such a prospect is seriously entertained is more than anything an index of a mentality, in all likelihood, inadequately seasoned by its *own* sexual experience.

If human enjoyment *per se* is not to be condemned then it is not too rash to say that we *know* pornography does good. We can easily produce our witnesses to testify to experiencing pleasure. If in the face of this — and no other favourable argument — we are unable to demonstrate a countervailing harm, then the case for easy availability of pornography is unassailable. If, in such circumstances, we find some people unconvinced it is futile to seek out further empirical data. Once we commit ourselves to the notion that the evil nature of something is axiomatic we tacitly concede that evidence is largely irrelevant to our position. If pornography never fails to fill us with predictable loathing then statistics on crime, or measured statements by careful specialists, will not be useful: our reactions will stay the same. But in this event we would do well to reflect on what our emotions tells us of our own mentality.

Viewed without moral preconception, pornography is nothing more than erotic art — sometimes of high quality, sometimes not. If art has a place in human life then so does erotic art. Some art plays on our drive for worldly success, our instinct for survival, our impulse to personal happiness: pornography plays on the sex drive — this being so, we should, if we value sexual feeling in human experience, liberate our pornography and insist (through argument and not the law) that our pornography be of good quality.

CATHARINE MACKINNON
Sex and Violence

CATHARINE MACKINNON *is a noted feminist and legal scholar who teaches at York University in Toronto. Her most recent book is* A Feminist Theory of the State *(1990).*

I WANT to raise some questions about the concept of this panel's title, "Violence against Women," as a concept that may coopt us as we attempt to formulate our own truths. I want to speak specifically about four issues: rape, sexual harassment, pornography, and battery. I think one of the reasons we say that each of these issues is an example of violence against women is to reunify them. To say that aggression against women has this unity is to criticize the divisions that have been imposed on that aggression by the legal system. What I see to be the danger of the analysis, what makes it potentially cooptive, is formulating it — and it *is* formulated this way — these are issues of violence, *not* sex: rape is a crime of violence, not sexuality; sexual harassment is an abuse of power, not sexuality; pornography is violence against women, it is not erotic. Although battering is not categorized so explicitly, it is usually treated as though there is nothing sexual about a man beating up a woman so long as it is with his fist. I'd like to raise some questions about that as well.

I hear in the formulation that these issues are violence against women, not sex, that we are in the shadow of Freud, intimidated at being called repressive Victorians. We're saying we're *op*pressed and they say we're *re*pressed. That is, when we say we're against rape, the immediate response is, "Does that mean you're against sex?" "Are you attempting to impose neo-Victorian prudery on sexual expression?" This comes up with sexual harassment as well. When we say we're against sexual harassment, the first thing people want to know is, "What's the difference between that and ordinary male-to-female sexual initiation?" That's a good question . . . The same is also true of criticizing pornography. "You can't be against erotica?" It's the latest version of the accusation that feminists are anti-male. To distinguish ourselves from this, and in reaction to it, we call these abuses violence. The attempt is to avoid the critique — we're not against sex — and at the same time retain our criticism of these practices. So we rename as violent those abuses that have been seen to be sexual, without saying that we have a very different perspective on violence and on sexuality and their relationship. I also think a reason we call these experiences violence

is to avoid being called lesbians, which for some reason is equated with being against sex. In order to avoid that, yet retain our opposition to sexual violation, we put this neutral, objective, abstract word *violence* on it all.

To me this is an attempt to have our own perspective on these outrages without owning up to having one. To have our point of view but present it as *not* a particular point of view. Our problem has been to label something as rape, as sexual harassment, as pornography in the face of a suspicion that it might be intercourse, it might be ordinary sexual initiation, it might be erotic. To say that these purportedly sexual events violate us, to be against them, we call them not sexual. But the attempt to be objective and neutral avoids owning up to the fact that women do have a specific point of view on these events. It avoids saying that from women's point of view, intercourse, sex roles, and eroticism can be and at times are violent to us as women.

My approach would claim our perspective; we are not attempting to be objective about it, we're attempting to represent the point of view of women. The point of view of men up to this time, called objective, has been to distinguish sharply between rape on the one hand and intercourse on the other; sexual harassment on the one hand and normal, ordinary sexual initiation on the other; pornography or obscenity on the one hand and eroticism on the other. The male point of view defines them by distinction. What women experience does not so clearly distinguish the normal, everyday things from those abuses from which they have been defined by distinction. Not just "Now we're going to take what *you* say as rape and call it violence"; "Now we're going to take what *you* say is sexual harassment and call it violence"; "Now we're going to take what *you* say is pornography and call it violence." We have a deeper critique of what has been done to women's sexuality and who controls access to it. What we are saying is that sexuality in exactly these normal forms often *does* violate us. So long as we say those things are abuses of violence, not sex, we fail to criticize what has been made of *sex*, what has been done to us *through* sex, because we leave the line between rape and intercourse, sexual harassment and sex roles, pornography and eroticism, right where it is.

I think it is useful to inquire how women and men (I don't use the term *persons*, I guess, because I haven't seen many lately) live through the meaning of their experience with these issues. When we ask whether rape, sexual harassment, and pornography are questions of violence or questions of sexuality, it helps to ask, to whom? What is the perspective of those who are involved, whose experience it is — to rape or to have been raped, to consume pornography or to be consumed through it. As to what these things *mean* socially, it is important whether they are about sexuality to women and men or whether they are instead about "violence," — or whether violence and sexuality can be distinguished in that way, as they are lived out.

The crime of rape — this is a legal and observed, not a subjective, individual, or feminist definition — is defined around penetration. That seems to me a very male point of view on what it means to be sexually violated. And it is exactly what heterosexuality as a social institution is fixated around, the penetration of the penis into the vagina. Rape is defined according to what men think violates women, and that is the same as what they think of as the *sine qua non* of sex. What women experience as degrading and defiling when we are raped includes as much that is distinctive to us as is our experi-

ence of sex. Someone once termed penetration a "peculiarly resented aspect" of rape — I don't know whether that meant it was peculiar that it was resented or that it was resented with heightened peculiarity. Women who have been raped often do resent having been penetrated. But that is not all there is to what was intrusive or expropriative of a woman's sexual wholeness.

I do think the crime of rape focuses more centrally on what men define as sexuality than on women's experience of our sexual being, hence its violation. A common experience of rape victims is to be unable to feel good about anything heterosexual thereafter — or anything sexual at all, or men at all. The minute they start to have sexual feelings or feel sexually touched by a man, or even a woman, they start to relive the rape. I had a client who came in with her husband. She was a rape victim, a woman we had represented as a witness. Her husband sat the whole time and sobbed. They couldn't have sex anymore because every time he started to touch her, she would flash to the rape scene and see his face change into the face of the man who had raped her. That, to me, is sexual. When a woman has been raped, and it is sex that she then cannot experience without connecting it to that, it was her sexuality that was violated.

Similarly, men who are in prison for rape think it's the dumbest thing that ever happened . . . It isn't just a miscarriage of justice; they were put in jail for something very little different from what most men do most of the time and call it sex. The only difference is they got caught. That view is nonremorseful and not rehabilitative. It may also be true. It seems to me we have here a convergence between the rapist's view of what he has done and the victim's perspective on what was done to her. That is, for both, their ordinary experiences of heterosexual intercourse and the act of rape have something in common. Now this gets us into intense trouble, because that's exactly how judges and juries see it who refuse to convict men accused of rape. A rape victim has to prove that it was not intercourse. She has to show that there was force and she resisted, because if there was sex, consent is inferred. Finders of fact look for "more force than usual during the preliminaries." Rape is defined by distinction from intercourse — not nonviolence, intercourse. They ask, does this event look more like fucking or like rape? But what is their standard for sex, and is this question asked from the *woman's point of view*? The level of force is not adjudicated at her point of violation; it is adjudicated at the standard of the normal level of force. Who sets this standard?

In the criminal law, we can't put everybody in jail who does an ordinary act, right? Crime is supposed to be deviant, not normal. Women continue not to report rape, and a reason is that they believe, and they are right, that the legal system will not see it from their point of view. We get very low conviction rates for rape. We also get many women who believe they have never been raped, although a lot of force was involved. They mean that they were not raped in a way that is legally provable. In other words, in all these situations, there was not *enough* violence against them to take it beyond the category of "sex"; they were not coerced enough. Maybe they were forced-fucked for years and put up with it, maybe they tried to get it over with, maybe they were coerced by something other than battery, something like economics, maybe even something like love.

What I am saying is that unless you make the point that there is much violence in intercourse, as a usual matter, none of that is changed. Also we continue to stigmatize the women who claim rape as hav-

ing experienced a deviant violation and allow the rest of us to go through life feeling violated but thinking we've never been raped, when there were a great many times when we, too, have had sex and didn't want it. What this critique does that is different from the "violence, not sex" critique is ask a series of questions about normal, heterosexual intercourse and attempt to move the line between heterosexuality on the one hand — intercourse — and rape on the other, rather than allow it to stay where it is.

Having done that so extensively with rape, I can consider sexual harassment more briefly. The way the analysis of sexual harassment is sometimes expressed now (and it bothers me) is that it is an abuse of power, not sexuality. That does not allow us to pursue whether sexuality, as socially constructed in our society through gender roles, is *itself* a power structure. If you look at sexual harassment as power, not sex, what is power supposed to be? Power is employer/employee, not because courts are marxist but because this is a recognized hierarchy. Among men. Power is teacher/student, because courts recognize a hierarchy there. Power is on one side and sexuality on the other. Sexuality is ordinary affection, everyday flirtation. Only when ordinary, everyday affection and flirtation and "I was just trying to be friendly" come into the context of *another* hierarchy is it considered potentially an abuse of power. What is not considered to be a hierarchy is women and men — men on top and women on the bottom. That is not considered to be a question of power or social hierarchy, legally or politically. A feminist perspective suggests that it is.

When we have examples of coequal sexual harassment (within these other hierarchies), worker to worker on the same level, involving women and men, we have a lot of very interesting, difficult questions about sex discrimination, which is supposed to be about gender difference, but does not conceive of gender as a social hierarchy. I think that implicit in race discrimination cases for a brief moment of light was the notion that there is a social hierarchy between Blacks and whites. So that presumptively it's an exercise of power for a white person to do something egregious to a Black person or for a white institution to do something egregious systematically to many Black people. Situations of coequal power — among coworkers or students or teachers — are difficult to see as examples of sexual harassment unless you have a notion of male power. I think we lie to women when we call it not power when a woman is come onto by a man who is not her employer, not her teacher. What do we labor under, what do we feel, when a man — any man — comes and hits on us? I think we require women to feel fine about turning down male-initiated sex so long as the man doesn't have some *other* form of power over us. Whenever — every and any time — a woman feels conflicted and wonders what's wrong with her that she can't decline although she has no inclination, and she feels open to male accusations, whether they come from women or men, of "why didn't you just tell him to buzz off?" we have sold her out, not named her experience. We are taught that we exist for men. We should be flattered or at least act as if we are — be careful about a man's ego because you never know what he can do to you. To flat out say to him, "You?" or "I don't want to" is not *in* most women's sex-role learning. To say it is, is bravado. And that's because he's a man, not just because you never know what he can do to you because he's your boss (that's two things — he's a man and he's the boss) or your teacher or in some other hierarchy. It seems to me that we haven't talked very

much about gender *as* a hierarchy, as a division of power, in the way that's expressed and acted out, primarily I think sexually. And therefore we haven't expanded the definition according to women's experience of sexuality, including our own sexual intimidation, of what things are sexual in this world. So men have also defined what can be called sexual about us. They say, "I was just trying to be affectionate, flirtatious and friendly," and we were just all felt up. We criticize the idea that rape comes down to her word against his — but it really *is* her perspective against his perspective, and the law has been written from *his* perspective. If he didn't mean to be sexual, it's not sexual. If he didn't see it as forced, it wasn't forced. Which is to say, only male sexual violations, that is, only male ideas of what sexually violates us as women are illegal. We buy into this when we say our sexual violations are abuses of power, not sex.

Just as rape is supposed to have nothing against intercourse, just as sexual harassment is supposed to have nothing against normal sexual initiation (men initiate, women consent — that's mutual?), the idea that pornography is violence against women, not sex, seems to distinguish artistic creation on the one hand from what is degrading to women on the other. It is candid and true but not enough to say of pornography, as Justice Stewart said, "I know it when I see it." *He* knows what he thinks it is when he sees it — but is that what *I* know? Is that the same "it"? Is he going to know what I know when I see it? I think pretty much not, given what's on the newsstand, given what is not considered hard-core pornography. Sometimes I think what is obscene is what does *not* turn on the Supreme Court — or what revolts them more. Which is uncommon, since revulsion is eroticized. We have to admit that pornography turns men on; it is therefore erotic. It is a lie to say that pornography is not erotic. When we say it is violence, not sex, we are saying, there is this degrading to women, over here, and this erotic, over there, without saying to whom. It is overwhelmingly disproportionately men to whom pornography is erotic. It is women, on the whole, to whom it is violent, among other things. And this is not just a matter or perspective, but a matter of reality.

Pornography turns primarily men on. Certainly they are getting something out of it. They pay incredible amounts of money for it; it's one of the largest industries in the country. If women got as much out of it as men do, we would buy it instead of cosmetics. It's a massive industry, cosmetics. We are poor but we have *some* money; we are some market. We spend our money to set ourselves up as the objects that emulate those images that are sold as erotic to men. What pornography says about us is that we enjoy degradation, that we are sexually turned on by being degraded. For me that obliterates the line, as a line at all, between pornography on one hand and erotica on the other, if what turns men on, what men find beautiful, is what degrades women. It is pervasively present in art, also, and advertising. But it is definitely present in eroticism, if that is what it is. It makes me think that women's sexuality as such is a stigma. We also sometimes have an experience of sexuality authentic somehow in all this. We are not allowed to have it; we are not allowed to talk about it; we are not allowed to speak of it or image it as from our own point of view. And, to the extent we try to assert that we are beings equal with men, we have to be either asexual or virgins.

To worry about cooptation is to realize that lies make bad politics. It is ironic that cooptation often results from an attempt to be "credible," to be strategically smart, to be "effective" on existing terms. Sometimes you become what you're fighting. Thinking about issues of sexual violation as issues of violence not sex could, if pursued legally, lead to opposing sexual harassment and pornography through morals legislation and obscenity laws. It is actually interesting that this theoretical stance has been widely embraced but these legal strategies have not been. Perhaps women realize that these legal approaches would not address the subordination of women to men, specifically and substantively. These approaches are legally as abstract as the "violence not sex" critique is politically abstract. They are both not enough and too much of the wrong thing. They deflect us from criticizing everyday behavior that is pervasive and normal and concrete and fuses sexuality with gender in violation and is not amenable to existing legal approaches. I think we need to think more radically in our legal work here.

Battering is called violence, rather than something sex-specific: this is done to women. I also think it is sexually done to women. Not only in where it is done — over half of the incidents are in the bedroom. Or the surrounding events — precipitating sexual jealousy. But when violence against women is eroticized as it is in this culture, it is very difficult to say that there is a major distinction in the level of sex involved between being assaulted by a penis and being assaulted by a fist, especially when the perpetrator is a man. If women as gender female are defined as sexual beings, and violence is eroticized, then men violating women has a sexual component. I think men rape women because they get off on it in a way that fuses dominance with sexuality. (This is different in emphasis from what Susan Brownmiller says.) I think that when men sexually harass women it expresses male control over sexual access to us. It doesn't mean they all want to fuck us, they just want to hurt us, dominate us, and control us, and that *is* fucking us. They want to be able to have that and to be able to say when they can have it, to *know* that. That is in itself erotic. The idea that opposing battering is about saving the family is, similarly, abstracted, gender-neutral. There are gender-neutral formulations of all these issues: law and order as opposed to derepression, Victorian morality as opposed to permissiveness, obscenity as opposed to art and freedom of expression. Gender-neutral, objective formulations like these avoid asking *whose* expression, from whose point of view? Whose law and whose order? It's not just a question of who is free to express ourselves; it's not just that there is almost no, if any, self-respecting women's eroticism. The fact is that what we do see, what we are allowed to experience, even in our own suffering, even in what we are allowed to complain about, is overwhelmingly constructed from the male point of view. Laws against sexual violation express what men see and do when they engage in sex with women; laws against obscenity center on the display of women's bodies in ways that men are turned on by viewing. To me, it not only makes us cooptable to define such abuses in gender-neutral terms like violence; when we fail to assert that we are fighting for the affirmative definition and control of our own sexuality, of our own lives as women, and that these experiences violate *that*, we have already been bought.

ELLEN WILLIS

Feminism, Moralism, and Pornography

ELLEN WILLIS *is a staff writer for the* Village Voice *who has also been published in* Rolling Stone *and the* New York Review of Books. *She writes about sex, the sixties, feminism, pornography, antisemitism, abortion, and family.*

THE emergence of pornography as a feminist issue fills me with ambivalence. Pornographic images that make women not only objects but specimens, and at worst are openly sadistic, have become a staple of popular culture. It pisses me off that men make fortunes selling these images and that they pass as respectable, chic, and even liberating; they're now so ubiquitous that they function as a form of psychological harassment. Yet the antiporn campaign raises disturbing political questions. Ironically, censorship is the least of them; at the moment there seems to be little sentiment for taking any kind of legal action against pornographers, as opposed to organizing demonstrations and other forms of public consciousness-raising. The most bothersome questions have to do with the issue itself.

When I first heard there was a group called Women Against Pornography, I twitched. Could I define myself as Against Pornography? Not really. In itself, pornography — which, my dictionary and I agree, means any image or description intended or used to arouse sexual desire — does not strike me as the proper object of a political crusade. Pornography is the return of the repressed, of feelings and fantasies driven underground by a culture that atomizes sexuality, defining love as a noble affair of the heart and mind, lust as a base animal urge centered in unmentionable organs. Prurience — the state of mind I associate with pornography — implies a sense of sex as forbidden, secretive pleasure, isolated from any emotional or social context. I imagine that in utopia, porn would wither away along with the state, heroin, and Coca-Cola. But for now the sexual impulses that pornography appeals to are part of virtually everyone's psychology. For obvious political and cultural reasons, nearly all porn is created by men for men; women are less likely to be consciously interested in pornography, or to indulge that interest, or to find porn that turns them on. But anyone who thinks women are simply indifferent to pornography has never watched a bunch of adolescent girls pass around a trashy novel. Over the years I've enjoyed various pieces of pornography — some of them of the sleazy 42nd Street paperback sort — and so have most women I know. If feminists define pornography, per se, as the enemy, the result will be to make a lot of women ashamed of their sexual feelings and afraid to be honest about them. And the last thing women need is more sexual shame, guilt, and hypocrisy — this time served up as feminism.

It seems to me that pornography is a plausible political target insofar as it contributes to larger patterns of oppression: the reduction of the female body to a commodity (the paradigm being prostitution); the sexual intimidation that makes women regard the public streets enemy territory (the paradigm being rape); sexist images and propaganda in general. Simple observation also suggests that some pornography is pernicious and some is more or less benign. So why concentrate on pornography, rather than its political context, and in effect condemn all pornography as equally bad? WAP organizers answer — or finesse — this question by redefining pornography. They maintain that pornography is not really about sex but about violence against women. Or, in a more colorful formulation, "Pornography is the theory, rape is the practice." Part of the argument is that pornography causes violence; much is made of the fact that Charles Manson and David Berkowitz had porn collections. This is the sort of inverted logic that presumes marijuana to be dangerous because most heroin addicts started with it. It is men's hostility toward women — combined with their power to express that hostility and for the most part get away with it — that causes sexual violence. Pornography that gives sadistic fantasies concrete shape–and, in today's atmosphere, social legitimacy — may well encourage suggestible men to act them out. But if *Hustler* were to vanish from the shelves tomorrow, I doubt that rape or wife-beating statistics would decline.

Even more problematic is the idea that pornography depicts violence rather than sex. Since porn is by definition overtly sexual, while most of it is not overtly violent, this equation requires some fancy explaining. The conference WAP held a few weeks ago was in part devoted to this task. Robin Morgan and Gloria Steinem, among others, addressed it by attempting to distinguish pornography from erotica. According to this argument, erotica (whose etymological root is eros, or sexual love) expresses an integrated sexuality based on mutual affection and desire between equals; pornography (which comes from another Greek root—porne, meaning prostitute) reflects a dehumanized sexuality based on male domination and exploitation of women. The distinction sounds promising, but it doesn't hold up. The accepted meaning of erotica is literature or pictures with sexual themes; it may or may not serve the essentially utilitarian function of pornography. Because it is less specific, less suggestive of actual sexual activity, "erotica" is regularly used as a euphemism for "classy porn." Pornography expressed in literary language or expensive photography and consumed by the upper middle class is "erotica"; the cheap stuff, which can't pretend to any purpose but getting people off, is smut. The erotica-versus-porn approach evades the (embarrassing) question of how porn is used. It endorses the portrayal of sex as we would like it to be, and condemns the portrayal of sex as it too often is, whether in action or only in fantasy. But if pornography is to arouse, it must appeal to the feelings we have, not those that by some utopian standard we ought to have. Sex in this culture has been so deeply politicized that it is impossible to make clear-cut distinctions between "authentic" sexual impulses and those conditioned by patriarchy. Between, say, *Ulysses* at one end and *Snuff* at the other, erotica/pornography conveys all sorts of mixed messages that elicit complicated and private responses. In practice, attempts to sort out good erotica from bad porn inevitably come down to "What turns me on is erotic; what turns you on is pornographic."

Another argument I heard at the conference (a minority view not, so far as I know, promoted by anyone in WAP) was that pornography reflects patriarchal sexual relations: patriarchal sexual relations are based on male power backed by force; ergo, pornography is violent. This dubious syllogism, which could as easily be applied to romantic novels, reduces the whole issue to hopeless mush. If all manifestations of patriarchal sexuality are violent, then opposition to violence cannot explain why pornography (rather than romantic novels) should be singled out as a target. Besides, such reductionism allows women no basis for distinguishing between consensual heterosexuality and rape. But this is precisely its point; as a number of women at the conference put it, "In a patriarchy, all sex with men is pornographic." Of course, to attack pornography, and at the same time equate it with heterosexual sex, is implicitly to criticize not only women who like pornography, but women who sleep with men. This is familiar ground. The pornography issue is providing a new focus for long-standing political differences among feminists. In part, these differences have to do with conflicting attitudes toward sex, men, heterosexuality, lesbian separatism, and "cultural feminism." In part, they reflect the tension that has always existed in the movement between moralism—the urge to define how good feminists should behave or feel—and materialism—the conviction that our politics must be rooted in a sympathetic understanding of how women do behave and feel. . . .

•   •   •

For women, life is an ongoing good cop–bad cop routine. The good cops are marriage, motherhood, and that courtly old gentleman, chivalry. Just cooperate, they say (crossing their fingers), and we'll go easy on you. You'll never have to earn a living or open a door. We'll even get you some romantic love. But you'd better not get stubborn, or you'll have to deal with our friend rape, and he's a real terror; we just can't control him.

Pornography often functions as a bad cop. If rape warns that without the protection of one man we are fair game for all, the hard-core pornographic image suggests that the alternative to being a wife is being a whore. As women become more "criminal" the cops call for nastier reinforcements; the proliferation of lurid, violent porn (symbolic rape) is a form of backlash. But one can be a solid citizen and still be shocked (naively or hypocritically) by police brutality. However widely condoned, rape is illegal. However loudly people proclaim that porn is as wholesome as granola, the essence of its appeal is that emotionally it remains taboo. It is from their very contempt for the rules that bad cops derive their power to terrorize (and the covert approbation of solid citizens who would love to break the rules themselves). The line between bad cop and outlaw is tenuous. Both rape and pornography reflect a male outlaw mentality that rejects the conventions of romance and insists, bluntly, that women are cunts. The crucial difference between the conservative's moral indignation at rape, or at *Hustler*, and the feminist's political outrage is the latter's understanding that the problem is not bad cops or outlaws but cops and the law.

What makes me nervous about the current feminist campaign against pornography is its tendency to blur this difference. Women Against Pornography has confused opposition to police brutality with opposition to the system: as a result, it is delivering a mixed political message that could end up reinforcing the very system it purports to fight. At the heart of the confusion is WAP's equation of porn with sexual violence. Even these days, most porn is not overtly violent, nor is there any hard evidence that it causes violence. Yet the idea that "Pornography is the theory, rape is the practice" speaks to powerful emotions in many women. As I've suggested, there is a social and psychic link between pornography and rape. In terms of patriarchal morality, both are expressions of men's innately vicious lust, and offenses to the sexual innocence of "good" women. But feminists supposedly begin with different assumptions—that men's confusion of sexual desire with predatory aggression reflects a sexist system, not male biology; that there are no good (chaste) or bad (lustful) women, just women who are, like men, sexual beings. From this standpoint, to lump pornography with rape is dangerously simplistic. Rape is a violent physical assault. Pornography can be a psychic assault, both in its content and in its public intrusions on our attention, but for women as for men it can also be a source of erotic pleasure. Though porn is generally the product of a male imagination, and in that sense is almost always sexist, fantasy is more flexible than reality; it is possible to shape someone else's fantasy to one's own needs. And though the pleasure porn affords is a compromise—at once protesting and acceding to a culture that segregates genital sex from the rest of life—compromised pleasure is still pleasure. I'll go further: for a woman to enjoy pornography, even if that means enjoying a rape fantasy, is less to collaborate in her oppression than to defy it, to insist on an aspect of her sexuality that has been defined as a male preserve. Insofar as pornography glorifies male supremacy and sexual alienation, it is deeply reactionary. But in rejecting sexual repression and hypocrisy—which have inflicted even more damage on women than on men—it expresses a radical impulse.

That this impulse still needs defending, even among feminists, is evident from the sexual attitudes that have surfaced in the anti-porn movement. In WAP's rhetoric, pornography is a code word for men's vicious lust. Anti-porn activists have redefined the word to mean not sexually arousing material, as such, but material that expresses (male) violence and domination. (To the objection that some women get off on porn, they reply that this only shows how deeply women have been brainwashed by male values. Note the good girl versus bad girl theme, reappearing as healthy versus sick; for "brainwashed" read "seduced.") The depiction of real sexuality is not pornography but "erotica." Unfortunately, the view of sex that too often emerges from talk about erotica is as sentimental and euphemistic as the word itself: lovemaking should be beautiful, romantic, soft, nice, and devoid of messiness, vulgarity, impulses to power, or indeed aggression of any sort. Above all, the emphasis should be on *relationships*, not (yuck) *organs*. This goody-goody concept of eroticism is not feminist but feminine. It is precisely sex as an aggressive unladylike activity, an expression of violent and unpretty emotion, an exercise of erotic power, and a specifically genital experience that has been taboo for women. Nor are we supposed to admit that we too have sadistic impulses, that our sexual fantasies may reflect forbidden urges to turn the tables and get revenge on men. (When a women is aroused by a rape fantasy, is she perhaps identifying with the rapist as well as the victim?) Sanitized feminine sexuality is as limited as the predatory masculine kind and as central to women's oppression; the whole purpose of *Hustler* is to scare us into embracing it. As a further incentive, the good cops stand ready to assure us that we are morally superior to men, that in our sweetness and nonviolence (read passivity and powerlessness) is our strength.

Women are understandably tempted to believe this comforting myth. Self-righteousness has always been a feminine weapon, a permissible way to make men feel bad. Ironically, it is socially acceptable for women to display fierce aggression in their crusades against male vice, which serve as an outlet for female anger without threatening male power. The temperance movement, which made alcohol the symbol of male violence, did not improve the position of women; substituting porn for demon rum won't work either. One reason it won't is that it bolsters the good girl–bad girl split. Overtly or by implication it isolates women who like porn, or who work in the sex industry. WAP has refused to take a position on prostitution, yet its activities—particularly its support for cleaning up Times Square—will affect prostitutes' lives. Prostitution raises its own set of complicated questions. But it is clearly not in women's interest to pit "good" feminists against "bad" whores (or topless dancers, or models for skin magazines).

In contrast to the abortion rights movement, which is struggling against a tidal wave of energy from the other direction, the anti-porn campaign is respectable. It gets approving press and cooperation from the city, which has its own stake (promoting tourism, making the Clinton area safe for gentrification) in cleaning up Times Square. Despite the insistence of WAP organizers that they support sexual freedom, their line appeals to the antisexual emotions that feed the backlash. Women who simply condemn pornography—rather than its specifically misogynist forms and uses—are doing the good cops' dirty work.

PART TWO

Individual Ethics

4

What Is Reproductive Freedom?

Frank and Gertrude fall in love. They talk about getting married, moving to California, getting good jobs, and several years later having two beautiful children. Their children will be three years apart in age. The little girl will look just like Gertrude; the little boy just like Frank.

The story of Frank and Gertrude is a fairly typical fantasy of the circumstances surrounding reproduction, at least in our culture. We tend to think of reproduction as a matter of choice. Most people, we imagine, want to have children and, when they are ready, they do; some people don't want to have children, and so they don't. Of course, a little reflection reminds us that this picture of reproduction is far from complete. It ignores the ways in which the complexities of human biology, individual wants and needs, and the constraints of human society affect our reproductive desires, choices, and possibilities. Pregnancy is not the result of an act of will alone. It requires the cooperation of two fully functioning reproductive systems. And, just as a woman can't get pregnant simply by *wanting* to, so can she get pregnant when she *doesn't* want to.

In this chapter, we explore two controversial issues concerning the nature and limits of reproductive freedom: abortion and surrogate motherhood. What we think is at stake morally with regard to these two issues is a function of what we think about sex, reproduction, responsibility, sexual equality, and religion. A philosophical point of view can help us sort out the principal moral questions that make these issues the subject of so much disagreement.

When thinking about abortion as a philosophical topic, it is helpful to begin by considering what a woman might actually think about as she decides whether or not to have an abortion. Obviously, the factors that a woman considers are a function of her particular circumstances. Sometimes, the pregnancy itself might present difficulties: for example, a teenager may feel that being pregnant while at school would cause enormous personal and social problems for her. Sometimes, the pregnancy itself is less of a problem than would be the child that will be its end result: a mother of two children, for instance, might feel that having a third child would impair her emotional and financial capacity to care for her existing ones. Whatever we ultimately decide about the morality of abortion, it is important to keep in mind that it is always a concrete act undertaken for particular reasons in particular circumstances.

Most opposition to abortion is based on the claim that human life begins at conception and thus a human embryo or fetus is a person like any of us and so has a right to life. While philosophers disagree as to all that a right to life involves, we can assume that at the very least it guarantees that one not be killed unjustifiably. Unwarranted or unjustified killing is murder; murder is not permissible. Those opposed to abortion typically believe that the killing of an "innocent" embryo is unwarranted. Abortion is therefore murder and is hence impermissible. When the problem of abortion is framed in this way, defenders of the practice of abortion are often forced to argue that personhood does not begin at conception but at some later stage of pregnancy, or at birth. Ann Druyan and Carl Sagan present the principal arguments for and against fetal personhood.

Judith Jarvis Thomson, on the other hand, urges us to avoid the entanglements of the debate over the beginnings of personhood. For the sake of argument, she grants those opposed to abortion their major premise, namely, that the fetus is a person from the moment of conception. She then proceeds to argue that, even if the fetus is a person, it does not follow that a woman is required to carry it to term. The woman's right to control her own body outweighs the rights of the fetus. Thomson hopes to set abortion in a context that displays clearly what she takes to be the central moral issue that it raises: does a woman have an *obligation* to maintain, for the sake of the fetus, an unwanted pregnancy to term? Thomson's example of the unconscious violinist who requires the use of your kidneys to stay alive has become legendary. It is up to you to decide whether you accept her analogy, or any of her other suggestive inferences, as persuasive. It is also useful to consider in the context of Thomson's claims both Mary Anne Warren's argument for and Alan Donagan's argument against the significance of birth in determining moral obligations to fetuses and infants.

Surrogate motherhood is in some ways the flip side of the abortion issue. The practice of surrogate motherhood is a "solution" to infertility. If one woman wants to have a baby but can't, for whatever reasons, another woman can have a baby for her. That sounds quite simple on the surface, but immediately beneath the happy picture of cooperative reproduction is a messy nest of controversial moral, legal, and political issues. Though they differ ultimately in their characterization of the ethics of surrogacy, the essays by Sara Ann Ketchum and by Meredith Michaels both refer to the famous case of "Baby M," the baby originally conceived as part of a surrogacy contract but whose biological mother then decided to keep her. The case has generated intense debate about whether surrogate motherhood is really a form of prostitution or baby-selling, or whether it is an exercise of reproductive freedom, both for those who make use of the services of the surrogate and for the surrogate herself. Whatever conclusion you yourself come to regarding surrogacy, in the process you will discover the enormous complexities involved both in making responsible reproductive choices and in establishing social policies of reproductive freedom and obligation.

ANN DRUYAN AND CARL SAGAN

The Question of Abortion

ANN DRUYAN is secretary of the Federation of American Scientists, founded in 1945 by the original atomic scientists to combat the misuse of science and technology. She is also a writer and television producer.

CARL SAGAN teaches and does research at Cornell University. The idea that fetal brain activity might help provide a rational compromise in the abortion debate was raised in his 1977 book, The Dragons of Eden, *for which he received the Pulitzer Prize.*

THE issue had been decided years ago. The court had chosen the middle ground. You'd think the fight was over. Instead, there are mass rallies, bombings and intimidation, arrests, intense lobbying, legislative drama, Congressional hearings, Supreme Court decisions and clerics threatening politicians with perdition. Partisans fling accusations of hypocrisy and murder. The intent of the Constitution and will of God are equally invoked. Doubtful arguments are trotted out as certainties. The contending factions call on science to bolster their positions. Families are divided, husbands and wives agree not to discuss it, old friends are no longer speaking. Politicians check the latest polls to discover the dictates of their consciences. Amid all the shouting, it is hard for the adversaries to hear one another. Opinions are polarized. Minds are closed.

Is it wrong to abort a pregnancy? Always? Sometimes? Never? How do we decide? We wrote this article to understand better what the contending views are and to see if we ourselves could find a position that would satisfy us both. We had to weigh the arguments of both sides for consistency and to pose test cases, some of which are purely hypothetical. If in some of these tests we seem to go too far, we ask the reader to be patient with us — we're trying to stress the various positions to the breaking point to see their weaknesses and where they fail.

In contemplative moments, nearly everyone recognizes that the issue is not wholly one-sided. Many partisans of differing views, we find, feel some disquiet, some unease when confronting what's behind the opposing arguments. (This is partly why such confrontations are avoided.) And the issue surely touches on deep questions: What are our responsibilities to one another? Should we permit the state to intrude into the most intimate and personal aspects of our lives? Where are the boundaries of freedom? What does it mean to be human?

Testing "Freedom of Choice"

Of the many actual points of view, it is widely held — especially in the media, which rarely have the time or the inclination to make fine distinctions — that there are only two: "pro-choice" and "pro-life." This is what the two principal warring camps like to call themselves, and that's what we'll call them here. In the simplest characterization, a pro-choicer would hold that the decision to abort a pregnancy is to be made only by the woman; the state has no right to interfere. And a pro-lifer would hold that, from the moment of conception, the embryo or fetus is alive; that this life imposes on us a moral obligation to preserve it; and that abortion is tantamount to murder. Both names — pro-choice and pro-life — were picked with an eye toward influencing those whose minds are not yet made up: Few people wish to be counted as being against freedom of choice or as opposed to life. Indeed, freedom and life are two of our most cherished values, and here they seem to be in fundamental conflict.

Let's consider these two absolutist positions in turn. A newborn baby is surely the same being it was just before birth. There is good evidence that a late-term fetus responds to sound — including music, but especially its mother's voice. It can suck its thumb or do a somersault. Occasionally, it generates adult brain wave patterns. Some people say they remember being born, or even the uterine environment. Perhaps there is thought in the womb. It's hard to maintain that a transformation to full personhood happens abruptly at the moment of birth. Why, then, should it be murder to kill an infant the day after it was born but not the day before?

As a practical matter, this isn't very important: less than one percent of all tabulated abortions in the United States are listed in the last three months of pregnancy (and, on closer investigation, most such reports turn out to be due to miscarriage or miscalculation). But third-trimester abortions provide a test of the limits of the pro-choice point of view. Does a woman's "innate right to control her own body" include the right to kill a near-term fetus who is, for all intents and purposes, identical to a newborn child?

We believe that many supporters of reproductive freedom are troubled at least occasionally by this question. But they are reluctant to raise it because it is the beginning of a slippery slope. If it is impermissible to abort a pregnancy in the ninth month, what about the eighth, seventh, sixth . . .? Once we acknowledge that the state can interfere at *any* time in the pregnancy, doesn't it follow that the state can interfere at all times?

This conjures up the specter of predominantly male, predominantly affluent legislators telling poor women they must bear and raise alone children they cannot afford to bring up; forcing teenagers to bear children they are not emotionally prepared to deal with; saying to women who wish for a career that they must give up their dreams, stay home and bring up babies; and, worst of all, condemning victims of rape and incest to carry and nurture the offspring of their assailants. Legislative prohibitions on abortion arouse the suspicion that their real intent is to control the independence and sexuality of women. Why should legislators have any right at all to tell women what to do with their bodies? To be deprived of reproductive freedom is demeaning. Women are fed up with being pushed around.

And yet, by consensus, all of us think it proper that there be prohibitions against, and penalties exacted for, murder. It would be a flimsy defense if the murderer pleads that this is just between him and his victim and none of the government's business. If killing a fetus is truly killing a human being, is it not the *duty* of the state to prevent it? Indeed, one of the chief functions of government is to protect the weak from the strong.

If we do not oppose abortion at *some* stage of pregnancy, is there not a danger of dismissing an entire category of human beings as unworthy of our protection and respect? And isn't that dismissal the hallmark of sexism, racism, nationalism and religious fanaticism? Shouldn't those dedicated to fighting such injustices be scrupulously careful not to embrace another?

Testing the "Right to Life"

There is no right to life in any society on Earth today, nor has there been at any former time (with a few rare exceptions, such as among the Jains of India): We raise farm animals for slaughter; destroy forests; pollute rivers and lakes until no fish can live there; kill deer and elk for sport, leopards for their pelts and whales for fertilizer; entrap dolphins, gasping and writhing, in great tuna nets; club seal pups to death; and render a species extinct every day. All these beasts and vegetables are as alive as we. What is (allegedly) protected is not life, but *human* life.

And even with that protection, casual murder is an urban commonplace, and we wage "conventional" wars with tolls so terrible that we are, most of us, afraid to consider them very deeply. (Tellingly, state-organized mass murders are often justified by redefining our opponents — by race, nationality, religion or ideology — as less than human.) That protection, that right to life, eluded the 40,000 children under 5 who died on our planet today — as every day — from preventable starvation, dehydration, disease and neglect.

Those who assert a "right to life" are for (at most) not just any kind of life, but for — particularly and uniquely — human life. So they too, like pro-choicers, must decide what distinguishes a human being from other animals, and when, during gestation, the uniquely human qualities — whatever they are — emerge.

Despite many claims to the contrary, life does not begin at conception: It is an unbroken chain that stretches back nearly to the origin of the Earth, 4.6 billion years ago. Nor does *human* life begin at conception: It is an unbroken chain dating back to the origin of our species, tens or hundreds of thousands of years ago. Every human sperm and egg is, beyond the shadow of a doubt, alive. They are not human beings, of course. However, it could be argued that neither is a fertilized egg.

In some animals, an egg develops into a healthy adult without benefit of a sperm cell. But not, so far as we know, among humans. A sperm and an unfertilized egg jointly comprise the full genetic blueprint for a human being. Under certain circumstances, after fertilization, they can develop into a baby. But most fertilized eggs are spontaneously miscarried. Development into a baby is by no means guaranteed. Neither a sperm and egg separately, nor a fertilized egg, is more than a *potential* baby or a *potential* adult. So if a sperm and an egg are as human as the fertilized egg produced by their union, and if it is murder to destroy a fertilized egg — despite the fact that it's only *potentially* a baby — why isn't it murder to destroy a sperm or an egg?

Hundreds of millions of sperm cells (top speed with tails lashing: 5 inches per hour) are produced in an average human ejaculation. A healthy young man can produce in a week or two enough spermatozoa to double the human population of the Earth. So is masturbation mass murder? How about nocturnal emissions or just plain sex? When the unfertilized egg is expelled each month, has someone died? Some lower animals can be grown in the laboratory from a single body cell. If such cloning technology were ever developed for humans, would we be committing genocide by shedding a drop of blood?

All human sperm and eggs are genetic halves of "potential" human beings. Should heroic efforts be made to save and preserve all of them, everywhere, because of this "potential"? Is failure to do so immoral or criminal? Of course, there's a difference between taking a life and failing to save it. And there's a big difference between the probability of survival of a sperm cell and that of a fertilized egg. But the absurdity of a corps of high-minded semen-preservers moves us to wonder whether a fertilized egg's mere "potential" to become a baby really does make destroying it murder.

Opponents of abortion worry that, once abortion is permissible immediately after conception, no argument will restrict it at any later time in the pregnancy. Then, they fear, one day it will be permissible to murder a fetus that is unambiguously a human being. Both pro-choicers and pro-lifers (at least some of them) are pushed toward absolutist positions by parallel fears of the slippery slope.

Another slippery slope is reached by those pro-lifers who are willing to make an exception in the agonizing case of a pregnancy resulting from rape or incest. But why should the right to live depend on the *circumstances* of conception? If the same child were to result, can the state ordain life for the offspring of a lawful union but death for one conceived by force or coercion? How can this be just? And if exceptions are extended to such a fetus, why should they be withheld from any other fetus? This is part of the reason some pro-lifers adopt what many others consider the outrageous posture of opposing abortions under any and all circumstances — only excepting, perhaps, when the life of the mother is in danger.

By far the most common reason for abortion is birth-control. So shouldn't opponents of abortion be handing out contraceptives? That would be an effective way to reduce the number of abortions. Instead, the United States is far behind other nations in the development of safe and effective methods of birth control — and, in many cases, opposition to such research (and to sex education) has come from the same people who oppose abortions.

When Do We Become Human?

The attempt to find an ethically sound and unambiguous judgment on when, if ever, abortion is permissible has deep historical roots. Often, especially in Christian tradition, such attempts were connected with the question of when the soul enters the body — a matter not readily amenable to scientific investigation and an issue of controversy even among learned theologians. Ensoulment has been asserted to occur in the sperm before conception, at conception, at the time of "quickening" (when the mother is first able to feel the fetus stirring within her) and at birth. Or even later.

Different religions have different teachings. Among hunter-gatherers, there are usually no prohibitions against abortion, and it was common in ancient Greece and Rome. The Assyrians impaled women on stakes for attempting abortions. The Jewish Talmud teaches that the fetus is not a person and has no rights. The Old and New Testaments — rich in detailed prohibitions on dress, diet and permissible words — contain not a word specifically prohibiting abortion. The only passage that's remotely relevant (*Exodus* 21:22) decrees that if there's a fight and a woman bystander is accidentally injured and made to miscarry, the assailant must pay a fine. The Catholic Church's first and longstanding collection of canon law (according to the leading historian of the Church's teachings on abortion, John Connery, S.J.) held that abortion was homicide only after the fetus was already "formed" — roughly, the end of the first trimester. It was not until 1869 that abortion at any time for any reason became grounds for excommunication.

If you deliberately kill a human being, it's called murder. If you deliberately kill a chimpanzee — biologically, our closest relative — whatever else it is, it's not murder. To date, murder uniquely applies to killing human beings. Therefore, the question of when personhood (or, if we like, ensoulment) arises is key to the abortion debate. When does the fetus become human? When do distinct and characteristic human qualities emerge?

We recognize that specifying a precise moment will overlook individual differences. Therefore, if we must draw a line, it ought to be drawn conservatively — that is, on the early side. There are people who object to having to set some numerical limit, and we share their disquiet; but if there is to be a law on this matter, and it is to effect some useful compromise between the two absolutist positions, it must specify, at least roughly, a time of transition to personhood.

Every one of us began from a dot. A fertilized egg is roughly the size of the period at the end of this sentence. The momentous meeting of sperm and egg generally occurs in one of the two fallopian tubes. One cell becomes two, two become four, and by the sixth day the fertilized egg has become a kind of hollow sphere wandering off to another realm: the womb. It destroys tissue in its path. It sucks blood from capillaries. It establishes itself as a kind of parasite on the walls of the uterus.

▶ By the third week, around the time of the first missed menstrual period, the forming embryo is about 2 millimeters long and is developing various body parts. But it looks a little like a segmented worm.

▶ By the end of the fourth week, it's approximately 5 millimeters (about ⅕ inch) long. It's recognizable as a vertebrate, its tube-shaped heart is beginning to beat, something like the gill arches of a fish or an amphibian have become conspicuous, and there is a pronounced tail. It looks something like a newt or a tadpole. This is the end of the first month after conception.

▶ By the fifth week, the gross divisions of the brain can be distinguished. What will later develop into eyes is apparent, and little buds appear — on their way to becoming arms and legs.

▶ By the sixth week, the embryo is 13 millimeters (about ½ inch) long. The eyes are still on the side of the head, as in most animals, and the reptilian face has connected slits where the mouth and nose eventually will be.

▶ By the end of the seventh week, the tail is almost gone, and sexual characteristics can be discerned (although both sexes look female). The face is mammalian but somewhat piglike.

▶ By the end of the eighth week, the face resembles a primate's but is still not quite human. Most of the human body parts are present in their essentials. Some lower brain anatomy is well-developed. The fetus shows some reflex response to delicate stimulation.

▶ By the tenth week, the face has an unmistakably human cast. It is beginning to be possible to distinguish males from females. Nails and major bone structures are not apparent until the third month.

▶ By the fourth month, you can tell the face of one fetus from that of another. Quickening is most often first felt in the fifth month. The bronchioles of the lungs do not begin developing until approximately the sixth month, the alveoli still later. Recognizably human brain activity begins intermittently around the middle of the seventh month.

So, if only a person can be murdered, when does the fetus attain personhood? When its face becomes distinctly human, near the end of the first trimester? When the fetus becomes responsive to stimuli —

again, at the end of the first trimester? When the fetus becomes active enough to be felt as quickening, typically in the middle of the second trimester? When the lungs have reached a stage of development sufficient that the fetus might, just conceivably, be able to breathe on its own in the outside air?

The trouble with such developmental milestones is not just that they're arbitrary. More troubling is the fact that none of them involves *uniquely human* characteristics — apart from the superficial matter of facial appearance. All animals respond to stimuli and move of their own volition. Large numbers are able to breathe. But that doesn't stop us from slaughtering them. Reflexes and motion and respiration are not what makes us human.

Other animals have advantages over us — in speed, strength, endurance, climbing or burrowing skills, camouflage, sight or smell or hearing, mastery of the air or water. Our one great advantage, the secret of our success, is thought — characteristically human thought. We are able to think things through, imagine events yet to occur, figure things out. That's how we invented agriculture and civilization. Thought is our blessing and our curse, and it makes us who we are.

Thinking occurs, of course, in the brain — principally in the top layers of the convoluted "gray matter" called the cerebral cortex. The roughly 100 billion neurons in the brain constitute the material basis of thought. The neurons are connected to each other, and their linkups play a major role in what we experience as thinking. But large-scale linking up of neurons doesn't begin until the 24th to 27th week of pregnancy — the sixth month.

By placing harmless electrodes on a subject's head, scientists can measure the electrical activity produced by the network of neurons inside the skull. Differ-

ent kinds of mental activity show different kinds of brain waves. But brain waves with regular patterns typical of adult human brains do not appear in the fetus until about the 30th week of pregnancy — near the beginning of the third trimester. Fetuses younger than this — however alive and active they may be — lack the necessary brain architecture. They cannot yet think.

Acquiescing in the killing of any living creature, especially one that might later become a baby, is troublesome and painful. But we've rejected the extremes of "always" and "never," and this puts us — like it or not — on the slippery slope. If we are forced to choose a developmental criterion, then this is where we draw the line: when the beginning of characteristically human thinking becomes barely possible. It is, in fact, a very conservative definition: Regular brain waves are rarely found in fetuses. More research would help. If we wanted to make the criterion still more stringent, to allow for precocious fetal brain development, we might draw the line at six months. This, it so happens, is where the Supreme Court drew it in 1973 — although for completely different reasons.

Viability and the Court

Its decision in the case of *Roe v. Wade* changed American law on abortion. It permits abortion at the request of the woman without restriction in the first trimester and, with some restrictions intended to protect her health, in the second trimester. It allows states to forbid abortion in the third trimester, except when there's a serious threat to the life or health of the woman. In a recent reassessment, the Supreme Court declined explicitly to overturn *Roe v. Wade* but in effect invited the 50 state legislatures to decide for themselves.

What was the reasoning in *Roe v. Wade*? There was no legal weight given to what happens to the children once they are born, or to the family. Instead, a woman's right to reproductive freedom is protected, the court ruled, by constitutional guarantees of privacy. But that right is not unqualified. The woman's guarantee of privacy and the fetus's right to life must be weighed — and when the court did the weighing, priority was given to privacy in the first trimester and to life in the third. The transition was decided not from any of the considerations we have been dealing with so far in this article — not when "ensoulment" occurs, not when the fetus takes on sufficient human characteristics to be protected by laws against murder. Instead, the criterion adopted was whether the fetus could live outside the mother. This is called "viability" and depends in part on the ability to breathe. The lungs are simply not developed, and the fetus cannot breathe — no matter how advanced an artificial lung it might be placed in — until about the 24th week, near the start of the sixth month. This is why *Roe v. Wade* permits states to prohibit abortions in the last trimester. It's a very pragmatic criterion.

If the fetus at a certain stage of gestation would be viable outside the womb, the argument goes, then the right of the fetus to life overrides the right of the woman to privacy. But just what does "viable" mean? Even a full-term newborn is not viable without a great deal of care and love. There was a time before incubators, only a few decades ago, when babies in their seventh month were unlikely to be viable. Would aborting in the seventh month have been permissible then? After the invention of incubators, did aborting pregnancies in the seventh month suddenly become immoral? What happens if, in the future, a new technology develops so that an artificial womb can sustain a fetus even before the sixth month by delivering oxygen and nutrients though the blood — as the mother does through the placenta and into the fetal blood system? We grant that this technology is unlikely to be developed soon or become available to many. But *if* it were available, does it then become immoral to abort earlier than the sixth month, when previously it was moral? A morality that depends on, and changes with, technology is a fragile morality; for some, it is also an unacceptable morality.

And why, exactly, should breathing (or kidney function, or the ability to resist disease) justify legal protection? If a fetus can be shown to think and feel but not be able to breathe, would it be all right to kill it? Do we value breathing more than thinking and feeling? Viability arguments cannot, it seems to us, coherently determine when abortions are permissible. Some other criterion is needed. Again, we offer for consideration the earliest onset of human thinking as that criterion.

Since, on average, fetal thinking occurs even later than fetal lung development, we find *Roe v. Wade* to be a good and prudent decision addressing a complex and difficult issue. With prohibitions on abortion in the last trimester — except in cases of grave medical necessity — it strikes a fair balance between the conflicting claims of freedom and of life.

JUDITH JARVIS THOMSON
A Defense of Abortion

JUDITH JARVIS THOMSON *teaches philosophy at the Massachusetts Institute of Technology. Some of her extensive writings on ethics are collected in* Rights, Restitution and Risk *(1986); her latest book is* The Realm of Rights *(1990).*

MOST opposition to abortion relies on the premise that the fetus is a human being, a person, from the moment of conception. The premise is argued for, but, as I think, not well. Take, for example, the most common argument. We are asked to notice that the development of a human being from conception through birth into childhood is continuous; then it is said that to draw a line, to choose a point in this development and say "before this point the thing is not a person, after this point it is a person" is to make an arbitrary choice, a choice for which in the nature of things no good reason can be given. It is concluded that the fetus is, or anyway that we had better say it is, a person from the moment of conception. But this conclusion does not follow. Similar things might be said about the development of an acorn into an oak tree, and it does not follow that acorns are oak trees, or that we had better say they are. Arguments of this form are sometimes called "slippery slope arguments" — the phrase is perhaps self-explanatory — and it is dismaying that opponents of abortion rely on them so heavily and uncritically.

I am inclined to agree, however, that the prospects for "drawing a line" in the development of the fetus look dim. I am inclined to think also that we shall probably have to agree that the fetus has already become a human person well before birth. Indeed, it comes as a surprise when one first learns how early in its life it begins to acquire human characteristics. By the tenth week, for example, it already has a face, arms and legs, fingers and toes; it has internal organs, and brain activity is detectable. On the other hand, I think that the premise is false, that the fetus is not a person from the moment of conception. A newly fertilized ovum, a newly implanted clump of cells, is no more a person than an acorn is an oak tree. But I shall not discuss any of this. For it seems to me to be of great interest to ask what happens if, for the sake of argument, we allow the premise. How, precisely, are we supposed to get from there to the conclusion that abortion is morally impermissible? Opponents of abortion commonly spend most of their time establishing that the fetus is a person, and hardly any time explaining the step from there to the impermissibility of abortion. Perhaps they think the step too simple and obvious to require much comment. Or perhaps instead they are simply being economical in argument. Many of those who defend abortion rely on the premise that the fetus is not a person, but only a bit of tissue that will become a person at birth; and why pay out more arguments than you have to? Whatever the explanation, I suggest that the step they take is neither easy nor obvious, that it calls for closer examination than it is commonly given, and that when we do give it this closer examination we shall feel inclined to reject it.

I propose, then, that we grant that the fetus is a person from the moment of conception. How does the argument go from here? Something like this, I take it. Every person has a right to life. So the fetus has a right to life. No doubt the mother has a right to decide what shall happen in and to her body; everyone would grant that. But surely a person's right to life is stronger and more stringent than the mother's right to decide what happens in and to her body, and so outweighs it. So the fetus may not be killed; an abortion may not be performed.

It sounds plausible. But now let me ask you to imagine this. You wake up in the morning and find yourself back to back in bed with an unconscious violinist. A famous unconscious violinist. He has been found to have a fatal kidney ailment, and the Society of Music Lovers has canvassed all the available medical records and found that you alone have the right blood type to help. They have therefore kidnapped you, and last night the violinist's circulatory system was plugged into yours, so that your kidneys can be used to extract poisons from his blood as well as your own. The director of the hospital now tells you, "Look, we're sorry the Society of Music Lovers did this to you — we would never have permitted it if we had known. But still, they did it, and the violinist now is plugged into you. To unplug you would be to kill him. But never mind, it's only for nine months. By then he will have recovered from his ailment, and can safely be unplugged from you." Is it morally incumbent on you to accede to this situation? No doubt it would be very nice of you if you did, a great kindness. But do you *have* to accede to it? What if it were not nine months, but nine years? Or longer still? What if the director of the hospital says, "Tough luck, I agree, but you've now got to stay in bed, with the violinist plugged into you, for the rest of your life. Because remember this. All persons have a right to life, and violinists

are persons. Granted you have a right to decide what happens in and to your body, but a person's right to life outweighs your right to decide what happens in and to your body. So you cannot ever be unplugged from him." I imagine you would regard this as outrageous, which suggests that something really is wrong with that plausible-sounding argument I mentioned a moment ago.

In this case, of course, you were kidnapped; you didn't volunteer for the operation that plugged the violinist into your kidneys. Can those who oppose abortion on the ground I mentioned make an exception for a pregnancy due to rape? Certainly. They can say that persons have a right to life only if they didn't come into existence because of rape; or they can say that all persons have a right to life, but that some have less of a right to life than others, in particular, that those who came into existence because of rape have less. But these statements have a rather unpleasant sound. Surely the question of whether you have a right to life at all, or how much of it you have, shouldn't turn on the question of whether or not you are the product of a rape. And in fact the people who oppose abortion on the ground I mentioned do not make this distinction, and hence do not make an exception in case of rape.

Nor do they make an exception for a case in which the mother has to spend the nine months of her pregnancy in bed. They would agree that would be a great pity, and hard on the mother; but all the same, all persons have a right to life, the fetus is a person, and so on. I suspect, in fact, that they would not make an exception for a case in which, miraculously enough, the pregnancy went on for nine years, or even the rest of the mother's life.

Some won't even make an exception for a case in which continuation of the pregnancy is likely to shorten the mother's life; they regard abortion as impermissible even to save the mother's life. Such cases are nowadays very rare, and many opponents of abortion do not accept this extreme view. All the same, it is a good place to begin: a number of points of interest come out in respect to it.

1. Let us call the view that abortion is impermissible even to save the mother's life "the extreme view." I want to suggest first that it does not issue from the argument I mentioned earlier without the addition of some fairly powerful premises. Suppose a woman has become pregnant, and now learns that she has a cardiac condition such that she will die if she carries the baby to term. What may be done for her? The fetus, being a person, has a right to life, but as the mother is a person too, so has she a right to life. Presumably they have an equal right to life. How is it supposed to come out that an abortion may not be performed? If mother and child have an equal right to life, shouldn't we perhaps flip a coin? Or should we add to the mother's right to life her right to decide what happens in and to her body, which everybody seems to be ready to grant — the sum of her rights now outweighing the fetus' right to life?

The most familiar argument here is the following. We are told that performing the abortion would be directly killing the child, whereas doing nothing would not be killing the mother, but only letting her die. Moreover, in killing the child, one would be killing an innocent person, for the child has committed no crime, and is not aiming at his mother's death. And then there are a variety of ways in which this might be continued. (1) But as directly killing an innocent person is always and absolutely impermissible, an abortion may not be performed. Or, (2) as directly killing an innocent person is murder, and murder is always and absolutely impermissible, an abortion may not be performed. Or, (3) as one's duty to refrain from directly killing an innocent person is more stringent than one's duty to keep a person from dying, an abortion may not be performed. Or, (4) if one's only options are directly killing an innocent person or letting a person die, one must prefer letting the person die, and thus an abortion may not be performed.

Some people seem to have thought that these are not further premises which must be added if the conclusion is to be reached, but that they follow from the very fact that an innocent person has a right to life. But this seems to me to be a mistake, and perhaps the simplest way to show this is to bring out that while we must certainly grant that innocent persons have a right to life, the theses in (1) through (4) are all false. Take (2), for example. If directly killing an innocent person is murder, and thus is impermissible, then the mother's directly killing the innocent person inside her is murder, and thus is impermissible. But it cannot seriously be thought to be murder if the mother performs an abortion on herself to save her life. It cannot seriously be said that she *must* refrain, that she *must* sit passively by and wait for her death. Let us look again at the case of you and the violinist. There you are, in bed with the violinist, and the director of the hospital says to you, "It's all most distressing, and I deeply sympathize, but you see this is putting an additional strain on your kidneys, and you'll be dead within the month. But you *have* to stay where you are all the same. Because unplugging you would be directly killing an innocent violinist, and that's murder, and that's impermissible." If anything in the world is true, it is that you do not commit murder, you do not do what is impermissible, if you reach around to your back and unplug yourself from that violinist to save your life.

The main focus of attention in writings on abortion has been on what a third party may or may not do in answer to a request from a woman for an abortion. This is in a way understandable. Things being as they are, there isn't much a woman can safely do to abort herself. So the question asked is what a third party may do, and what the mother may do, if it is mentioned at all, is deduced, almost as an afterthought, from what it is concluded that third parties may do. But it seems to me that to treat the matter in this way is to refuse to grant to the mother that very status of person which is so firmly insisted on for the fetus. For we cannot simply read off what a person may do from what a third party may do. Suppose you find yourself trapped in a tiny house with a growing child. I mean a very tiny house, and a rapidly growing child—you are already up against the wall of the house and in a few minutes you'll be crushed to death. The child on the other hand won't be crushed to death; if nothing is done to stop him from growing he'll be hurt, but in the end he'll simply burst open the house and walk out a free man. Now I could well understand it if a bystander were to say, "There's nothing we can do for you. We cannot choose between your life and his, we cannot be the ones to decide who is to live, we cannot intervene." But it cannot be concluded that you too can do nothing, that you cannot attack it to save your life. However innocent the child may be, you do not have to wait passively while it crushes you to death. Perhaps a pregnant woman is vaguely felt to have the status of house, to which we don't allow the right of self-defense. But if the woman houses the child, it should be remembered that she is a person who houses it.

I should perhaps stop to say explicitly that I am not claiming that people have a right to do anything whatever to save their lives. I think, rather, that there are drastic limits to the right of self-defense. If someone threatens you with death unless you torture someone else to death, I think you have not the right, even to save your life, to do so. But the case under consideration here is very different. In our case there are only two people involved, one whose life is threatened, and one who threatens it. Both are innocent: the one who is threatened is not threatened because of any fault, the one who threatens does not threaten because of any fault. For this reason we may feel that we bystanders cannot intervene. But the person threatened can.

In sum, a woman surely can defend her life against the threat to it posed by the unborn child, even if doing so involves its death. And this shows not merely that the theses in (1) through (4) are false; it shows also that the extreme view of abortion is false, and so we need not canvass any other possible ways of arriving at it from the argument I mentioned at the outset.

2. The extreme view could of course be weakened to say that while abortion is permissible to save the mother's life, it may not be performed by a third party, but only by the mother herself. But this cannot be right either. For what we have to keep in mind is that the mother and the unborn child are not like two tenants in a small house which has, by an unfortunate mistake, been rented to both: the mother *owns* the house. The fact that she does adds to the offensiveness of deducing that the mother can do nothing from the supposition that third parties can do nothing. But it does more than this: it casts a bright light on the supposition that third parties can do nothing. Certainly it lets us see that a third party who says "I cannot choose between you" is fooling himself if he thinks this is impartiality. If Jones has found and fastened on a certain coat,

which he needs to keep him from freezing, but which Smith also needs to keep him from freezing, then it is not impartiality that says "I cannot chose between you" when Smith owns the coat. Women have said again and again "This body is *my* body!" and they have reason to feel angry, reason to feel that it has been like shouting into the wind. Smith, after all, is hardly likely to bless us if we say to him, "Of course it's your coat anybody would grant that it is. But no one may choose between you and Jones who is to have it."

We should really ask what it is that says "no one may choose in the face of the fact that the body that houses the child is the mother's body. It may be simply a failure to appreciate this fact. But it may be something more interesting, namely the sense that one has a right to refuse to lay hands on people, even where it would be just and fair to do so, even where justice seems to require that somebody do so. This justice might call for somebody to get Smith's coat back from Jones and yet you have a right to refuse to be the one to lay hands on Jones, a right to refuse to do physical violence to him. This, I think, must be granted. But then what should be said is not "no one may choose, but only "*I* cannot choose," and indeed not even this, but "*I* will not *act*," leaving it open that somebody else can or should, and in particular that anyone in a position of authority, with the job of securing people's rights, both can and should. So this is no difficulty. I have not been arguing that any given third party must accede to the mother's request that he perform an abortion to save her life, but only that he may.

I suppose that in some views of human life the mother's body is only on loan to her, the loan not being one which gives her any prior claim to it. One who held this view might well think it impartiality to say "I cannot choose." But I shall simply ignore this possibility. My own view is that if a human being has any just, prior claim to anything at all, he has a just, prior claim to his own body. And perhaps this needn't be argued for here anyway, since, as I mentioned, the arguments against abortion we are looking at do grant that the woman has a right to decide what happens in and to her body.

But although they do grant it, I have tried to show that they do not take seriously what is done in granting it. I suggest the same thing will reappear even more clearly when we turn away from cases in which the mother's life is at stake, and attend, as I propose we now do, to the vastly more common cases in which a woman wants an abortion for some less weighty reason than preserving her own life.

3. Where the mother's life is not at stake, the argument I mentioned at the outset seems to have a much stronger pull. "Everyone has a right to life, so the unborn person has a right to life." And isn't the child's right to life weightier than anything other than the mother's own right to life, which she might put forward as ground for an abortion?

This argument treats the right to life as if it were unproblematic. It is not, and this seems to me to be precisely the source of the mistake.

For we should now, at long last, ask what it comes to, to have a right to life. In some views having a right to life includes having a right to be given at least the bare minimum one needs for continued life. But suppose that what in fact *is* the bare minimum a man needs for continued life is something he has no right at all to be given? If I am sick unto death, and the only thing that will save my life is the touch of Henry Fonda's cool hand on my fevered brow, then all the same, I have no right to be given the touch of Henry Fonda's cool hand on my fevered brow. It would be frightfully nice of him to fly in from the West Coast to provide it. It would be less nice, though no doubt well meant, if my friends flew out to the West Coast and carried Henry Fonda back with them. But I have no right at all against anybody that he should do this for me. Or again, to return to the story I told earlier, the fact that for continued life that violinist needs the continued use of your kidneys does not establish that he has a right to be given the continued use of your kidneys. He certainly has no right against you that *you* should give him continued use of your kidneys. For nobody has any right to use your kidneys unless you give him such a right; and nobody has the right against you that you shall give him this right—if you do allow him to go on using your kidneys, this is a kindness on your part, and not something he can claim from you as his due. Nor has he any right against anybody else that *they* should give him continued use of your kidneys. Certainly he had no right against the Society of Music Lovers that they should plug him into you in the first place. And if you now start to unplug yourself, having learned that you will otherwise have to spend nine years in bed with him, there is nobody in the world who must try to prevent you, in order to see to it that he is given something he has a right to be given.

Some people are rather stricter about the right to life. In their view, it does not include the right to be given anything, but amounts to, and only to, the right not to be killed by anybody. But here a related difficulty arises. If everybody is to refrain from killing that violinist, then everybody must refrain from doing a great many different sorts of things. Everybody must refrain from slitting his throat, everybody must refrain from shooting him—and

everybody must refrain from unplugging you from him. But does he have a right against everybody that they shall refrain from unplugging you from him? To refrain from doing this is to allow him to continue to use your kidneys. It could be argued that he has a right against us that *we* should allow him to continue to use your kidneys. That is, while he had no right against us that we should give him the use of your kidneys, it might be argued that he anyway has a right against us that we shall not now intervene and deprive him of the use of your kidneys. I shall come back to third-party interventions later. But certainly the violinist has no right against you that *you* shall allow him to continue to use your kidneys. As I said, if you do allow him to use them, it is a kindness on your part, and not something you owe him.

The difficulty I point to here is not peculiar to the right to life. It reappears in connection with all the other natural rights; and it is something which an adequate account of rights must deal with. For present purposes it is enough just to draw attention to it. But I would stress that I am not arguing that people do not have a right to life—quite to the contrary, it seems to me that the primary control we must place on the acceptability of an account of rights is that it should turn out in that account to be a truth that all persons have a right to life. I am arguing only that having a right to life does not guarantee having either a right to be given the use of or a right to be allowed continued use of another person's body—even if one needs it for life itself. So the right to life will not serve the opponents of abortion in the very simple and clear way in which they seem to have thought it would.

4. There is another way to bring out the difficulty. In the most ordinary sort of case, to deprive someone of what he has

a right to is to treat him unjustly. Suppose a boy and his small brother are jointly given a box of chocolates for Christmas. If the older boy takes the box and refuses to give his brother any of the chocolates, he is unjust to him, for the brother has been given a right to half of them. But suppose that, having learned that otherwise it means nine years in bed with that violinist, you unplug yourself from him. You surely are not being unjust to him, for you gave him no right to use your kidneys, and no one else can have given him any such right. But we have to notice that in unplugging yourself, you are killing him; and violinists, like everybody else, have a right to life, and thus in the view we were considering just now, the right not to be killed. So here you do what he supposedly has a right you shall not do, but you do not act unjustly to him in doing it.

The emendation which may be made at this point is this: the right to life consists not in the right not to be killed, but rather in the right not to be killed unjustly. This runs a risk of circularity, but never mind: it would enable us to square the fact that the violinist has a right to life with the fact that you do not act unjustly toward him in unplugging yourself, thereby killing him. For if you do not kill him unjustly, you do not violate his right to life, and so it is no wonder you do him no injustice.

But if this emendation is accepted, the gap in the argument against abortion stares us plainly in the face: it is by no means enough to show that the fetus is a person, and to remind us that all persons have a right to life — we need to be shown also that killing the fetus violates its right to life, i.e., that abortion is unjust killing. And is it?

I suppose we may take it as a datum that in a case of pregnancy due to rape the mother has not given the unborn person a right to the use of her body for food and shelter. Indeed, in what pregnancy could it be supposed that the mother has given the unborn person such a right? It is not as if there were unborn persons drifting about the world, to whom a woman who wants a child says "I invite you in."

But it might be argued that there are other ways one can have acquired a right to the use of another person's body than by having been invited to use it by that person. Suppose a woman voluntarily indulges in intercourse, knowing of the chance it will issue in pregnancy, and then she does become pregnant; is she not in part responsible for the presence, in fact the very existence, of the unborn person inside her? No doubt she did not invite it in. But doesn't her partial responsibility for its being there itself give it a right to the use of her body? If so, then her aborting it would be more like the boy's taking away the chocolates, and less like your unplugging yourself from the violinist — doing so would be depriving it of what it does have a right to, and thus would be doing it an injustice.

And then, too, it might be asked whether or not she can kill it even to save her own life: If she voluntarily called it into existence, how can she now kill it, even in self-defense?

The first thing to be said about this is that it is something new. Opponents of abortion have been so concerned to make out the independence of the fetus, in order to establish that it has a right to life, just as its mother does, that they have tended to overlook the possible support they might gain from making out that the fetus is *dependent* on the mother, in order to establish that she has a special kind of responsibility for it, a responsibility that gives it rights against her which are not possessed by any independent person—

such as an ailing violinist who is a stranger to her.

On the other hand, this argument would give the unborn person a right to its mother's body only if her pregnancy resulted from a voluntary act, undertaken in full knowledge of the chance a pregnancy might result from it. It would leave out entirely the unborn person whose existence is due to rape. Pending the availability of some further argument, then, we would be left with the conclusion that unborn persons whose existence is due to rape have no right to the use of their mothers' bodies, and thus that aborting them is not depriving them of anything they have a right to and hence is not unjust killing.

And we should also notice that it is not at all plain that this argument really does go even as far as it purports to. For there are cases and cases, and the details make a difference. If the room is stuffy, and I therefore open a window to air it, and a burglar climbs in, it would be absurd to say, "Ah, now he can stay, she's given him a right to the use of her house — for she is partially responsible for his presence there, having voluntarily done what enabled him to get in, in full knowledge that there are such things as burglars, and that burglars burgle." It would be still more absurd to say this if I had had bars installed outside my windows, precisely to prevent burglars from getting in, and a burglar got in only because of a defect in the bars. It remains equally absurd if we imagine it is not a burglar who climbs in, but an innocent person who blunders or falls in. Again, suppose it were like this: people-seeds drift about in the air like pollen, and if you open your windows, one may drift in and take root in your carpets or upholstery. You don't want children, so you fix up your windows with fine mesh screens, the very best you can buy. As can happen, however, and on

very, very rare occasions does happen, one of the screens is defective; and a seed drifts in and takes root. Does the person-plant who now develops have a right to the use of your house? Surely not — despite the fact that you voluntarily opened your windows, you knowingly kept carpets and upholstered furniture, and you knew that screens were sometimes defective. Someone may argue that you are responsible for its rooting, that it does have a right to your house, because after all you *could* have lived out your life with bare floors and furniture, or with sealed windows and doors. But this won't do — for by the same token anyone can avoid a pregnancy due to rape by having a hysterectomy, or anyway by never leaving home without a (reliable!) army.

It seems to me that the argument we are looking at can establish at most that there are *some* cases in which the unborn person has a right to the use of its mother's body, and therefore *some* cases in which abortion is unjust killing. There is room for much discussion and argument as to precisely which, if any. But I think we should sidestep this issue and leave it open, for at any rate the argument certainly does not establish that all abortion is unjust killing.

5. There is room for yet another argument here, however. We surely must all grant that there may be cases in which it would be morally indecent to detach a person from your body at the cost of his life. Suppose you learn that what the violinist needs is not nine years of your life, but only one hour: all you need do to save his life is to spend one hour in that bed with him. Suppose also that letting him use your kidneys for that one hour would not affect your health in the slightest. Admittedly you were kidnapped. Admittedly you did not give anyone permission to plug him into you. Nevertheless it seems to me plain you *ought* to allow him to use

your kidneys for that hour — it would be indecent to refuse.

Again, suppose pregnancy lasted only an hour, and constituted no threat to life or health. And suppose that a woman becomes pregnant as a result of rape. Admittedly she did not voluntarily do anything to bring about the existence of a child. Admittedly she did nothing at all which would give the unborn person a right to the use of her body. All the same it might well be said, as in the newly emended violinist story, that she *ought* to allow it to remain for that hour — that it would be indecent in her to refuse.

Now some people are inclined to use the term "right" in such a way that it follows from the fact that you ought to allow a person to use your body for the hour he needs, that he has a right to use your body for the hour he needs, even though he has not been given that right by any person or act. They may say that it follows also that if you refuse, you act unjustly toward him. This use of the term is perhaps so common that it cannot be called wrong; nevertheless it seems to me to be an unfortunate loosening of what we would do better to keep a tight rein on. Suppose that box of chocolates I mentioned earlier had not been given to both boys jointly, but was given only to the older boy. There he sits, stolidly eating his way through the box, his small brother watching enviously. Here we are likely to say "You ought not to be so mean. You ought to give your brother some of those chocolates." My own view is that it just does not follow from the truth of this that the brother has any right to any of the chocolates. If the boy refuses to give his brother any, he is greedy, stingy, callous — but not unjust. I suppose that the people I have in mind will say it does follow that the brother has a right to some of the chocolates, and thus that the boy does act unjustly if he refuses to give his

brother any. But the effect of saying this is to obscure what we should keep distinct, namely the difference between the boy's refusal in this case and the boy's refusal in the earlier case, in which the box was given to both boys jointly, and in which the small brother thus had what was from any point of view clear title to half.

A further objection to so using the term "right" that from the fact that A ought to do a thing for B, it follows that B has a right against A that A do it for him, is that it is going to make the question of whether or not a man has a right to a thing turn on how easy it is to provide him with it; and this seems not merely unfortunate, but morally unacceptable. Take the case of Henry Fonda again. I said earlier that I had no right to the touch of his cool hand on my fevered brow, even though I needed it to save my life. I said it would be frightfully nice of him to fly in from the West Coast to provide me with it, but that I had no right against him that he should do so. But suppose he isn't on the West Coast. Suppose he has only to walk across the room, place a hand briefly on my brow — and lo, my life is saved. Then surely he ought to do it, it would be indecent to refuse. Is it to be said "Ah, well, it follows that in this case she has a right to the touch of his hand on her brow, and so it would be an injustice in him to refuse"? So that I have a right to it when it is easy for him to provide it, though no right when it's hard? It's rather a shocking idea that anyone's rights should fade away and disappear as it gets harder and harder to accord them to him.

So my own view is that even though you ought to let the violinist use your kidneys for the one hour he needs, we should not conclude that he has a right to do so — we should say that if you refuse, you are, like the boy who owns all the chocolates and will give none away, self-centered and callous, indecent in fact, but not unjust. And similarly, that even supposing a case in which a woman pregnant due to rape ought to allow the unborn person to use her body for the hour he needs, we should not conclude that he has a right to do so; we should conclude that she is self-centered, callous, indecent, but not unjust, if she refuses. The complaints are no less grave; they are just different. However, there is no need to insist on this point. If anyone does wish to deduce "he has a right" from "you ought," then all the same he must surely grant that there are cases in which it is not morally required of you that you allow that violinist to use your kidneys, and in which he does not have a right to use them, and in which you do not do him an injustice if you refuse. And so also for mother and unborn child. Except in such cases as the unborn person has a right to demand it — and we were leaving open the possibility that there may be such cases — nobody is morally *required* to make large sacrifices, of health, of all other interests and concerns, of all other duties and commitments, for nine years, or even for nine months, in order to keep another person alive.

6. We have in fact to distinguish between two kinds of Samaritan: the Good Samaritan and what we might call the Minimally Decent Samaritan. The story of the Good Samaritan, you will remember, goes like this:

> A certain man went down from Jerusalem to Jericho, and fell among thieves, which stripped him of his raiment, and wounded him, and departed, leaving him half dead.
>
> And by chance there came down a certain priest that way; and when he saw him, he passed by on the other side.
>
> And likewise a Levite, when he was at the place, came and looked on him, and passed by on the other side.
>
> But a certain Samaritan, as he journeyed, came where he was; and when he saw him he had compassion on him.
>
> And went to him, and bound up his wounds, pouring in oil and wine, and set him on his own beast, and brought him to an inn, and took care of him.
>
> And on the morrow, when he departed, he took out two pence, and gave them to the host, and said unto him, "Take care of him; and whatsoever thou spendest more, when I come again, I will repay thee."   (Luke 10:30–35)

The Good Samaritan went out of his way, at some cost to himself, to help one in need of it. We are not told what the options were, that is, whether or not the priest and the Levite could have helped by doing less than the Good Samaritan did, but assuming they could have, then the fact they did nothing at all shows they were not even Minimally Decent Samaritans, not because they were not Samaritans, but because they were not even minimally decent.

These things are a matter of degree, of course, but there is a difference, and it comes out perhaps most clearly in the story of Kitty Genovese, who, as you will remember, was murdered while thirty-eight people watched or listened, and did nothing at all to help her. A Good Samaritan would have rushed out to give direct assistance against the murderer. Or perhaps we had better allow that it would have been a Splendid Samaritan who did this, on the ground that it would have involved a risk of death for himself. But the thirty-eight not only did not do this, they did not even trouble to pick up a phone to call the police. Minimally Decent Samaritanism would call for doing at least that, and their not having done it was monstrous.

After telling the story of the Good Samaritan, Jesus said "Go, and do thou likewise." Perhaps he meant that we are morally required to act as the Good Samaritan did. Perhaps he was urging people to do more than is morally required of them. At all events it seems plain that it was not morally required of any of the thirty-eight that he rush out to give direct assistance at the risk of his own life, and that it is not morally required of anyone that he give long stretches of his life — nine years or nine months — to sustaining the life of a person who has no special right (we were leaving open the possibility of this) to demand it.

Indeed, with one rather striking class of exceptions, no one in any country in the world is *legally* required to do anywhere near as much as this for anyone else. The class of exceptions is obvious. My main concern here is not the state of the law in respect to abortion, but it is worth drawing attention to the fact that in no state in this country is any man compelled by law to be even a Minimally Decent Samaritan to any person; there is no law under which charges could be brought against the thirty-eight who stood by while Kitty Genovese died. By contrast, in most states in this country women are compelled by law to be not merely Minimally Decent Samaritans, but Good Samaritans to unborn persons inside them. This doesn't by itself settle anything one way or the other, because it may well be argued that there should be laws in this country — as there are in many European countries — compelling at least Minimally Decent Samaritanism. But it does show that there is a gross injustice in the existing state of the law. And it shows also that the groups currently working against liberalization of abortion laws, in fact working toward having it declared unconstitutional for a state to permit abortion, had better start working for the adoption of Good Samaritan laws generally, or earn the charge that they are acting in bad faith.

I should think, myself, that Minimally Decent Samaritan laws would be one thing, Good Samaritan laws quite another, and in fact highly improper. But we are not here concerned with the law. What we should ask is not whether anybody should be compelled by law to be a Good Samaritan, but whether we must accede to a situation in which somebody is being compelled — by nature, perhaps — to be a Good Samaritan. We have, in other words, to look now at third-party interventions. I have been arguing that no person is morally required to make large sacrifices to sustain the life of another who has no right to demand them, and this even where the sacrifices do not include life itself; we are not morally required to be Good Samaritans or anyway Very Good Samaritans to one another. But what if a man cannot extricate himself from such a situation? What if he appeals to us to extricate him? It seems to me plain that there are cases in which we can, cases in which a Good Samaritan would extricate him. There you are, you were kidnapped, and nine years in bed with that violinist lie ahead of you. You have your own life to lead. You are sorry, but you simply cannot see giving up so much of your life to the sustaining of his. You cannot extricate yourself, and ask us to do so. I should have thought that — in light of his having no right to the use of your body — it was obvious that we do not have to accede to your being forced to give up so much. We can do what you ask. There is no injustice to the violinist in our doing so.

7. Following the lead of the opponents of abortion, I have throughout been speaking of the fetus merely as a person, and what I have been asking is whether or not the argument we began with, which proceeds only from the fetus' being a person, really does establish its conclusion. I have argued that it does not.

But of course there are arguments and arguments, and it may be said that I have simply fastened on the wrong one. It may be said that what is important is not merely the fact that the fetus is a person, but that it is a person for whom the woman has a special kind of responsibility issuing from the fact that she is its mother. And it might be argued that all my analogies are therefore irrelevant — for you do not have that special kind of responsibility for that violinist, Henry Fonda does not have that special kind of responsibility for me. And our attention might be drawn to the fact that men and women both *are* compelled by law to provide support for their children.

I have in effect dealt (briefly) with this argument in section 4 above; but a (still briefer) recapitulation now may be in order. Surely we do not have any such "special responsibility" for a person unless we have assumed it, explicitly or implicitly. If a set of parents do not try to prevent pregnancy, do not obtain an abortion, and then at the time of birth of the child do not put it out for adoption, but rather take it home with them, then they have assumed responsibility for it, they have given it rights, and they cannot *now* withdraw support from it at the cost of its life because they now find it difficult to go on providing for it. But if they have taken all reasonable precautions against having a child, they do not simply by virtue of their biological relationship to the child who comes into existence have a special responsibility for it. They may wish to assume responsibility for it, or they may not wish to. And I am suggesting that if assuming responsibility for it would require large sacrifices, then they may refuse. A Good Samaritan would not refuse — or anyway, a Splendid Samaritan, if the sacrifices that had to be made were enormous. But then so would a Good

Samaritan assume responsibility for that violinist; so would Henry Fonda, if he is a Good Samaritan, fly in from the West Coast and assume responsibility for me.

8. My argument will be found unsatisfactory on two counts by many of those who want to regard abortion as morally permissible. First, while I do argue that abortion is not impermissible, I do not argue that it is always permissible. There may well be cases in which carrying the child to term requires only Minimally Decent Samaritanism of the mother, and this is a standard we must not fall below. I am inclined to think it a merit of my account precisely that it does *not* give a general yes or a general no. It allows for and supports our sense that, for example, a sick and desperately frightened fourteen-year-old schoolgirl, pregnant due to rape, may *of course* choose abortion, and that any law which rules this out is an insane law. And it also allows for and supports our sense that in other cases resort to abortion is even positively indecent. It would be indecent in the woman to request an abortion, and indecent in a doctor to perform it, if she is in her seventh month, and wants the abortion just to avoid the nuisance of postponing a trip abroad. The very fact that the arguments I have been drawing attention to treat all cases of abortion, or even all cases of abortion in which the mother's life is not at stake, as morally on a par ought to have made them suspect at the outset.

Secondly, while I am arguing for the permissibility of abortion in some cases, I am not arguing for the right to secure the death of the unborn child. It is easy to confuse these two things in that up to a certain point in the life of the fetus it is not able to survive outside the mother's body; hence removing it from her body guarantees its death. But they are importantly different. I have argued that you are not morally required to spend nine months in bed, sustaining the life of that violinist; but to say this is by no means to say that if, when you unplug yourself, there is a miracle and he survives, you then have a right to turn round and slit his throat. You may detach yourself even if this costs him his life; you have no right to be guaranteed his death, by some other means, if unplugging yourself does not kill him. There are some people who will feel dissatisfied by this feature of my argument. A woman may be utterly devastated by the thought of a child, a bit of herself, put out for adoption and never seen or heard of again. She may therefore want not merely that the child be detached from her, but more, that it die. Some opponents of abortion are inclined to regard this as beneath contempt — thereby showing insensitivity to what is surely a powerful source of despair. All the same, I agree that the desire for the child's death is not one which anybody may gratify, should it turn out to be possible to detach the child alive.

At this place, however, it should be remembered that we have only been pretending throughout that the fetus is a human being from the moment of conception. A very early abortion is surely not the killing of a person, and so is not dealt with by anything I have said here.

MARY ANNE WARREN

The Moral Significance of Birth

MARY ANNE WARREN *currently teaches at San Francisco State University. She has published widely in applied ethics and feminist philosophy.*

ENGLISH common law treats the moment of live birth as the point at which a legal person comes into existence. Although abortion has often been prohibited, it has almost never been classified as homicide. In contrast, infanticide generally is classified as a form of homicide, even where (as in England) there are statutes designed to mitigate the severity of the crime in certain cases. But many people — including some feminists — now favor the extension of equal legal rights to some or all fetuses. The extension of legal personhood to fetuses would not only threaten women's right to choose abortion, but also undermine other fundamental rights. I will argue that because of these dangers, birth remains the most appropriate place to mark the existence of a new legal person. . . .

Speaking of Rights

. . . Some feminist philosophers have suggested that the very concept of a moral right may be inconsistent with the social nature of persons. Elizabeth Wolgast argues convincingly that this concept has developed within an atomistic model of the social world, in which persons are depicted as self-sufficient and exclusively self-interested individuals whose relationships with one another are essentially competitive. As Wolgast notes, such an atomistic model is particularly inappropriate in the context of pregnancy, birth, and parental responsibility. . . . But is the concept of a moral right necessarily incompatible with the social nature of human beings? Rights are indeed individualistic, in that they can be ascribed to individuals, as well as to groups. But respect for moral rights need not be based upon an excessively individualistic view of human nature. A more socially perceptive account of moral rights is possible, provided that we reject two common assumptions about the theoretical foundations of moral rights. These assumptions are widely accepted by mainstream philosophers, but rarely stated and still more rarely defended.

The first is what I shall call the intrinsic-properties assumption. This is the view that the only facts that can justify the ascription of basic moral rights or moral standing to individuals are facts about *the intrinsic properties of those individuals*. Philosophers who accept this view disagree about which of the intrinsic properties of individuals are relevant to the ascription of rights. They agree, however, that relational properties—such as being loved, or being part of a social community or biological ecosystem—cannot be relevant.

The second is what I shall call the single-criterion assumption. This is the view that there is some single property, the presence or absence of which divides the world into those things which have moral rights or moral standing, and those things which do not. Christopher Stone locates this assumption within a more general theoretical approach, which he calls "moral monism." Moral monists believe that the goal of moral philosophy is

the production of a coherent set of principles, sufficient to provide definitive answers to all possible moral dilemmas. Among these principles, the monist typically assumes, will be one that identifies some key property which is such that, "Those beings that possess the key property count morally . . . [while those] things that lack it are all utterly irrelevant, except as resources for the benefit of those things that do count."

Together, the intrinsic-properties and single-criterion assumptions preclude any adequate account of the social foundations of moral rights. The intrinsic-properties assumption requires us to regard all personal or other relationships among individuals or groups as wholly irrelevant to basic moral rights. The single-criterion assumption requires us to deny that there can be a variety of sound reasons for ascribing moral rights, and a variety of things and beings to which some rights may appropriately be ascribed. Both assumptions are inimical to a feminist approach to moral theory, as well as to approaches that are less anthropocentric and more environmentally adequate. The prevalence of these assumptions helps to explain why few mainstream philosophers believe that birth can in any way alter the infant's moral rights.

Protecting Nonpersons

If we are to justify a general moral distinction between abortion and infanticide, we must answer two questions. First, why should infanticide be discouraged, rather than treated as a matter for individual decision? And second, why should sentient fetuses not be given the same protections that law and common sense morality accord to infants? But before turning to these two questions, it is necessary to make a more general point.

Persons have sound reasons for treating

one another as moral equals. These reasons derive from both self-interest and altruistic concern for others — which, because of our social nature, are often very difficult to distinguish. Human persons — and perhaps all persons — normally come into existence only in and through social relationships. Sentience may begin to emerge without much direct social interaction, but it is doubtful that a child reared in total isolation from human or other sentient (or apparently sentient) beings could develop the capacities for self-awareness and social interaction that are essential to personhood. The recognition of the fundamentally social nature of persons can only strengthen the case for moral equality, since social relationships are undermined and distorted by inequalities that are perceived as unjust. There may be many nonhuman animals who have enough capacity for self-awareness and social interaction to be regarded as persons, with equal basic moral rights. But, whether or not this is true, it is certainly true that if any things have full and equal basic moral rights then persons do.

However we cannot conclude that, because all persons have equal basic moral rights, it is always wrong to extend strong moral protections to beings that are not persons. Those who accept the single-criterion assumption may find that a plausible inference. By now, however, most thoughtful people recognize the need to protect vulnerable elements of the natural world — such as endangered plant and animal species, rainforests, and rivers — from further destruction at human hands. . . . Although destroying them is not murder, it is an act of vandalism which later generations will mourn.

It is probably not crucial whether or not we say that endangered species and natural habitats have a moral right to our protection. What is crucial is that we recognize and act upon the need to protect them. Yet certain contemporary realities argue for an increased willingness to ascribe rights to impersonal elements of the natural world. Americans, at least, are likely to be more sensitive to appeals and demands couched in terms of rights than those that appeal to less familiar concepts, such as inherent value. So central are rights to our common moral idiom, that to deny that trees have rights is to risk being thought to condone the reckless destruction of rainforests and redwood groves. If we want to communicate effectively about the need to protect the natural world — and to protect it for its own sake as well as our own — then we may be wise to develop theories that permit us to ascribe at least some moral rights to some things that are clearly not persons.

Parallel issues arise with respect to the moral status of the newborn infant. As Wolgast argues, it is much more important to understand our responsibilities to protect and care for infants than to insist that they have exactly the same moral rights as older human beings. Yet to deny that infants have equal basic moral rights is to risk being thought to condone infanticide and the neglect and abuse of infants. Here too, effective communication about human moral responsibilities seems to demand the ascription of rights to beings that lack certain properties that are typical of persons. But, of course, that does not explain why we have these responsibilities towards infants in the first place.

Why Protect Infants?

. . . Although the human newborn may have no intrinsic properties that can ground a moral right to life stronger than that of a fetus just before birth, its emergence into the social world makes it appropriate to treat it as if it had such a stronger right. This, in effect, is what the law has done, through the doctrine that a person begins to exist at birth. Those who accept the intrinsic-properties assumption can only regard this doctrine as a legal fiction. However, it is a fiction that we would have difficulty doing without. If the line were not drawn at birth, then I think we would have to draw it at some point rather soon thereafter, as many other societies have done.

Another reason for condemning infanticide is that, at least in relatively privileged nations like our own, infants whose parents cannot raise them can usually be placed with people who will love them and take good care of them. This means that infanticide is rarely in the infant's own best interests, and would often deprive some potential adoptive individual or family of a great benefit. It also means that the prohibition of infanticide need not impose intolerable burdens upon parents (especially women). A rare parent might think it best to kill a healthy infant rather than permitting it to be reared by others, but a persuasive defense of that claim would require special circumstances. For instance, when abortion is unavailable and women face savage abuses for supposed sexual transgressions, those who resort to infanticide to conceal an "illegitimate" birth may be doing only what they must. But where enforcement of the sexual double standard is less brutal, abortion and adoption can provide alternatives that most women would prefer to infanticide.

Some might wonder whether adoption is really preferable to infanticide, at least from the parent's point of view. Judith Thomson notes that, "A woman may be utterly devastated by the thought of a child, a bit of herself, put out for adoption and never seen or heard of again." From the standpoint of narrow self-interest, it might not be irrational to prefer the death of the child to such a future. Yet few

would wish to resolve this problem by legalizing infanticide. The evolution of more open adoption procedures which permit more contact between the adopted child and the biological parent(s) might lessen the psychological pain often associated with adoption. But that would be at best a partial solution. More basic is the provision of better social support for child-rearers, so that parents are not forced by economic necessity to surrender their children for adoption.

These are just some of the arguments for treating infants as legal persons, with an equal right to life. A more complete account might deal with the effects of the toleration of infanticide upon other moral norms. But the existence of such effects is unclear. Despite a tradition of occasional infanticide, the Arapesh appear in Mead's descriptions as gentle people who treat their children with great kindness and affection. The case against infanticide need not rest upon the questionable claim that the toleration of infanticide inevitably leads to the erosion of other moral norms. It is enough that most people today strongly desire that the lives of infants be protected, and that this can now be done without imposing intolerable burdens upon individuals or communities. . . .

Why Birth Matters

I have defended what most regard as needing no defense, i.e., the ascription of an equal right to life to human infants. Under reasonably favorable conditions that policy can protect the rights and interests of all concerned, including infants, biological parents, and potential adoptive parents.

But if protecting infants is such a good idea, then why is it not a good idea to extend the same strong protections to sentient fetuses? The question is not whether sentient fetuses ought to be protected: of course they should. Most women readily accept the responsibility for doing whatever they can to ensure that their (voluntarily continued) pregnancies are successful, and that no avoidable harm comes to the fetus. Negligent or malevolent actions by third parties which result in death or injury to pregnant women or their potential children should be subject to moral censure and legal prosecution. A just and caring society would do much more than ours does to protect the health of all its members, including pregnant women. The question is whether the law should accord to late-term fetuses *exactly the same* protections as are accorded to infants and older human beings.

The case for doing so might seem quite strong. We normally regard not only infants, but all other postnatal human beings as entitled to strong legal protections *so long as they are either sentient or capable of an eventual return to sentience*. We do not also require that they demonstrate a capacity for thought, self-awareness, or social relationships before we conclude that they have an equal right to life. Such restrictive criteria would leave too much room for invidious discrimination. The eternal propensity of powerful groups to rationalize sexual, racial, and class oppression by claiming that members of the oppressed group are mentally or otherwise "inferior" leaves little hope that such restrictive criteria could be applied without bias. Thus, for human beings past the prenatal stage, the capacity for sentience — or for a return to sentience — may be the only pragmatically defensible criterion for the ascription of full and equal basic rights. If so, then both theoretical simplicity and moral consistency may seem to require that we extend the same protections to sentient human beings that have not yet been born as to those that have.

But there is one crucial consideration which this argument leaves out. It is impossible to treat fetuses *in utero* as if they were persons without treating women as if they were something less than persons. The extension of equal rights to sentient fetuses would inevitably license severe violations of women's basic rights to personal autonomy and physical security. In the first place, it would rule out most second-trimester abortions performed to protect the woman's life or health. Such abortions might sometimes be construed as a form of self-defense. But the right to self-defense is not usually taken to mean that one may kill innocent persons just because their continued existence poses some threat to one's own life or health. If abortion must be justified as self-defense, then it will rarely be performed until the woman is already in extreme danger, and perhaps not even then. Such a policy would cost some women their lives, while others would be subjected to needless suffering and permanent physical harm.

Other alarming consequences of the drive to extend more equal rights to fetuses are already apparent in the United States. In the past decade it has become increasingly common for hospitals or physicians to obtain court orders requiring women in labor to undergo Caesarean sections, against their will, for what is thought to be the good of the fetus. Such an extreme infringement of the woman's right to security against physical assault would be almost unthinkable once the infant has been born. No parent or relative can legally be forced to undergo any surgical procedure, even possibly to save the life of a child, once it is born. But pregnant women can sometimes be forced to undergo major surgery, for the supposed benefit of the fetus. As George Annas points out, forced Caesareans threaten to reduce women to the status of inanimate objects — containers which may be opened at the will of others in order to get at their contents.

Perhaps the most troubling illustration of this trend is the case of Angie Carder, who died at George Washington University Medical Center in June 1987, two days after a court-ordered Caesarean section. Ms. Carder had suffered a recurrence of an earlier cancer, and was not expected to live much longer. Her physicians agreed that the fetus was too undeveloped to be viable, and that Carder herself was probably too weak to survive the surgery. Although she, her family, and the physicians were all opposed to a Caesarean delivery, the hospital administration — evidently believing it had a legal obligation to try to save the fetus — sought and obtained a court order to have it done. As predicted, both Carder and her infant died soon after the operation. This woman's rights to autonomy, physical integrity, and life itself were forfeit — not just because of her illness, but because of her pregnancy.

Such precedents are doubly alarming in the light of the development of new techniques of fetal therapy. As fetuses come to be regarded as patients, with rights that may be in direct conflict with those of their mothers, and as the *in utero* treatment of fetuses becomes more feasible, more and more pregnant women may be subjected against their will to dangerous and invasive medical interventions. If so, then we may be sure that there will be other Angie Carders.

Another danger in extending equal legal protections to sentient fetuses is that women will increasingly be blamed, and sometimes legally prosecuted, when they miscarry or give birth to premature, sick, or abnormal infants. It is reasonable to hold to the caretakers of infants legally responsible if their charges are harmed because of their avoidable negligence. But when a woman miscarries or gives birth

to an abnormal infant, the cause of the harm might be traced to any of an enormous number of actions or circumstances which would not normally constitute any legal offense. She might have gotten too much exercise or too little, eaten the wrong foods or the wrong quantity of the right ones, or taken or failed to take certain drugs. She might have smoked, consumed alcohol, or gotten too little sleep. She might have "permitted" her health to be damaged by hard work, by unsafe employment conditions, by the lack of affordable medical care, by living near a source of industrial pollution, by a physically or mentally abusive partner, or in any number of other ways.

Are such supposed failures on the part of pregnant women potentially to be construed as child abuse or negligent homicide? If sentient fetuses are entitled to the same legal protections as infants, then it would seem so. The danger is not a merely theoretical one. Two years ago in San Diego, a woman whose son was born with brain damage and died several weeks later was charged with felony child neglect. It was said that she had been advised by her physician to avoid sex and illicit drugs, and to [go to] the hospital immediately if she noticed any bleeding. Instead, she had allegedly had sex with her husband, taken some inappropriate drug, and delayed getting to the hospital for what might have been several hours after the onset of bleeding.

In this case, the charges were eventually dismissed on the grounds that the child protection law invoked had not been intended to apply to cases of this kind. But the multiplication of such cases is inevitable if the strong legal protections accorded to infants are extended to sentient fetuses. A bill recently introduced in the Australian state of New South Wales would make women liable to criminal prosecution if they are found to have smoked during pregnancy, eaten unhealthful foods, or taken any other action which can be shown to have adversely affected the development of the fetus. Such an approach to the protection of fetuses authorizes the legal regulation of virtually every aspect of women's public and private lives, and thus is incompatible with even the most minimal right to autonomy. Moreover, such laws are apt to prove counterproductive, since the fear of prosecution may deter poor or otherwise vulnerable women from seeking needed medical care during pregnancy. I am not suggesting that women whose apparent negligence causes prenatal harm to their infants should always be immune from criticism. However, if we want to improve the health of infants we would do better to provide the services women need to protect their health, rather than seeking to use the law to punish those whose prenatal care has been less than ideal.

There is yet another problem, which may prove temporary but which remains significant at this time. The extension of legal personhood to sentient fetuses would rule out most abortions performed because of severe fetal abnormalities, such as Down's Syndrome or spina bifida. Abortions performed following amniocentesis are usually done in the latter part of the second trimester, since it is usually not possible to obtain test results earlier. Methods of detecting fetal abnormalities at earlier stages, such as chorion biopsy, may eventually make late abortion for reasons of fetal abnormality unnecessary; but at present the safety of these methods is unproven.

The elimination of most such abortions might be a consequence that could be accepted, were the society willing to provide adequate support for the handicapped children and adults who would come into being as a result of this policy. However, our society is not prepared to do this. In the absence of adequate communally-funded care for the handicapped, the prohibition of such abortions is exploitative of women. Of course, the male relatives of severely handicapped persons may also bear heavy burdens. Yet the heaviest portion of the daily responsibility generally falls upon mothers and other female relatives. If fetuses are not yet persons (and women are), then a respect for the equality of persons should lead to support for the availability of abortion in cases of severe fatal abnormality.

Such arguments will not persuade those who deeply believe that fetuses are already persons, with equal moral rights. How, they will ask, is denying legal equality to sentient fetuses different from denying it to any other powerless group of human beings? If some human beings are more equal than others, then how can any of us feel safe? The answer is twofold.

First, pregnancy is a relationship different from any other, including that between parents and already-born children. It is not just one of innumerable situations in which the rights of one individual may come into conflict with those of another; it is probably the *only* case in which the legal personhood of one human being is necessarily incompatible with that of another. Only in pregnancy is the organic functioning of one human individual biologically inseparable from that of another. This organic unity makes it impossible for others to provide the fetus with medical care or any other presumed benefit, except by doing something to or for the woman. To try to "protect" the fetus other than through her cooperation and consent is effectively to nullify her right to autonomy, and potentially to expose her to violent physical assaults such as would not be legally condoned in any other type of case. The uniqueness of pregnancy helps to explain why the toleration of abortion does not lead to the disenfranchisement of other groups of human beings, as opponents of abortion often claim. For biological as well as psychological reasons, "It is all but impossible to extrapolate from attitudes towards fetal life attitudes toward [other] existing human life."

But, granting the uniqueness of pregnancy, why is it *women's* rights that should be privileged? If women and fetuses cannot both be legal persons then why not favor fetuses, e.g., on the grounds that they are more helpless, or more innocent, or have a longer life expectancy? It is difficult to justify this apparent bias towards women without appealing to the empirical fact that women are already persons in the usual, nonlegal sense — already thinking, self-aware, fully social beings — and fetuses are not. Regardless of whether we stress the intrinsic properties of persons, or the social and relational dimensions of personhood, this distinction remains. Even sentient fetuses do not yet have either the cognitive capacities or the richly interactive social involvements typical of persons.

This "not yet" is morally decisive. It is wrong to treat persons as if they do not have equal basic rights. Other things being equal, it is worse to deprive persons of their most basic moral and legal rights than to refrain from extending such rights to beings that are not persons. This is one important element of truth in the self-awareness criterion. If fetuses were already thinking, self-aware, socially responsive members of communities, then nothing could justify refusing them the equal protection of the law. In that case, we would sometimes be forced to balance the rights of the fetus against those of the woman, and sometimes the scales might be almost equally weighted. However, if women are persons and fetuses are not, then the balance must swing towards women's rights.

Conclusion

Birth is morally significant because it marks the end of one relationship and the beginning of others. It marks the end of pregnancy, a relationship so intimate that it is impossible to extend the equal protection of the law to fetuses without severely infringing women's most basic rights. Birth also marks the beginning of the infant's existence as a socially responsive member of a human community. Although the infant is not instantly transformed into a person at the moment of birth, it does become a biologically separate human being. As such, it can be known and cared for as a particular individual. It can also be vigorously protected without negating the basic rights of women. There are circumstances in which infanticide may be the best of a bad set of options. But our own society has both the ability and the desire to protect infants, and there is no reason why we should not do so.

We should not, however, seek to extend the same degree of protection to fetuses. Both late-term fetuses and newborn infants are probably capable of sentience. Both are precious to those who want children; and both need to be protected from a variety of possible harms. All of these factors contribute to the moral standing of the late-term fetus, which is substantial. However, to extend equal legal rights to fetuses is necessarily to deprive pregnant women of the rights to personal autonomy, physical integrity, and sometimes life itself. *There is room for only one person with full and equal rights inside a single human skin.* That is why it is birth, rather than sentience, viability, or some other prenatal milestone that must mark the beginning of legal parenthood.

ALAN DONAGAN

The Moral Status of the Foetus

ALAN DONAGAN, *originally from Australia, now teaches philosophy at the California Institute of Technology in Pasadena. His latest works are* Choice: The Essential Element in Human Action *(1987) and* Spinoza *(1989).*

I N investigating duties to others, it is convenient to begin with those that can arise between one man and another independently of any institution with which either may be associated. . . . The most familiar institutions, like those of civil society, such as parliament and the legal system, invest certain official positions with certain rights, duties, and immunities; specify certain kinds of action as impermissible and others as permissible; and provide for the adjudication of whether the rules have been violated, and for the imposition of penalties if they have. However, I shall consider any system of constitutive rules whatever to be an institution, even that for a game of patience played by a solitary man, which he has invented and has divulged to nobody else.

The first set of noninstitutional duties to others to be considered are those having to do with force and violence. Since respect for human beings as rational creatures entails, in general, treating every normal adult as responsible for the conduct of his own affairs, to interfere by force with anybody else's conduct of his life, unless there is a special and adequate reason, is not to respect him as a rational creature. The principle may therefore be laid down that *it is impermissible for anybody at will to use force upon another*.

Not all human beings are normal, however, and not all are adult. . . .

Children also are rational creatures, whose reason is in process of develop-ment. Although it must be recognized that the power of normal children to look after themselves is constantly growing, while they remain children they are not fully capable of doing so: and, in a measure as they are not, those in charge of them may forcibly prevent them from harming themselves or others, and may compel them to submit to education reasonably thought to be of benefit to them.

The question of when a given human being's life as an individual begins is of great importance in the Hebrew-Christian system. The duties of human beings to others are duties to them as human beings, that is, as rational creatures of a certain kind. The forms which may be taken by the fundamental moral duty of respect for a rational creature as such will vary with the degree to which that creature is actually in possession of the reason a mature creature of that kind would normally possess; but such variations in no way annul the duty. In simpler ages, it was practically sufficient to treat duties to others as beginning with their birth. However, as medical knowledge has grown, and as techniques have been developed by which the unborn can be both benefited and injured, the theoretical issue cannot be set aside on the ground of practical unimportance.

The question of when the life of a human being begins is a biological one, since human beings are rational *animals*; and biology answers it simply and unequivocally: a human life begins at conception, when the new being receives the genetic code. Although a zygote does not, even when made visible through a microscope, look like a human being, and although adult human beings cannot have the kind of relations with it that they can have to other adults, or even to children, its status as a rational creature is in no way compromised. Attempts to deny the humanity of zygotes, by declaring that humanity begins at birth, or at viability (that is, at the point when an unborn child, extruded from the womb, could be kept alive) are scientifically obscurantist. An eight-month-old premature baby is biologically less mature than an eight-and-three-quarter-month-old unborn one; and viability has no biological significance. Whether an unborn child is viable or not depends on the state of medical technology. It is reasonable to forecast that, in a century or so, a zygote will be viable.

It follows that the principle *it is impermissible for anybody at will to use force upon another* applies to adult and child alike, to born and unborn. However, just as it is legitimate to use force on children for purposes for which it would not be legitimate to use it on adults, so very difficult questions are raised about the extent to which it is legitimate to use force upon an unborn child. . . . These questions bring into doubt the consistency of Hebrew-Christian morality. . . .

By far the most familiar charge of inconsistency against traditional Hebrew-Christian morality, and the only one that is plausible, has to do with its doctrine of the family. For, while its principle of parental responsibility presupposes . . . that it is impermissible voluntarily to become a parent of a child you cannot rear, traditional moralists have been agreed in condemning many of the methods by which a couple can limit the number of children they have. Now it is at least possible to argue that, in some societies at least, un-less the forbidden methods of limiting families are resorted to, in some cases individual parents, in others society at large, will not be able to discharge the duty owed to the children who will be born. Such problems are fittingly described as "Malthusian," after T. R. Malthus, whose *Essay on the Principle of Population as it Affects the Future Emprovement of Society* (1st ed., 1798) first persuasively presented the hypothesis that population always tends to outrun the growth of production.

Since the precepts of a moral system are inconsistent on a question only if they give rise to perplexity *simpliciter* with regard to it, in considering whether traditional Hebrew-Christian morality is inconsistent on Malthusian problems, attention must be confined to situations that can occur even though all its precepts have been observed. Hence only problems of overpopulation that could arise in a society in which the great majority of births occur in monogamous families are to be considered.

The precepts of traditional morality that bear upon Malthusian problems fall into two groups.

On one side, parents are held to have the duty of feeding, clothing, sheltering, and educating their children, and the right to noninterference in their doing so. Should either parent die or be incapacitated, the relatives of the bereaved children, and if they cannot or will not, society at large, must share or undertake the responsibility. In simpler times, any healthy laborer and his wife were supposed to be able to feed and clothe the children that would naturally be born to them, and to bring them up to be laborers or laborers' wives. That the supposition did not necessarily correspond to reality appears in many accounts of nineteenth-century England, such as this from Richard Jefferies' *Toilers of the Field*:

He minded when that sharp old Miss—
was always coming round with tracts
and blankets, like taking some straw to
a lot of pigs, and lecturing his missis
about economy. What a fuss she made,
and scolded his wife as if she were a
thief for having her fifteenth boy! His
missis turned on her at last and said:
"Lor miss, that's all the pleasure me an'
my old man got."

This anecdote places in an unlovely
light the presupposition of the Hebrew-
Christian precept of parental responsibility, that it is impermissible voluntarily to
become a parent of a child you cannot
rear. For the indomitable laborer's wife
also expresses a position sanctioned by
Hebrew-Christian morality, which from
the beginning has looked askance at any
requirement of prolonged continence in
marriage. Hence, without recent contraceptive techniques, in any society in
which most people are healthy and marry
young, a normal Jewish or Christian married life ensures that most families will be
large. And so inevitably, by Malthusian
calculations, a time will come of the kind
deplored by Jefferies' intrusive bringer of
tracts and blankets, when many parents
will not be able adequately to bring up
those children, and the population of the
society will outrun its natural resources.

Yet Hebrew-Christian morality condemns the most common practice by
which preindustrial societies have limited
their populations, namely, infanticide.
Sterilization is also rejected, as violating
the precept forbidding nontherapeutic mutilation. And, although not expressly prohibited, the method described in the
following grim passage from A. J. P. Taylor's *English History: 1914–1945* is undoubtedly contrary to the sexual ideal of
both Jewish and Christian marriage:

in the eighteen-eighties, when the decline in the birthrate first appears statis-

tically, the middle class, who were the
first to limit their families, simply ab-
stained from sexual intercourse.

Two methods of limiting families have
nevertheless been proposed as satisfying
the requirements of common morality.
One is to abstain from intercourse during
those days in the menstrual cycle in which
the wife is fertile; the other is to make the
act of intercourse infertile by physical
devices such as the sheath or diaphragm,
or by pharmacological treatments rendering either husband or wife temporarily
infertile.

The development of effective methods
of both kinds in the past fifty years has
posed a new set of problems for moralists.
At first contraceptive intercourse was condemned as perverse. . . . Jewish moralists seem to have found least difficulty in
drawing the necessary distinctions, but
Protestant opinion was not far behind. In
Protestantism, lay opinion makes itself
felt more promptly and directly than in
Roman Catholicism; and Protestant parents of modest means not only accepted it
as a duty to bring their children up in a
way that was not possible if they had
many, but also failed to see anything
wrong with the new contraceptive methods. In the Roman Catholic church, however, all forms of contraception remain
condemned. . . .

Yet even among Roman Catholics the
force of the argument [against contra-
ception] has widely been found obscure.
There is undoubtedly a genuine distinction between the approved "rhythm"
method of bringing it about that intercourse only takes place when the wife is
infertile, and the condemned contraceptive method of having intercourse only
when it has been brought about by one
of a variety of devices, that she, her
husband, or the act is infertile. The two
methods are not on a par. But what is

wrong with the second is not clear. . . . [I]ntercourse within marriage which is normal in every way, except for having been artificially made what most intercourse is naturally, may reasonably be held to have an erotic significance quite different from that of deviant sexual acts. If it does, and if the wrongness of deviant sexual acts derives from their significance and not from their merely physical character, a demonstration of their wrongness would be unlikely to apply also to contraceptive intercourse. And if that is so, it will be difficult to find any premise from which the impermissibility of contraception can be derived that anybody would take for a principle of common morality apart from his position on the issue in dispute.

Granting the legitimacy of contraception, any society which can produce contraceptive devices or medicines cheaply, and which can teach its members to use them, can solve Malthusian problems. But what of societies lacking those productive or educational capabilities?

The most common answer [is that] the duties of bringing up one's children well, and of promoting a reasonable balance between population and terrestrial resources, are duties of beneficence, and contain the qualification "by all lawful means in one's power." The duties not to commit abortion or infanticide, and not to mutilate oneself by sterilization, are all absolute prohibitions. Hence it is not inconsistent with the duty to bring up one's children adequately, or to contribute to the limitation of the population, to refuse to adopt unlawful means of doing so. Evil is not to be done that good may come of it.

Although this argument is logically adequate, its premises are disputable. To begin with, is it merely a duty of beneficence to bring one's children up adequately? Is it not rather an absolute

obligation, a perfect duty in Kant's sense, arising from the impermissibility of procreating any child who cannot be so brought up? If it is, and if every self-supporting couple is entitled to marry, and to have a normal sexual relationship in marriage, are there not possible situations in which perplexity *simpliciter* would arise?

It appears so; but, on closer scrutiny, the appearance begins to dissolve. Despite Malthus, human population generally did not outrun natural resources until technology had become advanced, and it did so partly because of it. . . . It is doubtful whether, in any environment in which a race of rational animals could naturally evolve, the societies formed by members of that race could not prevent overpopulation except by killing the innocent or invading morally legitimate forms of the family. In sum: it has not been shown that, if contraception is permissible, the traditional prohibitions of abortion, infanticide, and sterilization on the one side, and of invading legitimate forms of the family on the other, would give rise to perplexity *simpliciter* in any conceivable society of rational animals. Nor, if it were to be demonstrated that such a society is possible, would it follow that traditional common morality is inconsistent in principle. It is far more likely that the demonstration would disclose some flaw in the specificatory premises by which the traditional doctrine of the family is derived, and indicate how it may be corrected.

Finally, it should be mentioned that a further possible solution of Malthusian problems would be effected if the recent revival of the pagan doctrine that abortion is permissible could be reconciled with common morality. Two distinct lines of argument have been offered.

The first is that procuring an abortion does not, as was traditionally believed, violate the rights of a human child. This is sometimes asserted on the ground that a foetus is not a human being at all. But that is forced. It would be superfluous to rehearse the argument, neatly summed up in a brilliant if occasionally perverse paper by Roger Wertheimer, for the conclusion that "fertilization . . . [is] a non-aribitrary point marking the inception of a particular object, a human being." It is difficult, in view of modern scientific biology, to maintain that, although a newborn child, or a twenty-weeks-old unborn one, is a human being, a zygote is not.

Yet it is tautological to assert that the relations between a nonviable foetus and the world are different from those of a viable one or of a newborn child: namely, that the nonviable foetus can only survive in its mother's womb. And it has been argued that it has no absolute right to be there; and that the mother, under certain circumstances, has the right to have her womb evacuated. Judith Jarvis Thomson has put the matter thus:

> If a set of parents . . . have taken all reasonable precautions against having a child, they do not simply by virtue of their biological relationship to the child who comes into existence have a special responsibility for it. They may wish to assume responsibility for it, or they may not wish to. And . . . if assuming responsibility for it would require large sacrifices, then they may refuse.

As she recognizes, it may be objected that the parents of an unborn child brought into existence, although unintentionally, by their joint voluntary action, stand to it in a relation utterly different from that in which they would stand to a child left on their doorstep, or from that in which either would stand to another human being whose bloodstream had, without permission, been surgically connected with either of theirs, and who would die if the connection were broken.

That what matters here is not "simply . . . their biological relationship" is shown by the related case of a woman who has conceived as a result of rape. Here the unborn child has not been brought into existence by any voluntary action of hers. And so, in my opinion, for her to refuse to have it in her womb would not fail to respect it as a rational creature. Although the child is formally innocent, it is an involuntary intruder whom the mother may have removed from her body, even should that cause its death, without violating the prohibition of causing the death of the materially innocent. Of course, she would have no right to object to its being reared in an artificial womb, if that were possible, as presumably one day it will be. And it would be a super-erogatory act of great nobility for her to choose to give birth to it, out of reverence for its innocent humanity.

Accordingly, as Mary Anne Warren has acknowledged in a strong and original defence of abortion, if a foetus is human, and if moral duties are owed to human beings as such, then Thomson's argument "can provide a clear and persuasive defence of a woman's right to obtain an abortion only with respect to those cases in which the woman is in no way responsible for her pregnancy." If the absolute right of a pregnant woman to procure an abortion is to be sustained, it must be on the ground that a human being is not, as such, owed moral duties. That is the foundation of the second line of argument for the permissibility of abortion.

In Warren's version, that line is as follows. Only "full-fledged members of the moral community" have moral rights. A being becomes such a full-fledged member by virtue of being a person, not by virtue of being a member of the species *homo sapiens*, or of any other species of rational animal. The characteristics that make for personhood are: consciousness, developed reason, self-motivated activity, the power to communicate messages of an indefinite variety of types, and self-awareness. Hence "highly-advanced, self-aware robots or computers, should such be developed," would be persons, as would "intelligent inhabitants of other worlds." Unborn human children, human infants, and senile human dotards, would not — nor would their counterparts among non-terrestrial rational animals.

This argument implies that moral rights are acquired and lost according as one comes to be capable of certain sorts of mental activity, or ceases to be. To be a person, in Warren's sense, is not the nature of any being, but a stage through which some beings pass. And the concept of that stage varies with those who conceive it, despite Warren's belief that it "is very nearly universal (to people)" — that is, to persons. Michael Tooley, her ally in maintaining that moral rights go with personhood and not with membership of a rational species, let the cat out of the bag when he defined a person as a being having "a (serious) moral right to life." Tooley himself would grant this right to any organism that possesses the concept of a self as a continuing subject of experiences and other mental states, and that believes itself to be such a continuing entity. Hence his persons are not identical with Warren's. But that is the nature of our contemporary concept of personhood: it is a do-it-yourself kit for constructing a "moral community" to your own taste.

Yet within the concepts of traditional morality, could not the core of positions like Warren's and Tooley's be preserved without recourse to the factitious concept of personhood? A being whose actions are subject to moral judgement must be a full

rational agent; and is not full rational agency a stage through which rational animals pass? Why then, should not traditional morality be revised by recognizing only beings in a state of full rational agency as proper objects of moral duties, and possessors of moral rights?

Although it has been asserted that the dispute between those who take moral rights to go with a state ("personhood," or full moral agency, or what you will), and those who take them to go with membership of a rational species, probably cannot be settled objectively, there nevertheless seems to be an objective ground for settling it.

Duties owed to any being arise out of the respect that is owed to it. Let it, then, be provisionally conceded that, in the first instance, respect is recognized as owed to beings by virtue of a state they are in: say, that of rational agency. If there are beings who reach that state by a process of development natural to normal members of their species, given normal nurture, must not respect logically be accorded to them, whether they have yet reached that state or not? The principle underlying this reasoning is: if respect is owed to beings because they are in a certain state, it is owed to whatever, by its very nature, develops into that state. To reject this principle would be arbitrary, if indeed it would be intelligible. What could be made of somebody who professed to rate the state of rational agency as of supreme value, but who regarded as expendable any rational creature whose powers were as yet undeveloped?

Since it would be arbitrary to accord the respect that generates moral duties to beings in a state of developed rationality, while refusing it to beings who naturally develop into that state, there is a fundamental moral difference between a member of the species *homo sapiens*, or of any other species of rational animal there may be in the universe, and a cat or a sparrow. "Ye are of more value than many sparrows" even when your natural development is at the foetal stage.

Abortion is therefore not a possible solution of Malthusian problems within common morality.

***

SARA ANN KETCHUM
Selling Babies and Selling Bodies

SARA ANN KETCHUM *has written on philosophy, feminism, and medical ethics. She is currently attending Harvard Law School in Cambridge, Massachusetts, on leave from a position as Associate Professor of Philosophy at Rollins College.*

THE "Baby M" case has turned into something approaching a national soap opera, played out in newspapers and magazines. The drama surrounding the case tends to obscure the fact that the case raises some very abstract philosophical and moral issues. It forces us to examine questions about the nature and meaning of parenthood, of the limits of reproductive autonomy, of how the facts of pregnancy should affect our analysis of sexual equality, and of what counts as selling people and of what forms (if any) of selling people we should honor in law and what forms we should restrict. It is this last set of questions whose relevance I will be discussing here. One objection to what is usually called "surrogate motherhood" and which I will call "contracted motherhood" (CM) or "baby contracts" is that it commercializes reproduction and turns human beings (the mother and/or the baby) into objects of sale. If this is a compelling objection, there is a good argument for prohibiting (and/or not enforcing contracts for) com-

mercial CM. Such a prohibition would be similar to laws on black market adoptions and would have two parts, at least: 1) a prohibition of commercial companies who make the arrangements and/or 2) a prohibition on the transfer of money to the birth mother for the transfer of custody (beyond expenses incurred). I will also argue that CM law should follow adoption law in making clear that pre-birth agreements to relinquish parental rights are not binding and will not be enforced by the courts (the birth mother should not be forced to give up her child for adoption).

CM and AID:
The Real Difference Problem

CM is usually presented as a new reproductive technology and, moreover, as the female equivalent of AID (artificial insemination by donor) and, therefore, as an extension of the right to privacy or the right to make medical decisions about one's own life. There are two problems with this description: 1) CM uses the same technology as AID — the biological arrangements are exactly the same — but intends an opposite assignment of custody. 2) No technology is necessary for CM as is evidenced by the biblical story of Abraham and Sarah who used a "handmaid" as a birth mother. Since artificial insemination is virtually uncontroversial it seems clear that what makes CM controversial is not the technology, but the social arrangements — that is, the custody assignment. CM has been defended on the ground that such arrangements enable fertile men who are married to infertile women to reproduce and, thus, are parallel to AID which enables fertile women whose husbands are infertile to have children. It is difficult not to regard these arguments as somewhat disingenuous. The role of the sperm donor and the role of the egg donor/mother are distinguished by pregnancy, and pregnancy is, if anything is, a "real difference" which would justify us in treating women and men differently. To treat donating sperm as equivalent to biological motherhood would be as unfair as treating the unwed father who has not contributed to his children's welfare the same as the father who has devoted his time to taking care of them. At most, donating sperm is comparable to donating ova; however, even that comparison fails because donating ova is a medically risky procedure, donating sperm is not.

Therefore, the essential morally controversial features of CM have to do with its nature as a social and economic institution and its assignment of family relationships rather than with any technological features. Moreover, the institution of CM requires of contracting birth mothers much more time commitment, medical risk, and social disruption than AID does of sperm donors. It also requires substantial male control over women's bodies and time, while AID neither requires nor provides any female control over men's bodies. Christine Overall notes that when a woman seeks AID, she not only does not usually have a choice of donor, but she also may be required to get her husband's consent if she is married. The position of the man seeking CM is the opposite; he chooses a birth mother and his wife does not have to consent to the procedure (although the mother's husband does). The contract entered into by Mary Beth Whitehead and William Stern contains a number of provisions regulating her behavior, including: extensive medical examinations, an agreement about when she may or may not abort, an agreement to follow doctors' orders, and agreements not to take even prescription drugs without the doctor's permission. Some of these social and contractual provisions are eliminable. But the fact that CM requires a contract and AID does not reflects the differences between pregnancy and ejaculation. If the sperm donor wants a healthy child (a good product), he needs to control the woman's behavior. In contrast, any damage the sperm-donor's behavior will have on the child will be present in the sperm and could, in principle, be tested for before the woman enters the AID procedure. There is no serious moral problem with discarding defective sperm; discarding defective children is a quite different matter.

Commodification

There are three general categories of moral concern with commercializing either adoption (baby selling) or reproductive activities. The three kinds of argument are not always separated and they are not entirely separable:

1) There is the Kantian argument, based on a version of the Second Formulation of the Categorical Imperative. On

this argument, selling people is objectionable because it is treating them as means rather than as ends, as objects rather than as persons. People who can be bought and sold are being treated as being of less moral significance than are those who buy and sell. Allowing babies to be bought and sold adds an extra legal wedge between the status of children and that of adults, and allowing women's bodies to be bought and sold (or "rented" if you prefer) adds to the inequality between men and women. Moreover, making babies and women's bodies available for sale raises specters of the rich "harvesting" the babies of the poor. 2) Consequentialist objections are fueled by concern for what may happen to the children and women who are bought and sold, to their families, and to the society as a whole if we allow an area of this magnitude and traditional intimacy to become commercialized. 3) Connected to both 1 and 2 are concerns about protecting the birth mother and the mother–child relationship from the potential coerciveness of commercial transactions. These arguments apply slightly differently depending on whether we analyze the contracts as baby contracts (selling babies) or as mother contracts (as a sale of women's bodies), although many of the arguments will be very similar for both.

Selling Babies:

The most straightforward argument for prohibiting baby-selling is that it is selling a human being and that any selling of a human being should be prohibited because it devalues human life and human individuals. This argument gains moral force from its analogy with slavery. Defenders of baby contracts argue that baby selling is unlike selling slaves in that it is a transfer of parental rights rather than of ownership of the child — the adoptive parents cannot turn around and sell the baby to another couple for a profit. What the defenders of CM fail to do is provide an account of the wrongness of slavery such that baby-selling (or baby contracts) do not fall under the argument. Landes and Posner, in particular, would, I think, have difficulty establishing an argument against slavery because they are relying on utilitarian arguments. Since one of the classic difficulties with utilitarianism is that it cannot yield an argument that slavery is wrong in principle, it is hardly surprising that utilitarians will find it difficult to discover within that theory an argument against selling babies. Moreover, their economic argument is not even utilitarian because it only counts people's interest to the extent that they can pay for them.

Those who, unlike Landes and Posner, defend CM while supporting laws against baby-selling, distinguish CM from paid adoptions in that in CM the person to whom custody is being transferred is the biological (genetic) father. This suggests a parallel to custody disputes, which are not obviously any more appropriately ruled by money than is adoption. We could argue against the commercialization of either on the grounds that child-regarding concerns should decide child custody and that using market criteria or contract considerations would violate that principle by substituting another, unrelated, and possibly conflicting, one. In particular, both market and contract are about relations between the adults involved rather than about the children or about the relationship between the child and the adult.

Another disanalogy cited between preadoption contracts and CM is that, in preadoption contracts the baby is already there (that is, the preadoption contract is offered to a woman who is already pregnant, and, presumably, planning to have the child), while the mother contract is a contract to create a child who does not yet exist, even as an embryo. If our concern is the commodification of children, this strikes me as an odd point for the *defenders* of CM to emphasize. Producing a child to order for money is a paradigm case of commodifying children. The fact that the child is not being put up for sale to the highest bidder, but is only for sale to the genetic father, may reduce some of the harmful effects of an open market in babies but does not quiet concerns about personhood.

Arguments for allowing CM are remarkably similar to the arguments for legalizing black-market adoptions in the way they both define the problem. CM, like a market for babies, is seen as increasing the satisfaction and freedom of infertile individuals or couples by increasing the quantity of the desired product (there will be more babies available for adoption) and the quality of the product (not only more white healthy babies, but white healthy babies who are genetically related to one of the purchasers). These arguments tend to be based on the interests of infertile couples and obscure the relevance of the interests of the birth mothers (who will be giving the children up for adoption) and their families, the children who are produced by the demands of the market, and (the most invisible and most troubling group) needy children who are without homes because they are not "high-quality" products and because we are not, as a society, investing the time and money needed to place the hard to adopt children. If we bring these hidden interests to the fore, they raise a host of issues about consequences — both utilitarian issues and issues about the distribution of harms and benefits.

Perhaps the strongest deontological argument against baby selling is an objection to the characterization of the mother–child relationship (and, more generally, of the adult–child relationship) that it presupposes. Not only does the baby become an object of commerce, but the custody relationship of the parent becomes a property relationship. If we see parental custody rights as correlates of parental responsibility or as a right to maintain a relationship, it will be less tempting to think of them as something one can sell. We have good reasons for allowing birthmothers to relinquish their children because otherwise we would be forcing children into the care of people who either do not want them or feel themselves unable to care for them. However, the fact that custody may be waived in this way does not entail that it may be sold or transferred. If children are not property, they cannot be gifts either. If a mother's right is a right to maintain a relationship, it is implausible to treat it as transferrable; having the option of terminating a relationship with A does not entail having the option of deciding who A will relate to next — the right to a divorce does not entail the right to transfer one's connection to one's spouse to someone else. Indeed, normally, the termination of a relationship with A ends any right I have to make moral claims on A's relationships. Although in giving up responsibilities I may have a responsibility to see to it that someone will shoulder them when I go, I do not have a right to choose that person.

Selling Women's Bodies:

Suppose we do regard mother contracts as contracts for the sale or rental of reproductive capacities. Is there good reason for including reproductive capacities among those things or activities that ought not to be bought and sold? We might distinguish between selling reproductive capacities and selling work on a number of grounds. A conservative might argue against commercializing reproduction on the grounds that it disturbs family relationships, or on the grounds that there are some categories of human activities that should not be for sale. A Kantian might argue that there are some activities that are close to our personhood and that a commercial traffic in these activities constitutes treating the person as less than an end (or less than a person).

One interpretation of the laws prohibiting baby-selling is that they are an attempt to reduce or eliminate coercion in the adoption process, and are thus based on a concern for the birth mother rather than (or as well as) the child. All commercial transactions are at least potentially coercive in that the parties to them are likely to come from unequal bargaining positions and in that, whatever we have a market in, there will be some people who will be in a position such that they have to sell it in order to survive. Such concerns are important to arguments against an open market in human organs or in the sexual use of people's bodies as well as arguments against baby contracts of either kind.

As Margaret Radin suggests, the weakness of arguments of this sort—that relationships or contracts are exploitative on the grounds that people are forced into them by poverty—is that the real problem is not in the possibility of commercial transactions, but in the situation that makes these arrangements attractive by comparison. We do not end the feminization of poverty by forbidding prostitution or CM. Indeed, if we are successful in eliminating these practices, we may be reducing the income of some women (by removing ways of making money) and, if we are unsuccessful, we are removing these people from state protection by making their activities illegal. Labor legislation which

is comparably motivated by concern for unequal bargaining position (such as, for example, minimum wage and maximum hours laws, and health and safety regulations) regulates rather than prevents that activity and is thus less vulnerable to this charge. Radin's criticism shows that the argument from the coerciveness of poverty is insufficient as a support for laws rejecting commercial transactions in personal services. This does not show that the concern is irrelevant. The argument from coercion is still an appropriate response to simple voluntarist arguments—those that assume that these activities are purely and freely chosen by all those who participate in them. Given the coerciveness of the situation, we cannot assume that the presumed or formal voluntariness of the contract makes it nonexploitative.

If the relationship of CM is, by its nature, disrespectful of personhood, it can be exploitative despite short-term financial benefits to some women. The disrespect for women as persons that is fundamental to the relationship lies in the concept of the woman's body (and of the child and mother–child relationship) implicit in the contract. I have argued elsewhere that claiming a welfare right to another person's body is to treat that person as an object:

> An identity or intimate relation between persons and their bodies may or may not be essential to our metaphysical understanding of a person, but it is essential to a minimal moral conceptual scheme. Without a concession to persons' legitimate interests and concerns for their physical selves, most of our standard and paradigm moral rules would not make sense; murder might become the mere destruction of the body; assault, a mere interference with the body . . . and so on. We cannot make sense out of

the concept of assault unless an assault on S's body is ipso facto an assault on S. By the same token, treating another person's body as part of my domain — as among the things that I have a rightful claim to — is, if anything is, a denial that there is a person there.

This argument is, in turn, built on the analysis of the wrongness of rape developed by Marilyn Frye and Carolyn Shafer in "Rape and Respect":

> The use of a person in the advancement of interests contrary to its own is a limiting case of disrespect. It reveals the perception of the person simply as an object which can serve some purpose, a tool or a bit of material, and one which furthermore is dispensable or replaceable and thus of little value even as an object with a function.

We can extend this argument to the sale of persons. To make a person or a person's body an object of commerce is to treat the person as part of another person's domain, particularly if the sale of A to B gives B rights to A or to A's body. What is objectionable is a claim — whether based on welfare or on contract — to a right to another person such that that person is part of my domain. The assertion of such a right is morally objectionable even without the use of force. For example, a man who claims to have a *right* to sexual intercourse with his wife, on the grounds of the marriage relationship, betrays a conception of her body, and thus her person, as being properly within his domain, and thus a conception of her as an object rather than a person.

Susan Brownmiller, in *Against Our Will*, suggests that prostitution is connected to rape in that prostitution makes women's bodies into consumer goods that might — if not justifiably, at least understandably — be forcibly taken by those men who see themselves as unjustly deprived.

> When young men learn that females may be bought for a price, and that acts of sex command set prices, then how should they not also conclude that that which may be bought may also be taken without the civility of a monetary exchange? . . . legalized prostitution institutionalizes the concept that it is a man's monetary right, if not his divine right, to gain access to the female body, and that sex is a female service that should not be denied the civilized male.

The same can be said for legalized sale of women's reproductive services. The more hegemonic this commodification of women's bodies is, the more the woman's lack of consent to sex or to having children can present itself as unfair to the man because it is arbitrary.

A market in women's bodies — whether sexual prostitution or reproductive prostitution — reveals a social ontology in which women are among the things in the world that can be appropriately commodified — bought and sold and, by extension, stolen. The purported freedom that such institutions would give women to enter into the market by selling their bodies is paradoxical. Sexual or reproductive prostitutes enter the market not so much as *agents* or subjects, but as commodities or objects. This is evidenced by the fact that the pimps and their counterparts, the arrangers of baby contracts, make the bulk of the profits. Moreover, once there is a market for women's bodies, all women's bodies will have a price, and the woman who does not sell her body becomes a hoarder of something that is useful to other people and is financially valuable. The market is a hegemonic institution; it determines the meanings of actions of people who choose not to participate as well as those who choose to participate.

Contract:

The immediate objection to treating the Baby M case as a contract dispute is that the practical problem facing the court is a child custody problem and to treat it as a contract case is to deal with it on grounds other than the best interests of the child. That the best interests of the child count need not entail that contract does not count, although it helps explain one of the reasons we should be suspicious of this particular contract. There is still the question of whether the best interests of the child will trump contract considerations (making the contract nonbinding) or merely enter into a balancing argument in which contract is one of the issues to be balanced. However, allowing contract to count at all raises some of the same Kantian objections as the commodification problem. As a legal issue, the contract problem is more acute because the state action (enforcing the contract) is more explicit.

Any binding mother contract will put the state in the position of enforcing the rights of a man to a woman's body or to his genetic offspring. But this is to treat the child or the mother's body as objects of the sperm donor's rights, which, I argued above, is inconsistent with treating them as persons. This will be clearest if the courts enforce specific performance and require the mother to go through with the pregnancy (or to abort) if she chooses not to or requires the transfer of custody to the contracting sperm-donor on grounds other than the best interests of the child. In those cases, I find it hard to avoid the description that what is being awarded is a person and what is being affirmed is a right to a person. I think the Kantian argument still applies if the court refuses specific performance but awards damages. Damages compensate for the loss of something to which one has a right. A judge who awards damages to the contracting sperm donor for having been deprived of use of the contracting woman's reproductive capacities or for being deprived of custody of the child gives legal weight to the idea that the contracting sperm donor had a legally enforceable *right* to them (or, to put it more bluntly, to those commodities or goods).

The free contract argument assumes that Mary Beth Whitehead's claims to her daughter are rights (rather than, for example, obligations or a more complex relationship), and, moreover, that they are alienable, as are property rights. If the baby is not something she has an alienable right to, then custody of the baby is not something she can transfer by contract. In cases where the state is taking children away from their biological parents and in custody disputes, we do not want to appeal to some rights of the parents. However, I think it would be unfortunate to regard these rights as rights to the child, because that would be to treat the child as the object of the parents' rights and violate the principles that persons and persons' bodies cannot be the objects of other people's rights. The parents' rights in these cases should be to consideration, to nonarbitrariness and to respect for the relationship between the parent and the child.

Concluding Remarks

The Kantian, person-respecting arguments I have been offering do not provide an account of all of the moral issues surrounding CM. However, I think that they can serve as a counter-balance to arguments (also Kantian) for CM as an expression of personal autonomy. They might also add some weight to the empirical arguments against CM that are accumulating. There is increasing concern that women cannot predict in advance whether or not they and their family will form an attachment to the child they will bear nor can they promise not to develop such feelings (as some on the contracts ask them to do). There is also increasing concern for the birth-family and for the children produced by the arrangement (particularly where there is a custody dispute). A utilitarian might respond that the problems are outweighed by the joys of the adopting/sperm donor families, but, if so, we must ask: are we simply shifting the misery from wealthy (or wealthier) infertile couples to poorer fertile families and to the "imperfect" children waiting for adoption?

These considerations provide good reason for prohibiting commercialization of CM. In order to do that we could adopt new laws prohibiting the transfer of money in such arrangements or simply extend existing adoption laws, making the contracts non-binding as are pre-birth adoption contracts and limiting the money that can be transferred. There are some conceptual problems remaining about what would count as prohibiting commodification. I find the English approach very attractive. This approach has the following elements 1) it strictly prohibits third parties from arranging mother contracts; 2) if people arrange them privately, they are allowed, 3) the contracts are not binding. If the birth-mother decides to keep the baby, her decision is final (*and the father may be required to pay child-support; that may be too much for Americans*). 4) Although, in theory, CM is covered by limitations on money for adoption, courts have approved payments for contracted motherhood, and there is never criminal penalty on the parents for money payments.

MEREDITH MICHAELS

Conflicting Rights/ Conflicting Conceptions
The Case of Surrogate Motherhood

MEREDITH W. MICHAELS *teaches philosophy at Hampshire College in Massachusetts. Her work focuses on issues in feminist ethics and epistemology.*

M Y intention here is to provide an analysis of our current confusion over surrogacy and ultimately to suggest an alternative framework within which to refocus subsequent discussions about surrogacy and, perhaps, other reproductive practices. In what follows, I will introduce the practice of surrogacy by outlining the details of the Baby M case. I will then present a typology of responses to the case. The principal analysis of the paper, and the argument for its correctness, will begin in earnest when I then place the responses in the context of some recent work by Carol Gilligan. I will end with some reflections on the consequences of my analysis for our understanding and adjudication of the current debates over surrogacy. In addition, I will present an admittedly contentious proposal for recasting the *problem* of surrogacy.

The Case of "Baby M"

Here is how the story goes. Dr. and Mr. Stern were in their later thirties. When they discovered that Dr. Stern could not bear a child, they went to the New York Infertility Institute, an agency run by Noel Keane, who has been a vocal advocate of surrogacy arrangements. After qualifying as prospective parents, Mr. Stern was introduced to Mary Beth Whitehead, a potential surrogate who had answered an advertisement placed by the clinic. Based on her characteristics (similarity in appearance to Dr. Stern, age, previous successful pregnancies, etc.), the Sterns decided upon Mary Beth Whitehead, the then 27-year-old mother of two, married to a garbage collector. The parties signed a contract in which the Sterns agreed to pay Mary Beth Whitehead $10,000 upon receipt of a baby, the result of her impregnation with William Stern's sperm. In addition, the Sterns agreed to pay her medical expenses and a $7,500 finder's fee to the Institute. About a year and a half later, Mary Beth Whitehead gave birth to a baby, now known to us all as Baby M. Everything looked just fine, except that, after having the baby, Mary Beth Whitehead changed her mind. She said, effectively, you keep your money; I'll keep my baby. The Sterns decided to

hold her to her contract. She pleaded with them to let her keep the baby for a week, so that she could say "good-bye" to her. At the end of the week, Mary Beth Whitehead refused to give the baby to the Sterns. The Sterns went to court in New Jersey (where the Sterns and the Whiteheads live). The judge awarded temporary custody of the baby to the Sterns.

After fleeing to Florida with the baby for three months, Mary Beth Whitehead returned to New Jersey where she initiated a suit for custody of the baby. The judge who presided during the trial, Harvey Sorkow, held the surrogate contract to be valid; in addition, he awarded custody of the baby to Mr. Stern, on the grounds that he and his wife would provide better care for the child than would Mary Beth Whitehead. Shortly after the ruling, which denied all rights of visitation to Mary Beth Whitehead, Judge Sorkow signed the documents enabling Dr. Stern to adopt the baby. Eleven months later, the New Jersey Supreme Court, acting in response to an appeal of the lower court decision, overruled that decision. By declaring surrogate contracts illegal, they restored Mary Beth Whitehead's parental rights and so nullified Dr. Stern's adoption of the baby. Though the court allowed custody of the baby to remain with her father, the restoration of her parental rights meant that Mary Beth Whitehead could seek a new hearing on visitation. This, indeed, she did. Two months later, she was awarded "liberal visitation" in order, according to the deciding Judge Sween, to allow that mother and daughter "develop their own special relationship."

Those are, as they say, the bare facts of the case. As is true of any set of facts, they are susceptible to a variety of interpretations. For the moment, we can characterize the question around which the controversy centered as follows: was the contractual arrangement between Mary Beth Whitehead and William Stern fair? By providing a general characterization of five principal assessments of institutionalized surrogacy, I will describe a variety of responses to that question.

The Negative Feminist Response

On the one hand, a negative feminist response subsumes the practice of surrogacy under the umbrella of prostitution. According to it, women have been forced, under patriarchy, to sell their bodies for men's pleasure. Surrogate motherhood is simply an extension of this practice, though here the woman's body is sold not to ensure the man's sexual pleasure but rather to ensure his posterity. Just as women's sexual autonomy is sacrificed to that of men in the case of prostitution, so is women's reproductive autonomy sacrificed to that of men in the case of surrogate motherhood.

On the other hand, this response subsumes the practice of surrogate motherhood under the umbrella of coercive reproductive technology. Reproductive technology in general and surrogate motherhood in particular are seen as the contempory enforcement of women's traditional role as breeders for men. To ensure their posterity, and their continued control over nature, men manipulate women's reproductive capacities without regard to the consequences for women. In the case of surrogate motherhood, the role of woman as procreatrix plays itself out in the form of womb rental. The practice of surrogacy renders transparent the reproductive exploitation of women that is usually obscured by the veil of sex. Here, where there is reproduction without sex, the contours of that exploitation are rendered horrifyingly visible.

On this analysis, the question of the "fairness" of the surrogate contract is moot. The enforced alienation of women's reproductive labor, not to mention the "product" of her labor, is analogous to that of the worker under capitalism. A system of labor which is parasitic on relations of domination and subordination is a system within which any contractual arrangement between the worker and the capitalist is, by its nature, unfair. The same holds for the contractual arrangements between surrogates and those who seek their services. The Marxist analogy serves, too, to highlight the class structure of surrogacy arrangements. The high cost of surrogacy, coupled with the limited employment opportunities available to lower-class women, nestles the practice of surrogacy comfortably within a larger system of class exploitation. Indeed, in its ruling on the case, the New Jersey Supreme Court recognized that "it is unlikely that surrogate mothers will be as proportionately numerous among those women in the top 20 percent income bracket as among those in the bottom 20 percent." Whether we see surrogate mothers as analogous to prostitutes, or whether we see them as analogous to breeder cows, the inherently oppressive conditions of their labor puts them beyond the pale of contractual fairness, let alone legitimacy.

The Positive Feminist Response

There is, on the other side, a quite different feminist approach to the practice of surrogacy. According to this approach, we should see surrogate motherhood as falling under the umbrella of women's reproductive choice. Just as women have fought long and hard for the right to abortion, so too should women demand the right to choose for themselves whether to become surrogates. To outlaw surrogacy, then, is to restrict women's reproductive choice.

As a theoretical corollary to this line of reasoning, it is claimed that the opposition to surrogacy simply reinforces the connection between childbearing and childrearing that feminists have fought equally hard to sever. To privilege the connection between the two, by insisting that women who bear children must mother them, is to revert to a regressive, biologically essentialist procreative model.

The question of contractual fairness, then, becomes a question about particular contracts. In other words, while some surrogate contracts might not provide women with adequate protections against abuse or exploitation, it is possible, in principle, that a contractual agreement between a surrogate and a person seeking her services be fair. When a surrogate enters into such an agreement, she must abide by its terms. So, too, of course, must its cosignator or signators. From this feminist perspective, the purpose of contractual arrangements and of legislation governing their terms is precisely to protect women from incursions into their reproductive autonomy by the surrogate agency and its clients, once she has exercised her reproductive choice by agreeing to become a surrogate.

The Negative Moralist Response

Not surprisingly, the negative moralist response is best exemplified by a recent papal pronouncement. In 1987, the Vatican issued a major doctrinal statement condemning reproductive technology and surrogate motherhood. According to the statement:

> Surrogate motherhood represents an objective failure to meet the obligations of maternal love, of conjugal fidelity and of responsible motherhood; it offends the dignity and the right of the child to be conceived, carried in the womb, brought into the world and brought up by his own parents; it sets up, to the detriment of families, a division between the physical, psychological and moral elements which constitute those families.

The Vatican position represents a view that appears in more diffuse form in the secular community. Some opposition to surrogate motherhood seems to stem from a general worry about the simultaneous sanctity and fragility of marriage and the family. According to this view, artificial insemination is tantamount to adultery without sex. The relinquishing of the baby by the mother is tantamount to maternal abandonment. The mere consideration that she might do so is tantamount to a renunciation of the importance of maternal love. By severing the connections between sex and procreation, between procreation and marriage, between childbearing and childrearing, surrogate motherhood unravels the fabric in which biology and the social order have been so carefully woven. Placed in this context, the mere idea of a surrogate contract is anathema. It is an offense against the moral/social order.

The Positive Person-On-The-Street Response

The positive response of the person on the street is an admixture of various strains of political conservatism, pragmatism, and liberalism. The basic idea is this: there are a number of infertile couples who want babies. The availability of abortion, together with the relaxing of social sanctions against single motherhood, has created a "shortage" of babies available for adoption. In addition, many fathers, or couples, are attracted to the fact that surrogacy ensures genetic continuity between the father and the child. So, surrogacy is a relatively attractive choice for these infertile couples.

On the other side, there are women who view the option of being a surrogate favorably. Interviews appear to indicate that the decision to become a surrogate is often based on the desire to give the gift of a baby to a childless couple. Some women have indicated that they simply enjoy being pregnant and so are happy to get paid for it. Surrogate agencies encourage the view that the agreement between the surrogate and the infertile couple is a business deal like any other. If all parties consent to it voluntarily, then there should be no further questions asked. On this view, the contractual arrangement between Mary Beth Whitehead and William Stern is a reasonable one. Mary Beth reneged on a fair deal. In refusing to surrender the baby, she broke a contractually binding promise.

The Negative Baby-Selling Response

According to yet another, negative view, to legitimize surrogate motherhood is to legitimize baby-selling. The surrogate agency compels the woman to sell the product of her labor, thereby transforming the product, namely a baby, into a commodity. It is surely wrong to bring the production of children into the marketplace.

Another account, perhaps more in the spirit of the moralist, condemns surrogacy-as-baby-selling on moral grounds. Surrogacy replicates the structure of slavery. In the case of slavery, one human being is sold to another for the seller's profit and the buyer's use and enjoyment. Though the concepts of use and enjoyment may be different in the case of surrogate motherhood, the underlying structure of the transfer is the same. That

the father is paying for something other than the "services" of the woman is made evident by the clause in surrogate contracts that denies any compensation to the mother if she miscarries in the first five months. The $10,000 surrogate's fee is paid to her only upon the receipt of the baby by the father. She is not, for example, paid $1,100 per month of pregnancy. However hard the agencies might work to disguise the true nature of the transaction, the fact remains that one person is getting paid for making a baby for the other. To view a baby as a potentially transferable product is to fly in the face of our commitment to inviolable human dignity and respect. In terms of a Kantian morality, it treats a person as a means, rather than as an end. Every person, that is, has a moral right not to be bought and sold. On this view, surrogate contracts are inherently suspect, for they bring human beings into the marketplace, not merely as consumers, but as products.

Remapping Baby M

In her book *In a Different Voice: Psychological Theory and Women's Development*, Carol Gilligan argues that women's moral reasoning, based on an "ethic of care," has a different conceptual basis from that of men, which is based on an "ethic of justice." According to Gilligan, "the logic underlying an ethic of care is a psychological logic of relationships, which contrasts with the formal logic of fairness that informs the justice approach."

Each of these two ethics, she argues, contains within it a particular notion of responsibility. The ethic of justice privileges prior agreement by granting the importance and hence the authority of contractual arrangements. In contrast, the ethic of care privileges the capacity to respond to the needs of others, and of one-self, by maintaining a vigilance over the present. The first concept of responsibility can be illustrated by, for example, the importance of promise keeping. Promises are made in order to establish reasonable expectations. They are kept in order to see that those expectations are met. Those who fail to keep promises, who fail to honor obligations, undermine our capacity to live an ordered life. The second concept of responsibility can be illustrated by, for example, those sorts of cases in which the urgency of a unpredicted need compels our attention away from the tasks at hand. If my daughter's friend appears on our doorstep after having been battered by her mother, my responsibility is to come to her assistance. Whatever other obligations I may have incurred are suspended by her overriding need for help.

The Case of Baby M is difficult precisely because it appeals simultaneously to the two senses of responsibility, respectively associated with the ethic of care and the ethic of justice. At the center of the case is a contractual agreement, the one entered into by Mary Beth Whitehead and William Stern. But equally at its center is our strong sense that Mary Beth Whitehead's understandable desire to maintain a relationship with her child is based on a conception of maternal responsibility and need. The tension between these two moral frameworks and the concepts of responsibility unique to each, is manifest in the various responses to surrogacy that we have considered.

In the Negative Moralist Response, the possibility of a legitimate contractual arrangement is denied precisely because it subverts the ethic of care, narrowly circumscribed in this case by a regressive conception of maternal responsibility. On the other hand, the Negative Feminist Response denies to women the capacity to transcend that regressive concept of maternal responsibility by entering into contractual reproductive arrangements. What Gilligan refers to as the "psychological logic" of maternal responsibility binds women to their children in highly complex and deeply affective ways. In contrast, the ethic of justice permits relationships based on mutual interest, and hence often, disinterest. It is at least arguable that the ethic of care, constructed on the ground of maternal responsibility and connection, is itself responsible for the tenacity of a cultural commitment to woman-as-mother. In signing the surrogate contract, Mary Beth Whitehead challenged the romance of the maternal bond.

On the other hand, the Positive Feminist Response denies the actual hegemony of the ethic of care in maternal relationships. It asks us to subsume under the ethic of justice a relationship that does not, at least under the present conditions of mothering, have a happy home there. By insisting on the authority of the contractual arrangement, it diminishes the extent to which women's conception of procreative responsibility is governed by an ethic of care. The Positive Person-on-the-Street Response suffers from a conflation of the ethic of care and the ethic of contractual fairness. A gift, particularly a "gift of love" is typically viewed as an expression of care. To promise contractually to give a gift is to transform gift-giving into an obligation. The New Jersey Supreme Court alluded to the tension in this position when it claimed in its discussion of "The Factor of Money" that "first and perhaps most important, all parties concede that it is unlikely that surrogacy will survive without money. Despite the alleged selfless motivation of surrogate mothers, if there is no payment, there will be no surrogates, or very few." Altruism-for-Profit, the employment lure of the surrogate industry, precisely encodes the heterodoxy of its method of providing babies for those who can afford them.

Just as the two ethics inform and deform these responses to the institutionalized practice of surrogacy, so too do they inform and deform the ways in which the particular saga of Baby M unfolded. In distinguishing between the question of the legitimacy of the contract signed by Mary Beth Whitehead and William Stern and the question of custody, Judge Sorkow placed the case between the poles of the ethic of care and the ethic of justice. The evidence he garnered for the custody case is a compendium of stories designed to demonstrate the relative capacities of the Sterns and of Mary Beth Whitehead to care for the baby. The Sterns won because they succeeded in persuading the judge that their capacity to do so exceeded that of Mary Beth Whitehead. Portrayed as loving and caring parents, able to place the baby's needs before their own, they stood in sharp contrast to the picture painted of Mary Beth Whitehead by expert psychological witnesses. Characterized as "over identified, impulsive, egocentric, self-dramatized, manipulative," her "exploitative behavior" rendered her unable to adhere to the canons of maternal morality. She even, it turns out, gave Baby M the wrong toys to play with (a panda bear, instead of pots and pans). Though the New Jersey Supreme Court thought that Mary Beth Whitehead had been "rather harshly judged" during the course of the initial trial, they nevertheless agreed that "the Sterns promise a secure home, with an understanding relationship that allows nurturing and independent growth to develop together."

On the other hand, Judge Sorkow's ruling on the fairness of the contract sought to abstract from the human context those features of the situation deemed relevant to determining whether any legitimate obligation had been incurred by Mary Beth Whitehead. In arguing that indeed it had, Judge Sorkow seemed not the least troubled by the fact that he was thereby drawing motherhood into the sphere of rights, obligations, and contractual fairness. We have, he argued, a right to procreate noncoitally, a right, that is, to produce children outside the context of what have been, until now, ordinary human relationships. Holding fast to the ethic of justice that typically governs purely contractual relationships, Judge Sorkow essentially asked us to transform the dominant conception of maternal, and hence parental, relationships. At the very same time, in his determination of custody, he appealed to precisely the understanding of those relationships his contractual decision, in effect, undermined. The irony, of course, is that it is the father, and not the mother, who succeeded in demonstrating a superior capacity to embody the conditions of maternal morality.

What then of the higher court's "reversal" of Judge Sorkow's decision? In defending its judgment that surrogate contracts are illegal, the Court argued that,

> Under the contract, the natural mother is irrevocably committed before she knows the strength of her bond with the child. She never makes a totally voluntary, informed decision, for quite clearly any decision before the baby's birth is, in the most important sense, uninformed, and any decision after that, compelled by a pre-existing contractual agreement, the threat of a lawsuit, and the inducement of a $10,000 payment, is less than totally voluntary.

According to the Court, a surrogacy contract is invalid because the "natural mother" cannot enter into it voluntarily and adequately informed. She cannot be adequately informed because she cannot know, at the time that she signs the contract, how she will feel about the baby when she finally has it.

What is the principle of contractual fairness, or validity, underlying this bit of reasoning? The Court is claiming, first, that a person can't make a voluntary, informed decision in a case where she doesn't know, at the time that she makes the decision, what her relevant future feelings will be. Second, the Court is claiming that voluntariness and informedness are necessary conditions of contractual validity and fairness. Its conclusion, then, is that no contract is valid under circumstances where a person's relevant future feelings are unknown to her at the time of the contractual decision. The first of these claims, if true, would radically alter the prevailing notion of voluntary choice, both within and without the legal system. In claiming that, to be informed is to know *in advance* what your relevant future feelings will be, the Court renders involuntary many of decisions that we typically think of as voluntary. Take marriage, for example. In most cases, the decision to get married is based both on one's present feelings about another person and on some reasonable assessment of how one will feel about that person in the future (forever?). The fact that, in so many cases, those feelings take an unpredicted turn for the worse does not thereby render the initial decision to get married an involuntary one. The same reasoning applies in more clearly contractual cases. If I decide to sell you my house and thereby enter into a contractual relationship with you, the fact that I later discover that I have unanticipated feelings of regret about the sale does not reflect on the voluntariness of my initial decision. I could not declare the contract invalid on the grounds that I was inadequately informed about how I would feel. The notion of voluntariness to which the Court appeals in its claims about the surrogate contract is simply too strong to apply in ordinary cases of contractual obligation. Indeed, in the ordinary case, how a person *feels* about that to which a contract commits her is quite irrelevant to the validity of the contract.

It might be argued, however, that the Court does not intend this notion of voluntariness to apply in ordinary cases. If so, there must be something special about the surrogate contract that makes the inability to predict future feelings germane. The Court claims that the woman is "contractually committed before she knows the strength of the mother/child bond." It is in this particular sense that she is uninformed. In making this claim, the Court is presupposing that the affective ties between the woman and the child are constitutive of their relationship in a way that sets it apart from other legal relationships. So, in the absence of clear knowledge of her own future affective relationship to the child she will bear, the surrogate mother cannot make a voluntary decision about giving the child away.

Two features of this line of reasoning are worth noting. The Court, in attempting to determine the legitimacy of the surrogate *contract* must appeal to ethical notions, such as informedness and voluntariness, that typically define the terms and boundaries of contractual obligation. Not surprisingly, it is working within the framework of the ethic of justice characteristic of a legal system. On the other hand, the Court establishes the grounds for contractual legitimacy on the basis of affective ties and the knowledge thereof. In that regard, it is working within the framework of the ethic of care. The Court's particular and peculiar concept of voluntariness can be seen as an attempt to bridge the gap between these two moral paradigms.

It is important to note, however, that the strength of the bridge depends upon our willingness to concede that the mother/child bond is essentially affective in nature (even, as the Court indicates, immediately after birth). It is surely reasonable to claim that the relationship between women and their recently born children is usually affective. It is also possible to argue that it ought to be. But it is not at all clear either that it is essentially so, nor that it is, in this respect, different from other legal relationships. Because it views the mother/child relationship as essentially affective, the Court is thereby committed to the claim that a woman's affective states are relevant to determining her capacity to enter into contractual obligations. Since this is not true in ordinary cases of contractual obligation, the Court sets women apart from the usual workings of the contract system. The Court's excessively strong requirement on voluntariness, coupled with its excessively strong notion of the mother/child relationship, appears as a failed attempt to create an easy transition between discrepant moral frameworks. In addition, because it takes the Baby M case to be paradigmatic of the uncertainty of affective relationships between women and their recently born children, it rules out the possibility that any woman could rationally agree to give up her child before its birth. The dangers to women of entering into surrogacy arrangements are many. But the Court's argument against surrogacy relies on a fundamentally prescriptive account of the relationship between women and children that disguises itself as an accommodation to the ethic of care.

The Baby-Selling Response Reconsidered

Thus far, I have attempted to place the responses to the question about the fairness of the surrogate contract within the context of a bipolar moral edifice. I have omitted any mention of the Negative Baby-Selling Response. I should like to end with some reflections on that response. Unlike the other responses that I have considered, the Negative Baby-Selling Response, at least initially, fits quite comfortably in both the ethic of justice and the ethic of care. The moral force of the baby-selling objection rests on its assumption that to sell her is to undermine a baby's essential human dignity. Neither the ethic of care, nor the ethic of justice, it can be argued, lays special claim to the concept of human dignity or respect.

Central to the ethic of justice are the notions of individual autonomy and equality. Honoring those notions in the context of human relationships requires: 1) that we refrain from interfering with another person's capacity for self-determination, and 2) that we understand moral principles to apply equally to all people. Taken together, these propositions suggest a prohibition against baby-selling. Surely, the buying or selling of a person violates her autonomy. While someone might want to argue that the concept of autonomy makes no sense when applied to babies, the second proposition requires that the prohibition against the buying or selling of people extends to babies, as well as to adults.

The ethic of care, based on a psychological logic, locates the prohibition against baby-selling in the interdependence of human relationships. By focusing on dependence, rather than on autonomy, the ethic of care condemns baby-selling as a failure to acknowledge the importance of the affective ties that bind a child to her biological mother, even when the biological mother does not raise her. In addition, the financial transaction between the biological parents can only serve to distort the parental (especially maternal) responsibility on which the child's psychological nurturance depends.

While the other responses that we have considered exemplify the tension, even the clash, between two moral paradigms, the baby-selling objections seems to be quite consistent with each. One might, at this point, simply rest with that objection and so conclude that surrogacy is wrong precisely because it is an offense no matter which ethical framework one takes to be paramount.

Some Responses to the Negative Baby-Selling Response and an Immodest Proposal

Where, then, are we? There are, I think, three responses to the Negative Baby-Selling Response itself. None of them provides a definitive answer to the question that I, from the outset, wished to avoid, namely, Is surrogacy a good thing or a bad thing? Nevertheless, these responses provoke us to consider the ways in which surrogacy challenges given features of the moral and political landscape. I will take each one of them in turn.

First, considered in the context of the ethic of justice, the Negative Baby-Selling Response presupposes that there is no relevant moral distinction between babies and adult human beings. But it is not clear, without some further argument, that this is true. Though the ethic of justice requires respect for a person's autonomy, the concept of autonomy does not apply straightforwardly to infants. Those familiar with the abortion debate might recognize the dangers of relying too heavily on the assumed moral parity of adults and those who are not yet there. Thus, subsumed under the ethic of justice, the Negative Baby-Selling Response must establish that the reasons against the buying and selling of adult human beings apply equally in the case of infant human beings. This is not an easy task.

It might be argued at this point that the ethic of justice would do better to appeal to the Kantian distinction between treating a person as a means and treating her as an end. However, it is difficult to see how a baby is being used as a means in the case of surrogacy but not in the case of many ordinary adoptions. Moreover, our reasons for having and acquiring children are not so clearly independent of instrumental considerations. The ethic of justice must distinguish surrogacy from more familiar cases of child acquisition.

Second, the ethic of care rests its case against baby-selling on the prediction that the child's capacity to establish positive affective relationships may be undermined by his knowledge that his birth was the result of a financial relationship between his biological mother and father. In addition, it views surrogacy as undermining maternal responsibility by transplanting mother/child relationships into a financial context. This response brings with it a commitment to the traditional biological family as the principal site of healthy moral/psychological development. It ignores the possibility that alternatively constructed affective ties might serve to generate alternative, even progressive, notions of parental responsibility. Only in a social context that valorizes the psychology of the biological family to the exclusion of any alternatives do variations on its theme present themselves as psychologically, and hence morally, threatening.

The baby-selling objection to surrogacy based on the ethic of care should be particularly troubling to feminists who hold the biological family responsible for restricting the movement of women. Indeed, the ethic-of-care version of the baby-selling objection serves to highlight feminist objections to that moral paradigm. It may be that an affectively nuanced ethic has governed the relationship between women and children. But it may also be that such an ethic ties women to their children in undesirable ways. At the very least, feminist objections to surrogacy must face the extent to which their case rests on an adherence to precisely those features of the ethic of care that feminists have found most troubling.

Third, the baby-selling response might be dismissed, not for moral reasons, but rather on the grounds that it conflates a clear distinction between goods and services. In other words, the surrogate is being paid for her services and not for the product thereof. But the distinction between labor and the products of labor is not so clear in the context of a capitalist economy. The distinction between paying for labor and paying for the products produced by labor is a distinction without a difference. If I buy a pair of shoes, I am paying, at least in part, for the labor required to produce them. Shoes do not appear in the world *sui generis*; nor do babies. Conversely, if I were to claim that I am paying for the labor involved in producing the shoes, but not paying for the shoes themselves, I would be hard-pressed to see how I might sustain that alleged distinction. The distinction is equally implausible in the case of surrogacy.

In the end, however, the claim that surrogacy payments are for services, not babies, does little to dispel whatever qualms we might have about the commercialization of surrogacy. It is difficult to see precisely why reproductive labor and its products should escape the forces of commodification that leave so little untouched. In my discussion of the New Jersey Supreme Court's creation of a concept of voluntariness designed to apply uniquely to surrogates, and so uniquely to women, I suggested that women ought to say, in effect, "Thanks, but no thanks." The same response, it might be argued, is appropriate in the case of marketing of surrogacy and, perhaps, other reproductive services. And, yet, if the exclusion of such services from the marketplace serves to perpetuate a romantically regressive concept of maternal responsibility, then any attempt to create an acknowledged place for those services within the system of service and commodity exchange ought to focus on ways to resist the corruptions of that system. The specious moral arguments for and against surrogacy are caught in a messy, gerrymandered pastiche of ill-matched moral concepts, or so I have attempted to argue. My suggestion, then, is that we work toward developing a vision of surrogacy that brings it squarely within the marketplace. In so doing, it will be crucial that we avoid replicating the present system, which clearly leaves women and children at the mercy of those who, as the Supreme Court of New Jersey itself noted, have little real concern for their interests. As is the case with other workers whose employment options are limited, surrogates are presently susceptible to the exigencies of a marketplace that thrives on exploitation and mystification. Yet, even within a system so structured, workers have found ways to resist the forces of exploitation. If surrogates could do the same, they might transform, not the marketplace itself, but the position that reproductive practices and the ethics of reproductive practices have occupied within it.

Is my suggestion simply a replication of the Positive Feminist Response? I don't think so. Rather than simply insist that surrogacy meet the requirements of contractual fairness, surrogates should take economic matters into their collective hands. The contractual fairness demanded by liberal feminists itself does nothing to forge alliances between exploited workers. Collective action, on the other hand, holds some transformative promise.

5

Is It
Ever
Right to
Lie?

Have you told a lie in the past year? If you answer "no," you are probably lying (or at the very least engaged in self-deception!). While it is surely less than clear exactly what constitutes a lie, it is likely the case that sometime during the past year you deliberately deceived or misled someone by misrepresenting the truth in some way. A very few people may make it a practice never to lie. Depending upon the perspective from which we judge their behavior, and perhaps depending upon their motivations for adhering so strictly to truthfulness, we may consider them to be either saintly or just plain obnoxious.

Two things about lying are quite clear. On the one hand, lying is viewed as suspect; it is something that we are taught not to do as children and generally feel qualms about doing as adults. On the other, lying is a common human practice; most of us lie, in one way or another, quite often. Some of the lies that we tell we think of as harmless ("I overslept because my alarm clock is broken") or even kind ("Your hair looks really nice today"). Other lies seem designed to postpone the inevitable truth for some self-serving but in no way malicious reason ("The stork brought you"). Other lies are so commonplace that we hardly take them seriously ("With new Futz toothpaste, you'll never spend another Friday night alone"). Other lies appear plainly to be wrong ("There are no explosives in my luggage"). The range of assertions that can plausibly count as lying, together with the range of reasons people have for lying, make it extremely difficult for the philosopher to figure out just what is wrong with lying. Why is it that something that is such a common practice has such a bad reputation? Why is truth-telling so important? What exactly *is* a lie? Is it *always* wrong to lie? What *makes* lying wrong? If some lies are justified, then what excuses them?

In this chapter, you will discover that there is considerable disagreement among philosophers, first, as to whether lying is indeed wrong and, second, as to why it is wrong, if it is. Immanuel Kant argues the most extreme position on the wrongness of lying. According to him, lying is simply and absolutely wrong. Kant believes that telling an untruth to another is always injurious. Indeed, Kant defends the view that, for example, lying to a would-be murderer as to the whereabouts of his intended victim is wrong. Charles Fried, whose sympathies lie with Kant's position, provides a carefully articulated argument for what he calls the "evil" of lying. For Fried, lying is a breach of common trust. When I lie to someone, according to Fried, I act in such a way as to appropriate for myself another person's mind. Though Fried himself does not invoke the analogy of rape, he does claim that a person who lies violates the "moral personality" of the one lied to. For both Kant and Fried, something about the very nature of being human and being a member of the human community demands truth-telling. While their positions may strike you as extreme (especially Kant's), you might want to think about what it would be like to get from one end of the day to another if lying were to predominate as a practice. Try spending an hour systematically misleading — and being misled — and see how you and your companions fare. We begin to see how truth and honesty are necessary conditions for human communication.

Many lies are told because the liar believes that the lying protects someone from the hurtfulness of a particular truth. Lies told with the intention of doing good for another are benevolent lies. In his essay, Thomas E. Hill, Jr., questions whether benevolent lies are morally appropriate. He is particularly concerned with the sorts of lies that people in close or significant relationships tell one another. Should, for example, a doctor lie to a patient about her condition on the grounds that her final days will be happier if she does not know about her condition? Hill's position is that a lie is morally wrong, even if it brings about greater happiness, because it undermines the patient's autonomy.

In considering the merits of Hill's argument, you will be faced with the question whether the wrongness of lying is attributable to the negative consequences of particular lies, or whether it is attributable to the very nature of lying itself. Kant, Fried, and Hill differ by degrees on this question. Sidgwick, on the other hand, is a consequentialist, arguing that lying in and of itself is not wrong. Rather, we must judge, with respect to any particular lie, what its consequences are. In fact, according to him, some lies are required precisely because they have superior consequences to truth-telling. For Sidgwick, there is nothing intrinsically valuable about the truth.

Taking that position to an extreme, Mark Twain provides an engaging defense of what he calls the "art of lying." For Twain, the problem is not that people lie, but that they lie badly. Perhaps it is no surprise that such a master of fabrication should see little value in a blind adherence to the literal truth. And though it is clear that we must read Twain's essay through skeptical eyes, the essay does raise important questions about how precisely we draw the lines between truth and falsehood in the multiple contexts within which human communication takes place. It is precisely this issue that Harry Frankfurt takes up in his reflections on bullshit. According to Frankfurt, it is its programmatic nature that distinguishes bullshit from lying. Unlike the liar, the bullshitter constructs a whole world, at the center of which is a misrepresentation of what the bullshitter himself is up to. Both Twain and Frankfurt leave us wondering whether we have just been made victims of their own imaginative misrepresentations.

IMMANUEL KANT

On a Supposed Right to Tell Lies from Benevolent Motives

IMMANUEL KANT (1724–1804), *the great German philosopher, wrote his short* Foundations of the Metaphysics of Morals *as a summary of the more elaborate arguments in his* Critique of Practical Reason *(1788). In these books, he defends morality and moral principle as the product of practical reason, not feelings or "inclinations."*

IN the work called *France*, for the year 1797, Part VI., No. 1, on Political Reactions, by *Benjamin Constant*, the following passage occurs, p. 123: —

"The moral principle that it is one's duty to speak the truth, if it were taken singly and unconditionally, would make all society impossible. We have the proof of this in the very direct consequences which have been drawn from this principle by a German philosopher, who goes so far as to affirm that to tell a falsehood to a murderer who asked us whether our friend, of whom he was in pursuit, had not taken refuge in our house, would be a crime."

The French philosopher opposes this principle in the following manner, p. 124: — "It is a duty to tell the truth. The notion of duty is inseparable from the notion of right. A duty is what in one being corresponds to the right of another. Where there are no rights there are no duties. To tell the truth then is a duty, but only towards him who has a right to the truth. But no man has a right to a truth that injures others." The πρωτον ψευδος [false beginning] here lies in the statement that "*To tell the truth is a duty, but only towards him who has a right to the truth*."

It is to be remarked, first, that the expression "to have a right to the truth" is unmeaning. We should rather say, a man has a right to his own *truthfulness* (*veracitas*), that is, to subjective truth in his own person. For to have a right objectively to truth would mean that, as in *meum* and *tuum* generally, it depends on his *will* whether a given statement shall be true or false, which would produce a singular logic.

Now, the *first* question is whether a man — in cases where he cannot avoid answering Yes or No — has the *right* to be untruthful. The *second* question is whether, in order to prevent a misdeed that threatens him or some one else, he is not actually bound to be untruthful in a certain statement to which an unjust compulsion forces him.

Truth in utterances that cannot be avoided is the formal duty of a man to everyone, however great the disadvantage that may arise from it to him or any other; and although by making a false statement I do no wrong to him who unjustly compels me to speak, yet I do wrong to men in general in the most essential point of duty, so that it may be called a lie (though not in the jurist's sense), that is, so far as in me lies I cause that declarations in general find no credit, and hence that all rights founded on contract should lose their force; and this is a wrong which is done to mankind.

If, then, we define a lie merely as an intentionally false declaration towards another man, we need not add that it must injure another; as the jurists think proper to put in their definition (*mendacium est falsiloquium in praejudicium alterius*). For it always injures another; if not another individual, yet mankind generally, since it vitiates the source of justice. This benevolent lie *may*, however, by *accident* (*casus*) become punishable even by civil laws; and that which escapes liability to punishment only by accident may be condemned as a wrong even by external laws. For instance, if you have *by a lie* hindered a man who is even now planning a murder, you are legally responsible for all the consequences. But if you have strictly adhered to the truth, public justice can find no fault with you, be the unforeseen consequence what it may. It is possible that whilst you have honestly answered Yes to the murderer's question, whether his intended victim is in the house, the latter may have gone out unobserved, and so not have come in the way of the murderer, and the deed therefore have not been done; whereas, if you lied and said he was not in the house, and he had really gone out (though unknown to you), so that the murderer met him as he went, and executed his purpose on him, then you might with justice be accused as the cause of his death. For, if you had spoken the truth as well as you knew it, perhaps the murderer while seeking for his enemy in the house might have been caught by neighbours coming up and the deed been prevented. Whoever then *tells a lie*, however good his intentions may be, must answer for the consequences of it, even before the civil tribunal, and must pay the penalty for them, however unforeseen they may have been; because truthfulness is a duty that must be regarded as the basis of all duties founded on contract, the laws of which would be rendered uncertain and useless if even the least exception to them were admitted.

To be *truthful* (honest) in all declarations is therefore a sacred unconditional command of reason, and not to be limited to any expediency.

M. Constant makes a thoughtful and sound remark on the decrying of such strict principles, which it is alleged lose themselves in impracticable ideas, and are therefore to be rejected (p. 123): — "In every case in which a principle proved to be true seems to be inapplicable, it is because we do not know the *middle principle* which contains the medium of its application." He adduces (p. 121) the doctrine of *equality* as the first link forming the social chain (p. 121): "namely, that no man can be bound by any laws except those to the formation of which he has contributed. In a very contracted society this principle may be directly applied and become the ordinary rule without requiring any middle principle. But in a very numerous society we must add a new principle to that which we here state. This middle principle is, that the individuals may contribute to the formation of the laws either in their own person or by *representatives*. Whoever would try to apply the first principle to a numerous society without taking in the middle principle would infallibly bring about its destruction. But this circumstance, which would only show the ignorance or incompetence of the lawgiver, would prove nothing against the principle itself." He concludes (p. 125) thus: "A principle recognized as truth must, therefore, never be abandoned, however obviously danger may seem to be involved in it." (And yet the good man himself abandoned the unconditional principle of veracity on account of the danger to society, because he could not discover any middle principle which would serve to prevent this danger; and, in fact, no such principle is to be interpolated here.)

Retaining the names of the persons as they have been here brought forward, "the French philosopher" confounds the action by which one does harm (*nocet*) to another by telling the truth, the admission of which he cannot avoid, with the action by which he does him *wrong* (*lædit*). It was merely an *accident* (*casus*) that the truth of the statement did harm to the inhabitant of the house; it was not a free *deed* (in the juridical sense). For to admit his right to require another to tell a lie for his benefit would be to admit a claim opposed to all law. Every man has not only a right, but the strictest duty to truthfulness in statements which he cannot avoid, whether they do harm to himself or others. He himself, properly speaking, does not *do* harm to him who suffers thereby; but this harm is *caused* by accident. For the man is not free to choose, since (if he must speak at all) veracity is an unconditional duty. The "German philosopher" will therefore not adopt as his principle the proposition (p. 124): "It is a duty to speak the truth, but only to him who has *a right to the truth*," first on account of the obscurity of the expression, for truth is not a possession the right to which can be granted to one, and refused to another; and next and chiefly, because the duty of veracity (of which alone we are speaking here) makes no distinction between persons towards whom we have this duty, and towards whom we may be free from it; but is an *unconditional duty* which holds in all circumstances.

Now, in order to proceed from a *metaphysic* of Right (which abstracts from all conditions of experience) to a principle of *politics* (which applies these notions to cases of experience), and by means of this to the solution of a problem of the latter

in accordance with the general principle of right, the philosopher will enunciate: — 1. An *Axiom*, that is, an apodictically certain proposition, which follows directly from the definition of external right (harmony of the *freedom* of each with the freedom of all by a universal law). 2. A *Postulate* of external public *law* as the united will of all on the principle of *equality*, without which there could not exist the freedom of all. 3. A *Problem*; how it is to be arranged that harmony may be maintained in a society, however large, on principles of freedom and equality (namely, by means of a representative system); and this will then become a principle of the *political system*, the establishment and arrangement of which will contain enactments which, drawn from practical knowledge of men, have in view only the mechanism of administration of justice, and how this is to be suitably carried out. Justice must never be accommodated to the political system, but always the political system to justice.

"A principle recognized as true (I add, recognized *à priori*, and therefore apodictic) must never be abandoned, however obviously danger may seem to be involved in it," says the author. Only here we must not understand the danger of *doing harm* (accidentally), but of *doing wrong*; and this would happen if the duty of veracity, which is quite unconditional, and constitutes the supreme condition of justice in utterances, were made conditional and subordinate to other considerations; and although by a certain lie I in fact do no wrong to any person, yet I infringe the principle of justice in regard to all indispensably necessary statements *generally* (I do wrong formally, though not materially); and this is much worse than to commit an injustice to any individual, because such a deed does not presuppose any principle leading to it in the subject. The man who, when asked whether in the statement he is about to make he intends to speak truth or not, does not receive the question with indignation at the suspicion thus expressed towards him that he might be a liar, but who asks permission first to consider possible exceptions, is already a liar (*in potentia*), since he shows that he does not recognize veracity as a duty in itself, but reserves exceptions from a rule which in its nature does not admit of exceptions, since to do so would be self-contradictory.

All practical principles of justice must contain strict truths, and the principles here called middle principles can only contain the closer definition of their application to actual cases (according to the rules of politics), and never exceptions from them, since exceptions destroy the universality, on account of which alone they bear the name of principles.

CHARLES FRIED

The Evil of Lying

CHARLES FRIED *teaches at the Harvard University School of Law. He has written several books and articles on ethics.*

THE evil of lying is as hard to pin down as it is strongly felt. Is lying wrong or is it merely something bad? If it is bad, why is it bad — is it bad in itself or because of some tendency associated with it? Compare lying to physical harm. Harm is a state of the world and so it can only be classified as bad; the wrong I argued for was the *intentional doing* of harm. Lying, on the other hand, can be wrong, since it is an action. But the fact that lying is an action does not mean that it *must* be wrong rather than bad. It might be that the action of lying should be judged as just another state of the world — a time-extended state, to be sure, but there is no problem about that — and as such it would count as a negative element in any set of circumstances in which it occurred. Furthermore, if lying is judged to be bad it can be bad in itself, like something ugly or painful, or it can be bad only because of its tendency to produce results that are bad in themselves.

If lying were bad, not wrong, this would mean only that, other things being equal, we should avoid lies. And if lying were bad not in itself but merely because of its tendencies, we would have to avoid lies only when those tendencies were in fact likely to be realized. In either case lying would be permissible to produce a net benefit, including the prevention of more or worse lies. By contrast the categorical norm "Do not lie" does not evaluate states of affairs but is addressed to moral agents, forbidding lies. Now if lying is wrong it is also bad in itself, for the category of the intrinsically bad is weaker and more inclusive than the category of the wrong. And accordingly, many states of the world are intrinsically bad (such as destruction of valuable property) but intentional acts bringing them about are not necessarily wrong.

Bentham plainly believed that lying is neither wrong nor even intrinsically bad: "Falsehood, take it by itself, consider it as not being accompanied by any other material circumstances, nor therefore productive of any material effects, can never, upon the principle of utility, constitute any offense at all." By contrast, Kant and Augustine argued at length that lying is wrong. Indeed, they held that lying is not only wrong *unless* excused or justified in defined ways (which is my view) but that lying is always wrong. Augustine sees lying as a kind of defilement, the liar being tainted by the lie, quite apart from any consequences of the lie. Kant's views are more complex. He argues at one point that lying undermines confidence and trust among men generally: "Although by making a false statement I do no wrong to him who unjustly compels me to speak, yet I do wrong to men in general. . . . I cause that declarations in general find no credit, and hence all rights founded on contract should lose their force; and this is a wrong to mankind." This would seem to be a consequentialist argument, according to which lying is bad only insofar as it produces these bad results. But elsewhere he makes plain that he believes these bad consequences to be necessarily, perhaps even conceptually linked to lying. In this more rigoristic vein, he asserts that lying is a perversion of one's uniquely human capacities irrespective of any consequences of the lie, and thus lying is not only intrinsically bad but wrong.

Finally, a number of writers have taken what looks like an intermediate position: the evil of lying is indeed identified with its consequences, but the connection between lying and those consequences, while not a necessary connection, is close and persistent, and the consequences

themselves are pervasive and profound. Consider this passage from a recent work by G. F. Warnock:

> I do not necessarily do you any harm at all by deed or word if I induce you to believe what is not in fact the case; I may even do you good, possibly by way, for example, of consolation or flattery. Nevertheless, though deception is not thus necessarily directly damaging it is easy to see how crucially important it is that the natural inclination to have recourse to it should be counteracted. It is, one might say, not the implanting of false beliefs that is damaging, but rather the generation of the suspicion that they may be being implanted. For this undermines trust; and, to the extent that trust is undermined, all cooperative undertakings, in which what one person can do or has reason to do is dependent on what others have done, are doing, or are going to do, must tend to break down. . . . There is no sense in my asking you for your opinion on some point, if I do not suppose that your answer will actually express your opinion (verbal communication is doubtless the most important of all our co-operative undertakings).

Warnock does not quite say that truth-telling is good in itself or that lying is wrong, yet the moral quality of truth-telling and lying is not so simply instrumental as it is, for instance, for Bentham. Rather, truth-telling seems to bear a fundamental, pervasive relation to the human enterprise, just by lying appears to be fundamentally subversive of that enterprise. What exactly is the nature of this relation? How does truth-telling bear to human goods a relation which is more than instrumental but less than necessary?

The very definition of lying makes plain that consequences are crucial, for lying is intentional and the intent is an intent to produce a consequence: false belief. But how can I then resist the consequentialist analysis of lying? Lying is an attempt to produce a certain effect on another, and if that effect (consequence) is not bad, how can lying be wrong? I shall have to argue, therefore, that to lie is to intend to produce an effect which always has something bad about it, an effect moreover of the special sort that it is wrong to produce it intentionally. To lay that groundwork for my argument about lying, I must consider first the moral value of truth.

Truth and Rationality

A statement is true when the world is the way the statement says it is. Utilitarians insist (as in the quotation from Bentham above) that truth, like everything else, has value just exactly as it produces value — pleasure, pain, the satisfaction or frustration of desire. And of course it is easy to show that truth (like keeping faith, not harming the innocent, respecting rights) does not always lead to the net satisfactions of desire, to the production of utility. It may *tend* to do so, but that tendency explains only why we should discriminate between occasions when truth does and when it does not have value — an old story. It is an old story, for truth — like justice, respect, and self-respect — has a value which consequentialist analyses (utilitarian or any other) do not capture. Truth, like respect, is a foundational value.

The morality of right and wrong does not count the satisfaction of desire as the overriding value. Rather, the integrity of persons, as agents and as the objects of the intentional agency of others, has priority over the attainment of the goals which agents choose to attain. I have sought to show how respect for physical integrity is related to respect for the person. The person, I argued, is not just a locus of potential pleasure and pain but an entity with determinate characteristics. The person is, among other things, necessarily an incorporated, a physical, not an abstract entity. In relation to truth we touch another necessary aspect of moral personality: the capacity for judgment, and thus for choice. It is that aspect which Kant used to ground his moral theory, arguing that freedom and rationality are the basis for moral personality. John Rawls makes the same point, arguing that "moral personality and not the capacity for pleasure and pain . . . [is] the fundamental aspect of the self. . . . The essential unity of the self is . . . provided by the concept of right." The concept of the self is prior to the goods which the self chooses, and these goods gather their moral significance from the fact that they have been chosen by moral beings — beings capable of understanding and acting on moral principles.

In this view freedom and rationality are complementary capacities, or aspects of the same capacity, which is moral capacity. A man is free insofar as he is able to act on a judgment because he perceives it to be correct; he is free insofar as he may be moved to action by the judgments his reason offers to him. This is the very opposite of the Humean conception of reason as the slave of the passions. There is no slavery here. The man who follows the steps of a mathematical argument to its conclusion because he judges them to be correct is free indeed. To the extent that we choose our ends we are free; and as to objectively valuable ends which we choose because we see their value, we are still free.

Now, rational judgment is true judgment, and so the moral capacity for rational choice implies the capacity to recognize the matter on which choice is to act and to recognize the kind of result our choices will produce. This applies to judgments about other selves and to judgments in which one locates himself as a person among persons, a self among selves. These judgments are not just arbitrary suppositions: *they are judged to be true of the world*. For consider what the self would be like if these judgments were not supposed to be true. Maybe one might be content to be happy in the manner of the fool of Athens who believed all the ships in the harbor to be his. But what of our perceptions of other people? Would we be content to have those whom we love and trust the mere figments of our imaginations? The foundational values of freedom and rationality imply the foundational value of truth, for the rational man is the one who judges aright, that is, truly. Truth is not the same as judgment, as rationality; it is rather the proper subject of judgment. If we did not seek to judge truly, and if we did not believe we could judge truly, the act of judgment would not be what we know it to be at all.

Judgment and thus truth are *part* of a structure which as a whole makes up the concept of self. A person's relation to his body and the fact of being an incorporated self are another part of that structure. These two parts are related. The bodily senses provide matter for judgments of truth, and the body includes the physical organs of judgment.

The Wrong of Lying

So our capacity for judgment is foundational and truth is the proper object of that capacity, but how do we get to the badness of lying, much less its categorical wrongness? The crucial step to be supplied has to do not with the value of truth but with the evil of lying. We must show that to lie to someone is to injure him in a way that particularly touches his moral personality. From that, the passage is indeed easy to the conclusion that to inflict such injury intentionally (remember that all lying is by hypothesis intentional) is not only bad but wrong. It is this first, crucial step which is difficult. After all, a person's capacity for true judgment is not necessarily impaired by inducing in him a particular false belief. Nor would it seem that a person suffers a greater injury in respect to that capacity when he is induced to believe a falsity than when we intentionally prevent him from discovering the truth, yet only in the first case do we lie. Do we really do injury to a person's moral personality when we persuade him falsely that it rained yesterday in Bangkok—a fact in which he has no interest? And do we do him more injury than when we fail to answer his request for yesterday's football scores, in which he is mildly interested? Must we not calculate the injury by the *other* harm it does: disappointed expectations, lost property, missed opportunities, physical harm? In this view, lying would be a way of injuring a person in his various substantive interests—a way of stealing from him, hurting his feelings, perhaps poisoning him—but then the evil of lying would be purely instrumental, not wrong at all.

All truth, however irrelevant or trivial, has value, even though we may cheerfully ignore most truths, forget them, erase them as encumbrances from our memories. The value of every truth is shown just in the judgment that the only thing we must not do is falsify truth. Truths are like other people's property, which we can care nothing about but may not use for our own purposes. It is as if the truth were not ours (even truth we have discovered and which is known only to us), and so we may not exercise an unlimited dominion over it. Our relations to other people have a similar structure: we may perhaps have no duty to them, we may be free to put them out of our minds to make room for others whom we care about more, but we may not harm them. And so we may not falsify truth. But enough of metaphors — what does it mean to say that the truth is not ours?

The capacity for true judgment is the capacity to arrive at judgments which are in fact true of the world as it exists apart from our desires, our choices, our values. It is the world presented to us by true judgments — including true judgments about ourselves — which we then make the subject of our choices, our valuation. Now, if we treat the truth as our own, it must be according to desire or valuation. But for rational beings these activities are supposed to depend on truth; we are supposed to desire and choose according to the world as it is. To choose that something not be the case when it is in fact the case is very nearly self-contradictory — for choice is not *of* truth but *on the basis of* truth. To deliberate about whether to believe a truth (not whether it is indeed true — another story altogether) is like deciding whether to cheat at solitaire. All this is obvious. In fact I suppose one cannot even coherently talk about choosing to believe something one believes to be false. And this holds equally for all truths — big and little, useful, useless, and downright inconvenient. But we do and must calculate *about* (and not just *with*) truths all the time as we decide what truths to acquire, what to forget. We decide all the time not to pursue some inquiry because it is not worth it. Such calculations surely must go forward on the basis of what truths are useful, given one's plans and desires. Even when we pursue truth for its own sake, we distinguish between interesting and boring truths.

Considering what truth to acquire or retain differs, however, from deliberately acquiring false beliefs. All truths are acquired as propositions correctly (truly) corresponding to the world, and in this respect, all truths are equal. A lie, however, has the form and occupies the role of truth in that it too purports to be a proposition about the world; only the world does not correspond to it. So the choice of a lie is not like a choice among truths, for the choice of a lie is a choice to affirm as the basis for judgment a proposition which does not correspond to the world. So, when I say that truth is foundational, that truth precedes choice, what I mean is *not* that this or that truth is foundational but that judging according to the facts is foundational to judging at all. A scientist may deliberate about which subject to study and, having chosen his subject, about the data worth acquiring, but he cannot even deliberate as a scientist about whether to acquire false data. Clearly, then, there is something funny (wrong?) about lying to oneself, but how do we go from there to the proposition that it is wrong to lie to someone else? After all, much of the peculiarity about lying to oneself consists in the fact that it seems not so much bad as downright self-contradictory, logically impossible, but that does not support the judgment that it is wrong to lie to another. I cannot marry myself, but that hardly makes it wrong to marry someone else.

Let us imagine a case in which you come as close as you can to lying to yourself: You arrange some operation, some fiddling with your brain that has no effect other than to cause you to believe a proposition you know to be false and also to forget entirely the prior history of how you came to believe that proposition. It seems to me that you do indeed harm yourself in such an operation. This is because a free and rational person wishes to have a certain relation to reality: as nearly perfect as possible. He wishes to build his conception of himself and the world and his conception of the good on the basis of truth. Now if he affirms that the truth is available for fiddling in order to accommodate either his picture of the world or his conception of the good, then this affirms that reality is dependent on what one wants, rather than what one wants being fundamentally constrained by what there is. Rationality is the respect for this fundamental constraint of truth. This is just another way of saying that the truth is prior to our plans and prospects and must be respected whatever our plans might be. What if the truth we "destroy" by this operation is a very trivial and irrelevant truth — the state of the weather in Bangkok on some particular day? There is still an injury to self, because the fiddler must have some purpose in his fiddling. If it is a substantive purpose, then the truth is in fact relevant to that purpose, and my argument holds. If it is just to show it can be done, then he is only trying to show he can do violence to his rationality — a kind of moral blasphemy. Well, what if it is a very *little* truth? Why, then, it is a very little injury he does himself — but that does not undermine my point.

Now, when I lie to you, I do to you what you cannot actually do to yourself — brain-fiddling being only an approximation. The nature of the injury I would do to myself, if I could, explains why lying to you is to do you harm, indeed why it is wrong. The lie is an injury because it produces an effect (or seeks to) which a person as a moral agent should not wish to have produced in him, and thus it is as much an injury as any other effect which a moral agent would not wish to have produced upon his person. To be sure, some people may want to be lied to. That is a special problem; they are like people who want to suffer (not just are willing to risk)

physical injury. In general, then, I do not want you to lie to me in the same way that as a rational man I would not lie to myself if I could. But why does this make lying wrong and not merely bad?

Lying is wrong because when I lie I set up a relation which is essentially exploitative. It violates the principle of respect, for I must affirm that the mind of another person is available to me in a way in which I cannot agree my mind would be available to him — for if I do so agree, then I would not expect my lie to be believed. When I lie, I am like a counterfeiter: I do not want the market flooded with counterfeit currency; I do not want to get back my own counterfeit bill. Moreover, in lying to you, I affirm such an unfairly unilateral principle in respect to an interest and capacity which is crucial, as crucial as physical integrity: your freedom and your rationality. When I do intentional physical harm, I say that your body, your person, is available for my purposes. When I lie, I lay claim to your mind.

Lying violates respect and is wrong, as is any breach of trust. Every lie is a broken promise, and the only reason this seems strained is that in lying the promise is made and broken at the same moment. Every lie necessarily implies — as does every assertion — an assurance, a warranty of its truth. The fact that the breach accompanies the making should, however, only strengthen the conclusion that this is wrong. If promise-breaking is wrong, then a lie must be wrong, since there cannot be the supervening factor of changed circumstances which may excuse breaches of promises to perform in the future.

The final one of the convergent strands that make up the wrong of lying is the shared, communal nature of language. This is what I think Kant had in mind when he argued that a lie does wrong "to men in general." If whether people stood behind their statements depended wholly on the particular circumstances of the utterance, then the whole point of communication would be undermined. For every utterance would simply be the occasion for an analysis of the total circumstances (speaker's and hearer's) in order to determine what, if anything, to make of the utterance. And though we do often wonder and calculate whether a person is telling the truth, we do so from a baseline, a presumption that people do stand behind their statements. After all, the speaker surely depends on such a baseline. He wants us to think that he is telling the truth. Speech is a paradigm of communication, and all human relations are based on some form of communication. Our very ability to think, to conceptualize, is related to speech. Speech allows the social to penetrate the intimately personal. Perhaps that is why Kant's dicta seem to vacillate between two positions: lying as a social offense, and lying as an offense against oneself; the requirement of an intent to deceive another, and the insistence that the essence of the wrong is not injury to another but to humanity. Every lie violates the basic commitment to truth which stands behind the social fact of language.

I have already argued that bodily integrity bears a necessary relation to moral integrity, so that an attack upon bodily integrity is wrong, not just bad. The intimate *and* social nature of truth make the argument about lying stronger. For not only is the target aspect of the victim crucial to him as a moral agent but, by lying, we attack that target by a means which itself offends his moral nature; the means of attack are social means which can be said to belong as much to the victim as to his assailant. There is not only the attack at his moral vitals, but an attack with a weapon which belongs to him. Lying is, thus, a kind of treachery. (*Kind of* treachery? Why not treachery pure and simple?) It is as if we not only robbed a man of his treasure but in doing so used his own servants or family as our agents. That speech is our *common* property, that it belongs to the liar, his victim and all of us makes the matter if anything far worse.

So this is why lying is not only bad (a hurt), but wrong, why lying is wrong apart from or in addition to any other injury it does, and why lying seems at once an offense against the victim and against mankind in general, an offense against the liar himself, and against the abstract entity, truth. Whom do you injure when you pass a counterfeit bill?

What about little pointless lies? Do I really mean they are wrong? Well, yes, even a little lie is wrong, *if* it is a true piece of communication, an assertion of its own truth and not just a conventional way of asserting nothing at all or something else (as in the case of polite or diplomatic formulas). A little lie is a little wrong, but it is still something you must not do.

THOMAS E. HILL, JR.

Autonomy and Benevolent Lies

THOMAS E. HILL, JR., *teaches philosophy at the University of North Carolina at Chapel Hill. He is well known for his work in ethics and the philosophy of Kant.*

A former teacher related to me the following true story (which I have modified slightly). He had a student who showed in tutorial conversations signs of deep, suicidal depression. The student was later found dead, and the circumstances were such that others could easily have seen his death as accidental. The professor helped to gather up the boy's belongings to return to his mother, and no suicide note was found. But the mother, a devout Roman Catholic, was deeply worried about her son's soul, and she asked the professor point blank whether he had any reason to suspect suicide. The professor, an atheist, wanted to comfort her and so, by a quite deliberate lie, assured her that, as far as he knew, the boy had been in good spirits.

Another true story concerns a doctor who discovered that his mother, a very elderly but happy woman, had extremely advanced atherosclerosis. Her doctor had apparently chosen to treat the problem as best he could without informing the woman how near death she was. The son had no objection to the medical treatment or her doctor's decision to withhold information. Though he thought his mother psychologically and physically capable of handling the truth, he believed that her last days would be happier if she did not know. The problem arose when she asked her son directly, "Do you think the doctor is telling me everything?" The son lied; but since the question concerned his opinion and he had learned of her condition in ways she did not suspect and without anyone else knowing that he knew, he felt confident that she would never discover his lie. He lied to make her more comfortable, and she was in fact happy until her death.

Consider, lastly, a dilemma which could occur even if it has not. Mary has made a painful break from her ex-lover, John, and though pulled towards him, is on the mend. Her roommate is pleased for her, as she knows that John and Mary were, and will remain, painfully incompatible. She is fearful, though, that John and Mary will get together again, causing both unnecessary misery before the inevitable final separation. Overhearing John talking with a friend, she learns that John is ready to "start over" if only he receives an encouraging sign; and she expects that Mary, ever the optimist, would give the sign. Later Mary asks the roommate, "Do you think he would want to try again if I asked him?" As an act of kindness, the roommate replies, "No, I am sure he knows it would never work."

These examples illustrate the special sort of benevolent lies I want to consider. The lies are benevolent because they are intended to benefit the person deceived, for no ulterior motives, and they actually succeed in giving comfort without causing pain. Despite the benevolent motives, there is no denying that deliberate lies were told. We are not dealing with examples of mere silence, evasion, ambiguous response, and the like. The lies, moreover, are not designed to protect incompetents from truths beyond their capacities to handle sanely and responsibly. In our sample cases a lie will protect someone from avoidable pain, but it is not needed to prevent serious physical or psychological damage, violent outbursts, gross misperception of reality, and so on.

Our examples also fall outside a range of special problem situations. Some lies, for example, are told in a context where the liar has rather little chance of being believed; but in our cases there is sufficient credibility to make the deception effective. Other lies concern matters which are, intuitively, "none of the business" of the questioner: for example, a lie told to a curious student who asked his teacher about his private sex life. But the questions in our examples are clearly not "out of bounds" in this way. What is asked for is information or opinion about what deeply concerns the questioner's own life. Also the lies in our stories cannot be deemed trivial. Unlike "little white lies," they are about matters of the utmost importance to the deceived: heaven or hell, life or death, reunion or separation from a loved one. Further, our examples concern lies between individuals, not lies from public officials or to institutions, and so certain questions of public responsibility are left aside. Finally, let us imagine that the deceived has not forfeited a right to know, for example, by his own repeated lying or by having a plain intent to misuse the truth.

Lies are often wrong at least in part because they are breaches of a promise to be truthful, but, to simplify matters, let us suppose that there were no such promises in our examples. It is easy to imagine that the professor, the dying woman's son, and the roommate never made an *explicit* promise to tell the truth as, for example, one is required to do before testifying in court. The more difficult matter is to remove the suspicion that they made a tacit or implicit promise to be truthful. Ross maintained that we make such an implicit promise every time we make an assertion,

and so he viewed all lies as breaches of promise. But this position, surely, is implausible. Suppose, for example, two enemies distrust each other, have no desire to be honest with each other, and both know this. As seems to be common in international relations, they tell the truth to each other only when they expect that lying will not give them an advantage. In this situation when one asserts to the other, say, that he has documents damaging to the other's political ambitions, we cannot reasonably interpret this as a promise. Neither person believes that the speaker intends to put himself under obligation. Given their mutual understanding, the speaker cannot seriously intend to lead the other to believe that he is making it a matter of conscience to convey the truth. Furthermore if every assertion amounted to a promise to say what is true, we would not think, as in fact we do, that a lie preceded by an explicit promise to be truthful is usually worse than a lie not preceded by such a promise. There are, of course, implicit promises but it requires more than mere assertion to make one. Suppose, for example, Mary and her roommate had often discussed how they valued each other's honesty and frankness, and each had on other occasions insisted that the other tell the truth, however painful, and neither gave any hint of reservations about giving and counting on complete truthfulness between them. With this special background we might want to say that they had made implicit promises to tell each other the truth. However, to focus attention away from promises, let us suppose that in our examples there were no such special conditions to create implicit promises to be truthful.

Our examples are also meant to minimize the force of utilitarian considerations that so often tell against lying. Most importantly, the lies in our stories are extremely unlikely to be discovered. It is a moralist's fiction that lies can never remain hidden: perhaps a useful fiction, but untrue nonetheless. In each of our examples a person is asked about what he knows or believes, and if he is determined to stand by his response there is no practical way others can find out that he is lying. Even if the student's mother learns that her son committed suicide, she cannot know that the professor lied; the elderly woman can find out that she is seriously ill, but not that her son lied about his opinion; Mary may learn that John is still available, but she has no way of discovering that her roommate knew. There is, of course, always *some* chance, however remote, that those who lie will give themselves away; for example, they may talk in their sleep. If the discovery of the lie would be an utter disaster, then from a utilitarian point of view even this very small risk might not be warranted. But to simplify, let us suppose that in our cases discovery would not be disastrous. The persons deceived, let us say, have an unusually forgiving and trusting nature. If they realized the special circumstances and benevolent intent, they would forgive the lie; and, though disappointed, they would not become unreasonably suspicious and distrustful. Again, typical lies tend to multiply, one lie calling for another and each lie making successive ones easier; but we can imagine this not to be so in our example. Our professor, doctor/son, and roommate, let us suppose, are of firm character and would lie only in the special circumstances we have defined, and they do not need an entangled web of further deception to hide the first.

Lies of the sort pictured here are no doubt rare; but, by minimizing the usual considerations of utility and promises, they enable us to focus on other relevant considerations, which may be important in more typical cases as well. In particu-lar, we can reflect on how lies can fail to respect persons' autonomy. . . .

. . . Let us say that persons have autonomy, or live autonomously, . . . if the following is true: (1) They have the psychological capacities for rational decision making . . . ; (2) they actually use these capacities when they face important choice situations; (3) they have the right . . . to make morally and legally permissible decisions about matters deeply affecting their own lives free from threats and manipulation by others; (4) other people actually respect this right as well as their other rights; (5) they are able and disposed to have distinctly human values; (6) others respect this capacity by not presuming that they value only good experiences for themselves and by not counting their comfort more important than their declared values; and, finally, (7) they have ample opportunities to make use of these conditions in living a life over which they have a high degree of control. . . .

The ideal of developing the psychological capacities associated with autonomy may give some reason to hesitate to tell lies to protect people from painful realities, but not a reason that applies in all cases. Probably, as a rule, having to face unpleasant truths about matters deeply affecting one's life helps one to develop the capacity for mature, reflective decision making. If so, there would be a general presumption against benevolent lies, even if it would not always be persuasive as, for example, when we are dealing with the very elderly whose capacities have presumably already been developed as much as they will be.

If we believe in the *right* of autonomy, however, we have more reason to object to benevolent lies. This is most obvious in our example of the roommate lying to keep her friend from re-uniting with her ex-lover. The roommate manipulates her friend's decision (to call or not to call her "ex"-) by actively concealing pertinent information. If we accept the right of autonomy, this could only be justified if the reunion would have been so great a disaster that the right is over-ridden. In other cases the right of autonomy may be violated but in a less obvious way. The professor and the doctor/son, for example, did not lie in order to control the decisions of the people they deceived; they only wanted to spare them avoidable pain. Nevertheless, there were important, life-altering decisions which the deceived might have made if they had not been deprived of relevant information; and surely the professor and the doctor/son knew this. They knowingly prevented certain options presented by the real situation from ever being faced by the people they deceived; to pray or not, and, if so, how; to continue life as usual or to re-order one's priorities; to face death and tragedy stoically or to be open in a new way with friends.

Someone may object as follows: "Sometimes benevolent lies interfere with life-altering decisions, but not always; often benevolent lies merely keep people from suffering unnecessarily because of something which they can do nothing about. When, for example, a widow demands to know whether her husband suffered when he was killed in the war, there is little she can *do* if she is told truthfully that he died in horrible agony. And similarly, if the suicide's mother had been bed-ridden and terminally ill, the professor's lie would not have interfered with any important decisions."

The appropriate response, I think, is this: Benevolent lies do not necessarily or always violate the right of autonomy, but we should not be hasty in concluding that a particular lie does not concern any significant decisions. Good novelists and

biographers know what philosophers too easily forget, namely, that the most important decisions in life are not always about external behavior, about what to *do* in the public world. How we face death, family tragedy, our own successes and failures, and the way others treat us, is partly a matter of decision, as Sartreans knew but exaggerated. Even *whether* to see a situation as success or failure, tragic or routine, is not simply a matter of perception of fact. We can also interfere with these life-altering decisions or prevent a person from facing them, by keeping certain truths from him — even if he is immobile for the rest of his life.

Consider next the principles associated with autonomy as a capacity for distinctly human values. Their implications for benevolent lies depend upon what we know about the preferences of the person to be deceived. Suppose, first, that we have no reason to doubt that the questioner wants an honest answer. His question is in effect an expression of a desire to know the truth. To give him less because we want to spare him pain would be to count his comfort more important than what he himself professes to value more and so would be contrary to our principles.

Sometimes, of course, people ask questions wanting to be reassured rather than to learn the truth. What should we do if we have indirect evidence that the questioner does not really want to know? Much depends, I think, on the nature and strength of the evidence. Suppose, for example, the evidence is rather evenly mixed: the person often shrinks from painful realities but, on the other hand, he asked in a serious tone, he never said in advance not to reveal the sort of fact in question, and the truth is not outside the range of answers he could anticipate. Often when we are in doubt whether a person really prefers what he professes, we can remove the uncertainty by asking further questions; but the peculiarity of the dilemma of the would-be benevolent liar is that he cannot resolve the uncertainty this way. To ask, "Would you *really* prefer the truth even though it will hurt?" is in effect to give away the answer. When faced with such mixed evidence and unresolvable uncertainty, one guided by our principles of autonomy would, I believe, again be disposed to tell the truth; for respecting a person's capacity for distinctly human values implies that, other things equal, it is worse to presume that someone prefers comfort to some other declared value than to presume the opposite.

If there were definitive evidence that the questioner preferred not to learn the painful truth, then autonomy as a capacity for distinctly human values would not be relevant. This would be the case if, for example, the questioner had explicitly requested in advance not to be told the truth in specified circumstances, and then, later, those circumstances arose and ample evidence indicated that he had not changed his mind.

Such cases, however, are probably rare. Normally even if a person has previously asked not to be told the truth, his subsequent question raises legitimate doubts about his current preferences. Suppose the earlier request was not made in anticipation of a period of incompetence — like Ulysses' request to his crew before facing the sirens ("Don't listen to what I say later"). Then the would-be liar is apparently faced with two conflicting requests; an earlier request for deception, and a later request for truth. Unless there are independent reasons for discounting the latter, or for not treating the later question as a request for truth, then one might argue that respect for autonomy gives precedence to the more recent request. Other things equal, we respect a person's autonomy more by allowing changes of mind,

honoring what he *does* profess to value over what he *did* profess to value.

The many-sided *ideal* of autonomous living will usually give further reason for hesitating to tell benevolent lies. Even if benevolent lies do not violate a *right*, they still deprive people of a realistic picture of their situation. Insofar as having such a realistic picture is needed for genuine rational control over one's life, to that extent the benevolent liar fails to promote an ideal end.

It may be objected that this argument supports the desirability of volunteering the truth just as much as it supports the desirability of not actively depriving someone of the truth; and yet, it might be said, it is counter-intuitive to suppose that we have as much reason to volunteer painful truths as to tell them when directly asked. The ideal does give reason to volunteer the truth, I think, but there are also reasons why lying in response to a direct question is worse than merely not volunteering the truth. There is a general presumption that one should not cause avoidable pain to others, but this presumption is at least partially set aside when the person requests the painful treatment for the sake of something he wants: e.g. painful medical tests. Thus, although there is a general presumption against expressing truths which cause pain, this presumption is at least partially set aside when a competent person asks for truth; but the presumption is not set aside when one simply volunteers the truth without being asked. Thus, though the ideal of autonomy gives some reason for volunteering painful information about someone's life, the case for volunteering is not as strong as the case for telling the truth when asked.

Another objection might be this: "Sometimes we need to lie in order to increase the chances that a person will make his own decisions (and so live autonomously). For example, when my son asked me where I wanted him to go to college, I lied, telling him that I did not care. Actually I wanted very much for him to go where I went; but I figured that he could make up his own mind better if I kept my preference to myself."

The objection points to a practical problem difficult to resolve in real cases, but it does not, I think, show that the ideal of autonomy unequivocally recommends lying even in the example just presented. *One* aspect of ideal, to be sure, was encouraging people to make their important decisions in a rational way free from inner psychological obstacles such as neurotic need for a father's approval. Thus, if the son in our example was so dominated by his father's opinions that he could not make a rational choice once his father expressed his desires, then one aspect of the ideal of autonomy would urge the father to hide his opinion. But let us suppose, as in our previous examples, the person deceived is rationally competent with respect to his choice problem and so is not a slave to his father's wishes. In this case another aspect of the ideal of autonomy would urge the father to express his wishes: he should make clear both that he prefers his son to go to his old college and also that he wants his son to decide on the basis of what he, the son, most wants. This puts the pertinent facts on the table, giving the son an opportunity he would have otherwise lacked, namely, to choose whether to give weight to his father's wishes or not and, if so, which wish to count more important. By lying, the father would have helped the son make a self-interested choice; but, as we have seen, one's autonomous choice is not always self-interested. To "make up one's own mind" is not necessarily to decide without regard for others' wishes but to decide maturely in the light of the facts about the situation.

So far we have considered ways in which principles and ideals of autonomy help to explain why we view even benevolent lies as to some degree objectionable; but we also have intuitive opinions about which sort of lies (or deceptions) are worse than others. Let us consider, then, whether considerations of autonomy help to explain these intuitions as well.

To consider several factors together, I suppose it is commonly accepted that deceptive responses to questions are worse, other things equal, when (a) the response is a direct lie rather than a merely evasive, misleading, or deceptively ambiguous response, (b) the person deceived trusts the deceiver and was encouraged to do so, and (c) the lie concerns the life of the deceived rather than matters only remotely touching him. The lies of the roommate and the doctor/son described earlier exemplify the first sort. An example of the second, less significant sort of deception might be this: A person asks me, simply from curiosity, "Do you know whether so-and-so is gay?", and, though I know, I answer, "How would I know?"

Now utilitarians will have familiar explanations why the first sort of lie is regarded as more serious than the second; but it is worth nothing that our principles and ideals of autonomy provide an alternative, or additional, explanation. In brief, one's opportunity to live in rational control of one's life is increased when there are people one can unmistakenly identify as prepared to give straight, honest answers to direct pointed questions. If one does not want to know, one can refrain from asking; if the first answer is evasive or ambiguous, suggesting a reluctance on the other's part to reveal the truth, then one can choose to put the question again more pointedly or to back off; and if one does insist ("I want a straight, honest answer!"), then, while allowing for honest errors, one can make important decisions with more confidence that one understands the real situation. To live in a world without people we can rely on in this way would be to live in a world in which we have less control over our lives. Utilitarians often stress the unpleasantness that results when lies which violate trust become discovered, and for this reason our examples were designed to minimize the risk of discovery. But now it emerges that ideals of autonomy not only oppose undiscoverable benevolent lies; they also oppose lies which risk discovery of a breach of trust for discovery of such lies encourages us to be distrustful and suspicious and so less able to make use of even the honest answers trustworthy persons give us; and this limits our opportunities for rational control over our lives.

These conclusions, of course, are both hypothetical and intuitive: that is, the argument has been that if one accepts certain principles of autonomy, then one has reasons to refrain from benevolent lies. But imagine now an objection from a normative hedonist unwilling to rest the issue on intuitive principles. He argues that, intuitions aside, it is *irrational* to prefer truth to comfort, unless having the truth would maximize one's pleasure in the long run. Thus, he continues, when one aims to be benevolent towards another, it is *irrational* to give him the truth if a lie will contribute more to his total satisfaction.

The objection rests on the common, but mistaken, assumption that, at least when free from moral constraints, a fully rational person would always aim for his most favorable pleasure/pain ratio. But why so? As we have seen, people do in fact have (non-moral) concerns independent of any anticipated good experiences. Some, perhaps, make maximum pleasure their goal; and others do not. What deter-

mines whether one is rational is not, by itself, the content of one's aims, but how they are arrived at, how they fit into one's life plan, etc. More plausible than the hedonist's conception of rationality, I think, is that of John Rawls, who defines ideal rationality, roughly, as satisfying certain "counting principles" (means–end efficiency, inclusion, etc.) and then deciding in light of full information about one's desires, circumstances, etc. Given this conception and the falsity of *psychological* hedonism (i.e. that all seek only to maximize their pleasure), then the rational life will be different for different people. For some, maybe, it will be predominantly pursuit of pleasure; but, unless we suppose that all non-hedonistic desires would extinguish when exposed to more information, for many the rational life will include pursuit of other values, such as truth, independently of their pay-off in personal satisfaction.

The principles of autonomy which we have considered, though still un-unified in a general theory, point toward a conception of morality quite different in spirit from familiar forms of utilitarianism, hedonistic and otherwise. The latter start with views about what is intrinsically valuable as an end, and then define morality, in one way or another, as what promotes this end. A theory of autonomy, following Kant, Rawls, and others, would first define principles for moral institutions and personal interactions, leaving each person, within these constraints, the freedom to choose and pursue whatever ends they will. Such a theory would not oppose benevolent lies on the ground that truth-telling will maximize some intrinsic value other than pleasure (e.g. self-awareness); rather, it would encourage truthfulness as, in general, a way of respecting people as free to choose their own ends.

HENRY SIDGWICK
The Duty of Veracity

HENRY SIDGWICK (1828–1900) *was an English philosopher who taught at the University of Cambridge. He was a founding member and the first president of the Society for Psychical Research. Sidgwick's most noted work is his book* The Method of Ethics *(1874).*

§

1. It may easily seem that when we have discussed Benevolence, Justice, and the observance of Law and Contract, we have included in our view the whole sphere of social duty, and that whatever other maxims we find accepted by Common Sense must be subordinate to the principles which we have been trying to define.

For whatever we owe definitely to our fellow-men, besides the observance of special contracts, and of positive laws, seems — at least by a slight extension of common usage — to be naturally included under Justice: while the more indefinite obligations which we recognise seem to correspond to the goodwill which we think ought to exist among all members of the human family, together with the stronger affections appropriate to special relations and circumstances. And hence it may be thought that the best way of treating the subject would have been to divide Duty generally into Social and Self-regarding, and again to subdivide the former branch into heads which I have discussed one by one; afterwards adding such minor details of duty as have obtained special names and distinct recognition. And this is perhaps the proper place to explain why I did not adopt this course. The division of duties into Social and Self-regarding, though obvious, and acceptable enough as a rough *prima facie* classification, does not on closer examination seem exactly appropriate to the Intuitional Method. For these titles naturally suggest that the happiness or well-being, of the agent or of others, is always the end and final determinant of right action: whereas the Intuitional doctrine is, that at least certain kinds of conduct are prescribed absolutely, without reference to their ulterior consequences. And if a more general meaning be given to the terms, and by Social duties we understand those which consist in the production of certain effects upon others, while in the Self-regarding we aim at producing certain effects upon ourselves, the division is still an unsuitable one. For these consequences are not clearly recognised in the enunciation of common rules of morality: and in many cases we produce marked effects both on ourselves and on others, and it is not easy to say which (in the view of Common Sense) are most important: and again, this principle of division would sometimes make it necessary to cut in two the class of duties prescribed under some common notion; as the same rule may govern both our social and our solitary conduct. Take, for example, the acts morally prescribed under the head of Courage. It seems clear that the prominence given to this Virtue in historic systems of morality has been due to the great social importance that must always attach to it, so long as communities of men are continually called upon to fight for their existence and well-being: but still the quality of bravery is the same essentially, whether it be exhibited for selfish or social ends.

It is no doubt true that when we examine with a view to definition the kinds of conduct commended or prescribed in any list of Virtues commonly recognised, we find, to a great extent, that the maxims we obtain are clearly not absolute and independent; that the quality denoted by our term is admittedly only praiseworthy in so far as it promotes individual or general welfare, and becomes blameworthy — though remaining in other respects the same — when it operates adversely to these ends. We have already noticed this result in one or two instances, and it will be illustrated at length in the following chapters. But though this is the case to a great extent, it is, for our present purpose, of special importance to note the — real or apparent — exceptions to the rule; because they are specially characteristic of the method that we call Intuitionism.

One of the most important of these exceptions is Veracity: and the affinity in certain respects of this duty — in spite of fundamental differences — to the duty of Good Faith or Fidelity to Promises renders it convenient to examine the two in immediate succession. Under either head a certain correspondence between words and facts is prescribed: and hence the questions that arise when we try to make the maxims precise are somewhat similar in both cases. For example, just as the duty of Good Faith did not lie in conforming our acts to the *admissible* meaning of certain words, but to the meaning which we knew to be put on them by the promisee; so the duty of Truthspeaking is not to utter words which *might*, according to common usage, produce in other minds beliefs corresponding to our own, but words which we believe will have this effect on the persons whom we address. And this is usually a very simple matter,

as the natural effect of language is to convey our beliefs to other men, and we commonly know quite well whether we are doing this or not. A certain difficulty arises, as in the case of promises, from the use of set forms imposed either by law or by custom. . . . In the case of formulæ imposed by law — such (*e.g.*) as declarations of religious belief — it is doubtful whether we may understand the terms in any sense which they commonly bear, or are to take them in the sense intended by the Legislature that imposed them; and again, a difficulty is created by the gradual degradation or perversion of their meaning, which results from the strong inducements offered for their general acceptance; for thus they are continually strained and stretched until a new general understanding seems gradually to grow up as to the meaning of certain phrases; and it is continually disputed whether we may veraciously use the phrases in this new signification. A similar process continually alters the meaning of conventional expressions current in polite society. When a man declares that he 'has great pleasure in accepting' a vexatious invitation, or is 'the obedient servant' of one whom he regards as an inferior, he uses phrases which were probably once deceptive. If they are so no longer, Common Sense condemns as over-scrupulous the refusal to use them where it is customary to do so. But Common Sense seems doubtful and perplexed where the process of degradation is incomplete, and there are still persons who may be deceived: as in the use of the reply that one is 'not at home' to an inconvenient visitor from the country.

However, apart from the use of conventional phrases, the rule 'to speak the truth' is not generally difficult of application in conduct. And many moralists have regarded this, from its simplicity and definiteness, as a quite unexceptional instance of an ethical axiom. I think, however, that patient reflection will show that this view is not really confirmed by the Common Sense of mankind.

§

2. In the first place, it does not seem clearly agreed whether Veracity is an absolute and independent duty, or a special application of some higher principle. We find (*e.g.*) that Kant regards it as a duty owed to oneself to speak the truth, because 'a lie is an abandonment or, as it were, annihilation of the dignity of man.' And this seems to be the view in which lying is prohibited by the code of honour, except that it is not thought (by men of honour as such) that the dignity of man is impaired by *any* lying: but only that lying for selfish ends, especially under the influence of fear, is mean and base. In fact there seems to be circumstances under which the code of honour prescribes lying. Here, however, it may be said to be plainly divergent from the morality of Common Sense. Still, the latter does not seem to decide clearly whether truth-speaking is absolutely a duty, needing no further justification: or whether it is merely a general right of each man to have truth spoken to him by his fellows, which right however may be forfeited or suspended under certain circumstances. Just as each man is thought to have a natural right to personal security generally, but not if he is himself attempting to injure others in life and property: so if we may even kill in defence of ourselves and others, it seems strange if we may not lie, if lying will defend us better against a palpable invasion of our rights: and Common Sense does not seem to prohibit this decisively. And again, just as the orderly and systematic slaughter which we call war is thought perfectly right under certain circumstances, though painful and revolting: so in the word-contests of the law-courts, the lawyer is commonly held to be justified in untruthfulness within strict rules and limits: for an advocate is thought to be over-scrupulous who refuses to say what he knows to be false, if he is instructed to say it. Again, where deception is designed to benefit the person deceived, Common Sense seems to concede that it may sometimes be right: for example, most persons would not hesitate to speak falsely to an invalid, if this seemed the only way of concealing facts that might produce a dangerous shock: nor do I perceive that any one shrinks from telling fictions to children, on matters upon which it is thought well that they should not know the truth. But if the lawfulness of benevolent deception in any case be admitted, I do not see how we can decide when and how far it is admissible, except by considerations of expediency; that is, by weighing the gain of any particular deception against the imperilment of mutual confidence involved in all violation of truth.

The much argued question of religious deception ('pious fraud') naturally suggests itself here. It seems clear, however, that Common Sense now pronounces against the broad rule, that falsehoods may rightly be told in the interests of religion. But there is a subtler form in which the same principle is still maintained by moral persons. It is sometimes said that the most important truths of religion cannot be conveyed into the minds of ordinary men, except by being enclosed, as it were, in a shell of fiction; so that by relating such fictions as if they were facts, we are really performing an act of substantial veracity. Reflecting upon this argument, we see that it is not after all so clear wherein Veracity consists. For from the beliefs immediately communicated by any set of affirmations inferences are naturally drawn, and we may clearly foresee that they will be drawn. And though commonly we intend that both the beliefs immediately communicated and the inferences drawn from them should be true, and a person who always aims at this is praised as candid and sincere: still we find relaxation of the rule prescribing this intention claimed in two different ways by at least respectable sections of opinion. For first, as was just now observed, it is sometimes held that if a conclusion is true and important, and cannot be satisfactorily communicated otherwise, we may lead the mind of the hearer to it by means of fictitious premises. But the exact reverse of this is perhaps a commoner view: viz. that it is only an absolute duty to make our actual affirmations true; for it is said that though the ideal condition of human converse involves perfect sincerity and candour, and we ought to rejoice in exhibiting these virtues where we can, still in our actual world concealment is frequently necessary to the well-being of society, and may be legitimately effected by any means short of actual falsehood. Thus it is not uncommonly said that in defence of a secret we may not indeed *lie*, *i.e.* produce directly beliefs contrary to fact; but we may "turn a question aside," *i.e.* produce indirectly, by natural inference from our answer, a negatively false belief; or "throw the inquirer on a wrong scent," *i.e.* produce similarly a positively false belief. These two methods of concealment are known respectively as *suppressio veri* and *suggestio falsi*, and many think them legitimate under certain circumstances: while others say that if deception is to be practised at all, it is mere formalism to object to any one mode of effecting it more than another.

On the whole, then, reflection seems to show that the rule of Veracity, as commonly accepted, cannot be elevated into a definite moral axiom: for there is no real agreement as to how far we are bound to impart true beliefs to others: and while it is contrary to Common Sense to exact absolute candour under all circumstances, we yet find no self-evident secondary principle, clearly defining when it is not to be exacted.

§

3. There is, however, one method of exhibiting *a priori* the absolute duty of Truth, which we must not overlook; as, if it be valid, it would seem that the exceptions and qualifications above mentioned have been only admitted by Common Sense from inadvertence and shallowness of thought.

It is said that if it were once generally understood that lies were justifiable under certain circumstances, it would immediately become quite useless to tell the lies, because no one would believe them; and that the moralist cannot lay down a rule which, if generally accepted, would be suicidal. To this there seem to be three answers. In the first place it is not necessarily an evil that men's confidence in each other's assertions should, *under certain peculiar circumstances*, be impaired or destroyed: it may even be the very result which we should most desire to produce: *e.g.* it is obviously a most effective protection for legitimate secrets that it should be universally understood and expected that those who ask questions which they have no right to ask will have lies told them: nor, again, should we be restrained from pronouncing it lawful to meet deceit with deceit, merely by the fear of impairing the security which rogues now derive from the veracity of honest men. No doubt the ultimate result of general unveracity under the circumstances would be a state of things in which such falsehoods would no longer be told: but unless this ultimate result is undesirable, the prospect of it does not constitute a reason why the falsehoods should not be told so long as they are useful. But, secondly, since the beliefs of men in general are not formed purely on rational grounds, experience shows that unveracity may long remain partially effective under circumstances where it is generally understood to be legitimate. We see this in the case of the law-courts. For though jurymen are perfectly aware that it is considered the duty of an advocate to state as plausibly as possible whatever he has been instructed to say on behalf of any criminal he may defend, still a skilful pleader may often produce an impression that he sincerely believes his client to be innocent: and it remains a question of casuistry how far this kind of hypocrisy is justifiable. But, finally, it cannot be assumed as certain that it is never right to act upon a maxim of which the universal application would be an undoubted evil. This assumption may seem to be involved in what was previously admitted as an ethical axiom, that what is right for me must be right for 'all persons under similar conditions.' But reflection will show that there is a special case within the range of the axiom in which its application is necessarily self-limiting, and excludes the practical universality which the axiom appears to suggest: *i.e.* where the agent's conditions include (1) the knowledge that his maxim is not universally accepted, and (2) a reasoned conviction that his act will not tend to make it so, to any important extent. For in this case the axiom will practically only mean that it will be right for all persons to do as the agent does, if they are sincerely convinced that the act will not be widely imitated; and this conviction must vanish if it *is* widely imitated. It can hardly be said that these conditions are impossible: and if they are possible, the axiom that we are discussing can only serve, in its present application, to direct our attention to an important danger of unveracity, which constitutes a strong — but not formally conclusive — utilitarian ground for speaking the truth.

MARK TWAIN

On the Decay of the Art of Lying

MARK TWAIN (BORN SAMUEL LANGHORNE CLEMENS IN 1835) *was a noted humorist and novelist. He is especially known for his highly autobiographical stories of boyhood on the Mississippi:* The Adventures of Tom Sawyer *(1876) and* The Adventures of Huckleberry Finn *(1884).*

BSERVE, I do not mean to suggest that the *custom* of lying has suffered any decay or interruption — no, for the Lie, as a Virtue, a Principle, is eternal; the Lie, as a recreation, a solace, a refuge in time of need, the fourth Grace, the tenth Muse, man's best and surest friend, is immortal, and cannot perish from the earth while this Club remains. My complaint simply concerns the decay of the *art* of lying. No high-minded man, no man of right feeling, can contemplate the lumbering and slovenly lying of the present day without grieving to see a noble art so prostituted. In this veteran presence I naturally enter upon this scheme with diffidence; it is like an old maid trying to teach nursery matters to the mothers in Israel. It would not become me to criticise you, gentlemen, who are nearly all my elders — and my superiors, in this thing — and so, if I should here and there *seem* to do it, I trust it will in most cases be more in a spirit of admiration than of fault-finding; indeed, if this finest of the fine arts had everywhere received the attention, encouragement, and conscientious practice and development which this Club has devoted to it, I should not need to utter this lament, or shed a single tear. I do not say this to flatter: I say it in a spirit of just and appreciative recognition.

[It had been my intention, at this point, to mention names and give illustrative specimens, but indications observable about me admonished me to beware of particulars and confine myself to generalities.]

No fact is more firmly established than that lying is a necessity of our circumstances — the deduction that it is then a Virtue goes without saying. No virtue can reach its highest usefulness without careful and diligent cultivation — therefore, it goes without saying, that this one ought to be taught in the public schools — at the fireside — even in the newspapers. What chance has the ignorant, uncultivated liar against the educated expert? What chance have I against Mr. Per — against a lawyer? *Judicious* lying is what the world needs. I sometimes think it were even better and safer not to lie at all than to lie injudi-

ciously. An awkward, unscientific lie is often as ineffectual as the truth.

Now let us see what the philosophers say. Note that venerable proverb: Children and fools *always* speak the truth. The deduction is plain — adults and wise persons *never* speak it. Parkman, the historian, says, "The principle of truth may itself be carried into an absurdity." In another place in the same chapter he says, "The saying is old that truth should not be spoken at all times; and those whom a sick conscience worries into habitual violation of the maxim are imbeciles and nuisances." It is strong language, but true. None of us could *live* with an habitual truth-teller; but, thank goodness, none of us has to. An habitual truth-teller is simply an impossible creature; he does not exist; he never has existed. Of course there are people who *think* they never lie, but it is not so — and this ignorance is one of the very things that shame our so-called civilization. Everybody lies — every day; every hour; awake; asleep; in his dreams; in his joy; in his mourning; if he keeps his tongue still, his hands, his feet, his eyes, his attitude, will convey deception — and purposely. Even in sermons — but that is a platitude.

In a far country where I once lived the ladies used to go around paying calls, under the humane and kindly pretense of wanting to see each other; and when they returned home, they would cry out with a glad voice, saying, "We made sixteen calls and found fourteen of them out" — not meaning that they found out anything against the fourteen — no, that was only a colloquial phrase to signify that they were not at home — and their manner of saying it expressed their lively satisfaction in that fact. Now their pretense of wanting to see the fourteen — and the other two whom they had been less lucky with — was that commonest and mildest form of lying which is sufficiently described as a deflection from the truth. Is it justifiable? Most certainly. It is beautiful, it is noble; for its object is, *not* to reap profit, but to convey a pleasure to the sixteen. The iron-souled truth-monger would plainly manifest, or even utter the fact that he didn't want to see those people—and he would be an ass, and inflict a totally unnecessary pain. And next, those ladies in that far country—but never mind, they had a thousand pleasant ways of lying, that grew out of gentle impulses, and were a credit to their intelligence and an honor to their hearts. Let the particulars go.

The men in that far country were liars, every one. Their mere howdy-do was a lie, because *they* didn't care how you did, except they were undertakers. To the ordinary inquirer you lied in return; for you made no conscientious diagnosis of your case, but answered at random, and usually missed it considerably. You lied to the undertaker, and said your health was failing—a wholly commendable lie, since it cost you nothing and pleased the other man. If a stranger called and interrupted you, you said with your hearty tongue, "I'm glad to see you," and said with your heartier soul, "I wish you were with the cannibals and it was dinner-time." When he went, you said regretfully, "*Must* you go?" and followed it with a "Call again;" but you did no harm, for you did not deceive anybody nor inflict any hurt, whereas the truth would have made you both unhappy.

I think that all this courteous lying is a sweet and loving art, and should be cultivated. The highest perfection of politeness is only a beautiful edifice, built, from the base to the dome, of graceful and gilded forms of charitable and unselfish lying.

What I bemoan is the growing prevalence of the brutal truth. Let us do what we can to eradicate it. An injurious truth has no merit over an injurious lie. Neither should ever be uttered. The man who speaks an injurious truth, lest his soul be not saved if he do otherwise, should reflect that that sort of a soul is not strictly worth saving. The man who tells a lie to help a poor devil out of trouble, is one of whom the angels doubtless say, "Lo, here is an heroic soul who casts his own welfare into jeopardy to succor his neighbor's; let us exalt this magnanimous liar."

An injurious lie is an uncommendable thing; and so, also, and in the same degree, is an injurious truth—a fact which is recognized by the law of libel.

Among other common lies, we have the *silent* lie—the deception which one conveys by simply keeping still and concealing the truth. Many obstinate truth-mongers indulge in this dissipation, imagining that if they *speak* no lie, they lie not at all. In that far country where I once lived, there was a lively spirit, a lady whose impulses were always high and pure, and whose character answered to them. One day I was there at dinner, and remarked in a general way, that we are all liars. She was amazed, and said, "Not *all*?" It was before "Pinafore's" time, so I did not make the response which would naturally follow in our day, but frankly said, "Yes, *all*—we are all liars; there are no exceptions." She looked almost offended, and said, "Why, do you include *me*?" "Certainly," I said, "I think you even rank as an expert." She said, "'Sh—'sh! the children!" So the subject was changed in deference to the children's presence, and we went on talking about other things. But as soon as the young people were out of the way, the lady came warmly back to the matter and said, "I have made it the rule of my life to never tell a lie; and I have never departed from it in a single instance." I said, "I don't mean the least harm or disrespect, but really you have been lying like smoke ever since I've been sitting here. It has caused me a good deal of pain, because I am not used to it." She required of me an instance — just a single instance. So I said:

"Well, here is the unfilled duplicate of the blank which the Oakland hospital people sent to you by the hand of the sick-nurse when she came here to nurse your little nephew through his dangerous illness. This blank asks all manner of questions as to the conduct of that sick-nurse: 'Did she ever sleep on her watch? Did she ever forget to give the medicine?' and so forth and so on. You are warned to be very careful and explicit in your answers, for the welfare of the service requires that the nurses be promptly fined or otherwise punished for derelictions. You told me you were perfectly delighted with that nurse — that she had a thousand perfections and only one fault; you found you never could depend on her wrapping Johnny up half sufficiently while he waited in a chilly chair for her to rearrange the warm bed. You filled up the duplicate of this paper, and sent it back to the hospital by the hand of the nurse. How did you answer this question — 'Was the nurse at any time guilty of a negligence which was likely to result in the patient's taking cold?' Come — everything is decided by a bet here in California: ten dollars to ten cents you lied when you answered that question." She said, "I didn't; *I left it blank!*" "Just so — you have told a *silent* lie; you have left it to be inferred that you had no fault to find in that matter." She said, "Oh, was that a lie? And how *could* I mention her one single fault, and she so good? — it would have been cruel." I said, "One ought always to lie, when one can do good by it; your impulse was right, but your judgment was crude; this comes of unintelligent practice. Now observe the result of this inexpert deflection of yours. You know Mr. Jones's Willie is lying very low with scarlet fever; well, your rec-

ommendation was so enthusiastic that that girl is there nursing him, and the worn-out family have all been trustingly sound asleep for the last fourteen hours, leaving their darling with full confidence in those fatal hands, because you, like young George Washington, have a reputa — However, if you are not going to have anything to do, I will come around to-morrow and we'll attend the funeral together, for, of course, you'll naturally feel a peculiar interest in Willie's case — as personal a one, in fact, as the undertaker."

But that was all lost. Before I was half-way through she was in a carriage and making thirty miles an hour toward the Jones mansion to save what was left of Willie and tell all she knew about the deadly nurse. All of which was unnecessary, as Willie wasn't sick; I had been lying myself. But that same day, all the same, she sent a line to the hospital which filled up the neglected blank, and stated the *facts*, too, in the squarest possible manner.

Now, you see, this lady's fault was *not* in lying, but only in lying injudiciously. She should have told the truth, *there*, and made it up to the nurse with a fraudulent compliment further along in the paper. She could have said, "In one respect the sick-nurse is perfection — when she is on watch, she never snores." Almost any little pleasant lie would have taken the sting out of that troublesome but necessary expression of the truth.

Lying is universal — we *all* do it; we all *must* do it. Therefore, the wise thing is for us diligently to train ourselves to lie thoughtfully, judiciously; to lie with a good object, and not an evil one; to lie for others' advantage, and not our own; to lie healingly, charitably, humanely, not cruelly, hurtfully, maliciously; to lie gracefully and graciously, not awkwardly and clumsily; to lie firmly, frankly, squarely, with head erect, not haltingly, tortuously, with pusillanimous mien, as being ashamed of our high calling. Then shall we be rid of the rank and pestilent truth that is rotting the land; then shall we be great and good and beautiful, and worthy dwellers in a world where even benign Nature habitually lies, except when she promises execrable weather. Then— But I am but a new and feeble student in this gracious art; I cannot instruct *this* Club.

Joking aside, I think there is much need of wise examination into what sorts of lies are best and wholesomest to be indulged, seeing we *must* all lie and *do* all lie, and what sorts it may be best to avoid—and this is a thing which I feel I can confidently put into the hands of this experienced Club—a ripe body, who may be termed, in this regard, and without undue flattery, Old Masters.

HARRY FRANKFURT

On Bullshit

HARRY FRANKFURT *teaches philosophy at Princeton University. His most recent book is* The Importance of What We Care About *(1988).*

ONE of the most salient features of our culture is that there is so much bullshit. Everyone knows this. Each of us contributes his share. But we tend to take the situation for granted. Most people are rather confident of their ability to recognize bullshit and to avoid being taken in by it. So the phenomenon has not aroused much deliberate concern, nor attracted much sustained inquiry.

In consequence, we have no clear understanding of what bullshit is, why there is so much of it, or what functions it serves. And we lack a conscientiously developed appreciation of what it means to us. In other words, we have no theory. I propose to begin the development of a theoretical understanding of bullshit, mainly by providing some tentative and exploratory philosophical analysis. I shall not consider the rhetorical uses and mis-uses of bullshit. My aim is simply to give a rough account of what bullshit is and how it differs from what it is not. . . .

Bullshitting involves a kind of bluff. It is closer to bluffing, surely, than to telling a lie. But what is implied concerning its nature by the fact that it is more like the former than it is like the latter? Just what is the relevant difference here between a bluff and a lie?

Lying and bluffing are both modes of misrepresentation or deception. Now the concept most central to the distinctive nature of a lie is that of falsity: the liar is essentially someone who deliberately promulgates a falsehood. Bluffing too is typically devoted to conveying something false. Unlike plain lying, however, it is more especially a matter not of falsity but of fakery. This is what accounts for its nearness to bullshit. For the essence of bullshit is not that it is *false* but that it is *phony*. In order to appreciate this distinction, one must recognize that a fake or a phony need not be in any respect (apart from authenticity itself) inferior to the real thing. What is not genuine need not also be defective in some other way. It may be, after all, an exact copy. What is wrong with a counterfeit is not what it is like, but how it was made. This points to a similar and fundamental aspect of the essential nature of bullshit: although it is produced without concern with the truth, it need not be false. The bullshitter is faking things. But this does not mean that he necessarily gets them wrong.

In Eric Ambler's novel *Dirty Story*, a character named Arthur Abdel Simpson recalls advice that he received as a child from his father:

> Although I was only seven when my father was killed, I still remember him very well and some of the things he used to say. . . . One of the first things he taught me was, "*Never tell a lie when you can bullshit your way through*.". . .

The elder Simpson identifies the alternative to telling a lie as "bullshitting one's way through." This involves not merely producing one instance of bullshit; it involves a *program* of producing bullshit to whatever extent the circumstances require. This is a key, perhaps, to his preference. Telling a lie is an act with a sharp focus. It is designed to insert a particular falsehood at a specific point in a set or system of beliefs, in order to avoid the consequences of having that point occupied by the truth. This requires a degree of craftsmanship, in which the teller of the lie submits to objective constraints imposed by what he takes to be the truth. The liar is inescapably concerned with truth-values. In order to invent a lie at all, he must think he knows what is true. And

in order to invent an effective lie, he must design his falsehood under the guidance of that truth.

On the other hand, a person who undertakes to bullshit his way through has much more freedom. His focus is panoramic rather than particular. He does not limit himself to inserting a certain falsehood at a specific point, and thus he is not constrained by the truths surrounding that point or intersecting it. He is prepared to fake the context as well, so far as need requires. This freedom from the constraints to which the liar must submit does not necessarily mean, of course, that his task is easier than the task of the liar. But the mode of creativity upon which it relies is less analytical and less deliberative than that which is mobilized in lying. It is more expansive and independent, with more spacious opportunities for improvisation, color, and imaginative play. This is less a matter of craft than of art. Hence the familiar notion of the "bullshit artist.". . .

What bullshit essentially misrepresents is neither the state of affairs to which it refers nor the beliefs of the speaker concerning that state of affairs. Those are what lies misrepresent, by virtue of being false. Since bullshit need not be false, it differs from lies in its misrepresentational intent. The bullshitter may not deceive us, or even intend to do so, either about the facts or about what he takes the facts to be. What he does necessarily attempt to deceive us about is his enterprise. His only indispensably distinctive characteristic is that in a certain way he misrepresents what he is up to.

This is the crux of the distinction between him and the liar. Both he and the liar represent themselves falsely as endeavoring to communicate the truth. The success of each depends upon deceiving us about that. But the fact about himself that the liar hides is that he is attempting to lead us away from a correct apprehension of reality; we are not to know that he wants us to believe something he supposes to be false. The fact about himself that the bullshitter hides, on the other hand, is that the truth-values of his statements are of no central interest to him; what we are not to understand is that his intention is neither to report the truth nor to conceal it. This does not mean that his speech is anarchically impulsive, but that the motive guiding and controlling it is unconcerned with how the things about which he speaks truly are.

It is impossible for someone to lie unless he thinks he knows the truth. Producing bullshit requires no such conviction. A person who lies is thereby responding to the truth, and he is to that extent respectful of it. . . . For the bullshitter, however, all these bets are off: he is neither on the side of the true nor on the side of the false. His eye is not on the facts at all, as the eyes of the honest man and of the liar are, except insofar as they may be pertinent to his interest in getting away with what he says. . . .

For this reason, telling lies does not tend to unfit a person for telling the truth in the same way that bullshitting tends to. Through excessive indulgence in the latter activity, which involves making assertions without paying attention to anything except what it suits one to say, a person's normal habit of attending to the ways things are may become attenuated or lost. Someone who lies and someone who tells the truth are playing on opposite sides, so to speak, in the same game. Each responds to the facts as he understand them, although the response of the one is guided by the authority of the truth, while the response of the other defies that authority and refuses to meet its demands. The bullshitter ignores these demands altogether. He does not reject the authority of the truth, as the liar does, and oppose

himself to it. He pays no attention to it at all. By virtue of this, bullshit is a greater enemy of the truth than lies are.

One who is concerned to report or to conceal the facts assumes that there are indeed facts that are in some way both determinate and knowable. His interest in telling the truth or in lying presupposes that there is a difference between getting things wrong and getting them right, and that it is at least occasionally possible to tell the difference. Someone who ceases to believe in the possibility of identifying certain statements as true and others as false can have only two alternatives. The first is to desist both from efforts to tell the truth and from efforts to deceive. This would mean refraining from making any assertion whatever about the facts. The second alternative is to continue making assertions that purport to describe the way things are but that cannot be anything except bullshit.

Why is there so much bullshit? . . . Bullshit is unavoidable whenever circumstances require someone to talk without knowing what he is talking about. Thus the production of bullshit is stimulated whenever a person's obligations or opportunities to speak about some topic are more extensive than his knowledge of the facts that are relevant to that topic. This discrepancy is common in public life, where people are frequently impelled — whether by their own propensities or by the demands of others — to speak extensively about matters of which they are to some degree ignorant. Bullshit also arises from the widespread conviction that it is the responsibility of a citizen in a democracy to have opinions about everything, or at least everything that pertains to the conduct of his country's affairs.

The contemporary proliferation of bullshit also has deeper sources, in various forms of skepticism which deny that we can have any reliable access to an objective reality and which therefore reject the possibility of knowing how things truly are. These "anti-realist" doctrines undermine confidence in the value of disinterested efforts to determine what is true and what is false, and even in the intelligibility of the notion of objective inquiry. One response to this loss of confidence has been a retreat from the discipline required by dedication to the ideal of *correctness* to a quite different sort of discipline, which is imposed by pursuit of an alternative ideal of *sincerity*. Rather than seeking primarily to arrive at accurate representations of a common world, the individual turns toward trying to provide honest representations of himself. Convinced that reality has no inherent nature, which he might hope to identify as the truth about things, he devotes himself to being true to his own nature. It is as though he decides that since it makes no

sense to try to be true to the facts, he must therefore try instead to be true to himself.

But it is preposterous to imagine that we ourselves are determinate, and hence susceptible both to correct and to incorrect descriptions, while supposing that the ascription of determinacy to anything else has been exposed as a mistake. As conscious beings, we exist only in response to other things, and we cannot know ourselves at all without knowing them. Moreover, there is nothing in theory, and certainly nothing in experience, to support the extraordinary judgment that it is the truth about himself that is the easiest for a person to know. Facts about ourselves are not peculiarly solid and resistant to skeptical dissolution. Our natures are, indeed, elusively insubstantial — notoriously less stable and less inherent than the natures of other things. And insofar as this is the case, sincerity itself is bullshit.

6

How Should I Make Money?

Everyday life in America brings each of us into contact with many kinds of businesses: grocery stores, gasoline stations, convenience stores, restaurants, broadcasting networks — as well as countless advertisers. On an average day in the business week, the list might go on and on. Most of the time, though, you probably hardly notice the various businesses you interact with. But occasionally you do. And once in a while you might even have a moral response to your interaction with a given company: offense at a particular advertisement, perhaps, or approval that a fast-food restaurant has stopped using Styrofoam food packaging.

The ethics of the business world have an impact on all our lives, whether or not we personally have a career in business. As consumers, we expect and demand honesty in advertising, fair pricing, and reliable goods and services. The fact that these demands have in notorious cases not been met has led some people to question whether "business ethics" is a contradiction in terms. But the reactions of both the American public and the American legal system to such incidents as the insider-trading scandal on Wall Street and the *Valdez* oil-spill disaster indicate that ethical behavior still must be considered among the basic responsibilities of those engaged in business.

Nevertheless, such incidents have led some to question our basic way of doing business. Perhaps the pressures of the business world encourage questionable ethical practices. Some have argued that the profit motive, which is essential to the American form of capitalism, works as an incentive to low moral standards. If profits can be increased by selling goods of lesser quality, by bribing foreign (or American) officials, or by laying off workers in American factories in order to exploit cheap labor in Third World countries, doesn't the profit motive encourage such strategies? John Hospers, in "Profits and Liberty" makes the case for the profit motive. He argues that the right to profit from our labor is among the essential individual rights that government must not abridge. Moreover, he contends that utilitarian considerations support the protection of individuals' rights to profits, for the pursuit of profit has effects that are beneficial to society as a whole. (For a contrary perspective, see Michael Harrington's "Corporate Collectivism" in Chapter 12. Harrington takes issue with the status quo's protection of profits, and argues that our current system privileges corporations' interests, not the rights of individuals.)

Unlike Hospers, Christopher D. Stone believes that the profit motive may play a role in the development of unethical business practices. However, Stone argues that corporate practices are largely a result of basic attitudes, and that the attitudes that have promoted unethical practices can be changed within the system that currently exists. He suggests that those who seek to change business attitudes should recognize that the psychology of corporations is essentially the psychology of a culture. Not coercion, but an appeal to employees' sense of membership in a corporate culture is the most effective strategy for changing attitudes. Even when major change is desired, its achievement depends on awareness that the corporation is a complex community with its own collective attitudes and practices. Barbara Ehrenreich agrees that business in America has its own cultural practices. But unlike Stone, who emphasizes the unique cultural climate of individual corporations, Ehrenreich focuses on what corporations have in common. Her suggestion is that the population at large should realize that the language of people in business is different from that of the intelligentsia. The two groups now tend to feel suspicion toward each other, and political impasses frequently result. Such friction could be dispelled, Ehrenreich argues, if the groups made the effort to understand each other's language and focused more on shared concerns.

Carol Hymowitz and Timothy D. Schellhardt point to a disturbing feature of corporate culture, the "glass ceiling" phenomenon. This is the tendency of corporations to promote women only up to a point, and no higher. The effect is that even corporations who can take credit for promoting unprecedented numbers of women still have "a caste system of men at the top and women lower down." Hymowitz and Schellhardt place the blame for glass ceilings on stereotypes about women that endure despite increasing evidence that women manage as well as men.

Some ethical problems may stem largely from attitudes within corporate cultures, but other problems arise from questionable tactics within the practice of "business as usual." Albert Z. Carr considers the practice of business bluffing, a practice that some view as lying. Carr defends business bluffing, arguing that in the context of business it is as legitimate as bluffing in poker. The ethics of business, he argues, are "different from the ethics of religion."

The insider-trading scandal has led many to question the role that secret information plays in American business. Joanne B. Ciulla believes that, precisely because confidential information is vital to the conduct of business, the temptation to exploit information to unfair personal advantage is ever-present. She suggests that business education in America makes its students more vulnerable to the temptation to use secret information unethically by fostering the game-playing attitude that Carr defends. This attitude emphasizes technical excellence without consideration of the effects one's maneuvers may have on the complex social reality in which businesses operate. Business education, in Ciulla's view, should emphasize the impact that business has on societal life.

Robert C. Solomon and Kristine Hanson observe that even though occasional, well-publicized cases reveal the action of individuals within corporations to be sometimes appallingly irresponsible, most ethical problems in business are not of this sort. More often, a big problem for the whole corporation arises systemically, as a result of many small, intrinsically acceptable decisions that work together to produce bad results. Like Ciulla, Solomon and Hanson propose that business communities develop greater sensitivity to the social impact of their collective actions and strive to coordinate their efforts to achieve ethically desirable outcomes.

JOHN HOSPERS

Profits and Liberty

JOHN HOSPERS *teaches philosophy at the University of Southern California. He is editor of* The Monist *and author of* Libertarianism. *His publications span many areas of philosophy, including esthetics, ethics, and political philosophy.*

"HE'S earning too much—take it away from him!" "A hundred thousand a year while some people in the world are hungry? Nobody ought to be allowed to earn that much!" Such remarks are made, and they have a "humanitarian" sound. Yet, as I shall try to show, they result from ignorance of the functions of profits in an economy: and to the extent that the suggestion is followed, the result is poverty for everyone.

In a free economy—one in which wages, costs, and prices are left to the competitive market—profits have a very important function: they help to decide what products shall be made, of what kinds, and in what amounts. It is the hope of profits that leads people to make the products (or provide the services): if little or nothing can be made from producing them, or not enough to justify the risk of investing the capital, the product will not be made; but the more one hopes to make from it, the more people will bend over backwards to produce it. The hope of profits channels the factors of production, causing products to be made in whatever quantities the public demands. In a state-controlled economy, controlled by bureaucrats, nothing at all may be made of a certain product much in demand, because the ruling decision-makers have decided simply not to make it; and at the same time, millions of other things that nobody wants may be produced, again because of a bureaucratic decision. And the bureaucracy need not respond to public demand. But in a free-enterprise economy, the producer who does not respond to public demand will soon find his warehouse full of unsalable products and his business bankrupt.

The hope of profits also makes for an enormous increase in the efficiency of production, for, other things being equal, the most efficient producer—the one who can cut out waste and motivate his workers to produce the most and best products—will earn the highest profits. And is there any reason why these profits should not be applauded? To the consumer, these profits mean that the industry producing the goods he wants is healthy and nicely functioning—one that can continue to deliver the goods, and probably for at least as low a price as its competitors, since otherwise more customers would have turned to the competitor. To the workers, profits of their employer mean that the employer is doing a good job for his customers—good enough so that they keep buying his product—and thus that they, the employees, are more secure in their jobs, and are more likely to receive higher wages in the future than are the employees of a company that is just barely making it. And as for the enterprisers, who can honestly say that they do not deserve the profits they received? First, they are risk-takers: they risked their capital to start the business, and had they lost no one would have helped them. Second, they spent not only their money (and borrowed money) on the enterprise, but, in most cases, years of their lives, involving planning, down to the last detail of production, the solution of intractable problems having to do with materials, supplies, and availability of trained help. Third, they anticipated the market, and did so more expertly than their competitors, for in order to make profits they had to have the right amount of merchandise at the right places for sale at the right time. Fourth, they provided the consumer a product or service (they could not *force* the consumer to buy from them; the consumer voluntarily elected to buy), in quantity — for a price, of course (after all his time and effort, should the enterpriser give it away, or sell it without receiving a return on it?), but nevertheless they provided it at a price which the consumer was willing to pay.

But the public, or a large segment of it, becomes envious and bitter, seeing that the man makes a profit. Perhaps the envious man has tried to start a business himself and lost it; or perhaps he just lost his job or can't pay some of his bills, and sees the employer living in a large luxurious house; in any case, he doesn't understand what side his bread is buttered on, for he doesn't realize that if the employer couldn't keep going, he himself would have no job. For whatever reason, he curses the employer because the man has a larger annual income than he does. Never mind that the employer took the risks, made the innumerable decisions (any one of which could have wrecked the business), and made *his* job possible in the first place: he, the employer, must be brought down to the worker's level. So he curses him, envies him, and votes for higher taxes for his employer, which, if passed, will mean that the employer won't expand his business and hire extra employees, and in fact may even have to cut it down some, even including his (the worker's) job. Officially, his line is that the employer's profits are ill-got. And yet when one examines it carefully, the complaint is groundless and absurd.

Suppose that an enterprise can make a thousand dollars in profits by a certain amount of capital investment; let us call this amount of investment C. Suppose also there is a second enterprise, less efficiently run than the first, which can only make that same amount of profit by investing twice the capital — 2C. People will then say that the first, the efficient, manager, is reaping an excessive profit. For on the same investment of capital he can make twice the profits as his sloppy competitor; and for this his profits are branded as "excessive." But this is absurd: the efficient producer who gets more profits has more money to convert into plant expansion, more reserve for research so that he can improve his product, more wherewithal to reduce consumer prices and still make a healthy profit, thus benefiting the consumer with lower costs. The consumer ought to be anxious to have the most efficient producer possible; for only in that way can he be sure of getting the best possible product at the lowest possible price. By producing efficiently, the producer can undercut his competitors and thus benefit the consumer, while at the same time earning larger profits by capturing a larger share of the market for himself. We should applaud, not condemn, efficient production.

Add to this the fact that our present insane tax laws penalize the producer for his profits, and thus penalize efficiency. "Taxing profits is tantamount to taxing success in best serving the public. . . .

The smaller the input (of money) required for the production of an article becomes, the more of the scarce factors of production is left for the production of other articles. But the better an entrepreneur succeeds in this regard, the more he is vilified, and the more he is soaked by taxation. Increasing costs per unit of output, that is, waste, is praised as a virtue."

> There would not be any profits but for the eagerness of the public to acquire the merchandise offered for sale by the successful entrepreneur. But the same people who scramble for these articles vilify the businessman and call his profit ill-got.
>
> One of the main functions of profits is to shift the control of capital to those who know how to employ it in the best possible way for the satisfaction of the public. The more profits a man earns, the greater his wealth consequently becomes, the more influential does he become in the conduct of business affairs. Profit and loss are the instruments by means of which the consumers pass the direction of production activities into the hands of those who are best fit to serve them. Whatever is undertaken to curtail or to confiscate profits, impairs this function. The result of such measures is to loosen the grip the consumers hold over the course of production. The economic machine becomes, from the point of view of the people, less efficient and less responsive.

Many people are so envious of, and bitter against, the man who earns a large salary or makes large profits, that they are unable to stand back impartially and try to understand what the role of profit is in an economy, and how it tends to increase everyone's income, not merely that of the man who receives it.

• • •

Instead of resenting it when individuals or companies make a million dollars, we should be happy. That million dollars means that there is a prosperous enterpriser who has created many jobs for people and bought equipment and so on (which in turn requires jobs to produce) to keep the product going. A million dollars made on the free market means that a great deal of money has filtered down to a very large number of people in the economy — and that a product is available at a competitive price, else the consumers would not have bought it in sufficient quantity to make our company its million. By contrast, a million dollars earned in government jobs means a million dollars milked from the taxpayer, which he could have spent in other ways.

> The future prosperity of everyone — including the needy — depends on *encouraging* persons to become millionaires; to build railroads, houses, and power plants; to develop television, plastics, and new uses for atomic power. The reason is simple: *No man in a free country can make a million dollars through the machinery of production without producing something that we common men want at prices we are willing to pay.* And no man will continue to produce something we want at a price we are willing to pay unless he has the *chance* to make a profit, to become rich — yes, even to become a millionaire.

There is an old saying, "No one should have caviar until everyone has bread." This is, when one examines it, one of the most confused statements ever made, though it is easily mouthed and chanted and is useful for political campaigns. If the enterpriser were not permitted to have his caviar, he would have far less incentive (perhaps no incentive at all) to produce anything, with the result that in the end fewer people would have even bread. The correct slogan would be, "If no one were permitted to have caviar, finally not many people would have bread."

One of the prevailing impressions, which underlies many arguments in this area but seldom itself surfaces to the level of explicit argument, is that the riches of the rich are the cause of the poverty of the poor. The impression is one of a certain fixed quantity of wealth, and that if some persons have more, this must inevitably mean that others have less.

A little reflection is enough to refute this assertion. If there were only a fixed quantity of wealth, how is it that we have many hundreds of millionaires now, hundreds and even thousands of men with elaborate houses, cars, lands, and other possessions, whereas only a few kings and noblemen had anything like this in bygone ages? Where long ago only a comparative handful of people could live, at the borderline between existence and extinction, in a given area of land, today a thousand times that number live, and live so well that they need spend only 10 to 15 percent of their income on food and all the rest goes for other things, most of which were inconceivable to the population of centuries past.

What people do not comprehend is that wealth is not static, but *grows* as long as people are free to use their ingenuity to improve the quality of their life. Here are deposits of iron, lying in the ground century after century; they do no good to anyone as long as they are just lying there. Now someone devises an economical process for removing the iron from the ground; another devises a means for smelting it, and another for combining it with manganese and other metals to produce steel that can be used in buildings, railroad tracks, and countless other things. When all these factors of production are functioning and the steel is produced, the world's wealth has been increased. Consumers have something to use that they didn't have before, and workers have jobs that didn't exist before. Every party to the transaction is a gainer.

•   •   •

No, the world is not like a lifeboat. Wealth does increase, and it increases for all as a result of the efforts of a few creative men. The riches of the rich are not the cause of the poverty of the poor: the rich in a free enterprise society can become rich only (1) by hiring workers to produce something and (2) because these consumers on a free market choose to buy what the entrepreneur has offered. They are rich precisely *because* innumerable consumers have, through their purchases, voted for whatever product or service they have to offer. Not one penny of their income on the free market came from the taxed income of anyone else.

•   •   •

But perhaps the most telling argument for profits is that the hope of profit is the surest way to get increased production. Whenever the chance of profit is removed, production lags or ceases. And production is a basic human need: man must produce in order to live—that is an inescapable fact of man's situation on this planet. If some men do not produce, others must produce that much more if they are all to remain alive. A considerable amount of productive labor is required for the bare necessities of life; and if one desires more of life's goods than those required for subsistence, still more production is required.

When, in a free-enterprise economy, many thousands of kinds of items are produced, consumers scramble to buy them — if they didn't buy them, of course, they would not long continue to be produced. In practice, then, people do value the fruits of the productive process. But the moral code to which they give allegiance in their day-to-day talk puts no premium on production at all. According to popular morality, it is charity that is the supreme virtue. Presumably the production of the goods needed to sustain life is not considered virtuous because people produce to enhance their own lives and to make profits — all of which is selfish. And what is selfish, according to the popular morality, cannot be virtuous.

Yet charity is possible only from the surplus of production. Without production, there would be nothing for anyone to be charitable with. In a society on a bare subsistence level, charity would be near zero, for one could give food to another only by consigning oneself to starvation.

•   •   •

The producer, however, produces primarily for himself, and for his profit. Because of this fact, his activity — the supreme virtue of productivity — is not included on the popular list of virtues at all. Whatever his motives are, however, let us consider his deeds. His deeds, surely, are quite clear.

The man who perfects a method for taking materials out of the earth, and starts a factory to produce them, spends years of his time and thousands or millions in money, hoping quite properly to have a financial reward for his pains; and in the process he provides work for large numbers of people. Nevertheless, popular morality considers him an evil exploiter who deserves only to be taxed out of existence for the sake of the rest of us. And yet this man has, in all candor, probably done more good than any other kind of person in our society. The entrepreneur may not *want* to pay out money to get a product or hire workers; he would rather get the income without any effort, let us say: but he cannot get a product mass-produced without doing these things, so perforce he does them. And when he is left free to do these things, the economy of the nation flourishes; the system of free enterprise, that is economic freedom, has provided the highest standard of living ever known in the world to the degree to which nations have permitted economic freedom. In the nations which do not permit economic freedom, production stagnates, constant shortages appear, and the majority of the population fall well below the poverty level. Economic freedom, and the fruits of it, are perhaps the principal positive *moral* force in the history of America; to take just one example, the American supermarket, selling thousands of items at marginal profits per item, and making available thousands of items to thousands of people otherwise unable to buy them, has probably done more good than all the charitable schemes of the last two thousand years put together. And yet the professional do-gooders castigate and condemn the producer on whom they are dependent for the handouts they wish to give, and they praise their fellow do-gooders who, having taken it away from the producer, then undertakes to distribute these bounties to the needy — and what he is distributing isn't even his own money, but money taken by force from the men who produced the goods. Was there ever such a total inversion of moral values?

CHRISTOPHER D. STONE
The Culture of the Corporation

CHRISTOPHER D. STONE *teaches law at the University of Southern California and is the author of* Where the Law Ends: The Social Control of Corporate Behavior *(1975).*

W E . . . have some good clues as to how attitudinal changes can be brought about — clues that suggest two broad approaches suited to two distinguishable situations.

The key characteristic of the first situation is that the attitudes we want to inculcate can be connected with, and find support in, norms and/or subgroups that preexist in the organization. An example of this is provided in the aftermath of the electrical equipment conspiracy cases referred to earlier.

Price-fixing in the industry — certainly in the heavy-equipment section of the industry — had become so widespread as to constitute something of a behavioral norm. To change this corporate culture that had grown up within it, Westinghouse appointed an outside advisory panel.

The advisory panel insisted not merely on the company's instructing its employees that price-fixing was illegal. Despite all the industry protests about the "vagueness" of the antitrust laws, none of those involved in the secret meetings had any doubts about the illegality of price-fixing. And that knowledge, of itself, obviously had not pulled enough freight. Instead, the panel decided to aim for an affirmative demonstration "that competition, properly pursued, can produce far more consistent profits than . . . conspiracy."

In-house programs were established — management courses, workshops, conferences — all adopting the positive approach that the company's business success in the future, over the long haul, depended "to a considerable degree on the adoption . . . of policies of vigorous (and even aggressive) flexible, competitive initiative."

The presentation, in other words, was not that the company had to "submit" to a stronger, outside force — that is, the government. Rather, the price-fixing was depicted as itself a foreign element, inimical to the more fundamental corporate ideal of increasing one's share of the market through better salesmanship, superior design, and the like — the norm of competition. In fact, I am authoritatively informed that at discussions among employees, a sentiment emerged that the price-fixing had been "the sales force's thing: a way to avoid the hard work of really going after sales." The same source reports that the design engineers actually resented what had been going on. Their self-esteem had been based on their ability to build better mousetraps; suddenly they discovered that their share of the market for heavy equipment had been fixed at a ratio that had no real bearing on their own contribution.

This brings me to the second point. Securing conformity to the compliance norm was not based solely on demonstrating its link to a preexistent, supposedly dominant, corporate *ideal*. In addition, there already existed within the organization certain *groups* potentially more supportive of the desired attitude than the corporation as a whole. Part of the trick of changing the attitude manifested by the corporation as a whole is to locate the critical support group and strengthen its hand. (The engineers have already been mentioned.) In the example at hand, lawyers were particularly crucial. Company lawyers "look bad," both among their peers and their co-workers, when something like widespread price-fixing is revealed to have been going on under their noses. What is more, along with their other functions, they, in particular, symbolize law abidance within the organization. In such a context, making the desired attitude more acceptable involves placing the symbolic custodian of the attitude more prominently in the corporate hierarchy. This was accomplished in the Westinghouse situation by requiring other employees to, for example, file reports with the lawyers whenever certain questionable activity was undertaken. The practical virtues of this procedure have already been mentioned; what I am emphasizing here, though, is that in addition to its practical aspects, the underscoring of the lawyers' role had a significant symbolic component that may prove equally important. . . .

There are any number of roughly comparable situations where the same sort of approach should and could be invoked to alter unwanted attitudes. Insurance industry executives insist that a high percentage of worker injuries (and possibly product defects as well) are directly traceable to heavy drinking, and, increasingly, to drugs. The insurance industry wants, and management should want, to confront this problem and stamp it out. But the insurers have an almost impossible time getting the employer to discuss the problem. . . .

In a situation such as this, there is reason to hope for improving attitudes; the task is more one of changing perceptions and getting the problem into the open, rather than tampering with an underlying corporate goal (profits, prestige, expansion). And here, too, there are ready-made groups with which an alliance can be forged: the unions and insurance companies, especially. This does not mean that the task is easy. (If it were easy it would probably have been done.) But with some government encouragement, company bulletin boards could advertise and clarify the dangers, union executives could be called to Washington to discuss "their" interest in an airing of the drinking situation, in-plant worker meetings could be held (discussions among peer groups seem far more effective than hierarchical, "handed down" orders), and companies might set up alcoholic treatment programs (as some companies have done, but usually, to my understanding, solely for the executives).

In a second class of situation, however, the problem of dealing with the corporate culture is stickier. I am thinking now of the cases where the attitudes the society wants to inculcate are at odds with all the dominant norms of the corporation and can find no alliance with any of the attitudinal groups I mentioned (the work group, industry, business community).

For example, where worker-safety problems are concerned, we can at least consider mobilizing some internal alliance with the unions; for product quality and safety, with the engineers; for resource conservation (as through recycling energy), with the investors. But consider, by contrast, the problem of getting "insiders" to give notice of the company's pollution; to halt industrial espionage and campaign law violations; to keep clear of political adventures in foreign countries; to exercise concern for land use aesthetics. In these cases, the attitudes desired by the "outside" world have barely a toe-hold on the "inside."

When we move into this area what we are faced with is nothing less than providing the organization with a new *internal rhetoric* — the special "vocabulary of motives" that every culture, and every cultural subgroup, provides its members with as its own "legitimate" reasons for doing things. These varying vocabularies involve more than just different ways of interpreting and explaining an act already completed. The range of available motives imposes boundaries on the alternatives a member of the group is prepared to consider. Today, a lower-level executive who recommended against a program on the grounds that "it will cause a lot of noise in the neighborhood" would be rather unlikely to get his recommendation advanced very far up the corporate hierarchy — unless he could convincingly append something about "we are likely to get fined (or zoned out)."

That is why any program to shift basic corporate attitudes has to involve, not replacing the profit motive ("will it sell?"), but at least providing respectable alternate vocabularies that can effectively be invoked, within some range of profit constraint, in special circumstances.

How can such a change be brought about?

A good deal depends upon the sort of gradual social evolution that is out of the control of any of us. As the general public becomes more and more informed and concerned about the environment, for example, some of that concern will gradually work its way through the corporation's walls, with the result that explanations today unacceptable — "out of place" — will become persuasive in time.

On the other hand, while much is in the hands of this sort of evolution, there are some deliberate measures that we can take. These possibilities include the following.

Rewards for Excellence

At present, just about the only positive reward corporations achieve is in the form of profits (or sales, or other measures of financial growth). Essentially, all other social feedback is negative — public criticisms or legal punishments for doing things badly. This need not be the case. During World II, for example, "E" awards were bestowed on defense companies that had exceeded their allotted production. The presentation of the "E" to a qualifying corporation was the occasion of a high ceremony, at which government representatives, executives, and workers joined. The company would get a flag, and each of the workers an "E" pin. Why should not the Environmental Protection Agency, for example, be authorized to give out its own Environmental Protection "E"s to companies that accelerate beyond their "cleanup" timetables, or come up with ingenious new environment-protecting methods?

The Social Audit

A great deal has been written recently about devising a "social audit" for corporations to supplement their traditional financial audits. Their aim would be to represent on paper the total social costs and benefits of a corporation's activities, over and above those that are now reflected in its financial statements.

The problem with the traditional statements is that they developed to reflect the interests of the financial community. Investors — and potential investors — have no particular need for a breakdown of figures displaying, for example, how much the company has put into quality-control systems or how much it has done to increase minority worker mobility. A paper company's statement will reflect the cost of the lumber it consumes; but if it uses the local river as a sewer to carry away waste, and does not have to pay for the damages this causes downstream, those social costs will nowhere appear on the company's books. They don't affect earnings. . . .

I am inclined to agree with the suggestion of Bauer and Fenn that, at least while we are seeing what, if anything, corporate social audits may develop into, management ought to be encouraged to make them up for their own internal use only. I myself have doubts as to how successfully and far the social audit can evolve even in such a private and nurtured atmosphere. But to my mind, the key point is that even if these experiments never do produce anything terribly useful informationally, along the lines of a true audit, there is still a chance of success from our present viewpoint: from the point of developing a new internal vocabulary of motive that might compete with "profitability" and the profit constellation (sales, costs, etc.). What new constellations of motive would evolve, one cannot say. I would rather suspect that, in contrast with the true audit, different companies would design incommensurable categories and structures, each appropriate to its own fields of operation, capital intensivity, and so forth. Then these categories, in turn, could be worked into the internal evaluation process, so that those divisions and persons who performed in the appropriate way would stand a chance of reward.

Interchanges

There is no more primitive way to alter intergroup attitudes (hopefully, for the better) than to bring the groups together.

On an intracorporate scale, there have been a number of experiments in "sensitivity" confrontations among executives and, to a lesser extent I believe, among management and workers.

But insofar as the boundary between the corporation and the outside world is concerned, the exchanges could barely be worse. The government, for its part, relies largely on lawsuits and the threat of suits — certainly a less than ideal way to communicate values. The public at large — or, at least, the activist groups that purport to speak for it — maintain a shrill criticism that is just overstated enough that managers (even otherwise sympathetic managers) can find grounds to dismiss it in their own minds. The corporate response to the public is either a cynical PR bluff, or a defensiveness no less shrill and hysterical than the criticisms it receives. In a recent interview, Union Oil Company's president dismissed the environmental movement as "a question of people being irrational." Then, thinking a little further he added darkly, "It's more than that, actually. I don't know who's behind the Sierra Club, but it obviously isn't people of good will." . . .

What is called for, obviously, is some improved modes of communication and understanding — in both directions. Public criticism of corporate behavior certainly should be maintained. But it should be informed enough, and even sympathetic enough, that it does not induce so extreme and inflexible a defensiveness. . . .

Public Education

Part of the problem corporate reformers face in changing the corporate culture has been mentioned: that the shriller their criticisms, the more the corporate community inclines to discount them as "one-sided" and ill-informed. The reform movement has some particularly sensitive problems, too, in taking its case to the public. How the issues are handled is important, not only because of the obvious implications for garnering legislative support, but because the reactions of the outside world are themselves one of the more significant determinants of the corporation's internal culture. There is an interesting demonstration of this in a study of law violations among shoe manufacturers located in various New England communities. Though the companies studied were operating in the same industry, subject to the same laws, the variations in law obedience were dramatic. In Haverhill, Massachusetts, for example, 7 percent of the companies were law violators, while in Auburn, Maine, 44 percent were. The author concluded that "one of the reasons is the difference in attitude toward the law, the government, and the morality of illegality" that prevailed in the companies' various home communities.

The point is, altering corporate behavior may involve reexamining the views that prevail in the outside world. And in this regard, one has to be struck by the fact that while the public may be periodically exercised over corporations, corporate wrongdoing simply doesn't command the same dread and fascination as crimes committed by tangible human beings. To an extent, this difference in public reaction toward corporate as opposed to human wrongs probably owes to the different nature of the offenses that are typically involved, rather than to a difference in who the actor is. That is, the Boston Strangler commands headlines because strangulation (and rape) are embedded in the human psyche as particularly fearful acts, whereas price-fixing, stock frauds, and the range of most offenses associated with corporations seem more "technical."

On the other hand, I think we have to consider another factor that is at work, too — one that involves the nature of the corporation, as much as what the corporation is doing. I strongly suspect — although I cannot prove — that where a corporation rather than an identifiable person is the wrongdoer, the hostility that is aroused is less than even where the offense is more or less the same. For example, if we are subjected to the noise of a motorcyclist driving up and down our street at night, I think a deeper and more complex level of anger is tapped in us than if we are subjected to the same disturbance (decibelically measured) from an airline's operations overhead. It is not just that the one seems "uncalled for" while the other seems incidental to commerce and progress. It is also that where a tangible person is involved, we can picture him (even if that means only to fantasize him); whereas when the nuisances we are subjected to are corporate, there is no tangible target to fix our anger upon. And it all seems so hopeless anyway. The consequence, if I am right, is that while various small groups are turning increased publicity onto corporate wrongdoing, they are still a long way from bringing about effective changes in corporate laws and corporate performance. A reform movement, to be effective, needs both widespread indignation and widespread hope to sustain itself. Neither by itself will do. So long as the public continues to perceive the wrongs corporations do as impersonal, market-dictated, and somehow inevitable, the reformers will have as little success forcing a change in corporate consciousness as they will in marshaling a public opposition that can seriously challenge the corporation's legislative clout. In all events, those of us who aim to change things have a job to sort out and deal with the various reasons why corporate reform movements have not been more successful after so many decades of agitation.

BARBARA EHRENREICH

The Intelligentsia vs. the Suits

BARBARA EHRENREICH *is a social critic and theorist whose most recent book is* Fear of Falling: The Inner Life of the Middle Class *(1990).*

THERE are two cultures in the middle class. They inhabit the same neighborhood, sometimes even the same families, but with mutual suspicion and an ugly tinge of contempt. Consider an old friend's response when I asked how the kids were doing. "Oh, all right," she said, with a rueful little twist of the mouth. "But Melissa's thinking of law school. Public interest law, she says, but they all say that in the beginning. . . ." Most Americans would be proud to utter the words, "my daughter, the corporate lawyer." But my friend, a sociological researcher, believes there are better things to work for than money and better groups to join than "the suits." She could adjust to having her daughter be a dropout, I think, but not a *defector*.

Melissa's mother lives in one culture. Most of my children's friends have parents who live in another. I asked one of them recently how her son was doing in college and got the same twisted look. "He's taking a lot of lit," she said, in a tone you might employ for "doing a lot of dope." Interpreting my raised eyebrows as a sign of shared concern, she concluded, "But we're sure he'll settle down soon."

To accounting, she meant, or pre-law. We often trivialize this culture gap as yuppies vs. liberals or children of the '60s vs. people of the '80s. But there are those who take the split a lot more seriously, who see it as a clash, not of options or expectations, but of hard-edged social *classes*. Some of our most prominent conservative intellectuals, like Irving Kristol, for example, would label Melis-

sa's mother — and me — a member of the "intelligentsia," by which they mean any white-collared wage earner who works (or appears to work) for ideas or ideals as opposed to pure profit. This includes professors, journalists, public officials, foundation executives: occupants of the nonprofit sector, the media, and the education industry.

To conservative hard-liners, these are — collectively — the bad guys, disparaged as "the verbalists" (mere wordmongers) or "the non-producers" (they don't make anything, sometimes not even much money). There's a good reason why the conservative thinkers tend to look on members of the corporate culture with approval and lit majors with slightly narrowed eyes. Conservatives suspect that lit majors and their ilk are more likely to be liberals, or worse, troublemakers. They don't think the two cultures are capable of sharing the same social system. They may, in the long run, be right.

It's not just the political gap between these two classes. There are, after all, conservative spokespeople for the intelligentsia, such as Allan Bloom, just as there are liberal representatives of the corporate culture: Felix Rohatyn is a sterling example. But the *culture* gap is perilously wide. And as I recently had occasion to learn, it can be tougher to cross than New York's Holland Tunnel at Friday rush hour.

The occasion was an "executive enrichment" course, and I was an invited "resource person," there to lead seminars on social policy. For six days I was thrown in with 60 upper- and middle-level executives from the *Fortune* 500. We were isolated in a conference center, where we ate breakfast, lunch, and dinner together, slogged through six or more hours of seminars a day, and sometimes continued on over late-night pizza and beer. It took me about 45 minutes to realize I was seriously out of place.

To begin with, my "students" were all several significant digits richer than I, with average incomes well over $100,000 a year. Their lifestyles included country clubs, jaunts to Djakarta, and, among the overwhelmingly male majority, stay-at-home wives with an interest in gardening. I hesitated to say that I was a writer, because in this context it seemed insubstantial, almost frivolous — the kind of thing an executive wife might do when she wearied of gardening.

Our working sessions quickly cleared up one snobbish stereotype dear to the intelligentsia: These men were not Cro-Magnons whose brows and intellects had been flattened by the pressure of the bottom line. They were bright and verbal; they had done their assigned reading and still had time to scout out the local restaurants. But we had different concepts of what a "seminar" is meant to be: I envisioned impassioned discussions, wild speculation, creative clashes — the gourmet treats of the intelligentsia. But the executives wanted data, preferably in the form of long columns of numbers on the blackboard. In the face of ambiguity, speculation, or ideological tension, they simply shut down.

The reason, I finally figured out, had less to do with laziness than with loyalty. The corporate culture does not encourage non-conformity and positively scowls at dissent. When I cornered an official of Burroughs Wellcome, the manufacturer of AZT (a drug used for AIDS treatment), to

inquire gently why the company's life-giving product costs so much, he answered by reading from a public relations bulletin that seemed to be imprinted somewhere on his frontal lobe. Similarly, when I tried to question a representative of a notoriously untidy chemical firm, he excused himself to get another drink.

This would not happen in the intelligentsia. If I were to tell a professor friend that her university is a two-bit safety school with a reputation for academic fraud, she would most likely be delighted at my concern for her unenviable position. On the whole, members of the intelligentsia draw a very broad line between their employers and their egos. In fact, they (I should say "we") tend to get off on criticism. It's part of our conversational currency, sometimes even our job, as professional critics. And insofar as we're idealists, we see criticism and dissent as the first small steps toward a better world.

Four days into the enrichment course, I finally got up my nerve to reach out across the culture gap. At one of our obligatory evening cocktail hours I asked the cluster of men I was with, "Why do you guys get so defensive about your corporations — and the corporate world in general?" A Burt Reynolds look-alike spoke for the group: "It's our team, can't you see that?" Their faces glowed with something more deeply sustaining than gin and tonic. "Yeah," said the chorus. "We're part of a team!"

Their expressions gave me a moment of severe dislocation. I had seen this look of joyous submersion in a collective identity on the faces of reasonably powerful grown men only once before — on a visit to Mao's China 15 years ago, when I had asked some local bureaucrats about loyalty to Mao and the party. I stored this association away under the category of cross-cultural coincidences and returned, in a few days, to my life in the intelligentsia. Weeks later, post–Tiananmen Square, this momentary click of recognition began to seem less benignly coincidental. Consider: The Chinese rebels were university students, backed up by professors, scientists, and media professionals, as well as many blue-collar workers. In the pre-glasnost Soviet Union, the dissidents were, almost to a man and woman, writers, poets, scientists. Throughout the Communist world, democracy movements are being led by people who could be fairly described as the intelligentsia.

America's corporate executives are, of course, the political antithesis of Communist bureaucrats. They are champions of democracy, which they confuse, perhaps understandably from their point of view, with free enterprise and high profit margins. But, in some ways, their social role is not all that different from that of their white-collar counterparts in Bucharest or Beijing. They are our economic planners, administrators, and directors. They can decide to move a plant from Teaneck to Taiwan, or they can shut it down and put their assets into junk bonds and corporate mergers. They can manufacture life-saving technology or plastic pollutants. They are the bureaucrats, if you will, of our unelected, ordinarily invisible, corporate "government."

So I worry about the blind loyalty and intellectual timidity that I encounter in representatives of the corporate culture. No one ever claimed that corporations are models of internal democracy, but what matters is that they have the power to limit free expression for the rest of us. The magazine industry provides a case in point: If the editorial viewpoint offends the corporate culture, advertising can be withdrawn and the offending publication starved out of existence. One of our most prominent dissident publications — Ms. magazine — foundered for years because advertisers judged it too "radical."

At the end of the executive enrichment seminar, I was asked for ideas for the "next round." I suppressed an urge to say "leave me out of it" and suggested instead that the two cultures meet on a more equal basis: 60 from one side and 60 from the other, in a no-holds-barred encounter. Maybe the intelligentsia would become — from the corporate point of view — more hard-nosed and money-minded. Maybe the corporate types would — from my point of view — loosen up a little. Or maybe — as the conservative theorists might predict — the whole thing would break down into factions and fistfights.

But we ought to mix it up a little. Yuppie values have widened the gap between the two cultures, and — with the "suits" getting richer and more powerful by the day — we may have already begun the long slide toward the American version of Tiananmen Square.

CAROL HYMOWITZ AND TIMOTHY D. SCHELLHARDT

The Glass Ceiling

CAROL HYMOWITZ *is deputy chief of the* Wall Street Journal's *Pittsburgh Bureau and the author of* A History of Women in America *(1978).*

TIMOTHY D. SCHELLHARDT *is chief of the* Wall Street Journal's *Pittsburgh Bureau.*

LOOK at the names and pictures in almost any corporate annual report. Or consider the silence when a male executive is asked to name the women who hold policy-making positions in his company.

Notice how far women *haven't* come in corporate America.

More than a decade after large numbers of women joined American corporations as first-level managers, few have climbed as far or as fast as their male colleagues. Today, women fill nearly a third of all management positions (up from 19% in 1972), but most are stuck in jobs with little authority and relatively low pay. Even those few women who rose steadily through the ranks eventually crashed into an invisible barrier. The executive suite seemed within their grasp, but they just couldn't break through the glass ceiling.

To these women managers, the road to the top seems blocked by corporate tradition and prejudice. Women have a hard time finding the necessary sponsors in their companies. Furthermore, they often are thought to lack the right credentials and the appropriate drive and commitment to make it to the board room.

Unlike traditional male managers, women also are thought to be too easily diverted from their careers by family considerations. "One thing that worries top managers is that women take leaves of absence," says Alonzo McDonald, 57 years old, former White House staff director and now head of Avenir Group, a company that acquires troubled small businesses. "A month before battle, you can't afford to have your general do that."

Yet the biggest obstacle women face is also the most intangible: Men at the top feel uncomfortable with women beside them.

"Chief executives who are my age or even a little younger still feel uneasiness dealing with women," says David Maxwell, 57, chief executive officer of the Federal National Mortgage Association. "They're much more comfortable dealing with other men." Top executives, Mr. Maxwell adds, are often "quick to feel the woman who is tough isn't being womanly, while the woman who isn't tough isn't worth having around."

The result is that in spite of the extraordinary progress women have made in terms of numbers, a caste system of men at the top and women lower down still prevails in corporate America. Only 2% of 1,362 top executives surveyed by Korn/Ferry International last year were women. Just one woman — Katharine Graham of Washington Post Co. — heads a Fortune 500 company, and she acknowledges that she got the job because her family owns a controlling share of the corporation. Even women who seem very close to the top concede that they don't have a shot at sitting in the chief executive's chair.

"Where do CEO's come from?" asks Rosalie Wolf, treasurer of International Paper Co. and the corporation's only female officer. "Usually, they come out of the manufacturing and marketing ranks. There are very few women in meaningful middle-management jobs in those functions and hardly any in senior management." What can Ms. Wolf aspire to? "Maybe one day chief financial officer," she says. That would make her the only woman in that post among the top 200 U.S. companies.

The caste system undoubtedly will crumble more quickly in some fields than in others. It may disintegrate within a decade in financial services, insurance and retailing, where women make up a third to a half of all managers. It also could happen relatively soon in banking and communications, where sizable numbers of women hold top posts in middle-management. But in manufacturing and technology companies, women are a long way from the executive board room.

Right now, women in most fields hit the barrier well below the board-room level. "It often happens when a woman approaches a key managerial position where she'll affect company policy," says Nella Barkley, a New York management consultant. At manufacturing companies, that can happen even before a woman reaches the general manager level. On Wall Street, it happens when women approach the managing director or partnership slot; and in banking, the barrier usually appears when a woman becomes an operating vice president.

"Up to a certain point, brains and competence work," says Arlene Johnson, program director at Catalyst, a New York-based women's research group. "But then fitting in becomes very important. It's at that point that barriers against women set in."

Bumping the glass ceiling can be excruciatingly painful, especially for women who were early pioneers in their fields. Barbara Roberts, 38, started on Wall Street when the women who worked at what was then Blythe Eastman Dillon were required to use the back staircase. She spent 17 years moving up the ranks on Wall Street. In the five years Ms. Roberts spent at Dean Witter, she advanced from vice president and coordinator of research services to senior vice president and a member of the securities firm's board. "I worked extremely hard to get where I got," she says.

But then the annual promotions stopped. Instead of being considered for what seemed like the next logical post — executive vice president and director of marketing or research — Ms. Roberts was offered posts she judged to be lateral moves.

The explanations she got often sounded blatantly sexist, she says. One man above her in the hierarchy told her "it was his problem, but he couldn't make serious decisions if a woman was in the room." Another boss suggested that management at Sears Roebuck & Co., which acquired Dean Witter in 1982, "couldn't deal with a woman in the director's position."

Ms. Roberts resigned from Dean Witter in August to start her own marketing-consulting firm. She says she could have reconciled herself to not getting a promotion if the process had been fair. "What's so disturbing," she says, "is to know you have the credentials and aren't even being considered." Dean Witter officials declined to comment.

Corporate women say most of the discrimination they encounter is subtle, even unconscious. A bank vice president is excluded from a meeting to which all her male peers are invited. A marketing manager doesn't play golf with her boss and thus doesn't hear valuable industry scuttlebutt.

"A lot of male bonding and informal mentoring gets done on golf courses," says Allan Kennedy, co-author of "Corporate Cultures," a book about management. The result, he says, is that "senior male managers become much more comfortable with each other."

Frustrated by the strain of fighting what seems like unassailable barriers, hundreds of the brightest women managers are leaving corporations for smaller companies or to establish businesses of their own. Self-employed women are now increasing five times faster than self-employed men, according to a 1984 survey by Vogue magazine.

The exodus undoubtedly will disrupt some of the women's careers, but it also may threaten the future of the corporations, which are losing competent and experienced managers. "We're getting to the point where women are half the available talent," says Ms. Johnson of Catalyst. "If you can't make use of that talent, you're hampered. That has to be a concern to business."

But often it isn't. Many chief executives are oblivious to this brain drain because their women managers are pooled in low-visibility positions. Corporate women often complain that they're trapped in staff posts in which they don't have the opportunity to run a profit-and-loss center.

Companies seldom choose women for overseas jobs — experience considered essential for choice senior management posts. Many executives claim they don't mind sending women abroad, but they say foreign customers — or customs — preclude them from doing so.

Prevailing stereotypes — even when they're blatantly false — sometimes explain why women hit the glass ceiling. Among these biases: Women don't know how to get along in the business world, and women have ineffective management styles. A study last year by the Harvard Business Review of 1,900 male and female executives found that while these stereotypes had diminished since 1965, they were still widespread.

More than half of the men surveyed said they wouldn't feel comfortable working for a woman. Nearly one in five felt that women are "temperamentally unfit" for management. And more than half of all respondents, both men and women, said they thought women never would be wholly accepted in business.

Yet, recent research by the American Management Association indicates that women bosses don't manage any differently from men, and that women are more committed to their careers than men are. The association's survey, of 1,460 managers, found women more likely than men to relocate for promotions and, in conflicts between important home and business responsibilities, more likely to favor their jobs.

Executive women say they're intensely committed to their jobs because they have had to overcome more obstacles. "Men's track records come with them," but women repeatedly have to prove their competence, says Jan Johnson, who left her job as manager of marketing analysis at International Business Machines Corp. last year to start her own consulting business. Ms. Johnson recalls that at one meeting she chaired at IBM, financial managers kept addressing her male subordinates for answers only she could provide. The subordinates would then have to turn to her for the information.

Not only do senior women managers frequently find themselves pressing up against a glass ceiling, they also find themselves on display under glass. Often the lone woman at their level, they worry not just about performance but about how they dress, their political views and even the jokes they tell or laugh at on the job.

Many women who are now beginning their management careers or who have climbed quickly through the management ranks believe that changing times eventually will shatter the glass ceiling.

But it may be easier to reach that pinnacle by climbing off the corporate ladder and pursuing entrepreneurial goals. "A lot of us started out as high-risk ventures, but we've literally grown into corporations," says Marjorie Balazs, who left a management position in the semiconductor industry 11 years ago to found Balazs Analytical Laboratory Inc. in Mountain View, Calif. Today, her company does business with such giants as Du Pont Co. and Dow Chemical Co., "and the very top male executives I deal with treat me a lot more equally than the women they employ," she says.

Women like Ms. Balazs eventually could be offered top corporate posts, bypassing women trying to come up through the ranks, says Ms. Barkley, the management consultant. "Once there are enough women running powerful businesses of their own," she says, "the corporate barriers could begin to lift."

ALBERT Z. CARR

Is Business Bluffing Ethical?

ALBERT Z. CARR *was Assistant to the Chairman of the War Production Board during World War II and later served on the White House staff as a Special Consultant under Harry Truman. His books include* John D. Rockefeller's Secret Weapon *(1962),* Business as a Game *(1986) and* The Coming of War *(1960).*

A respected businessman with whom I discussed the theme of this article remarked with some heat, "You mean to say you're going to encourage men to bluff? Why, bluffing is nothing more than a form of lying! You're advising them to lie!"

I agreed that the basis of private morality is a respect for truth and that the closer a businessman comes to the truth, the more he deserves respect. At the same time, I suggested that most bluffing in business might be regarded simply as game strategy — much like bluffing in poker, which does not reflect on the morality of the bluffer.

I quoted Henry Taylor, the British statesman who pointed out that "falsehood ceases to be falsehood when it is understood on all sides that the truth is not expected to be spoken" — an exact description of bluffing in poker, diplomacy, and business. I cited the analogy of the criminal court, where the criminal is not expected to tell the truth when he pleads "not guilty." Everyone from the judge down takes it for granted that the job of the defendant's attorney is to get his client off, not to reveal the truth; and this is considered ethical practice. I mentioned Representative Omar Burleson, the Democrat from Texas, who was quoted as saying, in regard to the ethics of Congress, "Ethics is a barrel of worms" — a pungent summing up of the problem of deciding who is ethical in politics.

I reminded my friend that millions of businessmen feel constrained every day to say *yes* to their bosses when they secretly believe *no* and that this is generally accepted as permissible strategy when the alternative might be the loss of a job. The essential point, I said, is that the ethics of business are game ethics, different from the ethics of religion.

He remained unconvinced. Referring to the company of which he is president, he declared: "Maybe that's good enough for some businessmen, but I can tell you that we pride ourselves on our ethics. In 30 years not one customer has ever questioned my word or asked to check our figures. We're loyal to our customers and fair to our suppliers. I regard my handshake on a deal as a contract. I've never entered into price-fixing schemes with my competitors. I've never allowed my salesmen to spread injurious rumors about other companies. Our union contract is the best in our industry. And, if I do say so myself, our ethical standards are of the highest!"

He really was saying, without realizing it, that he was living up to the ethical standards of the business game — which are a far cry from those of private life.

Like a gentlemanly poker player, he did not play in cahoots with others at the table, try to smear their reputations, or hold back chips he owed them.

But this same fine man, at that very time, was allowing one of his products to be advertised in a way that made it sound a great deal better than it actually was. Another item in his product line was notorious among dealers for its "built-in-obsolescence." He was holding back from the market a much-improved product because he did not want it to interfere with sales of the inferior item it would have replaced. He had joined with certain of his competitors in hiring a lobbyist to push a state legislature, by methods that he preferred not to know too much about, into amending a bill then being enacted.

In his view these things had nothing to do with ethics; they were merely normal business practice. He himself undoubtedly avoided outright falsehoods — never lied in so many words. But the entire organization that he ruled was deeply involved in numerous strategies of deception.

Pressure to Deceive

Most executives from time to time are almost compelled, in the interests of their companies or themselves, to practice some form of deception when negotiating with customers, dealers, labor unions, government officials, or even other departments of their companies. By conscious misstatements, concealment of pertinent facts, or exaggeration — in short, by bluffing — they seek to persuade others to agree with them. I think it is fair to say that if the individual executive refuses to bluff from time to time — if he feels obligated to tell the truth, the whole truth, and nothing but the truth — he is ignoring opportunities permitted under the rules and is at a heavy disadvantage in his business dealings.

But here and there a businessman is unable to reconcile himself to the bluff in which he plays a part. His conscience, perhaps spurred by religious idealism, troubles him. He feels guilty; he may develop an ulcer or a nervous tic. Before any executive can make profitable use of the strategy of the bluff, he needs to make sure that in bluffing he will not lose self-respect or become emotionally disturbed. If he is to reconcile personal integrity and high standards of honesty with the practical requirements of business, he must feel that his bluffs are ethically justified. The justification rests on the fact that business, as practiced by individuals as well as by corporations, has the impersonal character of a game — a game that demands both special strategy and an understanding of its special ethics.

The game is played at all levels of corporate life, from the highest to the lowest. At the very instant that a man decides to enter business, he may be forced into a game situation, as is shown by the recent experience of a Cornell honor graduate who applied for a job with a large company:

◗ This applicant was given a psychological test which included the statement, "Of the following magazines, check any that you have read either regularly or from time to time, and double-check those which interest you most. *Reader's Digest, Time, Fortune, Saturday Evening Post, The New Republic, Life, Look, Ramparts, Newsweek, Business Week, U.S. News & World Report, The Nation, Playboy, Esquire, Harper's, Sports Illustrated.*"

His tastes in reading were broad, and at one time or another he had read almost all of these magazines. He was a subscriber to *The New Republic*, an enthusiast for *Ramparts*, and an avid student of the pictures in *Playboy*. He was not sure whether his interest in *Playboy* would be held against him, but he had a shrewd suspicion that if he confessed to an interest in *Ramparts* and *The New Republic*, he would be thought a liberal, a radical, or at least an intellectual, and his chances of getting the job, which he needed, would greatly diminish. He therefore checked five of the more conservative magazines. Apparently it was a sound decision, for he got the job.

He had made a game player's decision, consistent with business ethics.

A similar case is that of a magazine space salesman who, owing to a merger, suddenly found himself out of a job:

◗ This man was 58, and, in spite of a good record, his chance of getting a job elsewhere in a business where youth is favored in hiring practice was not good. He was a vigorous, healthy man, and only a considerable amount of gray in his hair suggested his age. Before beginning his job search he touched up his hair to confine the gray to his temples. He knew that the truth about his age might well come out in time, but he calculated that he could deal with that situation when it arose. He and his wife decided that he could easily pass for 45, and he so stated his age on his résumé.

This was a lie; yet within the accepted rules of the business game, no moral culpability attaches to it.

The Poker Analogy

We can learn a good deal about the nature of business by comparing it with poker. While both have a large element of chance, in the long run the winner is the man who plays with steady skill. In both games ultimate victory requires intimate knowledge of the rules, insight into the psychology of the other players, a bold front, a considerable amount of self-discipline, and the ability to respond swiftly and effectively to opportunities provided by chance.

No one expects poker to be played on the ethical principle preached in churches. In poker it is right and proper to bluff a friend out of the rewards of being dealt a good hand. A player feels no more than a slight twinge of sympathy, if that, when—with nothing better than a single ace in his hand—he strips a heavy loser, who holds a pair, of the rest of his chips. It was up to the other fellow to protect himself. In the words of an excellent poker player, former President Harry Truman, "If you can't stand the heat, stay out of the kitchen." If one shows mercy to a loser in poker, it is a personal gesture, divorced from the rules of the game.

Poker has its special ethics, and here I am not referring to rules against cheating. The man who keeps an ace up his sleeve or who marks the cards is more than unethical; he is a crook, and can be punished as such—kicked out of the game or, in the Old West, shot.

In contrast to the cheat, the unethical poker player is one who abiding by the letter of the rules, finds ways to put the other players at an unfair disadvantage. Perhaps he unnerves them with loud talk. Or he tries to get them drunk. Or he plays in cahoots with someone else at the table. Ethical poker players frown on such tactics.

Poker's own brand of ethics is different from the ethical ideals of civilized human relationships. The game calls for distrust of the other fellow. It ignores the claim of friendship. Cunning deception and concealment of one's strength and intentions, not kindness and openheartedness, are vital in poker. No one thinks any the worse of poker on that account. And no one should think any the worse of the game of business because its standards of right and wrong differ from the prevailing traditions of morality in our society. . . .

"We Don't Make the Laws"

Wherever we turn in business, we can perceive the sharp distinction between its ethical standards and those of the churches. Newspapers abound with sensational stories growing out of this distinction.

▶ We read one day that Senator Philip A. Hart of Michigan has attacked food processors for deceptive packaging of numerous products.

▶ The next day there is a Congressional to-do over Ralph Nader's book, *Unsafe At Any Speed*, which demonstrates that automobile companies for years have neglected the safety of car-owning families.

▶ Then another Senator, Lee Metcalf of Montana, and journalist Vic Reinemer show in their book, *Overcharge*, the methods by which utility companies elude regulating government bodies to extract unduly large payments from users of electricity.

These are merely dramatic instances of a prevailing condition; there is hardly a major industry at which a similar attack could not be aimed. Critics of business regard such behavior as unethical, but the companies concerned know that they are merely playing the business game.

Among the most respected of our business institutions are the insurance companies. A group of insurance executives meeting recently in New England was startled when their guest speaker, social critic Daniel Patrick Moynihan, roundly berated them for "unethical" practices. They had been guilty, Moynihan alleged, of using outdated actuarial tables to obtain unfairly high premiums. They habitually delayed the hearings of lawsuits against them in order to tire out the plaintiffs and win cheap settlements. In their employment policies they used ingenious devices to discriminate against certain minority groups.

It was difficult for the audience to deny the validity of these charges. But these men were business game players. Their reaction to Moynihan's attack was much the same as that of the automobile manufacturers to Nader, of the utilities to Senator Metcalf, and of the food processors to Senator Hart. If the laws governing their businesses change, or if public opinion becomes clamorous, they will make the necessary adjustments. But morally they have in their view done nothing wrong. As long as they comply with the letter of the law, they are within their rights to operate their businesses as they see fit.

The small business is in the same position as the great corporation in this respect. For example:

In 1967 a key manufacturer was accused of providing master keys for automobiles to mail-order customers, although it was obvious that some of the purchasers might be automobile thieves. His defense was plain and straightforward. If there was nothing in the law to prevent him from selling his keys to anyone who ordered them, it was not up to him to inquire as to his customers' motives. Why was it any worse, he insisted, for him to sell car keys by mail, than for mail-order houses to sell guns that might be used for murder? Until the law was changed, the key manufacturer could regard himself as being just as ethical as any other businessman by the rules of the business game.

Violations of the ethical ideals of society are common in business, but they are not necessarily violations of business principles. Each year the Federal Trade Commission orders hundreds of companies, many of them of the first magnitude, to "cease and desist" from practices which,

judged by ordinary standards, are of questionable morality but which are stoutly defended by the companies concerned.

In one case, a firm manufacturing a well-known mouthwash was accused of using a cheap form of alcohol possibly deleterious to health. The company's chief executive, after testifying in Washington, made this comment privately:

"We broke no law. We're in a highly competitive industry. If we're going to stay in business, we have to look for profit wherever the law permits. We don't make the laws. We obey them. Then why do we have to put up with this 'holier than thou' talk about ethics? It's sheer hypocrisy. We're not in business to promote ethics. Look at the cigarette companies, for God's sake! If the ethics aren't embodied in the laws by the men who made them, you can't expect businessmen to fill the lack. Why, a sudden submission to Christian ethics by businessmen would bring about the greatest economic upheaval in history!"

It may be noted that the government failed to prove its case against him.

Cast Illusions Aside

Talk about ethics by businessmen is often a thin decorative coating over the hard realities of the game:

Once I listened to a speech by a young executive who pointed to a new industry code as proof that his company and its competitors were deeply aware of their responsibilities to society. It was a code of ethics, he said. The industry was going to police itself, to dissuade constituent companies from wrongdoing. His eyes shone with conviction and enthusiasm.

The same day there was a meeting in a hotel room where the industry's top executives met with the "czar" who was to administer the new code, a man of high repute. No one who was present could doubt their common attitude. In their eyes the code was designed primarily to forestall a move by the federal government to impose stern restrictions on the industry. They felt that the code would hamper them a good deal less than new federal laws would. It was, in other words, conceived as a protection for the industry, not for the public.

The young executive accepted the surface explanation of the code; these leaders, all experienced game players, did not deceive themselves for a moment about its purpose.

The illusion that business can afford to be guided by ethics as conceived in private life is often fostered by speeches and articles containing such phrases as, "It pays to be ethical," or "Sound ethics is good business." Actually this is not an ethical position at all; it is a self-serving calculation in disguise. The speaker is really saying that in the long run a company can make more money if it does not antagonize competitors, suppliers, employees, and customers by squeezing them too hard. He is saying that oversharp policies reduce ultimate gains. That is true, but it has nothing to do with ethics. The underlying attitude is much like that in the familiar story of the shopkeeper who finds an extra $20 bill in the cash register, debates with himself the ethical problem — should he tell his partner — and finally decides to share the money because the gesture will give him an edge over the s.o.b. the next time they quarrel.

I think it is fair to sum up the prevailing attitude of businessmen on ethics as follows:

We live in what is probably the most competitive of the world's civilized societies. Our customs encourage a high degree of aggression in the individual's striving for success. Business is our main area of competition, and it has been ritualized into a game of strategy. The basic rules of the game have been set by the government, which attempts to detect and punish business frauds. But as long as a company does not transgress the rules of the game set by law, it has the legal right to shape its strategy without reference to anything but its profits. If it takes a long-term view of its profits, it will preserve amicable relations, so far as possible, with those with whom it deals. A wise businessman will not seek advantage to the point where he generates dangerous hostility among employees, competitors, customers, government, or the public at large. But decisions in this area are, in the final test, decisions of strategy, not of ethics. . . .

If a man plans to make a seat in the business game, he owes it to himself to master the principles by which the game is played, including its special ethical outlook. He can then hardly fail to recognize that an occasional bluff may well be justified in terms of the game's ethics and warranted in terms of economic necessity. Once he clears his mind on this point, he is in a good position to match his strategy against that of the other players. He can then determine objectively whether a bluff in a given situation has a good chance of succeeding and can decide when and how to bluff, without a feeling of ethical transgression

To be a winner, a man must play to win. This does not mean that he must be ruthless, cruel, harsh, or treacherous. On the contrary, the better his reputation for integrity, honesty, and decency, the better his chances of victory will be in the long run. But from time to time every businessman, like every poker player, is offered a choice between certain loss or bluffing within the legal rules of the game. If he is not resigned to losing, if he wants to rise in his company and industry, then in such a crisis he will bluff — and bluff hard.

Every now and then one meets a successful businessman who has conveniently forgotten the small or large deceptions that he practiced on his way to fortune. "God gave me my money," old John D. Rockefeller once piously told a Sunday school class. It would be a rare tycoon in our time who would risk the horse laugh with which such a remark would be greeted.

In the last third of the twentieth century even children are aware that if a man has become prosperous in business, he has sometimes departed from the strict truth in order to overcome obstacles or has practiced the more subtle deceptions of the half-truth or the misleading omission. Whatever the form of the bluff, it is an integral part of the game, and the executive who does not master its techniques is not likely to accumulate much money or power.

JOANNE B. CIULLA

Insider Trading
The Secret Seduction

JOANNE B. CIULLA *teaches business ethics at the University of Richmond. She is the author of* Honest Work *(1989).*

BEN Franklin once remarked, "Three may keep a secret if two of them are dead." If this were true, just think of how many dead people it would take to keep a secret on Wall Street. Consider, for example, the multi-service nature of the modern brokerage or banking firm. Underwriting, merger and acquisition advisory services, investment management, research, arbitrage, proprietary trading, program trading, broker and retail sales, and service on boards of directors all potentially provide broker dealers with inside information on the firm's clients. And, while the Glass-Steagall Act prohibits banking institutions from corporate underwriting activities, banks are, nonetheless, involved in a variety of securities industry functions, such as financial consulting, municipal bond underwriting, and corporate finance. Inside information from these activities can easily come in conflict with a bank's commercial lending and trust department activities. A list of institutions supplied with inside information could go on from insurance companies to law firms to newspapers. In this environment, the practice of trading on inside or secret information is not as surprising as its absence.

The current dialogue on insider trading generally focuses on the adequacy of current regulations and self-policing policies (such as "Chinese Walls"), and the ethics of individuals. Among these concerns, the moral flaws of people like Ivan Boesky and Dennis Levine capture the public's imagination most dramatically. Playing to the public, the media have put business ethics in the limelight and given the subject its fifteen minutes of fame. The publicity link between insider trading and business ethics courses has led some people to believe that our classes are nothing but discussions of the demonic Boesky and the greedy Levine. Those who blame business schools for producing amoral or immoral MBAs are often the same ones who oppose more government regulations of the securities industry — in other words, the system's ok, it's the people who are rotten.

As one who believes that research in business ethics should be more than just a rehash of the latest scandal, I begin by looking at the role of secrecy in business and the social impact of insider trading. I then argue that if one views secrecy as an attitude toward knowledge, then there are ways in which business schools might better prepare students to deal with the temptations of Wall Street.

Secrets and the Privacy of Property

Adam Smith recognized the utility of concealing information about prices, if only for a short period of time. In *The Wealth of Nations*, he tells us that when the market price of a commodity goes up substantially above the natural price, it is wise for those who supply the market with that commodity to conceal price change. According to Smith, if this change in price became known, rivals would enter the market, satiate demand, and knock the price down to its natural level. He says, "Secrets of this kind, however, it must be acknowledged, can seldom be long kept; and the extraordinary profit can last very little longer than they are kept." While, on the other hand, Smith notes

that secrets in manufacturers last longer than secrets in trade and can give a businessperson the competitive edge. Richard Posner, one of the many Smith clones around today, similarly argues that "some measure of privacy is necessary to enable people, by concealing their ideas from other people, to appropriate the social benefits of their discoveries and inventions."

Early on, Smith noticed that it is not just private use, but private knowledge that made property valuable. He saw that success in business can rest on the ability to keep some information secret, even while competing in a public market system. Ironically, the owner's prerogative to keep information private [militates] against the ability of the market to function according to Smith's rational ideal — making trade a bit more like gambling, because information is either uncertain or incomplete.

The privacy of private property troubled Karl Marx. In his early writings, he named private property as the root of alienation. Ownership of property gave a person the right to exclude others from it and do with it what he or she pleased. Factories could be moved, wages cut, people fired, work processes altered — all without mention to those affected. One ramification of alienation was that workers did not have control over their lives and well-being. The privacy of ownership and business decisions denied workers important knowledge of the future. This is especially true today. When a company faces a hostile takeover, employees suffer enormous stress because they are not given up-to-date information on the future of their jobs.

Writing at the turn of the century, German sociologist Georg Simmel argued that money, not property, allowed all exchanges to become secret and silent transactions. But, the concealability of money is, according to Simmel, "the symptom, or the extreme form of its relationship to private ownership." In his book *The Philosophy of Money*, Simmel says, "Money's formlessness and abstractness makes it possible to invest in the most varied and most remote value and thereby to remove it from the gaze of neighbors. Its anonymity and colorlessness does not reveal the source from which it came to the present owner." Simmel goes on to say that money hides many secrets as long as it is not transformed into property.

Investigators who work on Wall Street are well aware of the invisible properties of money. For example, Wall Street private investigator Jules B. Kroll has noted that Martin Siegel and Ivan Boesky were involved in cash transactions of which there was no record or system in the corporate structure to detect. As a result of this, he believes that when you are suspicious of employees, you need to look at their life-styles, not their bank books. Money itself is abstract and secretive; it only becomes public when it's transformed into goods and services.

To combat the dangers inherent in money, such as concealment, misleading estimates, and illegitimate use, Simmel points to laws that require public disclosure of the financial policies of the government and corporations. However, Simmel does not believe that the requirement for public disclosure really addresses the dangers of money. Rather, what the legal requirement for public disclosure actually does, according to him, is further differentiate public knowledge from private knowledge.

Smith, Marx, and Simmel present some interesting insights into the uses and problems of secrecy in business. Smith appreciates the usefulness of secrets as part of a business' competitive strategy, but also realizes that the lifetime of a se-

cret in a market setting is short-lived. Although I doubt that Marx would see it this way, in his early writings I see the worry that the secrecy allowed to private property under the capitalist system can and does lead to social irresponsibility. Simmel tells us openness (required by law) is one way to combat the danger of secrecy in business. However, he says that in its effect, mandatory disclosure actually creates even more secrets, by making a sharp distinction between the public and the private realms of knowledge.

These insights raise some provocative questions. For example, "Would more regulation concerning disclosure on Wall Street have the adverse affect of increasing stakes and making insider trading an even greater temptation?" If the question seems too farfetched we might ask, "Given the short life of a secret, such as one concerning a takeover, would regulations eliminate secrets or simply shorten their lives?"

Sissela Bok's distinction between privacy and private property sheds some light on these two questions. She defines 'secrecy' as intentional concealment and 'privacy' as "the condition of being protected from unwanted access by others—either physical access, personal information, or attention." So, according to Bok, a privately owned company is not a secretly owned one, and the privacy of this kind of private property is the right to limit access. The question that we have to ask today is, "What kind of privacy does a corporation have?"

Bok says secrecy and privacy do overlap in cases where secrecy must be used to guard against unwanted access. Hence, secrets can guard access to the private lives of individuals and corporations that are threatened by raiders. Secrets, then, tend to proliferate and become even more valuable in a dangerous environment.

Corporations today live under the threat of a hostile takeover. Do their secrets protect them from unwanted access? Since corporations are not privately owned, do they have a right to protect themselves from unwanted access with a cloak of secrecy? Or are they up for grabs by anyone who can pay the price of admission? These questions are outside the scope of this chapter, but are not unrelated to the ethical issues related to insider trading.

Secrets and Chinese Walls

If regulating secrecy from the outside is paradoxical, then consider how secrets are managed internally. In a *National Law Journal* article, Edward D. Herlihy argues that the internal self-policing systems that brokerage firms have used for the past fifty years, called "Chinese Walls," are effective. Herlihy defines a Chinese Wall as "a set of internal written policies designed to control and prevent the dissemination of non-public information acquired by one department to other separate departments of the organization."

In 1980 the SEC adopted Rule 14e-3, which prohibits insider trading while in possession of material information; however, Paragraph b of the rule provides for a safe-harbor exclusion of "the disclose or abstain from trading" proscription for multiservice firms who adopt a Chinese Wall and can show that individuals making investments have had no knowledge of inside information. Rule 17j-1, also adopted in 1980, requires every registered investment company and each investment advisor of, or principal underwriter for, such a company to adopt a written code of ethics.

Segregating people and information into departments has some obvious limitations, as do codes of ethics. Because of their bureaucratic nature, modern organizations all run the risk of, as Hannah Arendt once said, "looking like they're ruled by nobody," and this greatly obscures individual responsibility. Unless you literally lock your employees up every night and put Big Brother in the bathrooms, businesses are left depending on the morals of their employees.

Hence, in our world of fancy management systems, expensive consultants, behavioral psychologists and economists, pious CEOs, and complex rules and regulations, we still do not have complete control. In the end we are left hanging by the fragile threads of trust. These threads are crucial for the maintenance of social order in organizations and society. Since professionals are supposed to represent the height of trustworthiness with respect to technically competent performance and fiduciary obligation and responsibility, it was not unreasonable for the public eye to critically scrutinize the training ground for MBAs.

Ethics As An Attitude Toward Knowledge

Many different motifs have been used to explain insider trading. Some of the more common ones are: poor moral upbringing, ethical relativism or lack of shared moral values, amoral business schools, greed, lust for power, the Reagan era, deregulation, rapid growth in the securities industries, inadequate supervision, cracks in the Chinese Wall, and, just to round things out, secular humanism. In some ways, the publicity and concern over insider trading, although distant from most people's lives, has been a catalyst for moral, social, and legal soul searching.

The question that has intrigued me is, "Is there anything about the way that business schools train MBAs that makes them more prone to do something like trade on inside information?" Several press reports about Dennis Levine have said that for him money had become "a way of keeping score." Game theory and game analogies are often used in business schools to formulate strategies. But problems arise when people come to think of themselves as players. Viewing business as a game allows people to distance themselves from their actions and the effect of their actions on others. Game-playing engenders a delight in manipulation and technical expertise that is disjointed from responsibilities that one has to others and the organization. In particular, the game attitude fosters the development of technical excellence in isolation from any notion of moral excellence.

By compartmentalizing learning in business schools, teachers often fail to integrate how the "hard" areas like finance relate to the "soft" areas of management. For example, if, after two years at a top business school, the only way that a student can tell if a business is mismanaged is if its stock is undervalued, then I think that we've failed. What's at stake here is not just a matter of teaching values — it's a failure to give students an integrated understanding of business.

Some of our students who go on to work in the financial industry take with them a rationalist view of knowledge. They believe that quantitative methods and information (deductive knowledge) are superior to information collected through observation (inductive knowledge). Systems and models allow for deductive reasoning and yield information that has the sound ring of certainty and truth. I call this view "knowledge in a box." The problem with knowledge in a box is that it's not always clear whether what is true in the box is true in the world. So, for example, hostile takeovers might be shown to be good for the econ-

omy in one box, even if they don't appear to be good for the messy society in which the box sits.

If you look at insider trading from the perspective of finance, it may be hard to show that it does any harm; hence, so the argument goes, it may not be unethical. It is also difficult to demonstrate how insider trading violates current laws and regulations. But ethical thinking (and philosophical thinking in general) forces one to look at a far broader picture. For example, one might reasonably ask a transcendental question like "What are the ethical understandings that make business possible?" Here the harm is somewhat clearer. Business transactions cannot take place without trust. By betraying this trust, the inside trader causes social chaos. He or she is like a terrorist who sends the message that institutions do not have control. This shakes public confidence, not only in financial institutions, but in the ideals of fairness that underlie the market system.

Hence, an ethical attitude toward business requires that you clearly understand how your actions affect other people, your employer, the economic system, and society in general. Trading on inside information is a private action based on one area of expertise. There doesn't seem to be any harm or victim. It's an anonymous crime, if you haven't been trained to integrate what you know so as to understand the ramifications. Acts that "don't hurt anyone" are much easier to perform and rationalize than those that do.

One striking difference between graduate education in business and education in the liberal arts is the uncritical way in which information is presented and absorbed by students. With classes, cases to prepare, resumes to write, and the quest for the perfect job, students rarely take the time to reflect on or question what they've learned. The arrogance of some MBAs is often derived from the mistaken belief that they possess certain knowledge about how to get things done in the world. This special knowledge sets them apart from organizations and sometimes leads them to believe that they can outsmart everyone else. These unfortunate few have come to view knowledge only as a tool, not a guide.

Conclusion

As we have seen, secrets are seductive forms of knowledge that serve to hide, protect, and corrupt through unfair advantage. The law and Chinese Walls separate knowledge insofar as it is possible. These laws and policies need to be reassessed and refreshed; however, due to the privacy of secrets, not even more or tougher rules can completely control betrayal by insiders. Businesses will always have their secrets, and Wall Street will continue to offer new unethical schemes. Many will be tempted. However, one weapon against temptation is the ability to look it critically in the eye and have a clear picture of the impact of one's actions on others. Knowledge is an important part of conscience — it doesn't guarantee that a person will resist temptation, it just makes it tougher for a rational person to give in. When it comes to the building and development of character, moral struggle is almost as important as moral victory.

We don't really need to teach students that insider trading is wrong — they know that — it's yesterday's news. We won't be able to transform demons into saints. Courses in ethics and in social responsibility can be helpful, but students need to take away more than a bag full of case discussions. We need to give them the skills to think critically and philosophically about their work, their lives, and what they have learned.

ROBERT C. SOLOMON AND KRISTINE HANSON
The System Problem

ROBERT C. SOLOMON *teaches philosophy and business at the University of Texas at Austin. His books include* In the Spirit of Hegel *(1983),* From Hegel to Existentialism *(1987),* About Love *(1988),* It's Good Business *(1985), and* A Passion for Justice *(1990).*

KRISTINE HANSON *received her M.B.A. degree from Harvard University and now lives and works in Sydney, Australia.*

Los Angeles: The Collective Dilemma
Every person who lives in this basin knows that for twenty-five years he has been living through a disaster. We have all watched it happen, have participated in it with full

knowledge. . . . The smog is the result of ten million individual pursuits of private gratification. But there is absolutely nothing that any individual can do to stop its spread. An individual act of renunciation is now nearly impossible, and, in any case, would be meaningless unless everyone else did the same thing. But he has no way of getting everyone else to do it.

FRANCIS CARNEY
Harper's, 1974

A corporation is more than the sum of its parts. This is true not only in law (the corporation as a ficticious person); it is true in fact. A corporation can have power far greater than the collective powers of all of its employees, executives, and stockholders. The activities of a major corporation can change society, even if no one in or no one who owns the company can do so. Indeed, given the power of business in our society, the activities of any major corporation *will* change society, and the question is only whether it is for good or for ill. . . .

The issue is what we call the "system problem." In short, it is a collective dilemma in which bad consequences follow from no one's doing anything wrong.

The collective dilemma has become an essential feature of contemporary ethics — indeed, it may be *the* main problem of contemporary ethics. A collective dilemma is a situation in which an innocuous action, repeated many times by a great many people, produces results that are intolerable, perhaps even fatal. A moment's thought suggests a great many examples: traffic congestion, pollution, tax avoidance, and energy depletion, to name a few.

Consider the example of pollution. For hundreds of thousands of years, humans polluted the air with cooking fires and deposited their trash and excretions in nature, without noticing the consequences. We have discovered many more modes of combustion and, of necessity, developed artificial but more efficient ways of dealing with waste. Burning and producing waste are just as natural for an American family in 1985 as they were for an Egyptian family in 3000 B.C., but the collective consequences are very different. Can we say that a person is wrong, therefore, in driving a car that emits an unusually large amount of noxious exhaust fumes or in manufacturing a large number of not really necessary, hard to dispose of plastic containers for a fast-food product? Well, yes and no. In terms of the individual action, there is certainly nothing wrong. In view of the collective consequences, we have to say that there is something unethical here. "But my pollution and waste are minuscule, compared to the problem as a whole!" is the inevitable reply. But almost everyone else could say exactly the same.

The examples above concern the collective products of isolated activities of individuals. The power of the corporation, however, is not just the collected effort of hundreds or thousands of individuals. It is the coordinated and carefully controlled activity of an organization. The isolated effort of any one person — even the CEO — may not amount to much, but the collective commercial power generated by even a relatively inefficient corporation is immense. Again, any given employee, manager, executive, or (minor) stockholder can say — probably truthfully — "I don't have any control over what this company does," but, collectively, they all *are* the corporation. The system problem arises when there is a failure of unified vision, when the parts lose sight of the whole.

A decision at General Motors, which may require the input of thousands of employees and consultants and enough information to fill a good-size computer, can multiply small margins of error and uncertainty — or, worse, small margins of faked confidence — to disastrous proportions. Business ethicist Tom Donaldson points out that General Motors, like many large corporations, maintains a distinction between line and staff functions. Both report to the president, but communication between them is vague and often confused. The room for misunderstanding or lack of synchronization is considerable, and tragic errors are possible even when every single employee of the company is doing his or her job correctly.

The system problem is most of concern in ethics when the errors in question have to do with the safety of the product or its impact on the community in general. At General Motors, needless to say, safety is always a major consideration. So is the impact of automobiles on the environment. But there is a very real question as to how much essential ethical issues can be dealt with in a company so complicated. One can deal with specific safety or pollution-control features just as one can deal with any specific features of a car, but not all ethical issues are so specific. In an updated study of GM in 1970, Peter Drucker declared once again that General Motors had never yet managed to coordinate its decisions with concern for its environment and compassion for the community. The key word here is "coordinate," for it is not neglect or indifference that is responsible for General Motors' seemingly slow response to urgent ethical concerns. It is rather the system problem, lack of coordination in the system to deal with problems that are holistic rather than particular.

One of the most paradoxical functions of corporate organization, too rarely appreciated by efficiency-minded managers, is to make an organization sufficiently flexible and self-critical — which inevitably means less efficient — to prevent all of those small and possibly undetectable errors from adding up to one gigantic mistake. Ethical problems are typically of this sort. No senior executive orders anything unethical. No middle manager intends anything unethical. No employee does anything unethical. It is not even that everyone is "just a little unethical," bending the rule a bit or slightly cutting corners. And yet the net result is unethical because no one kept the entire system in perspective. No one in a company need discriminate against women or minorities, for instance, in order for the company as a whole to fall far short of a just distribution of jobs and promotions.

As often as not, unethical conduct itself is a function of the system problem. Consider the much-discussed case of B. F. Goodrich, which in the late 1960s had a contract with the Air Force to equip the new A7D planes with air brakes. The executives of the company had decided to go for the contract "at all costs," but there was too little communication between the policymakers who made that decision and the engineers and designers who had to produce the brakes themselves. The time period was too short. Early tests showed that the brakes were flawed. The due date came, and the brakes were delivered to the Air Force. The test plane crashed. An investigation showed that the flaws in the original design had never been fixed, and several otherwise responsible engineers had falsified the early test reports to meet their deadline. They all had done what they thought they were expected to do. Goodrich was another victim of the system problem.

We can understand how this happens if

we appreciate the extent to which American business is based on the idea of everyone's "just doing his job." What gets lost is the overview, the sense of how all of this will add up. No job is itself unethical. It simply consists of getting this contract, designing this product part, doing this market survey, and so on. But we should also ask what questions are *not* being asked, what concerns are *not* being raised by anyone. Are there matters of compliance to ecological and public demands that are something more (or less) than matters of law? What contributions can the company make — over and above the production of a reasonably priced, quality product? And, most difficult, what are the consequences, on the quality of life as well as on the quality of the product, of everyone's doing his or her job? All of those jobs can add up to an ethical embarrassment, just because of the lack of ethical coordination. To take an artistic analogue, one can draw a face with all perfect features but nevertheless emerge with the portrait of a monster.

7

What Are
My
Rights?

Suppose you are taking a course in which you think you are doing particularly well. You study hard for your final exam, and when you see the exam questions, you are certain that your study has paid off. You are confident that in this class you have earned an A. But when your grades arrive in the mail, you discover that your grade had been reported as C. You telephone the professor and are told that this reflects a new grading policy — Cs for everyone, because everyone is equal. You are furious. This is an absurd sense of equality, you think. You feel that your rights have been violated. Have they?

The concept of individual rights has been central to much political debate in America over the past several decades. Such diverse issues as gun control, school prayer, racial integration, and abortion have been articulated in terms of rights. A recent advertising slogan even claimed that we have a right to chicken prepared a certain way.

Probably few of us take such a slogan as a serious statement of our rights. But some current claims to rights are historically as novel as the right to well-prepared chicken. The last few decades have heard clamors that individuals should have the right to dress as they like, to control how their bodies are used, even to die when they want to. Many social and political activists suggest that our society should do more to guarantee all citizens rights to things that other societies have considered rights but that ours traditionally has not, for example, medical care and higher education. Obviously, such guarantees depend on monetary resources — and some would insist that taxation for the purpose of funding such programs deprives those taxed of a different kind of right, the right to keep the profits that stem from their own labor.

In the face of such varied and controversial interpretations of our rights, how can we determine what our rights are? Many of us probably have intuitions that converge with those of the framers of the U.S. Constitution, who held that all human beings, just by virtue of being human, are entitled to "certain unalienable rights." In the words of the Declaration of Independence, these included the rights to "life, liberty, and the pursuit of happiness." Whether or not the laws that our governments established actually protected the unalienable rights of all its citizens (and clearly, during the times of slavery, at least, they did not), the presumption in our society is that certain human rights are basic and self-evident. The same assumption lies behind the United Nations Universal Declaration of Human Rights, which articulates the human freedoms that no person or government, in the view of the United Nations, has the right to violate. The United States Bill of Rights articulates those rights that our government is not allowed to curtail.

The notion that government, in particular, should be prevented from interfering with personal rights is a fundamental premise of classical *liberalism*. John Stuart Mill, in one of the basic defenses of this position, argues that the government has no right to curtail human freedom except in cases in which such freedom impinges on another person's rights. Even if you engage in behavior harmful to yourself, the government has no right to interfere unless harm to other persons also results. This argument has been used to defend a wide range of alleged civil liberties, including rights to engage in sexual activity, to use recreational drugs, to opt not to use seatbelts or motorcycle helmets, or to sell and display pornography. Often, when the legitimacy of such alleged rights is debated, both sides of the argument accept Mill's notion that only harm to other persons justifies government interference. In such cases, the debate often revolves around the question of whether or not any harmful effects of the behavior in question actually are limited to the perpetrator.

Robert Nozick espouses *libertarianism*, a position whose upholders often take inspiration from Mill. Libertarians favor an extremely limited role for government (essentially, the role of "protector of liberties") and restrictions on what types of endeavors the government may tax its citizens to support. Because the libertarian position involves strong views about the individual's freedom regarding possessions, it requires a clear conception of what establishes legitimate possession. Nozick argues that the legitimacy of a claim to possession depends on how the possession was acquired. Nozick is not concerned to see that possessions are distributed in any particular way, for example, to ensure a particular level of material comfort for everyone. If people's rights to their legitimately acquired possessions are to be respected, governments must not meddle to try to ensure that a particular "fair" distribution will result.

On the other hand, John Rawls contends that distribution *must* be considered if one is to construct a government in which individuals are treated fairly. He argues that justice depends on two principles: (1) all individuals have equal rights to as much liberty as is compatible with the same degree of liberty for others, and (2) inequalities should be arbitrarily distributed, except in cases in which it is reasonable to expect that some other arrangement will work to everyone's advantage. Rawls contends that these are principles that rational persons would agree upon if they were in a position to set the basic rules for fairness without any advance knowledge of which particular advantages and disadvantages they would have in their own lives. He sees this sense of fairness as preeminently rational.

The fact that more and more sectors of society claim more and more rights has led some moral thinkers to question whether "rights" talk is still useful. Some have argued that framing our ethical discussions in terms of "duties" and "obligations" is more suitable for discussing many issues, since people who assert rights are effectively claiming that someone, perhaps the government, owes them certain things. Joel Feinberg considers the relationship between rights and duties and concludes that although rights and duties are intimately connected, the morality of rights cannot fully translate into duties and obligations. He also argues that a sense of rights is valuable for contributing to our sense of personal dignity and our respect for ourselves and for others.

This chapter closes with three readings pertaining to specific debates about rights. Amartya Sen's "The Right to Take Personal Risks" considers Mill's claim that one has the right to harm oneself so long as no one else is harmed. Sen accepts that right but questions how important it is in comparison with other, conflicting objectives. He proposes that in establishing laws that pertain to personal risks (for example, laws regarding the use of seatbelts), we evaluate the importance of the right to take risks in light of other goals. Public decisions must take the whole picture into account; while rights are important, they are only part of the picture.

Most Americans feel strongly about the individual's right to protection from government surveillance. Our law respects many rights of the individual to withhold information: consider, for instance, the Fifth Amendment in the Bill of Rights. Sissela Bok contends that our sense of the right to privacy is intimately linked with our sense of identity and freedom. However, she also itemizes a number of dangers that are linked to secrecy. Bok concludes that balancing our various intuitions about secrecy is necessarily complicated and requires sensitivity to the full range of intuitions we have on the subject.

The AIDS epidemic presents a case of contradictory intuitions regarding secrecy. While most of us probably feel that confidentiality between patient and doctor should be maintained, the public-health risk raises questions about whether this right should be maintained in AIDS cases. Do those who have been intimate with a person diagnosed as having AIDS have the right to know that they may have been infected? Certainly, their health and the health of any of their other sexual partners may depend on their awareness of the risks involved in their behavior. On the other hand, the cruel and prejudicial reactions against known victims of AIDS in many communities suggests that perhaps AIDS victims, in particular, should have their rights to privacy protected. Grant Gillett, arguing that the right to confidentiality in the doctor–patient relationship must be weighed against the duties and responsibilities required of the physician, concludes that, occasionally, the obligation to protect others from potential harm requires the physician to breach confidentiality. But he contends that, most often, the doctor's obligation can be fulfilled by guiding AIDS patients themselves to reveal their condition to those who need to know.

The United States Bill of Rights

THE UNITED STATES BILL OF RIGHTS *is the first ten amendments to the Constitution, which outline the individual's freedoms that cannot be infringed upon by governmental power. The document was ratified on December 15, 1791.*

AMENDMENT I

Congress shall make no law respecting an establishment of religion, or prohibiting the free exercise thereof; or abridging the freedom of speech, or of the press; or the right of the people peaceably to assemble, and to petition the Government for a redress of grievances.

AMENDMENT II

A well regulated Militia, being necessary to the security of a free State, the right of the people to keep and bear Arms, shall not be infringed.

AMENDMENT III

No Soldier shall, in time of peace be quartered in any house, without the consent of the Owner, nor in time of war, but in a manner to be prescribed by law.

AMENDMENT IV

The right of the people to be secure in their persons, houses, papers, and effects, against unreasonable searches and seizures, shall not be violated, and no Warrants shall issue, but upon probable cause, supported by Oath or affirmation, and particularly describing the place to be searched, and the persons or things to be seized.

AMENDMENT V

No person shall be held to answer for a capital, or otherwise infamous crime, un-less on a presentment or indictment of a Grand Jury, except in cases arising in the land or naval forces, or in the Militia, when in actual service in time of War or public danger; nor shall any person be subject for the same offence to be twice put in jeopardy of life or limb; nor shall be compelled in any criminal case to be a witness against himself, nor be deprived of life, liberty, or property, without due process of law; nor shall private property be taken for public use, without just compensation.

AMENDMENT VI

In all criminal prosecutions, the accused shall enjoy the right to a speedy and public trial, by an impartial jury of the State and district wherein the crime shall have been committed, which district shall have been previously ascertained by law, and to be informed of the nature and cause of the accusation; to be confronted with the witnesses against him; to have compulsory process for obtaining witnesses in his favor, and to have the Assistance of Counsel for his defence.

AMENDMENT VII

In suits at common law, where the value in controversy shall exceed twenty dollars, the right of trial by jury shall be preserved, and no fact tried by a jury, shall be otherwise reexamined in any Court of the United States, than according to the rules of the common law.

if your a criminal you shouddn't have rights

why do people get tortured? ~~gives~~ there guilty

cause

I wouldn't confess anything

the community should take care of elders.

There's volunteers out there you jest don't know it.

AMENDMENT VIII

Excessive bail shall not be required, nor excessive fines imposed, nor cruel and unusual punishments inflicted.

AMENDMENT IX

The enumeration in the Constitution, of certain rights, shall not be construed to deny or disparage others retained by the people.

AMENDMENT X

The powers not delegated to the United States by the Constitution, nor prohibited by it to the States, are reserved to the States respectively, or to the people.

The United Nations Universal Declaration of Human Rights

THE UNIVERSAL DECLARATION OF HUMAN RIGHTS *was adopted by the United Nations General Assembly on December 10, 1948.*

WHEREAS recognition of the inherent dignity and of the equal and inalienable rights of all members of the human family is the foundation of freedom, justice and peace in the world,

Whereas disregard and contempt for human rights have resulted in barbarous acts which have outraged the conscience of mankind, and the advent of a world in which human beings shall enjoy freedom of speech and belief and freedom from fear and want has been proclaimed as the highest aspiration of the common people,

Whereas it is essential, if man is not to be compelled to have recourse, as a last resort, to rebellion against tyranny and oppression, that human rights should be protected by the rule of law,

Whereas it is essential to promote the development of friendly relations between nations,

Whereas the peoples of the United Nations have in the Charter reaffirmed their faith in fundamental human rights, in the dignity and worth of the human person and in the equal rights of men and women and have determined to promote social progress and better standards of life in larger freedom,

Whereas Member States have pledged themselves to achieve, in co-operation with the United Nations, the promotion of universal respect for and observance of human rights and fundamental freedoms,

Whereas a common understanding of these rights and freedoms is of the greatest importance for the full realization of this pledge,

Now, therefore, **the General Assembly** *proclaims* **this Universal Declaration of Human Rights** as a common standard of achievement for all peoples and all nations, to the end that every individual and every organ of society, keeping this Declaration constantly in mind, shall strive by teaching and education to promote respect for these rights and freedoms and by progressive measures, national and international, to secure their universal and effective recognition and observance, both among the peoples of Member States themselves and among the peoples of territories under their jurisdiction.

Article 1

All human beings are born free and equal in dignity and rights. They are endowed with reason and conscience and should act towards one another in a spirit of brotherhood.

Article 2

Everyone is entitled to all the rights and freedoms set forth in this Declaration, without distinction of any kind, such as race, colour, sex, language, religion, political or other opinion, national or social origin, property, birth or other status.

Furthermore, no distinction shall be made on the basis of the political, jurisdictional or international status of the country or territory to which a person belongs, whether it be independent, trust, non-selfgoverning or under any other limitation of sovereignty.

Article 3

Everyone has the right to life, liberty and security of person.

Article 4

No one shall be held in slavery or servitude; slavery and the slave trade shall be prohibited in all their forms.

Article 5

No one shall be subjected to torture or to cruel, inhuman or degrading treatment or punishment.

Article 6

Everyone has the right to recognition everywhere as a person before the law.

Article 7

All are equal before the law and are entitled without any discrimination to equal protection of the law. All are entitled to equal protection against any discrimination in violation of this Declaration and against any incitement to such discrimination.

Article 8

Everyone has the right to an effective remedy by the competent national tribunals for acts violating the fundamental rights granted him by the constitution or by law.

Article 9

No one shall be subjected to arbitrary arrest, detention or exile.

Article 10

Everyone is entitled in full equality to a fair and public hearing by an independent and impartial tribunal, in the determination of his rights and obligations and of any criminal charge against him.

Article 11

(1) Everyone charged with a penal offence has the right to be presumed innocent until proved guilty according to law in a public trial at which he has had all the guarantees necessary for his defence.

(2) No one shall be held guilty of any penal offence on account of any act or omission which did not constitute a penal offence, under national or international law, at the time when it was committed.

Nor shall a heavier penalty be imposed than the one that was applicable at the time the penal offence was committed.

Article 12

No one shall be subjected to arbitrary interference with his privacy, family, home or correspondence, nor to attacks upon his honour and reputation. Everyone has the right to the protection of the law against such interference or attacks.

Article 13

(1) Everyone has the right to freedom of movement and residence within the borders of each State.

(2) Everyone has the right to leave any country, including his own, and to return to his country.

Article 14

(1) Everyone has the right to seek and to enjoy in other countries asylum from persecution.

(2) This right may not be invoked in the case of prosecutions genuinely arising from non-political crimes or from acts contrary to the purposes and principles of the United Nations.

Article 15

(1) Everyone has the right to a nationality.

(2) No one shall be arbitrarily deprived of his nationality nor denied the right to change his nationality.

Article 16

(1) Men and women of full age, without any limitation due to race, nationality or religion, have the right to marry and to found a family. They are entitled to equal rights as to marriage, during marriage and at its dissolution.

(2) Marriage shall be entered into only with the free and full consent of the intending spouses.

(3) The family is the natural and fundamental group unit of society and is entitled to protection by society and the State.

Article 17

(1) Everyone has the right to own property alone as well as in association with others.

(2) No one shall be arbitrarily deprived of his property.

Article 18

Everyone has the right to freedom of thought, conscience and religion; this right includes freedom to change his religion or belief, and freedom, either alone or in community with others and in public or private, to manifest his religion or belief in teaching, practice, worship and observance.

Article 19

Everyone has the right to freedom of opinion and expression; this right includes freedom to hold opinions without interference and to seek, receive and impart information and ideas through any media and regardless of frontiers.

Article 20

(1) Everyone has the right to freedom of peaceful assembly and association.

(2) No one may be compelled to belong to an association.

Article 21

(1) Everyone has the right to take part in the government of his country, directly or through freely chosen representatives.

(2) Everyone has the right of equal access to public service in his country.

(3) The will of the people shall be the basis of the authority of government; this will shall be expressed in periodic and genuine elections which shall be by universal and equal suffrage and shall be held by secret vote or by equivalent free voting procedures.

Article 22

Everyone, as a member of society, has the right to social security and is entitled to realization, through national effort and international co-operation and in accordance with the organization and resources of each State, of the economic, social and cultural rights indispensible for his dignity and the free development of his personality.

Article 23

(1) Everyone has the right to work, to free choice of employment, to just and favourable conditions of work and to protection against unemployment.

(2) Everyone, without any discrimination, has the right to equal pay for equal work.

(3) Everyone has the right to just and favourable remuneration ensuring for himself and his family an existence worthy of human dignity, and supplemented, if necessary, by other means of social protection.

(4) Everyone has the right to form and to join trade unions for the protection of his interests.

Article 24

Everyone has the right to rest and leisure, including reasonable limitation of working hours and periodic holidays with pay.

Article 25

(1) Everyone has the right to a standard of living adequate for the health and well-being of himself and of his family, including food, clothing, housing and medical care and necessary social services, and the right to security in the event of unemployment, sickness, disability, widowhood, old age or other lack of livelihood in circumstances beyond his control.

(2) Motherhood and childhood are entitled to special care and assistance. All children, whether born in or out of wedlock, shall enjoy the same social protection.

Article 26

(1) Everyone has the right to education. Education shall be free, at least in the elementary and fundamental stages. Elementary education shall be compulsory. Technical and professional education shall be made generally available and higher education shall be equally accessible to all on the basis of merit.

(2) Education shall be directed to the full development of the human personality and to the strengthening of respect for human rights and fundamental freedoms. It shall promote understanding, tolerance and friendship among all nations, racial or religious groups, and shall further the activities of the United Nations for the maintenance of peace.

(3) Parents have a prior right to choose the kind of education that shall be given to their children.

Article 27

(1) Everyone has the right to freely participate in the cultural life of the community, to enjoy the arts and to share in scientific advancement and its benefits.

(2) Everyone has the right to the protection of the moral and material interests

resulting from any scientific, literary or artistic production of which he is the author.

Article 28

Everyone is entitled to a social and international order in which the rights and freedoms set forth in this Declaration can be fully realized.

Article 29

(1) Everyone has duties to the community in which alone the free and full development of his personality is possible.

(2) In the exercise of his rights and freedoms, everyone shall be subject only to such limitations as are determined by law solely for the purpose of securing due recognition and respect for the rights and freedoms of others and of meeting the just requirements of morality, public order and the general welfare in a democratic society.

(3) These rights and freedoms may in no case be exercised contrary to the purposes and principles of the United Nations.

Article 30

Nothing in this Declaration may be interpreted as implying for any State, group or person any right to engage in any activity or to perform any act aimed at the destruction of any of the rights and freedoms set forth herein.

JOHN STUART MILL

The Authority of Society Over the Individual

JOHN STUART MILL (1806–1873) *was one of the documented geniuses of modern history. By the age of ten, he had accomplished more than most scholars do in a lifetime. He is best known for his moral and political writings, particularly* On Liberty *(1859) and* Utilitarianism *(1863).*

WHAT, then, is the rightful limit to the sovereignty of the individual over himself? Where does the authority of society begin? How much of human life should be assigned to individuality, and how much to society?

Each will receive its proper share, if each has that which more particularly concerns it. To individuality should belong the part of life in which it is chiefly the individual that is interested; to society, the part which chiefly interests society.

Though society is not founded on a contract, and though no good purpose is answered by inventing a contract in order to deduce social obligations from it, every one who receives the protection of society owes a return for the benefit, and the fact of living in society renders it indispensable that each should be bound to observe a certain line of conduct towards the rest. This conduct consists, first, in not injuring the interests of one another; or rather certain interests, which, either by express legal provision or by tacit understanding, ought to be considered as rights; and secondly, in each person's bearing his share (to be fixed on some equitable principle) of the labors and sacrifices incurred for defending the society or its members from injury and molestation. These conditions society is justified in enforcing at all costs to those who endeavor to withhold fulfilment. Nor is this all that society may do. The acts of an individual may be hurtful to others, or wanting in due consideration for their welfare, without going the length of violating any of their constituted rights. The offender may then be justly punished by opinion, though not by law. As soon as any part of a person's conduct affects prejudicially the interests of others, society has jurisdiction over it, and the question whether the general welfare will or will not be promoted by interfering with it, becomes open to discussion. But there is no room for entertaining any such question when a person's conduct affects the interests of no persons besides himself, or needs not affect them unless they like (all the persons concerned being of full age, and the ordinary amount of understanding). In all such cases there should be perfect freedom, legal and social, to do the action and stand the consequences.

It would be a great misunderstanding of this doctrine to suppose that it is one of selfish indifference, which pretends that human beings have no business with each other's conduct in life, and that they should not concern themselves about the well-doing or well-being of one another, unless their own interest is involved. Instead of any diminution, there is need of a great increase of disinterested exertion to promote the good of others. But disinterested benevolence can find other instruments to persuade people to their good, than whips and scourges, either of the literal or the metaphorical sort. I am the last person to undervalue the self-regarding virtues; they are only second in importance, if even second, to the social. It is equally the business of education to cultivate both. But even education works by conviction and persuasion as well as by compulsion, and it is by the former only that, when the period of education is past, the self-regarding virtues should be inculcated. Human beings owe to each other help to distinguish the better from the worse, and encouragement to choose the former and avoid the latter. They should be for ever stimulating each other to increased exercise of their higher faculties, and increased direction of their feelings and aims towards wise instead of foolish, elevating instead of degrading, objects and contemplations. But neither one person, nor any number of persons, is warranted in saying to another human creature of ripe years, that he shall not do with his life for his own benefit what he chooses to do with it. He is the person most interested in his own well-being: the interest which any other person, except in cases of strong personal attachment, can have in it, is trifling, compared with that which he himself has; the interest which society has in him individually (except as to his conduct to others) is fractional, and altogether indirect: while, with respect to his own feelings and circumstances, the most ordinary man or woman has means of knowledge immeasurably surpassing those that can be possessed by any one else. The interference of society to overrule his judgment and purposes in what only regards himself, must be grounded on general presumptions; which may be altogether wrong, and even if right, are as likely as not to be misapplied to individual cases, by persons no better acquainted with the circumstances of such cases than those are who look at them merely from without. In this department, therefore, of human affairs, Individuality has its proper field of action. In the conduct of human beings towards one another, it is necessary that general rules should for the most part be observed, in order that people may know what they have to expect; but in each person's own concerns, his individual spontaneity is entitled to free exercise. Considerations to aid his judgment, exhortations to strengthen his will, may be offered to him, even obtruded on him, by others; but he himself is the final judge. All errors which he is likely to commit against advice and warning, are far outweighed by the evil of allowing others to constrain him to what they deem his good.

I do not mean that the feelings with which a person is regarded by others, ought not to be in any way affected by his self-regarding qualities or deficiencies. This is neither possible nor desirable. If he is eminent in any of the qualities which conduce to his own good, he is, so far, a proper object of admiration. He is so much the nearer to the ideal perfection of human nature. If he is grossly deficient in those qualities, a sentiment the opposite of admiration will follow. There is a degree of folly, and a degree of what may be called (though the phrase is not unobjectionable) lowness or depravation of taste, which, though it cannot justify doing harm to the person who manifests it, renders him necessarily and properly a subject of distaste, or, in extreme cases, even of contempt: a person could not have the opposite qualities in due strength without entertaining these feelings. Though doing

no wrong to any one, a person may so act as to compel us to judge him, and feel to him, as a fool, or as a being of an inferior order: and since this judgment and feeling are a fact which he would prefer to avoid, it is doing him a service to warn him of it beforehand, as of any other disagreeable consequence to which he exposes himself. It would be well, indeed, if this good office were much more freely rendered than the common notions of politeness at present permit, and if one person could honestly point out to another that he thinks him in fault, without being considered unmannerly or presuming. We have a right, also, in various ways, to act upon our unfavorable opinion of any one, not to the oppression of his individuality, but in the exercise of ours. We are not bound, for example, to seek his society; we have a right to avoid it (though not to parade the avoidance), for we have a right to choose the society most acceptable to us. We have a right, and it may be our duty, to caution others against him, if we think his example or conversation likely to have a pernicious effect on those with whom he associates. We may give others a preference over him in optional good offices, except those which tend to his improvement. In these various modes a person may suffer very severe penalties at the hands of others, for faults which directly concern only himself; but he suffers these penalties only in so far as they are the natural, and, as it were, the spontaneous consequences of the faults themselves, not because they are purposely inflicted on him for the sake of punishment. A person who shows rashness, obstinacy, self-conceit—who cannot live within moderate means—who cannot restrain himself from hurtful indulgences—who pursues animal pleasures at the expense of those of feeling and intellect—must expect to be lowered in the opinion of others, and

"No Man is a Island" You can't do anything that won't effect other people.

to have a less share of their favorable sentiments; but of this he has no right to complain, unless he had merited their favor by special excellence in his social relations, and has thus established a title to their good offices, which is not affected by his demerits towards himself.

What I contend for is, that the inconveniences which are strictly inseparable from the unfavorable judgment of others, are the only ones to which a person should ever be subjected for that portion of his conduct and character which concerns his own good, but which does not affect the interests of others in their relations with him. Acts injurious to others require a totally different treatment. Encroachment on their rights; infliction on them of any loss or damage not justified by his own rights; falsehood or duplicity in dealing with them; unfair or ungenerous use of advantages over them; even selfish abstinence from defending them against injury — these are fit objects of moral reprobation, and, in grave cases, of moral retribution and punishment. And not only these acts, but the dispositions which lead to them, are properly immoral, and fit subjects of disapprobation which may rise to abhorrence. Cruelty of disposition; malice and ill nature; that most anti-social and odious of all passions, envy; dissimulation and insincerity; irascibility on insufficient cause, and resentment disproportioned to the provocation; the love of domineering over others; the desire to engross more than one's share of advantages . . . ; the pride which derives gratification from the abasement of others; the egotism which thinks self and its concerns more important than everything else, and decides all doubtful questions in its own favor; — these are moral vices, and constitute a bad and odious moral character: unlike the self-regarding faults previously mentioned, which are not properly immoralities, and to whatever pitch they may be carried, do not constitute wickedness. They may be proofs of any amount of folly, or want of personal dignity and self-respect; but they are only a subject of moral reprobation when they involve a breach of duty to others, for whose sake the individual is bound to have care for himself. . . .

The distinction between the loss of consideration which a person may rightly incur by defect of prudence or of personal dignity, and the reprobation which is due to him for an offense against the rights of others, is not a merely nominal distinction. It makes a vast difference both in our feelings and in our conduct towards him, whether he displeases us in things in which we think we have a right to control him, or in things in which we know that we have not. If he displeases us, we may express our distaste, and we may stand aloof from a person as well as from a thing that displeases us; but we shall not therefore feel called on to make his life uncomfortable. We shall reflect that he already bears, or will bear, the whole penalty of his error; if he spoils his life by mismanagement, we shall not, for that reason, desire to spoil it still further: instead of wishing to punish him, we shall rather endeavor to alleviate his punishment, by showing him how he may avoid or cure the evils his conduct tends to bring upon him. He may be to us an object of pity, perhaps of dislike, but not of anger or resentment; we shall not treat him like an enemy of society: the worst we shall think ourselves justified in doing is leaving him to himself, if we do not interfere benevolently by showing interest or concern for him. . . .

The distinction here pointed out between the part of a person's life which concerns only himself, and that which concerns others, many persons will refuse to admit. How (it may be asked) can any part of the conduct of a member of society be a matter of indifference to the other members? No person is an entirely isolated being; it is impossible for a person to do anything seriously or permanently hurtful to himself, without mischief reaching at least to his near connections, and often far beyond them. If he injures his property, he does harm to those who directly or indirectly derived support from it, and usually diminishes, by a greater or less amount, the general resources of the community. If he deteriorates his bodily or mental faculties, he not only brings evil upon all who depended on him for any portion of their happiness, but disqualifies himself for rendering the services which he owes to his fellow creatures generally; perhaps becomes a burthen on their affection or benevolence; and if such conduct were very frequent, hardly any offense that is committed would detract more from the general sum of good. Finally, if by his vices or follies a person does no direct harm to others, he is nevertheless (it may be said) injurious by his example; and ought to be compelled to control himself, for the sake of those whom the sight or knowledge of his conduct might corrupt or mislead.

And even (it will be added) if the consequences of misconduct could be confined to the vicious or thoughtless individual, ought society to abandon to their own guidance those who are manifestly unfit for it? If protection against themselves is confessedly due to children and persons under age, is not society equally bound to afford it to persons of mature years who are equally incapable of self-government? If gambling, or drunkenness, or incontinence, or idleness, or uncleanliness, are as injurious to happiness, and as great a hindrance to improvement, as many or most of the acts

prohibited by law, why (it may be asked) should not law, so far as is consistent with practicability and social convenience, endeavor to repress these also? And as a supplement to the unavoidable imperfections of law, ought not opinion at least to organize a powerful police against these vices, and visit rigidly with social penalties those who are known to practice them? There is no question here (it may be said) about restricting individuality, or impeding the trial of new and original experiments in living. The only things it is sought to prevent are things which have been tried and condemned from the beginning of the world until now; things which experience has shown not to be useful or suitable to any person's individuality. There must be some length of time and amount of experience, after which a moral or prudential truth may be regarded as established: and it is merely desired to prevent generation after generation from falling over the same precipice which has been fatal to their predecessors.

I fully admit that the mischief which a person does to himself may seriously affect, both through their sympathies and their interests, those nearly connected with him, and in a minor degree, society at large. When, by conduct of this sort, a person is led to violate a distinct and assignable obligation to any other person or persons, the case is taken out of the self-regarding class, and becomes amenable to moral disapprobation in the proper sense of the term. If, for example, a man, through intemperance or extravagance, becomes unable to pay his debts, or, having undertaken the moral responsibility of a family, becomes from the same cause incapable of supporting or educating them, he is deservedly reprobated, and might be justly punished; but it is for the breach of duty to his family or creditors, not for the extravagance. . . .

When is it exactly to kill Someone?

But with self defence or a dentist cause he with has you better

But with regard to the merely contingent, or, as it may be called, constructive injury which a person causes to society, by conduct which neither violates any specific duty to the public, nor occasions perceptible hurt to any assignable individual except himself; the inconvenience is one which society can afford to bear, for the sake of the greater good of human freedom. If grown persons are to be punished for not taking proper care of themselves, I would rather it were for their own sake, than under pretense of preventing them from impairing their capacity of rendering to society benefits which society does not pretend it has a right to exact. But I cannot consent to argue the point as if society had no means of bringing its weaker members up to its ordinary standard of rational conduct, except waiting till they do something irrational, and then punishing them, legally or morally, for it. Society has had absolute power over them during all the early portion of their existence: it has had the whole period of childhood and nonage in which to try whether it could make them capable of rational conduct in life. The existing generation is master both of the training and the entire circumstances of the generation to come; it cannot indeed make them perfectly wise and good, because it is itself so lamentably deficient in goodness and wisdom; and its best efforts are not always, in individual cases, its most successful ones; but it is perfectly well able to make the rising generation, as a whole, as good as, and a little better than, itself. If society lets any considerable number of its members grow up mere children, incapable of being acted on by rational consideration of distant motives, society has itself to blame for the consequences. . . .

But the strongest of all the arguments against the interference of the public with purely personal conduct, is that when it does interfere, the odds are that it interferes wrongly, and in the wrong place. On questions of social morality, of duty to others, the opinion of the public, that is, of an overruling majority, though often wrong, is likely to be still oftener right; because on such questions they are only required to judge of their own interests; of the manner in which some mode of conduct, if allowed to be practiced, would affect themselves. But the opinion of a similar majority, imposed as a law on the minority, on questions of self-regarding conduct, is quite as likely to be wrong as right; for in these cases public opinion means, at the best, some people's opinion of what is good or bad for other people; while very often it does not even mean that; the public, with the most perfect indifference, passing over the pleasure or convenience of those whose conduct they censure, and considering only their own preference. There are many who consider as an injury to themselves any conduct which they have a distaste for, and resent it as an outrage to their feelings; as a religious bigot, when charged with disregarding the religious feelings of others, has been known to retort that they disregard his feelings, by persisting in their abominable worship or creed. But there is no parity between the feeling of a person for his own opinion, and the feeling of another who is offended at his holding it; no more than between the desire of a thief to take a purse, and the desire of the right owner to keep it. And a person's taste is as much his own peculiar concern as his opinion or his purse.

ROBERT NOZICK

The Entitlement Theory

ROBERT NOZICK *teaches philosophy at Harvard University.*

THE subject of justice in holdings consists of three major topics. The first is the *original acquisition of holdings*, the appropriation of unheld things. This includes the issues of how unheld things may come to be held, the process, or processes, by which unheld things may come to be held, the things that may come to be held by these processes, the extent of what comes to be held by a particular process, and so on. We shall refer to the complicated truth about this topic, which we shall not formulate here, as the principle of justice in acquisition. The second topic concerns the *transfer of holdings* from one person to another. By what processes may a person transfer holdings to another? How may a person acquire a holding from another who holds it? Under this topic come general descriptions of voluntary exchange, and gift and (on the other hand) fraud, as well as reference to particular conventional details fixed upon in a given society. The complicated truth about this subject (with placeholders for conventional details) we shall call the principle of justice in transfer. (And we shall suppose it also includes principles governing how a person may divest himself of a holding, passing it into an unheld state.)

If the world were wholly just, the following inductive definition would exhaustively cover the subject of justice in holdings.

1.   A person who acquires a holding in accordance with the principle of justice in acquisition is entitled to that holding.

2.   A person who acquires a holding in accordance with the principle of justice in transfer, from someone else entitled to the holding, is entitled to the holding.

3.   No one is entitled to a holding except by (repeated) applications of 1 and 2.

The complete principle of distributive justice would say simply that a distribution is just if everyone is entitled to the holdings they possess under the distribution.

A distribution is just if it arises from another just distribution by legitimate means. The legitimate means of moving from one distribution to another are specified by the principle of justice in transfer. The legitimate first "moves" are specified by the principle of justice in acquisition. Whatever arises from a just situation by just steps is itself just. The means of change specified by the principle of justice in transfer preserve justice. As correct rules of inference are truth-preserving, and any conclusion deduced via repeated application of such rules from only true premises is itself true, so the means of transition from one situation to another specified by the principle of justice in transfer are justice-preserving, and any situation actually arising from repeated transitions in accordance with the principle from a just situation is itself just. The parallel between justice-preserving transformations and truth-preserving transformations illuminates where it fails as well as where it holds. That a conclusion could have been deduced by truth-preserving means from premises that are true suffices to show its truth. That from a just situation a situation *could* have arisen via justice-preserving means does *not* suffice to show its justice. The fact that a thief's victims voluntarily *could* have presented him with gifts does not entitle the thief to his ill-gotten gains. Justice in holdings is historical; it depends upon what actually has happened. We shall return to this point later.

Not all actual situations are generated in accordance with the two principles of justice in holdings: the principle of justice in acquisition and the principle of justice in transfer. Some people steal from others, or defraud them, or enslave them, seizing their product and preventing them from living as they choose, or forcibly exclude others from competing in exchanges. None of these are permissible modes of transition from one situation to another. And some persons acquire holdings by means not sanctioned by the principle of justice in acquisition. The existence of past injustice (previous violations of the first two principles of justice in holdings) raises the third major topic under justice in holdings: the rectification of injustice in holdings. If past injustice has shaped present holdings in various ways, some identifiable and some not, what now, if anything, ought to be done to rectify these injustices? What obligations do the performers of injustice have toward those whose position is worse than it would have been had the injustice not been done? Or, than it would have been had compensation been paid promptly? How, if at all, do things change if the beneficiaries and those made worse off are not the direct parties in the act of injustice, but, for example, their descendants? Is an injustice done to someone whose holding was itself based upon an unrectified injustice? How far back must one go in wiping clean the historical slate of injustices? What may victims of in-

justice permissibly do in order to rectify the injustices being done to them, including the many injustices done by persons acting through their government? I do not know of a thorough or theoretically sophisticated treatment of such issues. Idealizing greatly, let us suppose theoretical investigation will produce a principle of rectification. This principle uses historical information about previous situations and injustices done in them (as defined by the first two principles of justice and rights against interference), and information about the actual course of events that flowed from these injustices, until the present, and it yields a description (or descriptions) of holdings in the society. The principle of rectification presumably will make use of its best estimate of subjunctive information about what would have occurred (or a probability distribution over what might have occurred, using the expected value) if the injustice had not taken place. If the actual description of holdings turns out not to be one of the descriptions yielded by the principle, then one of the descriptions yielded must be realized.

The general outlines of the theory of justice in holdings are that the holdings of a person are just if he is entitled to them by the principles of justice in acquisition and transfer, or by the principle of rectification of injustice (as specified by the first two principles). If each person's holdings are just, then the total set (distribution) of holdings is just.

Historical Principles and End-Result Principles

The general outlines of the entitlement theory illuminate the nature and defects of other conceptions of distributive justice. The entitlement theory of justice in distribution is *historical*; whether a distribution is just depends upon how it came about. In contrast, *current time-slice principles* of justice hold that the justice of a distribution is determined by how things are distributed (who has what) as judged by some *structural* principle(s) of just distribution. A utilitarian who judges between any two distributions by seeing which has the greater sum of utility and, if the sums tie, applies some fixed equality criterion to choose the more equal distribution, would hold a current time-slice principle of justice. As would someone who had a fixed schedule of trade-offs between the sum of happiness and equality. According to a current time-slice principle, all that needs to be looked at, in judging the justice of a distribution, is who ends up with what; in comparing any two distributions one need look only at the matrix presenting the distributions. No further information need be fed into a principle of justice. It is a consequence of such principles of justice that any two structurally identical distributions are equally just. (Two distributions are structurally identical if they present the same profile, but perhaps have different persons occupying the particular slots. My having ten and your having five, and my having five and your having ten are structurally identical distributions.) Welfare economics is the theory of current time-slice principles of justice. The subject is conceived as operating on matrices representing only current information about distribution. This, as well as some of the usual conditions (for example, the choice of distribution is invariant under relabeling of columns), guarantees that welfare economics will be a current time-slice theory, with all of its inadequacies.

Most persons do not accept current time-slice principles as constituting the whole story about distributive shares. They think it relevant in assessing the justice of a situation to consider not only the distribution it embodies, but also how that distribution came about. If some persons are in prison for murder or war crimes, we do not say that to assess the justice of the distribution in the society we must look only at what this person has, and that person has, and that person has, . . . at the current time. We think it relevant to ask whether someone did something so that he *deserved* to be punished, deserved to have a lower share. Most will agree to the relevance of further information with regard to punishments and penalties. Consider also desired things. One traditional socialist view is that workers are entitled to the product and full fruits of their labor; they have earned it; a distribution is unjust if it does not give the workers what they are entitled to. Such entitlements are based upon some past history. No socialist holding this view would find it comforting to be told that because the actual distribution *A* happens to coincide structurally with the one he desires *D*, *A* therefore is no less just than *D*; it differs only in that the "parasitic" owners of capital receive under *A* what the workers are entitled to under *D*, and the workers receive under *A* what the owners are entitled to under *D*, namely very little. This socialist rightly, in my view, holds onto the notions of earning, producing, entitlement, desert, and so forth, and he rejects current time-slice principles that look only to the structure of the resulting set of holdings. (The set of holdings resulting from what? Isn't it implausible that how holdings are produced and come to exist has no effect at all on who should hold what?) His mistake lies in his view of what entitlements arise out of what sorts of productive processes.

We construe the position we discuss too narrowly by speaking of *current* time-slice principles. Nothing is changed if structural principles operate upon a time sequence of current time-slice profiles and, for example, give someone more now to counterbalance the less he has had earlier. A utilitarian or an egalitarian or any mixture of the two over time will inherit the difficulties of his more myopic comrades. He is not helped by the fact that *some* of the information others consider relevant in assessing a distribution is reflected, unrecoverably, in past matrices. Henceforth, we shall refer to such unhistorical principles of distributive justice, including the current time-slice principles, as *end-result principles* or *end-state principles*.

In contrast to end-result principles of justice, *historical principles* of justice hold that past circumstances or actions of people can create differential entitlements or differential deserts to things. An injustice can be worked by moving from one distribution to another structurally identical one, for the second, in profile the same, may violate people's entitlements or deserts; it may not fit the actual history. . . .

To think that the task of a theory of distributive justice is to fill in the blank in "to each according to his _____" is to be predisposed to search for a pattern; and the separate treatment of "from each according to his _____" treats production and distribution as two separate and independent issues. On an entitlement view these are *not* two separate questions. Whoever makes something, having bought or contracted for all other held resources used in the process (transferring some of his holdings for these cooperating factors), is entitled to it. The situation is *not* one of something's getting made, and there being an open question of who is to get it. Things come into the world already attached to people having entitlements over them. From the point of view of the historical entitlement conception of justice in holdings, those who start afresh to complete "to each according to his _____" treat objects as if they appeared from nowhere, out of nothing. A complete theory of justice might cover this limit case as well; perhaps here is a use for the usual conceptions of distributive justice.

So entrenched are maxims of the usual form that perhaps we should present the entitlement conception as a competitor. Ignoring acquisition and rectification, we might say:

> From each according to what he chooses to do, to each according to what he makes for himself (perhaps with the contracted aid of others) and what others choose to do for him and choose to give him of what they've been given previously (under this maxim) and haven't yet expended or transferred.

This, the discerning reader will have noticed, has its defects as a slogan. So as a summary and great simplification (and not as a maxim with any independent meaning) we have:

> *From each as they choose, to each as they are chosen.*

JOHN RAWLS

Justice as Fairness

JOHN RAWLS *teaches philosophy at Harvard University and is the author of*
A Theory of Justice *(1971).*

THE conception of justice which I want to develop may be stated in the form of two principles as follows: first, each person participating in a practice, or affected by it, has an equal right to the most extensive liberty compatible with a like liberty for all; and second, inequalities are arbitrary unless it is reasonable to expect that they will work out for everyone's advantage, and provided the positions and offices to which they attach, or from which they may be gained, are open to all. These principles express justice as a complex of three ideas: liberty, equality, and reward for services contributing to the common good.

The term "person" is to be construed variously depending on the circumstances. On some occasions it will mean human individuals, but in others it may refer to nations, provinces, business firms, churches, teams, and so on. The principles of justice apply in all these instances, although there is a certain logical priority to the case of human individuals. As I shall use the term "person," it will be ambiguous in the manner indicated.

The first principle holds, of course, only if other things are equal: that is, while there must always be a justification for departing from the initial position of equal liberty (which is defined by the pattern of rights and duties, powers and liabilities, established by a practice), and the burden of proof is placed on him who would depart from it, nevertheless, there can be, and often there is, a justification for doing so. Now, that similar particular cases, as defined by a practice, should be treated similarly as they arise, is part of the very concept of a practice; it is involved in the notion of an activity in accordance with rules. The first principle expresses an analogous conception, but as applied to the structure of practices themselves. It holds, for example, that there is a presumption against the distinctions and classifications made by legal systems and other practices to the extent that they infringe on the original and equal liberty of the persons participating in them. The second principle defines how this presumption may be rebutted.

It might be argued at this point that justice requires only an equal liberty. If, however, a greater liberty were possible for all without loss or conflict, then it would be irrational to settle on a lesser liberty. There is no reason for circumscribing rights unless their exercise would be incompatible, or would render the practice defining them less effective. Therefore no serious distortion of the concept of justice is likely to follow from including within it the concept of the greatest equal liberty.

The second principle defines what sorts of inequalities are permissible; it specifies how the presumption laid down by the first principle may be put aside. Now by inequalities it is best to understand not *any* differences between offices and positions, but differences in the benefits and burdens attached to them either directly or indirectly, such as prestige and wealth, or liability to taxation and compulsory services. Players in a game do not protest against there being different positions, such as batter, pitcher, catcher, and the like, nor to there being various privileges and powers as specified by the rules; nor do the citizens of a country object to there being the different offices of government such as president, senator, governor, judge, and so on, each with their special rights and duties. It is not differences of this kind that are normally thought of as inequalities, but differences in the resulting distribution established by a practice, or made possible by it, of the things men strive to attain or avoid. Thus they may complain about the pattern of honors and rewards set up by a practice (e.g., the privileges and salaries of government officials) or they may object to the distribution of power and wealth which results from the various ways in which men avail themselves of the opportunities allowed by it (e.g., the concentration of wealth which may develop in a free price system allowing large entrepreneurial or speculative gains).

It should be noted that the second principle holds that an inequality is allowed only if there is reason to believe that the practice with the inequality, or resulting in it, will work for the advantage of *every* party engaging in it. Here it is important to stress that *every* party must gain from the inequality. Since the principle applies to practices, it implies that the representative man in every office or position defined by a practice, when he views it as a going concern, must find it reasonable to prefer his condition and prospects with the inequality to what they would be under the practice without it. The principle excludes, therefore, the justification of inequalities on the grounds that the disadvantages of those in one position are outweighed by the greater advantages of those in another position. This rather sim-

ple restriction is the main modification I wish to make in the utilitarian principle as usually understood. . . .

Further, it is also necessary that the various offices to which special benefits or burdens attach are open to all. It may be, for example, to the common advantage, as just defined, to attach special benefits to certain offices. Perhaps by doing so the requisite talent can be attracted to them and encouraged to give its best efforts. But any offices having special benefits must be won in a fair competition in which contestants are judged on their merits. If some offices were not open, those excluded would normally be justified in feeling unjustly treated, even if they benefited from the greater efforts of those who were allowed to compete for them. Now if one can assume that offices are open, it is necessary only to consider the design of practices themselves and how they jointly, as a system, work together. It will be a mistake to focus attention on the varying relative positions of particular persons, who may be known to us by their proper names, and to require that each such change, as a once for all transaction viewed in isolation, must be in itself just. It is the system of practices which is to be judged, and judged from the general point of view: unless one is prepared to criticize it from the standpoint of a representative man holding some particular office, one has no complaint against it.

•   •   •

Imagine a society of persons amongst whom a certain system of practices is *already* well established. Now suppose that by and large they are mutually self-interested; their allegiance to their established practices is normally founded on the prospect of self-advantage. One need not assume that, in all senses of the term "person," the persons in this society are mutually self-interested. If the characterization as mutually self-interested applies when the line of division is the family, it may still be true that members of families are bound by ties of sentiment and affection and willingly acknowledge duties in contradiction to self-interest. Mutual self-interestedness in the relations between families, nations, churches, and the like, is commonly associated with intense loyalty and devotion on the part of individual members. Therefore, one can form a more realistic conception of this society if one thinks of it as consisting of mutually self-interested families, or some other association. Further, it is not necessary to suppose that these persons are mutually self-interested under all circumstances, but only in the usual situations in which they participate in their common practices.

Now suppose also that these persons are rational: they know their own interests more or less accurately; they are capable of tracing out the likely consequences of adopting one practice rather than another; they are capable of adhering to a course of action once they have decided upon it; they can resist present temptations and the enticements of immediate gain; and the bare knowledge or perception of the difference between their condition and that of others is not, within certain limits and in itself, a source of great dissatisfaction. Only the last point adds anything to the usual definition of rationality. This definition should allow, I think, for the idea that a rational man would not be greatly downcast from knowing, or seeing, that others are in a better position than himself, unless he thought their being so was the result of injustice, or the consequence of letting chance work itself out for no useful common purpose, and so on. So if these persons strike us as unpleasantly egoistic, they are at least free in some degree from the fault of envy.

Finally, assume that these persons have roughly similar needs and interests, or needs and interests in various ways complementary, so that fruitful cooperation amongst them is possible; and suppose that they are sufficiently equal in power and ability to guarantee that in normal circumstances none is able to dominate the others. This condition (as well as the others) may seem excessively vague; but in view of the conception of justice to which the argument leads, there seems no reason for making it more exact here.

Since these persons are conceived as engaging in their common practices, which are already established, there is no question of our supposing them to come together to deliberate as to how they will set these practices up for the first time. Yet we can imagine that from time to time they discuss with one another whether any of them has a legitimate complaint against their established institutions. Such discussions are perfectly natural in any normal society. Now suppose that they have settled on doing this in the following way. They first try to arrive at the principles by which complaints, and so practices themselves, are to be judged. Their procedure for this is to let each person propose the principles upon which he wishes his complaints to be tried with the understanding that, if acknowledged, the complaints of others will be similarly tried, and that no complaints will be heard at all until everyone is roughly of one mind as to how complaints are to be judged. They each understand further that the principles proposed and acknowledged on this occasion are binding on future occasions. Thus each will be wary of proposing a principle which would give him a peculiar advantage, in his present circumstances, supposing it to be accepted. Each person knows that he will be bound by it in future circumstances the peculiarities of which cannot be known, and which might well be such that the principle is then to his disadvantage. The idea is that everyone should be required to make *in advance* a firm commitment, which others also may reasonably be expected to make, and that no one be given the opportunity to tailor the canons of a legitimate complaint to fit his own special condition, and then to discard them when they no longer suit his purpose. Hence each person will propose principles of a general kind which will, to a large degree, gain their sense from the various applications to be made of them, the particular circumstances of which being as yet unknown. These principles will express the conditions in accordance with which each is the least unwilling to have his interests limited in the design of practices, given the competing interests of the others, on the supposition that the interests of others will be limited likewise. The restrictions which would so arise might be thought of as those a person would keep in mind if he were designing a practice in which his enemy were to assign him his place.

·   ·   ·

The two parts of the foregoing account are intended to mirror the kinds of circumstances in which questions of justice arise and the constraints which having a morality would impose upon persons so situated. In this way one can see how the acceptance of the principles of justice might come about, for given all these conditions as described, it would be natural

if the two principles of justice were to be acknowledged. Since there is no way for anyone to win special advantages for himself, each might consider it reasonable to acknowledge equality as an initial principle. There is, however, no reason why they should regard this position as final, for if there are inequalities which satisfy the second principle, the immediate gain which equality would allow can be considered as intelligently invested in view of its future return. If, as is quite likely, these inequalities work as incentives to draw out better efforts, the members of this society may look upon them as concessions to human nature: they, like us, may think that people ideally should want to serve one another. But as they are mutually self-interested, their acceptance of these inequalities is merely the acceptance of the relations in which they actually stand, and a recognition of the motives which lead them to engage in their common practices. *They* have no title to complain of one another. And so provided that the conditions of the principle are met, there is no reason why they should not allow such inequalities. Indeed, it would be short-sighted of them to do so, and could result, in most cases, only from their being dejected by the bare knowledge, or perception, that others are better situated. Each person will, however, insist on an advantage to himself, and so on a common advantage, for none is willing to sacrifice anything for the others.

These remarks are not offered as a proof that persons so conceived and circumstanced would settle on the two principles, but only to show that these principles could have such a background, and so can be viewed as those principles which mutually self-interested and rational persons, when similarly situated and required to make in advance a firm commitment, could acknowledge as restrictions governing the assignment of rights and duties in their common practices, and thereby accept as limiting their rights against one another. The principles of justice may, then, be regarded as those principles which arise when the constraints of having a morality are imposed upon parties in the typical circumstances of justice.

.   .   .

A practice is just or fair, then, when it satisfies the principles which those who participate in it could propose to one another for mutual acceptance under the afore-mentioned circumstances. Persons engaged in a just, or fair, practice can face one another openly and support their respective positions, should they appear questionable, by reference to principles which it is reasonable to expect each to accept.

It is this notion of the possibility of mutual acknowledgment of principles by free persons who have no authority over one another which makes the concept of fairness fundamental to justice. Only if such acknowledgment is possible can there be true community between persons in their common practices; otherwise their relations will appear in them as founded to some extent on force.

.   .   .

Now if the participants in a practice accept its rules as fair, and so have no complaint to lodge against it, there arises a prima facie duty (and a corresponding prima facie right) of the parties to each other to act in accordance with the prac-tice when it falls upon them to comply. When any number of persons engage in a practice, or conduct a joint undertaking according to rules, and thus restrict their liberty, those who have submitted to these restrictions when required have the right to a similar acquiescence on the part of those who have benefited by their submission. These conditions will obtain if a practice is correctly acknowledged to be fair, for in this case all who participate in it will benefit from it. The rights and duties so arising are special rights and duties in that they depend on previous actions voluntarily undertaken, in this case on the parties having engaged in a common practice and knowingly accepted its benefits. It is not, however, an obligation which presupposes a deliberate performative act in the sense of a promise, or contract, and the like. . . .

It is sufficient that one has knowingly participated in and accepted the benefits of a practice acknowledged to be fair. This prima facie obligation may, of course, be overridden: it may happen, when it comes one's turn to follow a rule, that other considerations will justify not doing so. But one cannot, in general, be released from this obligation by denying the justice of the practice only when it falls on one to obey. If a person rejects a practice, he should, so far as possible, declare his intention in advance, and avoid participating in it or enjoying its benefits.

This duty I have called that of fair play, but it should be admitted that to refer to it in this way is, perhaps, to extend the ordinary notion of fairness. Usually acting unfairly is not so much the breaking of any particular rule, even if the infraction is difficult to detect (cheating), but taking advantage of loop-holes or ambiguities in rules, availing oneself of unexpected or special circumstances which make it impossible to enforce them, insisting that rules be enforced to one's advantage when they should be suspended, and more generally, acting contrary to the intention of a practice. It is for this reason that one speaks of the sense of fair play: acting fairly requires more than simply being able to follow rules; what is fair must often be felt, or perceived, one wants to say. It is not, however, an unnatural extension of the duty of fair play to have it include the obligation which participants who have knowingly accepted the benefits of their common practice owe to each other to act in accordance with it when their performance falls due; for it is usu-ally considered unfair if someone accepts the benefits of a practice but refuses to do his part in maintaining it. Thus one might say of the tax-dodger that he violates the duty of fair play: he accepts the benefits of government but will not do his part in releasing resources to it; and members of labor unions often say that fellow workers who refuse to join are being unfair: they refer to them as "free riders," as persons who enjoy what are the supposed benefits of unionism, higher wages, shorter hours, job security, and the like, but who refuse to share in its burdens in the form of pay-ing dues, and so on.

JOEL FEINBERG

The Nature and Value of Rights

JOEL FEINBERG *teaches philosophy at the University of Arizona. He has written extensively in ethics, philosophy of law, and social philosophy.*

I would like to begin by conducting a thought experiment. Try to imagine Nowheresville — a world very much like our own except that no one, or hardly any one (the qualification is not important), has *rights*. If this flaw makes No-wheresville too ugly to hold very long in contemplation, we can make it as pretty as we wish in other moral respects. We can, for example, make the human beings in it as attractive and virtuous as possible without taxing our conceptions of the limits of human nature. In particular, let the virtues of moral sensibility flourish. Fill this imagined world with as much benev-olence, compassion, sympathy, and pity as it will conveniently hold without strain. Now we can imagine men helping one another from compassionate motives merely, quite as much or even more than they do in our actual world from a variety of more complicated motives.

This picture, pleasant as it is in some respects, would hardly have satisfied Im-manuel Kant. Benevolently motivated actions do good, Kant admitted, and therefore are better, *ceteris paribus*, than malevolently motivated actions; but no ac-tion can have supreme kind of worth — what Kant called "moral worth" — unless its whole motivating power derives from the thought that it is *required by duty*.

Accordingly, let us try to make Nowheresville more appealing to Kant by introducing the idea of duty into it, and letting the sense of duty be a sufficient motive for many beneficent and honorable actions. But doesn't this bring our original thought experiment to an abortive conclusion? If duties are permitted entry into Nowheresville, are not rights necessarily smuggled in along with them?

The question is well-asked, and requires here a brief digression so that we might consider the so-called "doctrine of the logical correlativity of rights and duties." This is the doctrine that (i) all duties entail other people's rights and (ii) all rights entail other people's duties. Only the first part of the doctrine, the alleged entailment from duties to rights, need concern us here. Is this part of the doctrine correct? It should not be surprising that my answer is: "In a sense yes and in a sense no." Etymologically, the word "duty" is associated with actions that are *due* someone else, the payments of debts *to* creditors, the keeping of agreements with promisees, the payment of club dues, or legal fees, or tariff levies to appropriate authorities or their representatives. In this original sense of "duty," all duties are correlated with the rights of those *to* whom the duty is owed. On the other hand, there seem to be numerous classes of duties, both of a legal and non-legal kind, that are *not* logically correlated with the rights of other persons. This seems to be a consequence of the fact that the word "duty" has come to be used for *any* action understood to be *required*, whether by the rights of others, or by law, or by higher authority, or by conscience, or whatever. When the notion of requirement is in clear focus it is likely to seem the only element in the idea of duty that is essential, and the other component notion — that a duty

is something *due* someone else — drops off. Thus, in this widespread but derivative usage, "duty" tends to be used for any action we feel we *must* (for whatever reason) do. It comes, in short, to be a term of moral modality merely; and it is no wonder that the first thesis of the logical correlativity doctrine often fails.

Let us then introduce duties into Nowheresville, but only in the sense of actions that are, or are believed to be, morally mandatory, but not in the older sense of actions that are due others and can be claimed by others as their right. Nowheresville now can have duties of the sort imposed by positive law. A legal duty is not something we are implored or advised to do merely; it is something the law, or an authority under the law, *requires* us to do whether we want to or not, under pain of penalty. When traffic lights turn red, however, there is no determinate person who can plausibly be said to claim our stopping as his due, so that the motorist owes it to *him* to stop, in the way a debtor owes it to his creditor to pay. In our own actual world, of course, we sometimes owe it to our *fellow motorists* to stop; but that kind of right-correlated duty does not exist in Nowheresville. There, motorists "owe" obedience to the Law, but they owe nothing to one another. When they collide, no matter who is at fault, no one is morally accountable to anyone else, and no one has any sound grievance or "right to complain."

When we leave legal contexts to consider moral obligations and other extra-legal duties, a greater variety of duties-without-correlative-rights present themselves. Duties of charity, for example, require us to contribute to one or another of a large number of eligible recipients, no one of whom can claim our contribution from us as his due. Charitable contributions are more like gratuitous services, favors, and gifts than like repayments of debts or reparations; and yet we do have duties to be charitable. Many persons, moreover, in our actual world believe that they are required by their own consciences to do more than that "duty" that *can* be demanded of them by their prospective beneficiaries. I have quoted elsewhere the citation from H. B. Acton of a character in a Malraux novel who "gave all his supply of poison to his fellow prisoners to enable them by suicide to escape the burning alive which was to be their fate and his." This man, Acton adds, "probably did not think that [the others] had more of a right to the poison than he had, though he thought it his duty to give it to them." I am sure that there are many actual examples, less dramatically heroic than this fictitious one, of persons who believe, rightly or wrongly, that they *must do* something (hence the word "duty") for another person in excess of what that person can appropriately demand of him (hence the absence of "right").

Now the digression is over and we can return to Nowheresville and summarize what we have put in it thus far. We now find spontaneous benevolence in somewhat larger degree than in our actual world, and also the acknowledged existence of duties of obedience, duties of charity, and duties imposed by exacting private consciences, and also, let us suppose, a degree of conscientiousness in respect to those duties somewhat in excess of what is to be found in our actual world. I doubt that Kant would be fully satisfied with Nowheresville even now that duty and respect for law and authority have been added to it; but I feel certain that he would regard their addition at least as an improvement. I will now introduce two further moral practices into Nowheres-

ville that will make that world very little more appealing to Kant, but will make it appear more familiar to us. These are the practices connected with the notions of *personal desert* and what I call a *sovereign monopoly of rights*.

When a person is said to deserve something good from us what is meant in part is that there would be a certain propriety in our giving that good thing to him in virtue of the kind of person he is, perhaps, or more likely, in virtue of some specific thing he has done. The propriety involved here is a much weaker kind than that which derives from our having promised him the good thing or from his having qualified for it by satisfying the well-advertised conditions of some public rule. In the latter case he could be said not merely to deserve the good thing but also to have a *right* to it, that is to be in a position to demand it as his due; and of course we will not have that sort of thing in Nowheresville. That weaker kind of propriety which is mere desert is simply a kind of *fittingness* between one party's character or action and another party's favorable response, much like that between humor and laughter, or good performance and applause.

The following seems to be the origin of the idea of deserving good or bad treatment from others: A master or lord was under no obligation to reward his servant for especially good service; still a master might naturally feel that there would be a special fittingness in giving a gratuitous reward as a grateful response to the good service (or conversely imposing a penalty for bad service). Such an act while surely fitting and proper was entirely supererogatory. The fitting response in turn from the rewarded servant should be gratitude. If the deserved reward had not been given him he should have had no complaint, since he only *deserved* the reward, as opposed to having a *right* to it, or a ground for claiming it as his due.

The idea of desert has evolved a good bit away from its beginnings by now, but nevertheless, it seems clearly to be one of those words J. L. Austin said "never entirely forget their pasts." Today servants qualify for their wages by doing their agreed upon chores, no more and no less. If their wages are not forthcoming, their contractual rights have been violated and they can make legal claim to the money that is their due. If they do less than they agreed to do, however, their employers may "dock" them, by paying them proportionately less than the agreed upon fee. This is all a matter of right. But if the servant does a splendid job, above and beyond his minimal contractual duties, the employer is under no further obligation to reward him, for this was not agreed upon, even tacitly, in advance. The additional service was all the servant's idea and done entirely on his own. Nevertheless, the morally sensitive employer may feel that it would be exceptionally appropriate for him to respond, freely on *his* own, to the servant's meritorious service, with a reward. The employee cannot demand it as his due, but he will happily accept it, with gratitude, as a fitting response to his desert.

In our age of organized labor, even this picture is now archaic; for almost every kind of exchange of service is governed by hard bargained contracts so that even bonuses can sometimes be demanded as a matter of right, and nothing is given for nothing on either side of the bargaining table. And perhaps that is a good thing; for consider an anachronistic instance of the earlier kind of practice that survives, at least as a matter of form, in the quaint old practice of "tipping." The tip was

originally conceived as a reward that has to be earned by "zealous service." It is not something to be taken for granted as a standard response to *any* service. That is to say that its payment is a "*gratuity*," not a discharge of obligation, but something given apart from, or in addition to, anything the recipient can expect as a matter of right. That is what tipping originally meant at any rate, and tips are still referred to as "gratuities" in the tax forms. But try to explain all that to a New York cab driver! If he has *earned* his gratuity, by God, he has it coming, and there had better be sufficient acknowledgment of his desert or he'll give you a piece of his mind! I'm not generally prone to defend New York cab drivers, but they do have a point here. There is the making of a paradox in the queerly unstable concept of an "earned gratuity." One can understand how "desert" in the weak sense of "propriety" or "mere fittingness" tends to generate a stronger sense in which desert is itself the ground for a claim of right.

In Nowheresville, nevertheless, we will have only the original weak kind of desert. Indeed, it will be impossible to keep this idea out if we allow such practices as teachers grading students, judges awarding prizes, and servants serving benevolent but class-conscious masters. Nowheresville is a reasonably good world in many ways, and its teachers, judges, and masters will generally try to give students, contestants, and servants the grades, prizes, and rewards they deserve. For this the recipients will be grateful; but they will never think to complain, or even feel aggrieved, when expected responses to desert fail. The masters, judges, and teachers don't *have* to do good things, after all, for *anyone*. One should be happy that they *ever* treat us well, and not grumble over their occasional lapses. Their hoped for responses, after all, are *gratuities*, and there is no wrong in the omission of what is merely gratuitous. Such is the response of persons who have no concept of *rights*, even persons who are proud of their own deserts.

Surely, one might ask, rights have to come in somewhere, if we are to have even moderately complex forms of social organization. Without rules that confer rights and impose obligations, how can we have ownership of property, bargains and deals, promises and contracts, appointments and loans, marriages and partnerships? Very well, let us introduce all of these social and economic practices into Nowheresville, but *with one big twist*. With them I should like to introduce the curious notion of a "sovereign right-monopoly." You will recall that the subjects in Hobbes's *Leviathan* had no rights whatever against their sovereign. He could do as he liked with them, even gratuitously harm them, but this gave them no valid grievance against him. The sovereign, to be sure, had a certain duty to treat his subjects well, but this duty was owed not to the subjects directly, but to God, just as we might have a duty to a person to treat his property well, but of course no duty to the property itself but only to its owner. Thus, while the sovereign was quite capable of *harming* his subjects, he could commit no wrong against them that they could complain about, since they had no prior claims against his conduct. The only party *wronged* by the sovereign's mistreatment of his subjects was God, the supreme lawmaker. Thus, in repenting cruelty to his subjects, the sovereign might say to God, as David did after killing Uriah, "to Thee only have I sinned."

Even in the *Leviathan*, however, ordinary people had ordinary rights *against one another*. They played roles, occupied offices, made agreements, and signed contracts. In a genuine "sovereign right-monopoly," as I shall be using that phrase, they will do all those things too, and thus incur genuine obligations toward one another; but the obligations (here is the twist) will not be owed directly *to* promisees, creditors, parents, and the like, but rather to God alone, or to the members of some elite, or to a single sovereign under God. Hence, the rights correlative to the obligations that derive from these transactions are all owned by some "outside" authority.

•   •   •

There will, of course, be delegated authorities in the imaginary world, empowered to give commands to their underlings and to punish them for their disobedience. But the commands are all given in the name of the right-monopoly who in turn are the only persons to whom obligations are owed. Hence, even intermediate superiors do not have claim-rights against their subordinates but only legal *powers* to create obligations in the subordinates *to* the monopolistic right-holders, and also the legal *privilege* to impose penalties in the name of that monopoly.

So much for the imaginary "world without rights." If some of the moral concepts and practices I have allowed into that world do not sit well with one another, no matter. Imagine Nowheresville with all of these practices if you can, or with any harmonious subset of them, if you prefer. The important thing is not what I've let into it, but what I have kept out. The remainder of this paper will be devoted to an analysis of what precisely a world is missing when it does not contain rights and why that absence is morally important.

The most conspicuous difference, I think, between the Nowheresvillians and ourselves has something to do with the activity of *claiming*. Nowheresvillians, even when they are discriminated against invidiously, or left without the things they need, or otherwise badly treated, do not think to leap to their feet and make righteous demands against one another, though they may not hesitate to resort to force and trickery to get what they want. They have no notion of rights, so they do not have a notion of what is their due; hence they do not claim before they take. The conceptual linkage between personal rights and claiming has long been noticed by legal writers and is reflected in the standard usage in which "claim-rights" are distinguished from the mere liberties, immunities, and powers, also sometimes called "rights," with which they are easily confused. When a person has a legal claim-right to X, it must be the case (i) that he is at liberty in respect to X, i.e., that he has no duty to refrain from or relinquish X, and also (ii) that his liberty is the ground of other people's *duties* to grant him X or not to interfere with him in respect to X. Thus, in the sense of claim-rights, it is true by definition that rights logically entail other people's duties. The paradigmatic examples of such rights are the creditor's right to be paid a debt by his debtor, and the landowner's right not to be interfered with by anyone in the exclusive occupancy of his land. The creditor's right against his debtor, for example, and the debtor's duty to his creditor, are precisely the same relation seen from two different vantage points, as inextricably linked as the two sides of the same coin.

•   •   •

A right *is* a kind of claim, and a claim is "an assertion of right," so that a formal definition of either notion in terms of the other will not get us very far. Thus if a "formal definition" of the usual philosophical sort is what we are after, the game is over before it has begun, and we can say that the concept of a right is a "simple, undefinable, unanalysable primitive." Here as elsewhere in philosophy this will have the effect of making the commonplace seem unnecessarily mysterious. We would be better advised, I think, not to attempt a formal definition of either "right" or "claim," but rather to use the idea of a claim in informal elucidation of the idea of a right. This is made possible by the fact that *claiming* is an elaborate sort of rule-governed *activity*. A claim is that which is claimed, the object of the act of claiming. There is, after all, a verb "to claim," but no verb "to right." If we concentrate on the whole activity of claiming, which is public, familiar, and open to our observation, rather than on its upshot alone, we may learn more about the generic nature of rights than we could ever hope to learn from a formal definition, even if one were possible. Moreover, certain facts about rights more easily, if not solely, expressible in the language of claims and claiming are essential to a full understanding not only of what rights are, but also why they are so vitally important.

•   •   •

Nearly all writers maintain that there is some intimate connection between having a claim and having a right. Some identify right and claim without qualification: some define "right" as justified or justifiable claim, others as recognized claim, still others as valid claim. My own preference is for the latter definition. Some writers, however, reject the identification of rights with valid claims on the ground that all claims as such are valid, so that the expression "valid claim" is redundant. These writers, therefore, would identify rights with claims *simpliciter*. But this is a very simple confusion. All claims, to be sure, are *put forward* as justified, whether they are justified in fact or not. A claim conceded even by its maker to have no validity is not a claim at all, but a mere demand. The highwayman, for example, *demands* his victim's money; but he hardly makes claim to it as rightfully his own.

But it does not follow from this sound point that it is redundant to qualify claims as justified (or as I prefer, valid) in the definition of a right; for it remains true that not all claims put forward as valid really are valid; and only the valid ones can be acknowledged as rights.

· · ·

Still, for all of that, I have a certain sympathy with the manifesto writers, and I am even willing to speak of a special "manifesto sense" of "right," in which a right need not be correlated with another's duty. Natural needs are real claims if only upon hypothetical future beings not yet in existence. I accept the moral principle that to have an unfulfilled need is to have a kind of claim against the world, even if against no one in particular. A natural need for some good as such, like a natural desert, is always a reason in support of a claim to that good. A person in need, then, is always "in a position" to make a claim, even when there is no one in the corresponding position to do anything about it. Such claims, based on need alone, are "permanent possibilities of rights," the natural seed from which rights grow. When manifesto writers speak of them as if already actual rights they are easily forgiven, for this is but a powerful way of expressing the conviction that they ought to be recognized by states here and now as potential rights and consequently as determinants of *present* aspirations and guides to *present* policies. That usage, I think, is a valid exercise of rhetorical licence.

I prefer to characterize rights as valid claims rather than justified ones, because I suspect that justification is rather too broad a qualification. "Validity," as I understand it, is justification of a peculiar and narrow kind, namely justification within a system of rules. A man has a legal right when the official recognition of his claim (as valid) is called for by the governing rules. This definition, of course, hardly applies to moral rights, but that is not because the genus of which moral rights are a species is something other than *claims*. A man has a moral right when he has a claim the recognition of which is called for—not (necessarily) by legal rules—but by moral principles, or the principles of an enlightened conscience.

· · ·

In brief conclusion: To have a right is to have a claim against someone whose recognition as valid is called for by some set of governing rules or moral principles. To have a *claim* in turn, is to have a case meriting consideration, that is, to have reasons or grounds that put one in a position to engage in performative and propositional claiming. The activity of claiming, finally, as much as any other thing, makes for self-respect and respect for others, gives a sense to the notion of personal dignity, and distinguishes this otherwise morally flawed world from the even worse world of Nowheresville.

AMARTYA SEN
The Right to Take Personal Risks

AMARTYA SEN *teaches economics at Harvard University. His recent publications in-clude* Commodities and Capabilities *(1985),* The Standard of Living *(1987), and* On Ethics and Economics *(1987). Sen has also conducted research on the role of rationality in social behavior.*

WHAT, then, are moral rights? These are rights that are intrinsically valuable, irrespective of whether they also have instrumental justification. There are at least two different ways of seeing moral rights. The constraint-based deontological way asserts that a person's moral rights impose constraints on what others may or may not do. If a person has a moral right to take a particular personal risk, then it would be morally wrong for anyone to stop him or her from taking that risk, no matter how good the consequences of stopping might be. "Individuals," as Robert Nozick puts it, "have rights, and there are things no person may do to them (without violating their rights)." Such "deontological rights" directly rule out certain actions, rather than being taken into account in the evaluation of states of affairs and then affecting actions through consequential links. In contrast, in the goal-based consequential view, moral rights *are* reflected in the evaluation of states of affairs—a right-fulfillment being favorable and a right-violation being unfavorable to the value of the state of affairs. Such "goal rights" influence actions through consequence-sensitive assessment. . . .

Goal rights can be characterized in several different ways. One particular view, which I have tried to explore elsewhere, is to see rights as "capabilities" — the capability to *do* this or that, or *be* this or that (such as free from hunger or free to move about). The failure to have such a capability, whether or not this is caused by the interference of others, makes the state of affairs worse, other things given. This fits into the general approach of valuing freedom *positively*. It contrasts with focusing on "negative freedom" — the right not to be prevented by others from doing things one can do. Negative freedom has been traditionally seen as imposing deontological constraints on others (stopping them from interfering), but if negative freedom, in the form of absence of interference, is *valued*, then it is natural to incorporate such freedom in a goal-rights system. This would imply attaching "disvalue" to interferences violating negative freedom. In assessing states of affairs, each agent should then have to consider the negative value of such interferences, and this applies not only to a person who may himself be interfering, but also to others whose actions could possibly prevent, or otherwise affect, such interferences.

Perhaps an example will help to bring out the contrasts involved. Consider the case in which person A bashes up person B. In the *deontological constraint formulation of negative freedom*, person A is asked not to do this, but other people, such as person C, are not asked to do anything at all in this context. In the *goal-rights formulation of negative freedom*, not only should A (the basher) take note of the disvalue of such violation of negative freedom, but so should others, such as C. A's violation of B's negative freedom in this view is a bad thing, and C may be required to consider what he can do to help stop this bad thing. . . .

Seat Belts and Other People

Take the issue of seat belts. A person, call him Hero, decides not to wear seat belts when driving and takes the additional risk of injury or death resulting from this courageous act. We have two immediate questions: (1) how important is this freedom for Hero's personal life and way of living? and (2) how are others affected?

On the first question, there is obviously quite a bit of person-to-person variation, but in most cases it probably is neither in itself a central concern nor a part of an important feature of one's life style. There are exceptions (I have heard some people — all Italian males, it so happens —

claim that going unbelted is indeed a matter of great personal importance), but they are relatively rare. Certainly, it will be difficult in this respect to compare the taking of risk involved in going unbelted with the taking of risk that a dedicated mountain climber deliberately chooses.

Insofar as most beltless drivers are beltless "simply to avoid bother," it is not clear that a moral right based on personal liberty is involved. But in refusing to accept the status of something as a moral right for members of a group, it is not enough to be sure that a majority of that group does not see anything of moment involved in the activity in question. The passionate involvement of a minority of the group cannot be ignored just because the majority sees things differently. It is possible that a minority group values a life style that includes going unbelted. In the decisions regarding regulations and rules, the numbers won't be irrelevant, but at this stage let us concede that possibly for a group, perhaps a relatively small group, going unbelted is important as a part of a life style, and that this makes it plausible to consider that a serious moral right might well be involved.

How are others affected? There are at least five different types of effects on others.

(1) *Injury effects*: It has been argued that a driver is in a better position to drive his car safely in case of minor accidents if he is wearing a seat belt, and thus the passengers benefit directly from the belting of the driver. Also, the belted passengers do not land on others, causing them injury. This may not be a common problem, but it obviously is of some relevance.

(2) *Psychological effects*: Other persons may possibly suffer from Hero's demise or injury, and the suffering might arise not only from sympathy for Hero but also from other causes: people might be

badly shocked and shaken by seeing a car crash and the resulting gore.

(3) *Opinion-offending effects*: Others, of more sedate temperament might disapprove of Hero's habit of going around without buckling his seat belt, and Hero's actions might well be offensive to them.

(4) *Medical effects*: Hero may need treatment when injured, and others may have to bear a part of the medical costs. Sometimes these might well be enormous.

(5) *Economic and social effects*: Hero's injury may affect his earning power and productivity, and a number of others might well be affected by these changes: members of Hero's family, the business in which Hero works, the public at large through the need to pay Hero Social Security benefits. Similarly, some people may be affected by social rather than economic links: friends losing someone to talk to, the local community losing a socially active member, children losing a loving parent.

Other possible effects are easy to think of, but let us confine ourselves to these. In this list of five different types of effects, only the third, the "opinion-offending effects," would involve an intrinsic conflict with Hero's moral right to go beltless as a part of his life style, since it is precisely that life style to which the others in question object. This is of course John Stuart Mill country. I have other issues to deal with, and so I choose not to pursue this particular question. I accept instead Mill's argument that the right to lead a particular type of life is not compromised by the existence of others who object to that life. I have pursued this issue elsewhere in essentially Millian lines, and the focus on risk in the pursuit of one's personal life does not alter the argument substantially.

It might be tempting to think that for similar reasons we must also ignore "psychological effects" in evaluating states of affairs. But this analogy does not hold. In asserting that one should ignore adverse opinion about a particular life style (in determining whether leading such a life can be a moral right), it was *not* also asserted that the suffering of those with an adverse opinion is morally irrelevant to the evaluation of states of affairs. It is indeed possible and plausible to take the view that given other things any suffering, no matter how caused, makes a state of affairs worse. The adverse opinion in question is intrinsically in conflict with the assertion of the right to lead such a life, and the Millian argument is primarily concerned with asserting the right despite that conflict. But when it comes to evaluating actions and rules by taking into account consequential links, the issue of whether or not to weigh the sufferings of others remains a separate question, requiring a treatment of its own. If all sufferings are accepted as disvaluable, then even the sufferings of the moral prig will come inter alia into the general evaluation.

This might look like a defeatist concession, through which authoritarianism might deeply compromise the exercise of liberty. In a system with trade-offs that possibility cannot indeed be fully ruled out, but three clarifying remarks are in order here. First, the alleged force of the position of "the guardians of public morality" does not rest on their personal disutilities (indeed, our "guardians" seem often enough to find much pleasure in fighting obscenity and such), but on the claim that the actions in question are intrinsically objectionable, or will in fact offend others "with good reason." The acceptance of the moral disvalue of any suffering thus does not amount at all to a concession to the authoritarian argument.

Second, to accept that any suffering is disvaluable (or that any pleasure is valuable) is not to limit all evaluations to computations of quantities of pleasure and pain. The latter is the prerogative of the utilitarian, and I am happy to leave him as the sole owner of that approach. What relative weights can be attached to suffering (and happiness) vis-à-vis other qualities of states of affairs remains an open question.

Third, even in weighing utilities vis-à-vis one another, one is not obliged to value them according to quantities only, and one can use differential weighting depending on the nonutility features associated with each case. Even Mill's utilitarianism — admittedly of a rather unusual kind — did not stop him from asserting that "there is no parity between the feeling of a person for his own opinion, and the feeling of another who is offended at his holding it."

The psychological effects on others might well be serious, and it would then be absurd to assert that the fulfillment of the moral right of an individual to take personal risks should invariably be judged more important than any suffering it might cause. The shocking experience of those who see someone's arm being chewed up by a tiger as he puts his hand into the cage might well be judged to be of greater disvalue than the violation of the person's right to put his hand in (if that is seen as a right in the first place). In other cases the balance may be seen as going the other way. One would certainly hesitate to give greater importance to the satisfaction of the "Jewish mother" than to the right of the adult son to diet if he so chooses.

The injury effects, the medical effects, and the economic and social effects typically arouse less suspicion than the psychological effects. If my driving without seat belts exposes you to greater danger of injury or death, or reduces your opportunities of getting medical attention, or harms you economically or socially, then it seems natural that these adverse effects must be weighed in the goal-rights system.

The sources of worry lie elsewhere. Three in particular may be taken up here. First, there is the problem of *robustness* of the right to take personal risks. This is a general worry about the nature of goal-rights systems. Since the acceptance of a moral right does not necessarily imply that the person having that right can do the thing he has a right to do, does this not make moral rights terribly flimsy? Do they have any bite at all? What sense does it make to say that we have a moral right to take personal risks, such as not to wear seat belts, and at the same time assert that it is morally appropriate to curb the exercise of that right, such as through seat-belt regulations? Hasn't the baby been thrown away with the bath water?

Second, there is the problem of *interactivity consistency*. If seat-belt wearing is made compulsory because of, say, the medical effects, then does this not threaten the right to undertake such activities as mountaineering? Might it not even compromise the right to drive a car (with or without seat belts), since driving also increases the chances of being injured and being in need of medical services?

Third, there is the problem of *interindividual sensitivity*. While the compulsory wearing of seat belts might be accepted to be more beneficial than harmful in most cases (taking into account all the effects, including the disvalue of violating a person's right to lead the kind of life he would like to lead), this would not be so in some cases, as when someone drives alone, has no dependents, and has private medical attention. Such a person's right might seem to require that he be exempted from the seat-belt regulations. And if no such concession can be made, then should one not see, on grounds of liberty, the seat-belt regulations as unacceptable? . . .

The constraint-based deontological formulation of moral rights has the great merit of simplicity: Either others are prohibited from doing certain things, or they are entirely free to do those things. Those who tend to think of rights in such all-or-nothing terms might feel that the framework of goal-rights does not give the robustness that is expected of rights. One should be able, it might be argued, to insist on one's rights come what may. Indeed, the familiar view of rights seems to demand an overwhelming, possibly irresistible, force, at least in some circumstances. The absence of such force might be seen as undermining the entire goal-rights approach and specifically the application of that approach to the right to take personal risks.

In taking up this question, I begin with a purely formal point. If irresistible force is sought, then that can be provided even *within* the goal-rights system by giving the fulfillment of the rights in question lexicographic priority over other goals. While goal-rights systems allow trade-offs, they also permit evaluations without trade-offs. I do not, however, intend to pursue this line further; one of the chief reasons for adopting the goal-rights approach is precisely the scope that it gives to the possibility of trade-offs.

Is it reasonable to expect that all moral rights must have irresistible force? Such a point of view immediately produces a problem of consistency, since conflicting rights cannot each have irresistible force. Your right not to be forced to wear seat belts might conflict with my right not to have you land on my shoulders at the touch of a brake. The problem is avoided either by formulating rights in such a way that they cannot possibly conflict (such as in terms of abstention from certain conscious actions), or by taking rights in the "everything considered" form, so that a right is not established until it wins, as it were, over all conflicting claims. The former procedure is very restrictive and permits only a narrow class of rights. The latter, if pursued fully, would make rights no more than "outputs" of moral arguments rather than being able to *influence* such arguments. Neither procedure is satisfactory. . . .

The apparent puzzles involving inter-activity consistency in the right to take risks arise from taking a nondiscriminating view of the role of rights in moral arguments. In the goal rights approach, which balances the pros and cons of restricting freedoms of different types, there is no general presumption that all cases with formal similarity would be assessed in the same way, since the assessment must go ultimately into the balancing of the relative weights of conflicting considerations. In terms of what is involved, seat-belt regulations are hardly comparable to prohibiting mountaineering or banning driving. . . .

What about Mahahero, the recluse millionaire whose taking of personal risks in not wearing seat belts would have little adverse effect on others and who, we assume, is bent on pursuing a life style involving beltless travel? Let us concede that to force him to be belted would involve a greater loss than gain from the moral point of view. Not only, like others, does he have the right to take personal risks, but that right in his case, unlike in those of others, is important when applied to beltless driving; and the adverse effects in his case, again unlike in those of others, are relatively tiny. There is a good case, then, for letting him go unbelted, if that can be done without the difference itself causing some adverse effects.

The rub, of course, is precisely there. It might be politically impossible to let our heroic recluse millionaire go unbelted while others are forced to belt up. Even if it is possible, it may be socially costly in terms causing resentment, misunderstanding, and *perceived* discrimination.

Suppose that a separate arrangement for Mahahero is not possible. What should be done then? In a "zero-one" system the barrier of Mahahero's personal right is of course hard to cross. But the goal-rights system permits trade-offs, and it is a question of interindividual balancing. The net disadvantage of violating Mahahero's right — a "winning" right if separate rules *were* costlessly possible — has to be compared with the net advantages, related to others, from enforcing seat-belt regulations.

So it is possible that *general* seat-belt regulations, applicable to all, are judged to be morally appropriate, and at the same time (1) everyone is acknowledged to have the moral right to take risks in these matters, and (2), furthermore, some people, such as Mahahero, have a moral right in this respect that outweighs the adverse effects of their not wearing seat belts. There is no real puzzle in this apparent oddity.

Concluding Remarks

Moral rights must be distinguished from rights with moral justification. If individual moral rights are admitted, it is difficult not to concede that people do have the moral right to take personal risks. The real issue, then, is not whether such rights exist, but how important they are vis-à-vis conflicting objectives.

The constraint-based deontological approach admits only all-conquering rights, although even there ad hoc compromises are made for the sake of plausibility. Such all-conquering rights lead to moral dilemmas that can be resolved only in a consequence-sensitive system with tradeoffs. The framework of goal-rights systems can provide systematic accounting of conflicting objectives to arrive at informed moral judgment.

In the goal-rights systems the fulfillment of the right to take personal risks can compete with other goals. Personal risks can rarely be taken without other important consequences. This fact does not in any way "cancel" the right to take personal risks, but it does make that right compete with other objectives. Much of this paper has been concerned with issues involved in the balancing of competing claims. The importance of the right to take risks varies with the nature of the activity involved. It also varies from person to person. Public decisions, such as seat-belt regulations, call for integrated assessment of pros and cons. In this calculus, rights do figure, but they are not irresistible: They win some and they lose some.

There are of course many apparent puzzles in attitudes toward the right to take personal risks, such as those involving interactivity consistency (between, say, beltless travel and mountaineering) or interindividual variation (between different roles of the same activity in the lives of different persons). These puzzles seem to arise from attempts to fit the right to take personal risks into a nondiscriminating framework. More room has to be made for sensitivity to different types of information. The notion of moral rights should help us to conduct informed moral arguments, rather than getting us tied up in knots in moral maneuvers in partial darkness. There is no escape from discriminating consequential calculation in assessing the implications of rights. The right to take personal risks is no exception.

SISSELA BOK
Secrecy and Moral Choice

SISSELA BOK *teaches philosophy at Brandeis University in Massachusetts.*

A *Thought-Experiment*

Imagine four different societies: two of them familiar from religious and mythological thinking, the other two closer to science fiction. To the extent that each reflects aspects of our own world, it will arouse the ambivalence and unease characteristic of conflicts over secrecy.

❱ In the first of the four imaginary societies, you and I cannot keep anything secret; but others, or at least someone, perhaps a deity, can. We are transparent to them, either because we are incapable of concealment or because they have means of penetrating all our defenses.

❱ In the second society, all is reversed. You and I can pierce all secrets. A magic ring and a coat of invisibility give us access to these secrets, unbeknownst to those on whom we focus our attention.

❱ In the third society, no one can keep secrets from anyone who desires to know them. Plans, actions, fears, and hopes are all transparent. Surprise and concealment are out of the question.

❱ In the fourth society, finally, everyone can keep secrets impenetrable at will. All can conceal innocuous as well as lethal plans, the noblest as well as the most shameful acts, and hatreds and conspiracies as much as generosity and self-sacrifice. Faces reveal nothing out of turn; secret codes remain unbroken. . . .

The *Need for Secrecy*

Secrecy is as indispensable to human beings as fire, and as greatly feared. Both enhance and protect life, yet both can stifle, lay waste, spread out of all control. Both may be used to guard intimacy or to invade it, to nurture or to consume. And each can be turned against itself; barriers of secrecy are set up to guard against secret plots and surreptitious prying, just as fire is used to fight fire. . . .

Control over secrecy provides a safety valve for individuals in the midst of communal life — some influence over transactions between the world of personal experience and the world shared with others. With no control over such exchanges, human beings would be unable to exercise choice about their lives. To restrain some secrets and to allow others freer play; to keep some hidden and to let others be known; to offer knowledge to some but not to all comers; to give and receive confidences and to guess at far more; these efforts at control permeate all human contact.

Those who lose all control over these relations cannot flourish in either the personal or the shared world, nor retain their sanity. If experience in the shared world becomes too overwhelming, the sense of identity suffers. Psychosis has been described as the breaking down of the delineation between the self and the outside world: the person going mad "flows out onto the world as through a broken dam." Conversely, experience limited to the inside world stunts the individual: at best it may lead to the aching self-exploration evoked by Nietzsche: "I am solitude become man. — That no word ever reached me forced me to reach myself."

In seeking some control over secrecy and openness, and the power it makes possible, human beings attempt to guard and to promote not only their autonomy but ultimately their sanity and survival itself. The claims in defense of this control, however, are not always articulated. Some take them to be so self-evident as to need no articulation; others subsume them under more general arguments about liberty or privacy. But it is important for the purposes of considering the ethics of secrecy to set forth these claims. Otherwise it will not be possible to ask, in particular cases, to what extent they should apply and what restraints they might require. Nor will it be possible to study the extrapolations made from them in support of collective practices of secrecy.

The claims in defense of some control over secrecy and openness invoke four different, though in practice inseparable, elements of human autonomy: identity, plans, action, and property. They concern protection of what we are, what we intend, what we do, and what we own.

The first of these claims holds that some control over secrecy and openness is needed in order to protect identity: the sense of what we identify ourselves as, through, and with. Such control may be needed to guard solitude, privacy, intimacy, and friendship. It protects vulnerable beliefs or feelings, inwardness, and the sense of being set apart: of having or belonging to regions not fully penetrable to scrutiny, including those of memory and dream; of being someone who is more, has become more, has more possibilities for the future than can ever meet the eyes of observers. Secrecy guards, therefore, not merely isolated secrets about the self but access to the underlying experience *of* secrecy.

Human beings can be subjected to every scrutiny, and reveal much about themselves; but they can never be entirely understood, simultaneously exposed from every perspective, completely transparent either to themselves or to other persons. They are not only unique but unfathomable. The experience of such uniqueness and depth underlies self-respect and what social theorists have called the sense of "the sacredness of the self." This sense also draws on group, familial, and societal experience of intimacy and sacredness, and may attach to individual as well as to collective identity. The growing stress in the last centuries on human dignity and on rights such as the right to privacy echoes it in secular and individualized language.

Without perceiving some sacredness in human identity, individuals are out of touch with the depth they might feel in themselves and respond to in others. Given such a sense, however, certain intrusions are felt as violations — a few even as desecrations. It is in order to guard against such encroachments that we recoil from those who would tap our telephones, read our letters, bug our rooms: no matter how little we have to hide, no matter how benevolent their intentions, we take such intrusions to be demeaning.

Not only does control over secrecy and openness preserve central aspects of identity; it also guards their *changes*, their growth or decay, their progress or backsliding, their sharing and transformation of every kind. Here as elsewhere, while secrecy can be destructive, some of it is indispensable in human lives. Birth, sexual intimacy, death, mourning, experiences of conversion or of efforts to transcend the purely personal are often surrounded by special protections, and with rituals that combine secrecy and openness in set proportions. . . .

The second and third claims to control over secrecy presuppose the first. Given the need to guard identity, they invoke, in addition, the need for such control in order to protect certain plans and actions.

Choice is future-oriented, and never fully expressed in present action. It requires what is most distinctive about human reasoning: intention — the capacity to envisage and to compare future possibilities, to make estimates, sometimes to take indirect routes to a goal or to wait. What is fragile, unpopular, perhaps threatened, such as Winston Smith's plan to express his views freely in his diary, seeks additional layers of secrecy. To the extent that it is possible to strip people of their capacity for secrecy about their intentions and their actions, their lives become more transparent and predictable; they can then the more easily be subjected to pressure and defeated.

Secrecy for plans is needed, not only to protect their formulation but also to develop them, perhaps to change them, at times to execute them, even to give them up. Imagine, for example, the pointlessness of the game of chess without secrecy on the part of the players. Secrecy guards projects that require creativity and prolonged work: the tentative and the fragile, unfinished tasks, probes and bargaining of all kinds. An elopement or a peace initiative may be foiled if prematurely suspected; a symphony, scientific experiment, or an invention falters if exposed too soon. In speaking of creativity, Carlyle stressed the need for silence and secrecy, calling them "the element in which great things fashion themselves together."

Joint undertakings as well as personal ones may require secrecy for the sharing and working out of certain plans and for cooperative action. Lack of secrecy would, for instance, thwart many negotiations, in which all plans cannot easily be revealed from the outset. Once projects

are safely under way, however, large portions of secrecy are often given up voluntarily, or dispelled with a flourish. Surprises are sprung and jokes explained. The result of the jury trial can be announced, the statue unveiled, the secretly negotiated treaty submitted for ratification, the desire to marry proclaimed. Here again, what is at issue is not secrecy alone, but rather the control over secrecy and openness. Many projects need both gestation and emergence, both confinement and publicity. Still others, such as certain fantasies and daydreams and hopes, may be too ephemeral or intimate, at times too discreditable, ever to see the light of day.

Secrecy about plans and their execution, therefore, allows unpredictability and surprise. These are often feared; yet without them human existence would not only be unfree but also monotonous and stifling. Secrecy heightens the value of revelations; it is essential for arousing suspense, whether through stories told, surprises prepared, or waiting times imposed. It can lend the joy of concentration and solemnity to the smallest matters. Secrecy may also lower intensity and provide relief, so that when a revelation is finally made — as after the death of those most intimately connected with events described in an author's private diaries — the anguish of exposure is lessened. In all these ways, secrecy is the carrier of texture and variety. Without it, and without the suspense and wit and unexpectedness it allows, communication would be oppressively dull — lifeless in its own right.

The fourth claim to control over secrecy concerns property. At its root, it is closely linked to identity, in that people take some secrets, such as hidden love letters, to *belong* to them more than to others, to be *proper* to them. We link such secrets with our identity, and resist intrusions into them. But the claim to own secrets about oneself is often far-fetched. Thus the school-bus driver who has a severe heart condition cannot rightfully claim to *own* this medical information, even though it concerns him intimately. Even when outsiders have less need to share the information than in such a case, the question who owns a secret may be hard to answer. Should one include only those "about whom" it is a secret, those who claim a right to decide whether or not to disclose it, or all who know it?

In addition to such questions of owning secrets, secrecy is invoked to protect what one owns. We take for granted the legitimacy of hiding silver from burglars and personal documents from snoopers and busybodies. Here, too, the link to identity is close, as is that to plans and their execution. For had we no belongings whatsoever, our identity and our capacity to plan would themselves be threatened, and in turn survival itself. As H. L. A. Hart points out, life depends on the respect for at least "some minimal form of the institution of property (though not necessarily individual property) and the distinctive kind of rule which requires respect for it." At the most basic level, if crops are to be grown, land must be secure from indiscriminate entry, and food must be safe from being taken by others.

The Dangers of Secrecy

Against every claim to secrecy stands, however, the awareness of its dangers. It is the experience of these dangers that has led so many to view secrecy negatively, and that underlies statements such as that by Lord Acton, that "every thing secret degenerates." Such categorical dismissals are too sweeping, but they do point to the harm that secrets can do both to those who keep them and to those from whom they are kept — harm that often thwarts and debilitates the very needs for which I have argued that control over secrecy is indispensable.

Secrecy can harm those who make use of it in several ways. I can debilitate judgment, first of all, whenever it shuts out criticism and feedback, leading people to become mired down in stereotyped, unexamined, often erroneous beliefs and ways of thinking. Neither their perception of a problem nor their reasoning about it then receives the benefit of challenge and exposure. Scientists working under conditions of intense secrecy have testified to its stifling effect on their judgment and creativity. And those who have written about their undercover work as journalists, police agents, and spies, or about living incognito for political reasons, have described similar effects of prolonged concealment on their capacity to plan and to choose, at times on their sense of identity.

Secrecy can affect character and moral choice in similar ways. It allows people to maintain façades that conceal traits such as callousness or vindictiveness — traits which can, in the absence of criticism or challenge from without, prove debilitating. And guilty or deeply embarrassing secrets can corrode from within before outsiders have a chance to respond or to be of help. This deterioration from within is the danger Acton referred to in his statement, and is at the root of the common view that secrecy, like other exercises of power, can corrupt.

These risks of secrecy multiply because of its tendency to spread. Aware of the importance of exercising control over secrecy and openness, people seek more control whenever they can, and rarely give up portions of it voluntarily. In imitation and in self-protection, others then seek more as well. The control shifts in the direction of secrecy whenever there is negligence or abuse to cover up; as a result, as Weber pointed out, bureaucracies and other organizations surround themselves with ever greater secrecy to the extent that circumstances permit.

As secrecy debilitates character and judgment, it can also lower resistance to the irrational and the pathological. It then poses great difficulties for individuals whose controls go awry. We know all the stifling rigidity that hampers those who become obsessed with secrecy. For them, secrecy no longer serves sanity and free choice. It shuts off the safety valve between the inner and the shared worlds. We know, too, the pathologies of prying into the private spheres of others, and of losing all protection for one's own: voyeurism and the corresponding hunger for self-exposure that destroy the capacity to discriminate and to choose.

The danger of secrecy, however, obviously goes far beyond risks to those who *keep* secrets. If they alone were at risk, we would have fewer reasons to try to learn about, and sometimes interfere with, their secret practices. Our attitude changes radically as soon as we suspect that these practices also hurt others. And because secrecy can debilitate judgment and choice, spread, and become obsessive, it often affects others even when it is not intended to. This helps explain why, in the absence of clear criteria for when secrecy is and is not injurious, many people have chosen to regard all secrecy as potentially harmful.

When the freedom of choice that secrecy gives one person limits or destroys that of others, it affects not only his own claims to respect for identity, plans, action, and property, but theirs. The power

of such secrecy can be immense. Because it bypasses inspection and eludes interference, secrecy is central to the planning of every form of injury to human beings. It cloaks the execution of these plans and wipes out all traces afterward. It enters into all prying and intrusion that cannot be carried out openly. While not all that is secret is meant to deceive — as jury deliberations, for instance, are not — all deceit does rely on keeping something secret. And while not all secrets are discreditable, all that is discreditable and all wrongdoing seek out secrecy (unless they can be carried out openly without interference, as when they are pursued by coercive means).

Such secrecy can hamper the exercise of rational choice at every step: by preventing people from adequately understanding a threatening situation, from seeing the relevant alternatives clearly, from assessing the consequences of each, and from arriving at preferences with respect to them. Those who have been hurt in such a way by the secrecy of others may in turn seek greater control over secrecy, and thus in turn experience its impairment of choice, its tendency to spread, its capacity to corrupt and to invite abuse.

Moral Considerations

I . . . rely on two presumptions that flow from the needs and dangers of secrecy that I have set forth. The first is one of *equality*. Whatever control over secrecy and openness we conclude is legitimate for some individuals should, in the absence of special considerations, be legitimate for all. If we look back at the four imaginary societies as illustrations, I can see no reason why some individuals should lack all such control, as in the first and second societies, and not others: no reason why, as in the first society, only you and I should be unable to keep anything secret or, as in the second, be able to penetrate all secrets. No just society would, if it had the choice, allocate controls so unequally. This is not to say that some people might not be granted limited powers for certain of those purposes under constraints that minimize the risks — in journalism, for instance, or government; but they would have to advance reasons sufficient to overcome the initial presumption favoring equality. On the basis of this presumption, I reject both the first and the second of the imaginary societies, and any others that come close to them even in part.

My second presumption is in favor of *partial individual control* over the degree of secrecy or openness about personal matters — those most indisputably in the private realm. (I shall leave for later consideration the question of large-scale collective control over secrecy and openness regarding personal matters, as well as individual *or* collective control over less personal matters, such as professional, business, or government secrets.) Without a premise supporting a measure of individual control over personal matters, it would be impossible to preserve the indispensable respect for identity, plans, action, and belongings that all of us need and should legitimately be able to claim.

Such individual control should extend, moreover, to what people choose to share with one another about themselves — in families, for example, or with friends and colleagues. Without the intimacy that such sharing makes possible, human relationships would be impossible, and identity and plans would themselves suffer. For these reasons, I reject also the third imaginary society, in which all is openness, and where people have no choice between such openness and secrecy, even in personal and intimate matters.

At the same time, however, it is important to avoid any presumption in favor of *full* control over such matters for individuals. Such full control is not necessary for the needs that I have discussed, and would aggravate the dangers. It would force us to disregard the legitimate claims of those persons who might be injured, betrayed, or ignored as a result of secrets inappropriately kept or revealed. I must therefore also reject the fourth imaginary society, in which all have such control and can exercise it at will.

Given these two presumptions, in favor of equal control over secrecy and openness among all individuals, and in favor of partial individual control over personal matters, exercised singly or shared with other individuals, I shall go on to ask: *What considerations override these presumptions?* This will require us to look at the reasons advanced in favor of unusual secrecy, probing, or revelation by some, and to ask when even the partial control exercised by an individual in personal matters must be overridden. It will also require us to examine the role of loyalty and promises in counteracting such reasons to override personal control; and the crucial difference it makes if it is one's own secret or that of another that one wonders whether to reveal. . . .

Such questions about the ethics of secrecy . . . mirror and shed light on aspects of ethics more generally. But these questions also create special difficulties; for no matter what moral principles one takes to be important in moral reasoning, they have a near-paradoxical relationship with secrecy. Thus secrecy both promotes and endangers what we think beneficial, even necessary for survival. It may prevent harm, but it follows maleficence like a shadow. Every misdeed cloaks itself in secrecy unless accompanied by such power that it can be performed openly.

And while secrecy may heighten a sense of equality and brotherhood among persons sharing the secret, it can fuel gross intolerance and hatred toward outsiders. At the heart of secrecy lies discrimination of some form, since its essence is sifting, setting apart, drawing lines. Secrecy, moreover, preserves liberty, yet this very liberty allows the invasion of that of others.

GRANT GILLETT

AIDS and Confidentiality

GRANT GILLETT *is both a doctor of philosophy and a surgeon. He teaches medicine and medical ethics at Otago University in Dunedin, New Zealand.*

DOES a doctor confronted by a patient with AIDS have a duty to maintain absolute confidentiality or could that doctor be considered to have some overriding duty to the sexual contacts of the AIDS sufferer? AIDS or Acquired Immune Deficiency Disease is a viral disease transmitted for the most part by sexual contact. It is fatal in the short or long term (i.e. nine months to six years) in those infected people who go on to develop the full-blown form of the disease.

Let us say that a 39 year old man goes to his family doctor with a dry persistent cough which has lasted three or four weeks and a 10 day history of night sweats. He admits that he is bisexually active. He is tested and found to have antibodies to HIV virus (indicating that he is infected with the virus that causes AIDS). In the setting of this clinical picture he must be considered to have the disease. He is told of his condition and also, in the course of a prolonged interview, of the risk to his wife and of the distinct possibility of his children aged one and three years old being left without parents should she contract the disease. He refuses to allow her to be told of his condition. The doctor finally accedes to his demand for absolute confidentiality. After one or two initial illnesses which are successfully combatted he dies some 18 months later. Over the last few weeks of his life he relents on his former demands and allows his wife to be informed of his problem. She is tested and, though asymptomatic, is found to be antibody positive. A year later she goes to the doctor with fever, dry cough and loss of appetite. Distraught on behalf of her children, she bitterly accuses the doctor of having failed her and them by allowing her husband to infect her when steps could have been taken to diminish the risk had she only known the truth.

In this case there is a powerful inclination to say that the wife is justified in her grievance. It seems just plain wrong for her doctor to sit back and allow her to fall victim to a fatal disease because of the wish of her husband. Against this intuition we can mobilise two powerful arguments — one deontological and the other utilitarian (of a rule or restricted utilitarian type).

(i) On a deontological view the practice of medicine will be guided by certain inviolate or absolute rules (not to harm, not to neglect the welfare of one's patients, etc.). Among these will be respect for confidentiality. Faced with this inviolable principle the deontologically inclined physician will not disclose what he has been told in confidence — he will regard the tacit agreement not to disclose his patient's affairs to others as tantamount to a substantive promise which he cannot break. Against this, in the present case, we might urge his *prima facie* duty not to neglect the welfare of his other patient, the young man's wife. His inaction has contributed to her death. In response to this he could both defend the absolute duty to respect confidentiality in general and urge some version of the doctrine of double effect, claiming that his clear duty was to honour his implicit vow of confidentiality but it had the unfortunate effect, which he had foreseen as possible but not intended, that it caused the death of his other patient. One is inclined to offer an intuitive response such as 'No moral duty is so binding that you can hazard another person's life in this manner'. It is a notorious feature of deontological systems that they involve conflicts of duties for which there exists no principled method of resolution.

(ii) A rule-utilitarian doctor can mount a more convincing case. He can observe that confidentiality is a cornerstone of a successful AIDS practice. Lack of confidentiality can cause the irrational victimisation of sufferers by a poorly educated public who are prone to witch-hunts of all kinds. The detection and treatment of AIDS, and the consequent protection of that large group of people who have contacts with the patients being treated depends on the patients who seek medical advice believing that medical confidentiality is inviolate. If confidentiality were seen as a relative duty only, suspended or breached at the discretion of the doctor, then far fewer cases would present for detection and crucial guidance about diminishing risks of spread would not be obtained. This would lead to more people suffering and dying. It may be hard on a few, unfortunate enough to be involved with people like the recalcitrant young husband, but the general welfare can only be served by a compassionate but resolute refusal to abandon sound principles in the face of such cases. Many find this a convincing argument but I will argue that it is superficial in the understanding of moral issues that it espouses.

Imagine, in order to soften the way for a rather less neatly argued position, a doctor confronted by a young man who has a scratched face and blood on his shirt and who wants to be checked for VD. In the course of the doctor's taking his history it emerges that he has forcibly raped two women and is worried that the second was a prostitute. He says to the doctor "Of course, I am telling you this in confidence, doc, because I know that you won't rat on me." Producing a knife, he then says, "See, this is the blade that I get them going with." Rather troubled, the doctor takes samples and tells the young man that there is no evidence of VD. He tries to talk his patient into giving himself up for some kind of psychiatric treatment but the young man is adamant. It becomes clear that he has certain delusional and persecutional ideas. Two days later the doctor reads that his patient has been arrested because after leaving the surgery he raped and savagely mutilated a young woman who, as a result, required emergency surgery for multiple wounds and remains in a critical condition.

Here we might well feel that any principle which dictates that it is the moral duty of the doctor to keep silent is wrong — but as yet no principles conflicting with or supplementing those above have been introduced. A possible loophole is introduced by the rapist's sadomasochism and probable psychosis but we need to spell out why this is relevant. In such a case we suspend our normal moral obligations to respect the avowed interests of the patient and claim that he is incompetent to make a responsible and informed assessment of his own interests and so we assume the right to make certain decisions on his behalf. In this case it would probably mean arranging for him to be given psychiatric help and society to be protected from him in the meantime. Notice that he may have demonstrated a 'lucid' and 'intelligent' grasp of his predicament, *vis-à-vis* his own wish to avoid detection but we discern that his instrumental rationality is deployed in service of a deep or moral insanity. His lack of awareness of the enormity of what he is doing to others counts as a sufficient basis to diagnose madness even in the face of astute inferential thought. He is insane because a normal person would never begin from the moral position he occupies and so his rights, including that to medical confidentiality, are suspended. He has moved outside the community of trust, mutual concern and non-malificence in which moral considerations for the preferences of others have their proper place. It is not that one 'contracts in' to such a community, nor that one in any sense volunteers, but rather one is a *de facto* member of it by virtue of possessing those human sensitivities and vulnerabilities which give moral predicates their meaning and importance. Such weight as one claims for one's own personal privileges and moral principles — such as the demand for confidentiality — is derived from a 'form of life' where the interpersonal transactions which define trust, respect, harm, and so on, are in play (it is important that no particular ideological overlay has been grafted on to these). Of the insane rapist we can say that he has excluded himself from that moral community by the very fact of his violation of certain of its most basic tenets and assumptions. He has no right to demand a full place in that structure where morally significant human exchanges are operative because his behaviour and attitudes do not fit the place to which he pretends. We are, of course, not released from a *prima facie* duty to try and help him in his odious predicament but we cannot be expected to accord him the full privileges of a member of the moral community as he persists, for whatever reason, in callously turning his back on the constraints normally operative there (albeit, perhaps, without reflective malevolence in its more usual forms). So, in this case, confidentiality can be suspended for legitimate moral reasons. The mad rapist has moved beyond the pale in terms of normal moral interactions and though we may have a duty to try and restore him to full participation within that order we are also entitled to protect ourselves in the interim at the expense of those considerations that would apply to a normal person. Notice again that the boundaries of our attitudes are not arbitrary or merely conventional but involve our most basic human feelings and reactions to one another.

We can now move from a case where insanity weights the decision in a certain direction to a case where the issues are more purely moral. Imagine that a 45-year-old man goes to see his family doctor and is also worried about a sexually transmitted disease. On being questioned he admits, in confidence, not only to intercourse with a series of prostitutes but also to forced sexual intercourse with his daughter. He is confident that she will not tell anyone what is happening because she is too ashamed and scared. After counselling he gives no sign of a wish to change his ways but rather continues to justify himself because of his wife's behaviour. The doctor later hears from the school psychological service that the daughter is showing some potentially serious emotional problems.

Here, it seems to me, we have few compunctions about setting in motion that machinery to deal with child abuse, even though the sole source of our information is what was said, in medical confidence, by the father. The justification we might give for the doctor's actions is illuminating. We are concerned for the actual harm being done to the child, both physical and psychological, and we overturn the father's injunction to confidence in order to prevent further harm being done. In so doing we class the situation as one in which a *prima facie* moral claim can be suspended because of the actions and attitudes involved. I believe that we do so because we implicitly realise that here also the agent has acted in such a way as to put himself beyond the full play of moral consideration and to justify our withholding certain of his moral 'dues'. Confidentiality functions to allow the patient to be honest with the doctor and to put trust in him. Trust is (at least in part) a two-way thing and can only exist between morally sensitive human beings (this, of course, blurs a vast range of distinctions between degrees of sensitivity). A basic element of such moral attitudes is the responsiveness of the agents concerned to the moral features of human interactions. The legitimate expectation that a doctor be trustworthy and faithful to his patient's wishes regardless of the behaviour of that patient is undermined when the patient abuses the relationship so formed in ways which show a lack of these basic human reactions because it is just these reactions which ground the importance of confidentiality in general. Therefore, if the father in this example refuses to accept the enormity of what he is doing to his daughter, he thereby casts doubt upon his standing as a moral agent. Stated baldly, that sounds like an open warrant for moralistic medical paternalism, but I do not think it need be. In asking that his affairs be concealed from others, a person is demanding *either* the right to preserve himself from the harms that might befall him if the facts about his life were generally known, *or* that his sensitivity as an individual be respected and protected. On either count it is inconsistent for him to claim some moral justification for that demand when it is made solely with the aim of allowing him to inflict comparable disregard or harm upon another. By his implicit intention to use a position, which only remains tenable with the collusion of the doctor, callously to harm another individual, the father undermines the moral force of his own appeal. His case is only worsened by the fact that from any moral perspective he would be considered to have a special and protective obligation toward his own offspring.

Implicit within what I have said is a reappraisal of the nature of medical confidentiality. I have argued that it is not to be treated as an absolute duty but is rather to rank among other *prima facie* duties and responsibilities of the doctor–patient relationship. Just as the performance of a lifesaving procedure can be vetoed by the patient's choice to forgo treatment, even though it is a doctor's duty to strive for his patient's life, so each of these duties can be negated by certain considerations. One generally attempts to prevent a fatal illness overtaking a patient but in the case of a deformed neonate or an elderly and demented patient often the attempt is not made. In the case of confidentiality, I have claimed that we recognise the right of a patient to preserve his own personal life as inviolate. We accept that patients can and should share with a doctor details which it would not be right to disclose to other people. But we must also recognise that implicit within this recognition is the assumption that the patient is one of us, morally speaking. Our attitude to him and his rights assumes that he is one of or a participant in a community of beings who matter (or are morally interacting individuals like himself to whom the same considerations apply). We could offer a superficial and rather gross systematisation of this assumption in the universalisability test. The patient in the last two cases applies a standard to his own human concerns which he is not prepared to extend to others involved with him in relevant situations. We must therefore regard his moral demands as spurious; we are not at liberty to harm him but we are bound to see that his cynical abuse of the moral code within which he lives does not harm others. At this point it might be objected that we are on a 'slippery slope'. Will any moral transgression suffice to undermine the moral privileges of the patient? I do not think that this extreme conclusion can be supported from what I have said. Williams, remarking on the tendency to slide down 'slippery slopes', observes, "that requires that there should be some motive to move from one step to the next" and "Possible cases are not enough, and the situation must have some other feature which means that those cases have to be confronted." Here we are not in such a position. Doctors in general have a strong tendency to protect their patients and keep their confidences. They require strong moral pressures to contemplate doing otherwise. All I have sought to do is to make explicit the moral justification upon which these exceptions can be seen to rest. I have not spelled out any formal decision-making procedure whereby the right answer will be yielded in each case. Indeed it is possible that whereas grounds and reasons recommending a certain course of action are the lifeblood of moral philosophy, such clearcut principles and derivations are a 'will o' the wisp'.

Now we can return to the AIDS patient. From what I have said it becomes clear that it is only the moral intransigent who forces us to breach confidentiality. In most cases it will be possible to guide the patient into telling those who need to know or allowing them to be told (and where it is possible to so guide him it will be mandatory to involve him in an informed way). In the face of an expressed disregard for the harm being caused to those others concerned, we will be morally correct in abandoning what would otherwise be a binding obligation. We should and do feel the need to preserve and protect the already affected life of the potential victim of his deception and in this feeling we exhibit a sensitivity to moral rectitude. Of course, it is only the active sexual partners of the patient who are at risk and thus it is only to them that we and the patient have a moral duty (in this respect talk of 'society at large' is just rhetoric). If it is the case that sexual activity, as Nagel claims, involves a mutual openness in those who have intercourse, one could plausibly argue that the cynical moral and interpersonal attitudes here evinced undermined the patient's sexual rights (assuming that people have such).

The sexual activity of this individual is aberrant or perverted in the important respect that it involves a harmful duplicity toward or deception of his sexual partner. Whereas people may have a right to sexual fulfilment in general, they can hardly be said to have a right to perverted sexual fulfilment; but both Nagel's contentions and this talk of rights are contentious and it is outside my present brief to discuss them.

The doctor's obligation to inform, in the face of an enjoinder to keep his confidence, can, even if I am right, be seen to be restricted to those in actual danger and would in no wise extend to employers, friends or non-sexually interacting relatives of the patient or any other person with an even more peripheral interest. His duty extends only so far as to avert the actual harm that he can reasonably expect to arise from his keeping confidence.

Given the intransigent case, one further desideratum presents itself. I believe that doctors should be open with their patients and that therefore the doctor is bound to share his moral dilemma with the patient and inform him of his intention to breach confidentiality. I think he can legitimately claim a pre-emptive duty to prevent harm befalling his patients and should do so in the case of the abuse of others which the patient intends. It may be the case, with the insane rapist for instance, that the doctor will need to deceive in order to carry out his prevailing duty but this will hardly ever be so, and

should, I believe, be regarded as unacceptable in general.

One thorny problem remains — the possible deleterious effect on the detection and treatment of AIDS if confidentiality is seen as only a relative principle in medical practice. Clearly, if the attitude were ever to take root that the medical profession could not be trusted to 'keep their mouths shut' then the feared effect would occur. I believe that where agencies and informal groups were told of the *only* grounds on which confidentiality would be breached and the *only* people who would be informed then this effect would not occur.

It seems to me that the remarkable intensification of one's sensitivity to personal and ethical values that is produced by contact with life-threatening or 'abyss' situations means that the cynical abuse of confidentiality by the patient which I have sought to address is likely to be both rare and transient. The greatest resource available to any of us in 'the valley of the shadow' is the closeness of those who will walk alongside us, and for many that will be a close spiritual and sexual partner. Confidentiality within the mutuality of that relationship rather than interpersonal dishonesty would thus seem to be vital to the welfare not only of the co-respondent but also of the patient himself as he struggles to cope with the disease that has him in its grip. To foster that welfare seems to me to be as close as a doctor can ever come to an absolute duty.

PART THREE

Social
Ethics

8

How Does
Racism
Affect
My Life?

While you were growing up, your parents probably reminded you again and again that you should not talk to strangers or accept rides from them. For your safety, you were taught to trust people you know and to mistrust people you don't know. This simplistic distinction was useful for making you less vulnerable as a small child. Your parents were no doubt confident that in time you would outgrow it and achieve a more subtle understanding of circumstances in which it is or is not appropriate to trust.

Racism is built on the unsophisticated distinction btween those who are familiar and those who are not. It is a defensive and immature approach to humanity, which divides the trustworthy from the untrustworthy on the basis of oversimple and unreasonable criteria. So understood, racism is morally objectionable by that definition alone. That racism is wrong implies that actions motivated by racism — perhaps with the intent to accomplish racist goals — are wrong. But our motives are not always obvious, even to ourselves. Determining whether our motivations are racist requires considerable self-awareness.

Kant points out that it is not always easy for the individual to know his or her own intentions, and this fact complicates ethical reflection on racism. It is possible to be racist in one's assumptions and motivations without realizing it. Many moral thinkers concerned with racism therefore focus on the importance of consciousness-raising, of becoming more aware of ways in which racism may affect one's own orientation.

Investigations of the psychological mechanisms involved in racism can assist our awareness of the nature of the problem. Jean-Paul Sartre considers anti-Semitism and explains it as a guiding passion that organizes the anti-Semite's life. Sartre suggests that the passionate hatred involved in anti-Semitism allows the anti-Semite to fortify his own self-perception. Sartre claims that the anti-Semite is able to take pleasure in his or her own sense of mediocrity, enhancing self-esteem through hatred of Jews.

Jorge Valadez considers the psychology of more subtle kinds of racism. Valadez suggests that many Americans, perhaps unwittingly, take the perspective that the American way of life — often understood in terms of economic, technological, and military advantages — is superior to that of their Latin American neighbors, and conclude that the United States can boast a superior worldview in all respects. Valadez observes that this amounts to metaphysical imperialism. He proposes that philosophical reflection can help overcome the patterns of oppression imbedded in such imperialism by helping us to develop a "multi-cultural perspective," a perspective that values the contributions that various particular cultures can make to our understanding of reality in a global society.

Elizabeth V. Spelman argues that the dominant tradition of philosophy in the West has also subtly assisted the formation of racist attitudes. Spelman argues that Western philosophy has encouraged simplistic dualisms in our basic evaluations of human beings. It is particularly easy, Spelman argues, to distinguish groups of people on the basis of the kind of bodies they have. She believes that because the white male has been taken as the standard, those whose bodies are significantly different from those of white males — women and nonwhites — are frequently seen as inferior or deviant. Spelman argues that this perspective has even invaded philosophical feminism, and she suggests that the feminist agenda should reassert the value of female and nonwhite bodies.

Unlike Kant, who emphasizes intention alone in his moral theory, utilitarians approach moral questions connected with racism — and all other moral questions — in terms of consequences. Utilitarians stress the impact that racism has on society and contend that our moral response to racism should focus on actions that will actually do some good.

What is the impact of racism on society? Clearly, racism has harmful effects on the individuals who are its targets. The opening of Ralph Ellison's *The Invisible Man* portrays in striking metaphors the damage that racism does to its victims' self-concepts and sense of participation in society.

It is valuable for nonvictims to empathize with victims of racism, but bell hooks reminds everyone of the dangers of relying on customary metaphors to interpret the relationship between the powerful and the powerless. She observes that the American feminist movement has taken the experiences of the middle-class white woman as paradigm, and as a consequence has reproduced the perspective of the privileged, even in its efforts to counter oppressive patterns in society. hooks insists on the importance of voices from "the margins," as well as from the center of power, for the creation of a less oppressive world.

Lisa H. Newton, George Sher, and Tom L. Beauchamp each consider the effectiveness and appropriateness of policies of reverse discrimination — practices that give preferred status to members of groups that have been previously discriminated against. Newton argues that reverse discrimination is difficult to justify, because it cannot truly compensate for a past violation of rights, and because it undermines the basic ideal it allegedly promotes, the ideal of equality. Sher contends further that even if reverse discrimination is defended in terms of some future good that will result, the inequalities that necessarily result from such discrimination are not morally more acceptable or defensible than the problems purportedly redressed. Beauchamp argues, by contrast, that even though all discrimination, including reverse discrimination is *prima facie* immoral, this does not establish that reverse discrimination is always wrong. Under certain circumstances, other considerations may override a *prima facie* duty, such as the duty to avoid discrimination. He concludes that considerations of utility and justice are sufficiently compelling to justify certain policies of reverse discrimination.

JEAN-PAUL SARTRE

Anti-Semite and Jew

JEAN-PAUL SARTRE (1905–1980) *was a French novelist, playwright, and philosopher. He is closely associated with the twentieth-century existentialist movement, and was a Communist Party supporter until 1956. His works examine philosophical notions of freedom, political philosophy, and philosophy of the mind. His publications include* Being and Nothingness *(1948) and* Nausea *(1949), and he was the founder of the philosophical periodical* Les Temps Modernes.

I F the Jew did not exist, the anti-Semite would invent him. . . .

Anti-Semitism is a free and total choice of oneself, a comprehensive attitude that one adopts not only toward Jews but toward men in general, toward history and society; it is at one and the same time a passion and a conception of the world. . . .

Ordinarily hate and anger have a *provocation*: I hate someone who has made me suffer, someone who contemns or insults me. . . .

Anti-Semitic passion could not have such a character. It precedes the facts that are supposed to call it forth: it seeks them out to nourish itself upon them; it must even interpret them in a special way so that they may become truly offensive. Indeed, if you so much as mention a Jew to an anti-Semite, he will show all the signs of a lively irritation. If we recall that we must always *consent* to anger before it can manifest itself and that, as is indicated so accurately by the French idiom, we "put ourselves" into anger, we shall have to agree that the anti-Semite has *chosen* to live on the plane of passion. It is not unusual for people to elect to live a life of passion rather than one of reason. But ordinarily they love the *objects* of passion: women, glory, power, money. Since the anti-Semite has chosen hate, we are forced to conclude that it is the *state* of passion that he loves. . . .

How can one choose to reason falsely? It is because of a longing for impenetrability. The rational man groans as he gropes for the truth; he knows that his reasoning is no more than tentative, that other considerations may supervene to cast doubt on it. He never sees very clearly where he is going; he is "open"; he may even appear to be hesitant. But there are people who are attracted by the durability of a stone. They wish to be massive and impenetrable; they wish not to change. Where, indeed, would change take them? We have here a basic fear of oneself and of truth. What frightens them is not the content of truth, of which they have no conception, but the form itself of truth, that thing of indefinite approximation. It is as if their own existence were in continual suspension. But they wish to exist all at once and right away. They do not want any acquired opinions: they want them to be innate. Since they are afraid of reasoning, they wish to lead the kind of life wherein reasoning and research play only a subordinate role, wherein one seeks only what he has already found, wherein one becomes only what he already was. This is nothing but passion. . . .

If then, as we have been able to observe, the anti-Semite is impervious to reason and to experience, it is not because his conviction is strong. Rather his conviction is strong because he has chosen first of all to be impervious.

He has chosen also to be terrifying. People are afraid of irritating him. No one knows to what lengths the aberrations of his passion will carry him — but he knows, for this passion is not provoked by something external. He has it well in hand; it is obedient to his will: now he lets go the reins and now he pulls back on them. He is not afraid of himself, but he sees in the eyes of others a disquieting image — his own — and he makes his words and gestures conform to it. Having this external model, he is under no necessity to look for his personality within himself. He has chosen to find his being entirely outside himself, never to look within, to be nothing save the fear he inspires in others. What he flees even more than Reason is his intimate awareness of himself. . . .

The anti-Semite has no illusions about what he is. He considers himself an average man, modestly average, basically mediocre. There is no example of an anti-Semite's claiming individual superiority over the Jews. But you must not think that he is ashamed of his mediocrity; he takes pleasure in it; I will even assert that he has chosen it. This man fears every kind of solitariness, that of the genius as much as that of the murderer; he is the man of the crowd. However small his stature, he takes every precaution to make it smaller, lest he stand out from the herd and find himself face to face with himself. He has made himself an anti-Semite because that is something one cannot be alone. The phrase, "I hate the Jews," is one that is uttered in chorus; in pronouncing it, one attaches himself to a tradition and to a community — the tradition and community of the mediocre.

We must remember that a man is not necessarily humble or even modest because he has consented to mediocrity. On the contrary, there is a passionate pride among the mediocre, and anti-Semitism is an attempt to give value to mediocrity as such, to create an elite of the ordinary. To the anti-Semite, intelligence is Jewish; he can thus disdain it in all tranquility, like all the other virtues which the Jew possesses. They are so many ersatz attributes that the Jew cultivates in place of that balanced mediocrity which he will never have. . . .

Thus I would call anti-Semitism a poor man's snobbery. . . . Anti-Semitism is not merely the joy of hating; it brings positive pleasures too. By treating the Jew as an inferior and pernicious being, I affirm at the same time that I belong to the elite. This elite, in contrast to those of modern times which are based on merit or labor, closely resembles an aristocracy of birth. There is nothing I have to do to merit my superiority, and neither can I lose it. It is given once and for all. It is a *thing*. . . .

We begin to perceive the meaning of the anti-Semite's choice of himself. He chooses the irremediable out of fear of being free; he chooses mediocrity out of fear of being alone, and out of pride he makes of this irremediable mediocrity a rigid aristocracy. To this end he finds the existence of the Jew absolutely necessary. Otherwise to whom would he be superior? Indeed, it is vis-à-vis the Jew and the Jew alone that the anti-Semite realizes that he has rights. If by some miracle all the Jews were exterminated as he wishes, he would find himself nothing but a concierge or a shopkeeper in a strongly hierarchical society in which the quality of "true Frenchman" would be at a low valuation, because everyone would possess it. He would lose his sense of rights over the country because no one would any longer contest them, and that profound equality which brings him close to the nobleman and the man of wealth would disappear all of a sudden, for it is primarily negative. His frustrations, which he has attributed to the disloyal competition of the Jew, would have to be imputed to some other cause, lest he be forced to look within himself. He would run the risk of falling into bitterness, into a melancholy hatred of the privileged classes. Thus the anti-Semite is in the unhappy position of having a vital need for the very enemy he wishes to destroy.

JORGE VALADEZ

The Metaphysics of Oppression

JORGE VALADEZ *teaches philosophy at Southwest Texas State University in San Marcos, Texas. His primary philosophical interests are in the field of ontology.*

CONSUELO had been living at a frantic pace for months. She was deeply involved in an organization of mothers who were demanding that the Guatemalan government account for their sons and daughters who had disappeared. Many of the mothers believed that their sons or daughters had probably already been killed by the government security forces, but they continued to hope that perhaps they might be alive and jailed with other political prisoners. The crimes of their loved ones consisted of their having protested and opposed the policies of the militarily controlled government. In Guatemala the degree of poverty and human suffering is staggering and many of the people from the poor and disfranchised classes had finally decided that it was necessary to speak up against the government, even if it meant placing themselves and others close to them in danger.

Consuelo knew all of this, and she also knew that the bloated bodies of some of the disappeared were sometimes found floating in a river or buried in shallow graves. But despite it all she felt that it was preferable for her to know what had happened to her twenty year old son. Even the knowledge that he was dead was better than this insufferable uncertainty that weighed down her waking hours and haunted her dreams. At least the body could then receive a proper burial.

Early on in her life Consuelo had learned about responsibility and about hardship, and the latter she had come to accept as an inevitable aspect of her existence. She was the eldest child, and by age twelve she had assumed the duties of an adult. She had married while still an adolescent. Later, in her tenth year of marriage her husband left to seek work in the U.S. Whether he actually ever made it across the border she never knew, since she had not heard from him since. Through the years, she had convinced herself that it was best to think of him only as part of those joyful scenes that she stored in her memory like precious secret jewels.

Nothing in her life, however, had prepared her for what occurred that warm Sunday evening when the four armed men broke into her house. The organization of mothers which she headed had been particularly vocal during the last few months and the government wanted to set an example. While two of the men held her, the others grabbed her six year old child. One of them took out a pointed pair of pliers and in a savagely methodical motion pulled out the fingernail from one of the horrified child's fingers. The image of her son's contorted face and the sound of his uncontrolled screams pierced and bored into her brain. The child kicked and twisted his whole body in a crazed effort to get free, but the butchers had had practice. One of them put his knee on the boy's chest and pinned him against the floor, while holding down the other small flailing arm. His partner then completed the gruesome task.

The event just described actually occurred, and incidents of this degree of brutality are not rare in Guatemala and other Central American countries. In recent years the United States had provided tens of millions of dollars in military aid to the Guatemalan government. Even though that government has an elected civilian president, the real power is in the hands of the military, for the most powerful appointed officials in the government are military officers. Death squads and special security forces play a crucial role in the maintenance of power by the military. In Guatemala approximately two percent of the population own about 75 percent of the country's land and resources. It is a country where great inequalities of wealth exist between the privileged few and the mostly poor Indian population. About 73 percent of all children under the age of five are malnourished and, for every 1,000 births, 270 will die before reaching the age of five. The national illiteracy rate is 65 percent. Government violence has been responsible for more than 100,000 deaths in the last 30 years.

The problems faced by the Guatemalan people are not unique; they are shared by people in many other Third World countries. These problems could no doubt be analyzed from a variety of perspectives, including the sociological, political, epidemiological, etc. A question which I want to consider here is whether there are certain insights which a distinctively philosophical perspective could give us into the problem of oppression. Are there some elements of this problem which could be elucidated by taking the peculiarly general and abstract position of the philosopher? I believe the answer is yes. In what follows, I will try to show that certain of our philosophical orientations restrict and limit our understanding of Third World oppression.

In attempting to establish the need for our changing the way in which we understand oppression in underdeveloped countries, especially in Latin America, I will first discuss some pragmatic or instrumental considerations that should be taken into account and then I will discuss those issues which are of a more properly philosophical nature. Drawing the connection between the pragmatic and the philosophical reasons for reorienting our perspectives should enable us to make a more compelling case for our position, especially if it can be shown that these two types of reasons ultimately coalesce and reinforce one another.

One of the important factors to consider in analyzing the situation from an instrumental viewpoint is the economic factor. Countries like Guatemala, Mexico, Brazil, Peru, and Argentina have collective foreign debts that total in the hundreds of billions of dollars. These foreign debts are primarily the result of an inequitable system of international trade. Third World countries sell their raw materials and cash crops to industrialized countries at prices which are often determined by these industrialized countries themselves — in fact, in some cases foreign companies control the production process in Third World countries. In turn, the industrialized countries like the U.S. sell them manufactured goods (tractors, factory machinery, etc.) at a relatively higher price. The profit margin for manufactured goods is greater than that of raw or unprocessed goods. The manufactured/raw goods exchange creates an economic imbalance which is getting worse for Third World countries. In 1960 it took one hundred pound bags of coffee for a country like Costa Rica to buy a tractor, and by 1977 it took 400 bags of coffee to buy that same tractor. In order to obtain the needed manufactured goods, Third World countries had to borrow from the industrialized countries. They had to pay interest on these loans, but the inequitable terms of international trade made it practically impossible for them to keep up the interest payments without borrowing more to do so. In 1973 the trade deficit of Third World countries was about nine billion dollars. In 1989 it is well over three hundred billion.

The result of this degree of indebtedness is that much needed resources that could be used for health care, education, etc. are channeled into the payment of the foreign debt. This in turn creates more misery and poverty for the majority of the population, who remain undernourished, illiterate, and with inadequate medical care. And it gets worse. The dire conditions under which the people are forced to live create an atmosphere of political instability which is exacerbated by the realization that the wealth in their countries is concentrated in a few hands. The wealthy classes and the high ranking military and government officials who benefit from the unjust distribution of resources want to maintain the status quo. In order to suppress the demands of the populace for better wages, improved working conditions, etc., the governments of many of these countries use a significant portion of their economic resources to strengthen the military and to create specialized security forces trained in intelligence and internal security operations (intimidation techniques, torture, etc.). Thus more of these countries' funds are used in areas that do not improve the living conditions of the people. The vicious cycle of poverty and oppression is reinforced — the demands of the poor for the alleviation of their misery lead to their political oppression, and the mechanisms that implement this oppression in turn increase their poverty.

In addition, the inability of these countries to pay back the money that they owe presents a serious problem for the lending institutions, many of which are American banks. And the possibility that the economies of these countries, after being declared bankrupt, may be taken over by American banks is politically, socially, and ethically unsettling. This possible scenario could be seen as the modern day equivalent of colonialism. It would validate in a frighteningly concrete way many of the fears and resentments that Latin Americans share toward the U.S. This scenario would be a clear and undeniable manifestation of the economic control that the industrialized nations have over the Third World.

Two questions which Americans should pose for themselves are these: First, at a time when our own social problems demand a wise and effective use of our economic resources, can we afford to spend many hundreds of millions of dollars in military aid to countries where the ruling classes seek to perpetuate their positions of privilege, to the detriment of the rest of the population? Second, what can be done to lessen the oppression in these countries and to strengthen their economies?

It is highly instructive to analyze the usual or official answers to these questions, i.e., the answers given by the government officials responsible for formulating our foreign policies. In regard to the first question, the position taken by the U.S. administration over the last decade is that we must keep the armies of the "democratically" elected governments of Latin America strong so that they can repel externally instigated communist threats. The idea here is that the demands which the people of El Salvador or Guatemala, for example, make of their governments for better living conditions and respect of their human rights are the result of external communist interference and not the result of the poverty and oppression which they suffer. Democracy is so far superior to a communist system of government, so the argument goes, that almost no price is too high to pay to keep communism away from this hemisphere. This position is bolstered by the alleged threat posed by communism to our own national security. Finally, our continued support of these military regimes is justified by either denying or de-emphasizing the human rights abuses which they perpetrate.

I will now provide a philosophical analysis of these questions in order to identify certain tacit metaphysical assumptions which affect the way in which we conceptualize the issues under consideration. Several orientations and perspectives can be seen as underlying the answer to our first question. In the first place, the assumption is made that Americans have the right to interfere with and determine the internal politics of Latin American countries. The last century provides us with numerous examples of such interference, including the overthrow of established, elected governments (e.g., Chile under Allende) and the invasion of countries like Nicaragua and Mexico. What is important to note here is that this assumption of the right of interference is an expression of our supposed right to impose our visions of reality on Latin America. It is *our* perception of the world that counts. It is Americans who should determine how other people are to live, how they are to organize their governments, and how they are to choose their values and priorities. This perspective is in effect a kind of metaphysical imperialism, i.e., an imperialism that involves the forced imposition of a dominant culture's vision of reality on another culture.

Most Americans are so convinced of the metaphysical imperialist perspective that it is almost impossible for us to question the basis of this perspective or to think of entering into a real and equal dialogue with the people of Latin America. Instead of engaging in an egalitarian effort to understand the world from their point of view, our attitude is that we have the right to impose our own visions of reality (through armed invasion if necessary). When dealing with under-developed countries, the notion that political truth is something that emerges as the result of a negotiated, open interchange of perspectives and ideas is foreign to most of us. And the belief that we have the right to impose our way of looking at the world on others is based on an even more deeply rooted philosophical view, namely, that those who are economically, technologically, and militarily superior, and are assumed to be intellectually and morally superior, have the right to control those who are inferior in these same respects. The history of Latin America can be seen as example of the concrete implementation of this philosophical principle, first at the hands of Western European countries and then at the hands of the United States.

It is difficult to overemphasize the importance and influence of this last philosophical principle for understanding the historical relationships between Latin America and Western Europe, and in contemporary times, between Latin America and the United States. America has, to a large extent, inherited its intellectual and philosophical traditions from Western Europe, including its attitudes towards underdeveloped or Third World nations. A common thread running through these attitudes is not only the metaphysical imperialist appropriation of the "truth" but also the above mentioned principle that those who are in possession of this "truth" have the moral right, and in some cases (like that of Christianity), even the moral obligation to impose their vision of reality on others. This principle works by assigning an inferior status to those who fail to meet our criteria of intellectual and moral worth. And once they have been categorized as inferior, it is an easy step towards the attitude that it is the task of their "superiors" either to subjugate them or to transform their perspectives of reality to conform with the ideals of their "superiors." We find an example of this in the attitudes of Anglo-Americans towards the Mexicans living in south Texas during the late 1800s and the early 1900s. According to Carey McWilliams, "To the early American settlers, the Mexicans were lazy, shiftless, jealous, cowardly, bigoted, superstitious, backward, and immoral." It is important to note that, as pointed out by McWilliams,

the inferior status of the Mexicans made it easier for the American settlers to accept the practice of killing Mexicans with impunity and without due process of law.

Other examples of the oppression of cultures, and of the forced imposition of a view of reality on them, can be readily acknowledged: the conquest of Mexico, which involved not only a military conquest, but also the destruction of an indigenous metaphysical and religious worldview; the long and well-documented history of racial subjugation of blacks and Native Americans in the United States; the oppression of women and their categorization as secondary and marginal beings, etc. We can elaborate briefly on one of these cases. The refusal to recognize that women have a status equal to that of men is a phenomenon that is deeply entrenched within our historical and cultural traditions. Aristotle, one of the most influential thinkers in Western intellectual history, thought that "the slave has absolutely no deliberative faculty; the woman has but its authority is imperfect; so has the child, but in this case it is immature." The implication here is that women's rational capacity is not on an equal par with that of men, i.e., that it lacks full legitimacy or authority.

It can be said without fear of exaggeration that understanding the phenomenon of oppression is crucial for an adequate understanding of Western history and civilization. Unfortunately, such an analysis is usually neglected, especially at the metaphysical level. A philosophical approach to the phenomenon of oppression helps us to see its scope as well as its deep roots within our intellectual traditions.

Probably all cultures are, to some degree or another, ethnocentric and even predisposed to believe that others see the world as they do. But what makes the Western European culture distinctive is its excessive emphasis on control and its systematic attempts to prove the alleged inferiority of various oppressed groups. Even though in most of these attempts there may have been no conscious intention to justify oppression, nevertheless the actual impact of several prominent Western theoretical traditions has been to reinforce attitudes which make oppressive behavior toward these groups appear reasonable and justifiable. The [above mentioned] Aristotelian view of women, the early views of some Spanish conquistadores that Indians did not possess souls, and the pseudoscientific attempts throughout history to establish the "natural" inferiority of blacks are all examples of theories which have complemented and sometimes justified the control, subjugation, and/or indoctrination of these groups.

Even today there are widespread misconceptions regarding discrimination and oppression of minority groups. One of the most disturbing experiences I have had [teaching college students] dealt with the dogmatic refusal of white students to recognize that racism exists in American society. There is a commonly held perception that racism and discrimination are problems that were resolved in the 1960s. In fact, some students feel that too much is being done for minorities, i.e., that minorities are getting a "free ride" and that they "have it made." There is resentment that whites are being treated unfairly when minorities are given preferential consideration. What is so ironic about this situation is that most of these white students are almost totally ignorant of the mass of statistical facts that show that economically, socially, and educationally things are worse for minorities, in relation to whites, than they were ten years ago. A larger percentage of black women and children are living in poverty today than a decade ago. Between 1969 and 1979 the expected life-time earnings of black men was about 57 percent that of white men, and in 1984 that percentage had actually decreased to 56 percent. Also, a proportionately lower number of black men are attending college today than ten years ago. The high school dropout rate is almost fifty percent for Hispanics nationwide and more Hispanics are living in poverty than ever before. A recent study showed that blacks were widely discriminated against when applying for housing loans.

It is an interesting fact that when discussing racism some of those Anglo students who do recognize that racism is a significant factor in society quickly exempt themselves by saying or implying "some Anglos are racist, but not me." Even though there are surely some Anglo students who can truthfully say this about themselves, I suspect that for some others this statement simply represents a refusal to reflect on racist attitudes which they might have. Students usually get very defensive when issues of racism are discussed. Perhaps this is because feelings of resentment or guilt emerge during such discussions. It is unfortunate that most students do not realize that recognizing prejudiced attitudes that one may have is not a sign of weakness or moral deficiency, but is rather a sign of an emerging intellectual and emotional maturity. It is the first step towards dealing with and eliminating such attitudes. By refusing to reflect openly and honestly on their own prejudices students miss an important opportunity to grow and develop as human beings.

The second question I proposed we Americans ask ourselves was, What should be done to alleviate the problems of poverty, oppression, and underdevelopment in Latin America? The conventional answers is also very revealing of the ontocentrism* that is so characteristic of our culture. Secretary of State James Baker recently gave succinct expression to the present administration's solution to these problems. According to Baker, the solution is greater foreign investment and ownership of businesses in Latin America and the lifting of trade restrictions. No mention was made of encouraging economic self-sufficiency, of dismantling the military units that help perpetuate corruption and oppression, of a more equitable distribution of resources, or of the need to respect human rights.

In proposing solutions to the problems of poverty and oppression, Americans ignore the need of Latin Americans to live in a manner that respects their values and traditions; instead, our solutions call for their becoming more like us; i.e., more technocratic, more modern, more socially mobile, etc., even if this entails a weakening of their cultural heritage and values. To be sure, there are some technological advances that all Third World countries would benefit from, especially regarding medical care and education, but Third World nations can enjoy these advances without having to transform their value system into one which prizes materialism, depersonalization, hierarchical rigidity, efficiency, and egocentrism over community relationships, rootedness in history and cultural tradition, economic decentralization and self-sufficiency, and an integrative approach to life. The assumption that people of a different culture can deal with the problems of poverty and economic underdevelopment only by adopting our values and way of life once again

betrays the ontocentrism of our conceptual framework.

Just as the philosophical point of view has deepened our understanding of oppression, can it now offer us some insights that can serve as a starting point for resolving the problem of oppression in the Third World and in Latin America? Even though philosophical reflection by itself will certainly not resolve this problem, philosophy can nevertheless help us to formulate a useful approach to dealing with this issue. The approach which I want to propose can be called the multi-cultural perspective. According to this perspective, an adequate understanding of reality is one which emerges as the result of an open, mutually liberated dialogue between the participants of different cultural traditions. This multi-cultural context of dialogue and interaction would make possible the recognition and removal of the cultural blinders of each of the participants. Thus, one of the first goals of this dialogue would be for the participants to understand and appreciate the perspectives from which the others perceive reality. The articulation and negotiation of their different needs and concerns would then be based on this prior understanding. None of the perspectives would have an initial or *a priori* privileged status, nor would there be an initial hierarchical differentiation between perspectives or between the elements of the perspectives.

It is important to note that there would be certain normative principles implicit in the adoption of this multi-cultural perspective. The liberated dialogue would in essence be free from ideological distor-

---

Ontocentrism can be defined as the conviction held by a group that its conception of reality is superior to all others.

tions; its participants would have an equal access to information (and would have developed the critical understanding necessary for evaluating that information); and there would be a lack of hierarchical controls in the exchange of information, etc. The practical and political implications of these principles are profound and wide-ranging. Consider the second of the conditions just mentioned. If the participants in the dialogue are to have an equal access to as well as a critical understanding of any information that may be relevant for the negotiation of a case at hand, then this implies at least an approximate parity in the educational preparation of the participants, as well as an elimination of economic restrictions that would impose arbitrary limitations on the use of available information. Furthermore, a critical understanding of this information presupposes an absence of sexist, racist, classist, and other ideological factors that may distort its meaning and interpretation. It is important to note that putting these normative principles into practice will take work and effort, and that we should not be discouraged by the realization that these principles will not be implemented simply by adopting the multi-cultural perspective. Attaining educational parity, for example, or developing modes of communication that are free of ideological distortions and biases, will take strong efforts to achieve.

The satisfaction of these conditions for liberated dialogue implies the elimination of substantial differences in the economic and educational status of the participants. In the multi-cultural perspective the connection between the socioeconomic position of the participants of a political community and their capacity to participate meaningfully in the decision making process of that community are empha-

sized. This perspective thus avoids the naive viewpoint of classical liberal political theory that severs the connection between political and economic power and the capacity to equally exercise one's civil rights in a real political setting.

Finally, I want to clarify the multi-cultural perspective by saying what it is not. It is not a relativistic or perspectival approach according to which all cultural perspectives are "equally valid." It is entirely possible that the participants in the open liberated dialogue may determine that certain cultural practices are oppressive or unethical (traditional views of women are a case in point). Thus we do not naively idealize or romanticize other cultures. This perspective does not tell us ahead of time which practices of what culture are oppressive or not. Instead, what it does is to give us a methodology by which the identification of such practices is to be achieved. Also, the multi-cultural perspective is not a Marxist perspective, because, although it recognizes the important role of economic factors in oppression, it leaves it as an open question whether it is in the best interests of the members of a community (either local, national, or international) to adopt a capitalist, socialist, communist, or mixed economic system. It is certainly logically possible that one or another of these systems may be more effective and desirable to different communities at different points in time.

It is unlikely that we will be able to deal adequately with the issues of poverty and oppression in the Third World until we recognize the philosophical assumptions which shape the way in which we understand these issues. In our dealings with the Third World and in our own domestic policies we should have the moral courage to strive for economic and social justice, for this is the ethically correct thing to do. But in addition to this compelling moral reason, we have strong practical reasons to do so. We can no longer afford not to. The facts that the population of the U.S. is becoming increasingly multi-cultural and that we live in an increasingly interdependent world, make it necessary for us to adopt the multi-cultural perspective in order to function effectively, at a political and eco-nomic level, in the future. We must re-evaluate the philosophy of egoism and ontocentrism which is so central to our conceptual orientations. And, most importantly, we must realize that refusing to deal with oppression involves an alienation from our own humanity and compassion. The struggle with the problem of oppression is not to be taken lightly, for ultimately the battle is to reclaim our own souls.

ELIZABETH V. SPELMAN

The Erasure of Black Women

ELIZABETH V. SPELMAN *teaches philosophy at Smith College and has written extensively on issues of feminist theory. Her book* Inessential Woman: Problems of Exclusion in Feminist Thought *was published in 1988.*

RECENT feminist theory has not totally ignored white racism, though white feminists have paid much less attention to it than have black feminists. Nor have white feminists explicitly enunciated and espoused positions of white superiority. Yet much of feminist theory has reflected and contributed to what Adrienne Rich has called "white solipsism":

to think, imagine, and speak as if whiteness described the world.

not the consciously held *belief* that one race is inherently superior to all others, but a tunnel-vision which simply does not see nonwhite experience or existence as precious or significant, unless in spasmodic, impotent guilt-reflexes, which have little or no long-term, continuing momentum or political usefulness.

In this essay, I shall focus on what I take to be instances and sustaining sources of such solipsism in recent theoretical works by, or of interest to, feminists — in particular, certain ways of comparing sexism and racism, and some well-ingrained habits of thought about the source of women's oppression and the possibility of our liberation. . . . To begin, I will examine some recent prominent claims to the effect that sexism is more fundamental than racism. . . . Before turning to the evidence that has been given in behalf of that claim, we need to ask what it means to say that sexism is more fundamental than racism. It has meant or might mean several different though related things:

▶ It is harder to eradicate sexism than it is to eradicate racism.

▶ There might be sexism without racism but not racism without sexism: any social and political changes which eradicate sexism will have eradicated racism, but social and political changes which eradicate racism will not have eradicated sexism.

▶ Sexism is the first form of oppression learned by children.

▶ Sexism is historically prior to racism.

▶ Sexism is the cause of racism.

▶ Sexism is used to justify racism.

In the process of comparing racism and sexism, Richard Wasserstrom describes ways in which women and blacks have been stereotypically conceived of as less fully developed than white men. "Men and women are taught to see men as independent, capable, and powerful; men and women are taught to see women as dependent, limited in abilities, and passive. . . ." But who is taught to see black men as "independent, capable, and powerful," and by whom are they taught? Are black men taught that? Black women? White men? White women? Similarly, who is taught to see black women as "dependent, limited in abilities, and passive"? If this stereotype is so prevalent, why then have black women had to defend themselves against the images of matriarch and whore?
Wasserstrom continues:

As is true for race, it is also a significant social fact that to be a female is to be an entity or creature viewed as different from the standard, fully developed person who is male as well as white. *But to be female, as opposed to being black*, is not to be conceived of as simply a creature of less worth. That is one important thing that differentiates sexism from racism: the ideology of sex, as opposed to the ideology of race, is a good deal more complex and confusing. *Women are both put on a pedestal* and deemed not fully developed persons. (emphasis mine)

In this brief for the view that sexism is a "deeper phenomenon" than racism, Wasserstrom leaves no room for the black woman. For a black woman cannot be "female, as opposed to being black"; she is female *and* black. Since Wasserstrom's argument proceeds from the assumption that one is either female or black, it cannot be an argument that applies to black women. Moreover, we cannot generate a composite image of the black women from the above, since the description of women as being put on a pedestal, or being dependent, never generally applied to black women in the United States and was never meant to apply to them.

Wasserstrom's argument about the priority of sexism over racism has an odd result, which stems from the erasure of black women in his analysis. He wishes to claim that in this society sex is a more fundamental fact about people than race. Yet his description of woman does not apply to the black woman, which implies that being black is a more fundamental fact about her than being a woman. I am not saying that Wasserstrom actually believes this is true, but that paradoxically the terms of his theory force him into that position. . . .

Additive Analyses

Sexism and racism do not have different "objects" in the case of black women. Moreover, it is highly misleading to say, without further explanation, that black women experience sexism and racism. For to say *merely* that suggests that black women experience one form of oppression, *as blacks* — the same thing black men experience — and that they experience another form of oppression, *as women* — the same thing white women experience. But this way of describing and analyzing black women's experience seems to me to be inadequate. For while it is true that images and institutions that are described as sexist affect both black and white women, they are affected in different ways, depending upon the extent to which they are affected by other forms of oppression.

For example, . . . it will not do to say that women are oppressed by the image of the "feminine" woman as fair, delicate, and in need of support and protection by men. While all women are oppressed by the use of that image, we are not oppressed in the same ways. As Linda Brent puts it so succinctly, "That which commands admiration in the white woman only hastens the degradation of the female slave." More specifically, as Angela Davis reminds us, "the alleged benefits of the ideology of femininity did not accrue" to the black female slave — she was expected to toil in the fields for just as long and hard as the black male was.

Reflection on the experience of black women also shows that it is not as if one form of oppression is merely piled upon another. As Barbara Smith has remarked, the effect of multiple oppression "is not merely arithmetic." Such an "additive" analysis informs, for example, Gerda Lerner's remark about the nature of the oppression of black women under slavery: "Their work and duties were the same as that of the men, while childbearing and rearing fell upon them as an added burden." But, as Angela Davis has pointed out, the mother/housewife role (even the words seem inappropriate) doesn't have the same *meaning* for women who experience racism as it does for those who are not so oppressed:

> . . . . In the infinite anguish of ministering to the needs of the men and children around her (who were not necessarily members of her immediate family), she was performing the *only* labor of the slave community which could not be directly and immediately claimed by the oppressor . . . . Even as she was suffering from her unique oppression as female, she was thrust by the force of circumstances into the center of the slave community.

The meaning and the oppressive nature of the "housewife" role has to be understood in relation to the roles against which it is contrasted. The work of mate/mother/nurturer has a different meaning depending on whether it is contrasted to work which has high social value and ensures economic independence, or to labor which is forced, degrading and unpaid. All of these factors are left out in a simple additive analysis. How one form of oppression (e.g., sexism) is experienced, is influenced by and influences how another form (i.e., racism) is experienced. So it would be quite misleading to say simply that black women and white women both are oppressed *as women,* and that a black woman's oppression as a black is thus separable from her oppression as a woman because she shares the latter but not the former with the white woman. An additive analysis treats the oppression of a black woman in a sexist and racist society as if it were a *further* burden than her oppression in a sexist but non-racist society, when, in fact, it is a *different* burden. As the article by Davis, among others, shows, to ignore the difference is to deny or obscure the particular reality of the black woman's experience.

If sexism and racism must be seen as interlocking, and not as piled upon each other, serious problems arise for the claim that one of them is more fundamental than the other. As we saw, one meaning of the claim that sexism is more fundamental than racism is that sexism causes racism: racism would not exist if sexism did not, while sexism could and would continue to exist even in the absence of racism. In this connection, racism is sometimes seen as something which is both derivative from sexism and in the service of it: racism keeps women from uniting in alliance against sexism. This view has been articulated by Mary Daly in *Beyond God the Father*. According to Daly, sexism is "root and paradigm" of other forms of oppression such as racism. Racism is a "deformity *within* patriarchy. . . It is most unlikely that racism will be eradicated as long as sexism prevails."

Daly's theory relies on an additive analysis, and we can see again why such an analysis fails to describe adequately black women's experience. Daly's analysis makes it look simply as if both black and white women experience sexism, while black women also experience racism. Black women should realize, Daly says, that they must see what they have in common with white women — shared sexist oppression — and see that black and white women are "pawns in the racial struggle, which is basically not the struggle that will set them free as *women*." The additive analysis obscures the differences between black and white women's struggles. Insofar as she is oppressed by racism in a sexist context and sexism in a racist context, the black woman's struggle cannot be compartmentalized into two struggles — one *as a black* and one *as a woman*. But that way of speaking about her struggle is required by a theory which insists not only that sexism and racism are distinct but that one might be eradicated before the other. Daly rightly points out that the black woman's struggle can easily be, and has usually been, subordinated to the black man's struggle in anti-racist organizations. But she does not point out that the black woman's struggle can easily be, and usually has been, subordinated to the white woman's struggle in anti-sexist organizations.

Daly's line of thought also promotes the idea that, were it not for racism, there would be no important differences between black and white women. Since sexism is the fundamental form of oppression, and racism works in its service, the only significant differences between black and white women are differences which men have created and which are the source of antagonism between women. What is really crucial about us is our sex; racial distinctions are one of the many products of sexism, of patriarchy's attempt to keep women from uniting. It is through our shared sexual identity that we are oppressed together; it is through our shared sexual identity that we shall be liberated together.

A serious problem in thinking or speaking this way, however, is that it seems to deny or ignore the positive aspects of "racial" identities. It ignores the fact that being black is a source of pride, as well as an occasion for being oppressed. It suggests that once racism is eliminated (!), black women no longer need be concerned about or interested in their blackness — as if the only reason for paying attention to one's blackness is that it is the source of pain and sorrow and agony. But that is racism pure and simple, if it assumes that there is nothing positive about having a black history and identity. . . .

Racism and Somatophobia

Feminist theorists as politically diverse as Simone de Beauvoir, Betty Friedan and Shulamith Firestone have described the conditions of women's liberation in terms which suggest that the identification of woman with her body has been the source of our oppression, and that, hence, the source of our liberation lies in sundering that connection. For example, de Beauvoir introduces *The Second Sex* with the comment that woman has been regarded as "womb"; woman is thought of as planted firmly in the world of "immanence," that is, the physical world of nature, her life defined by the dictates of her "biologic fate." In contrast, men live in the world of "transcendence," actively using their minds to create "values, mores, religions," the world of culture as opposed to the world of nature. Among Friedan's central messages is that women should be allowed and encouraged to be "culturally" as well as "biologically" creative, because the former activities, which are "mental," are of "highest value to society" in comparison to childbearing and rearing — "mastering the secrets of atoms, or the stars, composing symphonies, pioneering a new concept in government or society.". . .

I bring up the presence of somatophobia in the work of Firestone and others because I think it is a force that contributes to white solopsism in feminist thought, in at least three related ways.

First, insofar as feminists do not examine somatophobia, but actually accept it and embrace it in prescriptions for women's liberation, we will not be examining what often has been an important element in racist thinking. For the superiority of men to women is not the only hierarchical relationship that has been linked to the superiority of the mind to the body. Certain kinds, or "races," of people have been held to be more body-like than others, and this has been meant as more animal-like and less god-like.

For example, in *The White Man's Burden*, Winthrop Jordan describes ways in which white Englishmen portrayed black Africans as beastly, dirty, highly sexed beings. Lillian Smith tells us in *Killers of the Dream* how closely run together were her lessons about the evil of the body and the evil of blacks.

Derogatory stereotypes of blacks versus whites (as well as of manual workers versus intellectuals) have been very similar to the derogatory stereotypes of women versus men. Indeed, the grounds on which Plato ridiculed women were so similar to those on which he ridiculed slaves, beasts and children that he typically ridiculed them in one breath. He also thought it sufficient ridicule of one such group to accuse it of being like another (women are like slaves, slaves are like children, etc.). Aristotle's defense of his claim about the inferiority of women to men in the *Politics* is almost the same as his defense of the view that some people are meant to be slaves. (Aristotle did not identify what he called the natural class of slaves by skin color, but he says that identifying that class would be much easier if there were readily available physical characteristics by which one could do that.) Neither in women nor in slaves does the rational element work the way it ought to. Hence women and slaves are, though in different ways, to attend to the physical needs of the men/masters/intellectuals. . . .

So we need to examine and understand somatophobia and look for it in our own thinking, for the idea that the work of the body and for the body has no part in real human dignity has been part of racist as well as sexist ideology. That is, oppressive stereotypes of "inferior races" and of women have typically involved images of their lives as determined by basic bodily functions (sex, reproduction, appetite, secretions and excretions) and as given over to attending to the bodily functions of others (feeding, washing, cleaning, doing the "dirty work"). Superior groups, we have been told from Plato on down, have better things to do with their lives. As Hannah Arendt has pointed out, the position of women and slaves has been directly tied to the notion that their lives are to be devoted to taking care of bodily functions. It certainly does not follow from the presence of somatophobia in a person's writings that she or he is a racist or a sexist. But somatophobia historically has been symptomatic of sexist and racist (as well as classist) attitudes.

Human groups know that the work of the body and for the body is necessary for human existence, and they make provisions for that fact. And so even when a group views its liberation in terms of being free of association with, or responsibility for, bodily tasks, explicitly or implicitly, its own liberation may be predicated on the oppression of other groups — those assigned to do the body work. For example, if feminists decide that women are not going to be relegated to doing such work, who do we think is going to do it? Have we attended to the role that racism (and classism) historically has played in settling that question?

Finally, if one thinks — as de Beauvoir, Friedan and Firestone do — that the liberation of women requires abstracting the notion of woman from the notion of woman's body, then one perhaps also will think that the liberation of blacks requires abstracting the notion of a black person from the notion of a black body. Since the body is thought to be the culprit (or anyway certain aspects of the body are thought to be the culprits), the solution may seem to be: keep the person and leave the occasion for oppression behind. Keep the woman, somehow, but leave behind her woman's body; keep the black person but leave the blackness behind. . . .

Once the concept of woman is divorced from the concept of woman's body, conceptual room is made for the idea of a woman who is no particular historical woman — she has no color, no accent, no particular characteristics that require having a body. She is somehow all and only woman; that is her only identifying feature. And so it will seem inappropriate or beside the point to think of women in terms of any physical characteristics, especially if it has been in the name of such characteristics that oppression has been rationalized. . . .

Rich on Embodiment

Adrienne Rich is perhaps the only well-known white feminist to have noted "white solipsism" in feminist theorizing and activity. I think it is no coincidence that she also noticed and attended to the strong strain of somatophobia in feminist theory. . . .

Both de Beauvoir and Firestone wanted to break it by insisting that women need be no more connected — in thought or deed — with the body than men have been. De Beauvoir and Firestone more or less are in agreement, with the patriarchal cultural history they otherwise question, that embodiment is a drag. Rich, however, insists that the negative connection between woman and body be broken along other lines. She asks us to think about whether what she calls "flesh-loathing" is the only attitude it is possible to have toward our bodies. Just as she explicitly distinguishes between motherhood as experience and motherhood as institution, so she implicitly asks us to distinguish between embodiment as experience and embodiment as institution. Flesh-loathing is part of the well-entrenched beliefs, habits and practices epitomized in the treatment of pregnancy as a disease. But we need not experience our flesh, our body, as loathsome. . . .

I think it is not a psychological or historical accident that having reflected so thoroughly on flesh-loathing, Rich focused on the failure of white women to see black women's experiences as different from their own. For looking at embodiment is one way (though not the only one) of coming to note and understand the *particularity* of experience. Without bodies we could not have personal histories, for without them we would not live at a particular time nor in a particular place. Moreover, without them we could not be identified as woman or man, black or white. This is not to say that reference to publicly observable bodily characteristics settles the question of whether someone is woman or man, black or white; nor is it to say that being woman or man, black or white, just means having certain bodily characteristics. But different meanings are attached to having those characteristics, in different places and at different times and by different people, and those differences make a huge difference in the kinds of lives we lead or experiences we have. Women's oppression has been linked to the meanings assigned to having a woman's body by male oppressors. Blacks' oppression has been linked to the meanings assigned to having a black body by white oppressors. We cannot hope to understand the meaning of a person's experiences, including her experiences of oppression, without first thinking of her as embodied, and second thinking about the particular meanings assigned to that embodiment. If, because of somatophobia, we think and write as if we are not embodied, or as if we would be better off if we were not embodied, we are likely to ignore the ways in which different forms of embodiment are correlated with different kinds of experience. . . .

Rich does not run away from the fact that women have bodies, nor does she wish that women's bodies were not so different from men's. That healthy regard for the ground of our differences from men is logically connected — though of course does not ensure — to a healthy regard for the ground of the differences between black women and white women.

RALPH ELLISON
The Invisible Man

RALPH ELLISON, *originally from Oklahoma, has taught at a number of colleges and universities, including the University of Chicago and New York University. He is the author of* The Invisible Man *(1952), which won the National Book Award.*

I am an invisible man. No, I am not a spook like those who haunted Edgar Allan Poe; nor am I one of your Hollywood-movie ectoplasms. I am a man of substance, of flesh and bone, fiber and liquids — and I might even be said to possess a mind. I am invisible, understand, simply because people refuse to see me. Like the bodiless heads you see sometimes in circus sideshows, it is as though I have been surrounded by mirrors of hard, distorting glass. When they approach me they see only my surroundings, themselves, or figments of their imagination — indeed, everything and anything except me.

Nor is my invisibility exactly a matter of a biochemical accident to my epidermis. That invisibility to which I refer occurs because of a peculiar disposition of the eyes of those with whom I come in contact. A matter of the construction of their *inner* eyes, those eyes with which they look through their physical eyes upon reality. I am not complaining, nor am I protesting either. It is sometimes advantageous to be unseen, although it is most often rather wearing on the nerves. Then too, you're constantly being bumped against by those of poor vision. Or again, you often doubt if you really exist. You wonder whether you aren't simply a phantom in other people's minds. Say, a figure in a nightmare which the sleeper tries with all his strength to destroy. It's when you feel like this that, out of resentment, you begin to bump people back. And, let me confess, you feel that way most of the time. You ache with the need to convince yourself that you do exist in the real world, that you're a part of all the sound and anguish, and you strike out with your fists, you curse and you swear to make them recognize you. And, alas, it's seldom successful.

One night I accidentally bumped into a man, and perhaps because of the near darkness he saw me and called me an insulting name. I sprang at him, seized his coat lapels and demanded that he apologize. He was a tall blond man, and as my face came close to his he looked insolently out of his blue eyes and cursed me, his breath hot in my face as he struggled. I pulled his chin down sharp upon the crown of my head, butting him as I had seen the West Indians do, and I felt his flesh tear and the blood gush out, and I yelled, "Apologize! Apologize!" But he continued to curse and struggle, and I butted him again and again until he went down heavily, on his knees, profusely bleeding. I kicked him repeatedly, in a frenzy because he still uttered insults though his lips were frothy with blood. Oh yes, I kicked him! And in my outrage I got out my knife and prepared to slit his throat, right there beneath the lamplight in the deserted street, holding him in the collar with one hand, and opening the knife with my teeth — when it occurred to me that the man had not *seen* me, actually; that he, as far as he knew, was in the midst of a walking nightmare! And I stopped the blade, slicing the air as I

Do you have an invisible pop.? well, how could you know, cause you know what you know and you don't know what you don't know.

pushed him away, letting him fall back to the street. I stared at him hard as the lights of a car stabbed through the darkness. He lay there, moaning on the asphalt; a man almost killed by a phantom. It unnerved me. I was both disgusted and ashamed. I was like a drunken man myself, wavering about on weakened legs. Then I was amused: Something in this man's thick head had sprung out and beaten him within an inch of his life. I began to laugh at this crazy discovery. Would he have awakened at the point of death? Would Death himself have freed him for wakeful living? But I didn't linger. I ran away into the dark, laughing so hard I feared I might rupture myself. The next day I saw his picture in the *Daily News*, beneath a caption stating that he had been "mugged." Poor fool, poor blind fool, I thought with sincere compassion, mugged by an invisible man!

Most of the time (although I do not choose as I once did to deny the violence of my days by ignoring it) I am not so overtly violent. I remember that I am invisible and walk softly so as not to awaken the sleeping ones. Sometimes it is best not to awaken them; there are few things in the world as dangerous as sleepwalkers. I learned in time though that it is possible to carry on a fight against them without their realizing it. For instance, I have been carrying on a fight with Monopolated Light & Power for some time now. I use their service and pay them nothing at all, and they don't know it. Oh, they suspect that power is being drained off, but they don't know where. All they know is that according to the master meter back there in their power station a hell of a lot of free current is disappearing somewhere into the jungle of Harlem. The joke, of course, is that I don't live in Harlem but in a border area. Several years ago (before I discovered the advantages of being invisible)

I went through the routine process of buying service and paying their outrageous rates. But no more. I gave up all that, along with my apartment, and my old way of life: That way based upon the fallacious assumption that I, like other men, was visible. Now, aware of my invisibility, I live rent-free in a building rented strictly to whites, in a section of the basement that was shut off and forgotten during the nineteenth century. . . .

The point now is that I found a home—or a hole in the ground, as you will. Now don't jump to the conclusion that because I call my home a "hole" it is damp and cold like a grave; there are cold holes and warm holes. Mine is a warm hole. And remember, a bear retires to his hole for the winter and lives until spring; then he comes strolling out like the Easter chick breaking from its shell. I say all this to assure you that it is incorrect to assume that, because I'm invisible and live in a hole, I am dead. I am neither dead nor in a state of suspended animation. Call me Jack-the-Bear, for I am in a state of hibernation.

My hole is warm and full of light. Yes, *full* of light. I doubt if there is a brighter spot in all New York than this hole of mine, and I do not exclude Broadway. Or the Empire State Building on a photographer's dream night. But that is taking advantage of you. Those two spots are among the darkest of our whole civilization—pardon me, our whole *culture* (an important distinction, I've heard)—which might sound like a hoax, or a contradiction, but that (by contradiction, I mean) is how the world moves: Not like an arrow, but a boomerang. (Beware of those who speak of the *spiral* of history; they are preparing a boomerang. Keep a steel helmet handy.) I know; I have been boomeranged across my head so much that I now can see the darkness of lightness. And I

why would someone get a regular job when they can go on a corner and have a *merandos* by the end of the week?

love light. Perhaps you'll think it strange that an invisible man should need light, desire light, love light. But maybe it is exactly because I *am* invisible. Light confirms my reality, gives birth to my form. A beautiful girl once told me of a recurring nightmare in which she lay in the center of a large dark room and felt her face expand until it filled the whole room, becoming a formless mass while her eyes ran in bilious jelly up the chimney. And so it is with me. Without light I am not only invisible, but formless as well; and to be unaware of one's form is to live a death. I myself, after existing some twenty years, did not become alive until I discovered my invisibility.

That is why I fight my battle with Monopolated Light & Power. The deeper reason, I mean: It allows me to feel my vital aliveness. I also fight them for taking so much of my money before I learned to protect myself. In my hole in the basement there are exactly 1,369 lights. I've wired the entire ceiling, every inch of it. And not with fluorescent bulbs, but with the older, more-expensive-to-operate kind, the filament type. An act of sabotage, you know. I've already begun to wire the wall. A junk man I know, a man of vision, has supplied me with wire and sockets. Nothing, storm or flood, must get in the way of our need for light and ever more and brighter light. The truth is the light and light is the truth. When I finish all four walls, then I'll start on the floor. Just how that will go, I don't know. Yet when you have lived invisible as long as I have you develop a certain ingenuity. I'll solve the problem. And maybe I'll invent a gadget to place my coffee pot on the fire while I lie in bed, and even invent a gadget to warm my bed — like the fellow I saw in one of the picture magazines who made himself a gadget to warm his shoes! Though invisible, I am in the great Amer-

ican tradition of tinkers. That makes me kin to Ford, Edison and Franklin. Call me, since I have a theory and a concept, a "thinker-tinker." Yes, I'll warm my shoes; they need it, they're usually full of holes. I'll do that and more. . . .

Please, a definition: A hibernation is a covert preparation for a more overt action. . . .

Meanwhile I enjoy my life with the compliments of Monopolated Light & Power. Since you never recognize me even when in closest contact with me, and since, no doubt, you'll hardly believe that I exist, it won't matter if you know that I tapped a power line leading into the building and ran it into my hole in the ground. Before that I lived in the darkness into which I was chased, but now I see. I've illuminated the blackness of my invisibility — and vice versa. And so I play the invisible music of my isolation. The last statement doesn't seem just right, does it? But it is; you hear this music simply because music is heard and seldom seen, except by musicians. Could this compulsion to put invisibility down in black and white be thus an urge to make music of invisibility? But I am an orator, a rabble rouser — Am? I *was*, and perhaps shall be again. Who knows? All sickness is not unto death, neither is invisibility.

I can hear you say, "What a horrible, irresponsible bastard!" And you're right. I leap to agree with you. I am one of the most irresponsible beings that ever lived. Irresponsibility is part of my invisibility; any way you face it, it is a denial. But to whom can I be responsible, and why should I be, when you refuse to see me? And wait until I reveal how truly irresponsible I am. Responsibility rests upon recognition, and recognition is a form of agreement. Take the man whom I almost killed: Who was responsible for that near murder — I? I don't think so, and I refuse it. I won't buy it. You can't give it to me. *He* bumped *me*, *he* insulted *me*. Shouldn't he, for his own personal safety, have recognized my hysteria, my "danger potential"? He, let us say, was lost in a dream world. But didn't *he* control that dream world — which, alas, is only too real! — and didn't *he* rule me out of it? And if he had yelled for a policeman, wouldn't *I* have been taken for the offending one? Yes, yes, yes! Let me agree with you, I was the irresponsible one; for I should have used my knife to protect the higher interests of society. Some day that kind of foolishness will cause us tragic trouble. All dreamers and sleepwalkers must pay the price, and even the invisible victim is responsible for the fate of all. But I shirked that responsibility; I became too snarled in the incompatible notions that buzzed within my brain. I was a coward . . .

BELL HOOKS

Black Women
Shaping Feminist Theory

BELL HOOKS *teaches at Yale University. She has published several books on black women and feminism, the most recent of which is* Yearning *(1990).*

FEMINISM in the United States has never emerged from the women who are most victimized by sexist oppression; women who are daily beaten down, mentally, physically, and spiritually — women who are powerless to change their condition in life. They are a silent majority. A mark of their victimization is that they accept their lot in life without visible question, without organized protest, without collective anger or rage. Betty Friedan's *The Feminine Mystique* is still heralded as having paved the way for contemporary feminist movement — it was written as if these women did not exist. Friedan's famous phrase, "the problem that has no name," often quoted to describe the condition of women in this society, actually referred to the plight of a select group of college-educated, middle and upper class, married white women — housewives bored with leisure, with the home, with children, with buying products, who wanted more out of life. Friedan concludes her first chapter by stating: "We can no longer ignore that voice within women that says: 'I want something more than my husband and my children and my house.'" That "more" she defined as careers. She did not discuss who would be called in to take care of the children and maintain the home if more women like herself were freed from their house labor and given equal access with white men to the professions. She did not speak of the needs of women without men, without children, without homes. She ignored the existence of all non-white women and poor white women. She did not tell readers whether it was more fulfilling to be a maid, a babysitter, a factory worker, a clerk, or a prostitute, than to be a leisure class housewife.

She made her plight and the plight of white women like herself synonymous with a condition affecting all American women. In so doing, she deflected attention away from her classism, her racism, her sexist attitudes towards the masses of American women. In the context of her book, Friedan makes clear that the women she saw as victimized by sexism were college-educated, white women who were compelled by sexist conditioning to remain in the home. She contends:

> It is urgent to understand how the very condition of being a housewife can create a sense of emptiness, non-existence, nothingness in women. There are aspects of the housewife role that make it almost impossible for a woman of adult intelligence to retain a sense of human identity, the firm core of self or "I" without which a human being, man or woman, is not truly alive. For women of ability, in America today, I am convinced that there is something about the housewife state itself that is dangerous.

Specific problems and dilemmas of leisure class white housewives were real concerns that merited consideration and change but they were not the pressing political concerns of masses of women. Masses of women were concerned about economic survival, ethnic and racial discrimination, etc. When Friedan wrote *The Feminine Mystique*, more than one third of all women were in the work force. Although many women longed to be housewives, only women with leisure time and money could actually shape their identities on the model of the feminine mystique. They were women who, in Friedan's words, were "told by the most advanced thinkers of our time to go back and live their lives as if they were Noras, restricted to the doll's house by Victorian prejudices."

From her early writing, it appears that Friedan never wondered whether or not the plight of college-educated, white housewives was an adequate reference point by which to gauge the impact of sexism or sexist oppression on the lives of women in American society. Nor did she move beyond her own life experience to acquire an expanded perspective on the lives of women in the United States. I say this not to discredit her work. It remains a useful discussion of the impact of sexist discrimination on a select group of women. Examined from a different perspective, it can also be seen as a case study of narcissism, insensitivity, sentimentality, and self-indulgence which reaches its peak when Friedan, in a chapter titled "Progressive Dehumanization," makes a comparison between the psychological effects of isolation on white housewives and the impact of confinement on the self-concept of prisoners in Nazi concentration camps.

Friedan was a principal shaper of contemporary feminist thought. Significantly, the one-dimensional perspective on women's reality presented in her book became a marked feature of the contemporary feminist movement. Like Friedan before them, white women who dominate feminist discourse today rarely question whether or not their perspective on women's reality is true to the lived experiences of women as a collective group. Nor are they aware of the extent to which their perspectives reflect race and class biases,

although there has been a greater awareness of biases in recent years. Racism
abounds in the writings of white feminists, reinforcing white supremacy and
negating the possibility that women will
bond politically across ethnic and racial
boundaries. Past feminist refusal to draw
attention to and attack racial hierarchies
suppressed the link between race and
class. Yet class structure in American society has been shaped by the racial politic
of white supremacy; it is only by analyzing racism and its function in capitalist
society that a thorough understanding of
class relationships can emerge. Class
struggle is inextricably bound to the
struggle to end racism. Urging women to
explore the full implication of class in an
early essay, "The Last Straw," Rita Mae
Brown explained:

> Class is much more than Marx's defini-
> tion of relationship to the means of pro-
> duction. Class involves your behavior,
> your basic assumptions about life. Your
> experience (determined by your class)
> validates those assumptions, how you
> are taught to behave, what you expect
> from yourself and from others, your
> concept of a future, how you understand
> problems and solve them, how you
> think, feel, act. It is these behavioral
> patterns that middle class women resist
> recognizing although they may be per-
> fectly willing to accept class in Marxist
> terms, a neat trick that helps them avoid
> really dealing with class behavior and
> changing that behavior in themselves. It
> is these behavioral patterns which must
> be recognized, understood, and changed.

White women who dominate feminist discourse, who for the most part make and
articulate feminist theory, have little or no
understanding of white supremacy as a racial politic, of the psychological impact of
class, of their political status within a racist, sexist, capitalist state.

.   .   .

A central tenet of modern feminist
thought has been the assertion that "all
women are oppressed." This assertion implies that women share a common lot, that
factors like class, race, religion, sexual
preference, etc. do not create a diversity
of experience that determines the extent
to which sexism will be an oppressive
force in the lives of individual women.
Sexism as a system of domination is institutionalized but it has never determined in
an absolute way the fate of all women in
this society. Being oppressed means the
absence of choices. It is the primary point
of contact between the oppressed and the
oppressor. Many women in this society do
have choices (as inadequate as they are),
therefore exploitation and discrimination
are words that more accurately describe
the lot of women collectively in the
United States. Many women do not join
organized resistance against sexism precisely because sexism has not meant an
absolute lack of choices. They may know
they are discriminated against on the basis
of sex, but they do not equate this with
oppression. Under capitalism, patriarchy
is structured so that sexism restricts wom-
en's behavior in some realms even as freedom from limitations is allowed in other
spheres. The absence of extreme restrictions leads many women to ignore the
areas in which they are exploited or discriminated against; it may even lead them
to imagine that no women are oppressed.

There are oppressed women in the
United States, and it is both appropriate
and necessary that we speak against such
oppression. French feminist Christine
Delphy makes the point in her essay, "For
a Materialist Feminism," that the use of
the term oppression is important because
it places feminist struggle in a radical political framework:

The rebirth of feminism coincided with the use of the term "oppression." The ruling ideology, i.e. common sense, daily speech, does not speak about oppression but about a "feminine condition." It refers back to a naturalist explanation: to a constraint of nature, exterior reality out of reach and not modifiable by human action. The term "oppression," on the contrary, refers back to a choice, an explanation, a situation that is political. "Oppression" and "social oppression" are therefore synonyms or rather social oppression is a redundance: the notion of a political origin, i.e. social, is an intregral part of the concept of oppression.

Had middle class black women begun a movement in which they had labeled themselves "oppressed," no one would have taken them seriously. Had they established public forums and given speeches about their "oppression," they would have been criticized and attacked from all sides. This was not the case with white bourgeois feminists for they could appeal to a large audience of women, like themselves, who were eager to change their lot in life. Their isolation from women of other class and race groups provided no immediate comparative base by which to test their assumptions of common oppression.

•   ,   •

However, feminist emphasis on "common oppression" in the United States was less a strategy for politicization than an appropriation by conservative and liberal women of a radical political vocabulary that masked the extent to which they shaped the movement so that it addressed and promoted their class interests.

Although the impulse towards unity and empathy that informed the notion of common oppression was directed at building solidarity, slogans like "organize around your own oppression" provided the excuse many privileged women needed to ignore the differences between their social status and the status of masses of women. It was a mark of race and class privilege, as well as the expression of freedom from the many constraints sexism places on working class women, that middle class white women were able to make their interests the primary focus of feminist movement and employ a rhetoric of commonality that made their condition synonymous with "oppression." Who was there to demand a change in vocabulary? What other group of women in the United States had the same access to universities, publishing houses, mass media, money?

The ideology of "competitive, atomistic liberal individualism" has permeated feminist thought to such an extent that it undermines the potential radicalism of feminist struggle. The usurpation of feminism by bourgeois women to support their class interests has been to a very grave extent justified by feminist theory as it has so far been conceived. (For example, the ideology of "common oppression.") Any movement to resist the co-optation of feminist struggle must begin by introducing a different feminist perspective — a new theory — one that is not informed by the ideology of liberal individualism.

The exclusionary practices of women who dominate feminist discourse have made it practically impossible for new and varied theories to emerge. Feminism has its party line and women who feel a need for a different strategy, a different foundation, often find themselves ostracized and silenced. Criticisms of or alternatives to established feminist ideas are not encouraged, e.g. recent controversies about expanding feminist discussions of sexuality. Yet groups of women who feel excluded from feminist discourse and praxis can make a place for themselves only if they first create, via critiques, an awareness of the factors that alienate them. Many individual white women found in the women's movement a liberatory solution to personal dilemmas. Having directly benefited from the movement, they are less inclined to criticize it or to engage in rigorous examination of its structure than those who feel it has not had a revolutionary impact on their lives or the lives of masses of women in our society. Nonwhite women who feel affirmed within the current structure of feminist movement (even though they may form autonomous groups) seem to also feel that their definitions of the party line, whether on the issue of black feminism or on other issues, is the only legitimate discourse. . . .

•   •   •

We resist hegemonic dominance of feminist thought by insisting that it is a theory in the making, that we must necessarily criticize, question, re-examine, and explore new possibilities. My persistent critique has been informed by my status as a member of an oppressed group, experience of sexist exploitation and discrimination, and the sense that prevailing feminist analysis has not been the force shaping my feminist consciousness. This is true for many women. There are white women who had never considered resisting male dominance until the feminist movement created an awareness that they could and should. My awareness of feminist struggle was stimulated by social circumstance. Growing up in a Southern, black, father-dominated, working class household, I experienced (as did my mother, my sisters, and my brother) varying degrees of patriarchal tyranny and it made me angry—it made us all angry. Anger led me to question the politics of male dominance and enabled me to resist sexist socialization. Frequently, white feminists act as if black women did not know sexist oppression existed until they voiced feminist sentiment. They believe they are providing black women with "the" analysis and "the" program for liberation. They do not understand, cannot even imagine, that black women, as well as other groups of women who live daily in oppressive situations, often acquire an awareness of patriarchal politics from their lived experience, just as they develop strategies of resistance (even though they may not resist on a sustained or organized basis).

These black women observed white feminist focus on male tyranny and women's oppression as if it were a "new" revelation and felt such a focus had little impact on their lives. To them it was just another indication of the privileged living conditions of middle and upper class white women that they would need a theory to inform them that they were "oppressed." The implication being that people who are truly oppressed know it even though they may not be engaged in organized resistance or are unable to articulate in written form the nature of their oppression. These black women saw nothing liberatory in party line analysis of women's oppression. Neither the fact that black women have not organized collectively in huge numbers around the issues of "feminism" (many of us do not know or use the term) nor the fact that we have not had access to the machinery of power that would allow us to share our analyses or theories about gender with the American public negate its presence in our lives or place us in a position of dependency in relationship to those white and non-white feminists who address a larger audience.

The understanding I had by age thirteen of patriarchal politics created in me expectations of the feminist movement that were quite different from those of young, middle class, white women. When I entered my first women's studies class at Stanford University in the early 1970s, white women were revelling in the joy of being together—to them it was an important, momentous occasion. I had not known a life where women had not been together, where women had not helped, protected, and loved one another deeply. I had not known white women who were ignorant of the impact of race and class on their social status and consciousness (Southern white women often have a more realistic perspective on racism and classism than white women in other areas of the United States.) I did not feel sympathetic to white peers who maintained that I could not expect them to have knowledge of or understand the life experiences of black women. Despite my background (living in racially segregated communities) I knew about the lives of white women, and certainly no white women lived in our neighborhood, attended our schools, or worked in our homes.

When I participated in feminist groups, I found that white women adopted a condescending attitude towards me and other non-white participants. The condescension they directed at black women was one of the means they employed to remind us that the women's movement was "theirs"—that we were able to participate because they allowed it, even encouraged it; after all, we were needed to legitimate the process. They did not see us as equals. They did not treat us as equals. And though they expected us to provide first hand accounts of black experience, they felt it was their role to decide if these experiences were authentic. Frequently, college-educated black women (even those from poor and working class backgrounds) were dismissed as mere imitators. Our presence in movement activities did not count, as white women were convinced that "real" blackness meant speaking the patois of poor black people, being uneducated, streetwise, and a variety of other stereotypes. If we dared to criticize the movement or to assume responsibility for reshaping feminist ideas and introducing new ideas, our voices were turned out, dismissed, silenced. We could be heard only if our statements echoed the sentiments of the dominant discourse.

Attempts by white feminists to silence black women are rarely written about. All too often they have taken place in conference rooms, classrooms, or the privacy of cozy living room settings, where one lone black woman faces the racist hostility of a group of white women. From the time the women's liberation movement began, individual black women went to groups. Many never returned after a first meeting. Anita Cornwall is correct in "Three for the Price of One: Notes from a Gay Black Feminist," when she states, ". . . sadly enough, fear of encountering racism seems to be one of the main reasons that so many black women refuse to join the women's movement." Recent focus on the issue of racism has generated discourse but has had little impact on the behavior of white feminists towards black women. Often the white women who are busy publishing papers and books on "unlearning racism" remain patronizing and condescending when they relate to black women. This is not surprising given that frequently their discourse is aimed solely in the direction of a white audience and the focus solely on changing attitudes rather than addressing racism in a historical and political context. They make us the "objects" of their privileged discourse on race. As "objects," we remain unequals, inferiors. Even though they may be sincerely concerned about racism, their methodology suggests they are not yet free of the type of paternalism endemic to white supremacist ideology. Some of these women place themselves in the position of "authorities" who must mediate communication between racist white women (naturally they see themselves as having come to terms with their racism) and angry black women whom they believe are incapable of rational discourse. Of course, the system of racism, classism, and educational elitism remain intact if they are to maintain their authoritative positions.

·   ·   ·

Racist stereotypes of the strong, superhuman black woman are operative myths in the minds of many white women, allowing them to ignore the extent to which black women are likely to be victimized in this society and the role white women may play in the maintenance and perpetuation of that victimization. In Lillian Hellman's autobiographical work *Pentimento*, she writes, "All my life, beginning at birth, I have taken orders from black women, wanting them and resenting them, being superstitious the few times I disobeyed." The black women Hellman describes worked in her household as family servants and their status was never that of an equal. Even as a child, she was always in the dominant position as they questioned, advised, or guided her; they were free to exercise these rights because

she or another white authority figure allowed it. Hellman places power in the hands of these black women rather than acknowledge her own power over them; hence she mystifies the true nature of their relationship. By projecting onto black women a mythical power and strength, white women both promote a false image of themselves as powerless, passive victims and deflect attention away from their aggressiveness, their power, (however limited in a white supremacist, male-dominated state) their willingness to dominate and control others. These unacknowledged aspects of the social status of many white women prevent them from transcending racism and limit the scope of their understanding of women's overall social status in the United States.

Privileged feminists have largely been unable to speak to, with, and for diverse groups of women because they either do not understand fully the inter-relatedness of sex, race, and class oppression or refuse to take this inter-relatedness seriously. Feminist analyses of woman's lot tend to focus exclusively on gender and do not provide a solid foundation on which to construct feminist theory. They reflect the dominant tendency in Western patriarchal minds to mystify woman's reality by insisting that gender is the sole determinant of woman's fate. Certainly it has been easier for women who do not experience race or class oppression to focus exclusively on gender. Although socialist feminists focus on class and gender, they tend to dismiss race or they make a point of acknowledging that race is important and then proceed to offer an analysis in which race is not considered.

As a group, black women are in an unusual position in this society, for not only are we collectively at the bottom of the occupational ladder, but our overall social status is lower than that of any other group. Occupying such a position, we bear the brunt of sexist, racist, and classist oppression. At the same time, we are the group that has not been socialized to assume the role of exploiter/oppressor in that we are allowed no institutionalized "other" that we can exploit or oppress. (Children do not represent an institutionalized other even though they may be oppressed by parents.) White women and black men have it both ways. They can act as oppressor or be oppressed. Black men may be victimized by racism, but sexism allows them to act as exploiters and oppressors of women. White women may be victimized by sexism, but racism enables them to act as exploiters and oppressors of black people. Both groups have led liberation movements that favor their interests and support the continued oppression of other groups. Black male sexism has undermined struggles to eradicate racism just as white female racism undermines feminist struggle. As long as these two groups or any group defines liberation as gaining social equality with ruling class white men, they have a vested interest in the continued exploitation and oppression of others.

Black women with no institutionalized "other" that we may discriminate against, exploit, or oppress often have a lived experience that directly challenges the prevailing classist, sexist, racist social structure and its concomitant ideology. This lived experience may shape our consciousness in such a way that our world view differs from those who have a degree of privilege (however relative within the existing system). It is essential for continued feminist struggle that black women recognize the special vantage point our marginality gives us and make use of this perspective to criticize the dominant racist, classist, sexist hegemony as well as to envision and create a counter-hegemony. I am suggesting that we have a central role to play in the making of feminist theory and a contribution to offer that is unique and valuable. The formation of a liberatory feminist theory and praxis is a collective responsibility, one that must be shared. Though I criticize aspects of feminist movement as we have known it so far, a critique which is sometimes harsh and unrelenting, I do so not in an attempt to diminish feminist struggle but to enrich, to share in the work of making a liberatory ideology and a liberatory movement.

LISA H. NEWTON

Reverse Discrimination as Unjustified

LISA H. NEWTON *teaches philosophy at Fairfield University in Fairfield, Connecticut. She specializes in political and social philosophy and has published a book of readings on ethics in America.*

I have heard it argued that "simple justice" requires that we favor women and blacks in employment and educational opportunities, since women and blacks were "unjustly" excluded from such opportunities for so many years in the not so distant past. It is a strange argument, an example of a possible implication of a true proposition advanced to dispute the proposition itself, like an octopus absent-mindedly slicing off his head with a stray tentacle. A fatal confusion underlies this argument, a confusion fundamentally relevant to our understanding of the notion of the rule of law.

Two senses of justice and equality are involved in this confusion. The root notion of justice, progenitor of the other, is the one that Aristotle (*Nichomachean Ethics* 5. 6; *Politics* 1. 2; 3. 1) assumes to be the foundation and proper virtue of the political association. It is the condition which free men establish among themselves when they "share a common life in order that their association bring them self-sufficiency" — the regulation of their relationship by law, and the establishment, by law, of equality before the law. Rule of law is the name and pattern of this justice; its equality stands against the inequalities — of wealth, talent, etc. — otherwise obtaining among its participants, who by virtue of that equality are called "citizens." It is an achievement — complete, or, more frequently, partial — of certain people in certain concrete situations. It is fragile and easily disrupted by powerful individuals who discover that the blind equality of rule of law is inconvenient for their interests. Despite its obvious instability, Aristotle assumed that the establishment of justice in this sense, the creation of citizenship, was a permanent possibility for men and that the resultant association of citizens was the natural home of the species. At levels below the political association, this rule-governed equality is easily found; it is exemplified by any group of children agreeing together to play a game. At the level of the political association, the attainment of this justice is more difficult, simply because the stakes are so much higher for each participant. The equality of citizenship is not something that happens of its own accord, and without the expenditure of a fair amount of effort it will collapse into the rule of a powerful few over an apathetic many. But at least it has been achieved, at some times in some places; it is always worth trying to achieve, and eminently worth trying to maintain, wherever and to whatever degree it has been brought into being.

Aristotle's parochialism is notorious; he really did not imagine that persons other than Greeks could associate freely in justice, and the only form of association he had in mind was the Greek *polis.*

With the decline of the *polis* and the shift in the center of political thought, his notion of justice underwent a sea change. To be exact, it ceased to represent a political type and became a moral ideal: the ideal of equality as we know it. This ideal demands that all men be included in citizenship—that one Law govern all equally, that all men regard all other men as fellow citizens, with the same guarantees, rights, and protections. Briefly, it demands that the circle of citizenship achieved by any group be extended to include the entire human race. Properly understood, its effect on our association can be excellent: it congratulates us on our achievement of rule of law as a process of government but refuses to let us remain complacent until we have expanded the associations to include others within the ambit of the rules, as often and as far as possible. While one man is a slave, none of us may feel truly free. We are constantly prodded by this ideal to look for possible unjustifiable discrimination, for inequalities not absolutely required for the functioning of the society and advantageous to all. And after twenty centuries of pressure, not at all constant, from this ideal, it might be said that some progress has been made. To make the cases in point for this problem, we are now prepared to assert, as Aristotle would never have been, the equality of sexes and of persons of different colors. The ambit of American citizenship, once restricted to white males of property, has been extended to include all adult free men, then all adult males including ex-slaves, then all women. The process of acquisition of full citizenship was for these groups a sporadic trail of half-measures, even now not complete; the steps on the road to full equality are marked by legislation and judicial decisions which are only recently concluded and still often not enforced. But the fact

that we can now discuss the possibility of favoring such groups in hiring shows that over the area that concerns us, at least, full equality is presupposed as a basis for discussion. To that extent, they are full citizens, fully protected by the law of the land.

It is important for my argument that the moral ideal of equality be recognized as logically distinct from the condition (or virtue) of justice in the political sense. Justice in this sense exists *among* a citizenry, irrespective of the number of the populace included in that citizenry. Further, the moral ideal is parasitic upon the political virtue, for "equality" is unspecified—it means nothing until we are told in what respect that equality is to be realized. In a political context, "equality" is specified as "equal rights"—equal access to the public realm, public goods and offices, equal treatment under the law—in brief, the equality of citizenship. If citizenship is not a possibility, political equality is unintelligible. The ideal emerges as a generalization of the real condition and refers back to that condition for its content.

Now, if justice (Aristotle's justice in the political sense) is equal treatment under law for all citizens, what is injustice? Clearly, injustice is the violation of that equality, discriminating for or against a group of citizens, favoring them with special immunities and privileges or depriving them of those guaranteed to the others. When the southern employer refuses to hire blacks in white-collar jobs, when Wall Street will only hire women as secretaries with new titles, when Mississippi high schools routinely flunk all black boys above ninth grade, we have examples of injustice, and we work to restore the equality of the public realm by ensuring that equal opportunity will be provided in such cases in the future. But of course, when the employers and the schools *favor* women and blacks, the same injustice is done. Just as the previous discrimination did, this reverse discrimination violates the public equality which defines citizenship and destroys the rule of law for the areas in which these favors are granted. To the extent that we adopt a program of discrimination, reverse or otherwise, justice in the political sense is destroyed, and none of us, specifically affected or not, is a citizen, a bearer of rights — we are all petitioners for favors. And to the same extent, the ideal of equality is undermined, for it has content only where justice obtains, and by destroying justice we render the ideal meaningless. It is, then, an ironic paradox, if not a contradiction in terms, to assert that the ideal of equality justifies the violation of justice; it is as if one should argue, with William Buckley, that an ideal of humanity can justify the destruction of the human race.

Logically, the conclusion is simple enough: all discrimination is wrong prima facie because it violates justice, and that goes for reverse discrimination too. No violation of justice among the citizens may be justified (may overcome the prima facie objection) by appeal to the ideal of equality, for that ideal is logically dependent upon the notion of justice. Reverse discrimination, then, which attempts no other justification than an appeal to equality, is wrong. But let us try to make the conclusion more plausible by suggesting some of the implications of the suggested practice of reverse discrimination in employment and education. My argument will be that the problems raised there are insoluble, not only in practice but in principle.

We may argue, if we like, about what "discrimination" consists of. Do I discriminate against blacks if I admit none to my school when none of the black applicants are qualified by the tests I always give? How far must I go to root out cultural bias from my application forms and tests before I can say that I have not discriminated against those of different cultures? Can I assume that women are not strong enough to be roughnecks on my oil rigs, or must I test them individually? But this controversy, the most popular and well-argued aspect of the issue, is not as fatal as two others which cannot be avoided: if we are regarding the blacks as a "minority" victimized by discrimination, what is a "minority"? And for any group — blacks, women, whatever — that has been discriminated against, what amount of reverse discrimination wipes out the initial discrimination? Let us grant as true that women and blacks were discriminated against, even where laws forbade such discrimination, and grant for the sake of argument that a history of discrimination must be wiped out by reverse discrimination. What follows?

First, are there other groups which have been discriminated against? For they should have the same right of restitution. What about American Indians, Chicanos, Appalachian Mountain whites, Puerto Ricans, Jews, Cajuns, and Orientals? And if these are to be included, the principle according to which we specify a "minority" is simply the criterion of "ethnic (sub) group," and we're stuck with every hyphenated American in the lower-middle class clamoring for special privileges for *his* group — and with equal justification. For be it noted, when we run down the Harvard roster, we find not only a scarcity of blacks (in comparison with the proportion in the population) but an even more striking scarcity of those second-, third-, and fourth-generation ethnics who make up the loudest voice of Middle America. Shouldn't they demand *their* share? And eventually, the WASPs will have to form their own lobby, for they too are a minority. The point is simply this: there is no "majority" in America who will not mind giving up just a bit of their rights to make room for a favored minority. There are only other minorities, each of which is discriminated against by the favoring. The initial injustice is then repeated dozens of times, and if each minority is granted the same right of restitution as the others, an entire area of rule governance is dissolved into a pushing and shoving match between self-interested groups. Each works to catch the public eye and political popularity by whatever means of advertising and power politics lend themselves to the effort, to capitalize as much as possible on temporary popularity until the restless mob picks another group to feel sorry for. Hardly an edifying spectacle, and in the long run no one can benefit: the pie is no larger — it's just that instead of setting up and enforcing rules for getting a piece, we've turned the contest into a free-for-all, requiring much more effort for no larger a reward. It would be in the interests of all the participants to re-establish an objective rule to govern the process, carefully enforced and the same for all.

Second, supposing that we do manage to agree in general that women and blacks (and all the others) have some right of restitution, some right to a privileged place in the structure of opportunities for a while, how will we know when that while is up? How much privilege is enough? When will the guilt be gone, the price paid, the balance restored? What recompense is right for centuries of exclusion? What criterion tells us when we are done? Our experience with the Civil Rights movement shows us that agreement on these terms cannot be presupposed: a process that appears to some to be going at a mad gallop into a black take-

over appears to the rest of us to be at a standstill. Should a practice of reverse discrimination be adopted, we may safely predict that just as some of us begin to see "a satisfactory start toward righting the balance," others of us will see that we "have already gone too far in the other direction" and will suggest that the discrimination ought to be reversed again. And such disagreement is inevitable, for the point is that we could not *possibly* have any criteria for evaluating the kind of recompense we have in mind. The context presumed by any discussion of restitution is the context of rule of law: law sets the rights of men and simultaneously sets the method for remedying the violation of those rights. You may exact suffering from others and/or damage payments for yourself if and only if the others have violated your rights; the suffering you have endured is not sufficient reason for them to suffer. And remedial rights exist only where there is law: primary human rights are useful guides to legislation but cannot stand as reasons for awarding remedies for injuries sustained. But then, the context presupposed by any discussion of restitution is the context of preexistent full citizenship. No remedial rights could exist for the excluded; neither in law nor in logic does there exist a right to *sue* for a standing to sue.

From these two considerations, then, the difficulties with reverse discrimination become evident. Restitution for a disadvantaged group whose rights under the law have been violated is possible by legal means, but restitution for a disadvantaged group whose grievance is that there was no law to protect them simply is not. First, outside of the area of justice defined by the law, no sense can be made of "the group's rights," for no law recognizes that group or the individuals in it, qua members, as bearers of rights (hence *any* group can constitute itself as a disadvantaged minority in some sense and demand similar restitution). Second, outside of the area of protection of law, no sense can be made of the violation of rights (hence the amount of the recompense cannot be decided by any objective criterion). For both reasons, the practice of reverse discrimination undermines the foundation of the very ideal in whose name it is advocated; it destroys justice, law, equality, and citizenship itself, and replaces them with power struggles and popularity contests.

GEORGE SHER

Reverse Discrimination, the Future, and the Past

GEORGE SHER *teaches philosophy at the University of Vermont in Burlington, Vermont. He publishes in the areas of ethics and social and political philosophy.*

THERE exist in our society some groups whose members, in the past, were discriminatorily denied jobs, admission to educational institutions, and others goods; and many people believe that members of these groups should be given special preference in these areas now. Although the groups most often mentioned in this connection are blacks and women, the current affirmative action guidelines list also American Indians and Alaskan natives, certain Asians and Pacific Islanders, and persons of Hispanic background; and I suspect that most proponents of a policy of reverse discrimination which follows group lines would want it to apply to these groups as well. For simplicity, I will use the term "minority" to designate all the groups except women for which preference is advocated. Because the areas in which preference is urged are so closely related to those in which the initial discrimination took place, it is natural to view the proponents of reverse discrimination as arguing not merely that it will improve the lot of the current group members, but rather that in doing so it will compensate for the earlier discrimination. To the extent that the argument for reverse discrimination is a compensatory one, that argument will involve an essential reference to the unjust actions of the past, and so will be fundamentally backward-looking.

Although explicitly backward-looking justifications of reverse discrimination are common enough, they have tended to call forth an equally common objection. Put simply, the objection is that the current beneficiaries of reverse discrimination are not often the same persons as those who were harmed by the original discrimination, and those who now bear the burden of reverse discrimination are seldom the same persons as those who practiced the original discrimination. Because of this, reverse discrimination is said to be both irrelevant to the aim of compensating for past injustices and unfair to those whose superior qualifications are bypassed. To meet this objection, the backward-looking defender of reverse discrimination may elaborate his position in one of three ways. He may hold either that (1) every woman and minority group member has suffered and every nonminority male has benefited at least indirectly from the effects of past discrimination; or that (2) the entities to be compensated are not individuals at all but rather the groups to which the initial victims belonged; or that (3) we should extend preference not to every woman and minority group member but rather only to those group members who have actually suffered from past discrimination. However, (1) and (2) raise obvious and well-known difficulties in their turn, and (3) represents what many regard as an intolerable weakening of the original thesis.

In light of these difficulties, some defenders of reverse discrimination have attempted to justify that practice in what appears to be a different way altogether. On the alternative justification they propose, the aim of reverse discrimination is not to compensate anyone for any harm caused by past wrongdoing, but rather simply to promote certain highly desirable forms of social change. Although the details of this account have tended to vary, its fundamental thrust is that reverse discrimination is a necessary tool for improving the socioeconomic position of minorities and for providing role-models for both members of minority groups and women, and that these results are in turn essential steps toward bringing the present and future members of these groups into society's mainstream. The fundamental

point is that reverse discrimination should be seen not primarily as redressing past wrongs, but rather simply as breaking what would otherwise be an endlessly continuing cycle of poverty and subservience. Since the latter aim seems compelling independently of any historical considerations, a strong policy of preferential treatment for all members of the affected groups is said to be justified in a purely forward-looking way.

It must be conceded that a genuinely forward-looking justification of reverse discrimination would avoid the need to establish what must be the extremely complicated causal connections between past wrongs and the current positions of particular individuals. However, the advantage gained here may be more apparent than real; for in place of this task, the forward-looking justification will face the equally difficult challenge of marshalling enough detailed social scientific evidence to show that reverse discrimination would indeed disrupt the relevant cycles of disadvantage, and that no other, fairer way of doing so would be as effective. Moreover, even if such empirical evidence could be mustered, a deeper difficulty with the forward-looking approach to reverse discrimination would remain. If that approach is to be genuinely acceptable, then the disruption of the relevant cycles of disadvantage will itself have to be called for by some independently grounded and forward-looking moral principle. However, although the principles of utility and equality have both been invoked in this connection, I shall argue in what follows that neither of them could plausibly be said to justify a policy with just the effects that reverse discrimination is claimed to have. If this contention is correct, then the forward-looking approach to reverse discrimination will be considerably more problematic than it first appears to be.

Let us begin by examining the appeal to utility. In its most basic form, a utilitarian defense of reverse discrimination will consist simply of the claim that interrupting the ongoing cycles of disadvantage would bring more overall benefit than allowing those cycles to continue; while a more sophisticated version will supplement this utility claim with a further argument that qualifications of the traditional sort do not themselves confer any right to a contested good. Assuming that the relevant factual claims are correct, such utilitarian arguments may appear to offer a quick and decisive justification for a sustained policy of reverse discrimination. However, a closer look reveals that on either formulation, the utilitarian defense is vulnerable to a simple but serious objection. Put briefly, the objection is that if it is acceptable to discriminate in *favor* of minorities and women when doing so maximizes utility, then it is hard to see why it should not also be acceptable to discriminate *against* minorities and women when *that* policy maximizes utility. However, the possibility that racial, ethnic, or sexual discrimination might be legitimate is surely not one that any defender of reverse discrimination could accept.

The force of this objection has not been lost on the utilitarian defenders of reverse discrimination. One of these defenders, Thomas Nagel, has attempted to rebut the objection by contending that racial and sexual discrimination, unlike reverse discrimination, "has no social advantages . . . and attaches a sense of reduced worth to a feature with which people are born." Moreover, another utilitarian defender, Ronald Dworkin, has attempted to bolster the utilitarian defense by distin-

guishing between two sorts of preferences. According to Dworkin: "The preferences of an individual for the consequences of a particular policy may be seen to reflect, on further analysis, either a *personal* preference for his own enjoyment of some goods or opportunities, or an *external* preference for the assignment of goods and opportunities to others, or both." To whatever extent a utility claim rests on external preferences, it will tie someone's chances of satisfaction to "the respect or affection [others] have for him or for his way of life," and so will not be legitimate. Thus, since utilitarian arguments for racial (and, we may add, ethnic and sexual) discrimination are evidently based on just such external preferences while utilitarian arguments for reverse discrimination are not, Dworkin concludes that we may safely accept the latter arguments without being forced to accept the former also.

Nagel and Dworkin have both attempted to show how the utilitarian can avoid the charge that his principle cuts two ways. However, even if we accept both Nagel's empirical claim and Dworkin's distinction between personal and external preferences, it will remain doubtful whether either has successfully answered the difficulty. What Nagel and Dworkin have shown is that no legitimate utilitarian argument can justify a policy of racial, ethnic, or sexual discrimination under the conditions which now prevail. However, it is one thing to show this, and quite another to show that no legitimate utilitarian argument could justify such discrimination under *any circumstances at all*. As far as I can see, Nagel has offered us no reason to believe that there could never be alternative circumstances in which racial, ethnic, or sexual discrimination had social advantages which *did* outweigh the sense of reduced worth it produced; and neither, despite his bare assertion to the contrary, has Dworkin produced any reason to suppose that such discrimination could never maximize the satisfaction of purely personal preferences. Because these possibilities still remain open, the utilitarian will still have to regard the wrongness of racial, ethnic, and sexual discrimination as fundamentally an empirical accident. However, this claim is precisely the one which the proponent of reverse discrimination will presumably be unwilling to accept. Because this is so, a viable forward-looking defense of reverse discrimination will evidently have to appeal to some principle other than that of mere utility.

The other main consequentialist principle that has been invoked to support reverse discrimination is the principle of equality. By breaking the existing cycles of disadvantage, reverse discrimination is said to be a way of eliminating the gaps which now separate the different races, sexes, and ethnocultural groups, and so of promoting greater social equality. By thus appealing to the aim of equality, the defender of reverse discrimination can avoid the failure of generalization which vitiates the utilitarian approach. However, by making such an appeal, he will raise a further problem in its turn. This further problem stems from the fact that even if he is committed to the ideal of equality among races, sexes, and other groups, the proponent of reverse discrimination must *ex hypothesi* continue to accept a framework of *inequality* among individuals. This acceptance of inequality follows directly from the nature of reverse discrimination itself. To practice reverse discrimination is just to award certain contested goods to women and minority group members in preference to other, more traditionally qualified claimants;

and to award goods in this way is not to abolish, but merely to rearrange, the inequalities of distribution that now prevail. Moreover, since the goods to be awarded preferentially are themselves instrumental to the procuring of further goods, it is clear that any inequalities which are perpetuated by reverse discrimination must result in yet further inequalities in the future. Because this is so, and because many other egalitarian strategies (for example, the direct redistribution of wealth) are likely not to have this consequence to the same degree, any egalitarian who argues for reverse discrimination will have to explain why we should stop at just the amount of equality which that practice would produce. If he cannot answer this question, then the egalitarian's refusal to tolerate racial, ethnic, and sexual inequalities will be flatly inconsistent with his willingness to tolerate the other inequalities which reverse discrimination perpetuates.

One possible way for the egalitarian proponent of reverse discrimination to defend his stopping point would be for him to maintain that more equality would indeed be desirable, but that no alternative strategy for achieving it is politically and economically feasible. If this claim were correct, then the egalitarian's willingness to settle for the amount of equality which can be achieved through reverse discrimination could be defended on pragmatic grounds. However, anyone who pursued this line would have to assume that reverse discrimination is in fact the most effective egalitarian strategy now available; and in light of the many possible alternative strategies and the open-ended time period which reverse discrimination is said to require to work its effects, this unproven factual assumption is even more problematical than the others already encountered. Perhaps because of this, few egalitarians have tried to defend reverse discrimination in this way. Instead, the prevailing egalitarian view appears to be that racial, ethnic, and sexual inequalities are somehow especially wrong, and so are especially deserving of eradication. But how, exactly, is this further claim to be supported in its turn?

One way of showing that continuing racial, ethnic, and sexual inequalities are worse than others would be to argue that the former inequalities deprive groups as well as individuals of equal shares of goods, and so violate the principle of equality twice over. However, to make this argument, one would have to presuppose that the relevant groups are themselves proper candidates for equal treatment; and this supposition seems no more supportable in a forward-looking context than it is in a backward-looking one. Moreover, neither could it be argued that at least racial and sexual inequalities are especially wrong because they are based on morally arbitrary or unchangeable characteristics; for if these inequalities are genuinely self-perpetuating, then they will persist independently of any future discriminatory acts, and so will not be based on any personal characteristics at all. In light of these facts, the only remotely plausible forward-looking way of showing that racial, ethnic, and sexual inequalities are especially wrong is to reinvoke Nagel's observation that these inequalities, unlike others, are apt to lead to further inequalities of self-respect. A white who is poor and uneducated is not likely to despise himself for belonging to an inferior group, while even an affluent and well-educated black may think badly of himself because so many other blacks have occupied inferior positions; and something similar may hold, *mutatis mutandis*, for members of other minorities and women as well. We saw above that such observations do not rescue the utilitarian from the charge that his principle might sometimes justify racial, ethnic, or sexual discrimination. However, they may appear far more effective when they are marshalled to show that racial, ethnic, and sexual inequalities are decisively worse than others.

It must be acknowledged that any distributional inequality which leads to a further inequality in self-respect is *ceteris paribus* worse than one which does not. However, properly understood, this fact offers little comfort to the egalitarian defender of reverse discrimination. What that defender needs to show is that it is consistent to denounce whichever inequalities follow racial, ethnic, or sexual lines, while at the same time *not* denouncing those other inequalities which reverse discrimination inevitably perpetuates. However, the fact that racial, ethnic, and sexual inequalities are accompanied by further psychological inequalities while others are not simply does not yield this conclusion. At best, it shows only that the former inequalities would have first claim on our attention if we were forced to choose among inequalities — which, as we have seen, there is not good reason to think we are. It does not show, and no further argument *could* show, that any consistent egalitarian could ignore the import of the other inequalities altogether. Because this is so, the appeal to equality is in the end just as dubious as the previous appeal to utility.

We have now examined the two most common forward-looking defenses of reverse discrimination. Although there is plainly more to be said about each, we have seen enough to show that both are vulnerable to what is at bottom the same objection. To the utilitarian defense, the objection is that it is merely a logical accident that the principle of utility now dictates practices which favor women and minority group members instead of nonminority males; while for the egalitarian defense, the difficulty is to explain why we should adopt a policy which equalizes only the positions of women and the specified minorities. Because neither forward-looking principle tells us why we should restrict our attention to the members of these groups, it is reasonable to seek the justification for this restriction in some further premise which has hitherto been suppressed. Moreover, given the context in which the whole discussion has taken place, the relevant suppressed premise is not difficult to find. Because the most salient fact about blacks, women, American Indians, Hispanics, etc., is just that they *were* so often discriminated against in the past, the suppressed reason for focusing attention on them now can hardly fail to be that they, unlike the others, are now deserving of compensation.

If this suggestion is correct, of course, then even those defenses of reverse discrimination which at first appear to be entirely forward-looking will in the end not be purely forward-looking at all. They will indeed be forward-looking to the extent that they attempt to justify reverse discrimination by claiming that it will maximize future utility or equality for women and members of the specified minorities; but their concentration on women and members of these minorities will itself by warranted by the fact that these persons' lack of goods or unequal status is likely to call for compensation if it does occur. They will indeed shift the emphasis from the amelioration of harms already done to prophylaxis to avoid future harms; but the future harms which they aim at avoiding will themselves be singled out by their immoral causal antecedents. Because the scope of the proposed arguments will thus be determined by the demands created by past wrongs, the arguments in question will reach no further than those future persons who are genuinely in danger of suffering compensable harms. These persons will undoubtedly include many blacks and members of the other official minorities; but there is little reason to believe that they will include all the members of these groups. Moreover, to be consistent, we should also expect them to include a good many Italians, Jews, Slavs, and members of the various other groups which have suffered past discrimination, but which are not included in the official list. Because so many groups have been subjected to active discrimination, any attempt to single out the endangered future members of some few of them is likely to be quite arbitrary. All in all, therefore, the proposed arguments do not avoid, but rather actually extend, the crucial question of which individuals deserve compensation for past discrimination.

TOM L. BEAUCHAMP

The Justification of Reverse Discrimination

TOM L. BEAUCHAMP *teaches philosophy at Georgetown University. He has published widely on ethics. Among his books are* Principles of Biomedical Ethics *(1989) and* Ethics and Public Policy *(1983).*

MY moral argument is intended to show that policies productive of reverse discrimination are compatible with basic principles of justice and utility. This is not to say that no injustices result from the occurrence of reverse discrimination, but it is to say that these injustices can be justified.

• • •

An initial difficulty must be faced in any appeal to principles of justice. Since there are different theories of justice, and different kinds of justice recognized within the different theories, it might be thought that a comprehensive theory of justice must be defended before problems of reverse discrimination can be intelligently discussed. Fortunately, for our purposes, this difficulty may be largely ignored for two reasons. First, we can without prejudicing the arguments successfully operate with two rather minimal principles of justice, both of which derive from Aristotle and both of which receive wide acceptance as at least necessary, even if not sufficient, conditions of justice. The first is the principle of *formal equality*. It says that equals must be treated equally and unequals unequally; or, more fully stated, it says that "No person should be treated unequally, despite all differences with other persons, until such time as it has been shown that there is a difference between them relevant to the treatment at stake." One demand of the principle is the egalitarian ideal of equal consideration of persons: Every person is to be evaluated on his or her merit when there is equal opportunity to compete. The problem with the principle is notoriously more in its abstractness than in any deficiency of content. That equals ought to be treated equally, by law and elsewhere, is not likely to stir disagreement. But who is equal and who unequal? Presumably all citizens should have equal political rights, equal access to public services, and should receive equal treatment under the law. But almost all would allow that distinctions based on experience, merit, and position do sometimes introduce criteria justifying differential treatment. Whether race, sex, and religion similarly justify differential treatment under some conditions is more controversial. This issue of the appropriate *application* of the principle of formal equality is one that we shall be considering.

The second principle of justice deserving explicit statement is the principle of *compensatory justice*. It says that whenever an injustice has been committed, just compensation or reparation is owed the injured parties. The idea is to restore, so far as possible, the state of affairs prior to the injury or injustice which created the need for compensation, and also to benefit the injured parties in a manner proportional to the injury or loss suffered. The compensation might be to groups or to individuals, but in either case the same justifying principle is used. It is now a widespread view that groups invidiously discriminated against in the proximate and remote past, including women, blacks, North American Indians, and French Canadians, should be recompensed for these injustices by compensatory policies, at least in those cases where injury is traceable to particular persons. . . .

Compensatory justice both (1) demands that we make an especially vigorous attempt to discover *present* discrimination against classes of persons discriminated against in the past and (2) creates a *special* obligation to eliminate such present discriminatory treatment wherever it is found. I will take for granted that this weakened claim about obligations generated by compensatory justice is reasonable, and that any society which fails to act on this obligation is an unjust society, whether or not this failure is intentional.

Recently a rather large literature has emerged in which the attempt is made to show that policies causing reverse discrimination violate the above (and perhaps other) principles of justice. . . .

Among reasons proposed as supplementary to this primary argument are the following: (1) Some who are innocent of and not responsible for the past invidious discrimination pay the price (e.g., qualified young white males); but this treatment is discriminatory because such persons are penalized solely on the basis of their race. (2) Male members of minority groups such as Poles, Irish, and Italians — themselves discriminated against in the past — will bear a heavy burden of the cost of compensating women and minority groups such as blacks. (3) Many members of the *class* selected for preferential treatment will have never themselves been unjustly treated and will not deserve preferential policies. (4) There are some relevant differences between the sexes which justify differential expectations and treatment (men are naturally better at some things, women at others). (5) Compensation can be provided to *individuals* treated unfairly in the past without resort to reverse discrimination, which is the result of blanket treatment for groups. The least reason (5) is presumably not only a reason against reverse discrimination, but an alternative *policy,* as well.

• • •

I find these reasons against allowing reverse discrimination to occur both thoughtful and tempting, and I want to concede from the outset that policies of reverse discrimination can create serious and perhaps even tragic injustices. One must be careful, however, not to draw an overzealous conclusion from this admission. Those who argue that reverse discrimination creates injustices often say that, because of the injustice, such policies are *unjust.* I think by this use of "unjust" they generally mean "not justified" (rather than "not sanctioned by justice"). But this conclusion does not follow merely from the arguments thus far mentioned. A policy can create and even perpetuate injustices, as violations of the principle of formal equality, and yet be justified by other reasons. It would be an injustice in this sense to fire either one of two assistant professors with exactly similar professional credentials, while retaining the other of the two; yet the financial condition of the university or compensation owed the person retained might provide compelling reasons which justify the action. The first reason supporting the dismissal is utilitarian in character, and the other derives from the principle of compensatory justice. This shows both that there can be conflicts between different justice-regarding reasons and also that violations of the principle of formal equality are not in themselves sufficient to render an action unjustifiable.

A proper conclusion, then — and one which I accept — is that all discrimination, including reverse discrimination, is *prima facie* immoral, because a basic principle of justice creates a *prima facie* duty to abstain from such treatment of persons. But no absolute duty is created come what may, for we might have conflicting duties of sufficient weight to justify such injustices. The latter is the larger thesis I wish to defend: Considerations of compensatory justice and utility are conjointly of sufficient weight in contemporary society to neutralize and overcome the quite proper presumption of immorality in the case of some policies productive of reverse discrimination.

.   .   .

My argument is motivated by the belief that racial, sexual, and no doubt other forms of discrimination are not antique relics but are living patterns which continue to warp selection and ranking procedures. In my view the difference between the present and the past is that discriminatory treatment is today less widespread and considerably less blatant. But its reduction has produced apathy; its subtleness has made it less visible and considerably more difficult to detect.

Largely because of the reduced visibility of racism and sexism, I suggest, reverse discrimination now strikes us as all too harsh and unfair. After all, quotas and preferential treatment have no appeal if one assumes a just, primarily nondiscriminatory society. Since the presence or absence of seriously discriminatory conditions in our society is a factual matter, empirical evidence must be adduced to show that the set of discriminatory attitudes and selection procedures I have alleged to exist do in fact exist.

.   .   .

A massive body of statistics constituting *prima facie* evidence of discrimination has been assembled in recent years. Here is a tiny but diverse fragment of some of these statistical findings. (1) Women college teachers with identical credentials in terms of publications and experience are promoted at almost exactly one-half the rate of their male counterparts. (2) In the United States women graduates of medical schools in 1965 stood at 7%, as compared with 36% in Germany. The gap in the number of women physicians was similar. (3) Of 3,000 leading law firms surveyed in 1957 only 32 reported a woman partner, and even these women were paid much less (increasingly so for every year of employment) than their male counterparts. (4) 40% of the white-collar positions in the United States are presently held by women, but only 10% of the management positions are held by women, and their pay again is significantly less (70% of clerical workers are women). (5) 8,000 workers were employed in May 1967 in the construction of BART (Bay Area Rapid Transit), but not a single electrician, ironworker, or plumber was black. (6) In the population as a whole in the

United States, 3 out of 7 employees hold white-collar positions, but only 1 of 7 blacks holds such a position, and these latter jobs are clustered in professions which have the fewest jobs to offer in top-paying positions.

In a number of decisions of the Equal Employment Opportunity Commission, it has been shown that the interviewers have racially biased attitudes and that the applications of blacks and women are systematically handled in unusual ways, such as never even being filed. So serious and consistent have such violations been that the EEOC has publicly stated its belief that word-of-mouth recruitment policies without demonstrable supplementary and simultaneous recruitment in minority group communities is in itself a "prima facie violation of Title VII." Gertrude Erorsky has argued, convincingly I believe, that this pattern of "special ties" is no less present in professional white collar hiring, which is neither less discriminatory nor more sensitive to hiring strictly on the basis of merit.

The Carnegie Commission and others have assembled statistical evidence to show that in even the most favorable construal of relevant variables, women teachers have been discriminated against in hiring, tenuring, and ranking. But instead of summarizing this mountain of material, I wish here to take a particular case in order to illustrate the difficulty in determining, on the basis of statistics and similar empirical data, whether discrimination is occurring even where courts have been forced to find satisfactory evidence of discrimination. In December 1974 a decision was reached by the Commission against Discrimination of the Executive Department of the State of Massachusetts regarding a case at Smith College where the two complainants were women who were denied tenure and dismissed by the English Department. The

women claimed sex discrimination and based their case on the following: (1) Women at the full professor level in the college declined from 54% in 1958 to 21%, and in the English department from 57% in 1960 to 11% in 1972. These statistics compare unfavorably at all levels with Mt. Holyoke's, a comparable institution (since both have an all female student body and are located in Western Massachusetts). (2) Thirteen of the department's fifteen associate and full professorships at Smith belonged to men. (3) The two tenured women had obtained tenure under "distinctly peculiar experiences" including a stipulation that one be only part-time and that the other not be promoted when given tenure. (4) The department's faculty members conceded that tenure standards were applied subjectively, were vague, and lacked the kind of precision which would avoid discriminatory application. (5) The women denied tenure were at no time given advance warning that their work was deficient. Rather, they were given favorable evaluations of their teaching and were encouraged to believe they would receive tenure. (6) Some stated reasons for the dismissals were later demonstrated to be rationalizations, and one letter from a senior member to the tenure and promotion committee contradicted his own appraisal of teaching ability filed with the department. (7) The court accepted expert testimony that any deficiencies in the women candidates were also found in male candidates promoted and given tenure during this same period, and that the women's positive credentials were at least as good as the men's.

The commissioner's opinion found that "the Complainants properly used statistics to demonstrate that the Respondents' practices operate with a discriminatory effect." Citing *Parham* v. *Southwestern Bell Telephone Co.,* the commissioner argued that "in such cases extreme statistics may establish discrimination as a matter of law, without additional supportive evidence." But in this case the commissioner found abundant additional evidence in the form of "the historical absence of women," "word-of-mouth recruitment policies" which operate discriminatorily, and a number of "subtle and not so subtle, societal patterns" existing at Smith. On December 30, 1974 the commissioner ordered the two women reinstated with tenure and ordered the department to submit an affirmative action program within 60 days.

This case is interesting because there is little in the way of clinching proof that the members of the English Department actually held discriminatory attitudes. Yet so consistent a pattern of *apparently* discriminatory treatment must be regarded, according to this decision, as *de facto* discrimination. The commissioner's ruling and other laws are quite explicit that "intent or lack thereof is of no consequence." If a procedure constitutes discriminatory treatment, then the parties discriminated against must be recompensed. Here we have a case where irresistible statistics and other sociological evidence of "social exclusion" and "subtle societal patterns" provide convincing evidence that strong, court backed measures must be taken because nothing short of such measures is sufficiently strong to overcome the discriminatory pattern, as the Respondents' testimony in the case verifies.

•   •   •

Some contemporary government programs are conceived as compensatory programs, whereas others are construed as non-compensatory legal means of ensuring equal treatment. I am not concerned with this distinction, except that where the programs are expressly compensatory I construe government intent as that of providing compensatory programs which do not permit reverse discrimination. This is the stated intent of those who administer such programs in the United States, and I believe this statement of intent is generally consistent with their practice. There has, however, been considerable confusion over the meaning and content of various government "regulations" and "guidelines" for enforcing federal laws, and a moment must be spent on this interpretative problem.

•   •   •

For further clarification, I mention a sample of the affirmative action guidelines, as understood by those who administer them. I use the example of HEW guidelines for educational institutions receiving federal financial aid. These guidelines cover three areas: admission, treatment of students, and employment. A sample of the sorts of requirements universities are under includes: (1) They may not advertise vacant positions as open only to or preferentially to a particular race or sex, except where sex is a legitimate occupational requirement. (2) The university sets standards and criteria for employment, but if these effectively work to exclude women or minorities as a class, the university must justify the job requirements. (3) An institution may not set different standards of admission for one sex, race, etc. (4) There must be active recruitment where there is an under-representation of women and minorities, as gauged by the availability of qualified members of these classes. However, the relevant government officials have from time to time made it clear that (1) quotas are unacceptable, either for admission or employment, though target goals and timetables intended to correct deficiencies are acceptable and to be encouraged. (2) A university is never under any obligation to dilute legitimate standards, and hence there is no conflict with merit hiring. (3) Reserving positions for members of a minority group (and presumably for the female sex) is "an outrageous and illegal form of reverse bias" (as one former director of the program wrote). By affirmative action requirements I mean this latter interpretation and nothing stronger (though I have given only a sample set of qualifications, of course).

The question I am currently asking is whether these guidelines, assuming they will be vigorously pursued, can reasonably be expected to bring about their goal, which is the social circumstance of nondiscriminatory treatment of persons. If they *are* strong enough, then Cohen, Blackstone, and others are right: Reverse discrimination is not under such circumstances justified. Unfortunately the statistical and linguistic evidence previously adduced indicates otherwise. The *Smith College* case is paradigmatic of the concealed yet serious discrimination which occurs through the network of subtle distortions, old-boy procedures, and prejudices we have accumulated. Only when the statistics become egregiously out of proportion is action taken or a finding of mistreatment possible. And that is one reason why it seems unlikely that substantial progress can be made, in any realistic sense of "can," by current government measures not productive of reverse discrimination. According to Peter Holmes, currently the Director of HEW's Office for Civil Rights and in charge of interpreting affirmative action guidelines: "It has been our policy that it is the institutions' respon-

sibility to determine non-discriminatory qualifications in the first instance, and that such qualifications, in conjunction with other affirmative action steps, should yield results." This is the received HEW view, but the last sentence contains an ambiguous use of the word "should." If the "should" in this statement is a moral "should," none will disagree. But if it is an empirical, predictive "should," as I take Mr. Holmes to intend, we are back to the core of the difficulty.

·　　·　　·

No one could be happy about the conclusions I have reached or about the depressing and disturbing facts on which they are based. But I do take it to be a *factual* and not an *evaluative* conclusion both (1) that the camouflaged attitudes I have discussed exist and affect the social position of minority groups and women and (2) that they will in all likelihood continue to have this influence. It is, of course, an evaluative conclusion that we are morally permitted and even required to remedy this situation by the imposition of quotas, target goals, and timetables. But anyone who accepts my *interpretation* of the facts bears a heavy burden of moral argument to show that we ought not to use such means to that end upon which I take it we all agree, viz., the equal consideration of persons irrespective of race, sex, religion, or nationality.

By way of conclusion, it is important to set my arguments in the framework of a distinction between real reverse discrimination and merely apparent reverse discrimination. My evidence demonstrates present, ongoing barriers to the removal of discriminatory practices. My contentions set the stage for showing that *because* of the existence of what Thalberg calls "visceral racism," and because of visceral sexism as well, there will be many occasions on which we can only avoid inevitable discrimination by policies productive of reverse discrimination. Sometimes, however, persons will be hired or admitted — on a quota basis, for example — who appear to be displacing better applicants, but the appearance is the result of visceral discriminatory perceptions of the person's qualifications. In this case there will certainly appear to the visceral racist or sexist to be reverse discrimination, and this impression will be reinforced by knowl-edge that quotas were used; yet the allegation of reverse discrimination will be a mistaken one. On other occasions there will be genuine reverse discrimination, and on many occasions it will be impossible to determine whether or not this consequence is occurring. The evidence I have adduced is, of course, intended to support the contention that real and not merely apparent reverse discrimination is justified. But it is justified only as a means to the end of ensuring genuinely non-discriminatory treatment of all persons.

9

Can There Be Equality Between Men and Women?

Story 1: Driving the truck to work one day, Lee noticed somebody by the side of the road with a flat tire. Lee stopped and got out to help fix the flat. Because neither of them had a jack, Lee had to hold up the rear end of the *car while the owner replaced the tire. When they were done, Lee reminded herself to buy a new jack on her way home.*

Story 2: Pat was putting the finishing touches on the pie when the kids rushed in the door. "What's for dinner? We're starved." "Wash your hands, kids, and set the table," Pat replied. "We'll be eating as soon as Mom gets home from work."

It is a rare person indeed who would read either of these stories without experiencing a "gender jolt" at the end of them. No matter what your views about sexual equality, it is nevertheless true that we tend to make certain associations when it comes to gender. Even if your mother is a body builder who rides a Harley, you probably assumed that the person holding up the rear of the car was a man. Similarly, even if your father does the cooking every night, you probably assumed that the person putting the finishing touches on the pie was a woman.

While we do make such characteristic gender associations, it is far from clear whether they are rooted in fundamental, irreversible differences between men and women, or whether they are a function of changeable social practices. Look around the world. How many women are steamroller operators? Heads of state? CIA agents? Garage mechanics? Nuclear physicists? How many men are elementary school teachers? Secretaries? Nurses? Homemakers? It is important to notice two things. First, men and women tend to occupy different roles in our culture. Second, the roles that women occupy tend to be subordinate to those of men.

These facts often lead people to conclude that gender differences are "natural," that they are part of the order of things and hence cannot in any significant way be changed. John Stuart Mill argues that the conceptions that we have of the alleged "natures" of men and women are the result of taking facts about the way things *are* as equivalent to facts about the way things *must be*. Suppose that you are in the hospital for a week and during that time, you never encounter a male nurse. Are you entitled to conclude that men can't, by their very nature, be nurses? Or that women, by their very nature, are suited to nursing? Mill cautions us against making inferences like these.

Writing a hundred years after John Stuart Mill, Simone de Beauvoir sought to provide a more complete account of the causes and effects of women's oppression. Beauvoir argues that men have constructed women as what she calls "the Other" in order to establish the superiority of their own characteristics. The human tendency toward self-importance takes the form, in men, of casting feminine characteristics in a negative light. The feminine becomes the negative, that which is not male. By denying women the capacity to make sound judgments, men ensure that whatever resistance women might show to this negative assessment of their abilities is itself dismissed as yet another error in judgment. Left with no other resources, women come to see themselves as men want them to be seen. They expect to be weak, silly, emotional, powerless, and dependent. They, too, see themselves as the Other.

The remaining essays in this chapter take up in various ways the challenge posed by Beauvoir's original, illuminating, though rather dismal, depiction of women's consciousness of themselves as inferior to men. If Beauvoir is correct in her assertion that women's consciousness is constructed by men, then it looks as though women have no feelings, thoughts or desires that are truly their own. In her essay, Jean Grimshaw explores the differences between the Beauvoirean view and that of other feminists who have argued that, lying underneath the encrustations of male dominance, there is an authentic female self waiting to be discovered. She finds both views to be inadequate and proposes a way of thinking about the self that avoids what she takes to be the philosophical and political dangers of each.

Marilyn Frye is concerned to provide a rigorous analysis of the term *sexism* in order to render sexist institutions, people, and actions more visible. The fact that sexism is not always apparent, either to those who suffer from it or to those who perpetrate it, is part of what allows sexism to prosper. According to Frye, sexism is the result of a particular system of "sex-marking." She asks us to think about the variety of ways in which sex differences are reinforced by clothing and by manners of walking and speaking. By continuing, as a culture, to emphasize the importance of sex differences, we further reinforce the relationship of domination and subordination whose purpose it serves.

María C. Lugones and Elizabeth V. Spelman's dialogue furthers Frye's analysis by placing the issue of sexism in a larger social context. They allow us to see the ways in which feminist theory and practice exclude issues of racism by assuming that white women speak for all women. They emphasize the importance of acknowledging the diversity of the women engaged in the common struggle for women's equality.

JOHN STUART MILL

The Subjection of Women

JOHN STUART MILL (1806–1873) *was one of the documented geniuses of modern history. By the age of ten, he had accomplished more than most scholars do in a lifetime. He is best known for his moral and political writings, particularly* On Liberty *(1859) and* Utilitarianism *(1863).*

NEITHER does it avail anything to say that the *nature* of the two sexes adapts them to their present functions and position, and renders these appropriate to them. Standing on the ground of common sense and the constitution of the human mind, I deny that any one knows, or can know, the nature of the two sexes, as long as they have only been seen in their present relation to one another. If men had ever been found in society without women, or women without men, or if there had been a society of men and women in which the women were not under the control of the men, something might have been positively known about the mental and moral differences which may be inherent in the nature of each. What is now called the nature of women is an eminently artificial thing — the result of forced repression in some directions, unnatural stimulation in others. It may be asserted without scruple, that no other class of dependents have had their character so entirely distorted from its natural proportions by their relation with their masters; for, if conquered and slave races have been, in some respects, more forcibly repressed, whatever in them has not been crushed down by an iron heel has generally been let alone, and if left with any liberty of development, it has developed itself according to its own laws; but in the case of women, a hot-house and stove cultivation has always been carried on of some of the capabilities of their nature, for the benefit and pleasure of their masters. Then, because certain products of the general vital force sprout luxuriantly and reach a great development in this heated atmosphere and under this active nurture and watering, while other shoots from the same root, which are left outside in the wintry air, with ice purposely heaped all around them, have a stunted growth, and some are burnt off with fire and disappear; men, with that inability to recognize their own work which distinguishes the unanalytic mind, indolently believe that the tree grows of itself in the way they have made it grow, and that it would die if one half of it were not kept in a vapour bath and the other half in the snow.

Of all difficulties which impede the progress of thought, and the formation of well-grounded opinions on life and social arrangements, the greatest is now the unspeakable ignorance and inattention of mankind in respect to the influences which form human character. Whatever any portion of the human species now are, or seem to be, such, it is supposed, they have a natural tendency to be: even when the most elementary knowledge of the circumstances in which they have been placed, clearly points out the causes that made them what they are. . . . Because the Greeks cheated the Turks, and the Turks only plundered the Greeks, there are persons who think that the Turks are naturally more sincere: and because women, as is often said, care nothing about politics except their personalities, it is supposed that the general good is naturally less interesting to women than to men. History, which is now so much better understood than formerly, teaches another lesson: if only by showing the extraordinary susceptibility of human nature to external influences, and the extreme variableness of those of its manifestations which are supposed to be most universal and uniform. But in history, as in travelling, men usually see only what they already had in their own minds; and few learn much from history, who do not bring much with them to its study.

Hence, in regard to that most difficult question, what are the natural differences between the two sexes — a subject on which it is impossible in the present state of society to obtain complete and correct knowledge — while almost everybody dogmatizes upon it, almost all neglect and make light of the only means by which any partial insight can be obtained into it. This is, an analytic study of the most important department of psychology, the laws of the influence of circumstances on character. For, however great and apparently ineradicable the moral and intellectual differences between men and women might be, the evidence of there being natural differences could only be negative. Those only could be inferred to be natural which could not possibly be artificial — the residuum, after deducting every characteristic of either sex which can admit of being explained from education or external circumstances. The profoundest knowledge of the laws of the formation of character is indispensable to entitle any one to affirm even that there is any difference, much more what the difference is, between the two sexes considered as moral and rational beings; and since no one, as yet, has that knowledge (for there is hardly any subject which, in proportion to its importance, has been so little studied), no one is thus far entitled to any positive opinion on the subject. Conjectures are all that can at present be made; conjectures more or less probable, according as more or less authorized by such knowledge as we yet have of the laws of psychology, as applied to the formation of character.

Even the preliminary knowledge, what the differences between the sexes now are, apart from all question as to how they are made what they are, is still in the crudest and most incomplete state. Medical practitioners and physiologists have ascertained, to some extent, the differences in bodily constitution; and this is an important element to the psychologist: but hardly any medical practitioner is a psychologist. Respecting the mental characteristics of women; their observations are of no more worth than those of common men. It is a subject on which nothing final can be known, so long as those who alone can really know it, women themselves, have given but little testimony, and that little, mostly suborned. It is easy to know stupid women. Stupidity is much the same all the world over. A stupid person's notions and feelings may confidently be inferred from those which prevail in the circle by which the person is surrounded. Not so with those whose opinions and feelings are an emanation from their own nature and faculties. It is only a man here and there who has any tolerable knowledge of the character even of the women of his own family. I do not mean, of their capabilities; these nobody knows, not even themselves, because most of them have never been called out. I mean their actually existing thoughts and feelings. Many a man thinks he perfectly understands women, because he has had amatory relations with several, perhaps with many of them. If he is a good observer, and his experience extends to quality as well as quantity, he may have learnt something of one narrow department of their nature — an important department, no doubt. But of all the rest of it, few persons are generally more ignorant, because there are few from whom it is so carefully hidden. The most favorable case which a man can generally have for studying the character of a woman, is that of his own wife: for the opportunities are greater, and the cases of complete sympathy not so unspeakably rare. And in fact, this is the source from which any knowledge worth having on the subject has, I believe, generally come. But most men have not had the opportunity of studying in this way more than a single case: accordingly one can, to an almost laughable degree, infer what a man's wife is like, from his opinions about women in general. To make even this one case yield any results, the woman must be worth knowing, and the man not only a competent judge, but of a character so sympathetic in itself, and so well adapted to hers, that he can either read her mind by sympathetic intuition, or has nothing in himself which makes her shy of disclosing it. Hardly anything, I believe, can be more rare than this conjunction. It often happens that there is the most complete unity of feeling and community of interests as to all external things, yet the one has as little admission into the internal life of the other as if they were common acquaintance. Even with true affection, authority on the one side and subordination on the other prevent perfect confidence. Though nothing may be intentionally withheld, much is not shown. In the analogous relation of parent and child, the corresponding phenomenon must have been in the observation of every one. As between father and son, how many are the cases in which the father, in spite of real affection on both sides, obviously to all the world does not know, nor suspect, parts of the son's character familiar to his companions and equals. The truth is, that the position of looking up to another is extremely unpropitious to complete sincerity and openness with him. The fear of losing ground in his opinion or in his feelings is so strong, that even in an upright character, there is an unconscious tendency to show only the best side, or the side which, though not the best, is that which he most likes to see: and it may be confidently said that thorough knowledge of one another hardly ever exists, but between persons who, besides being intimates, are equals. How much more true, then, must all this be, when the one is not only under the authority of the other, but has it inculcated on her as a duty to reckon everything else subordinate to his comfort and pleasure, and to let him neither see nor feel anything coming from her, except what is agreeable to him. All these difficulties stand in the way of a man's obtaining any thorough knowledge even of the one woman whom alone, in general, he has sufficient opportunity of studying. When we further consider that to understand one woman is not necessary to understand any other woman; that even if he could study many women of one rank, or of one country, he would not thereby understand women of other ranks or countries; and even if he did, they are still only the women of a single period of history; we may safely assert that the knowledge which men can acquire of women, even as they have been and are, without reference to what they might be, is wretchedly imperfect and superficial, and always will be so, until women themselves have told all that they have to tell.

And this time has not come; nor will it come otherwise than gradually. It is but of yesterday that women have either been qualified by literary accomplishments, or permitted by society, to tell anything to the general public. As yet very few of them dare tell anything, which men, on whom their literary success depends, are unwilling to hear. Let us remember in which manner, up to a very recent time, the expression, even by a male author, of uncustomary opinions, or what are deemed eccentric feelings, usually was, and in some degree still is, received; and we may form some faint conception under what impediments a woman, who is brought up to think custom and opinion her sovereign rule, attempts to express in books anything drawn from the depths of her own nature. The greatest woman who has left writings behind her sufficient to give her an eminent rank in the literature of her country, thought it necessary to prefix as a motto to her boldest work, 'A man dares to have an opinion; a woman must submit to it.' The greater part of what women write about women is mere sycophancy to men. In the case of unmarried women, much of it seems only intended to increase their chance of a husband. Many, both married and unmarried, overstep the mark, and inculcate a servility beyond what is desired or relished by any man, except the very vulgarest. But this is not so often the case as, even at a quite late period, it still was. Literary women are becoming more freespoken, and more willing to express their real sentiments. Unfortunately, in this country especially, they are themselves such artificial products, that their sentiments are compounded of a small element of individual observation and consciousness, and a very large one of acquired associations. This will be less and less the case, but it will remain true to a great extent, as long as social institutions do not admit the same free development of originality in women which is possible to men. When that time comes, and not before, we shall see, and not

merely hear, as much as it is necessary to know of the nature of women, and the adaptation of other things to it.

I have dwelt so much on the difficulties which at present obstruct any real knowledge by men of the true nature of women, because in this as in so many other things 'opinio copiae inter maximas causas inopiae est'; and there is little chance of reasonable thinking on the matter, while people flatter themselves that they perfectly understand a subject of which most men know absolutely nothing, and of which it is at present impossible that any man, or all men taken together, should have knowledge which can qualify them to lay down the law to women as to what is, or is not, their vocation. Happily, no such knowledge is necessary for any practical purpose connected with the position of women in relation to society and life. For, according to all the principles involved in modern society, the question rests with women themselves — to be decided by their own experience, and by the use of their own faculties. There are no means of finding what either one person or many can do, but by trying — and no means by which any one else can discover for them what it is for their happiness to do or leave undone.

One thing we may be certain of — that what is contrary to women's nature to do, they never will be made to do by simply giving their nature free play. The anxiety of mankind to interfere in behalf of nature, for fear lest nature should not succeed in effecting its purpose, is an altogether unnecessary solicitude. What women by nature cannot do, it is quite superfluous to forbid them from doing. What they can do, but not so well as the men who are their competitors, competition suffices to exclude them from; since nobody asks for protective duties and bounties in favour of women; it is only asked that the present bounties and protective duties in favour of men should be recalled. If women have a greater natural inclination for some things than for others, there is no need of laws or social inculcation to make the majority of them do the former in preference to the latter. Whatever women's services are most wanted for, the free play of competition will hold out the strongest inducements to them to undertake. And, as the words imply, they are most wanted for the things for which they are most fit; by the apportionment of which to them, the collective faculties of the two sexes can be applied on the whole with the greatest sum of valuable result.

The general opinion of men is supposed to be, that the natural vocation of a woman is that of a wife and mother. I say, is supposed to be, because, judging from acts — from the whole of the present constitution of society — one might infer that their opinion was the direct contrary. They might be supposed to think that the alleged natural vocation of women was of all things the most repugnant to their nature; insomuch that if they are free to do anything else — if any other means of living, or occupation of their time and faculties, is open, which has any chance of appearing desirable to them — there will not be enough of them who will be willing to accept the condition said to be natural to them. If this is the real opinion of men in general, it would be well that it should be spoken out. I should like to hear somebody openly enunciating the doctrine (it is already implied in much that is written on the subject) — 'It is necessary to society that women should marry and produce children. They will not do so unless they are compelled. Therefore it is necessary to compel them.' The merits of the case would then be clearly defined. It would be exactly that of the slaveholders of South Carolina and Louisiana. 'It is necessary that cotton and sugar should be grown.

White men cannot produce them. Negroes will not, for any wages which we choose to give. *Ergo* they must be compelled.' An illustration still closer to the point is that of impressment. Sailors must absolutely be had to defend the country. It often happens that they will not voluntarily enlist. Therefore there must be the power of forcing them. How often has this logic been used! and, but for one flaw in it, without doubt it would have been successful up to this day. But it is open to the retort — First pay the sailors the honest value of their labour. When you have made it as well worth their while to serve you, as to work for other employers, you will have no more difficulty than others have in obtaining their services. To this there is no logical answer except 'I will not': and as people are now not only ashamed, but are not desirous, to rob the labourer of his hire, impressment is no longer advocated. Those who attempt to force women into marriage by closing all other doors against them, lay themselves open to a similar retort. If they mean what they say, their opinion must evidently be, that men do not render the married condition so desirable to women, as to induce them to accept it for its own recommendations. It is not a sign of one's thinking the boon one offers very attractive, when one allows only Hobson's choice, 'that or none.' And here, I believe, is the clue to the feelings of those men, who have a real antipathy to the equal freedom of women. I believe they are afraid, not lest women should be unwilling to marry, for I do not think that any one in reality has that apprehension; but lest they should insist that marriage should be on equal conditions; lest all women of spirit and capacity should prefer doing almost anything else, not in their own eyes degrading, rather than marry, when marrying is giving themselves a master, and a master too of all their earthly possessions. And truly, if this consequence were necessarily incident to marriage, I think that the apprehension would be very well founded. I agree in thinking it probable that few women, capable of anything else, would, unless under an irresistible *entraînement*, rendering them for the time insensible to anything but itself, choose such a lot, when any other means were open to them of filling a conventionally honourable place in life: and if men are determined that the law of marriage shall be a law of despotism, they are quite right, in point of mere policy, in leaving to women only Hobson's choice. But, in that case, all that has been done in the modern world to relax the chain on the minds of women, has been a mistake. They never should have been allowed to receive a literary education. Women who read, much more women who write, are, in the existing constitution of things, a contradiction and a disturbing element: and it was wrong to bring women up with any acquirements but those of an odalisque, or of a domestic servant. . . .

When we consider how vast is the number of men, in any great country, who are little higher than brutes, and that this never prevents them from being able, through the law of marriage, to obtain a victim, the breadth and depth of human misery caused in this shape alone by the abuse of the institution swells to something appalling. Yet these are only the extreme cases. They are the lowest abysses, but there is a sad succession of depth after depth before reaching them. In domestic as in political tyranny, the case of absolute monsters chiefly illustrates the institution by showing that there is scarcely any horror which may not occur under it if the despot pleases, and thus setting in a strong light what must be the terrible frequency of things only a little less atrocious. Absolute fiends are as rare as angels, perhaps rarer: ferocious savages, with occasional touches of humanity, are,

however, very frequent: and in the wide interval which separates these from any worthy representatives of the human species, how many are the forms and gradations of animalism and selfishness, often under an outward varnish of civilization and even cultivation, living at peace with the law, maintaining a creditable appearance to all who are not under their power, yet sufficient often to make the lives of all who are so, a torment and a burthen to them! It would be tiresome to repeat the commonplaces about the unfitness of men in general for power, which, after the political discussions of centuries, every one knows by heart, were it not that hardly any one thinks of applying these maxims to the case in which above all others they are applicable, that of power, not placed in the hands of a man here and there, but offered to every adult male, down to the basest and most ferocious. . . . I know that there is another side to the question. I grant that the wife, if she cannot effectually resist, can at least retaliate; she, too, can make the man's life extremely uncomfortable, and by that power is able to carry many points which she ought, and many which she ought not, to prevail in. But this instrument of self-protection — which may be called the power of the scold, or the shrewish sanction — has the fatal defect, that it avails most against the least tyrannical superiors, and in favor of the least deserving dependants. It is the weapon of irritable and self-willed women; of those who would make the worst use of power if they themselves had it, and who generally turn this power to a bad use. The amiable cannot use such an instrument, the high-minded disdain it. And on the other hand, the husbands against whom it is used most effectively are the gentler and more inoffensive; those who cannot be induced, even by provocation, to resort to any very harsh exercise of authority. The wife's power of being disagreeable generally only establishes a counter-tyranny, and makes victims in their turn chiefly of those husbands who are least inclined to be tyrants. . . .

With regard to the fitness of women, not only to participate in elections, but themselves to hold offices or practise professions involving important public responsibilities; I have already observed that this consideration is not essential to the practical question in dispute: since any woman, who succeeds in an open profession, proves by that very fact that she is qualified for it. And in the case of public offices, if the political system of the country is such as to exclude unfit men, it will equally exclude unfit women: while if it is not, there is no additional evil in the fact that the unfit persons whom it admits may be either women or men. As long therefore as it is acknowledged that even a few women may be fit for these duties, the laws which shut the door on those exceptions cannot be justified by any opinion which can be held respecting the capacities of women in general. But, though this last consideration is not essential, it is far from being irrelevant. An unprejudiced view of it gives additional strength to the arguments against the disabilities of women, and reinforces them by high consideration of practical utility.

Let us at first make entire abstraction of all psychological considerations tending to show, that any of the mental differences supposed to exist between women and men are but the natural effect of the differences in their education and circumstances, and indicate no radical difference, far less radical inferiority, of nature. Let us consider women only as they already are, or as they are known to have been; and the capacities which they have already practically shown. What they have done, that at least, if nothing else, it is proved that they can do. When we con-

sider how sedulously they are all trained away from, instead of being trained towards, any of the occupations or objects reserved for men, it is evident that I am taking a very humble ground for them, when I rest their case on what they have actually achieved. For, in this case, negative evidence is worth little, while any positive evidence is conclusive. It cannot be inferred to be impossible that a woman should be a Homer, or an Aristotle, or a Michelangelo, or a Beethoven, because no woman has yet actually produced works comparable to theirs in any of those lines of excellence. This negative fact at most leaves the question uncertain, and open to psychological discussion. But it is quite certain that a woman can be a Queen Elizabeth, or a Deborah, or a Joan of Arc, since this is not inference, but fact. Now it is a curious consideration, that the only things which the existing law excludes women from doing, are the things which they have proved that they are able to do. There is no law to prevent a woman from having written all the plays of Shakespeare, or composed all the operas of Mozart. But Queen Elizabeth or Queen Victoria, had they not inherited the throne, could not have been entrusted with the smallest of the political duties, of which the former showed herself equal to the greatest.

If anything conclusive could be inferred from experience, without psychological analysis, it would be that the things which women are not allowed to do are the very ones for which they are peculiarly qualified; since their vocation for government has made its way, and become conspicuous, through the very few opportunities which have been given; while in the lines of distinction which apparently were freely open to them, they have by no means so eminently distinguished themselves. We know how small a number of reigning queens history presents, in comparison with that of kings. Of this smaller number a far larger proportion have shown talents for rule; though many of them have occupied the throne in difficult periods. It is remarkable, too, that they have, in a great number of instances, been distinguished by merits the most opposite to the imaginary and conventional character of women: they have been as much remarked for the firmness and vigour of their rule, as for its intelligence. When, to queens and empresses, we add regents, and viceroys of provinces, the list of women who have been eminent rulers of mankind swells to a great length. . . .

Exactly where and in proportion as women's capacities for government have been tried, in that proportion have they been found adequate.

This fact is in accordance with the best general conclusions which the world's imperfect experience seems as yet to suggest, concerning the peculiar tendencies and aptitudes characteristic of women, as women have hitherto been. I do not say, as they will continue to be; for, as I have already said more than once, I consider it presumption in any one to pretend to decide what women are or are not, can or cannot be, by natural constitution. They have always hitherto been kept, as far as regards spontaneous development, in so unnatural a state, that their nature cannot but have been greatly distorted and disguised; and no one can safely pronounce that if women's nature were left to choose its direction as freely as men's, and if no artificial bent were attempted to be given to it except that required by the conditions of human society, and given to both sexes alike, there would be any material difference, or perhaps any difference at all, in the character and capacities which would unfold themselves. . . . Even the least contestable of the differences which now exist, are such as may very well have been produced merely by circumstances, without any difference of natural capacity.

SIMONE DE BEAUVOIR
The Second Sex

SIMONE DE BEAUVOIR (1908–1986) *was a French philosopher best known for her extensive contributions to the development of feminist thought. A life-long companion of Jean-Paul Sartre, her philosophical roots are in the existentialist tradition. Her book* The Second Sex *(1952) is a classic of feminist philosophy.*

FOR a long time I have hesitated to write a book on woman. The subject is irritating, especially to women; and it is not new. Enough ink has been spilled in the quarreling over feminism, now practically over, and perhaps we should say no more about it. It is still talked about, however, for the voluminous nonsense uttered during the last century seems to have done little to illuminate the problem. After all, is there a problem? And if so, what is it? Are there women, really?

Most assuredly the theory of the eternal feminine still has its adherents who will whisper in your ear: "Even in Russia women still are *women*"; and other erudite persons — sometimes the very same — say with a sigh: "Woman is losing her way, woman is lost." One wonders if women still exist, if they will always exist, whether or not it is desirable that they should, what place they occupy in this world, what their place should be. "What has become of women?" was asked recently in an ephemeral magazine.

But first we must ask: what is a woman? "*Tota mulier in utero*," says one, "woman is a womb." But in speaking of certain women, connoisseurs declare that they are not women, although they are equipped with a uterus like the rest. All agree in recognizing the fact that females exist in the human species; today as always they make up about one half of humanity. And yet we are told that femininity is in danger; we are exhorted to be women, remain women, become women. It would appear, then, that every female human being is not necessarily a woman; to be so considered she must share in that mysterious and threatened reality known as femininity. Is this attribute something secreted by the ovaries? Or is it a Platonic essence, a product of the philosophic imagination? Is a rustling petticoat enough to bring it down to earth? Although some women try zealously to incarnate this essence, it is hardly patentable. It is frequently described in vague and dazzling terms that seem to have been borrowed from the vocabulary of the seers, and indeed in the times of St. Thomas it was considered an essence as certainly defined as the somniferous virtue of the poppy.

But conceptualism has lost ground. The biological and social sciences no longer admit the existence of unchangeable fixed entities that determine given characteristics, such as those ascribed to woman, the Jew, or the Negro. Science regards any characteristic as a reaction dependent in part upon a *situation*. If today femininity no longer exists, then it never existed. But does the word *woman*, then, have no specific content? This is stoutly affirmed by those who hold to the philosophy of the enlightenment, of rationalism, of nominalism; women, to them, are merely the human beings arbitrarily designated by the word *woman*. Many American women particularly are prepared to think that there is no longer any place for woman as such; if a backward individual still takes herself for a woman, her friends advise her to be psychoanalyzed and thus get rid of this obsession. In regard to a work, *Modern Woman: The Lost Sex*, which in other respects has its irritating features, Dorothy Parker has written: "I cannot be just to books which treat of woman as woman. . . . My idea is that all of us, men as well as women, should be regarded as human beings." But nominalism is a rather inadequate doctrine, and the antifemininists have had no trouble in showing that woman simply *are not* men. Surely woman is, like man, a human being; but such a declaration is abstract. The fact is that every concrete human being is always a singular, separate individual. To decline to accept such notions as the eternal feminine, the black soul, the Jewish character, is not to deny that Jews, Negroes, women exist today — this denial does not represent a liberation for those concerned, but rather a flight from reality. Some years ago a well-known woman writer refused to permit her portrait to appear in a series of photographs especially devoted to women writers; she wished to be counted among the men. But in order to gain this privilege she made use of her husband's influence! Women who assert that they are men lay claim none the less to masculine consideration and respect. I recall also a young Trotsky-ite standing on a platform at a boisterous meeting and getting ready to use her fists, in spite of her evident fragility. She was denying her feminine weakness; but it was for love of a militant male whose equal she wished to be. The attitude of defiance of many American women proves that they are haunted by a sense of their femininity. In truth, to go for a walk with one's eyes open is enough to demonstrate that human-ity is divided into two classes of individ-uals whose clothes, faces, bodies, smiles, gaits, interests,and occupations are mani-festly different. Perhaps these differences are superficial, perhaps they are destined to disappear. What is certain is that right now they do most obviously exist.

If her functioning as a female is not enough to define woman, if we decline also to explain her through "the eternal feminine," and if nevertheless we admit, provisionally, that women do exist, then we must face the question: what is a woman?

To state the question is, to me, to sug-gest, at once, a preliminary answer. The fact that I ask it is in itself significant. A man would never get the notion of writing a book on the peculiar situation of the human male. But if I wish to define my-self, I must first of all say: "I am a woman"; on this truth must be based all further discussion. A man never begins by presenting himself as an individual of a certain sex; it goes without saying that he is a man. The terms *masculine* and *femi-nine* are used symmetrically only as a matter of form, as on legal papers. In ac-tuality the relation of the two sexes is not quite like that of two electrical poles, for man represents both the positive and the neutral, as is indicated by the common use of *man* to designate human beings in general; whereas woman represents only

the negative, defined by limiting criteria, without reciprocity. In the midst of an abstract discussion it is vexing to hear a man say: "You think thus and so because you are a woman"; but I know that my only defense is to reply: "I think thus and so because it is true," thereby removing my subjective self from the argument. It would be out of the question to reply: "And you think the contrary because you are a man," for it is understood that the fact of being a man is no peculiarity. A man is in the right in being a man; it is the woman who is in the wrong. It amounts to this: just as for the ancients there was an absolute vertical with reference to which the oblique was defined, so there is an absolute human type, the masculine. Woman has ovaries, a uterus; these pecu-liarities imprison her in her subjectivity, circumscribe her within the limits of her own nature. It is often said that she thinks with her glands. Man superbly ignores the fact that his anatomy also includes glands, such as the testicles, and that they secrete hormones. He thinks of his body as a di-rect and normal connection with the world, which he believes he apprehends objec-tively, whereas he regards the body of woman as a hindrance, a prison, weighed down by everything peculiar to it. "The female is a female by virtue of a certain *lack* of qualities," said Aristotle; "we should regard the female nature as af-flicted with a natural defectiveness." And St. Thomas for his part pronounced woman to be an "imperfect man," an "in-cidental" being. This is symbolized in Genesis where Eve is depicted as made from what Bossuet called "a supernumer-ary bone" of Adam.

Thus humanity is male and man de-fines woman not in herself but as relative to him; she is not regarded as an autono-mous being. Michelet writes: "Woman, the relative being. . . ." And Benda is most positive in his *Rapport d'Uriel*: "The body of man makes sense in itself quite apart from that of woman, whereas the latter seems wanting in significance by itself. . . . Man can think of himself without woman. She cannot think of herself without man." And she is simply what man decrees; thus she is called "the sex," by which is meant that she appears essentially to the male as a sexual being. For him she is sex—absolute sex, no less. She is defined and differentiated with reference to man and not he with reference to her; she is the incidental, the inessential as opposed to the essential. He is the Subject, he is the Absolute—she is the Other.

The category of the *Other* is as primordial as consciousness itself. In the most primitive societies, in the most ancient mythologies, one finds the expression of a duality—that of the Self and the Other. This duality was not originally attached to the division of the sexes; it was not dependent upon any empirical facts. It is revealed in such works as that of Granet on Chinese thought and those of Dumézil on the East Indies and Rome. The feminine element was at first no more involved in such pairs as Varuna-Mitra, Uranus-Zeus, Sun-Moon, and Day-Night than it was in the contrasts between Good and Evil, lucky and unlucky auspices, right and left, God and Lucifer. Otherness is a fundamental category of human thought.

Thus it is that no group ever sets itself up as the One without at once setting up the Other over against itself. If three travelers chance to occupy the same compartment, that is enough to make vaguely hostile "others" out of all the rest of the passengers on the train. In small-town eyes all persons not belonging to the village are "strangers" and suspect; to the native of a country all who inhabit other countries are "foreigners"; Jews are "different" for the anti-Semite, Negroes are "inferior" for American racists, aborigines are "natives" for colonists, proletarians are the "lower class" for the privileged. . . .

The native traveling abroad is shocked to find himself in turn regarded as a "stranger" by the natives of neighboring countries. As a matter of fact, wars, festivals, trading, treaties, and contests among tribes, nations, and classes tend to deprive the concept *Other* of its absolute sense and to make manifest its relativity; willy-nilly, individuals and groups are forced to realize the reciprocity of their relations. How is it, then, that this reciprocity has not been recognized between the sexes, that one of the contrasting terms is set up as the sole essential, denying any relativity in regard to its correlative and defining the latter as pure otherness? Why is it that women do not dispute male sovereignty? No subject will readily volunteer to become the object, the inessential; it is not the Other who, in defining himself as the Other, establishes the One. The Other is posed as such by the One in defining himself as the One. But if the Other is not to regain the status of being the One, he must be submissive enough to accept this alien point of view. Whence comes this submission in the case of woman? . . .

History has shown us that men have always kept in their hands all concrete powers; since the earliest days of the patriarchate they have thought best to keep woman in a state of dependence; their codes of law have been set up against her; and thus she has been definitely established as the Other. This arrangement suited the economic interests of the males; but it conformed also to their ontological and moral pretensions. Once the subject seeks to assert himself, the Other, who limits and denies him, is none the less a necessity to him: he attains himself only through that reality which he is not, which is something other than himself. That is why man's life is never abundance and quietude; it is dearth and activity, it is struggle. Before him, man encounters Nature; he has some hold upon her, he endeavors to mold her to his desire. But she cannot fill his needs. Either she appears simply as a purely impersonal opposition, she is an obstacle and remains a stranger; or she submits passively to man's will and permits assimilation, so that he takes possession of her only through consuming her — that is, through destroying her. In both cases he remains alone; he is alone when he touches a stone, alone when he devours a fruit. There can be no presence of an other unless the other is also present in and for himself: which is to say that true alterity — otherness — is that of a consciousness separate from mine and substantially identical with mine.

It is the existence of other men that tears each man out of his immanence and enables him to fulfill the truth of his being, to complete himself through transcendence, through escape toward some objective, through enterprise. But this liberty not my own, while assuring mine, also conflicts with it: there is the tragedy of the unfortunate human consciousness; each separate conscious being aspires to set himself up alone as sovereign subject. Each tries to fulfill himself by reducing the other to slavery. But the slave, though he works and fears, senses himself somehow as the essential; and, by a dialectical inversion, it is the master who seems to be the inessential. It is possible to rise above this conflict if each individual freely recognizes the other, each regarding himself and the other simultaneously as object and as subject in a reciprocal manner. But friendship and generosity, which alone permit in actuality this recognition of free beings, are not facile virtues; they are assuredly man's highest achievement, and

through that achievement he is to be found in his true nature. But this true nature is that of a struggle unceasingly begun, unceasingly abolished; it requires man to outdo himself at every moment. We might put it in other words and say that man attains an authentically moral attitude when he renounces *mere being* to assume his position as an existent; through this transformation also he renounces all possession, for possession is one way of seeking mere being; but the transformation through which he attains true wisdom is never done, it is necessary to make it without ceasing, it demands a constant tension. And so, quite unable to fulfill himself in solitude, man is incessantly in danger in his relations with his fellows: his life is a difficult enterprise with success never assured.

But he does not like difficulty; he is afraid of danger. He aspires in contradictory fashion both to life and to repose, to existence and to merely being; he knows full well that "trouble of spirit" is the price of development, that his distance from the object is the price of his nearness to himself; but he dreams of quiet in disquiet and of an opaque plenitude that nevertheless would be endowed with consciousness. This dream incarnated is precisely woman; she is the wished-for intermediary between nature, the stranger to man, and the fellow being who is too closely identical. She opposes him with neither the hostile silence of nature nor the hard requirement of a reciprocal relation; through a unique privilege she is a conscious being and yet it seems possible to possess her in the flesh. Thanks to her, there is a means for escaping that implacable dialectic of master and slave which has its source in the reciprocity that exists between free beings.

We have seen that there were not at first free women whom the males had enslaved nor were there even castes based on sex. To regard woman simply as a slave is a mistake; there were women among the slaves, to be sure, but there have always been free women — that is, women of religious and social dignity. They accepted man's sovereignty and he did not feel menaced by a revolt that could make of him in turn the object. Woman thus seems to be the inessential who never goes back to being the essential, to be the absolute Other, without reciprocity. This conviction is dear to the male, and every creation myth has expressed it, among others the legend of Genesis, which, through Christianity, has been kept alive in Western civilization. Eve was not fashioned at the same time as the man; she was not fabricated from a different substance, nor of the same clay as was used to model Adam: she was taken from the flank of the first male. Not even her birth was independent; God did not spontaneously choose to create her as an end in herself and in order to be worshipped directly by her in return for it. She was destined by Him for man; it was to rescue Adam from loneliness that He gave her to him, in her mate was her origin and her purpose; she was his complement on the order of the inessential. Thus she appeared in the guise of privileged prey. She was nature elevated to transparency of consciousness; she was a conscious being, but naturally submissive. And therein lies the wondrous hope that man has often put in woman: he hopes to fulfill himself as a being by carnally possessing a being, but at the same time confirming his sense of freedom through the docility of a free person. No man would consent to be a woman, but every man wants women to exist. "Thank God for having created woman." "Nature is good since she has given women to men." In such expressions man once more asserts with naïve

arrogance that his presence in this world is an ineluctable fact and a right, that of woman a mere accident — but a very happy accident. Appearing as the Other, woman appears at the same time as an abundance of being in contrast to that existence the nothingness of which man senses in himself; the Other, being regarded as the object in the eyes of the subject, is regarded as *en soi*; therefore as a being. In woman is incarnated in positive form the lack that the existent carries in his heart, and it is in seeking to be made whole through her that man hopes to attain self-realization. . . .

Perhaps the myth of woman will some day be extinguished; the more women assert themselves as human beings, the more the marvelous quality of the Other will die out in them. But today it still exists in the heart of every man.

A myth always implies a subject who projects his hopes and his fears toward a sky of transcendence. Women do not set themselves up as Subject and hence have erected no virile myth in which their projects are reflected; they have no religion or poetry of their own: they still dream through the dreams of men. Gods made by males are the gods they worship. Men have shaped for their own exaltation great virile figures: Hercules, Prometheus, Parsifal; woman has only a secondary part to play in the destiny of these heroes. No doubt there are conventional figures of man caught in his relations to woman: the father, the seducer, the husband, the jealous lover, the good son, the wayward son; but they have all been established by men, and they lack the dignity of myth, being hardly more than clichés. Whereas woman is defined exclusively in her relation to man. The asymmetry of the categories — male and female — is made manifest in the unilateral form of sexual myths. We sometimes say "the sex" to designate woman; she is the flesh, its delights and dangers. The truth that for woman man is sex and carnality has never been proclaimed because there is no one to proclaim it. Representation of the world, like the world itself, is the work of men; they describe it from their own point of view, which they confuse with absolute truth.

It is always difficult to describe a myth; it cannot be grasped or encompassed; it haunts the human consciousness without ever appearing before it in fixed form. The myth is so various, so contradictory, that at first its unity is not discerned: Delilah and Judith, Aspasia and Lucretia, Pandora and Athena—woman is at once Eve and the Virgin Mary. She is an idol, a servant, the source of life, a power of darkness; she is the elemental silence of truth, she is artifice, gossip, and falsehood; she is healing presence and sorceress; she is man's prey, his downfall, she is everything that he is not and that he longs for, his negation and his *raison d'être*. . . .

Man seeks in woman the Other as Nature and as his fellow being. But we know what ambivalent feelings Nature inspires in man. He exploits her, but she crushes him, he is born of her and dies in her; she is the source of his being and the realm that he subjugates to his will; Nature is a vein of gross material in which the soul is imprisoned, and she is the supreme reality; she is contingence and Idea, the finite and the whole; she is what opposes the Spirit, and the Spirit itself. Now ally, now enemy, she appears as the dark chaos from whence life wells up, as this life itself, and as the over-yonder toward which life

tends. Woman sums up nature as Mother, Wife, and Idea; these forms now mingle and now conflict, and each of them wears a double visage. . . .

This, then, is the reason why woman has a double and deceptive visage: she is all that man desires and all that he does not attain. She is the good mediatrix between propitious Nature and man; and she is the temptation of unconquered Nature, counter to all goodness. She incarnates all moral values, from good to evil, and their opposites; she is the substance of action and whatever is an obstacle to it, she is man's grasp on the world and his frustration; as such she is the source and origin of all man's reflection on his existence and of whatever expression he is able to give to it; and yet she works to divert him from himself, to make him sink down in silence and in death. She is servant and companion, but he expects her also to be his audience and critic and to confirm him in his sense of being; but she opposes him with her indifference, even with her mockery and laughter. He projects upon her what he desires and what he fears, what he loves and what he hates. And if it is so difficult to say anything specific about her, that is because man seeks the whole of himself in her and because she is All. She is All, that is, on the plane of the inessential; she is all the Other. And, as the other, she is other than herself, other than what is expected of her. Being all, she is never quite *this* which she should be; she is everlasting deception, the very deception of that existence which is never successfully attained nor fully reconciled with the totality of existents.

JEAN GRIMSHAW

Autonomy and Identity in Feminist Thinking

JEAN GRIMSHAW *teaches philosophy and cultural studies at Bristol Polytechnic in England. She is the author of* Feminist Philosophers: Women's Perspectives on Philosophical Traditions *(1986).*

ISSUES about women's autonomy have been central to feminist thinking and action. Women have so often been in situations of powerlessness and dependence that any system of belief or programme of action that could count as 'feminist' must in some way see this as a central concern. But what is meant by 'autonomy' and under what conditions is it possible? This has been an important and contentious question in philosophy. But questions about autonomy, and related questions about self and identity have also been important to feminism, and within feminist thinking it is possible to find radically different ways of thinking about these things. In this paper, I want to look at one kind of way in which some feminists have tried to conceptualize what it is for a woman to be 'autonomous', and at the implications this has for ways of thinking about the human self. I shall argue that this conception is not only philosophically problematic, but also has an implicit politics which is potentially damaging. And I shall try to suggest some ways of beginning to think about 'autonomy' which seem to me to be more fruitful and adequate, and to draw on different traditions of thinking about the self which have become influential in some recent feminist thinking.

Feminist thinking does not, of course, exist in a vacuum, and in thinking about women's autonomy, feminists have drawn on different (and conflicting) approaches to questions about the human self, some of which have a long history. I want to begin by going back to an argument that Aristotle put forward in the *Ethics*, since I think that the point at which his argument breaks down can illuminate the nature of the problem some feminist thinking has faced.

Aristotle's argument concerns the question of what it is that makes an action 'voluntary', done of a person's own free will, and in order to answer this question, he distinguished between actions whose origin was 'inside' a person, and those whose origin was 'outside', which resulted from external influences or pressure or compulsion. He discussed at some length the problems that arise over trying to define ideas such as 'compulsion', and in estimating the degree of severity of pressure that could make an action not voluntary. But in this sort of model of autonomy, what defines an action as autonomous is seen as its point of *origin*; it must have an 'immaculate conception', as it were, from *within* the self.

Now ultimately I think that it is this definition of 'autonomy' in terms of origin, and the associated distinction between an 'inner' self which can in some way spontaneously generate its 'own' actions, and 'external' influences which are not 'part' of the self, that will need challenging. But I think it is possible to defend the Aristotelian version of autonomy up to a point, provided notions of 'inside' and 'outside' the self are defined in a certain way. If a person is prevented from doing what they would otherwise intend or desire to do, or if they are coerced into doing what they would *not* otherwise want or desire to do, they are not acting autonomously. Under this interpretation, actions which originate from 'inside' the self are those which are seen as in accordance with conscious desires or intentions, and those which originate from 'outside' the self are those which one would not do if one were not coerced. The pressure here is to consider the sorts of circumstances which do, in fact, coerce people in these sorts of ways. And, of course, a central concern of feminism has been to identify and fight against the kinds of coercion to which women have been subjected, including things like physical violence and economic dependence.

But it is at this point that an Aristotelian-type argument fails to be able to deal with the most difficult questions about autonomy. The Aristotelian view, as I have interpreted it, 'works' only to the extent that it is assumed that there is no problem about what I shall call 'the autonomy of desires'. Autonomy is defined as acting in accordance with desire (or intention). But what of the desires themselves? Are there *desires* (or intentions) which are not 'autonomous', which do not originate from 'within' the self, which are not authentic, not really 'one's own'?

Feminist writers have wanted, of course, to indict the various forms of brutality and coercion from which women have suffered. But this brutality and coercion has been seen not merely as a question of physical or 'external' coercion or constraint; the force of subjection has also been seen as a psychic one, invading women's very selves. The language of 'conditioning', 'brainwashing', 'indoctrination', and so forth, has been used to describe this force. The female self, under male domination, is riddled through and through with false or conditioned desires. But set against this conditioned, non-autonomous female self are various images of a female self that would be authentic, that would transcend or shatter this conditioning. I want now to look at some of these images of the female self in feminist discourse: my particular examples are from the work of Mary Daly, Marilyn Frye and Kate Millett.

Daly, Frye and Millett all stress the way in which women have been subject to the *power* of men. Much of Daly's book, *Gyn/Ecology* (1979), is an account of the barbarities inflicted on women such as suttee, clitorectomy, foot-binding and other forms of mutilation. Millett, in *Sexual Politics* (1977), sees patriarchal power as something so historically all-embracing that it has totally dominated women's lives. Frye, in *The Politics of Reality* (1983), uses the situation of a young girl sold into sexual slavery and then systematically brutalized and brainwashed into a life of service to her captors as an analogy for the situation of all women. And all three writers stress the way in which they see the female self as 'invaded' by patriarchal conditioning. Millett writes:

> When, in any group of persons, the ego is subjected to such invidious versions of itself through social beliefs, ideology and tradition, the effect is bound to be pernicious. This should make it no very special cause for surprise that women develop group characteristics common to those who suffer minority status and a marginal existence.

Women, she argues, are deprived of all but the most trivial sources of dignity or self-respect. In her discussion of Lawrence's depiction of Connie in *Lady Chatterley's Lover*, what she sees Connie as relinquishing is 'self, ego, will, individuality', all those things which, Millett argues, women had but recently achieved, (and for which Lawrence had a profound distaste).

Mary Daly's picture of the way in which women's selves are invaded by patriarchal conditioning is even more striking. She describes women, for example, as 'moronised', 'robotised', 'lobotomised', as 'the puppets of Papa'. At times she seems to see women as so 'brainwashed' that they are scarcely human; thus she describes them as 'fembots', even as 'mutants'. In Millett, Daly and Frye, women are seen primarily as *victims*: the monolithic brutality and psychological pressures of male power have reduced women almost to the state of being 'non-persons'. And indeed, as Daly sees women as having become 'mutants' or 'fembots', so Millett sees them as not having been allowed to participate in fully 'human' activities (which she characterises as those that are most remote from the biological contingencies of life), and Frye sees them as simply 'broken' and then 'remade' in the way that suits their masters.

But behind this victimised female self, whose actions and desires are assumed to be not truly 'her own', since they derive from processes of force, conditioning or psychological manipulation, there is seen to be an authentic female self, whose recovery or discovery it is one of the aims of feminism to achieve. The spatial metaphor implicit in the word 'behind' is not accidental, since this model of self is premised on the possibility of making a distinction between an 'inner' and an 'outer' self. . . . In *Gyn/Ecology*, discov-

ering or recovering one's own self is seen as akin to a process of salvation or religious rebirth, and Daly writes of what she calls the unveiling or unwinding of the 'shrouds' of patriarchy to reveal the authentic female Spirit-Self underneath. And this Self is seen as a unitary and harmonious one. Splits and barriers within the psyche, she argues, as well as those between Selves, are the result of patriarchal conditioning. In the unitary and harmonious female Spirit-Self there will be no such splits.

Millett's picture of the authentic female self is rather different from that of Daly. It does not draw, as Daly's does, on religious metaphors of salvation and rebirth. It derives, rather, from a picture of the self as fundamentally a unitary, conscious and rational thing, a picture which, in Western philosophy, can be traced back to Descartes. It emerges most clearly in her discussion of Freud. She describes Freud's theory of the Unconscious as a major contribution to human understanding, but her account of the self owes, in fact, scarcely anything to Freud. She is scathingly critical of Freud's theory of penis envy: Freud, she argued, 'did not accept his patient's symptoms as evidence of a justified dissatisfaction with the limiting circumstances imposed on them by society, but as symptomatic of an independent and universal feminine tendency'. He made a major (and foolish) confusion between biology and culture. Girls, Millett argues, are fully cognisant of male supremacy long before they see their brother's penis; and what they envy is not the penis, but the things to which having a penis gives the boy access — power, status and rewards. Freud ignored the more likely 'social' hypothesis for feminine dissatisfaction, preferring to ascribe it to a biologically based female nature. What we should be studying, Millett argues, are the effects of male-supremacist culture on the female ego. And what will undo these effects, she writes in the Postscript, is altered consciousness, and a process of 'human growth and true re-education'.

The 'social' factors of which Millett writes are here seen as pressures which are 'external' to the self, and which have the effect of thwarting the conscious and unitary rationality of female individuality, or the female ego. And the task is that of *removing* their influence. . . .

The paradigm of coercion, writes Frye, is *not* the direct application of physical force. Rather, it is a situation in which choice and action *do* take place, and in which the victim acts under her own perception and judgement. Hence, what the exploiter needs is that

> the will and intelligence of the victim be disengaged from the projects of resistance and escape but that they not be simply broken or destroyed. Ideally, the disintegration and misintegration of the victim should accomplish the detachment of the victim's will and intelligence from the victim's own interests and their attachment to the interests of the exploiter. This will effect a displacement or dissolution of self-respect and will undermine the victim's intolerance of coercion. With that, the situation transcends the initial paradigmatic form or structure or coercion; for if people don't mind doing what you want them to do, you can't really be *making* them do it.

And, she writes:

> The health and integrity of an organism is a matter of its being organised largely towards its own interests and welfare. *She* is healthy and 'working right' when her substance is organised primarily on principles which align it to *her* interests

and welfare. Co-operation is essential of course, but it will not do that I arrange everything so that *you* get enough exercise: for me to be healthy, *I* must get enough exercise. My being adequately exercised is logically independent of your being so.

Frye is writing here as if it were possible to distinguish the interests of one self sharply from those of another, and as if, were the effects of male domination to be undone, it would not be too much of a problem for the self to know what its interests were.

In various ways then, underlying much of the work of these three writers is a set of assumptions about the self. First, that it is, at least potentially, a unitary, rational thing, aware of its interests. Second, that 'splits' within the psyche should be seen as resulting from the interference of patriarchal or male-dominated socialisation or conditioning. Third, that the task of undoing this conditioning is one that can be achieved solely by a rational process of learning to understand and fight against the social and institutional effects of male domination. And implicit in these assumptions about the self, I think, is a conception of autonomy. Frye writes that 'left to themselves' women would not want to serve men. Daly writes of unveiling or unwinding the 'shrouds' of patriarchy. Millett writes of the individuality and ego that women can discover in themselves once they recognise the effects of their patriarchal socialisation. And in all three, what is autonomous (or authentic) is what is seen as originating in some way from *within* the self; what is in some way *untainted* by the conditioning or manipulation to which a woman has previously been subjected.

Before I come to discuss the philosophical problems that are raised by this sort of account of self and autonomy, I want to look at what I have called its implicit politics; and what I mean by this primarily is its possible consequences for the way in which women might think about their relationships to each other, and the way in which they might think about themselves. The first consequence seems to me to be this. Any view which see self-affirmation in terms of an 'authentic' inner self arising from the smashing of a socially conditioned 'false self', or which sees autonomy as a question of the origin of actions from 'inside' rather than 'outside', is almost bound to adopt, however implicitly, a derogatory attitude towards those who are not yet 'authentic'. The precise nature and tone of this attitude may vary. But Mary Daly, for example, in *Gyn/Ecology*, sometimes writes as if most women were really little more than the programmed, robotic puppets. . . . And this is related, for example, to Daly's scorn for 'tokenism' — for those women who participate in what are seen as patriarchal institutions. Kate Millett's language is less obviously extreme. But the picture she paints of women is nevertheless often a derogatory one. She describes them, for example, as 'infantilised'; she accepts without question research which purported to show that most women despised each other; she sees women as having little 'self-respect', and as devoting almost all their time and attention to pleasing and flattering men.

This implicitly derogatory attitude to women is linked both to an overmonolithic account of male power, and to a failure to give much attention to the ways in which women have, in fact, often spent much of their lives, and to the activities which have been particularly theirs (such as the rearing of children, for example). Sometimes women are depicted almost as a caricature of a male stereotype of themselves — they *are* servile, weak, powerless etc.

Mary Daly's indictment of male power and brutality similarly allows little space for a consideration of the patterns of women's lives, or the strengths and capacities that these might have enabled them to develop. Her female Spirit-Self simply seems to rise mysteriously like a phoenix from the ashes of patriarchal conditioning. And Frye is sceptical about the possibility of women looking to their foremothers as a source of inspiration; of seeing some women, at least, as having led lives that were not wholly male-mediated. Feminist vision or imagination has no real resource to turn to.

Now these kinds of accounts (or perhaps one might say *failures* to give an adequate account?) of women's lives are implicitly divisive and threatening. They are divisive because they have a tendency to divide women into two camps; those who have and those who have not shaken the dust of patriarchal conditioning from their feet. And they are threatening, because it is offensive and undermining to be told that the life one has led has merely been one of servility, that it has not been of truly 'human' value, that one has been a 'fembot' or a 'puppet'. I think that one important strand in the rejection of feminism by many women has been a feeling that feminists are saying that their lives have been of no value, and that their activities and concerns have been trivial.

But this image of autonomy and of the self can be threatening, too, to women who *do* have a strong allegiance to feminism; and the threat intersects with assumptions that have been made in some feminist discourse about who is or is not 'really' a feminist. The threat arises because this account of autonomy is in fact often a strongly *normative* one; it presents an image of what a 'feminist self' should be like. To be autonomous or authentic one should be strong, independent, rational, coherent or consistent, able to distinguish clearly those aspects of one's previous self which derive from male-dominated conditioning and reject them. If one is ambivalent, conflicted, uncertain, confused, unwilling to make wholesale rejections, one stands to be accused, whether by oneself or by others, of bad faith, of lack of courage, of 'selling out', of tokenism.

I am here giving an account of just one (influential) strand in feminist discourse. There are other strands which have rejected this account of self and autonomy. As I have said before, a picture of the self as conscious, unitary and rational can be traced back, in Western philosophy, to Descartes. . . .

Now any adequate account of self needs to be able, I think, to encompass and try to make intelligible the ways in which women and men experience themselves. And the central reasons for rejecting the 'humanist' paradigm of the self — as I have outlined it above — are, firstly, that there may be aspects of the development of self which are not easily accessible to consciousness, and secondly, that there are conscious experiences which are not easy to make intelligible within the humanist paradigm. I want now to look at some aspects of self-experience that I think should be central to any theory of self, and hence to any discussion of women's autonomy. . . .

There is a type of feminist criticism, both in literature and other media (and in fields such as education), which has been called 'Images of Women' criticism. This has supposed that feminist effort should be devoted, first, to showing how the 'images' in question oppress or denigrate women, and second, to offering positive images of women to replace these. One problem with this kind of criticism is that the 'images' in question have often been misinterpreted, since they have been discussed without reference to the context or

narrative structure in which they may appear. But there are two other problems with this type of criticism which I want to focus on here. First, what this approach often fails to recognise is the importance of understanding the *appeal* of the 'images' that are criticised; the relations they may have to women's pleasures, desires, fantasies, fears and conceptions of themselves. Second, it fails to recognise what is signally obvious in the experience of many women, myself of course included, namely that it is perfectly possible to agree 'in one's head' that certain images of women might be reactionary or damaging or oppressive, while remaining committed to them in emotion and desire. I suspect that this 'split' happens at times in all women, and perhaps particularly in those who have some commitment to feminism. And what it suggests is that structures of desire, emotion and fantasy have deep roots of some sort in the self which are not necessarily amenable in any simple way to processes of conscious rational argument. An adequate theory of subjectivity has to recognise and try to understand these roots. . . .

In his *Introductory Lectures on Psychoanalysis* (1973), Freud discussed the way in which symptoms are experienced in certain forms of obsessional neurosis. He wrote:

Obsessional neurosis is shown in the patient's being occupied with thoughts in which he is in fact not interested, in his being aware of impulses which appear very strange to him and his being led to actions the performance of which give him no enjoyment, but which it is quite impossible for him to omit. The thoughts (obsessions) may be senseless in themselves, or merely a matter of indifference to the subject; often they are completely silly, and invariably they are the starting-point of a strenuous mental activity, which exhausts the patient and to which he only surrenders himself most unwillingly.

Obsessional neurosis is characterized, Freud argued, by the fact that the symptoms are not only debilitating, but are experienced by the person as *alien*; they do not seem 'part' of him or her, and they seem discrepant with an everyday or normal sense of the self. In the case of many of Freud's patients the disruption and debilitation caused by the symptoms was so extreme that they were scarcely able to carry on their lives adequately at all. But Freud insisted that there was no sharp dividing line between 'normal' and 'neurotic' people, and would have argued that similar, though less extreme, obsessions and apparently inexplicable compulsions can be found in all of us. In these cases, the self is, as it were, split against itself, subject to desires and impulses that seem 'out of character'.

But one cannot assume that an everyday 'coherent' sense of self is readily available. One reason for this is that women (and men, of course) are often faced with the problem of negotiating contradictory or conflicting conceptions of themselves. Women may, for example, be required to be *both* sexually exciting and available, *and* modest and chaste. And gender relationships may be subject to the problems that can arise from conflicting discourses about femininity or masculinity. Men may, for example, *both* see themselves as 'stronger' than women and tend to see women as more weak and passive, but *also* see women as having a power over them that can seem to engulf the man in forms of emotional dependence by which he may feel threatened. Discourse about femininity and masculinity is by no means a homogeneous or stable thing.

In the twentieth century, the advent of a 'consumer culture' and of mass communications has given questions about self and identity a peculiar intensity and difficulty in some respects. They have led, for example, to a focus on appearance and 'style', and the way in which these may 'express' one's individuality, that is historically novel. The clothes one wears, the 'room of one's own' in the Sunday Supplements: one may, apparently, now 'try on' identities as if they really were clothes. And women have often tended to be the main target of fashion and 'lifestyle' talk. For all the rejection of what was sometimes called 'woman garbage' by American feminists, the issue of appearance is something that no woman can wholly avoid. Feminists too, of course, have used style of dress and demeanour to express a sense of self and of political commitment. . . .

The concept of self-deception is one that has constantly puzzled philosophers. How can one both know and yet not know something about oneself. I do not have space here to discuss the question of self-deception in detail. But an important thing to recognise at the outset is that knowing about oneself can never be a matter of 'mere information'. One cannot be distanced from or emotionally neutral about issues of self-knowledge. (Freud stressed this in his account of the transference in the analytic situation.) Herbert Fingarette uses the concept of 'avowal' to give an account of the concept of self-deception. We do not see everything that we think or do or fantasise or desire as equally 'central' to ourselves. It is quite common, in everyday discourse, to say things like 'I wasn't really myself' or 'It wasn't like *me* to do that'. Sometimes this process of rejection, of not avowing, is quite conscious. At other times it may be barely admitted to consciousness, if whatever it was is seen as threatening to the self. And sometimes it is, I think, not conscious at all. Psychoanalysts have talked, for example, about the process of 'projection', in which aspects of oneself of which one is fearful may be projected on to other people. (A number of writers have seen 'projection' as involved in the problem of masculinity, and have suggested that men may sometimes project their own fears of such things as emotional intimacy on to women, who are then seen as 'bad' because they cause these problems.)

Self-knowledge can never be a matter of easy or immediate introspection. This is partly because aspects of oneself may be disavowed, sometimes unconsciously, and partly because the 'meaning' of the deliverances of introspection is always dependent on an interpretation. One may be *aware* of feelings, sexual ones for example, that one is not able to conceptualize *as* sexual at the time. Freud believed that at the root of all neuroses lay repressed sexual desires, but even if one does not follow him in this, it would be hard to resist the conclusion that this was true of some of his patients. Sometimes his patients lacked the kind of knowledge that would have enabled them to interpret the experience as 'sexual' at all. Sometimes they possessed knowledge about sex, but could not admit that *this* was sexual, or that *they* had those sorts of desires.

I have outlined above some of the experiences and the problems about subjectivity that any adequate theory of self must be able to encompass, in a way that the 'humanist' paradigm is, I think, unable to do. There are approaches to understanding and theorizing self which depart radically from the humanist paradigm. I shall not attempt to enumerate them all here, nor do I think that feminism should accept any of them uncritically. What they share, despite their differences, is an insistence that there is no 'original' wholeness or unity in the self, nor a 'real self' which can be thought of as in some way *underlying* the self of everyday life. The self is *always* a more or less precarious and conflictual construction out of, and compromise between, conflicting and not always conscious desires and experiences, which are born out of the ambivalences and contradictions in human experience and relationships with others. . . .

Feminism, as I have said, needs to preserve a critical distance from all theories of self. But it needs also to engage with those theories which deconstruct the distinction between the 'individual' and the 'social', which recognise the power of desire and fantasy and the problems of supposing any 'original' unity in the self, while at the same time preserving its concern with lived experience and the practical and material struggles of women to achieve more autonomy and control over their lives.

MARILYN FRYE

Sexism

MARILYN FRYE *teaches feminist philosophy at Michigan State University. Some of her extensive contributions to feminist thought are collected in her book* The Politics of Reality *(1983).*

THE first philosophical project I undertook as a feminist was that of trying to say carefully and persuasively what sexism is, and what it is for someone, some institution or some act to be sexist. This project was pressed on me with considerable urgency because, like most women coming to a feminist perception of themselves and the world, I was seeing sexism everywhere and trying to make it perceptible to others. I would point out, complain and criticize, but most frequently my friends and colleagues would not see that what I declared to be sexist was sexist, or at all objectionable.

As the critic and as the initiator of the topic, I was the one on whom the burden of proof fell — it was I who had to explain and convince. Teaching philosophy had already taught me that people cannot be persuaded of things they are not ready to be persuaded of; there are certain complexes of will and prior experience which will inevitably block persuasion, no matter the merits of the case presented. I knew that even if I could explain fully and clearly what I was saying when I called something sexist, I would not necessarily be able to convince various others of the correctness of this claim. But what troubled me enormously was that I could not explain it in any way which satisfied *me*. It is this sort of moral and intellectual frustration which, in my case at least, always generates philosophy.

The following was the product of my first attempt to state clearly and explicitly what sexism is:

The term 'sexist' in its core and perhaps most fundamental meaning is a term which characterizes anything whatever which creates, constitutes, promotes or exploits any irrelevant or impertinent marking of the distinction between the sexes.

When I composed this statement, I was thinking of the myriads of instances in which persons of the two sexes are treated differently, or behave differently, but where nothing in the real differences between females and males justifies or explains the difference of treatment or behavior. I was thinking, for instance, of the tracking of boys into Shop and girls into Home Ec, where one can see nothing about boys or girls considered in themselves which seems to connect essentially with the distinction between wrenches and eggbeaters. I was thinking also of sex discrimination in employment — cases where someone otherwise apparently qualified for a job is not hired because she is a woman. But when I tried to put this definition of 'sexist' to use, it did not stand the test.

Consider this case: If a company is hiring a supervisor who will supervise a group of male workers who have always worked for male supervisors, it can scarcely be denied that the sex of a candidate for the job is relevant to the candidate's prospects of moving smoothly and successfully into an effective working relationship with the supervisees (though the point is usually exaggerated by those looking for excuses not to hire women). Relevance is an intrasystematic thing. The patterns of behavior, attitude and custom within which a process goes on determine what is relevant to what in matters of describing, predicting or evaluating. In the case at hand, the workers' attitudes and the surrounding customs of the culture make a difference to how they interact with their supervisor and, in particular, *make* the sex of the supervisor a relevant factor in predicting how things will work out. So then, if the company hires a man, in preference to a more experienced and knowledgeable woman, can we explain our objection to the decision by saying it involved distinguishing on the basis of sex when sex is irrelevant to the ability to do the job? No: sex is relevant here.

So, what did I mean to say about 'sexist'? I was thinking that in a case of a candidate for a supervisory job, the reproductive capacity of the candidate has nothing to do with that person's knowing what needs to be done and being able to give properly timed, clear and correct directions. What I was picturing was a situation purified of all sexist perception and reaction. But, of course, *If* the whole context were not sexist, sex would not be an issue in such a job situation; indeed, it might go entirely unnoticed. It is precisely the fact that the sex of the candidate *is* relevant that is the salient symptom of the sexism of the situation.

I had failed, in that first essay, fully to grasp or understand that the locus of sexism is primarily in the system or framework, not in the particular act. It is not accurate to say that what is going on in cases of sexism is that distinctions are made on the basis of sex when sex is irrelevant; what is wrong in cases of sexism is, in the first place, that sex *is* relevant; and then that the making of distinctions on the basis of sex reinforces the patterns which make it relevant.

In sexist cultural/economic systems,

sex is always relevant. To understand what sexism is, then, we have to step back and take a larger view.

Sex-identification intrudes into every moment of our lives and discourse, no matter what the supposedly primary focus or topic of the moment is. Elaborate, systematic, ubiquitous and redundant marking of a distinction between the two sexes of humans and most animals is customary and obligatory. One *never* can ignore it.

Examples of sex-marking behavior patterns abound. A couple enters a restaurant; the headwaiter or hostess addresses the man and does not address the woman. The physician addresses the man by surname and honorific (Mr. Baxter, Rev. Jones) and addresses the woman by given name (Nancy, Gloria). You congratulate your friend—a hug, a slap on the back, shaking hands, kissing; one of the things which determines which of these you do is your friend's sex. In everything one does one has two complete repertoires of behavior, one for interactions with women and one for interactions with men. Greeting, storytelling, order-giving and order-receiving, negotiating, gesturing deference or dominance, encouraging, challenging, asking for information: one does all of these things differently depending upon whether the relevant others are male or female.

That this is so has been confirmed in sociological and socio-linguistic research, but it is just as easily confirmed in one's own experience. To discover the differences in how you greet a woman and how you greet a man, for instance, just observe yourself, paying attention to the following sorts of things: frequency and duration of eye contact, frequency and type of touch, tone and pitch of voice, physical distance maintained between bodies, how and whether you smile, use of slang or swear words, whether your body dips into a shadow curtsy or bow. That I have two repertoires for handling introductions to people was vividly confirmed for me when a student introduced me to his friend, Pat, and I really could not tell what sex Pat was. For a moment I was stopped cold, completely incapable of action. I felt myself helplessly caught between two paths — the one I would take if Pat were female and the one I would take if Pat were male. Of course the paralysis does not last. One is rescued by one's ingenuity and good will; one can invent a way to behave as one says "How do you do?" to a human being. But the habitual ways are not for humans: they are one way for women and another for men. . . .

In order to behave "appropriately" toward women and men, we have to know which of the people we encounter are women and which are men. But if you strip humans of most of their cultural trappings, it is not always that easy to tell without close inspection which are female, which are male. The tangible and visible physical differences between the sexes are not particularly sharp or numerous and in the physical dimensions we associate with "sex differences," the range of individual variation is very great. The differences between the sexes could easily be, and sometimes are, obscured by bodily decoration, hair removal and the like. So the requirement of knowing everyone's sex in every situation and under almost all observational conditions generates a requirement that we all let others know our sex in every situation. And we do. We announce our sexes in a thousand ways. We deck ourselves from head to toe with garments and decorations which serve like badges and buttons to announce our sexes. For every type of occasion there are distinct clothes, gear and accessories, hairdos, cosmetics and scents, labeled as "ladies'" or "men's" and labeling us as

females or males, and most of the time most of us choose, use, wear or bear the paraphernalia associated with our sex. It goes below the skin as well. There are different styles of gait, gesture, posture, speech, humor, taste and even of perception, interest and attention that we learn as we grow up to be women or to be men and that label and announce us as women or as men. It begins early in life: even infants in arms are color coded.

That we wear and bear signs of our sexes, and that this is absolutely compulsory, is made clearest in the relatively rare cases when we do not do so, or not enough. Responses ranging from critical to indignant to hostile meet mothers whose babies are not adequately coded; one of the most agitated criticisms of the sixties' hippies was that "you can't tell the boys from the girls." The requirement of sex-announcement is laden, indeed, with all the urgency of the taboo against homosexuality. One appears heterosexual by informing people of one's sex *very* emphatically and *very* unambiguously, and lesbians and homosexuals who wish *not* to pass as heterosexual generally can accomplish this just by cultivating ambiguous sex-indicators in clothes, behavior and style. The power of this ambiguity to generate unease and punitive responses in others mirrors and demonstrates the rigidity and urgency of this strange social rule that we all be and assertively act "feminine" or "masculine" (and not both) — that we flap a full array of sex-signals at all times.

The intense demand for marking and for asserting what sex each person is adds up to a strenuous requirement that there *be* two distinct and sharply dimorphic sexes. But, in reality, there are not. There are people who fit on a biological spectrum between two not-so-sharply defined poles. In about 5 percent of live births, possibly more, the babies are in some degree and way not perfect exemplars of male and female. There are individuals with chromosome patterns other than XX or YY and individuals whose external genitalia at birth exhibit some degree of ambiguity. There are people who are chromosomally "normal" who are at the far ends of the normal spectra of secondary sex characteristics — height, musculature, hairiness, body density, distribution of fat, breast size, etc. — whose overall appearance fits the norm of people whose chromosomal sex is the opposite of theirs.

These variations not withstanding, persons (mainly men, of course) with the power to do so actually *construct* a world in which men are men and women are women and there is nothing in between and nothing ambiguous; they do it by chemically and/or surgically altering people whose bodies are indeterminate or ambiguous with respect to sex. Newborns with "imperfectly formed" genitals are immediately "corrected" by chemical or surgical means, children and adolescents are given hormone "therapies" if their bodies seem not to be developing according to what physicians and others declare to be the norm for what has been declared to be that individual's sex. Persons with authority recommend and supply cosmetics and cosmetic regimens, diets, exercises and all manner of clothing to revise or disguise the too-hairy lip, the too-large breast, the too-slender shoulders, the too-large feet, the too-great or too-slight stature. Individuals whose bodies do not fit the picture of exactly two sharply dimorphic sexes are often enough quite willing to be altered or veiled for the obvious reason that the world punishes them severely for their failure to be the "facts" which would verify the doctrine of two sexes. The demand that the world be a world in which there are exactly two sexes is inexorable, and we are all compelled to answer to it emphatically, unconditionally, repetitiously and unambiguously.

Even being physically "normal" for one's assigned sex is not enough. One must *be* female or male, actively. Again, the costumes and performances. Pressed to acting feminine or masculine, one colludes (co-lude: play along) with the doctors and counselors in the creation of a world in which the apparent dimorphism of the sexes is so extreme that one can only think there is a great gulf between female and male, that the two are, essentially and fundamentally and naturally, utterly different. One helps to create a world in which it seems to us that we *could* never mistake a woman for a man or a man for a woman. We never need worry.

Along with all the making, marking and announcing of sex-distinction goes a strong and visceral feeling or attitude to the effect that sex-distinction is the most important thing in the world: that it would be the end of the world if it were not maintained, clear and sharp and rigid; that a sex-dualism which is rooted in the nature of the beast is absolutely crucial and fundamental to all aspects of human life, human society and human economy. . . .

It is a general and obvious principle of information theory that when it is very, very important that certain information be conveyed, the suitable strategy is redundancy. If a message *must* get through, one sends it repeatedly and by as many means or media as one has at one's command. On the other end, as a receiver of information, if one receives the same information over and over, conveyed by every medium one knows, another message comes through as well, and implicitly: the message that this information is very, very important. The enormous frequency with which information about people's sexes is conveyed conveys implicitly the message that this topic is enormously important. I suspect that this is the single topic on which we most frequently receive information from others throughout our entire lives. If I am right, it would go part way to explaining why we end up with an almost irresistible impression, unarticulated, that the matter of people's sexes is the most important and most fundamental topic in the world.

We exchange sex-identification information, along with the implicit message that it is very important, in a variety of circumstances in which there really is no concrete or experientially obvious point in having the information. There are reasons, as this discussion has shown, why you should want to know whether the person filling your water glass or your tooth is male or female and why that person wants to know what you are, but those reasons are woven invisibly into the fabric of social structure and they do not have to do with the bare mechanics of things being filled. Furthermore, the same culture which drives us to this constant information exchange also simultaneously enforces a strong blanket rule requiring that the simplest and most nearly definitive physical manifestations of sex difference be hidden from view in all but the most private and intimate circumstances. The double message of sex-distinction and its pre-eminent importance is conveyed, in fact, in part *by* devices which systematically and deliberately cover up and hide from view the few physical things which do (to a fair extent) distinguish two sexes of humans. The messages are overwhelmingly dissociated from the concrete facts they supposedly pertain to, and from matrices of concrete and sensible reasons and consequences. . . .

If one is made to feel that a thing is of prime importance, but common sensory experience does not connect it with things of obvious concrete and practical impor-

tance, then there is mystery, and with that a strong tendency to the construction of mystical or metaphysical conceptions of its importance. If it is important, but not of mundane importance, it must be of transcendent importance. All the more so if it is *very* important.

This matter of our sexes must be very profound indeed if it must, on pain of shame and ostracism, be covered up and must, on pain of shame and ostracism, be boldly advertised by every means and medium one can devise.

There is one more point about redundancy that is worth making here. If there is one thing more effective in making one believe a thing than receiving the message repetitively, it is rehearsing it repetitively. Advertisers, preachers, teachers, all of us in the brainwashing professions, make use of this apparently physical fact of human psychology routinely. The redundancy of sex-marking and sex-announcing serves not only to make the topic seem transcendently important, but to make the sex-duality it advertises seem transcendently and unquestionably *true*. . . .

Sex-marking and sex-announcing are equally compulsory for males and females; but that is as far as equality goes in this matter. The meaning and import of this behavior is profoundly different for women and for men.

Whatever features an individual male person has which tend to his social and economic disadvantage (his age, race, class, height, etc.), one feature which never tends to his disadvantage in the society at large is his maleness. The case for females is the mirror image of this. Whatever features an individual female person has which tend to her social and economic advantage (her age, race, etc.), one feature which always tends to her disadvantage is her femaleness. Therefore, when a male's sex-category is the thing about him that gets first and most repeated notice, the thing about him that is being framed and emphasized and given primacy is a feature which in general is an asset to him. When a female's sex-category is the thing about her that gets first and most repeated notice, the thing about her that is being framed and emphasized and given primacy is a feature which in general is a liability to her. Manifestations of this divergence in the meaning and consequences of sex-announcement can be very concrete.

Walking down the street in the evening in a town or city exposes one to some risk of assault. For males the risk is less; for females the risk is greater. If one announces oneself male, one is presumed by potential assailants to be more rather than less likely to defend oneself or be able to evade the assault and, if the male-announcement is strong and unambiguous, to be a noncandidate for sexual assault. If one announces oneself female, one is presumed by potential assailants to be less rather than more likely to defend oneself or to evade the assault and, if the female-announcement is strong and unambiguous, to be a prime candidate for sexual assault. Both the man and the woman "announce" their sex through style of gait, clothing, hair style, etc., but they are not equally or identically affected by announcing their sex. The male's announcement tends toward his protection or safety, and the female's announcement tends toward her victimization. It could not be more immediate or concrete; the meaning of the sex-identification could not be more different.

The sex-marking behavioral repertoires are such that in the behavior of almost all people of both sexes addressing or responding to males (especially within their own culture/race) generally is done in a manner which suggests basic respect, while addressing or responding to females is done in a manner that suggests the females' inferiority (condescending tones,

presumptions of ignorance, overfamiliarity, sexual aggression, etc.). So, when one approaches an ordinary well-socialized person in such cultures, if one is male, one's own behavioral announcement of maleness tends to evoke supportive and beneficial response and if one is female, one's own behavioral announcement of femaleness tends to evoke degrading and detrimental response.

The details of the sex-announcing behaviors also contribute to the reduction of women and the elevation of men. The case is most obvious in the matter of clothing. As feminists have been saying for two hundred years or so, ladies' clothing is generally restrictive, binding, burdening and frail; it threatens to fall apart and/or to uncover something that is supposed to be covered if you bend, reach, kick, punch or run. It typically does not protect effectively against hazards in the environment, nor permit the wearer to protect herself against the hazards of the human environment. Men's clothing is generally the opposite of all this — sturdy, suitably protective, permitting movement and locomotion. The details of feminine manners and postures also serve to bind and restrict. To be feminine is to take up little space, to defer to others, to be silent or affirming of others, etc. It is not necessary here to survey all this, for it has been done many times and in illuminating detail in feminist writings. My point here is that though both men and women must behave in sex-announcing ways, the behavior which announces femaleness is in itself both physically and socially binding and limiting as the behavior which announces maleness is not.

The sex-correlated variations in our behavior tend systematically to the benefit of males and the detriment of females. The male, announcing his sex in sex-identifying behavior and dress, is both announcing and acting on his membership in a dominant caste — dominant within his subculture and to a fair extent across subcultures as well. The female, announcing her sex, is both announcing and acting on her membership in the subordinated caste. She is obliged to inform others constantly and in every sort of situation that she is to be treated as inferior, without authority, assaultable. She cannot move or speak within the usual cultural norms without engaging in self-deprecation. The male cannot move or speak without engaging in self-aggrandizement. Constant sex-identification both defines and maintains the caste boundary without which there could not be a dominance–subordination structure. . . .

The cultural and economic structures which create and enforce elaborate and rigid patterns of sex-marking and sex-announcing behavior, that is, create gender as we know it, mold us as dominators and subordinates (I do not say "mold our minds" or "mold our personalities"). They construct two classes of animals, the masculine and the feminine, where another constellation of forces might have constructed three or five categories, and not necessarily hierarchically related. Or such a spectrum of sorts that we would not experience them as "sorts" at all.

The term 'sexist' characterizes cultural and economic structures which create and enforce the elaborate and rigid patterns of sex-marking and sex-announcing which divide the species, along lines of sex, into dominators and subordinates. Individual act and practices are sexist which reinforce and support those structures, either as culture or as shapes taken on by the enculturated animals. Resistance to sexism is that which undermines those structures by social and political action and by projects of reconstruction and revision of ourselves.

MARÍA C. LUGONES AND ELIZABETH V. SPELMAN

Have We Got a Theory for You!
Feminist Theory, Cultural Imperialism, and the Demand for "The Woman's Voice"

MARÍA C. LUGONES *teaches philosophy at Carleton College in Minnesota and radical grassroots politics at Escuela Popular Norteña. She is working on a book on pluralist feminism.*

ELIZABETH V. SPELMAN *teaches philosophy at Smith College and has written extensively on issues of feminist theory. Her book* Inessential Woman: Problems of Exclusion in Feminist Thought *was published in 1988.*

Prologue

[IN AN HISPANA VOICE]

A veces quisiera mezclar en una voz el sonido canyenge, tristón y urbano del porteñismo que llevo adentro con la cadencia apacible, serrana y llena de corage de la hispana nuevo mejicana. Contrastar y unir

> el piolín y la cuerda
> el traé y el pepéname
> el camión y la troca
> la lluvia y el llanto

Pero este querer se me va cuando veo que he confundido la solidaridad con la falta de diferencia. La solidaridad requiere el reconocer, comprender, respetar y amar lo que nos lleva a llorar en distintas cadencias. El imperialismo cultural desea lo contrario, por eso necesitamos muchas voces. Porque una sola voz nos mata a las dos.

No quiero hablar por ti sino contigo. Pero si no aprendo tus modos y tu los mios la conversación es sólo aparente. Y la apariencia se levanta como una barrera sin sentido entre las dos. Sin sentido y sin sentimiento. Por eso no me debes dejar que te dicte tu ser y no me dictes el mio. Porque entonces ya no dialogamos. El diálogo entre nosotras requiere dos voces y no una.

Tal vez un día jugaremos juntas y nos hablaremos no en una lengua universal sino que vos me hablarás mi voz y yo la tuya.

Preface

This paper is the result of our dialogue, of our thinking together about differences among women and how these differences are silenced. (Think, for example, of all the silences there are connected with the fact that this paper is in English — for that is a borrowed tongue for one of us.) In the process of our talking and writing together, we saw that the differences between us did not permit our speaking in one voice. For example, when we agreed we expressed the thought differently; there were some things that both of us thought were true but could not express as true of each of us; sometimes we could not say 'we'; and sometimes one of us could not express the thought in the first person singular, and to express it in the third person would be to present an outsider's and not an insider's perspective. Thus the use of two voices is central both to the process of constructing this paper and to the substance of it. We are both the authors of this paper and not just sections of it but we write together without presupposing unity of expression or of experience. So when we speak in unison it means just that — there are two voices and not just one.

Introduction

[IN THE VOICE OF A WHITE/ANGLO WOMAN WHO HAS BEEN TEACHING AND WRITING ABOUT FEMINIST THEORY]

Feminism is, among other things, a response to the fact that women either have been left out of, or included in demeaning and disfiguring ways in what has been an almost exclusively male account of the world. And so while part of what feminists want and demand for women is the right to move and to act in accordance with our own wills and not against them, another part is the desire and insistence that we give our *own* accounts of these movements and actions. For it matters to us what is said about us, who says it, and to whom it is said: having the opportunity to talk about one's life, to give an account of it, to interpret it, is integral to leading that life rather than being led through it; hence our distrust of the male monopoly over accounts of women's lives. To put the same point slightly differently, part of human life, human living, is talking about it, and we can be sure that being silenced in one's own account of one's life is a kind of amputation that signals oppression. Another reason for not divorcing life from the telling of it or talking about it is that as humans our experiences are deeply influenced by what is said about them, by

ourselves or powerful (as opposed to significant) others. Indeed, the phenomenon of internalized oppression is only possible because this is so; one experiences her life in terms of the impoverished and degrading concepts others have found it convenient to use to describe her. We can't separate lives from the accounts given of them; the articulation of our experience is part of our experience.

Sometimes feminists have made even stronger claims about the importance of speaking about our own lives and the destructiveness of others presuming to speak about us or for us. First of all, the claim has been made that on the whole men's accounts of women's lives have been at best false, a function of ignorance; and at worst malicious lies, a function of a knowledgeable desire to exploit and oppress. Since it matters to us that falsehood and lies not be told about us, we demand, of those who have been responsible for those falsehoods and lies, or those who continue to transmit them, not just that we speak but that they learn to be able to hear us. It has also been claimed that talking about one's life, telling one's story, in the company of those doing the same (as in consciousness-raising sessions), is constitutive of feminist method.

And so the demand that the woman's voice be heard and attended to has been made for a variety of reasons: not just so as to greatly increase the chances that true accounts of women's lives will be given, but also because the articulation of experience (in myriad ways) is among the hallmarks of a self-determining individual or community. There are not just epistemological, but moral and political reasons for demanding that the woman's voice be heard, after centuries of androcentric din.

But what more exactly is the feminist demand that the woman's voice be heard? There are several crucial notes to make about it. First of all, the demand grows out of a complaint, and in order to understand the scope and focus of the demand we have to look at the scope and focus of the complaint. The complaint does not specify *which* women have been silenced, and in one way this is appropriate to the conditions it is a complaint about: virtually no women have had a voice, whatever their race, class, ethnicity, religion, sexual alliance, whatever place and period in history they lived. And if it is as women that women have been silenced, then of course the demand must be that women as women have a voice. But in another way the complaint is very misleading, insofar as it suggests that it is women as women who have been silenced, and that whether a woman is rich or poor, Black, brown or white, etc. is irrelevant to what it means for her to be a woman. For the demand thus simply made ignores at least two related points: (1) it is only possible for a woman who does not feel highly vulnerable with respect to other parts of her identity, e.g. race, class, ethnicity, religion, sexual alliance, etc., to conceive of her voice simply or essentially as a 'woman's voice'; (2) just because not all women are equally vulnerable with respect to race, class, etc., some women's voices are more likely to be heard than others by those who have heretofore been giving — or silencing — the accounts of women's lives. For all these reasons, the women's voices most likely to come forth and the women's voices most likely to be heard are, in the US anyway, those of white, middle-class, heterosexual Christian (or anyway not self-identified non-Christian) women. Indeed, many Hispanas, Black women, Jewish women — to name a few groups — have felt it an invitation to silence rather than speech to be requested — if they are requested at all — to speak about being 'women' (with the plain wrapper — as if there were one) in distinction from speaking about being Hispana, Black, Jewish, working-class, etc., women.

The demand that the 'woman's voice' be heard, and the search for the 'woman's voice' as central to feminist methodology, reflects nascent feminist theory. It reflects nascent empirical theory insofar as it presupposes that the silencing of women is systematic, shows up in regular, patterned ways, and that there are discoverable causes of this widespread observable phenomenon; the demand reflects nascent political theory insofar as it presupposes that the silencing of women reveals a systematic pattern of power and authority; and it reflects nascent moral theory insofar as it presupposes that the silencing is unjust and that there are particular ways of remedying this injustice. Indeed, whatever else we know feminism to include — e.g. concrete direct political action — theorizing is integral to it: theories about the nature of oppression, the causes of it, the relation of the oppression of women to other forms of oppression. And certainly the concept of the woman's voice is itself a theoretical concept, in the sense that it presupposes a theory according to which our identities as human beings are actually compound identities, a kind of fusion or confusion of our otherwise separate identities as women or men, as Black or brown or white, etc. That is no less a theoretical stance than Plato's division of the person into soul and body or Aristotle's parcelling of the soul into various functions.

The demand that the 'woman's voice' be heard also invites some further directions in the exploration of women's lives and discourages or excludes others. For reasons mentioned above, systematic, sustained reflection on being a woman — the kind of contemplation that 'doing theory' requires—is most likely to be done by women who vis-à-vis other women enjoy a certain amount of political, social and economic privilege because of their skin color, class membership, ethnic identity. There is a relationship between the content of our contemplation and the fact that we have the time to engage in it at some length—otherwise we shall have to say that it is a mere accident of history that white middle-class women in the United States have in the main developed 'feminist theory' (as opposed to 'Black feminist theory', 'Chicana feminist theory', etc.) and that so much of the theory has failed to be relevant to the lives of women who are not white or middle class. Feminist theory—of all kinds—is to be based on, or anyway touch base with, the variety of real life stories women provide about themselves. But in fact, because, among other things, of the structural political and social and economic inequalities among women, the tail has been wagging the dog: feminist theory has not for the most part arisen out of a medley or women's voices; instead, the theory has arisen out of the voices, the experiences, of a fairly small handful of women, and if other women's voices do not sing in harmony with the theory, they aren't counted as women's voices—rather, they are the voices of the woman as Hispana, Black, Jew, etc. There is another sense in which the tail is wagging the dog, too: it is presumed to be the case that those who do the theory know more about those who are theorized than vice versa: hence it ought to be the case that if it is white/Anglo women who write for and about all other women, then white/Anglo women must know more about all other women than other women know about them. But in fact just in order to survive, brown and Black women have to know a lot more about white/Anglo women—not

through the sustained contemplation theory requires, but through the sharp observation stark exigency demands.

[IN AN HISPANA VOICE]

I think it necessary to explain why in so many cases when women of color appear in front of white/Anglo women to talk about feminism and women of color, we mainly raise a complaint: the complaint of exclusion, of silencing, of being included in a universe we have not chosen. We usually raise the complaint with a certain amount of disguised or undisguised anger. I can only attempt to explain this phenomenon from a Hispanic viewpoint and a fairly narrow one at that: the viewpoint of an Argentinian woman who has lived in the US for 16 yr, who has attempted to come to terms with the devaluation of things Hispanic and Hispanic people in 'America' and who is most familiar with Hispano life in the Southwest of the US. I am quite unfamiliar with daily Hispano life in the urban centers, though not with some of the themes and some of the salient experiences of urban Hispano life.

When I say 'we', I am referring to Hispanas. I am accustomed to use the 'we' in this way. I am also pained by the tenuousness of this 'we' given that I am not a native of the US. Through the years I have come to be recognized and I have come to recognize myself more and more firmly as part of this 'we'. I also have a profound yearning for this firmness since I am a displaced person and I am conscious of not being of and I am unwilling to make myself of—even if this were possible—the white/Anglo community.

When I say 'you' I mean not the non-Hispanic but the white/Anglo women that I address. 'We' and 'you' do not capture my relation to other non-white women. The complexity of that relation is not addressed here, but it is vivid to me as I write down my thoughts on the subject at hand.

I see two related reasons for our complaint-full discourse with white/Anglo women. Both of these reasons plague our world, they contaminate it through and through. It takes some hardening of oneself, some self-acceptance of our own anger to face them, for to face them is to decide that maybe we can change our situation in self-constructive ways and we know fully well that the possibilities are minimal. We know that we cannot rest from facing these reasons, that the tenderness towards others in us undermines our possibilities, that we have to fight our own niceness because it clouds our minds and hearts. Yet we know that a thoroughgoing hardening would dehumanize us. So, we have to walk through our days in a peculiarly fragile psychic state, one that we have to struggle to maintain, one that we do not often succeed in maintaining.

We and you do not talk the same language. When we talk to you we use your language: the language of your experience and of your theories. We try to use it to communicate our world of experience. But since your language and your theories are inadequate in expressing our experiences, we only succeed in communicating our experience of exclusion. We cannot talk to you in our language because you do not understand it. So the brute facts that we understand your language and that the place where most theorizing about women is taking place is your place, both combine to require that we either use your language and distort our experience not just in the speaking about it, but in the living of it, or that we remain silent. Complaining about exclusion is a way of remaining silent.

You are ill at ease in our world. You are ill at ease in our world in a very dif-ferent way than we are ill at ease in yours. You are not of our world and again, you are not of our world in a very different way than we are not of yours. In the intimacy of a personal relationship we appear to you many times to be wholly there, to have broken through or to have dissipated the barriers that separate us because you are Anglo and we are raza. When we let go of the psychic state that I referred to above in the direction of sympathy, we appear to ourselves equally whole in your presence but our intimacy is thoroughly incomplete. When we are in your world many times you remake us in your own image, although sometimes you clearly and explicitly acknowledge that we are not wholly there in our being with you. When we are in your world we ourselves feel the discomfort of having our own being Hispanas disfigured or not understood. And yet, we have had to be in your world and learn its ways. We have to participate in it, make a living in it, live in it, be mistreated in it, be ignored in it, and rarely, be appreciated in it. In learning to do these things or in learning to suffer them or in learning to enjoy what is to be enjoyed or in learning to understand your conception of us, we have had to learn your culture and thus your language and self-conceptions. But there is nothing that necessitates that you understand our world: understand, that is, not as an observer understands things, but as a participant, as someone who has a stake in them understands them. So your being ill at ease in our world lacks the features of our being ill at ease in yours precisely because you can leave and you can always tell yourselves that you will be soon out of there and because the wholeness of your selves is never touched by us, we have no tendency to remake you in our image.

But you theorize about women and we are women, so you understand yourselves to be theorizing about us and we understand you to be theorizing about us. Yet none of the feminist theories developed so far seem to me to help Hispanas in the articulation of our experience. We have a sense that in using them we are distorting our experiences. Most Hispanas cannot even understand the language used in these theories — and only in some cases the reason is that the Hispana cannot understand English. We do not recognize ourselves in these theories. They create in us a schizophrenic split between our concern for ourselves as women and ourselves as Hispanas, one that we do not feel otherwise. Thus they seem to us to force us to assimilate to some version of Anglo culture, however revised that version may be. They seem to ask that we leave our communities or that we become alienated so completely in them that we feel hollow. When we see that you feel alienated in your own communities, this confuses us because we think that maybe every feminist has to suffer this alienation. But we see that recognition of your alienation leads many of you to be empowered into the remaking of your culture, while we are paralyzed into a state of displacement with no place to go.

So I think that we need to think carefully about the relation between the articulation of our own experience, the interpretation of our own experience, and theory making by us and other non-Hispanic women about themselves and other 'women'.

The only motive that makes sense to me for your joining us in this investigation is the motive of friendship, out of friendship. A non-imperialist feminism requires that you make a real space for our articulating, interpreting, theorizing and reflecting about the connections among them — a real space must be a non-coerced space — and/or that you follow us

into our world out of friendship. I see the 'out of friendship' as the only sensical motivation for this following because the task at hand for you is one of extraordinary difficulty. It requires that you be willing to devote a great part of your life to it and that you be willing to suffer alienation and self-disruption. Self-interest has been proposed as a possible motive for entering this task. But self-interest does not seem to me to be a realistic motive, since whatever the benefits you may accrue from such a journey, they cannot be concrete enough for you at this time and they not be worth your while. I do not think that you have any obligation to understand us. You do have an obligation to abandon your imperialism, your universal claims, your reduction of us to your selves simply because they seriously harm us.

I think that the fact that we are so ill at ease with your theorizing in the ways indicated above does indicate that there is something wrong with these theories. But what is it that is wrong? Is it simply that the theories are flawed if meant to be universal but accurate so long as they are confined to your particular group(s)? Is it that the theories are not really flawed but need to be translated? Can they be translated? Is it something about the process of theorizing that is flawed? How do the two reasons for our complaint-full discourse affect the validity of your theories? Where do *we* begin? To what extent are our experience and its articulation affected by our being a colonized people, and thus by your culture, theories and conceptions? Should we theorize in community and thus as part of community life and outside the academy and other intellectual circles? What is the point of making theory? Is theory making a good thing for us to do at this time? When are we making theory and when are we just articulating and/ or interpreting our experiences?

Some Questionable Assumptions about Feminist Theorizing

[UNPROBLEMATICALLY IN VICKY'S & MARIA'S VOICE]

Feminist theories aren't just about what happens to the female population in any given society or across all societies; they are about the meaning of those experiences in the lives of women. They are about beings who give their own accounts of what is happening to them or of what they are doing, who have culturally constructed ways of reflecting on their lives. But how can the theorizer get at the meaning of those experiences? What should the relation be between a woman's own account of her experiences and the theorizer's account of it?

Let us describe two different ways of arriving at an account of another woman's experience. It is one thing for both me and you to observe you and come up with our different accounts of what you are doing; it is quite another for me to observe myself and others much like me culturally and in other ways and to develop an account of myself and then use that account to give an account of you. In the first case you are the 'insider' and I am the 'outsider'. When the outsider makes clear that she is an outsider and that this is an outsider's account of your behavior, there is a touch of honesty about what she is doing. Most of the time the 'interpretation by an outsider' is left understood and most of the time the distance of outsidedness is understood to mark objectivity in the interpretation. But why is the outsider as an outsider interpreting your behavior? Is she doing it so that you can understand how she sees you? Is she doing it so that other outsiders will understand how you *are*? Is she doing it so that *you* will understand how you are? It would seem that if the outsider wants you to understand how she sees you and you have given your account of how you see yourself to her, there is a possibility of genuine dialogue between the two. It also seems that the lack of reciprocity could bar genuine dialogue. For why should you engage in such a one-sided dialogue? As soon as we ask this question, a host of other conditions for the possibility of a genuine dialogue between us arise: conditions having to do with your position relative to me in the various social, political and economic structures in which we might come across each other or in which you may run face to face with my account of you and my use of your account of yourself. Is this kind of dialogue necessary for me to get at the meaning of your experiences? That is, is this kind of dialogue necessary for feminist theorizing that is not seriously flawed?

Obviously the most dangerous of the understandings of what I — an outsider — am doing in giving an account of your experience is the one that describes what I'm doing as giving an account of who and how you are whether it be given to you or to other outsiders. Why should you or anyone else believe me; that is why should you or anyone else believe that you are as I say you are? Could I be right? What conditions would have to obtain for my being right? That many women are put in the position of not knowing whether or not to believe outsiders' accounts of their experiences is clear. The pressures to believe these accounts are enormous even when the woman in question does not see herself in the account. She is thus led to doubt her own judgment and to doubt all interpretation of her experience. This leads her to experience her life differently. Since the consequences of outsiders' accounts can be so significant, it is crucial that we reflect on whether or not this type of account can ever be right and if so, under what conditions.

The last point leads us to the second way of arriving at an account of another woman's experience, viz. the case in which I observe myself and others like me culturally and in other ways and use that account to give an account of you. In doing this, I remake you in my own image. Feminist theorizing approaches this remaking insofar as it depends on the concept of women as women. For it has not arrived at this concept as a consequence of dialogue with many women who are culturally different, or by any other kind of investigation of cultural differences which may include different conceptions of what it is to be a woman; it has simply presupposed this concept.

Our suggestion in this paper, and at this time it is no more than a suggestion, is that only when genuine and reciprocal dialogue takes place between 'outsiders' and 'insiders' can we trust the outsider's account. At first sight it may appear that the insider/outsider distinction disappears in the dialogue, but it is important to notice that all that happens is that we are now both outsider and insider with respect to each other. The dialogue puts us both in position to give a better account of each other's and our own experience. Here we should again note that white/Anglo women are much less prepared for this dialogue with women of color than women of color are for dialogue with them in that women of color have had to learn white/Anglo ways, self-conceptions, and conceptions of them.

But both the possibility and the desirability of this dialogue are very much in question. We need to think about the possible motivations for engaging in this dialogue, whether doing theory jointly would be a good thing, in what ways and for whom, and whether doing theory is in itself a good thing at this time for women

of color or white/Anglo women. In motivating the last question let us remember the hierarchical distinctions between theorizers and those theorized about and between theorizers and doers. These distinctions are endorsed by the same views and institutions which endorse and support hierarchical distinctions between men/women, master race/inferior race, intellectuals/manual workers. Of what use is the activity of theorizing to those of us who are women of color engaged day in and day out in the task of empowering women and men of color face to face with them? Should we be articulating and interpreting their experience for them with the aid of theories? Whose theories?

Ways of Talking or Being Talked About That Are Helpful, Illuminating, Empowering, Respectful

[UNPROBLEMATICALLY IN MARIA'S & VICKY'S VOICE]

Feminists have been quite diligent about pointing out the ways in which empirical, philosophical and moral theories have been androcentric. They have thought it crucial to ask, with respect to such theories: who makes them? for whom do they make them? about what or whom are the theories? why? how are theories tested? what are the criteria for such tests and where did the criteria come from? Without posing such questions and trying to answer them, we'd never have been able to begin to mount evidence for our claims that particular theories are androcentric, sexist, biased, paternalistic, etc. Certain philosophers have become fond of—indeed, have made their careers on—pointing out that characterizing a statement as true or false is only one of many ways possible of characterizing it; it might also be, oh, rude, funny, disarming, etc.; it may be intended to soothe or to hurt; or it may have the effect, intended or not, of soothing or hurting. Similarly, theories appear to be the kinds of things that are true or false; but they also are the kinds of things that can be, e.g. useless, arrogant, disrespectful, ignorant, ethnocentric, imperialistic. The immediate point is that feminist theory is no less immune to such characterizations than, say, Plato's political theory, or Freud's theory of female psychosexual development. Of course this is not to say that if feminist theory manages to be respectful or helpful it will follow that it must be true. But if, say, an empirical theory is purported to be about 'women' and in fact is only about certain women, it is certainly false, probably ethnocentric, and of dubious usefulness except to those whose position in the world it strengthens (and theories, as we know, don't have to be true in order to be used to strengthen people's positions in the world).

Many reasons can be and have been given for the production of accounts of people's lives that plainly have nothing to do with illuminating those lives for the benefit of those living them. It is likely that both the method of investigation and the content of many accounts would be different if illuminating the lives of the people the accounts are about were the aim of the studies. Though we cannot say ahead of time how feminist theory-making would be different if all (or many more) of those people it is meant to be about were more intimately part of the theory-making process, we do suggest some specific ways being talked about can be helpful:

(1) The theory or account can be helpful if it enables one to see how parts of one's life fit together, for example, to see connec-tions among parts of one's life one hasn't seen before. No account can do this if it doesn't get the parts right to begin with, and this cannot happen if the concepts used to describe a life are utterly foreign.

(2) A useful theory will help one locate oneself concretely in the world, rather then add to the mystification of the world and one's location in it. New concepts may be of significance here, but they will not be useful if there is no way they can be translated into already existing concepts. Suppose a theory locates you in the home, because you are a woman, but you know full well that is not where you spend most of your time? Or suppose you can't locate yourself easily in any particular class as defined by some version of marxist theory?

(3) A theory or account not only ought to accurately locate one in the world but also enable one to think about the extent to which one is responsible or not for being in that location. Otherwise, for those whose location is as oppressed peoples, it usually occurs that the oppressed have no way to see themselves as in any way self-determining, as having any sense of being worthwhile or having grounds for pride, and paradoxically at the same time feeling at fault for the position they are in. A useful theory will help people sort out just what is and is not due to themselves and their own activities as opposed to those who have power over them.

It may seem odd to make these criteria criteria of a useful theory, if the usefulness is not to be at odds with the issue of the truth of the theory: for the focus on feeling worthwhile or having pride seems to rule out the possibility that the truth might just be that such-and-such a group of people has been under the control of others for centuries and that the only explanation of that is that they are worthless and weak people, and will never be able to change that. Feminist theorizing seems implicitly if not explicitly committed to the moral view that women *are* worthwhile beings, and the metaphysical theory that we are beings capable of bringing about a change in our situations. Does this mean feminist theory is 'biased'? Not any more than any other theory, e.g. psychoanalytic theory. What is odd here is not the feminist presupposition that women are worthwhile but rather that feminist theory (and other theory) often has the effect of empowering one group and demoralizing another.

Aspects of feminist theory are as unabashedly value-laden as other political and moral theories. It is not just an examination of women's positions, for it includes, indeed begins with, moral and political judgements about the injustice (or, where relevant, justice) of them. This means that there are implicit or explicit judgements also about what kind of changes constitute a better or worse situation for women.

(4) In this connection a theory that is useful will provide criteria for change and make suggestions for modes of resistance that don't merely reflect the situation and values of the theorizer. A theory that is respectful of those about whom it is a theory will not assume that changes that are perceived as making life better for some women are changes that will make, and will be perceived as making, life better for other women. This in NOT to say that if some women do not find a situation oppressive, other women ought never to suggest to the contrary that there might be very good reasons to think that the situation nevertheless *is* oppressive. But it is to say that, e.g. the prescription that life for women will be better when we're in the workforce rather than at home, when we are completely free of religious beliefs

with patriarchal origins, when we live in complete separation from men, etc., are seen as slaps in the face to women whose life would be better if they could spend more time at home, whose identity is inseparable from their religious beliefs and cultural practices (which is not to say those beliefs and practices are to remain completely uncriticized and unchanged), who have ties to men — whether erotic or not — such that to have them severed in the name of some vision of what is 'better' is, at that time and for those women, absurd. Our visions of what is better are always informed by our perception of what is bad about our present situation. Surely we've learned enough from the history of clumsy missionaries, and the white suffragists of the 19th century (who couldn't imagine why Black women 'couldn't see' how crucial getting the vote for 'women' was) to know that we can clobber people to destruction with our visions, our versions, of what is better. BUT: this does not mean women are not to offer supportive and tentative criticism of one another. But there is a very important difference between (a) developing ideas together, in a 'pre-theoretical' stage, engaged as equals in joint enquiry, and (b) one group developing, on the basis of their own experience, a set of criteria for good change for women — and then reluctantly making revisions in the criteria at the insistence of women to whom such criteria seem ethnocentric and arrogant. The deck is stacked when one group takes it upon itself to develop the theory and then have others criticize it. Categories are quick to congeal, and the experiences of women whose lives do not fit the categories will appear as anomalous when in fact the theory should have grown out of them as much as others from the beginning. This, of course, is why any organization or conference having to do with 'women' — with no qualification — that seriously does not want to be 'solipsistic' will from the beginning be multi-cultural or state the appropriate qualifications. How we think and what we think about does depend in large part on who is there — not to mention who is expected or encouraged to speak. (Recall the boys in the *Symposium* sending the flute girls out.) Conversations and criticism take place in particular circumstances. Turf matters. So does the fact of who if anyone already has set up the terms of the conversations.

(5) Theory cannot be useful to anyone interested in resistance and change unless there is reason to believe that knowing what a theory means and believing it to be true have some connection to resistance and change. As we make theory and offer it up to others, what do we assume is the connection between theory and consciousness? Do we expect others to read theory, understand it, believe it, and have their consciousness and lives thereby transformed? If we really want theory to make a difference to people's lives, how ought we to present it? Do we think people come to consciousness by reading? only by reading? Speaking to people through theory (orally or in writing) is a *very* specific context-dependent activity. That is, theory-makers and their methods and concepts constitute a community of people and of shared meanings. Their language can be just as opaque and foreign to those not in the community as a foreign tongue or dialect. Why do we engage in *this* activity and what effect do we think it ought to have? As Helen Longino has asked: 'Is, "doing theory" just a bonding ritual for academic or educationally privileged feminists/women?' Again, whom does our theory-making serve?

Some Suggestions About How to Do Theory That Is Not Imperialistic, Ethnocentric, Disrespectful

[PROBLEMATICALLY IN THE VOICE OF A WOMAN OF COLOR]

What are the things we need to know about others, and about ourselves, in order to speak intelligently, intelligibly, sensitively, and helpfully about their lives? We can show respect, or lack of it, in writing theoretically about others no less than in talking directly with them. This is not to say that here we have a well-worked out concept of respect, but only to suggest that together all of us consider what it would mean to theorize in a respectful way.

When we speak, write, and publish our theories, to whom do we think we are accountable? Are the concerns we have in being accountable to 'the profession' at odds with the concerns we have in being accountable to those about whom we theorize? Do commitments to 'the profession', method, getting something published, getting tenure, lead us to talk and act in ways at odds with what we ourselves (let alone others) would regard as ordinary, decent behavior? To what extent do we presuppose that really understanding another person or culture requires our behaving in ways that are disrespectful, even violent? That is, to what extent do we presuppose that getting and/or publishing the requisite information requires or may require disregarding the wishes of others, lying to them, wresting information from them against their wills? Why and how do we think theorizing about others provides *understanding* of them? Is there any sense in which theorizing about others is a short-cut to understanding them?

Finally, if we think doing theory is an important activity, and we think that some conditions lead to better theorizing than others, what are we going to do about creating those conditions? If we think it not just desirable but necessary for women of different racial and ethnic identities to create feminist theory jointly, how shall that be arranged for? It may be the case that at this particular point we ought not even try to do that—that feminist theory by and and for Hispanas needs to be done separately from feminist theory by and for Black women, white women, etc. But it must be recognized that white/Anglo women have more power and privilege than Hispanas, Black women, etc., and at the very least they can use such advantage to provide space and time for other women to speak (with the above caveats about implicit restrictions on what counts as 'the woman's voice'). And once again it is important to remember that the power of white/Anglo women vis-à-vis Hispanas and Black women is in inverse proportion to their working knowledge of each other.

This asymmetry is a crucial fact about the background of possible relationships between white women and women of color, whether as political co-workers, professional colleagues, or friends.

If white/Anglo women and women of color are to do theory jointly, in helpful, respectful, illuminating and empowering ways, the task ahead of white/Anglo women because of this asymmetry, is a very hard task. The task is a very complex one. In part, to make an analogy, the task can be compared to learning a text without the aid of teachers. We all know the lack of contact felt when we want to discuss a particular issue that requires knowledge of a text with someone who does not know the text at all. Or the discomfort and impatience that arise in us when we are discussing an issue that presupposes a text and someone walks into the conversation who does not know the text. That person is either left out or will impose herself on us and either try to engage in the discussion or try to change the subject. Women of color are put in these situations by white/Anglo women and men constantly. Now imagine yourself simply left out but wanting to do theory with us. The first thing to recognize and accept is that you disturb our own dialogues by putting yourself in the left-out position and not leaving us in some meaningful sense to ourselves.

You must also recognize and accept that you must learn the text. But the text is an extraordinarily complex one: viz. our many different cultures. You are asking us to make ourselves more vulnerable to you than we already are before we have any reason to trust that you will not take advantage of this vulnerability. So you need to learn to become unintrusive, unimportant, patient to the point of tears, while at the same time open to learning any possible lessons. You will also have to come to terms with the sense of alienation, of not belonging, of having your world thoroughly disrupted, having it criticized and scrutinized from the point of view of those who have been harmed by it, having important concepts central to it dismissed, being viewed with mistrust, being seen as of no consequence except as an object of mistrust.

Why would any white/Anglo woman engage in this task? Out of self-interest? What in engaging in this task would be, not just in her interest, but perceived as such by her before the task is completed or well underway? Why should we want you to come into our world out of self-interest? Two points need to be made here. The task as described could be entered into with the intention of finding out as much as possible about us so as to better dominate us. The person engaged in this task would act as a spy. The motivation is not unfamiliar to us. We have heard it said that now that Third World countries are more powerful as a bloc, westerners need to learn more about them, that it is in their self-interest to do so. Obviously there is no reason why people of color should welcome white/Anglo women into their world for the carrying out of this intention. It is also obvious that white/Anglo feminists should not engage in this task under this description since the task under this description would not lead to joint theorizing of the desired sort: respectful, illuminating, helpful and empowering. It would be helpful and empowering only in a one-sided way.

Self-interest is also mentioned as a possible motive in another way. White/Anglo women sometimes say that the task of understanding women of color would entail self-growth or self-expansion. If the task is conceived as described here, then one should doubt that growth or expansion will be the result. The severe self-disruption that the task entails should place a doubt in anyone who takes the task seriously about her possibilities of coming out of the task whole, with a self that is not as fragile as the selves of those who have been the victims of racism. But also, why should women of color embrace white/Anglo women's self-betterment without reciprocity? At this time women of color cannot afford this generous affirmation of white/Anglo women.

Another possible motive for engaging in this task is the motive of duty, 'out of obligation', because white/Anglos have done people of color wrong. Here again two considerations: coming into Hispano, Black, Native American worlds out of obligation puts white/Anglos in a morally self-righteous position that is inappropriate. You are active, we are passive. We become the vehicles of your own redemption. Secondly, we couldn't want you to come into our worlds 'out of obligation'. That is like wanting someone to make love to you out of obligation. So, whether or not you have an obligation to do this (and we would deny that you do), or whether this task could even be done out of obligation, this is an inappropriate motive.

Out of obligation you should stay out of our way, respect us and our distance, and forgo the use of whatever power you have over us — for example, the power to use your language in our meetings, the power to overwhelm us with your education, the power to intrude in our communities in order to research us and to record the supposed dying of our cultures, the power to engrain in us a sense that we are members of dying cultures and are doomed to assimilate, the power to keep us in a defensive posture with respect to our own cultures.

So the motive of friendship remains as both the only appropriate and understandable motive for white/Anglo feminists engaging in the task as described above. If you enter the task out of friendship with us, then you will be moved to attain the appropriate reciprocity of care for your and our wellbeing as whole beings, you will have a stake in us and in our world, you will be moved to satisfy the need for reciprocity of understanding that will enable you to follow us in our experiences as we are able to follow you in yours.

We are not suggesting that if the learning of the text is to be done out of friendship, you must enter into a friendship with a whole community and for the purpose of making theory. In order to understand what it is that we are suggesting, it is important to remember that during the description of her experience of exclusion, the Hispana voice said that Hispanas experience the intimacy of friendship with white/Anglo women friends as thoroughly incomplete. It is not until this fact is acknowledged by our white/Anglo women friends and felt as a profound lack in our experience of each other that white/Anglo women can begin to see us. Seeing us in our communities will make clear and concrete to you how incomplete we really are in our relationships with you. It is this beginning that forms the proper background for the yearning to understand the text of our cultures that can lead to joint theory-making.

Thus, the suggestion made here is that if white/Anglo women are to understand our voices, they must understand our communities and us in them. Again, this is not to suggest that you set out to make friends with our communities, though you may become friends with some of the members, nor is it to suggest that you should try to befriend us for the purpose of making theory with us. The latter would be a perversion of friendship. Rather, from within friendship you may be moved by friendship to undergo the very difficult task of understanding the text of our cultures by understanding our lives in our communities. This learning calls for circumspection, for questioning of yourselves and your roles in your own culture. It necessitates a striving to understand while in the comfortable position of not having an official calling card (as 'scientific' observers of our communities have); it demands recognition that you do not have the authority of knowledge; it requires coming to the task without ready-made theories to frame our lives. This learning is then extremely hard because it requires openness (including openness to severe criticism of the white/Anglo world), sensitivity, concentration, self-questioning, circumspection. It should be clear that it does not consist in a passive immersion in our cultures, but in a striving to understand what it is that our voices are saying. Only then can we engage in a mutual dialogue that does not reduce each one of us to instances of the abstraction called 'woman'.

10

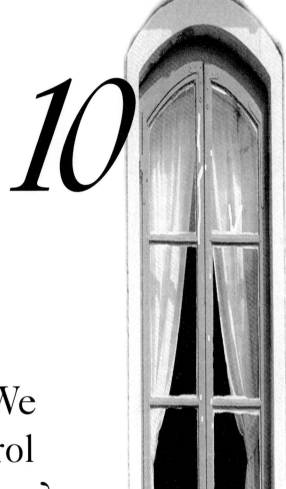

Can We
Control
Violence?

Imagine the worst day that you have had this semester, one of those days when everything seems to be going wrong: the alarm clock didn't ring; the traffic was hectic on the way to class; you ran into someone who annoys you. On days like that, irritations that would be easy enough to handle on ordinary occasions seem insurmountable challenges. Suppose that on that worst day of the semester, someone bumps into you on the sidewalk and starts yelling at you. Do you yell back? Do you hurl every insult you can recall at the person? Do you get out of that person's way but explode later when you discover that your roommate has thrown out the leftovers you planned to eat for dinner? Would any of these scenarios make the world a more violent place in which to live?

Violence is often held up as an indicator of societal malaise. Acts commonly agreed to be wrong typically include certain violent acts: murder, torture, child-molestation. In fact, "violence" is sometimes taken to be almost synonymous with wrongdoing: one is said to "do violence to" someone or something when one has done wrong.

At the same time, much of our entertainment is seasoned with violence, so much so that the motion picture industry feels compelled to indicate whether the level of violence in a given film exceeds what a young child should be permitted to see. Rock videos commonly allude to violence as a part of their esthetic. Capital punishment is legal in a majority of states. Aside from total pacifists, most people believe that violence is sometimes justified — in law enforcement, perhaps, or in waging a "moral" war.

Still most Americans believe that there is far too much violence in our country and in our world. Ethics has a role to play in our reflections on violence. Moral philosophy ponders questions such as the following: When, if ever, is violence morally appropriate? Are human beings inherently violent? If so, can we control or limit our expressions of violence? If not, is violence dispensable? Are certain ways of thinking inherently violent? Can we eliminate violence by changing the ways we think?

Sigmund Freud's psychoanalytic theory defends the view that human nature is essentially violent. Among our basic instincts are drives toward aggression which human societies must channel if they are to survive. In general, civilized society depends on the repression of sexual and aggressive instincts. The result is that human beings enjoy the security of civilized life only by forfeiting the happiness of much instinctual gratification. Moreover, no organization of society can entirely harness our inclinations toward violence. Ethical precepts attempt to control violence by means of conscience, the "superego" of the Freudian system. But the emphatic demands of the superego cannot be met, and the person who does not get the superego to moderate its demands becomes neurotic.

Sam Keen argues that our tendency to see other groups of people as enemies is a product of habits of thought entrenched in our own and other societies. We have been taught to see our enemies as "inhuman" and therefore as not deserving of the respect to which human beings are entitled. Unfortunately, the means of modern warfare have made it easier to dehumanize "the enemy." Because violent attitudes toward an enemy are not essential aspects of human beings, such thinking, and the violence it facilitates, can be eradicated. But this overcoming of socially cultivated habits must begin within the individual's own mind.

Like Keen, Hannah Arendt believes that the structure of our modern society and the metaphors that frame our thought contribute to the widespread violence of our world. Arendt observes that violence is, in its very nature, the opposite of power: violence is typically employed by those who lack or are losing power. Nonetheless, violence is fostered by instrumental thinking and by metaphors that license our tendency to imagine that the ends justify the means. It is also encouraged by the increasing bureaucratization of public life. Bureaucracy frustrates the individual's sense of power in action, with the result that violence becomes a more tempting option for those who have grievances.

William James agrees with Freud that deep-seated human needs have been satisfied by war. War, in his view, has provided the circumstances for developing valor and other virtues among individuals, as well as the possibility of changing the world in decisive, dramatically satisfying ways. But James denies that war is inevitable. He proposes an alternative: a conscription of all young people to be part of an army "against Nature." This army that would work to control nature to serve human beings, and thus to achieve desirable civic goals. Such a conscription, James argues, would provide the benefits that war has conferred on societies without entailing the violence and horror of war.

War, however, is not the only kind of violence that ethical reflection should address. While it is arguable that the violence of war might sometimes be justified, certain kinds of violence are wrong by definition. And some of these, unlike war, are domestic and personal concerns. Date rape is among these. Lois Pineau believes that a mythology of rape undercuts legal protection for victims of date rape. In such cases, the point of view on which the legal system depends — that of the "reasonable man" — is biased by mythological ideas: for instance, the idea that women often say "no" when they mean "yes." In order for victims of date rape to be adequately protected by the law, Pineau concludes, the law must recognize criteria for consent that conform to the point of view of the "reasonable woman."

Do we have a moral obligation to prevent violence? Presumably, there are cases when our failure to attempt to prevent violence ought to be considered a moral failure. The case of the New York woman who was stabbed to death while more than twenty people simply looked on is a case in point. But what one is morally obligated to do depends on one's ability to do something. "Ought implies can," a premise of most moral theorists, makes precisely this point.

But if ought implies can, then we need some factual information if we are to know what we ought to do. The question "What can we do?" is relevant. Ernest van den Haag considers the implications of certain facts for moral judgment in the case of the death penalty. The death penalty is considered by some to be a legitimate use of violence. Kant even argues that it is sometimes morally obligatory to execute; he considers the death penalty for murderers, for instance, to be in accordance with moral law. Others consider the death penalty to be murder that is only considered respectable because it is committed by the government. Van den Haag considers whether the death penalty actually deters criminals from committing acts of violence. The question of deterrence is important to utilitarians, who would weigh the good for society achieved by deterring crime against the harms to the criminal and society that are produced by an execution. Van den Haag finds that statistical means are inadequate to establish whether the death penalty is really a deterrent. He argues, however, that, despite our uncertainty, we should allow the death penalty in the case of murder because it might be a deterrent; we have no right to risk the lives of persons whose lives might be forfeited if this possible deterrent effect were eliminated.

Albert Camus takes issue with this view. He is unpersuaded that capital punishment deters crime. Moreover, he sees the government's action in capital cases to be essentially murder, often the murder of innocents, and he observes that capital cases typically involve psychological cruelty as well. He also worries about the societal effects of the government's open endorsement of the principle of retaliation.

Another case in which the justification of violence is hotly debated is the case of terrorism. Many people believe that terrorism is always unjustifiable — even that it is wrong to negotiate with terrorists. (The latter position often rests on utilitarian grounds: it would be wrong to negotiate with terrorists because to do so would be to recognize terrorism as a legitimate strategic ploy and thereby encourage potential terrorists in the belief that terrorism is useful to them.) On the other hand, those who think that the unequal distribution of power among nations and among ethnic groups is wrong sometimes argue that terrorism seems the only available tactic for disenfranchised groups. Virginia Held finds that terrorism should be considered morally akin to war. Thus, if war can sometimes be justified, so can terrorism. She goes on to suggest that limited terrorism may be morally preferable to war, in that war typically involves far more killing than terrorism.

SIGMUND FREUD

On Inclination Toward Aggression

SIGMUND FREUD (1856–1939), *the founder of psychoanalysis, lived most of his life in Vienna. A physician by training, Freud sought to explain the existence and nature of mental phenomena. His clinical and theoretical work in this area was supplemented by numerous reflections on cultural and social matters. Virtually nothing escaped his fierce intelligence.*

I think I can now hear a dignified voice admonishing me: 'It is precisely because your neighbour is not worthy of love, and is on the contrary your enemy, that you should love him as yourself'. . . .

Now it is very probable that my neighbour, when he is enjoined to love me as himself, will answer exactly as I have done and will repel me for the same reasons. I hope he will not have the same objective grounds for doing so, but he will have the same idea as I have. Even so, the behaviour of human beings shows differences, which ethics, disregarding the fact that such differences are determined, classifies as 'good' or 'bad'. So long as these undeniable differences have not been removed, obedience to high ethical demands entails damage to the aims of civilization, for it puts a positive premium on being bad. . . .

The element of truth behind all this, which people are so ready to disavow, is that men are not gentle creatures who want to be loved, and who at the most can defend themselves if they are attacked; they are, on the contrary, creatures among whose instinctual endowments is to be reckoned a powerful share of aggressiveness. As a result, their neighbour is for them not only a potential helper or sexual object, but also someone who tempts them to satisfy their aggressiveness on him, to exploit his capacity for work without compensation, to use him sexually without his consent, to seize his possessions, to humiliate him, to cause him pain, to torture and to kill him. Who, in the face of all his experience of life and of history, will have the courage to dispute this assertion? As a rule this cruel aggressiveness waits for some provocation or puts itself at the service of some other purpose, whose goal might also have been reached by milder measures. In circumstances that are favourable to it, when the mental counter-forces which ordinarily inhibit it are out of action, it also manifests itself spontaneously and reveals man as a savage beast to whom consideration towards his own kind is something alien. Anyone who calls to mind the atrocities committed during the racial migrations or the invasions of the Huns, or by the people known as Mongols under Jenghiz Kahn and Tamerlane, or at the capture of Jerusalem by the pious Crusaders, or even, indeed, the horrors of the recent World War — anyone who calls these things to mind will have to bow humbly before the truth of this view.

The existence of this inclination to aggression, which we can detect in ourselves and justly assume to be present in others, is the factor which disturbs our relations with our neighbour and which forces civilization into such a high expenditure [of energy]. In consequence of this primary mutual hostility of human beings, civilized society is perpetually threatened with disintegration. The interest of work in common would not hold it together; instinctual passions are stronger than reasonable interests. Civilization has to use its utmost efforts in order to set limits to a man's aggressive instincts and to hold the manifestations of them in check by psychical reaction-formations. Hence, therefore, the use of methods intended to incite people into identifications and aim-inhibited relations of love, hence the restriction upon sexual life, and hence too the ideal's commandment to love one's neighbour as oneself—a commandment which is really justified by the fact that nothing else runs so strongly counter to the original nature of man. In spite of every effort, these endeavours of civilization have not so far achieved very much. . . .

It is clearly not easy for men to give up the satisfaction of this inclination to aggression. They do not feel comfortable without it. The advantage which a comparatively small cultural group offers of allowing this instinct an outlet in the form of hostility against intruders is not to be dispised. It is always possible to bind together a considerable number of people in love, so long as there are other people left over to receive the manifestations of their aggressiveness. I once discussed the phenomenon that it is precisely communities with adjoining territories, and related to each other in other ways as well, who are engaged in constant feuds and in ridiculing each other—like the Spaniards and Portuguese, for instance, the North Germans and South Germans, the English and Scotch, and so on. I gave this phenomenon the name of 'the narcissism of minor differences', a name which does not do much to explain it. We can now see that it is a convenient and relatively harmless satisfaction of the inclination to aggression, by means of which cohesion

between the members of the community is made easier. . . .

If civilization imposes such great sacrifices not only on man's sexuality but on his aggressivity, we can understand better why it is hard for him to be happy in that civilization. In fact, primitive man was better off in knowing no restrictions of instinct. To counterbalance this, his prospects of enjoying this happiness for any length of time were very slender. Civilized man has exchanged a portion of his possibilities of happiness for a portion of security. We must not forget, however, that in the primal family only the head of it enjoyed this instinctual freedom; the rest lived in slavish suppression. In that primal period of civilization, the contrast between a minority who enjoyed the advantages of civilization and a majority who were robbed of those advantages was, therefore, carried to extremes. As regards the primitive peoples who exist today, careful researches have shown that their instinctual life is by no means to be envied for its freedom. It is subject to restrictions of a different kind but perhaps of greater severity than those attaching to modern civilized man.

When we justly find fault with the present state of our civilization for so inadequately fulfilling our demands for a plan of life that shall make us happy, and for allowing the existence of so much suffering which could probably be avoided— when, with unsparing criticism, we try to uncover the roots of its imperfection, we are undoubtedly exercising a proper right and are not showing ourselves enemies of civilization. We may expect gradually to carry through such alterations in our civilization as will better satisfy our needs and will escape our criticisms. But perhaps we may also familiarize ourselves with the idea that there are difficulties attaching to the nature of civilization which will not yield to any attempt at reform. . . .

Starting from speculations on the beginning of life and from biological parallels, I drew the conclusion that, besides the instinct to preserve living substance and to join it into ever larger units, there must exist another, contrary instinct seeking to dissolve those units and to bring them back to their primaeval, inorganic state. That is to say, as well as Eros there was an instinct of death. The phenomena of life could be explained from the concurrent or mutually opposing action of these two instincts. It was not easy, however, to demonstrate the activities of this supposed death instinct. The manifestations of Eros were conspicuous and noisy enough. It might be assumed that the death instinct operated silently within the organism towards its dissolution, but that, of course, was no proof. A more fruitful idea was that a portion of the instinct is diverted towards the external world and comes to light as an instinct of aggressiveness and destructiveness. In this way the instinct itself could be pressed into the service of Eros, in that the organism was destroying some other thing, whether animate or inanimate, instead of destroying its own self. Conversely, any restriction of this aggressiveness directed outwards would be bound to increase the self-destruction, which is in any case proceeding. At the same time one can suspect from this example that the two kinds of instinct seldom — perhaps never — appear in isolation from each other, but are alloyed with each other in varying and very different proportions and so become unrecognizable to our judgement. . . .

I adopt the standpoint, therefore, that the inclination to aggression is an original, self-subsisting instinctual disposition in man, and I return to my view that it constitutes the greatest impediment to civilization. At one point in the course of this enquiry I was led to the idea that civilization was a special process which mankind undergoes, and I am still under the influence of that idea. I may now add that civilization is a process in the service of Eros, whose purpose is to combine single human individuals, and after that families, then races, peoples and nations, into one great unity, the unity of mankind. Why this has to happen, we do not know; the work of Eros is precisely this. These collections of men are to be libidinally bound to one another. Necessity alone, the advantages of work in common, will not hold them together. But man's natural aggressive instinct, the hostility of each against all and of all against each, opposes this programme of civilization. This aggressive instinct is the derivative and the main representative of the death instinct which we have found alongside of Eros and which shares world-dominion with it. And now, I think, the meaning of the evolution of civilization is no longer obscure to us. It must present the struggle between Eros and Death, between the instinct of life and the instinct of destruction, as it works itself out in the human species. This struggle is what all life essentially consists of, and the evolution of civilization may therefore be simply described as the struggle for life of the human species. And it is this battle of the giants that our nurse-maids try to appease with their lullaby about Heaven. . . .

The cultural super-ego has developed its ideals and set up its demands. Among the latter, those which deal with the relations of human beings to one another are comprised under the heading of ethics. People have at all times set the greatest value on ethics, as though they expected that it in particular would produce especially important results. And it does in fact deal with a subject which can easily be recognized as the sorest spot in every civilization. Ethics is thus to be regarded as a therapeutic attempt — as an endeavour to achieve, by means of a command of the super-ego, something which has so far not been achieved by means of any other cultural activities. As we already know, the problem before us is how to get rid of the greatest hindrance to civilization — namely, the constitutional inclination of human beings to be aggressive towards one another; and for that very reason we are especially interested in what is probably the most recent of the cultural commands of the super-ego, the commandment to love one's neighbour as oneself. In our research into, and therapy of, a neurosis, we are led to make two reproaches against the super-ego of the individual. In the severity of its commands and prohibitions it troubles itself too little about the happiness of the ego, in that it takes insufficient account of the resistances against obeying them — of the instinctual strength of the id [in the first place], and of the difficulties presented by the real external environment [in the second]. Consequently we are very often obliged, for therapeutic purposes, to oppose the super-ego, and we endeavour to lower its demands. Exactly the same objections can be made against the ethical demands of the cultural super-ego. It, too, does not trouble itself enough about the facts of the mental constitution of human beings. It issues a command and does not ask whether it is possible for people to obey it. On the contrary, it assumes that a man's ego is psychologically capable of anything that is required of it, that his ego has unlimited mastery over his id. This is a mistake; and even in what are known as normal people the id cannot be controlled beyond certain limits. If more is demanded of a man, a revolt will be produced in him or a neurosis, or he will be made unhappy. The commandment, 'Love thy neighbour as thyself', is the strongest defence against human aggressiveness and an excellent example of the unpsychological proceedings of the cultural super-ego. The commandment is impossible to fulfil; such an enormous inflation of love can only lower its value, not get rid of the difficulty. Civilization pays no attention to all this; it merely admonishes us that the harder it is to obey the precept the more meritorious it is to do so. But anyone who follows such a precept in present-day civilization only puts himself at a disadvantage *vis-à-vis* the person who disregards it. What a potent obstacle to civilization aggressiveness must be, if the defence against it can cause as much unhappiness as aggressiveness itself! 'Natural' ethics, as it is called, has nothing to offer here except the narcissistic satisfaction of being able to think oneself better than others. At this point the ethics based on religion introduces its promises of a better after-life. But so long as virtue is not rewarded here on earth, ethics will, I fancy, preach in vain.

SAM KEEN

The Enemy as Abstraction

SAM KEEN *is a contributing editor for* Psychology Today. *He is author of* The Passionate Life *(1983),* Faces of the Enemy *(1986), and* Fire in the Belly *(1991). He lives and raises horses in Sonoma, California, and he consults with a number of corporations.*

The execution of the Air-Land Battle doctrine will depend on our ability to distribute the information gained in microprocessors, embedded computers and data processing devices which are integral to the new system. The chip is the technological key to the new doctrine — the counterpart to the blitzkrieg's use of the gasoline engine.

MAJ. GEN. JOHN WOODMANSEE, JR.

MODERN technological warfare is gradually changing the way we think about the enemy. Both the heroic and the vitriolic images are being replaced by sterile concepts as the long reach of our weapons no longer makes it necessary for us to respect or hate those we intend to kill. The missile technician or the bomber pilot is so far removed from his "target" that he need not confront the carnage he inflicts. As one pilot who served in Vietnam told me, "I was OK so long as I was conducting high altitude missions, but when I had to come in and strafe and I could see the faces of the people I was killing, I got very disturbed." The ancient warrior needed massive physical strength and agility, a passionate hatred, and an ability to relish killing. He was either fierce, proud, arrogant, dominating, boastful, comfortable with cruelty, or dead. The modern warrior, by contrast, must be a specialist, coolheaded and emotionally detached. He prevails only if his calculations are accurate and his mind uncluttered by any passion save the love of efficiency. It has not escaped the attention

of the Army that the now and future warrior will have all the virtues of a computer expert and video game player.

The change from heroic tradition to modern warrior is from

Intimacy	to	Distance
Hot	to	Cool
Courage	to	Calculation
Hate	to	Feelinglessness
Physical fierceness	to	Intellectual accuracy
Individual initiative	to	Bureaucratic cooperation
Daring	to	Obedience

In the past when decisive victory was the point of war, a warrior needed to be aggressive, impatient, and ready for immediate action. Today stalling, posturing, rendering the threat of nuclear annihilation credible and creating stalemates is the essence of warfare. Hence another type of military personality is needed. The National War College has a course called "Executive Skills Development" that is directed at developing a personality called ISTJ (introverted, sensing, thinking judging), and students are tested by using the Myers-Briggs Type Indicator, a test based on the work of Jung, that measures whether one is introverted or extroverted, intuitive or sensing, thinking or feeling, and judging or perceptive. The ISTJs like to look for canned answers, they want to know the right answer. This personality type is the same as the corporate executive — objective decision makers. According to psychologist Otto Kroeger, a consultant to the U.S. Army,

> This corporate personality is something fairly new in the military, and it helps explain why during war games, the students prefer deterrence to destruction. The peacetime Army does not have the George Patton type. They've been weeded out. I know a number who have early-outed in the last ten years. The action types, the hard-nosed risk-taking daredevils, said, "I didn't come to push papers. I joined the action Army and there's no action."

As the modern warrior has become increasingly disembodied and warfare an intellectual and technological matter, the enemy has been progressively reduced to an abstraction.

The process began with the introduction of the drum and the uniform. Forcing men to march to a single cadence and to dress in ways that eradicated all distinctions, removed the element of individuality that was essential to heroic warfare. Enemies and allies alike are all pretty much olive drab or dull gray. Like a unit in a society governed by mass production, the soldier has been reduced to standardized functionary. He is a part of a well-oiled war machine, and his highest virtue is to function efficiently, which involves obeying the orders of his superiors. And the enemy is merely an impediment, an obstacle to be removed.

Occasionally we use machine images to dehumanize the enemy. We suggest that he is an automaton, a mindless being who is programmed by some higher, but demonic, intelligence. The enemy as automaton is an updated version of the enemy as puppet. In both cases what is central is the notion that he has no independent will and is controlled by something beyond himself. Hence we should have no more compunction in dispatching him than we would in destroying a robot. There is no soul in the machine.

More often than lending the enemy even the slight dignity we accord to machines, we simply erase him from our field of vision and act as if he is not there. Robert Bathurst reports that in the 1970s the U.S. Naval War College got the idea "that the study of war can be abstracted from people." After Vietnam there was a feeling that the language of war and enemies was immoral and old-fashioned, and that these subjects could be made more agreeable by being denationalized and universalized. Thus all specific references to the Soviets as enemies were deleted from textbooks, and men were told that they would be fighting to defend "land areas." "With such planning armed forces tend to become transformed into enormous riot squads being sent to a neighborhood they don't know to fight an enemy difficult to recognize, an enemy with technological characteristics, but no human face."

Nowhere has the statistical, abstract concept of the enemy become more obvious than in the American practice in Vietnam of determining "progress" in war by announcing daily "body counts." Under such conditions all it took to define an enemy was a body. As the popular saying went, "If it's dead, it's Viet Cong." The enemy is only a number used in our mathematical calculations. He is one of 6 million Jews killed, 20 million Soviets, 8,000 Sandinistas, 36 Arab terrorists, 250,000 Hindus, and so forth.

One professional soldier with much combat experience, Col. Anthony Herbert, translates the pathetic language of abstraction into its tragic reality:

> To say that it had not been a very important day because the Second Battalion had but two NVA kills now seems ludicrous; it was a damned important day for those two dead men. When even just one man died or got his fingers blown off or his leg shattered or his hearing impaired or his eyes bloodied and blinded, it was one hell of a costly battle — especially if you happened to be the guy who got it that day. It's something generals and presidents can never understand — only mothers, fathers, brothers, sons and daughters, and wives. . . . If anything has happened to our country as a result of the Vietnam War, it is our national infection with the sickness of the numbers game. We reduced the blood and suffering and the death and destruction to mere ciphers, and in so doing we reduced our own souls. Numbers don't die; people do. Columns of figures don't disintegrate in the explosion of a bomb; human beings do. Statistics don't bleed, and if you can make your war a war of numbers, you have no trouble sleeping. Most generals and presidents sleep well.

. . . To see how completely we have dehumanized and eliminated the enemy, even to the point of not dignifying him with an image we can hate, we must look at the euphemistic language of modern warfare. Our weapons have become so indiscriminate and omnicidal that we dare not look specifically at the enemy on whom they will fall. To imagine what nuclear weapons will do would require the "nice" technician, the computer specialist, the games theorist, the modern human general, to admit that he is contemplating a crime against humanity that makes Hitler's extermination camps appear small scale. To visualize the millions of Soviet or American men, women, and children who would be incinerated by even a small atomic "device" might upset our digestion. So long as we want to kill from a distance with clean hands, we must refrain from imagining the consequences of our weapons, and must completely eliminate any awareness of the enemy as human. Our new language of warfare is not accidental. The Air Force colonel who described the Titan II missile with a nine-megaton warhead as "a potentially disruptive re-entry system" (and was awarded the National Association of English Teacher's American Doublespeak Award in 1983), should have also gotten the Adolph Eichmann Memorial Prize. When a missile warhead becomes a "reentry vehicle," when killing civilians becomes "collateral damage," when the destruction of cities becomes "countervalue," when an MX missile becomes "Peacemaker," when combat becomes "violence processing," when destroying entire areas with Agent Orange becomes "an environmental adjustment," and peace becomes "permanent pre-hostility," we have reached the end of the line of dehumanization: 100 on a scale of 100. (Incidentally, the Grenada "invasion" was changed by the U.S. State Department first to a "rescue mission" and then to "a pre-dawn vertical insertion.") When the warrior makes only technical decisions with no reference to moral considerations, the enemy is reduced to a cipher, a statistical unit. Both the warrior and the enemy have disappeared. No living, feeling, agonizing, tragic, cruel, compassionate, courageous, fearful, anxious person is left on the battlefield, which has now become the entire world. Only machines fighting other machines. Little wonder that when Army futurists speculate about the human aspects of Airland Battle 2000 they present us with the ultimate triumph and nemesis of the historical union of *Homo faber* and *Homo hostilis*:

> The human aspects of Airland Battle 2000 are of genuine concern for which we have far more questions than answers. Will soldiers be able to exist on the battlefield of the year 2000? Or are we imagining such a technologically hostile environment that soldiers themselves will not be accommodated? We expect, in addition to more and worse physical wounds, more psychological stress casualties. Whole battle staffs of professional officers may collapse; commanders may have to be replaced or dual command instituted. Human engineering to immunize our soldiers against stress may be required, just as we now immunize against disease.

When war has become so terrible that we can no longer bear to think about those we destroy and when we must think of "engineering" a new breed of man to withstand the horror, it should be clear that *Homo hostilis* has reached the end of the line.

We are faced with choices so radical that any one of them will completely change the way we think about ourselves. We may resign from all hope of remaining human and alive and accept our fate as anonymous victims of "potentially dangerous re-entry systems." If we refuse this path of impotent despair, we may control our technology, run the arms race backward, and learn to fight limited wars with minimal weapons. Or we may undertake the heroic psychological, political, and spiritual task of transforming our ancient habit of enmity.

Realistically, most of what has masqueraded as practical politics and rational warfare has been mass madness, corporate schizophrenia. Rarely is warfare an effective solution to conflict. Therefore we will fall far short of investigating promising solutions to the problem of war if we limit ourselves to looking for rational, exterior, political means for adjudicating conflict. No doubt, the habit of warfare will not be ended without an effective international law and enforcement agency and the creation of new political institutions both within and between nations. But even less will it be ended without a psychological transformation of large numbers of individuals.

Healing begins when we cease playing the blame game, when we stop assigning responsibility for war to some mysterious external agency and dare to become conscious of our violent ways. . . .

If we desire peace, each of us must begin to demythologize the enemy; cease politicizing psychological events; re-own our shadows; make an intricate study of the myriad ways in which we disown, deny, and project our selfishness, cruelty, greed, and so on onto others; be conscious of how we have unconsciously created a warrior psyche and have perpetuated warfare in its many modes:

1. *The civil war within the self*—the enemy within, agonizing self-consciousness, the struggle between "I should" and "I want," the battle between "good" and "evil" parts of the self

2. *The war between the sexes*—combat in the erogenous zones, the creation of familiar enemies, the practice of seduction, rape, one-upmanship. The sadistic-masochistic element in sexual and familiar relationships, the practice of superiority–inferiority, winners and victims

3. *The political war between Us and Them*—how our psyches have been shaped by the consensual paranoia and the standard propaganda of our society and by the barrage of images of the enemy

4.   *The battle against nature, life* — the measure in which we have a propensity to identify ourselves "against," to assume that we must struggle, control, dominate, in order to be safe; the mistrust of self, others, life.

It should go without saying that individuals dealing with their personal enmity will not automatically solve the problem of warfare. But it is likewise certain that the politics of the warrior will not change without a constituency of individuals who have made the solitary decision to follow the path of metanoia rather than paranoia and to begin the practice of compassion rather than competition. Or, as the matter was stated a long time ago, "Remove first the beam from your own eye and then you will see more clearly to remove the mote from your brother's eye."

I believe the initiative for world peace at this time in history rests primarily with North Americans. Our repentance will be the major factor in determining the future of enmity. To use an analogy, every family therapist knows that the healthiest person in a diseased family system bears the most responsibility for changing the conflict and pathology of the system. For various historical reasons, the Soviet Union is an exceptionally paranoid nation. The United States is slightly less paranoid. Therefore, we have a greater responsibility to introduce sanity, to be willing to repent of our mistakes, to de-escalate our propaganda, to demythologize the "communist" as enemy. Our blame for world conflict is not greater, but our psychological opportunity for resolution is greater. When it comes to the individual task of reowning the enemy, of practicing metanoia, we are all equal. The journey into the wilderness of the shadow requires a heroic and solitary effort of anyone who would make it. But Americans, at least, have a wide access to alternative media, to information, and therapeutic help which is necessary to become genuinely self-critical, to jump outside the prison of the tribal or national psyche. . . .

HANNAH ARENDT
Violence, Power, and Bureaucracy

HANNA ARENDT (1906–1975) *was born and educated in Germany but fled to France in 1933, eventually becoming an American citizen in 1951. She taught in various American universities and is the author of many books on social and political theory, including* The Origins of Totalitarianism *(1973),* On Revolution *(1982), and* Men in Dark Times *(1968).*

POWER is indeed of the essence of all government, but violence is not. Violence is by nature instrumental; like all means, it always stands in need of guidance and justification through the end it pursues. And what needs justification by something else cannot be the essence of anything. The end of war—

end taken in its twofold meaning — is peace or victory; but to the question And what is the end of peace? there is no answer. Peace is an absolute, even though in recorded history periods of warfare have nearly always outlasted periods of peace. Power is in the same category; it is, as they say, "an end in itself." (This, of course, is not to deny that governments pursue policies and employ their power to achieve prescribed goals. But the power structure itself precedes and outlasts all aims, so that power, far from being the means to an end, is actually the very condition enabling a group of people to think and act in terms of the means–end category.) And since government is essentially organized and institutionalized power, the current question What is the end of government? does not make much sense either. The answer will be either question-begging — to enable men to live together — or dangerously utopian — to promote happiness or to realize a classless society or some other nonpolitical ideal, which if tried out in earnest cannot but end in some kind of tyranny.

Power needs no justification, being inherent in the very existence of political communities; what it does need is legitimacy. The common treatment of these two words as synonyms is no less misleading and confusing than the current equation of obedience and support. Power springs up whenever people get together and act in concert, but it derives its legitimacy from the initial getting together rather than from any action that then may follow. Legitimacy, when challenged, bases itself on an appeal to the past, while justification relates to an end that lies in the future. Violence can be justifiable, but it never will be legitimate. Its justification loses in plausibility the farther its intended end recedes into the future. No one

questions the use of violence in self-defense, because the danger is not only clear but also present, and the end justifying the means is immediate. . . .

In a head-on clash between violence and power, the outcome is hardly in doubt. If Gandhi's enormously powerful and successful strategy of nonviolent resistance had met with a different enemy — Stalin's Russia, Hitler's Germany, even prewar Japan, instead of England — the outcome would not have been decolonization, but massacre and submission. However, England in India and France in Algeria had good reasons for their restraint. Rule by sheer violence comes into play where power is being lost; it is precisely the shrinking power of the Russian government, internally and externally, that became manifest in its "solution" of the Czechoslovak problem — just as it was the shrinking power of European imperialism that became manifest in the alternative between decolonization and massacre. To substitute violence for power can bring victory, but the price is very high; for it is not only paid by the vanquished, it is also paid by the victor in terms of his own power. This is especially true when the victor happens to enjoy domestically the blessings of constitutional government. Henry Steele Commager is entirely right: "If we subvert world order and destroy world peace we must inevitably subvert and destroy our own political institutions first. . . .

Politically speaking, the point is that loss of power becomes a temptation to substitute violence for power — in 1968 during the Democratic convention in Chicago we could watch this process on television — and that violence itself results in impotence. Where violence is no longer backed and restrained by power, the well-known reversal in reckoning with means and ends has taken place. The means, the means of destruction, now determine the end — with the consequence that the end will be the destruction of all power.

Nowhere is the self-defeating factor in the victory of violence over power more evident than in the use of terror to maintain domination, about whose weird successes and eventual failures we know perhaps more than any generation before us. Terror is not the same as violence; it is, rather, the form of government that comes into being when violence, having destroyed all power, does not abdicate but, on the contrary, remains in full control. It has often been noticed that the effectiveness of terror depends almost entirely on the degree of social atomization. Every kind of organized opposition must disappear before the full force of terror can be let loose. This atomization — an outrageously pale, academic word for the horror it implies — is maintained and intensified through the ubiquity of the informer, who can be literally omnipresent because he no longer is merely a professional agent in the pay of the police but potentially every person one comes into contact with. How such a fully developed police state is established and how it works — or rather, how nothing works where it holds sway — can now be learned in Aleksandr I. Solzhenitsyn's *The First Circle*, which will probably remain one of the masterpieces of twentieth-century literature and certainly contains the best documentation on Stalin's regime in existence. The decisive difference between totalitarian domination, based on terror, and tyrannies and dictatorships, established by violence, is that the former turns not only against its enemies but against its friends and supporters as well, being afraid of all power, even the power of its friends. The climax of terror is reached when the police state begins to devour its own children, when yesterday's executioner becomes today's victim. And this is also the moment when power disappears entirely. There exist now a great many plausible explanations for the de-Stalinization of Russia — none, I believe, so compelling as the realization by the Stalinist functionaries themselves that a continuation of the regime would lead, not to an insurrection, against which terror is indeed the best safeguard, but to paralysis of the whole country.

To sum up: politically speaking, it is insufficient to say that power and violence are not the same. Power and violence are opposites; where the one rules absolutely, the other is absent. Violence appears where power is in jeopardy, but left to its own course it ends in power's disappearance. This implies that it is not correct to think of the opposite of violence as nonviolence; to speak of nonviolent power is actually redundant. Violence can destroy power; it is utterly incapable of creating it. Hegel's and Marx's great trust in the dialectical "power of negation," by virtue of which opposites do not destroy but smoothly develop into each other because contradictions promote and do not paralyze development, rests on a much older philosophical prejudice: that evil is no more than a private *modus* of the good, that good can come out of evil; that, in short, evil is but a temporary manifestation of a still-hidden good. Such time-honored opinions have become dangerous. They are shared by many who have never heard of Hegel or Marx, for the simple reason that they inspire hope and dispel fear — a treacherous hope used to dispel legitimate fear. By this, I do not mean to equate violence with evil; I only want to stress that violence cannot be derived from its opposite, which is power, and that in order to understand it for what it is, we shall have to examine its roots and nature. . . .

Nothing, in my opinion, could be theoretically more dangerous than the tradition of organic thought in political matters by which power and violence are interpreted in biological terms. As these terms are understood today, life and life's alleged creativity are their common denominator, so that violence is justified on the ground of creativity. The organic metaphors with which our entire present discussion of these matters, especially of the riots, is permeated—the notion of a "sick society," of which riots are symptoms, as fever is a symptom of disease—can only promote violence in the end. Thus the debate between those who propose violent means to restore "law and order" and those who propose nonviolent reforms begins to sound ominously like a discussion between two physicians who debate the relative advantages of surgical as opposed to medical treatment of their patient. The sicker the patient is supposed to be, the more likely that the surgeon will have the last word. Moreover, so long as we talk in nonpolitical, biological terms, the glorifiers of violence can appeal to the undeniable fact that in the household of nature destruction and creation are but two sides of the natural process, so that collective violent action, quite apart from its inherent attraction, may appear as natural a prerequisite for the collective life of mankind as the struggle for survival and violent death for continuing life in the animal kingdom. . . .

Violence, being instrumental by nature, is rational to the extent that it is effective in reaching the end that must justify it. And since when we act we never know with any certainty the eventual consequences of what we are doing, violence can remain rational only if it pursues short-term goals. Violence does not promote causes, neither history nor revolution, neither progress nor reaction; but it can serve to dramatize grievances and bring them to public attention. As Conor Cruise O'Brien (in a debate on the legitimacy of violence in the Theatre of Ideas) once remarked, quoting William O'Brien, the nineteenth-century Irish agrarian and nationalist agitator: Sometimes "violence is the only way of ensuring a hearing for moderation." To ask the impossible in order to obtain the possible is not always counterproductive. And indeed, violence, contrary to what its prophets try to tell us, is more the weapon of reform than of revolution. France would not have received the most radical bill since Napoleon to change its antiquated education system if the French students had not rioted; if it had not been for the riots of the spring term, no one at Columbia University would have dreamed of accepting reforms; and it is probably quite true that in West Germany the existence of "dissenting minorities is not even noticed unless they engage in provocation." No doubt, "violence pays," but the trouble is that it pays indiscriminately, for "soul courses" and instruction in Swahili as well as for real reforms. And since the tactics of violence and disruption make sense only for short-term goals, it is even more likely, as was recently the case in the United States, that the established power will yield to nonsensical and obviously damaging demands—such as admitting students without the necessary qualifications and instructing them in nonexistent subjects—if only such "reforms" can be made with comparative ease, than that violence will be effective with respect to the relatively long-term objective of structural change. Moreover, the danger of violence, even if it moves consciously within a nonextremist framework of short-term goals, will always be that the means overwhelm to the end. If goals are not achieved rapidly, the result will be not merely defeat but the introduction of the practice of violence into the whole body politic. Action is irreversible, and a return to the *status quo* in case of defeat is always unlikely. The practice of violence, like all action, changes the world, but the most probable change is to a more violent world.

Finally — to come back to Sorel's and Pareto's earlier denunciation of the system as such — the greater the bureaucratization of public life, the greater will be the attraction of violence. In a fully developed bureaucracy there is nobody left with whom one can argue, to whom one can present grievances, on whom the pressures of power can be exerted. Bureaucracy is the form of government in which everybody is deprived of political freedom, of the power to act; for the rule by Nobody is not no-rule, and where all are equally powerless we have a tyranny without a tyrant. The crucial feature in the student rebellions around the world is that they are directed everywhere against the ruling bureaucracy. . . .

What makes man a political being is his faculty of action; it enables him to get together with his peers, to act in concert, and to reach out for goals and enterprises that would never enter his mind, let alone the desires of his heart, had he not been given this gift — to embark on something new. Philosophically speaking, to act is the human answer to the condition of natality. Since we all come into the world by virtue of birth, as newcomers and beginnings, we are able to start something new; without the fact of birth we would not even know what novelty is, all "action" would be either mere behavior or preservation. No other faculty except language, neither reason nor consciousness, distinguishes us so radically from all animal species. To act and to begin are not the same, but they are closely interconnected. . . .

Whatever the administrative advantages and disadvantages of centralization may be, its political result is always the same: monopolization of power causes the drying up or oozing away of all authentic power sources in the country. In the United States, based on a great plurality of powers and their mutual checks and balances, we are confronted not merely with the disintegration of power structures, but with power, seemingly still intact and free to manifest itself, losing its grip and becoming ineffective. To speak of the impotence of power is no longer a witty paradox. . . .

Again, we do not know where these developments will lead us, but we know, or should know, that every decrease in power is an open invitation to violence — if only because those who hold power and feel it slipping from their hands, be they the government or be they the governed, have always found it difficult to resist the temptation to substitute violence for it.

WILLIAM JAMES
The Moral Equivalent of War

WILLIAM JAMES (1842–1910) *was one of the greatest American philosophers. He graduated from Harvard with a medical degree but decided to teach (at Harvard) rather than practice medicine. A founder of modern pragmatism, he also established himself as one of the fathers of modern psychology with his* Principles of Psychology *(1890).*

REFLECTIVE apologists for war at the present day all take it religiously. It is a sort of sacrament. Its profits are to the vanquished as well as to the victor; and quite apart from any question of profit, it is an absolute good, we are told, for it is human nature at its highest dynamic. Its "horrors" are a cheap price to pay for rescue from the only alternative supposed, of a world of clerks and teachers, of co-education and zoophily, of "consumer's leagues" and "associated charities," of industrialism unlimited, and feminism unabashed. No scorn, no hardness, no valor any more! Fie upon such a cattleyard of a planet!

So far as the central essence of this feeling goes, no healthy minded person, it seems to me, can help to some degree partaking of it. Militarism is the great preserver of our ideals of hardihood, and human life with no use for hardihood would be comtemptible. Without risks or prizes for the darer, history would be insipid indeed; and there is a type of military character which every one feels that the race should never cease to breed, for every one is sensitive to its superiority. The duty is incumbent on mankind, of keeping military characters in stock — of keeping them, if not for use, then as ends in themselves and as pure pieces of perfection — so that Roosevelt's weaklings and mollycoddles may not end by making everything else disappear from the face of nature.

This natural sort of feeling forms, I think, the innermost soul of army-writings. Without any exception known to me, militarist authors take a highly mystical view of their subject, and regard war as a biological or sociological necessity, uncontrolled by ordinary psychological checks and motives. When the time of development is ripe the war must come, reason or no reason, for the justifications pleaded are invariably fictitious. War is, in short, a permanent human *obligation*. . . .

Turn the fear over as I will in my mind, it all seems to lead back to two unwillingnesses of the imagination, one aesthetic, and the other moral: unwillingness, first to envisage a future in which army-life, with its many elements of charm, shall be forever impossible, and in which the destinies of peoples shall nevermore be decided quickly, thrillingly, and tragically, by force, but only gradually and insipidly by "evolution"; and, secondly, unwillingness to see the supreme theatre of human strenuousness closed, and the splendid military aptitudes of men doomed to keep always in a state of latency and never show themselves in action. These insistent unwillingnesses, no less than other esthetic and ethical insistencies have, it seems to me, to be listened to and respected. One cannot meet them effectively by mere counter-insistency on war's expensiveness and horror. The horror makes the thrill; and when the question is of getting the extremest and supremest out of human nature, talk of expense sounds ignominious. The weakness of so much merely negative criticism is evident — pacificism makes no converts from the military party. The military party denies neither the bestiality nor the horror, nor the expense; it only says that these things tell but half the story. It only says that war is *worth* them; that, taking human nature as a whole, its wars are its best protection against its weaker and more cowardly self, and that mankind cannot *afford* to adopt a peace-economy. . . .

Having said thus much in preparation, I will now confess my own utopia. I devoutly believe in the reign of peace and in the gradual advent of some sort of a socialistic equilibrium. The fatalistic view of the war-function is to me nonsense, for I know that war-making is due to definite motives and subject to prudential checks and reasonable criticisms, just like any other form of enterprise. And when whole nations are the armies, and the science of destruction vies in intellectual refinement with the sciences of production, I see that war becomes absurd and impossible from its own monstrosity. Extravagant ambitions will have to be replaced by reasonable claims, and nations must make common cause against them. I see no reason why all this should not apply to yellow as well as to white countries, and I look forward to a future when acts of war shall be formally outlawed as between civilized peoples.

All these beliefs of mine put me squarely into the anti-militarist party. But I do not believe that peace either ought to be or will be permanent on this globe, unless the states pacifically organized preserve some of the old elements of army-discipline. A permanently successful peace-economy cannot be a simple pleasure-economy. In the more or less socialistic future towards which mankind seems drifting we must still subject ourselves collectively to those severities which answer to our real position upon this only partly hospitable globe. We must make new energies and hardihoods continue the manliness to which the military mind so faithfully clings. Martial virtues must be the enduring cement; intrepidity, contempt of softness, surrender of private interest, obedience to command, must still remain the rock upon which states are built — unless, indeed, we wish for dangerous reactions against commonwealths fit only for contempt, and liable to invite attack whenever a centre of crystallization for military-minded enterprise gets formed anywhere in their neighborhood.

The war-party is assuredly right in affirming and reaffirming that the martial virtues, although originally gained by the race through war, are absolute and permanent human goods. Patriotic pride and ambition in their military form are, after all, only specifications of a more general competitive passion. They are its first form, but that is no reason for supposing them to be its last form. Men now are proud of belonging to a conquering nation, and without a murmur they lay down their persons and their wealth, if by so doing they may fend off subjection. But who can be sure that *other aspects of one's country* may not, with time and education and suggestion enough, come to be regarded with similarly effective feelings of pride and shame? Why should men not some day feel that it is worth a blood-tax to belong to a collectivity superior in *any* ideal respect? Why should they not blush with indignant shame if the community that owns them is vile in any way whatsoever? Individuals, daily more numerous, now feel this civic passion. It is only a question of blowing on the spark till the whole population gets incandescent, and on the ruins of the old morals of military honour, a stable system of morals of civic honour builds itself up. What the whole community comes to believe in grasps the individual as in a vise. The war-function has graspt us so far; but constructive interests may some day seem no less imperative, and impose on the individual a hardly lighter burden.

Let me illustrate my idea more concretely. There is nothing to make one indignant in the mere fact that life is hard, that men should toil and suffer pain. The planetary conditions once for all are such, and we can stand it. But that so many men, by mere accidents of birth and opportunity, should have a life of *nothing else* but toil and pain and hardness and inferiority imposed upon them, should have *no* vacation, while others natively no more deserving never get any taste of this campaigning life at all, — *this* is capable of arousing indignation in reflective minds. It may end by seeming shameful to all of us that some of us have nothing but campaigning, and others nothing but unmanly ease. If now — and this is my idea — there were, instead of military conscription a conscription of the whole youthful population to form for a certain number of years a part of the army enlisted against *Nature*, the injustice would tend to be evened out, and numerous other goods to the commonwealth would follow. The military ideals of hardihood and discipline would be wrought into the growing fibre of the people; no one would remain blind as the luxurious classes now are blind, to man's real relations to the globe he lives on, and to the permanently sour and hard foundations of his higher life. To coal and iron mines, to freight trains, to fishing fleets in December, to dish-washing, clothes-washing, and window-washing, to road-building and tunnel-making, to foundries and stoke-holes, and to the frames of skyscrapers,

would our gilded youths be drafted off, according to their choice, to get the childishness knocked out of them, and to come back into society with healthier sympathies and soberer ideas. They would have paid their blood-tax, done their own part in the immemorial human warfare against nature, they would tread the earth more proudly, the women would value them more highly, they would be better fathers and teachers of the following generation.

Such a conscription, with the state of public opinion that would have required it, and the many moral fruits it would bear, would preserve in the midst of a pacific civilization the manly virtues which the military party is so afraid of seeing disappear in peace. We should get toughness without callousness, authority with as little criminal cruelty as possible, and painful work done cheerily because the duty is temporary, and threatens not, as now, to degrade the whole remainder of one's life. I spoke of the "moral equivalent" of war. So far, war has been the only force that can discipline a whole community, and until an equivalent discipline is organized, I believe that war must have its way. But I have no serious doubt that the ordinary prides and shames of social man, once developed to a certain intensity, are capable of organizing such a moral equivalent as I have sketched, or some other just as effective for preserving manliness of type. It is but a question of time, of skillful propagandism, and of opinion-making men seizing historic opportunities.

The martial type of character can be bred without war. Strenuous honour and disinterestedness abound elsewhere. Priests and medical men are in a fashion educated to it, and we should all feel some degree of it imperative if we were conscious of our work as an obligatory service to the state. We should be *owned*, as soldiers are by the army, and our pride would rise accordingly. We could be poor, then, without humiliation, as army officers now are. The only thing needed henceforward is to inflame the civic temper as past history has inflamed the military temper. H. G. Wells, as usual, sees the centre of the situation. "In many ways," he says, "military organization is the most peaceful of activities. When the contemporary man steps from the street, of clamorous insincere advertisement, push, adulteration, underselling and intermittent employment, into the barrack-yard, he steps on to a higher social plane, into an atmosphere of service and co-operation and of infinitely more honourable emulations. Here at least men are not flung out of employment to degenerate because there is no immediate work for them to do. They are fed and drilled and trained for better services. Here at least a man is supposed to win promotion by self-forgetfulness and not by self-seeking. And beside the feeble and irregular endowment of research by commercialism, its little short-sighted snatches at profit by innovation and scientific economy, see how remarkable is the steady and rapid development of method and appliances in naval and military affairs! Nothing is more striking than to compare the progress of civil conveniences which has been left almost entirely to the trader, to the progress in military apparatus during the last few decades. The house-appliances of to-day for example, are little better than they were fifty years ago. A house of to-day is still almost as ill-ventilated, badly heated by wasteful fires, clumsily arranged and furnished as the house of 1858. Houses a couple of hundred years old are still satisfactory places of residence, so little have our standards risen. But the rifle or battleship of fifty years ago was beyond all comparison inferior to those we possess; in power, in speed, in convenience alike. No one has a use now for such superannuated things."

Wells adds that he thinks that the conceptions of order and discipline, the tradition of service and devotion, of physical fitness, unstinted exertion, and universal responsibility, which universal military duty is now teaching European nations, will remain a permanent acquisition, when the last ammunition has been used in the fireworks that celebrate the final peace. I believe as he does. It would be simply preposterous if the only force that could work ideals of honour and standards of efficiency into English or American natures should be the fear of being killed by the Germans or the Japanese. Great indeed is Fear; but it is not, as our military enthusiasts believe and try to make us believe, the only stimulus known for awakening the higher ranges of men's spiritual energy. The amount of alteration in public opinion which my utopia postulates is vastly less than the difference between the mentality of those black warriors who pursued Stanley's party on the Congo with their cannibal war-cry of "Meat! Meat!" and that of the "general-staff" of any civilized nation. History has seen the latter interval bridged over: the former one can be bridged over much more easily.

LOIS PINEAU

Date Rape
A Feminist Analysis

LOIS PINEAU *teaches philosophy at Kansas State University in Manhattan, Kansas. She publishes in the areas of ethics, philosophy of language, and feminism.*

D ATE rape is nonaggravated sexual assault, nonconsensual sex that does not involve physical injury, or the explicit threat of physical injury. But because it does not involve physical injury, and because physical injury is often the only criterion that is accepted as evidence that *actus reas* is nonconsensual, what is really sexual assault is often mistaken for seduction. The replacement of the old rape laws with the new laws on sexual assault have done nothing to resolve this problem.

Rape, defined as nonconsensual sex, usually involving penetration by a man of a woman who is not his wife, has been replaced in some criminal codes with the charge of sexual assault. This has the advantage both of extending the range of possible victims of sexual assault, the manner in which people can be assaulted, and replacing a crime which is exclusive of consent, with one for which consent is a defence. But while the consent of a woman is now consistent with the conviction of her assailant in cases of aggravated assault, nonaggravated sexual assault is still distinguished from normal sex solely by the fact that it is not consented to. Thus the question of whether someone has consented to a sexual encounter is still important, and the criteria for consent continues to be the central concern of discourse on sexual assault.

However, if a man is to be convicted, it does not suffice to establish that the *actus reas* was nonconsensual. In order to be guilty of sexual assault a man must have the requisite *mens rea*, i.e., he must either have believed that his victim did not consent or that she was probably not consenting. In many common law jurisdictions a man who sincerely believes that a woman consented to a sexual encounter is deemed to lack the required *mens rea*, even though the woman did not consent, and even though his belief is not reasonable. Recently, strong dissenting voices have been raised against the sincerity condition, and the argument made that *mens rea* be defeated only if the defendant has a reasonable belief that the plaintiff consented. The introduction of legislation which excludes 'honest belief' (unreasonable sincere belief) as a defence, will certainly help to provide women with greater protection against violence. But while this will be an important step forward, the question of what constitutes a reasonable belief, the problem of evidence when rapists lie, and the problem of the entrenched attitudes of the predominantly male police, judges, lawyers, and jurists who handle sexual assault cases, remains.

The criteria for *mens rea*, for the reasonableness of belief, and for consent are closely related. For although a man's sincere belief in the consent of his victim may be sufficient to defeat *means rea*, the court is less likely to believe his belief is sincere if his belief is unreasonable. If his belief is reasonable, they are more likely to believe in the sincerity of his belief. But evidence of the reasonableness of his belief is also evidence that consent really did take place. For the very things that make it reasonable for *him* to believe that the defendant consented are often the very things that incline the court to believe that she consented. What is often missing is the voice of the woman herself, an account of what it would be reasonable for *her* to agree to, that is to say, an account of what is reasonable from *her* standpoint.

Thus, what is presented as reasonable has repercussions for four separate but related concerns: (1) the question of whether a man's belief in a woman's consent was reasonable; (2) the problem of whether it is reasonable to attribute *mens rea* to him; (3) the question of what could count as reasonable from the woman's point of view, (4) the question of what is reasonable from the court's point of view. These repercussions are of the utmost practical concern. In a culture which contains an incidence of sexual assault verging on epidemic, a criterion of reasonableness which regards mere submission as consent fails to offer persons vulnerable to those assaults adequate protection.

The following statements by self-confessed date rapists reveal how our lack of a solution for dealing with date rape protects rapists by failing to provide their victims with legal recourse:

> All of my rapes have been involved in a dating situation where I've been out with a woman I know. . . . I wouldn't take no for an answer. I think it had something to do with my acceptance of rejection. I had low self-esteem and not much self-confidence and when I was rejected for something which I considered to be rightly mine, I became angry and I went ahead anyway. And this was

the same in any situation, whether it was rape or it was something else.

•   •   •

> When I did date, when I was younger, I would pick up a girl and if she didn't come across I would threaten her or slap her face then tell her she was going to fuck — that was it. But that's because I didn't want to waste time with any come-ons. It took too much time. I wasn't interested because I didn't like them as people anyway, and I just went with them just to get laid. Just to say that I laid them.

There is, at this time, nothing to protect women from this kind of unscrupulous victimization. A woman on a casual date with a virtual stranger has almost no chance of bringing a complaint of sexual assault before the courts. One reason for this is the prevailing criterion for consent. According to this criterion, consent is implied unless some emphatic episodic sign of resistance occurred, and its occurrence can be established. But if no episodic act occurred, or if it did occur, and the defendant claims that it didn't, or if the defendant threatened the plaintiff but won't admit it in court, it is almost impossible to find any evidence that would support the plaintiff's word against the defendant. This difficulty is exacerbated by suspicion on the part of the courts, police, and legal educators that even where an act of resistance occurs, this act should not be interpreted as a withholding of consent, and this suspicion is especially upheld where the accused is a man who is known to the female plaintiff.

In Glanville William's classic textbook on criminal law we are warned that where a man is unknown to a woman, she does not consent if she expresses her rejection in the form of an episodic and vigorous act at the 'vital moment'. But if the man is known to the woman she must, according to Williams, make use of "all means available to her to repel the man". Williams warns that women often welcome a 'mastery advance' and present a token resistance. He quotes Byron's couplet,

> A little still she strove, and much repented
> And whispering 'I will ne'er consent' —
> consented

by way of alerting law students to the difficulty of distinguishing real protest from pretence. Thus, while in principle, a firm unambiguous stand, or a healthy show of temper ought to be sufficient, if established, to show nonconsent, in practice the forceful overriding of such a stance is apt to be taken as an indication that the resistance was not seriously intended, and that the seduction had succeeded. The consequence of this is that it is almost impossible to establish the defendant's guilt beyond a reasonable doubt.

Thus, on the one hand, we have a situation in which women are vulnerable to the most exploitive tactics at the hands of men who are known to them. On the other hand, almost nothing will count as evidence of their being assaulted, including their having taken an emphatic stance in withholding their consent. The new laws have done almost nothing to change this situation. Yet clearly, some solution must be sought. Moreover, the road to that solution presents itself clearly enough as a need for a reformulation of the criterion of consent. It is patent that a criterion that collapses whenever the crime itself succeeds will not suffice. . . .

The reasoning that underlies the present criterion of consent is entangled in a number of mutually supportive mythologies which see sexual assault as masterful seduction, and silent submission as sexual enjoyment. Because the prevailing ideology has so much informed our conceptualization of sexual interaction, it is extraordinarily difficult for us to distinguish between assault and seduction, submission and enjoyment, or so we imagine. At the same time, this failure to distinguish has given rise to a network of rationalizations that support the conflation of assault which seduction, submission and enjoyment. . . .

Rape Myths

The belief that the natural aggression of men and the natural reluctance of women somehow makes date rape understandable underlies a number of prevalent myths about rape and human sexuality. These beliefs maintain their force partly on account of a logical compulsion exercised by them at an unconscious level. The only way of refuting them effectively, is to excavate the logical propositions involved, and to expose their misapplication to the situations to which they have been applied. In what follows, I propose to excavate the logical support for popular attitudes that are tolerant of date rape. These myths are not just popular, however, but often emerge in the arguments of judges who acquit date rapists, and policemen who refuse to lay charges.

The claim that the victim provoked a sexual incident, that 'she asked for it', is by far the most common defence given by men who are accused of sexual assault. Feminists, rightly incensed by this response, often treat it as beneath contempt, singling out the defence as an argument against it. On other fronts, sociologists have identified the response as part of an overall tendency of people to see the world as just, a tendency which disposes them to conclude that people for the most part deserve what they get. However, an inclination to see the world as just requires us to construct an account which yields this outcome, and it is just such an account that I wish to examine with regard to date rape.

The least sophisticated of the 'she asked for it' rationales, and in a sense, the easiest to deal with, appeals to an injunction against sexually provocative behaviour on the part of women. If women should not be sexually provocative, then, from this standpoint, a woman who is sexually provocative deserves to suffer the consequences. Now it will not do to respond that women get raped even when they are not sexually provocative, or that it is men who get to interpret (unfairly) what counts as sexually provocative. The question should be: Why shouldn't a woman be sexually provocative? Why should this behaviour warrant any kind of aggressive response whatsoever?

Attempts to explain that women have a right to behave in sexually provocative ways without suffering dire consequences still meet with surprisingly tough resistance. Even people who find nothing wrong or sinful with sex itself, in any of its forms, tend to suppose that women must not behave sexually unless they are prepared to carry through on some fuller course of sexual interaction. The logic of this response seems to be that at some point a woman's behaviour commits her to following through on the full course of a sexual encounter as it is defined by her assailant. At some point she has made an agreement, or formed a contract, and once that is done, her contractor is entitled to demand that she satisfy the terms of that contract. Thus, this view about sexual responsibility and desert is supported by other assumptions about contracts and

agreement. But we do not normally suppose that casual nonverbal behaviour generates agreements. Nor do we normally grant private persons the right to enforce contracts. What rationale would support our conclusion in this case?

The rationale, I believe, comes in the form of a belief in the especially insistent nature of male sexuality, an insistence which lies at the foot of natural male aggression, and which is extremely difficult, perhaps impossible to contain. At a certain point in the arousal process, it is thought, a man's rational will gives way to the prerogatives of nature. His sexual need can and does reach a point where it is uncontrollable, and his natural masculine aggression kicks in to assure that this need is met. Women, however, are naturally more contained, and so it is their responsibility not to provoke the irrational in the male. If they do go so far as that, they have both failed in their responsibilities, and subjected themselves to the inevitable. One does not go into the lion's cage and expect not to be eaten. Natural feminine reluctance, it is thought, is no protection against a sexually aroused male.

This belief about the normal aggressiveness of male sexuality is complemented by common knowledge about female gender development. Once, women were taught to deny their sexuality and to aspire to ideals of chastity. Things have not changed so much. Women still tend to eschew conquest mentalities in favour of a combination of sex and affection. Insofar as this is thought to be merely a cultural requirement, however, there is an expectation that women will be coy about their sexual desire. The assumption that women both want to indulge sexually, and are inclined to sacrifice this desire for higher ends, gives rise to the myth that they want to be raped. After all, doesn't rape give them the sexual enjoyment they *really* want, at the same time that it relieves them of the responsibility for admitting to and acting upon what they want? And how then can we blame men, who have been socialized to be aggressively seductive precisely for the purpose of overriding female reserve? If we find fault at all, we are inclined to cast our suspicions on the motives of the woman. For it is on her that the contradictory roles of sexual desirer and sexual denier has been placed. Our awareness of the contradiction expected of her makes us suspect her honesty. In the past, she was expected to deny her complicity because of the shame and guilt she felt at having submitted. This expectation persists in many quarters today, and is carried over into a general suspicion about her character, and the fear that she might make a false accusation out of revenge, or some other low motive.

But if women really want sexual pleasure, what inclines us to think that they will get it through rape? This conclusion logically requires a theory about the dynamics of sexual pleasure that sees that pleasure as an emergent property of overwhelming male insistence. For the assumption that a raped female experiences sexual pleasure implies that the person who rapes her knows how to cause that pleasure independently of any information she might convey on that point. Since her ongoing protest is inconsistent with requests to be touched in particular ways in particular places, to have more of this and less of that, then we must believe that the person who touches her knows these particular ways and places instinctively, without any directives from her.

Thus, we find, underlying and reinforcing this belief in incommunicative male prowess, a conception of sexual pleasure that springs from wordless interchanges, and of sexual success that occurs

in a place of meaningful silence. The language of seduction is accepted as a tacit language: eye contact, smiles, blushes, and faintly discernible gestures. It is, accordingly, imprecise and ambiguous. It would be easy for a man to make mistakes about the message conveyed, understandable that he should mistakenly think that a sexual invitation has been made, and a bargain struck. But honest mistakes, we think, must be excused.

In sum, the belief that women should not be sexually provocative is logically linked to several other beliefs, some normative, some empirical. The normative beliefs are that (1) people should keep the agreements they make (2) that sexually provocative behaviour, taken beyond a certain point, generates agreements (3) that the peculiar nature of male and female sexuality places such agreements in a special category, one in which the possibility of retracting an agreement is ruled out, or at least made highly unlikely, (4) that women are not to be trusted, in sexual matters at least. The empirical belief, which turns out to be false, is that male sexuality is not subject to rational and moral control.

Dispelling the Myths

The 'she asked for' justification of sexual assault incorporates a conception of a contract that would be difficult to defend in any other context and the presumptions about human sexuality which function to reinforce sympathies rooted in the contractual notion of just deserts are not supported by empirical research.

The belief that a woman generates some sort of contractual obligation whenever her behaviour is interpreted as seductive is the most indefensible part of the mythology of rape. In law, contracts are not legitimate just because a promise has been made. In particular, the use of pressure tactics to extract agreement is frowned upon. Normally, an agreement is upheld only if the contractors were clear on what they were getting into, and had sufficient time to reflect on the wisdom of their doing so. Either there must be a clear tradition in which the expectations involved in the contract are fairly well known (marriage), or there must be an explicit written agreement concerning the exact terms of the contract and the expectations of the persons involved. But whatever the terms of a contract, there is no private right to enforce it. So that if I make a contract with you on which I renege, the only permissible recourse for you is through due legal process.

Now it is not clear whether sexual contracts can be made to begin with, or if so, what sort of sexual contracts would be legitimate. But assuming that they could be made, the terms of those contracts would not be enforceable. To allow public enforcement would be to grant the State the overt right to force people to have sex, and this would clearly be unacceptable. Granting that sexual contracts are legitimate, state enforcement of such contracts would have to be limited to ordering non-sexual compensation for breaches of contract. So it makes no difference whether a sexual contract is tacit or explicit. There are no grounds whatsoever that would justify enforcement of its terms.

Thus, even if we assume that a woman has initially agreed to an encounter, her agreement does not automatically make all subsequent sexual activity to which she submits legitimate. If during coitus a woman should experience pain, be suddenly overcome with guilt or fear of pregnancy, or simply lose her initial desire, those are good reasons for her to change her mind. Having changed her mind, neither her partner nor the state has any right

to force her to continue. But then if she is forced to continue she is assaulted. Thus, establishing that consent occurred at a particular point during a sexual encounter should not conclusively establish the legitimacy of the encounter. What is needed is a reading of whether she agreed throughout the encounter.

If the 'she asked for it' contractual view of sexual interchange has any validity, it is because there is a point at which there is no stopping a sexual encounter, a point at which that encounter becomes the inexorable outcome of the unfolding of natural events. If a sexual encounter is like a slide on which I cannot stop halfway down, it will be relevant whether I enter the slide of my own free will, or am pushed.

But there is no evidence that the entire sexual act is like a slide. While there may be a few seconds in the 'plateau' period just prior to orgasm in which people are 'swept' away by sexual feelings to the point where we could justifiably understand their lack of heed for the comfort of their partner, the greater part of a sexual encounter comes well within the bounds of morally responsible control of our own actions. Indeed, the available evidence shows that most of the activity involved in sex has to do with building the requisite level of desire, a task that involves the proper use of foreplay, the possibility of which implies control over the form that foreplay will take. Modern sexual therapy assumes that such control is universally accessible, and so far there has been no reason to question that assumption. Sexologists are unanimous, moreover, in holding that mutual sexual enjoyment requires an atmosphere of comfort and communication, a minimum of pressure, and an ongoing check-up on one's partner's state. They maintain that different people have different predilections, and that what is pleasurable for one person is very often anathema to another. These findings show that the way to achieve sexual pleasure, at any time at all, let alone with a casual acquaintance, decidedly does not involve overriding the other person's express reservations and providing them with just any kind of sexual stimulus. And while we do not want to allow science and technology a voice in which the voices of particular women are drowned, in this case science seems to concur with women's perception that aggressive incommunicative sex is not what they want. But if science and the voice of women concur, if aggressive seduction does not lead to good sex, if women do not like it, or want it, then it is not rational to think that they would agree to it. Where such sex takes place, it is therefore rational to presume that the sex was not consensual.

The myth that women like to be raped, is closely connected, as we have seen, to doubt about their honesty in sexual matters, and this suspicion is exploited by defence lawyers when sexual assault cases make it to the courtroom. It is an unfortunate consequence of the presumption of innocence that rape victims who end up in court frequently find that it is they who are on trial. For if the defendant is innocent, then either he did not intend to do what he was accused of, or the plaintiff is mistaken about his identity, or she is lying. Often the last alternative is the only plausible defence, and as a result, the plaintiff's word seldom goes unquestioned. Women are frequently accused of having made a false accusation, either as a defensive mechanism for dealing with guilt and shame, or out of a desire for revenge.

Now there is no point in denying the possibility of false accusation, though there are probably better ways of seeking revenge on a man than accusing him of rape. However, we can now establish a logical connection between the evidence that a woman was subjected to high-pressure aggressive 'seduction' tactics, and her claim that she did not consent to that encounter. Where the kind of encounter is not the sort to which it would be reasonable to consent, there is a logical presumption that a woman who claims that she did not consent is telling the truth. Where the kind of sex involved is not the sort of sex we would expect a woman to like, the burden of proof should not be on the woman to show that she did not consent, but on the defendant to show that contrary to every reasonable expectation she did consent. The defendant should be required to convince the court that the plaintiff persuaded him to have sex with her even though there are no visible reasons why she should.

In conclusion, there are no grounds for the 'she asked for it' defence. Sexually provocative behaviour does not generate sexual contracts. Even where there are sexual agreements, they cannot be legitimately enforced either by the State, or by private right, or by natural prerogative. Secondly, all the evidence suggests that neither women nor men find sexual enjoyment in rape or in any form of non-communicative sexuality. Thirdly, male sexual desire is containable, and can be subjected to moral and rational control. Fourthly, since there is no reason why women should not be sexually provocative, they do not 'deserve' any sex they do not want. This last is a welcome discovery. The taboo on sexual provocativeness in women is a taboo both on sensuality and on teasing. But sensuality is a source of delight, and teasing is playful and inspires wit. What a relief to learn that it is not sexual provocativeness, but its enemies, that constitutes a danger to the world. . . .

In thinking about sex we must keep in mind its sensual ends, and the facts show that aggressive high-pressure sex contradicts those ends. Consensual sex in dating situations is presumed to aim at mutual enjoyment. It may not always do this, and when it does, it might not always succeed. There is no logical incompatibility between wanting to continue a sexual encounter, and failing to derive sexual pleasure from it.

But it seems to me that there is a presumption in favour of the connection between sex and sexual enjoyment, and that if a man wants to be sure that he not forcing himself on a woman, he has an obligation either to ensure that the encounter really is mutually enjoyable, or to know the reasons why she would want to continue the encounter in spite of her lack of enjoyment. A closer investigation of the nature of this obligation will enable us to construct a more rational and more plausible norm of sexual conduct.

Onara O'Neill has argued that in intimate situations we have an obligation to take the ends of others as our own, and to promote those ends in a non-manipulative and non-paternalistic manner. Now it seems that in honest sexual encounters just this is required. Assuming that each person enters the encounter in order to seek sexual satisfaction, each person engaging in the encounter has an obligation to help the other seek his or her ends. To do otherwise is to risk acting in opposition to what the other desires, and hence to risk acting without the other's consent.

But the obligation to promote the sexual ends of one's partner implies that obligation to know what those ends are, and also the obligation to know how those ends are attained. Thus, the problem comes down to a problem of epistemic responsibility, the responsibility to know. The solution, in my view, lies in the practice of a communicative sexuality, one which combines the appropriate knowledge of the other with respect for the dialectics of desire. . . .

Cultural Presumptions

Now it may well be that we have no obligation to care for strangers, and I do not wish to claim that we do. Nonetheless, it seems that O'Neill's point about the special moral duties we have in certain intimate situations is supported by a conceptual relation between certain kinds of personal relationships and the expectation that it should be a communicative relation. Friendship is a case in point. It is a relation that is greatly underdetermined by what we usually include in our sets of rights and obligations. For the most part, rights and obligations disappear as terms by which friendship is guided. They are still there, to be called upon, in case the relationship breaks down, but insofar as the friendship is a friendship, it is concerned with fostering the quality of the interaction and not with standing on rights. Thus, because we are friends, we share our property, and property rights between us are not invoked. Because we are friends, privacy is not an issue. Because we are friends we may see to each other's needs as often as we see to our own. The same can be said for relations between lovers, parents and dependent children, and even between spouses, at least when interaction is functioning at an optimal level. When such relations break down to the point that people must stand on their rights, we can often say that the actors ought to make more of an effort, and in many instances fault them for their lack of charity, tolerance, or benevolence. Thus, although we have a right to end friendships, it may be a reflection on our lack of virtue that we do so, and while we cannot be criticized for violating other people's rights, we can be rightfully deprecated for lacking the virtue to sustain a friendship.

But is there a similar conceptual relation between the kind of activity that a date is, and the sort of moral practice that it requires? My claim is that there is, and that this connection is easily established once we recognize the cultural presumption that dating is a gesture of friendship and regard. Traditionally, the decision to date indicates that two people have an initial attraction to each other, that they are disposed to like each other, and look forward to enjoying each other's company. Dating derives its implicit meaning from this tradition. It retains this meaning unless other aims are explicitly stated, and even then it may not be possible to alienate this meaning. It is a rare woman who will not spurn a man who states explicitly, right at the onset, that he wants to go out with her solely on the condition that he have sexual intercourse with her at the end of the evening, and that he has no interest in her company apart from gaining that end, and no concern for mutual satisfaction.

Explicit protest to the contrary aside, the conventions of dating confer on it its social meaning, and this social meaning implies a relationship which is more like friendship than the cutthroat competition of opposing teams. As such, it requires that we do more than stand on our rights with regard to each other. As long as we are operating under the auspices of a dating relationship, it requires that we behave in the mode of friendship and trust. But if a date is more like a friendship than a business contract, then clearly respect for the dialectics of desire is incompatible with the sort of sexual pressure that is inclined to end in date rape. And clearly, also, a conquest mentality which exploits

a situation of trust and respect for purely selfish ends is morally pernicious. Failure to respect the dialectics of desire when operating under the auspices of friendship and trust is to act in flagrant disregard of the moral requirement to avoid manipulative, coercive, and exploitive behaviour. Respect for the dialectics of desire is *prima facie* inconsistent with the satisfaction of one person at the expense of the other. The proper end of friendship relations is mutual satisfaction. But the requirement of mutuality means that we must take a communicative approach to discovering the ends of the other, and this entails that we respect the dialectics of desire.

But now that we know what communicative sexuality is, and that it is morally required, and that it is the only feasible means to mutual sexual enjoyment, why not take this model as the norm of what is reasonable in sexual interaction. The evidence of sexologists strongly indicates that women whose partners are aggressively uncommunicative have little chance of experiencing sexual pleasure. But it is not reasonable for women to consent to what they have little chance of enjoying. Hence it is not reasonable for women to consent to aggressive noncommunicative sex. Nor can we reasonably suppose that women have consented to sexual encounters which we know and they know they do not find enjoyable. With the communicative model as the norm, the aggressive contractual model should strike us as a model of deviant sexuality, and sexual encounters patterned on that model should strike us as encounters to which *prima facie* no one would reasonably agree. But if acquiescence to an encounter counts as consent only if the acquiescence is reasonable, something to which a reasonable person, in full possession of knowledge relevant to the encounter, would agree, then acquiescence to aggressive noncommunicative sex is not reasonable. Hence, acquiescence under such conditions should not count as consent.

Thus, where communicative sexuality does not occur, we lack the main ground for believing that the sex involved was consensual. Moreover, where a man does not engage in communicative sexuality, he acts either out of reckless disregard, or out of willful ignorance. For he cannot know, except through the practice of communicative sexuality, whether his partner has any sexual reason for continuing the encounter. And where she does not, he runs the risk of imposing on her what she is not willing to have. All that is needed then, in order to provide women with legal protection from 'date rape' is to make both reckless indifference and willful ignorance a sufficient condition of *mens rea* and to make communicative sexuality the accepted norm of sex to which a reasonable woman would agree. Thus, the appeal to communicative sexuality as a norm for sexual encounters accomplishes two things. It brings the aggressive sex involved in 'date rape' well within the realm of sexual assault, and it locates the guilt of date rapists in the failure to approach sexual relations on a communicative basis.

ERNEST VAN DEN HAAG

On Deterrence and the Death Penalty

ERNEST VAN DEN HAAG *is a psychoanalyst who lives and practices in New York.*

I

If rehabilitation and the protection of society from unrehabilitated offenders were the only purposes of legal punishment the death penalty could be abolished: it cannot attain the first end, and is not needed for the second. No case for the death penalty can be made unless "doing justice," or "deterring others," are among our penal aims. Each of these purposes can justify capital punishment by itself; opponents, therefore, must show that neither actually does, while proponents can rest their case on either.

Although the argument from justice is intellectually more interesting, and, in my view, decisive enough, utilitarian arguments have more appeal: the claim that capital punishment is useless because it does not deter others, is most persuasive. I shall, therefore, focus on this claim. Lest the argument be thought to be unduly narrow, I shall show, nonetheless, that some claims of injustice rest on premises which the claimants reject when arguments for capital punishment are derived therefrom; while other claims of injustice have no independent standing: their weight depends on the weight given to deterrence.

II

Capital punishment is regarded as unjust because it may lead to the execution of innocents, or because the guilty poor (or disadvantaged) are more likely to be executed than the guilty rich.

Regardless of merit, these claims are relevant only if "doing justice" is one purpose of punishment. Unless one regards it as good, or, at least, better, that the guilty be punished rather than the innocent, and that the equally guilty be punished equally, unless, that is, one wants penalties to be just, one cannot object to them because they are not. However, if one does include justice among the purposes of punishment, it becomes possible to justify any one punishment — even death — on grounds of justice. Yet, those who object to the death penalty because of its alleged injustice, usually deny not only the merits, or the sufficiency, of specific arguments based on justice, but the propriety of justice as an argument: they exclude "doing justice" as a purpose of legal punishment. If justice is not a purpose of penalties, injustice cannot be an objection to the death penalty, or to any other; if it is, justice cannot be ruled out as an argument for any penalty.

Consider the claim of injustice on its merits now. A convicted man may be found to have been innocent; if he was executed, the penalty cannot be reversed. Except for fines, penalties never can be reversed. Time spent in prison cannot be returned. However a prison sentence may be remitted once the prisoner serving it is found innocent; and he can be compensated for the time served (although compensation ordinarily cannot repair the harm). Thus, though (nearly) all penalties are irreversible, the death penalty, unlike others, is irrevocable as well.

Despite all precautions, errors will occur in judicial proceedings: the innocent may be found guilty; or the guilty rich may more easily escape conviction, or receive lesser penalties than the guilty poor.

However, these injustices do not reside in the penalties inflicted but in their maldistribution. It is not the penalty — whether death or prison — which is unjust when inflicted on the innocent. Inequity between poor and rich also involves distribution, not the penalty distributed. Thus injustice is not an objection to the death penalty but to the distributive process — the trial. Trials are more likely to be fair when life is at stake — the death penalty is probably less often unjustly inflicted than others. It requires special consideration not because it is more, or more often, unjust than other penalties, but because it is always irrevocable. . . .

In general, the possibility of injustice argues against penalization of any kind only if the suspected usefulness of penalization is less important than the probable harm (particularly to innocents) and the probable inequities. The possibility of injustice argues against the death penalty only inasmuch as the added usefulness (deterrence) expected from irrevocability is thought less important than the added harm. (Were my argument specifically concerned with justice, I could compare the injustice inflicted by the courts with the injustice — outside the courts — avoided by the judicial process. *I.e.*, "important" here may be used to include everything to which importance is attached.)

We must briefly examine now the general use and effectiveness of deterrence to decide whether the death penalty could add enough deterrence to be warranted.

III

Does any punishment "deter others" at all? Doubts have been thrown on this effect because it is thought to depend on the incorrect rationalistic psychology of some of its 18th and 19th century proponents.

Actually deterrence does not depend on rational calculation, on rationality or even on capacity for it; nor do arguments for it depend on rationalistic psychology. Deterrence depends on the likelihood and on the regularity — not on the rationality — of human responses to danger; and further on the possibility of reinforcing internal controls by vicarious external experiences.

.   .   .

Unlike natural dangers, legal threats are constructed deliberately by legislators to restrain actions which may impair the social order. Thus legislation transforms social into individual dangers. Most people further transform external into internal danger: they acquire a sense of moral obligation, a conscience, which threatens them, should they do what is wrong. Arising originally from the external authority of rulers and rules, conscience is internalized and becomes independent of external forces. However, conscience is constantly reinforced in those whom it controls by the coercive imposition of external authority on recalcitrants and on those who have not acquired it. Most people refrain from offenses because they feel an obligation to behave lawfully. But this obligation would scarcely be felt if those who do not feel or follow it were not to suffer punishment.

Although the legislators may calculate their threats and the responses to be produced, the effectiveness of the threats neither requires nor depends on calculations by those responding. The predictor (or producer) of effects must calculate; those whose responses are predicted (or produced) need not. Hence, although legislation (and legislators) should be rational,

subjects, to be deterred as intended, need not be: they need only be responsive.

Punishments deter those who have not violated the law for the same reasons — and in the same degrees (apart from internalization: moral obligation) as do natural dangers. Often natural dangers — all dangers not deliberately created by legislation (*e.g.*, injury of the criminal inflicted by the crime victim) are insufficient. Thus, the fear of injury (natural danger) does not suffice to control city traffic; it must be reinforced by the legal punishment meted out to those who violate the rules. These punishments keep most people observing the regulations. However, where (in the absence of natural danger) the threatened punishment is so light that the advantage of violating rules tends to exceed the disadvantage of being punished (divided by the risk), the rule is violated (*i.e.*, parking fines are too light). In this case the feeling of obligation tends to vanish as well. Elsewhere punishment deters.

To be sure, not everybody responds to threatened punishment. Non-responsive persons may be a) self-destructive or b) incapable of responding to threats, or even of grasping them. Increases in the size, or certainty, of penalties would not affect these two groups. A third group c) might respond to more certain or more severe penalties. . . . There is no reason to believe that all present and future offenders belong to the *a priori* non-responsive groups, or that all penalties have reached the point of diminishing, let alone zero returns. . . .

IV

The foregoing suggests the question posed by the death penalty: is the deterrence added (return) sufficiently above zero to warrant irrevocability (or other, less clear, disadvantages)? The question is not only whether the penalty deters, but whether it deters more than alternatives and whether the difference exceeds the cost of irrevocability. (I shall assume that the alternative is actual life imprisonment so as to exclude the complication produced by the release of the unrehabilitated.)

In some fairly infrequent but important circumstances the death penalty is the only possible deterrent. Thus, in case of acute *coups d'état*, or of acute substantial attempts to overthrow the government, prospective rebels would altogether discount the threat of any prison sentence. They would not be deterred because they believe the swift victory of the revolution will invalidate a prison sentence and turn it into an advantage. Execution would be the only deterrent because, unlike prison sentences, it cannot be revoked by victorious rebels. The same reasoning applies to deterring spies or traitors in wartime. Finally, men who, by virtue of past acts, are already serving, or are threatened, by a life sentence, could be deterred from further offenses only by the threat of the death penalty.

What about criminals who do not fall into any of these (often ignored) classes? Prof. Thorsten Sellin has made a careful study of the available statistics: he concluded that they do not yield evidence for the deterring effect of the death penalty. Somewhat surprisingly, Prof. Sellin seems to think that this lack of evidence for deterrence is evidence for the lack of deterrence. It is not. It means that deterrence has not been demonstrated statistically — not that non-deterrence has been.

It is entirely possible, indeed likely (as Prof. Sellin appears willing to concede), that the statistics used, though the best available, are nonetheless too slender a reed to rest conclusions on. They indicate that the homicide rate does not vary greatly between similar areas with or without the death penalty, and in the same area before and after abolition. However, the similar areas are not similar enough; the periods are not long enough; many social differences and changes, other than the abolition of the death penalty, may account for the variation (or lack of) in homicide rates with and without, before and after abolition; some of these social differences and changes are likely to have affected homicide rates. I am unaware of any statistical analysis which adjusts for such changes and differences. And logically, it is quite consistent with the postulated deterrent effect of capital punishment that there be less homicide after abolition: with retention there might have been still less.

Homicide rates do not depend exclusively on penalties any more than do other crime rates. A number of conditions which influence the propensity to crime, demographic, economic or generally social, changes or differences — even such matters as changes of the divorce laws or of the cotton price — may influence the homicide rate. Therefore variation or constancy cannot be attributed to variations or constancy of the penalties, unless we know that no other factor influencing the homicide rate has changed. Usually we don't. To believe in the death penalty deterrent does not require one to believe that the death penalty, or any other, is the only, or the decisive causal variable; this would be as absurd as the converse mistake that "social causes" are the only, or always the decisive factor. To favor capital punishment, the efficacy of neither variable need be denied. It is enough to affirm that the severity of the penalty may influence some potential criminals, and that the added severity of the death penalty adds to deterrence, or may do so. It is quite possible that such a deterrent effect may be offset (or intensified) by non-penal factors which affect propensity; its presence of absence therefore may be hard, and perhaps impossible to demonstrate.

Contrary to what Prof. Sellin *et al.* seem to presume, I doubt that offenders are aware of the absence or presence of the death penalty state by state or period by period. Such unawareness argues against the assumption of a calculating murderer. However, unawareness does not argue against the death penalty if by deterrence we mean a preconscious, general response to a severe, but not necessarily specifically and explicitly apprehended or calculated threat. A constant homicide rate, despite abolition, may occur because of unawareness and not because of lack of deterrence: people remain deterred for a lengthy interval by the severity of the penalty in the past, or by the severity of penalties used in similar circumstances nearby.

I do not argue for a version of deterrence which would require me to believe that an individual shuns murder while in North Dakota, because of the death penalty, and merrily goes to it in South Dakota since it has been abolished there; or that he will start the murderous career from which he had hitherto refrained, after abolition. I hold that the generalized threat of the death penalty may be a deterrent, and the more so, the more generally applied. Deterrence will not cease in the particular areas of abolition or at the particular times of abolition. Rather, general deterrence will be somewhat weakened, through local (partial) abolition. Even such weakening will be hard to detect owing to changes in many offsetting, or reinforcing, factors.

For all of these reasons, I doubt that the presence or absence of a deterrent effect of the death penalty is likely to be demonstrable by statistical means. . . . It is on our uncertainty that the case for deterrence must rest.

V

If we do not know whether the death penalty will deter others, we are confronted with two uncertainties. If we impose the death penalty, and achieve no deterrent effect thereby, the life of a convicted murderer has been expended in vain (from a deterrent viewpoint). There is a net loss. If we impose the death sentence and thereby deter some future murderers, we spared the lives of some future victims (the prospective murderers gain too; they are spared punishment because they were deterred). In this case, the death penalty has led to a net gain, unless the life of a convicted murderer is valued more highly than that of the unknown victim, or victims (and the non-imprisonment of the deterred non-murderer).

The calculation can be turned around, of course. The absence of the death penalty may harm no one and therefore produce a gain — the life of the convicted murderer. Or it may kill future victims of murderers who could have been deterred, and thus produce a loss — their life.

To be sure, we must risk something certain — the death (or life) of the convicted man, for something uncertain — the death (or life) of the victims of murderers who may be deterred. This is in the nature of uncertainty — when we invest, or gamble, we risk the money we have for an uncertain gain. Many human actions, most commitments — including marriage and crime — share this characteristic with the deterrent purpose of any penalization, and with its rehabilitative purpose (and even with the protective).

More proof is demanded for the deterrent effect of the death penalty than is demanded for the deterrent effect of other penalties. This is not justified by the absence of other utilitarian purposes such as protection and rehabilitation; they involve no less uncertainty than deterrence.

Irrevocability may support a demand for some reason to expect more deterrence than revocable penalties might produce, but not a demand for more proof of deterrence, as has been pointed out above. The reason for expecting more deterrence lies in the greater severity, the terrifying effect inherent in finality. Since it seems more important to spare victims than to spare murderers, the burden of proving that the greater severity inherent in irrevocability adds nothing to deterrence lies on those who oppose capital punishment. Proponents of the death penalty need show only that there is no more uncertainty about it than about greater severity in general.

The demand that the death penalty be proved more deterrent than alternatives can not be satisfied any more than the demand that six years in prison be proved to be more deterrent than three. But the uncertainty which confronts us favors the death penalty as long as by imposing it we might save future victims of murder. This effect is as plausible as the general idea that penalties have deterrent effects which increase with their severity. Though we have no proof of the positive deterrence of the penalty, we also have no proof of zero, or negative effectiveness. I believe we have no right to risk additional future victims of murder for the sake of sparing convicted murderers; on the contrary, our moral obligation is to risk the possible ineffectiveness of executions. However rationalized, the opposite view appears to be motivated by the simple fact that executions are more subjected to social control than murder. However, this applies to all penalties and does not argue for the abolition of any.

ALBERT CAMUS

Reflections on the Guillotine

ALBERT CAMUS (1913–1960), *a leading French intellectual, was a political activist and an associate of Jean-Paul Sartre. Awarded the Nobel Prize for Literature in 1957, Camus' philosophical concerns were often expressed in fiction.*

WE all know that the great argument of those who defend capital punishment is the exemplary value of the punishment. Heads are cut off not only to punish but to intimidate, by a frightening example, any who might be tempted to imitate the guilty. Society is not taking revenge; it merely wants to forestall. It waves the head in the air so that potential murderers will see their fate and recoil from it.

This argument would be impressive if we were not obliged to note:

1) that society itself does not believe in the exemplary value it talks about;

2)   that there is no proof that the death penalty ever made a single murderer recoil when he had made up his mind, whereas clearly it had no effect but one of fascination on thousands of criminals;

3)   that in other regards, it constitutes a repulsive example, the consequences of which cannot be foreseen.

To begin with, society does not believe in what it says. If it really believed what it says, it would exhibit the heads. Society would give executions the benefit of the publicity it generally uses for national bond issues or new brands of drinks. But we know that executions in our country, instead of taking place publicly, are now perpetrated in prison courtyards before a limited number of specialists. . . .

How can a furtive assassination committed at night in a prison courtyard be exemplary? At most, it serves the purpose of periodically informing the citizens that they will die if they happen to kill — a future that can be promised even to those who do not kill. For the penalty to be truly exemplary it must be frightening. . . .

But, after all, why should society believe in that example when it does not stop crime, when its effects, if they exist, are invisible? To begin with, capital punishment could not intimidate the man who doesn't know that he is going to kill, who makes up his mind to it in a flash and commits his crime in a state of frenzy or obsession, nor the man who, going to an appointment to have it out with someone, takes along a weapon to frighten the faithless one or the opponent and uses it although he didn't want to or didn't think he wanted to. In other words, it could not intimidate the man who is hurled into crime as if into a calamity. This is tantamount to saying that it is powerless in the majority of cases. It is only fair to point out that in our country capital punishment is rarely applied in such cases. But the word "rarely" itself makes one shudder.

Does it frighten at least that race of criminals on whom it claims to operate and who live off crime? Nothing is less certain. We can read in Koestler that at a time when pickpockets were executed in England, other pickpockets exercised their talents in the crowd surrounding the scaffold where their colleague was being hanged. Statistics drawn up at the beginning of the century in England show that out of 250 who were hanged, 170 had previously attended one or more executions. And in 1886, out of 167 condemned men who had gone through the Bristol prison, 164 had witnessed at least one execution. . . .

If fear of death is, indeed, a fact, another fact is that such fear, however great it may be, has never sufficed to quell human passions. Bacon is right in saying that there is no passion so weak that it cannot confront and overpower fear of death. Revenge, love, honor, pain, another fear manage to overcome it. How could cupidity, hatred, jealousy fail to do what love of a person or a country, what a passion for freedom manage to do? For centuries the death penalty, often accompanied by barbarous refinements, has been trying to hold crime in check; yet crime persists. Why? Because the instincts that are warring in man are not, as the law claims, constant forces in a state of equilibrium. They are variable forces constantly waxing and waning, and their repeated lapses from equilibrium nourish the life of the mind as electrical oscillations, when close enough, set up a current. . . . But it may happen that one of the soul's forces breaks loose until it fills the whole field of consciousness; at such a moment no instinct, not even that of life, can oppose the tyranny of that irresistible force. For capital punishment to be really intimidating, human nature would have to be different; it would have to be as stable and serene as the law itself. But then human nature would be dead.

It is not dead. This is why, however surprising this may seem to anyone who has never observed or directly experienced human complexity, the murderer, most of the time, feels innocent when he kills. Every criminal acquits himself before he is judged. He considers himself, if not within his right, at least excused by circumstances. He does not think or foresee; when he thinks, it is to foresee that he will be forgiven altogether or in part. How could he fear what he considers highly improbable? He will fear death after the verdict but not before the crime. Hence the law, to be intimidating, should leave the murderer no chance, should be implacable in advance and particularly admit no extenuating circumstance. But who among us would dare ask this?

If anyone did, it would still be necessary to take into account another paradox of human nature. If the instinct to live is fundamental, it is no more so than another instinct of which the academic psychologists do not speak: the death instinct, which at certain moments calls for the destruction of oneself and of others. It is probable that the desire to kill often coincides with the desire to die or to annihilate oneself. Thus, the instinct for self-preservation is matched, in variable proportions, by the instinct for destruction. The latter is the only way of explaining altogether the various perversions which, from alcoholism to drugs, lead an individual to his death while he knows full well what is happening. Man wants to live, but it is useless to hope that this desire will dictate all his actions. He also wants to be nothing; he wants the irreparable, and death for its own sake. So it

happens that the criminal wants not only the crime but the suffering that goes with it, even (one might say, especially) if that suffering is exceptional. When that odd desire grows and becomes dominant, the prospect of being put to death not only fails to stop the criminal, but probably even adds to the vertigo in which he swoons. Thus, in a way, he kills in order to die.

Such peculiarities suffice to explain why a penalty that seems calculated to frighten normal minds is in reality altogether unrelated to ordinary psychology. All statistics without exception, those concerning countries that have abolished execution as well as the others, show that there is no connection between the abolition of the death penalty and criminality. Criminal statistics neither increase nor decrease. The guillotine exists, and so does crime; between the two there is no other apparent connection than that of the law. . . .

"Nothing proves, indeed," say the conservatives, "that the death penalty is exemplary; as a matter of fact, it is certain that thousands of murderers have not been intimidated by it. But there is no way of knowing those it has intimidated; consequently, nothing proves that it is not exemplary." Thus, the greatest of punishments, the one that involves the last dishonor for the condemned and grants the supreme privilege to society, rests on nothing but an unverifiable possibility. Death, on the other hand, does not involve degrees or probabilities. It solidifies all things, culpability and the body, in a definitive rigidity. Yet it is administered among us in the name of chance and a calculation. Even if that calculation were reasonable, should there not be a certainty to authorize the most certain of deaths? However, the condemned is cut in two, not so much for the crime he committed but by virtue of all the crimes that might have been and were not committed, that can be and will not be committed. The most sweeping uncertainty in this case authorizes the most implacable certainty. . . .

What will be left of that power of example if it is proved that capital punishment has another power, and a very real one, which degrades men to the point of shame, madness, and murder? . . .

What can we think of those officials who call the guillotine "the shunting engine," the condemned man "the client" or "the parcel"? The priest Bela Just, who accompanied more than thirty condemned men writes: "The slang of the administrators of justice is quite as cynical and vulgar as that of the criminals." And here are the remarks of one of our assistant executioners on his journeys to the provinces: "When we would start on a trip, it was always a lark, with taxis and the best restaurants part of the spree!" The same one says, boasting of the executioner's skill in releasing the blade: "You could *allow yourself the fun* of pulling the client's hair." The dissoluteness expressed here has other, deeper aspects. The clothing of the condemned belongs in principle to the executioner. The elder Deibler used to hang all such articles of clothing in a shed and *now and then would go and look at them*. But there are more serious aspects. Here is what our assistant executioner declares: "The new executioner is batty about the guillotine. He sometimes spends days on end at home sitting on a chair, ready with hat and coat on, waiting for a summons from the Ministry." . . .

The fine and solemn example, thought up by our legislators, at least produces one sure effect — to depreciate or to destroy all humanity and reason in those who take part in it directly. But, it will be said, these are exceptional creatures who find a vocation in such dishonor. They

seem less exceptional when we learn that hundreds of persons offer to serve as executioners without pay. The men of our generation, who have lived through the history of recent years, will not be astonished by this bit of information. They know that behind the most peaceful and familiar faces slumbers the impulse to torture and murder. The punishment that aims to intimidate an unknown murderer certainly confers a vocation of killer on many another monster about whom there is no doubt. And since we are busy justifying our cruelest laws with probable considerations, let there be no doubt that out of those hundreds of men whose services were declined, one at least must have satisfied otherwise the bloodthirsty instincts the guillotine excited in him.

If, therefore, there is a desire to maintain the death penalty, let us at least be spared the hypocrisy of a justification by example. Let us be frank about that penalty which can have no publicity, that intimidation which works only on respectable people, so long as they are respectable, which fascinates those who have ceased to be respectable and debases or deranges those who take part in it. It is a penalty, to be sure, a frightful torture, both physical and moral, but it provides no sure example except a demoralizing one. It punishes, but it forestalls nothing; indeed, it may even arouse the impulse to murder. It hardly seems to exist, except for the man who suffers it — in his soul for months and years, in his body during the desperate and violent hour when he is cut in two without suppressing his life. Let us call it by the name which, for lack of any other nobility, will at least give the nobility of truth, and let us recognize it for what it is essentially: a revenge. . . .

Many laws consider a premeditated crime more serious than a crime of pure violence. But what then is capital punishment but the most premeditated of murders, to which no criminal's deed, however calculated it may be, can be compared? For there to be equivalence, the death penalty would have to punish a criminal who had warned his victim of the date at which he would inflict a horrible death on him and who, from that moment onward, had confined him at his mercy for months. Such a monster is not encountered in private life.

VIRGINIA HELD

Violence, Terrorism, and Moral Inquiry

VIRGINIA HELD *teaches philosophy at Hunter College and at the Graduate School of the City University of New York. She is the author of many books, including* Rights and Goods: Justifying Social Action *(1984).*

Violence

It is sometimes suggested that violence is by definition wrong, but to maintain this is not a satisfactory position. It is easy enough to think of examples of acts of violence of which it is meaningful to ask whether they were wrong or not. One of the clearest examples would be the 1944 bomb plot against Hitler. To answer questions about the justifiability of acts of violence requires that the issues not be construed as ones which can be settled merely by appealing to a definition.

Violence can be defined as action, usually sudden, predictably and coercively inflicting injury upon or damage harming a person. The threat of such action is a violent threat. Property damage is sometimes called "violence" by those who deplore it, but should only be included insofar as it risks injury or harm to persons.

Some hold that failures to act can also be instances of violence, as when persons are harmed by being deprived of food. But it might be more accurate to see the violence involved as the injury inflicted when those who are deprived attempt to change their position. And failures to act can certainly be morally outrageous without being violent. To starve a person slowly may be as blameworthy as, or sometimes even more blameworthy than, killing the person quickly. But it is not more violent.

Harm can be inflicted through psychological as well as physical pressure, and the injury caused by violence may be physical or psychological.

A dissident who blows up a car, intentionally killing its occupants, is violent. The police who capture him with guns threaten violence to do so. If he is wounded or killed in the capture, violence has been used against him. A competent doctor operating on a patient is not inflicting harm. An honest tennis player injuring another does not do so predictably. Automobile driving predictably risks injury, but to the extent that it is voluntarily engaged in, it does not do so coercively.

Violence is distinct from force and coercion, since force may be used to coerce without violence, and coercion is not always violent, though violence is always coercive. Force is power to cause someone to do something against his or her will. Coercion is the activity of causing someone to do something against his or her will, whether that will is actual, or what the person would will if the person knew what was going to happen to him or to her or to others, and still had what could be described as a capacity to will.

The use of force to coerce may often be justified where the use of violence for the same purpose would not be. For instance, a parent may coerce a child to surrender a dangerous object by gently forcing the child's fingers open, where to retrieve the object by a violent blow would not be justified.

If we agree with Plato that it can never be right to injure or harm anyone, we will be back with the view, rejected at the outset, that violence is by definition unjustifiable. But we can retain a meaning of "inflicting injury" which is descriptive, and morally indeterminate, and that does not allow us to call every form of causing pain a kind of violence. To injure someone in self-defense, or in the upholding of a just law, may be not only a legally allowed but a morally justifiable case of injuring.

The legal rules of almost any legal system permit the use of violence to preserve and enforce the laws, whether these laws are just or not, but forbid most other uses of violence. Where laws are morally un-

justified, the use of violence to uphold them will be morally unjustified even if legally permitted. And sometimes legal rules permit the use of violence to uphold highly corrupt and harmful political power. Violence is also often used in the enforcement of law in excess of what might be needed for this purpose, and in excess of what the law allows.

In an improving political system, violence not allowed by law will seldom be found legal by new judicial decisions, so we can rarely speak of illegal violence as coming to be *legally* justified, at least not without becoming, first, politically acceptable. But it is not unusual for illegal violence to become politically justified in the sense that within the political system it will come to be taken as justified. Let's examine these issues.

If we have made a higher-level moral judgment that a given political system is worthy of existence, or that it is satisfactory enough for us to consider ourselves to be members of it, that it ought to be changed rather than destroyed, but that it cannot be adequately changed within its existing legal forms and legally allowed political processes, we may consider engaging in acts of violence which are illegal but which will come to be seen as justifiable on political grounds. And if we consider a given political system so thoroughly corrupt and productive of harm that it cannot be repaired, we may consider whether we would be morally justified in engaging in violence to rid human beings of the violence it inflicts or to express our outrage. . . .

Violence and the Self

The argument is made, particularly by Sartre and by Fanon, that violence can contribute significantly to the psychological health of the oppressed. They argue that through the commission of a violent act, a subjugated person can come to recognize his human freedom. Sartre writes, "We only become what we are by the radical and deep-seated refusal of that which others have made of us. . . ." Writing of the Algerians' struggle for independence, he says,

> First, the only violence is the settler's; but soon (the rebels) will make it their own; that is to say, the same violence is thrown back upon us. . . . By this mad fury, by this bitterness and spleen, by their ever-present desire to kill us . . . they have become men: men *because of* the settler, who wants to make beasts of burden of them—because of him, and against him. . . . This irrepressible violence is neither sound and fury, not the resurrection of savage instincts, nor even the effect of resentment: it is man recreating himself."

One may respond that the capacity to say "no" to the command of one's oppressor may indeed be an essential part of the process by which a person becomes aware of her freedom, but that the form of the refusal need not therefore be violent. It may even be asserted that the awareness of freedom is greater when a person recognizes that she possesses a capacity for violent action, and also a capacity to refrain from using it. She may become conscious of a higher degree of freedom by defying those who taunt her to prove herself through violence as well as by defying those who oppress her.

If, however, an existing political system refuses to allow the expression of moral arguments designed to transform it, and if an act of political violence can constitute such an expression, it may be morally justifiable. There will be grave danger

that any violent political act will cause unforeseeable consequences, and even graver danger that a violent action intended to change a political system will instead be seen as, and unleash the responses that would attend, an action intended to destroy that system. Then the consequence may be to entrench repression rather than to shake it. If any such acts are to have any chance of achieving their purposes it will be necessary to evolve tacit rules to keep them within bounds and make their intentions clear. As in the case of civil disobedience, there will have to be an understanding of the possible moral sincerity of both the actor and those members of the political system faced with responding to such action, both of whom may be acting in accordance with what they conscientiously consider to be their moral obligations. In the case of civil disobedience, the sincerity of the actor can sometimes be demonstrated by his willingness to limit himself to non violent actions. Sometimes, but not always, a willingness to accept the penalty which the legal system decides upon, or to perform the action in public, can contribute to a demonstration of sincerity. Comparable evidence of sincerity is much more difficult to offer in the case of violent action that is not justifiable within the political system, but it is not impossible. The provision of fair warning to minimize unnecessary injury, the offering of unmistakable evidence of restraint that the violence can be ended in as disciplined a way as it is being taken, may all contribute.

When those to whom a political system fails to give a voice constitute a large number of that system's members, the argument may be persuasive that an act of violence which warns that system of possible danger to itself, may have to be justifiable within that political system or it will not be justifiable at all. But when those to whom a political system denies a voice are too small a minority or too powerless to represent a significant threat to the existence or even the health of that system, the requirement that for an act of violence to be morally justifiable it must also be politically justifiable, may be mistaken. Political systems have been known to be long-lived though highly immoral.

Can Terrorism be Justified?

Do the arguments I have considered concerning violence apply also to terrorism? Terrorism is sometimes defined as "the systematic use of murder, injury, and destruction" to create terror and despair through "indiscriminate" attacks in which "no distinction" is made that might exempt the innocent from being targets of such attacks. Terrorists are sometimes said to "sacrifice all moral and humanitarian considerations for the sake of some political end." If terrorism is defined this way, we may be unable even to raise the question of whether it could be justifiable. As with violence, the question should be open, not shut by definition. Any adequate definition of terrorism must be able to include terrorism carried out by a government as well as by its opponents. If, as some report, terrorist acts "are often viewed in many Third World countries as noble acts of 'freedom fighters,'" we should be able to examine the reasons without having precluded them by definitional fiat.

Robert Young, in an article on terrorism, agrees with most definitions that terrorism is "intimidatory in intent," but does not agree that terrorist attacks need be "indiscriminate." The targets of terrorism may be the armed forces, the police, and those with political power responsible for repression. Although surprise is "central to the potency of terrorism," this is not inconsistent with warnings to minimize harm to the innocent. In Young's view, terrorism should only be tactic of last resort where other means of political action are not available. However, as part of an ideological "program of revolutionary struggle," it may be justified, he thinks, as certain wars can be. Its casualties and violence are very limited compared to war. A program including terrorist acts may in his view be the only realistic means to counter state-inspired terrorism, and, if its cause is just and success likely, terrorism may thus be justified.

In one of the most comprehensive discussions, Grant Wardlaw defines political terrorism as "the systematic threat of violence to secure political goals." The purposes may be varied: "Whilst the primary effect is to create fear and alarm the objectives may be to gain concessions, obtain maximum publicity for a cause, provoke repression, break down social order, build morale in the movement or enforce obedience to it. Several of the objectives may be accomplished simultaneously by a single incident."

Amar Ouzegane, a leader of the Algerian FLN movement trying to gain Algerian independence against the French, wrote of the functions of terrorism that "urban terrorism, our liberating terrorism, functioned as a safety valve. It permitted patriots ulcerated by the unequal struggle, revolted by French injustice . . . , to liberate themselves from an unconscious psychological complex, to keep cool heads, to respect revolutionary discipline."

Interestingly, those who defend terrorism often employ arguments familiar from "just war" discussions. John Dugard writes that "The Third World argument is based largely on a Western philosophical tradition: that of the 'just war.'" He points out that many states "including the major Western powers, have on occasion engaged in acts of terror against civilian populations which completely overshadow the acts of terror committed by national liberation movements . . ." While prohibitions against state terrorism remain unenforced, "it is asking too much," he thinks, "of Third World countries to collaborate in the suppression of the most effective means to counter terror available to national liberation movements."

We might conclude that *if* war can be justified, terrorist acts can be also, if they have certain characteristics. But if terrorism includes, not by definition but in fact, the unnecessary killing of the innocent, it is at least not more justified than war in doing so, though the scale may be smaller. And if comparable good results can be accomplished with far less killing, an alternative to war that would achieve these results through acts intrinsically no worse than those that occur in war would be more justifiable.

But it is almost always possible to show that as limited terrorism is better than war, less violent alternatives to terrorism are better than terrorism, and non violent pressures are better than violent ones. We might agree that the causing of war, whether through aggression, violent repression, the extermination or expulsion of unwanted populations, or by depriving people of the means to maintain life, is the ultimate crime of violence. If war to prevent the success of those who cause war can be justified, lesser uses of terror and violence can also, sometimes, be justified. But the more tyrants and torturers depend on the support of those around them, the better may be the chances of eroding that support through non violent pressure. The opponents of evil should not have to sacrifice their lives. But those who use violence must also be prepared to risk their lives. To risk one's life in non violent protest, if the risk is no greater, and the chance of success and the rightness of the cause are only no less, is surely more justifiable.

11

What
Should We
Sacrifice for
Animals
and the
Environment?

Should we do more than we are doing to protect our natural environment? Fifty years ago most people would have been relatively unconcerned about the environment. But we live today in an age in which most people believe it is important to devote time and resources to the protection of the environment. But if most people already agree that we should do more, then what philosophical problems could there be about environmental issues? Similarly, most people would agree we shouldn't be cruel to animals — what then is philosophically perplexing about the treatment of animals?

Interestingly, both of these areas raise a host of important and perplexing philosophical issues. The most obvious of these is the question of the *extent* of our obligations toward animals and the environment. Several years ago a dam project undertaken by the Tennessee Valley Authority was temporarily halted when it was discovered that a small fish called a "snail darter" had as its only habitat some of the marshes that were to be submerged by the dam project. The dilemma was this: the dam would bring significant economic improvement to thousands of people, but the snail darter would become extinct as its habitat was flooded. More recently, vast tracts of forest in the Pacific Northwest have been declared off-grounds for lumbering because they provide the only habitat for the spotted owl, an endangered species. Protecting the spotted owl will put thousands of people out of work. It is arguable in both of these cases that some human lives might be lost because people will be less able to pay for food, health care, automobile maintenance, and safety measures. Is it right to save animals, or animal species, when doing so costs people their jobs, or even their lives? What is the extent of our obligation? How much must we sacrifice?

Obviously it is not possible to answer questions like these by setting some amount in dollars, pesos, or person-hours that each person must sacrifice for animals and the environment. Even to approach such a question, we need to have some idea of what basis there is for valuing the environment and the interests of animals. In his article, Tom Regan distinguishes three kinds of justification we might appeal to for valuing the environment. The first, a *management ethic*, holds that animals and the environment are valuable because they benefit humans. In this view, we must protect animals and the environment to the extent that it is in our (human) interest to do so. For example, one might argue that we should not build a dam because it will prevent fish migration and harm the fishing industry, or because it will drown scenic land that could be used for recreation. One could argue that biological diversity is important on ecological grounds, and that we ultimately are beneficiaries of such diversity. A management ethic might well question whether the snail darter was valuable enough to warrant canceling a significant river project.

A second justification is a *kinship ethic*, which holds that we value things that bear a "kinship" relationship to us. In most versions of this view, our kinship is to other creatures that are sentient (capable of thought), or to creatures that can suffer; these, in addition to ourselves, are the creatures we feel impelled to protect. Peter Singer, an influential animal-rights theorist, argues in his selection that it is wrong of us to raise animals in harsh conditions for food, but that there is no need to sacrifice a river project for the snail darter. Similarly, we have no special obligation to protect endangered *species*, so long as we do not cause the suffering of any particular members of those species.

The third justification is what Regan claims as a true *environmental ethic*, namely one that holds that nonsentient beings — animals, plants, and even natural formations — have inherent value and moral standing independent of their value, or kinship, to us humans. Just as it is racist to hold that the interests of whites count more than the interests of other races, and just as it is sexist to hold that the interests of men count more than the interests of women, it is *speciesist* of us to hold that the interests of humans (and of animals that are relevantly like humans) count for more than the interests of snail darters, plants or deserts. In a classic statement, Aldo Leopold argues eloquently that we must stop seeing land-use as a narrowly economic problem and see it rather as a problem of environmental ethics. On the other hand, Mark Sagoff claims in his article that you can't be both an environmentalist and in favor of animal rights. If he is right, then we cannot agree both with Leopold and with Singer.

One principal reason for protecting the environment is that, if we do not, future generations will inherit an inhospitable, perhaps unlivable, planet. For example, plutonium waste created by nuclear power plants is deathly poisonous in even minute quantities, and takes over 20,000 years to lose even half of its toxicity. The loss of rain forests contributes to the greenhouse effect, and once a critical mass of them has been lost, they cannot be restored by replanting. But people living on the planet often feel that they need to use these resources now. Most future generations don't even exist yet. To what extent must we sacrifice our well-being to protect the interests of people who don't even exist?

In her selection, Annette Baier focuses on what has been called the *futurity problem*. Here is an example of the futurity problem in an individual case. Suppose that a couple decides to have a baby. Out of concern for their future child's health, they agree to stop drinking alcohol during the entire course of the pregnancy — even before conceiving a child. Because they have stopped consuming alcohol, they go to bed at 10 P.M. — earlier than they would have if they had gone out drinking. The sperm that therefore fertilizes the egg is different than the one that would have fertilized the egg if the couple had gone to bed at 11 P.M. after drinking. It is possibly even a different egg that is fertilized. Let's call the baby that *would* have been conceived at 11 P.M. *Sue* and call the baby that *was* conceived in an alcohol-free body at 10 P.M. *Mike*.

Remember that the couple decided to stop drinking out of concern for their child's health, and that the child who would have been born if they had continued drinking would have been Sue. But now that they have stopped drinking, Sue will not be born more healthy — Sue will not be born at all. Rather, it is Mike who will be born. Mike may well be healthier than Sue would have been, but that is hardly a benefit to Sue, who will not exist. Accordingly, if the couple had *not* stopped drinking, and if Sue had been born with alcohol-related birth defects, Sue would hardly seem in a position to complain about her parents' drinking; she would not exist at all if her parents had stopped drinking. Baier tries to show how a person could coherently complain that her interests had not been served even if serving them better would have caused her never to exist.

Marti Kheel claims that the very structures of thought that have brought us such staggering environmental problems are now being invoked in an effort to solve them. In an attempt to reframe completely the discussion of environmental issues, she argues that we must turn to a feminist conception of environmental ethics. Such a framework would offer hope of a truly holist approach toward the environment, one based less on the dualistic discussion of rights and principles that has caused the problems in the first place and that will prevent their resolution.

The chapter opens with a wry poem by Allen Ginsberg, a chronicle of environmental woes. It closes, too, on a wry note by John Stuart Mill, written well over a century ago, reminding us not to be uncritical in our glorification of nature.

ALLEN GINSBERG
Ballade of Poisons

ALLEN GINSBERG *is a poet, photographer, and musician associated with the Beat generation poets of the 1950s and the antiwar movement of the 1960s. He is the author of many books, including* The Fall of America: Poems of These States, *which won the 1974 National Book Award.*

> With oil that streaks streets a magic color,
> With soot that falls on city vegetables
> With basement sulfurs & coal black odor
> With smog that purples suburbs' sunset hills
> With Junk that feebles black & white men's wills
> With plastic bubbles aeons will dissolve
> With new plutoniums that only resolve
> Their poison heat in quarter million years,
> With pesticides that round food Chains revolve
> May your soul make home, may your eyes weep tears.
>
> With freak hormones in chicken & soft egg
> With panic red dye in cow meat burger
> With mummy med'cines, nitrate in sliced pig

With sugar'd cereal kids scream for murder,
With Chemic additives that cause Cancer
With bladder and mouth in your salami,
With Strontium Ninety in milks of Mommy,
With sex voices that spill beer thru your ears
With Cups of Nicotine till you vomit
May your soul make home, may your eyes weep tears.

With microwave toaster television
With Cadmium lead in leaves of fruit trees
With Trade Center's nocturnal emission
With Coney Island's shore plopped with Faeces
While blue Whales sing in high infrequent seas
With Amazon worlds with fish in ocean
Washed in Rockefellers greasy Potion
With oily toil fueled with atomic fears
With CIA tainting World emotion
May your soul make home, may your eyes weep tears.

Envoi

President, 'spite cockroach devotion,
Folk poisoned with radioactive lotion,
'Spite soulless bionic energy queers
May your world move to healthy emotion,
Make your soul at home, let your eyes weep tears.

TOM REGAN

The Nature and Possibility of an Environmental Ethic

TOM REGAN *teaches philosophy at North Carolina State University and has published widely in ethics. He is best known as a defender of animal rights.*

I. Introduction

Is an environmental ethic possible? Answers to this question presuppose that we have an agreed upon understanding of the nature of an environmental ethic. Evidently we do not, and one fundamental problem for this burgeoning area of ethics is to say what such an ethic must be like. In this essay, I characterize and defend, although incompletely, a particular conception of an environmental ethic. My modest objective is to show that there is something worth thinking about completing.

II. *Two Conditions of an Environmental Ethic*

The conception I favor accepts the following two conditions:

1. An environmental ethic must hold that there are nonhuman beings that have moral standing.
2. An environmental ethic must hold that the class of those beings that have moral standing includes but is larger than the class of conscious beings — that is, all conscious beings and some nonconscious beings must be held to have moral standing.

If both conditions are accepted, then a theory that satisfies neither of them is not a false environmental ethic; it is not an environmental ethic at all. Any theory that satisfies (1), but does not satisfy (2) might be regarded as a theory "on the way to becoming" such an ethic, in that it satisfies a necessary condition, but, since it fails to satisfy condition (2), it fails to qualify as a genuine environmental ethic. Only theories that satisfy (2), on the conception advanced here, can properly be regarded as environmental ethics, whether true, reasonable, or otherwise.

Though only a necessary condition, (1) assists us in distinguishing between (*a*) an ethic *of* the environment, and (*b*) an ethic *for the use* of the environment. Suppose we think that only the interests of human beings matter morally. Then it certainly would be possible to develop a homocentric ethic for the use of the environment. Roughly speaking, such an ethic would declare that the environment ought to be used so that the quality of human life, including possibly that of future generations, ought to be enhanced. I do not say developing such an ethic (what I shall call "a management ethic") would be simple or unimportant, but a management ethic falls short of an ethic of the environment, given the conditions stated earlier. It restricts the loci of value to the lives and interests of *human* beings, whereas an environmental ethic requires that we recognize the moral standing of nonhumans.

L. W. Sumner advances considerations that, if accepted, would lead us to an ethical theory that satisfies condition (1) and thereby takes us beyond a management ethic. Sumner argues that the lives and interests of nonhuman animals, not just those of human beings, ought to be taken into account in their own right. Recognition of this fact, he states, marks "the beginning of a genuine environmental consciousness." Other thinkers have advanced similar arguments. Despite many differences, these thinkers share the belief that only *conscious* beings can have moral standing. I refer to theories that embody this belief as *kinship theories* because they grow out of the idea that beings resembling humans in the quite fundamental way of being conscious, and thus to this extent kin to us, have moral standing. I have more to say about kinship theories below (Section IV).

Management and kinship theories are clearly distinct. Management theories direct us, for example, to preserve wildlife if this is in the interest of human beings, including (possibly) the interest of generations yet unborn. Animals in the wild are not themselves recognized as having interests or value that ought to be taken into account. Given a kinship ethic, however, wild animals, in their own right, figure in the moral arithmetic, though precisely how we are to carry out the required computations is unclear. When, for example, there is a clash between the preservation of wild animals and the economic development of the wilderness, it is unclear how conflicting interests are to be weighed. The value of survival of how many caribou, for example, equals the disvalue of how much financial loss to oil investors in Northern Canada?

Whatever difficulties may exist for management or kinship theories in weighing conflicting claims, however, these difficulties seem to be compounded if we move beyond these theories to ones that meet condition (2), for then we are required, it appears, to deal with the possibility that human and animal interests might come into conflict with the survival or flourishing of nonconscious beings, and it is extremely doubtful whether such conflicts can *in principle* admit of rational adjudication.

I do not wish to minimize the difficulties that attend the development of an environmental ethic that is consequentialist in nature (e.g., some form of utilitarianism). There are difficulties of comparison, perhaps themselves great enough to foreclose the possibility of developing a consequentialist environmental ethic. I have more to say on this matter as we proceed. First, though, a more fundamental problem requires our attention. Is it even logically possible for a theory to meet both the conditions I have recommended for an environmental ethic? The answer clearly is no if compelling reasons can be given for limiting moral standing *only* to conscious beings. In the following section I reject three arguments that attempt to establish this restriction.

III. Arguments against the Possibility of an Environmental Ethic

The first argument to be considered I call the "interest argument":

The Interest Argument

1. The only beings that can have moral standing are those beings that can have interests.
2. The only beings that can have interests

are those that have the capacity for consciousness.
3. Therefore, the only beings that can have moral standing are beings having the capacity for consciousness.

Now, this argument, as I have argued elsewhere against a similar argument, has apparent plausibility because it exploits an ambiguity in the concept of something having interests. To speak of A's interests in x might mean either (a) that A is interested in (wants, desires, hopes for, cares about, etc.) x, or (b) that x is in A's interest (that x will contribute to A's good, or well-being, or welfare). Clearly *if* the only beings that can have moral standing are those that can be interested in things (have desires, wants, etc.), then only conscious beings can have moral standing. The idea of nonconscious beings having desires, or wants, at least in any literal sense, seems plainly unintelligible. If, however, we mean beings that can be benefited or harmed by what is given or denied them, then it is an open question whether the class of beings which can have moral standing is coextensive with the class of beings having the capacity for consciousness. Perhaps other beings can have a good or value that can be advanced or retarded depending on what is done to them. The interest argument provides us with no resolution of this question, and so fails to demonstrate the impossibility of an environmental ethic.

A second argument, which I shall call the "sentience argument," closely resembles the interest argument and is vulnerable to the same type of objection:

The Sentience Argument

1. The only beings that can have moral standing are those that are sentient.
2. The only beings that are sentient are those that have the capacity for consciousness.

3. Therefore, the only beings that can have moral standing are those that have the capacity for consciousness.

I limit my critical remarks to step (1). How might it be supported? First, one might argue that only sentient beings have interests; that is, one might seek to support the sentience argument by invoking the interest argument, but since we have shown this latter argument is incomplete, at best, this defense of the sentience argument must bear the same diagnosis. A second defense consists in claiming that it is "meaningless" to think that nonconscious beings possibly have moral standing. This is unconvincing. *If* it is meaningless, there ought to be some way of illuminating why this is so, and this illumination is not provided by the mere charge of meaninglessness itself. Such a defense has more the aura of rhetoric than of philosophy.

A third defense consists in arguing that the only beings having moral standing are those having value in their own right, *and* that only sentient beings have value of this kind. This defense, as I argue in a moment, is a token of the argument type I call the "goodness argument." Its major liability is that by itself it provides no justification for its two central claims — namely, (*a*) that only beings that can have value in their own right can have moral standing, and (*b*) that only sentient beings have value in their own right. For reasons to which I come below, I believe (*b*) is false while (*a*) is true. Meanwhile, neither is self-evident and so each stands in need of rational defense, something not provided by the sentience argument itself.

The final argument to be considered is the goodness argument:

The Goodness Argument

1. The only beings that can have moral standing are those that can have a good of their own.

2. The only beings that can have a good of their own are those capable of consciousness.
3. Therefore, the only beings that can have moral standing are those capable of consciousness.

Premise (1) of the goodness argument seems to identify a fundamental presupposition of an environmental ethic. The importance of this premise is brought out when we ask for the grounds on which we might rest the obligation to preserve any existing x. Fundamentally, two types of answer are possible. First, preserving x is necessary to bring about future good or prevent future evil for beings other than x; on this account x's existence has instrumental value. Second, the obligation we have might be to x itself, independently of x's instrumental value, because x has a good or value in its own right. Given our conditions for an environmental ethic, not all of the values recognized in nonconscious nature can be instrumental. Only if we agree with premise (1) of the goodness argument, therefore, can we have a necessary presupposition of an environmental ethic. How inherent goodness or value can be intelligibly ascribed to nonconscious beings is a difficult question, one we shall return to later (Section V). At present, we must consider the remainder of the goodness argument, since if sound, it rules out the logical possibility of nonconscious beings having a good or value of their own.

"The only beings that have a good of their own," premise (2) states, "are those capable of consciousness." What arguments can be given to support this view? I have examined suggested answers elsewhere at length. What these arguments come to in the end, if I am right, is the thesis that consciousness is a logically necessary condition of having only *a certain kind* of good of one's own, happiness. Thus, though we may speak metaphorically of a "happy azalea" or a "contented broccoli," the only sorts of beings that literally can have happiness are conscious beings. There is no disputing this. What is disputable is the tacit assumption that this is the *only* kind of good or value a given *x* can have in its own right. Unless or until a compelling supporting argument is supplied, for limiting inherent goodness to happiness, the goodness argument falls short of limiting moral standing to just those beings capable of consciousness.

Four truths result if the argument of this section is sound. First, an environmental ethic must recognize that the class of beings having moral standing is larger than the class of conscious beings. Second, the basis on which an environmental ethic must pin this enlargement is the idea that nonconscious beings can have a good or value in their own right. Third, though it remains to be ascertained what this goodness or value is, it is not happiness; and fourth, efforts to show that nonconscious beings cannot have moral standing fail to show this. The conclusion we guardedly reach, then, is that the impossibility of an environmental ethic has not been shown.

IV. Arguments against the Necessity of an Environmental Ethic

We turn now to a second series of objections against an environmental ethic, all of which concede that it is *possible* that nonconscious beings may have value in themselves, and thus that it is *possible* to develop an environmental ethic, but which all deny, nonetheless, that there are good enough reasons for holding that nonconscious beings *do* have a good or value in their own right. There are, these objections hold in common, alternative ways of accounting for the moral dimensions of our relationship to the environment which

are rationally preferable to postulating inherent value in it. Thus, while granting the possibility of an environmental ethic, the four views about to be considered deny its necessity.

The Corruption of Character Argument

Advocates of this argument insist that it is wrong to treat nonconscious nature in certain ways — for example, unchecked strip mining — but account for this by urging that people who engage in such activities tend to become similarly ruthless in their dealings with people. Just as Kant speculated that those who act cruelly to animals develop the habit of cruelty, and so are likely to be cruel to their fellow man, so similarly those who indiscriminately destroy the natural environment will develop destructive habits that will in time wreak havoc on their neighbor. Our duties to act toward the environment in certain ways are thus explained without our having to postulate value *in* the environment.

This argument cannot be any stronger than its central empirical thesis that those who treat the environment in certain ways will be inclined to treat their fellow humans in analogous ways. I do not believe there is any hard empirical evidence at hand which supports this hypothesis. Comparing the crime rates of strip miners and accountants would probably provide much hard empirical data against it. Indeed, one cannot help wondering if the very reverse habits might not be fostered by instructing persons to do anything they want to the environment, if no person is harmed, while insisting on strict prohibitions in our dealings with persons. There would appear to be just as much (or just as little) empirical data to support this hypothesis as there is to support the hypothesis central to the corruption of character argument. On empirical grounds, the argument lacks credibility.

The Utilitarian Argument

To speak of *the* utilitarian argument is misleading. A wide variety of utilitarian arguments is possible, even including positions that hold that some nonconscious beings do have value in their own right. I restrict my attention to forms of utilitarianism that deny this, focusing mainly on hedonistic utilitarianism.

Abstractly and roughly, hedonistic utilitarianism holds that an action is right if no alternative action produces a better balance of pleasure over pain for all those affected. A theory of this type is "on the way to becoming" an environmental ethic if, as utilitarians since Bentham have argued, animals are sentient, and thus, given the utilitarian criteria, have moral standing. But hedonistic utilitarianism fails to satisfy the second condition of an environmental ethic and thus fails to qualify as an ethic of the environment. Its shortcomings are highlighted by asking, "Why not plastic trees? Why not lawns of astro-turf, or mountains of papier-mâché suitably coated with vinyl to withstand harsh weather?" Stories find their way almost daily into the popular press which illustrate that a plastic environment is increasingly within the reach of modern technology. If, as Martin Krieger argues, "the demand for rare environments is a learned one," then "conscious public choice can manipulate this learning so that the environments which people learn to use and want reflect environments which are likely to be available at low cost." Thus, as Mark Sagoff sees it, "This is the reason that the redwoods are (given Krieger's position) replaceable by plastic trees." "The advertising that created rare environments," Krieger writes, "can create plentiful (e.g., plastic) substitutes."

A hedonistic utilitarianism cannot quarrel over the *source* of environmentally based pleasures, whether they arise from real stands of redwoods or plastic replicas. Provided only that the pleasures are equal in the relevant respects (e.g., of equal duration and intensity), both are of equal value. To the suggestion that pleasures rooted in real redwoods are "higher" or "nobler" than those rooted in plastic ones, the reply must be that there is a long, untold story surrounding the idea of "higher" and "lower" pleasures, that no hedonistic utilitarian has yet succeeded in telling this story, and, indeed, that it may be inconsistent for a hedonistic utilitarian to believe this. Other things being equal, if a plastic environment can give rise to pleasures equal in value to those arising out of a natural environment, we will have just as much or as little reason to preserve the latter as to manufacture the former. Moreover, if the pleasures flowing from the manufactured environment should happen to outweigh those accompanying the natural environment, we would then have greater reason to enlarge the world of plastic trees and reduce that of living ones.

The Embodiment of Cultural Values Argument

According to this argument, the natural environment, or certain parts of it, symbolize or express certain of our culture's values. In Sagoff's words, "Our rivers, forests, and wildlife . . . serve our society as paradigms of concepts we cherish," for example, freedom, integrity, power. "A wild area may be powerful, majestic, free; an animal may express courage, innocence, purpose, and strength. As a nation we value these qualities: the obligation toward nature is an obligation toward them." Thus, we are to preserve the environment because in doing so we preserve these natural expressions of the values of our culture.

This argument is not intended to be utilitarian. The claim is not made that the consequences of natural preservation will be better, all considered, if we preserve wilderness areas, for example, than if we allow their development for commercial purposes. Whether we ought to preserve wilderness is not to be settled by cost–benefit analysis. Rather, since our obligation is to the cultural values themselves embodied in nature, our obligation to preserve the natural environment cannot be overridden by or, for that matter, based upon calculations about the comparative value of the consequences of respecting them. The propriety of respect for cultural values is not a consequence of its being useful to respect them. . . .

What the embodiment argument has in common with the other arguments considered here is the view that environmental objects have no value in their own right. This view is perhaps not so clear in this case because the embodiment argument carries with it "objectivist" presuppositions. Advocates of this argument do hold that the environment itself has certain objective qualities — for example, majesty, power, freedom. These *qualities* are *in* nature no less than are, say, chromosomes. But the *value* these qualities have is no less than are, say, chromosomes. But the *value* these qualities have is not something else that is *in them* independently of the dominant interest of a given culture ("our cultural heritage"). On the contrary, what qualities in nature are valuable is a consequence of what qualities are essential in one's cultural heritage. For example, if freedom is a dominant cultural

value, then, since animals or rivers in the wild embody this quality, they have value and ought to be preserved. What *qualities* a natural object expresses is an objective question, but the *value* a natural object has is not something it has objectively in its own right, but only as it happens to embody those qualities valued by one's culture.

The embodiment argument provides an enormously important and potentially powerful basis for a political-legal argument on behalf of the preservation of American wilderness. It is easy to see how one may use it to argue for "what is best" in American society: freedom, integrity, independence, loyalty, and so on. It is the speculative developer rather than the conservationist who seems to be running roughshod over our nation's values. On this view, Disneyland, not Yosemite, seems un-American. Moreover, by insisting that such values as freedom and integrity cannot be trumped even if the consequences of doing so are utilitarian, advocates of the embodiment argument strike a blow that helps to counter the developer's argument that the commercial development of the wilderness will bring about better consequences, more pleasure to more people, than leaving it undeveloped. The embodiment argument replies that, though this may be true, it just so happens to be irrelevant. Given the nature of values such as freedom, integrity, and the like, it is inappropriate to destroy their expression in nature in the name of utilitarian consequences. The rhetorical force of such arguments can be great, and can be a powerful practical weapon in the war for the preservation of nature.

But the embodiment argument does not have comparable philosophical strength. Two problems in particular haunt it. First, how are we to establish what our culture's values are? Sagoff states that we are to do this by consulting our artistic (cultural) history. If we do this, however, we do not hear a chorus singing the same tune; on the contrary, there is much dissonance, some of which Sagoff himself mentions (e.g., the view of wilderness as an adversary to be tamed versus the view that it is to be cherished). Moreover, even if we were to arrive at a cultural consensus, the basis that Sagoff recommends is suspiciously elitist, reminding one of Ross's reference to "the judgment of the best people" in the determination of what is valuable. Implicit in Sagoff's way of establishing what our cultural values are is an evaluative estimate of whose judgment to trust. The cards are stacked against the developer from the outset, since developers normally do not have the time or inclination to dabble in arts, history, and letters. It is not surprising, therefore, that developers take a back seat to the values of freedom and integrity. The argument is indeed potentially a powerful political weapon, but fundamental questions go begging.

A second problem is no less severe. Cultural values can be relative, both between different cultures and within the same culture at different times. Thus, even were we to concede that *our* cultural values up to now call for the preservation of nature, that would entail nothing whatever about what environmental policies ought to be pushed in *other* countries (e.g., in Kenya or India, where many species of wild animals are endangered). Nor would it guarantee even in our own country that future environmental policy should continue to be protectionist. If plastic trees are possible, our culture might evolve to prefer them over real ones, in which case the embodiment of cultural values argument would sanction replacing natural with plastic flora and fauna.

Sagoff recognizes the possibility of significant changes in a culture's dominant values. He observes that we might "change the nature of our cultural heritage" and then goes on to imagine what a changed cultural heritage might be like — for example, imagining a four-lane highway painted through *Christina's World*. But I do not believe he realizes the full significance of the issues at hand. If, as he supposes, hedonistic utilitarianism falls victim to a *reductio* by allowing that a plastic environment might be just as good or better than a living one, consistency requires that we reach the same judgment *re* the embodiment of cultural values argument. That argument, too, allows that a plastic environment might be just as good or better than a natural one, *if* the dominant values of our culture were to become plasticized.

I conclude this section, therefore, not by claiming to have shown that nonconscious natural objects do have a good or value of their own, independent of human interests. I only conclude that the principal arguments that might be advanced for thinking that we can reasonably account for our duties regarding the environment short of postulating such value in nature fail to do so. Thus, neither the possibility of, nor the need for, postulating that nonconscious natural objects have a value that is independent of human interests, has been rationally undermined.

V. Inherent Goodness?

In this final section, I offer some tentative remarks about the nature of inherent goodness, emphasizing their tentativeness and incompleteness. I comment first on five different but related ideas.

1.   *The presence of inherent value in a natural object is independent of any awareness, interest,*

or appreciation of it by any conscious being.

This does not tell us what objects are inherently good or why, only that *if* an object is inherently good its value must *inhere in (be in)* the object itself. Inherent value is not conferred upon objects in the manner of an honorary degree. Like other properties in nature, it must be discovered. . . . There is value *in* the world, if natural objects are inherently valuable.

2. *The presence of inherent value in a natural object is a consequence of its possessing those other properties that it happens to possess.*

This follows from (1), given the further assumption that inherent goodness is a consequential or supervenient property. By insisting that inherent goodness depends on an object's *own* properties, the point made in (1), that inherent goodness is a value possessed by the object independently of any awareness, is reemphasized. *Its* goodness depends on *its* properties.

3. *The inherent value of a natural object is an objective property of that object.*

This differs from but is related to Sagoff's objectivity of the freedom and majesty of natural objects. Certain stretches of the Colorado River, for example, are free, not subjectively, but objectively. The freedom expressed by (or in) the river is an objective fact. But this goes beyond Sagoff's position by insisting that *the value of the river's being free* also is an objective property of the river. If the river is inherently good, in the sense explained in (1), then it is a *fact about the river* that it is good inherently.

4. *The inherent value of a natural object is such that toward it the fitting attitude is one of admiring respect.*

This brings out the appropriateness of regarding what is inherently valuable in a certain way and thus provides a way of connecting what is inherently valuable in the environment with an ideal of human nature. In part, the ideal in question bids us be appreciative of the values nature holds, not merely as a resource to be used in the name of human interests, but inherently. The ideal bids us, further, to regard what is inherently valuable with both admiration and respect. Admiration is fitting because not everything in nature is inherently valuable (what *is* is to be admired both because of its value *and* because of its comparative uniqueness). Respect is appropriate because this is a fitting attitude to have toward whatever has value in its own right. One must realize that its being valuable is not contingent on one's happening to value it, so that to treat it *merely* as a means to human ends is to mistreat it. Such treatment shows a lack of respect for its being something that has value independently of these ends. Thus, I fall short of the ideal if I gratuitously destroy what has inherent value, or even if I regard it merely as having value only relative to human desires. But half the story about ideals of human nature remains untold if we leave out the part about the value inherent in those things toward which we can act in the ideal way. So it is vital to insist that our having ideals is neither to deny nor diminish the further point that this ideal requires postulating inherent value in nature, independently of these ideals.

5. *The admiring respect of what is inherently valuable in nature gives rise to the preservation principle.*

By the "preservation principle" I mean a principle of nondestruction, noninterference, and, generally, nonmeddling. By characterizing this in terms of a principle, moreover, I am emphasizing that preservation (letting be) be regarded as a moral imperative. Thus, if I regard wild stretches of the Colorado River as inherently valuable and regard these sections with admiring respect, I also think it is wrong to destroy these sections of the river; I think one ought not to meddle in the river's affairs, as it were.

A difficult question to answer is whether

the preservation principle gives us a principle of absolute or of prima facie duty. It is unclear how it can be absolute, for it appears conceivable that in some cases letting be what is at present inherently good in nature may lead to value diminution or loss in the future. For example, because of various sedimentary changes, a river that is now wild and free might in time be transformed into a small, muddy creek; thus, it might be necessary to override the preservation principle to preserve or increase what is inherently valuable in nature. Even if the preservation principle is regarded as being only prima facie, however, it is still possible to agree on at least one point with those who regard it as absolute, that is, the common rejection of the "human interests principle," which says:

> Whenever human beings can benefit more from overriding the preservation principle than if they observe it, the preservation principle ought to be overridden.

This principle *must* be rejected by anyone who accepts the preservation principle because it distorts the very conception of goodness underlying that principle. If the sort of value natural objects possess is inherent, then one fails to show a proper respect for these objects if one is willing to destroy them merely on the grounds that this would benefit human beings. Since such destruction is precisely what the human interests principle commits one to, one cannot *both* accept the preservation principle, absolute or prima facie, *and* also accept the human interests principle. The common enemies of all preservationists are those who accept the human interests principle.

This brief discussion of the preservation principle may also cast some light on the problem of making intelligible cross-species value comparisons, for example, in the case of the survival of caribou versus the economic development of wilderness. The point preservationists must keep in mind is that to ask how many caribou lives equal in value the disvalue of how much economic loss is unanswerable because it is an improper question. It confounds two incommensurable kinds of good, the inherent good of the caribou with the noninherent good of economic benefits. Indeed, because these kinds of good are incommensurable, a utilitarian or consequentialist environmental ethic, which endeavors to accommodate both kinds of goodness, is doomed to fail. The inherent value of the caribou cannot be cashed in terms of human economic benefit, and such a theory ends up providing us with no clear moral direction. For the preservationist, the proper philosophical response to those who would uproot the environment in the name of human benefit is to say that they fail to understand the very notion of something being inherently good.

Two questions that I have not endeavored to answer are: (*a*) what, if anything in general, makes something inherently good, and (*b*) how can we know, if we can, what things are inherently good? The two questions are not unrelated. If we could establish that there is something (*x*) such that, whenever any object (*y*) has *x* it is inherently good, we could then go on to try to establish how we can know that any object has *x*. Unfortunately, I now have very little to say about these questions, and what little I do have to say concerns only how not to answer them.

Two possible answers to question (*a*) merit mention. The first is that an object (*x*) is inherently good if it is good of its kind. This is a view I have assumed and argued for elsewhere, but it now appears to me to be completely muddled. The concept of inherent goodness cannot be reduced to the notion of something being good of its kind, for though I believe that we can conceive of the goodness any *x* has, if *x* is good of its kind, as a value it has in its own right, there is no reason to believe that we ought to have the attitude of admiring respect toward what is (merely) good of its kind. A good murderer is good-of-his-kind, but is not thereby a proper object of admiring respect, and similarly in the case of natural objects. The type of inherent goodness required by an environmental ethic is conceptually distinct from being good of its kind.

The second possible answer to (*a*) is that life makes something inherently good. To what extent this view is connected with Schweitzer's famous ethic of reverence for life, or with Kenneth Goodpaster's recent argument for considering life as a necessary and sufficient condition of something being "morally considerable," I do not know, and I cannot here explore these matters in detail. But limiting the class of beings that have inherent value to the class of living beings seems to be an arbitrary decision and one that does not serve well as a basis for an environmental ethic. That it appears arbitrary is perhaps best seen by considering the case of beauty, since in nature, as in art, it is not essential to the beauty of an object to insist that something living be involved.

As for question (*b*), I have even less to say and that is negative also. My one point is that we cannot find out what is inherently good merely by finding out what those things are toward which we have admiring respect. All that this tells us is facts about the people who have this attitude. It does not tell us whether it is the fitting attitude to have. To put the point differently, we can be as mistaken in our judgment that something is inherently good as we can be in our judgment about how old or how heavy it is. Our feeling one way or another does not settle matters one way or the other.

How, then, are we to settle these matters? I wish I knew. I am not even certain that they can be settled in a rationally coherent way, and hence the tentativeness of my closing remarks. But more fundamentally, there is the earlier question about the very possibility of an environmental ethic. If I am right, the development of what can properly be called an environmental ethic requires that we postulate inherent value in nature. I have tried to say something about this variety of goodness as well as something about its role in an ethic of the environment. If my remarks have been intelligible and my arguments persuasive, then, though the project is far from complete, we at least know the direction in which we must move to make headway in environmental ethics. And that is no small advantage.

PETER SINGER

Not for Humans Only
The Place of Nonhumans in Environmental Issues

PETER SINGER *teaches philosophy and directs the Center for Human Bioethics at Monash University in Australia. His best-known work is* Animal Liberation *(1975). He has written widely on civil disobedience and medical ethics.*

WHEN we humans change the environment in which we live, we often harm ourselves. If we discharge cadmium into a bay and eat shellfish from that bay, we become ill and may die. When our industries and automobiles pour noxious fumes into the atmosphere, we find a displeasing smell in the air, the long-term results of which may be every bit as deadly as cadmium poisoning. The harm that humans do the environment, however, does not rebound solely, even chiefly, on humans. It is nonhumans who bear the most direct burden of human interference with nature.

By "nonhumans" I mean to refer to all living things other than human beings, though for reasons to be given later, it is with nonhuman animals, rather than plants, that I am chiefly concerned. It is also important, in the context of environmental issues, to note that living things may be regarded either collectively or as individuals. In debates about the environment the most important way of regarding living things collectively has been to regard them as species. Thus, when environmentalists worry about the future of the blue whale, they usually are thinking of the blue whale as a species, rather than of individual blue whales. But this is not, of course, the only way in which one can think of blue whales, or other animals,

and one of the topics I shall discuss is whether we should be concerned about what we are doing to the environment primarily in so far as it threatens entire species of nonhumans, or primarily insofar as it affects individual nonhuman animals.

The general question, then, is how the effects of our actions on the environment of nonhuman beings should figure in our deliberations about what we ought to do. There is an unlimited variety of contexts in which this issue could arise. To take just one: Suppose that it is considered necessary to build a new power station, and there are two sites, A and B, under consideration. In most respects the sites are equally suitable, but building the power station on site A would be more expensive because the greater depth of shifting soil at that site will require deeper foundations; on the other hand to build on site B will destroy a favored breeding ground for thousands of wildfowl. Should the presence of the wildfowl enter into the decision as to where to build? And if so, in what manner should it enter, and how heavily should it weigh?

In a case like this the effects of our actions on nonhuman animals could be taken into account in two quite different ways: directly, giving the lives and welfare of nonhuman animals an intrinsic significance which must count in any moral calculation; or indirectly, so that the effects of our actions on nonhumans are morally significant only if they have consequences for humans.

It is the latter view which has been predominant in the Western tradition. Aristotle was among the founders of this tradition. He regarded nature as a hierarchy, in which the function of the less rational and hence less perfect beings was to serve the more rational and more perfect. So, he wrote:

> Plants exist for the sake of animals, and brute beasts for the sake of man — domestic animals for his use and food, wild ones (or at any rate most of them) for food and other accessories of life, such as clothing and various tools.
>
> Since nature makes nothing purposeless or in vain, it is undeniably true that she has made all animals for the sake of man.

If one major strain of Western thought came from Greece, the other dominant influence was that of Christianity. The early Christian writers were no more ready than Aristotle to give moral weight to the lives of non-human animals. When St. Paul, in interpreting the old Mosaic law against putting a muzzle on the ox that treads out the corn, asked: "Doth God care for oxen?" it is clear that he was asking a rhetorical question, to which the answer was "No"; the law must have somehow been meant "altogether for our sakes." Augustine agreed, using as evidence for the view that there are no common rights between humans and lesser living things, the incidents in the Gospels when Jesus sent devils into a herd of swine, causing them to hurl themselves into the sea, and with a curse withered a fig tree on which he had found no fruit.

It was Thomas Aquinas, blending Aristotle and the Christian writings, who put most clearly the view that any consideration of the lives or welfare of animals must be because of the indirect consequences of such consideration for humans. Echoing Aristotle, he maintained that plants exist for the sake of animals, and animals for the sake of man. Sins can only be against God, one's human neighbors, or against oneself. Even charity does not extend to "irrational creatures," for, among other things, they are not included in "the fellowship of everlasting happiness." We can love animals only "if we regard them as the good things that we desire for others," that is, "to God's honor and man's use." Yet if this was the correct view, as Aquinas thought, there was one problem that needed explaining: Why does the Old Testament have a few scattered injunctions against cruelty to animals, such as "The just man regardeth the life of his beast, but the bowels of the wicked are cruel?" Aquinas did not overlook such passages, but he did deny that their intention was to spare animals pain. Instead, he wrote, "it is evident that if a man practices a pitiable affection for animals, he is all the more disposed to take pity on his fellow-men." So, for Aquinas, the only sound reason for avoiding cruelty to animals was that it could lead to cruelty to humans.

The influence of Aquinas has been strong in the Roman Catholic church. Not even that oft-quoted exception to the standard Christian view of nature, Francis of Assisi, really broke away from the orthodox theology of his co-religionists. Despite his legendary kindness to animals, Francis could still write: "every creature proclaims: 'God made me for your sake, O man!'" As late as the nineteenth century, Pope Pius IX gave evidence of the continuing hold of the views of Paul, Augustine, and Aquinas by refusing to allow a society for the prevention of cruelty to animals to be established in Rome because to do so would imply that humans have duties toward animals.

It is not, however, only among Roman Catholics that a view like that of Aquinas has found adherents. Calvin, for instance, had no doubt that all of nature was created specifically for its usefulness to man; and in the late eighteenth century, Immanuel Kant, in lecturing on ethics, considered the question of our duties to animals, and told his students: "So far as animals are concerned, we have no direct duties. Animals are not self-conscious and are there merely as a means to an end. That end is man." And Kant then repeated the line that cruelty to animals is to be avoided because it leads to cruelty to humans.

The view that the effects of our actions on other animals has no direct moral significance is not as likely to be openly advocated today as it was in the past; yet it is likely to be accepted implicitly and acted upon. When planners perform cost-benefit studies on new projects, the costs and benefits are costs and benefits for human beings only. This does not mean that the impact of the power station or highway on wildlife is ignored altogether, but it is included only indirectly. That a new reservoir would drown a valley teeming with wildlife is taken into account only under some such heading as the value of the facilities for recreation that the valley affords. In calculating this value, the cost-benefit study will be neutral between forms of recreation like hunting and shooting and those like bird watching and bush walking — in fact hunting and shooting are likely to contribute more to the benefit side of the calculations because larger sums of money are spent on them, and they therefore benefit manufacturers and retailers of firearms as well as the hunters and shooters themselves. The suffering experienced by the animals whose habitat is flooded is not reckoned into the costs of the operation; nor is the recreational value obtained by the hunters and shooters offset by the cost to the animals that their recreation involves.

Despite its venerable origins, the view that the effects of our actions on nonhuman animals have no intrinsic moral significance can be shown to be arbitrary and morally indefensible. If a being suffers, the fact that it is not a member of our own species cannot be a moral reason for failing to take its suffering into account. This becomes obvious if we consider the analogous attempt by white slaveowners to deny consideration to the interests of blacks. These white racists limited their moral concern to their own race, so the suffering of a black did not have the same moral significance as the suffering of a white. We now recognize that in doing so they were making an arbitrary distinction, and that the existence of suffering, rather than the race of the sufferer, is what is really morally significant. The point remains true if "species" is substituted for "race." The logic of racism and the logic of the position we have been discussing, which I have elsewhere referred to as "speciesism," are indistinguishable; and if we reject the former then consistency demands that we reject the latter too.

It should be clearly understood that the rejection of speciesism does not imply that the different species are in fact equal in respect of such characteristics as intelligence, physical strength, ability to communicate, capacity to suffer, ability to damage the environment, or anything else. After all, the moral principle of human equality cannot be taken as implying that all humans are equal in these respects either — if it did, we would have to give up the idea of human equality. That one being is more intelligent than another does not entitle him to enslave, exploit, or disregard the interests of the less intelligent being. The moral basis of equality among humans is not equality in fact, but the principle of equal consideration of interests, and it is this principle that, in consistency, must be extended to any nonhumans who have interests.

There may be some doubt about whether any nonhuman beings have interests. This doubt may arise because of uncertainty about what it is to have an interest, or because of uncertainty about the nature of some nonhuman beings. So far as the concept of "interest" is the cause of doubt, I take the view that only a being with subjective experiences, such as the experience of pleasure or the experience of pain, can have interests in the full sense of the term; and that any being with such experiences does have at least one interest, namely, the interest in experiencing pleasure and avoiding pain. Thus consciousness, or the capacity for subjective experience, is both a necessary and a sufficient condition for having an interest. While there may be a loose sense of the term in which we can say that it is in the interests of a tree to be watered, this attenuated sense of the term is not the sense covered by the principle of equal consideration of interests. All we mean when we say that it is in the interests of a tree to be watered is that the tree needs water if it is to continue to live and grow normally; if we regard this as evidence that the tree has interests, we might almost as well say that it is in the interests of a car to be lubricated regularly because the car needs lubrication if it is to run properly. In neither case can we really mean (unless we impute consciousness to trees or cars) that the tree or car has any preference about the matter.

The remaining doubt about whether nonhuman beings have interests is, then, a doubt about whether nonhuman beings have subjective experiences like the experience of pain. I have argued elsewhere that the commonsense view that birds and mammals feel pain is well founded; but more serious doubts arise as we move down the evolutionary scale. Vertebrate animals have nervous systems broadly similar to our own and behave in ways that resemble our own pain behavior when subjected to stimuli that we would find painful; so the inference that vertebrates are capable of feeling pain is a reasonable one, though not as strong as it is if limited to mammals and birds. When we go beyond vertebrates to insects, crustaceans, mollusks and so on, the existence of subjective states becomes more dubious, and with very simple organisms it is difficult to believe that they could be conscious. As for plants, though there have been sensational claims that plants are not only conscious, but even psychic, there is no hard evidence that supports even the more modest claim.

The boundary of beings who may be taken as having interests is therefore not an abrupt boundary, but a broad range in which the assumption that the being has interests shifts from being so strong as to be virtually certain to being so weak as to be highly improbable. The principle of equal consideration of interests must be applied with this in mind, so that where there is a clash between a virtually certain interest and a highly doubtful one, it is the virtually certain interest that ought to prevail.

In this manner our moral concern ought to extend to all beings who have interests. Unlike race or species, this boundary does not arbitrarily exclude any being; indeed it can truly be said that it excludes nothing at all, not even "the most contemptible clod of earth" from equal consideration of interests — for full consideration of no interests still results in no weight being given to whatever was considered, just as multiplying zero by a million still results in zero.

Giving equal consideration to the interests of two different beings does not mean treating them alike or holding their lives to be of equal value. We may recognize that the interests of one being are greater than those of another, and equal consideration will then lead us to sacrifice the being with lesser interests, if one or the other must be sacrificed. For instance, if for some reason a choice has to be made between saving the life of a normal human being and that of a dog, we might well decide to save the human because he, with his greater awareness of what is going to happen, will suffer more before he dies; we may also take into account the likelihood that it is the family and friends of the human who will suffer more; and finally, it would be the human who had the greater potential for future happiness. This decision would be in accordance with the principle of equal consideration of interests, for the interests of the dog get the same consideration as those of the human, and the loss to the dog is not discounted because the dog is not a member of our species. The outcome is as it is because the balance of interests favors the human. In a different situation — say, if the human were grossly mentally defective and without family or anyone else who would grieve for it — the balance of interests might favor the nonhuman.

The more positive side of the principle of equal consideration is this: where interests are equal, they must be given equal weight. So where human and nonhuman animals share an interest — as in the case of the interest in avoiding physical pain — we must give as much weight to violations of the interest of the nonhumans as we do to similar violations of the human's interest. This does not mean, of course, that it is as bad to hit a horse with a stick as it is to hit a human being, for the same blow would cause less pain to the animal with the tougher skin. The principle holds between similar amounts of felt pain, and what this is will vary from case to case.

It may be objected that we cannot tell exactly how much pain another animal is suffering, and that therefore the principle is impossible to apply. While I do not deny the difficulty and even, so far as precise measurement is concerned, the impossibility of comparing the subjective experiences of members of different species, I do not think that the problem is different in kind from the problem of comparing the subjective experiences of two members of our own species. Yet this is something we do all the time, for instance when we judge that a wealthy person will suffer less by being taxed at a higher rate than a poor person will gain from the welfare benefits paid for by the tax; or when we decide to take our two children to the beach instead of to a fair, because although the older one would prefer the fair, the younger one has a stronger preference the other way. These comparisons may be very rough, but since there is nothing better, we must use them; it would be irrational to refuse to do so simply because they are rough. Moreover, rough as they are, there are many situations in which we can be reasonably sure which way the balance of interests lies. While a difference of species may make comparisons rougher still, the basic problem is the same, and the comparisons are still often good enough to use, in the absence of anything more precise. . . .

We can now draw at least one conclusion as to how the existence of nonhuman living things should enter into our deliberations about actions affecting the environment: Where our actions are likely to make animals suffer, that suffering must count in our deliberations, and it should count equally with a like amount of suffering by human beings, insofar as rough comparisons can be made.

The difficulty of making the required comparison will mean that the application of this conclusion is controversial in many cases, but there will be some situations in which it is clear enough. Take, for instance, the wholesale poisoning of animals that is euphemistically known as "pest control." The authorities who conduct these campaigns give no consideration to the suffering they inflict on the "pests," and invariably use the method of slaughter they believe to be cheapest and most effective. The result is that hundreds of millions of rabbits have died agonizing deaths from the artificially introduced disease, myxomatosis, or from poisons like "ten-eighty"; coyotes and other wild dogs have died painfully from cyanide poisoning; and all manner of wild animals have endured days of thirst, hunger, and fear with a mangled limb caught in a leg-hold trap. Granting, for the sake of argument, the necessity for pest control—though this has rightly been questioned—the fact remains that no serious attempts have been made to introduce alternative means of control and thereby reduce the incalculable amount of suffering caused by present methods. It would not, presumably, be beyond modern science to produce a substance which, when eaten by rabbits or coyotes, produced sterility instead of a drawn-out death. Such methods might be more expensive, but can anyone doubt that if a similar amount of human suffering were at stake, the expense would be borne?

Another clear instance in which the principle of equal consideration of interests would indicate methods different from those presently used is in the timber industry. There are two basic methods of obtaining timber from forests. One is to cut only selected mature or dead trees, leaving the forest substantially intact. The other, known as clear-cutting, involves chopping down everything that grows in a given area, and then reseeding. Obviously when a large area is clear-cut, wild animals find their whole living area destroyed in a few days, whereas selected felling makes a relatively minor disturbance. But clear-cutting is cheaper, and timber companies therefore use this method and will continue to do so unless forced to do otherwise.

This initial conclusion about how the effects of our actions on nonhuman animals should be taken into account is the only one which follows directly from the argument that I have given against the view that only actions affecting our own species have intrinsic moral significance. There are, however, other suggestions which I shall make more tentatively which are at least consistent with the preceding argument, although much more discussion would be needed to establish them.

The first of these suggestions is that while the suffering of human and nonhuman animals should, as I have said, count equally, the killing of nonhuman animals is in itself not as significant as the killing of normal human beings. Some of the reasons for this have already been discussed—the probable greater grief of the family and friends of the human, and the human's greater potential. To this can be added the fact that other animals will not be made to fear for their own lives, as humans would, by the knowledge that others of their species have been killed. There is also the fact that normal humans are beings with foresight and plans for the future, and to cut these plans off in midstream seems a greater wrong than that which is done in killing a being without the capacity for reflection on the future.

All these reasons will seem to some not to touch the heart of the matter, which is the killing itself and not the circumstances surrounding it; and it is for this reason that I have put forward this view as a suggestion rather than a firm conclusion. For it might be held that the taking of life is intrinsically wrong — and equally wrong whatever the characteristics of the life that was taken. This, perhaps, was the view that Schweitzer held and which has become famous under his memorable if less than crystal-clear phrase, "reverence for life." If this view could be supported, then of course we would have to hold that the killing of nonhuman animals, however painless, is as serious as the killing of humans. Yet I find Schweitzer's position difficult to justify. What is it that is so valuable in the life of, say, a fly, which presumably does not itself have any awareness of the value of its own life, and the death of which will not be a source of regret to any member of its own species or of any other species? . . .

For Schweitzer, life itself is sacred, not even consciousness being necessary. So the truly ethical man, he says, will not tear a leaf from a tree or break off a flower unnecessarily. Not surprisingly, given the breadth of its coverage, it is impossible for the ethic of reverence for life to be absolute in its prohibitions. We must take plant life, at least, if we are to eat and live. Schweitzer therefore accepts the taking of one form of life to preserve another form of life. Indeed, Schweitzer's whole life as a doctor in Africa makes no sense except on the assumption that the lives of the human beings he was saving are more valuable than the lives of the germs and parasites he was destroying in their bodies, not to mention the plants and probably animals that those humans would kill and eat after Schweitzer had cured them. So I suggest that the idea that all life has equal value, or is equally sacred, lacks a plausible theoretical basis and was not, in practice, adhered to even by the man whose name is most often linked with it. . . .

To this point we have been discussing the place of individual nonhuman animals in environmental issues, and we have seen that an impartial consideration of their interests provides sufficient reason to show that present human attitudes and practices involving environmental issues are morally unjustifiable. Although this conclusion is, I think, obvious enough to anyone who thinks about the issue along the lines just discussed, there is one aspect of it that is in sharp contrast to an underlying assumption of much environmental debate, an assumption accepted even by many who consider themselves for animals and against the arrogant "human chauvinism" that sees all of nature as a resource to be harvested or a pit for the disposal of wastes. This assumption is that concern for nonhuman animals is appropriate when a whole species is endangered, but not when the threat is only to individual animals. It is in accordance with this assumption that the National Wildlife Federation has sought and obtained a court injunction preventing the U.S. Department of Transportation from building an interstate highway interchange in an area frequented by the extremely rare Mississippi sandhill crane, while the same organization openly supports what it calls "the hunter-sportsman who, during legal hunting seasons, crops surplus wildlife." Similarly the National Audubon Society has fought to preserve rare birds and other animals but opposed moves to stop the annual slaughter of 40,000 seals on the Pribilof Islands of Alaska on the grounds that this "harvest" could be sustained indefinitely, and the protests were thus "without foundation from a conservation and biological viewpoint." Other "environmentalist" organizations which either actively support or refuse to oppose hunting include the Sierra Club, the Wilderness Society, and the World Wildlife Fund.

Since we have already seen that animals' interests in avoiding suffering are to be given equal weight to our own, and since it is sufficiently obvious that hunting makes animals suffer—for one thing, no hunter kills instantly every time—I shall not discuss the ethics of hunting, though I cannot resist inviting the reader to think about the assumptions behind the use of such images as the "cropping" of "surplus wildlife" or the "harvesting" of seals. The remaining ethical issue that needs to be discussed is whether it is still worse to hunt or otherwise to kill animals of endangered species than it is to kill those of species that are plentiful. In other words, suppose that groups like the National Wildlife Federation were to see the error of their prohunting views, and swing round to opposition to hunting. Would they nevertheless be justified in putting greater efforts into stopping the shooting of the Mississippi sandhill crane than into stopping duck-shooting? If so, why?

Some reasons for an affirmative answer are not hard to find. For instance, if we allow species to become extinct, we shall deprive ourselves and our descendants of the pleasures of observing all of the variety of species that we can observe today. Anyone who has ever regretted not being able to see a great auk must have some sympathy with this view. Then again, we never know what ecological role a given species plays, or may play under some unpredictable change of circumstances. Books on ecology are full of stories about how farmers/the health department/the army/the Forestry Commission decided to get rid of a particular rodent/ bird/fish/insect because it was a bit of a nuisance, only to find that that particular animal was the chief restraint on the rate of increase of some much nastier and less easily eradicated pest. Even if a species has already been reduced to the point where its total extinction could not have much "environmental impact" in the sense of triggering off other changes, it is always possible that in the future conditions will change, the species will prove better adapted to the new conditions than its rivals, and will flourish, playing an important part in the new ecological balance in its area to the advantage of humans living there. Yet another reason for seeking to preserve species is that, as is often said, the removal of a species depletes the "gene pool" and thus reduces the possibility of "improving" existing domestic or otherwise useful animals by crossbreeding with related wild animals. We do not know what qualities we may want domestic animals to have in the future. It may be that existing breeds lack resistance to a build-up of toxic chemicals or to a new disease that may break out in some remote place and sweep across our planet; but by interbreeding domestic animals with rare wild varieties, we might be able to confer greater resistance on the former, or greater usefulness to humans on the latter.

These reasons for preserving animals of endangered species have something in common: They are all concerned with benefits or dangers for humans. To regard these as the only reasons for preserving species is to take a position similar to that of Aquinas and Kant, who, as we saw earlier, thought cruelty to animals wrong only because it might indirectly harm human beings. We dismissed that argument on the grounds that if human suffering is intrinsically bad, then it is arbitrary to maintain that animal suffering is of no intrinsic significance. Can we similarly dismiss the view that species should be preserved only because of the benefits of preservation to humans? It might seem that we should, but it is not easy to justify doing so. While individual animals have interests, and no morally defensible line can be drawn between human interests and the interests of nonhuman animals, species as such are not conscious entities and so do not have interests above and beyond the interests of the individual animals that are members of the species. These individual interests are certainly potent reasons against killing rare animals, but they are no more potent in the case of rare animals than in the case of common animals. The rarity of the blue whale does not cause it to suffer any more (nor any less) when harpooned than the more common sperm whale. On what basis, then, other than the indirect benefits to humans, can we justifiably give preference to the preserving of animals of endangered species rather than animals of species that are not in any danger?

One obvious answer, on the basis of the foregoing, is that we ought to give preference to preserving animals of endangered species if so doing will have indirect benefits for nonhuman animals. This may sometimes be the case, for if the extinction of a species can lead to far-reaching ecological damage, this is likely to be bad for nonhuman animals as well as for humans. Yet this answer to our question, while extending the grounds for preserving species beyond the narrow limits of human benefits, still provides no basis for attributing intrinsic value to preservation. To find such a basis we need an answer to the following modified version of the question asked above: On what basis, other than the indirect benefits to humans or other animals, can we justifiably give preference to the preserving of animals of endangered species rather than animals of species that are not in danger?

To this question I can find no satisfactory answer. The most promising suggestion, perhaps, is that the destruction of a whole species is the destruction of something akin to a great work of art; that the tiger, or any other of the "immensely complex and inimitable items produced in nature" has its own, noninstrumental value, just as a great painting or cathedral has value apart from the pleasure and inspiration it brings to human beings. On this view, to exterminate a species is to commit an act of vandalism, like setting about Michelangelo's *Pietà* with a hammer; while allowing an endangered species to die out without taking steps to save it is like allowing Angkor Wat to fall into ruins and be obliterated by the jungle.

My difficult with this argument is a difficulty with the allegedly less controversial case on which the analogy is built. If the analogy is to succeed in persuading us that there may be intrinsic value quite independently of any benefits for sentient beings in the existence of a species, we must believe that there is this kind of intrinsic value in the existence of works of art; but how can it be shown that the *Pietà* has value independently of the appreciation of those who have seen or will see it? If, as philosophers are fond of asking, I were the last sentient being on earth, would it matter if, in a moment of boredom, I entertained myself by making a bonfire of all the paintings in the Louvre? My own view is that it would not matter — provided, of course, I really could exclude the possibility that, as I stood around the dying embers, a flying saucer would not land and disgorge a load of tourists from Alpha Centauri who had come all the way solely in order to see the Mona Lisa. But there are those who take the opposite view, and I would agree that *if* works of art have intrinsic value, then it is plausible to suppose that species have too.

I conclude, then, that unless or until better grounds are advanced, the only reasons for being more concerned about the interests of animals from endangered species than about other animals are those which relate the preservation of species to benefits for humans and other animals. The significance of these reasons will vary from case to case, depending on such factors as just how different the endangered species really is from other nonendangered species. For instance, if it takes an expert ornithologist to tell a Mississippi sandhill crane from other, more common cranes (and I have no knowledge of whether this is so), then the argument for preservation based on the pleasures of observing a variety of species cannot carry much weight in this case, for this pleasure would be available only to a few people. Similarly, the value of retaining species that perhaps will one day be usefully crossbred with domestic species will not apply to species that have no connection with any domestic animal; and the importance we place on this reason for preserving species will also depend on the importance we place on domestic animals. If, as I have argued elsewhere, it is generally both inefficient and inhumane to raise animals for food, we are not going to be greatly moved by the thought of "improving" our livestock. Finally, although the argument that the greater the variety of species, the better the chances of a smooth adjustment to environmental changes, is usually a powerful one, it has little application to endangered species that differ only marginally and in ecologically insignificant ways — like minor differences in the markings of birds — from related, nonendangered species.

This conclusion may seem unfavorable to the efforts of environmental groups to preserve endangered species. I would not wish it to be taken in that way. Often the indirect reasons for preservation will make an overwhelming case for preservation; and in any case we must remember that what we have been discussing is not whether to defend animals against those who would kill them and deprive them of their habitat but whether to give preference to defending animals of endangered species. Defending endangered species is, after all, defending individual animals too. If we are more likely to stop the cruel form of commercial hunting known as whaling by pointing out that blue whales may become extinct than by pointing out that blue whales are sentient creatures with lives of their own to lead, then by all means let us point out that blue whales may become extinct. If, however, the commercial whalers should limit their slaughter to what they call the "maximum sustainable yield" and so cease to be a threat to blue whales as a species, let us not forget that they remain a threat to thousands of individual blue whales. My aim throughout this essay has been to increase the importance we give to individual animals when discussing environmental issues, and not to decrease the importance we presently place on defending animals which are members of endangered species.

ALDO LEOPOLD

The Land Ethic

ALDO LEOPOLD (1887–1948) *was a pioneer in the field of wildlife conservation. He was a scientist and author of over 350 articles on science and wildlife management. He is best known for* A Sand County Almanac *(1948), from which this selection is taken, and for the text* Game Management, *which is still in use today. His articulation of the environmental ethic is considered by many to be the classic statement on that subject. He died of a heart attack while helping his neighbors fight a grass fire.*

WHEN god-like Odysseus returned from the wars in Troy, he hanged all on one rope a dozen slave-girls of his household whom he suspected of misbehavior during his absence.

This hanging involved no question of propriety. The girls were property. The disposal of property was then, as now, a matter of expediency, not of right and wrong.

Concepts of right and wrong were not lacking from Odysseus' Greece: witness the fidelity of his wife through the long years before at last his black-prowed galleys clove the wine-dark seas for home. The ethical structure of that day covered wives, but had not yet been extended to human chattels. During the three thousand years which have since elapsed, ethical criteria have been extended to many fields of conduct, with corresponding shrinkages in those judged by expediency only.

The Ethical Sequence

This extension of ethics, so far studied only by philosophers, is actually a process in ecological evolution. Its sequences may be described in ecological as well as in philosophical terms. An ethic, ecologically, is a limitation on freedom of action in the struggle for existence. An ethic, philosophically, is a differentiation of social from anti-social conduct. These are two definitions of one thing. The thing has its origin in the tendency of interdependent individuals or groups to evolve modes of co-operation. The ecologist calls these symbioses. Politics and economics are advanced symbioses in which the original free-for-all competition has been replaced, in part, by co-operative mechanisms with an ethical content.

The complexity of co-operative mechanisms has increased with population density, and with the efficiency of tools. It was simpler, for example, to define the anti-social uses of sticks and stones in the days of the mastodons than of bullets and billboards in the age of motors.

The first ethics dealt with the relation between individuals; the Mosaic Decalogue [the Ten Commandments] is an example. Later accretions dealt with the relation between the individual and society. The Golden Rule tries to integrate the individual to society; democracy to integrate social organization to the individual.

There is as yet no ethic dealing with man's relation to land and to the animals and plants which grow upon it. Land, like Odysseus' slave-girls, is still property. The land-relation is still strictly economic, entailing privileges but not obligations.

The extension of ethics to this third element in human environment is, if I read the evidence correctly, an evolutionary possibility and an ecological necessity. It is the third step in a sequence. The first two have already been taken. Individual thinkers since the days of Ezekel and Isaiah have asserted that the despoliation of land is not only inexpedient but wrong. Society, however, has not yet affirmed their belief. I regard the present conservation movement as the embryo of such an affirmation.

An ethic may be regarded as a mode of guidance for meeting ecological situations so new or intricate, or involving such deferred reactions, that the path of social expediency is not discernible to the average individual. Animal instincts are modes of guidance for the individual in meeting such situations. Ethics are possibly a kind of community instinct in-the-making.

The Community Concept

All ethics so far evolved rest upon a single premise: that the individual is a member of a community of interdependent parts. His instincts prompt him to compete for his place in that community, but his ethics prompt him also to cooperate (perhaps in order that there may be a place to compete for).

The land ethic simply enlarges the boundaries of the community to include soils, waters, plants, and animals, or collectively: the land.

This sounds simple: do we not already sing our love for and obligation to the land of the free and the home of the brave? Yes, but just what and whom do we love? Certainly not the soil, which we are sending helter-skelter downriver. Certainly not the waters, which we assume have no function except to turn turbines, float barges, and carry off sewage. Certainly not the plants, of which we exterminate

whole communities without batting an eye. Certainly not the animals, of which we have already extirpated many of the largest and most beautiful species. A land ethic of course cannot prevent the alteration, management, and use of these 'resources,' but it does affirm their right to continued existence, and, at least in spots, their continued existence in a natural state.

In short, a land ethic changes the role of *Homo sapiens* from conqueror of the land-community to plain member and citizen of it. It implies respect for his fellow-members, and also respect for the community as such.

In human history, we have learned (I hope) that the conqueror role is eventually self-defeating. Why? Because it is implicit in such a role that the conqueror knows, *ex cathedra*, just what makes the community clock tick, and just what and who is valuable, and what and who is worthless, in community life. It always turns out that he knows neither, and this is why his conquests eventually defeat themselves.

In the biotic community, a parallel situation exists. Abraham knew exactly what the land was for: it was to drip milk and honey into Abraham's mouth. At the present moment, the assurance with which we regard this assumption is inverse to the degree of our education.

The ordinary citizen today assumes that science knows what makes the community clock tick; the scientist is equally sure that he does not. He knows that the biotic mechanism is so complex that its workings may never be fully understood.

That man is, in fact, only a member of a biotic team is shown by an ecological interpretation of history. Many historical events, hitherto explained solely in terms of human enterprise, were actually biotic interactions between people and land. The characteristics of the land determined the facts quite as potently as the characteristics of the men who lived on it.

Consider, for example, the settlement of the Mississippi valley. In the years following the Revolution, three groups were contending for its control: the native Indian, the French and English traders, and the American settlers. Historians wonder what would have happened if the English at Detroit had thrown a little more weight into the Indian side of those tipsy scales which decided the outcome of the colonial migration into the cane-lands of Kentucky. It is time now to ponder the fact that the cane-lands, when subjected to the particular mixture of forces represented by the cow, plow, fire, and axe of the pioneer, became bluegrass. What if the plant succession inherent in this dark and bloody ground had, under the impact of these forces, given us some worthless sedge, shrub, or weed? Would Boone and Kenton have held out? Would there have been any overflow into Ohio, Indiana, Illinois, and Missouri? Any Louisiana Purchase? Any transcontinental union of new states? Any Civil War?

Kentucky was one sentence in the drama of history. We are commonly told what the human actors in this drama tried to do, but we are seldom told that their success, or the lack of it, hung in large degree on the reaction of particular soils to the impact of the particular forces exerted by their occupancy. In the case of Kentucky, we do not even know where the bluegrass came from — whether it is a native species, or a stowaway from Europe.

Contrast the cane-lands with what hindsight tells us about the Southwest, where the pioneers were equally brave, resourceful, and persevering. The impact of occupancy here brought no bluegrass, or other plant fitted to withstand the bumps and buffetings of hard use. This region, when grazed by livestock, reverted through a series of more and more worthless grasses, shrubs, and weeds to a condition of unstable equilibrium. Each recession of plant types bred erosion; each increment to erosion bred a further recession of plants. The result today is a progressive and mutual deterioration, not only of plants and soils, but of the animal community subsisting thereon. The early settlers did not expect this: on the ciénegas [marshes] of New Mexico some even cut ditches to hasten it. So subtle has been its progress that few residents of the region are aware of it. It is quite invisible to the tourist who finds this wrecked landscape colorful and charming (as indeed it is, but it bears scant resemblance to what it was in 1848). . . .

In short, the plant succession steered the course of history; the pioneer simply demonstrated, for good or ill, what successions inhered in the land. Is history taught in this spirit? It will be, once the concept of land as a community really penetrates our intellectual life.

The Ecological Conscience

Conservation is a state of harmony between men and land. Despite nearly a century of propaganda, conservation still proceeds at a snail's pace; progress still consists largely of letterhead pieties and convention oratory. On the back forty we still slip two steps backward for each forward stride.

The usual answer to this dilemma is 'more conservation education.' No one will debate this, but is it certain that only the *volume* of education needs stepping up? Is something lacking in the *content* as well?

It is difficult to give a fair summary of its content in brief form, but, as I understand it, the content is substantially this:

obey the law, vote right, join some organizations, and practice what conservation is profitable on your own land; the government will do the rest.

Is not this formula too easy to accomplish anything worth-while? It defines no right or wrong, assigns no obligation, calls for no sacrifice, implies no change in the current philosophy of values. In respect of land-use, it urges only enlightened self-interest. Just how far will such education take us? . . .

No important change in ethics was ever accomplished without an internal change in our intellectual emphasis, loyalties, affections, and convictions. The proof that conservation has not yet touched these foundations of conduct lies in the fact that philosophy and religion have not yet heard of it. In our attempt to make conservation easy, we have made it trivial.

Substitutes for a Land Ethic

When the logic of history hungers for bread and we hand out a stone, we are at pains to explain how much the stone resembles bread. I now describe some of the stones which serve in lieu of a land ethic.

One basic weakness in a conservation system based wholly on economic motives is that most members of the land community have no economic value. Wildflowers and songbirds are examples. Of the 22,000 higher plants and animals native to Wisconsin, it is doubtful whether more than 5 per cent can be sold, fed, eaten, or otherwise put to economic use. Yet these creatures are members of the biotic community, and if (as I believe) its stability depends on its integrity, they are entitled to continuance.

When one of these non-economic categories is threatened, and if we happen to love it, we invent subterfuges to give it economic importance. At the beginning of the century songbirds were supposed to be disappearing. Ornithologists jumped to the rescue with some distinctly shaky evidence to the effect that insects would eat us up if birds failed to control them. The evidence had to be economic on order to be valid.

It is painful to read these circumlocutions today. We have no land ethic yet, but we have at least drawn nearer the point of admitting that birds should continue as a matter of biotic right, regardless of the presence or absence of economic advantage to us.

A parallel situation exists in respect of predatory mammals, raptorial birds, and fish-eating birds. Time was when biologists somewhat overworked the evidence that these creatures preserve the health of game by killing weaklings, or that they control rodents for the farmer, or that they prey only on 'worthless' species. Here again, the evidence had to be economic in order to be valid. It is only in recent years that we hear the more honest argument that predators are members of the community, and that no special interest has the right to exterminate them for the sake of a benefit, real or fancied, to itself. Unfortunately this enlightened view is still in the talk stage. In the field the extermination of predators goes merrily on: witness the impending erasure of the timber wolf by fiat of Congress, the Conservation Bureaus, and many state legislatures. . . .

When the private landowner is asked to perform some unprofitable act for the good of the community, he today assents only with outstretched palm. If the act costs him cash this is fair and proper, but when it costs only forethought, open-mindedness, or time, the issue is at least debatable. The overwhelming growth of land-use subsidies in recent years must be ascribed, in large part, to the government's own agencies for conservation education: the land bureaus, the agricultural colleges, and the extension services. As far as I can detect, no ethical obligation toward land is taught in these institutions.

To sum up: a system of conservation based solely on economic self-interest is hopelessly lopsided. It tends to ignore, and thus eventually to eliminate, many elements in the land community that lack commercial value, but that are (as far as we know) essential to its healthy functioning. It assumes, falsely, I think, that the economic parts of the biotic clock will function without the uneconomic parts. It tends to relegate to government many functions eventually too large, too complex, or too widely dispersed to be performed by government.

An ethical obligation on the part of the private owner is the only visible remedy for these situations. . . .

Land Health and the A-B Cleavage

A land ethic, then, reflects the existence of an ecological conscience, and this in turn reflects a conviction of individual responsibility for the health of the land. Health is the capacity of the land for self-renewal. Conservation is our effort to understand and preserve this capacity.

Conservationists are notorious for their dissensions. Superficially these seem to add up to mere confusion, but a more careful scrutiny reveals a single plane of cleavage common to many specialized fields. In each field one group (A) regards the land as soil, and its function as commodity-production; another group (B) regards the land as a biota, and its function as something broader. How much broader is admittedly in a state of doubt and confusion.

In my own field, forestry, group A is quite content to grow trees like cabbages,

with cellulose as the basic forest commodity. It feels no inhibition against violence; its ideology is agronomic. Group B, on the other hand, sees forestry as fundamentally different from agronomy because it employs natural species, and manages a natural environment rather than creating an artificial one. Group B prefers natural reproduction on principle. It worries on biotic as well as economic grounds about the loss of species like chestnut, and the threatened loss of the white pines. It worries about a whole series of secondary forest functions: wildlife, recreation, watersheds, wilderness areas. To my mind, Group B feels the stirrings of an ecological conscience.

In the wildlife field, a parallel cleavage exists. For Group A the basic commodities are sport and meat; the yardsticks of production are ciphers of take in pheasants and trout. Artificial propagation is acceptable as a permanent as well as a temporary recourse — if its unit costs permit. Group B, on the other hand, worries about a whole series of biotic side-issues. What is the cost in predators of producing a game crop? Should we have further recourse to exotics? How can management restore the shrinking species, like prairie grouse, already hopeless as shootable game? How can management restore the threatened rarities, like trumpeter swan and whooping crane? Can management principles be extended to wildflowers? Here again it is clear to me that we have the same A–B cleavage as in forestry. . . .

In all of these cleavages, we see repeated the same basic paradoxes: man the conqueror *versus* man the biotic citizen; science the sharpener of his sword *versus* science the searchlight on his universe; land the slave and servant *versus* land the collective organism. Robinson's injunction to Tristram may well be applied, at this juncture, to *Homo sapiens* as a species in geological time:

Whether you will or not
You are a King, Tristram, for you are one
Of the time-tested few that leave the world,
When they are gone, not the same place
   it was.
Mark what you leave.

The Outlook

It is inconceivable to me that an ethical relation to land can exist without love, respect, and admiration for land, and a high regard for its value. By value, I of course mean something far broader than mere economic value; I mean value in the philosophical sense.

Perhaps the most serious obstacle impeding the evolution of a land ethic is the fact that our educational and economic system is headed away from, rather than toward, an intense consciousness of land. Your true modern is separated from the land by many middlemen, and by innumerable physical gadgets. He has no vital relation to it; to him it is the space between cities on which crops grow. Turn him loose for a day on the land, and if the spot does not happen to be a golf links or a 'scenic' area, he is bored stiff. If crops could be raised by hydroponics instead of farming, it would suit him very well. Synthetic substitutes for wood, leather, wool, and other natural land products suit him better than the originals. In short, land is something he has 'outgrown.'

Almost equally serious as an obstacle to a land ethic is the attitude of the farmer for whom the land is still an adversary, or a taskmaster that keeps him in slavery. Theoretically, the mechanization of farming ought to cut the farmer's chains, but whether it really does is debatable.

One of the requisites for an ecological comprehension of land is an understanding of ecology, and this is by no means co-extensive with 'education'; in fact, much higher education seems deliberately to avoid ecological concepts. An understanding of ecology does not necessarily originate in courses bearing ecological labels; it is quite as likely to be labeled geography, botany, agronomy, history, or economics. This is as it should be, but whatever the label, ecological training is scarce.

The case for a land ethic would appear hopeless but for the minority which is in obvious revolt against these 'modern' trends.

The 'key-log' which must be moved to release the evolutionary process for an ethic is simply this: quit thinking about decent land-use as solely an economic problem. Examine each question in terms of what is ethically and esthetically right, as well as what is economically expedient. A thing is right when it tends to preserve the integrity, stability, and beauty of the biotic community. It is wrong when it tends otherwise.

It of course goes without saying that economic feasibility limits the tether of what can or cannot be done for land. It always has and it always will. The fallacy the economic determinists have tied around our collective neck, and which we now need to cast off, is the belief that economics determines *all* land-use. This is simply not true. An innumerable host of actions and attitudes, comprising perhaps the bulk of all land relations, is determined by the land-users' tastes and predilections, rather than by his purse. The bulk of all land relations hinges on investments of time, forethought, skill, and faith rather than on investments of cash. As a land-user thinketh, so is he.

I have purposely presented the land ethic as a product of social evolution because nothing so important as an ethic is ever 'written.' Only the most superficial student of history supposes that Moses 'wrote' the Decalogue; it evolved in the minds of a thinking community, and Moses wrote a tentative summary of it for a 'seminar.' I say tentative because evolution never stops.

The evolution of a land ethic is an intellectual as well as emotional process. Conservation is paved with good intentions which prove to be futile, or even dangerous, because they are devoid of critical understanding either of the land, or of economic land-use. I think it is a truism that as the ethical frontier advances from the individual to the community, its intellectual content increases.

The mechanism of operation is the same for any ethic: social approbation for right actions: social disapproval for wrong actions.

By and large, our present problem is one of attitudes and implements. We are remodeling the Alhambra with a steamshovel, and we are proud of our yardage. We shall hardly relinquish the shovel, which after all has many good points, but we are in need of gentler and more objective criteria for its successful use.

MARK SAGOFF

Animal Liberation and Environmental Ethics
Bad Marriage, Quick Divorce

MARK SAGOFF *works at the Center for Philosophy and Public Policy at the University of Maryland at College Park.*

"THE land ethic," Aldo Leopold wrote in *A Sand County Almanac*, "simply enlarges the boundaries of the community to include soils, waters, plants, and animals, or collectively, the land." What kind of community does Leopold refer to? He might mean a *moral* community, a group of individuals who respect each other's right to treatment as equals or who regard one another's interests with equal respect and concern. Leopold may also mean an *eco-logical* community, a community tied together by biological relationships in interdependent webs of life.

Let us suppose, for a moment, that Leopold has a *moral* community in mind; he would expand our *moral* boundaries to include soils, waters, plants, and animals, as well as human beings. Leopold's view, then, might not differ in principle from that of Christopher Stone, who has suggested that animals and even trees be given legal standing, so that their interests may be represented in court. Stone sees the expansion of our moral consciousness in this way as part of a historical progress in which societies have recognized the equality of groups of oppressed people, notably blacks, women, and children.

Peter Singer, perhaps more than any other writer, has emphasized the analogy between human liberation movements (e.g., abolitionism and suffragism) and "animal liberation" or the "expansion of our moral horizons" to include members of other species in "the basic principle of equality." Singer differs from Stone in arguing that the question whether animals have *rights* is less important than it appears: "what matters is how we think animals ought to be treated, and not how we employ the concept of a right." He also confines membership in the moral community to beings with the "capacity for subjective experience, such as the experience of pleasure or the experience of pain." But Stone and Singer agree that we have a moral obligation to minimize the suffering of animals and to balance their interests against our own.

Mother Nature vs. Frank Perdue

What practical course of action should we take once we have climbed the spiral of moral evolution high enough to recognize our obligation to value the rights, interests, or welfare of animals equally with our own? In discussing the rights of human beings, Henry Shue describes two that are basic in the sense that "the enjoyment of them is essential to the enjoyment of all other rights." These are the right to physical security and the right to minimum subsistence. These, surely, are basic to animal rights as well. To allow animals to be killed, to permit them to die of disease or starvation, when it is within our

power to prevent it, surely seems not to balance their interests with our own.

Where, then, shall we begin to provide for the basic welfare — the security and subsistence — of animals? Plainly, where they most lack this security, where their basic rights, needs, or interests are most thwarted and where their suffering is the most intense. This is in nature. Ever since Darwin, we have been aware that few organisms survive to reach sexual maturity; most are quickly annihilated in the struggle for existence.

Consider this rough but reasonable statement of the facts, given by Fred Hapgood: "All species reproduce to excess, way past the carrying capacity of their niche. In her lifetime a lioness might have 20 cubs; a pigeon, 150 chicks; a mouse, 1,000 kits; a trout, 20,000 fry; a tuna or cod, a million fry or more; an elm tree, several million seeds; and an oyster, perhaps a hundred million spat. If one assumes that the population of each of these species is, from generation to generation, roughly equal, then on the average only one offspring will survive to replace each parent. All the other thousands and millions will die, one way or another."

The way creatures in nature die are typically violent: predation, starvation, disease, parasitism, cold. If the dying animal in the wild understood his condition, what would he think? Surely, he would prefer to be raised on a farm, where his chances of survival would be good and to escape from the wild, where they are negligible. Either way, the animal will be killed; few die of old age. The path from birth to slaughter, however, is nearly always longer and less painful in the barnyard than in the woods. The misery of animals in nature beggars by comparison every other form of suffering in the world. Mother Nature is so cruel to her children she makes [chicken magnate] Frank Perdue look like a saint.

I do not know how animal liberationists, such as Singer, propose to relieve animal suffering in nature, but there are many ways we could greatly improve the situation at little cost to ourselves. It may not be beyond the reach of science to attempt a broad program of contraceptive care for animals in nature so that fewer will fall victim to an early and horrible death. One may propose, with all modesty, the conversion of our national wilderness areas, especially our national parks, into farms in order to replace violent wild areas with humane, managed environments. Animals and trees would then benefit from the same efficient and productive technology that benefits us.

My point in raising this argument is to suggest that the thesis that animals have important rights and interests that command our respect has little bearing on the policies it is supposed by some to support, in particular, policies intended to preserve and protect the natural environment. We must ask ourselves whether in fact the kind of policies environmentalists recommend would make animals better off in the long run. I see no reason at all to suppose that they would.

Can Environmentalists Be Hunters?

In a persuasive essay, J. Baird Callicott describes a number of differences between the ideas of Aldo Leopold and those of Peter Singer — differences, which suggest Leopold's environmental ethic and Singer's humanitarianism lead in opposite directions. First, while Singer and other animal liberationists deplore the suffering of domestic animals, "Leopold manifests an attitude that can only be described as

indifference." Second, while Leopold expresses an urgent concern about the disappearance of species, Singer, consistently with his premises, is concerned with the welfare of individual animals, without special regard to their status as endangered species.

Third, wilderness, according to Leopold, provides "a means of perpetuating, in sport form, the more virile and primitive skills. . . ." He had hunting in mind. Hunters, since top predators are gone, may serve an important ecological function. Leopold was himself an enthusiastic hunter and wrote unabashedly about his exploits pursuing game. The term "game" as applied to animals, Callicott wryly comments, "appears to be morally equivalent to referring to a sexually appealing young woman as a 'piece' or to a strong, young black man as a 'buck' — if animal rights, that is, are to be considered on a par with women's rights and the rights of formerly enslaved races."

Hunting is what disturbs animal liberationists as much as any other human activity. Singer expresses disdain and chagrin at what he calls "'environmentalist'" organizations which actively support or refuse to oppose hunting, such as the Sierra Club and the World Wildlife Fund. I can appreciate Singer's aversion to hunting, but why does he place the word "environmentalist" in shudder quotes when he refers to organizations like the Sierra Club? Environmentalist and conservationist organizations traditionally have been concerned with ecological, not with humanitarian, issues. They make no pretense to improving the lot of individual animals; they attempt rather to maintain the diversity, integrity, beauty, and authenticity of the natural environment. These goals are ecological, not eleemosynary. They are entirely consistent with licensing hunters to shoot animals whose populations exceed the carrying capacity of their habitats.

I do not in any way mean to support the practice of hunting; nor am I advocating environmentalism at this time. I merely want to point out that groups like the Sierra Club, the Wilderness Society, and the World Wildlife Fund do not fail in their mission insofar as they devote themselves to causes other than the happiness or welfare of individual creatures; that never was their mission. These organizations, which promote a love and respect for the functioning of natural ecosystems, differ ideologically from organizations that make the suffering of animals their primary concern — groups like the Fund for Animals, the Animal Protection Institute, Friends of Animals, the American Humane Association, and various single issue groups such as Friends of the Sea Otter, Beaver Defenders, Friends of the Earthworm, and Worldwide Fair Play for Frogs.

I proposed earlier that Aldo Leopold views the community of nature as a *moral* community — one in which we, as members, have obligations to all other animals, presumably to minimize their pain. I suggested that Leopold, like Singer, may be committed to the idea that we should preserve and respect the natural environment only insofar as that promotes the welfare of the individual animals nature contains. This is plainly not Leopold's view, however. The principle of natural selection is not a humanitarian principle; the predator–prey relation does not depend on moral empathy. Nature ruthlessly limits animal populations by doing violence to virtually every individual before it reaches maturity. These conditions respect animal equality only in the darkest sense. Yet these are precisely the ecological relationships which Leopold admires;

they are the conditions which he would not interfere with, but protect. Leopold, apparently, does not think that an ecological system has to be a moral system in order to deserve our love. An ecological system has a beauty and an authenticity we can admire — but not on humanitarian grounds.

Animal Liberation and Environmental Law

Muckraking journalists, thank God for them, who depict the horrors that all too often occur in laboratories and on farms, appeal, quite properly, to our conviction that mankind should never inflict needless pain on animals, especially for the sake of profit. When we read stories about man's cruelty to domestic animals, we respond, as we should, with moral outrage and revulsion. When we read accounts of natural history, which reveal as much suffering and slaughter, we do not respond with outrage or indignation. Why not? The reason is plain. It is not suffering per se that concerns us. What outrages us is human responsibility for that suffering.

Moral obligations to animals may arise in either of two ways. Our duties to nonhuman animals may be based on the principle that cruelty to animals is obnoxious, a principle nobody denies. These obligations, however, might rest instead on the stronger contention that we are obliged to prevent and to relieve animal suffering wherever it occurs and however it is caused; that we are obliged to protect the welfare of *all* animals just because they are sentient beings.

Animal liberationists insist, as Singer does, that moral obligations to animals are justified by their distress and by our ability to relieve that distress. Accordingly, the liberationist must ask: how can I most efficiently relieve animal suffering? The answer must be: by getting animals out of the natural environment. Starving deer in the woods might be adopted as pets; they might be fed in kennels. Birds that now kill earthworms may repair instead to birdhouses stocked with food — including textured soybean protein that looks and smells like worms. And to protect the brutes from cold, we might heat their dens or provide shelter for the all too many who freeze.

Now, whether you believe that this harangue is a *reductio ad absurdum* of Singer's position or whether you think it should be taken seriously as an ideal is no concern to me. I merely wish to point out that an environmentalist must take what I have said as a *reductio* whereas an animal liberationist must regard it as stating a serious position. An environmentalist cannot be an animal liberationist; nor may animal liberationists be environmentalists. The environmentalist would sacrifice the welfare of individual creatures to preserve the authenticity, integrity, and complexity of ecological systems. The liberationist must be willing to sacrifice the authenticity, integrity, and complexity of ecosystems for the welfare of animals. A humanitarian ethic will not help us to understand or to justify an environmental ethic. It will not provide new foundations for environmental law.

ANNETTE BAIER

For the Sake of Future Generations

ANNETTE BAIER *teaches at the University of Pittsburgh. Her interests are the history of modern philosophy, especially Hume's philosophy, ethics, and philosophy of mind. Some of her most important essays are collected in her book* Postures of the Mind *(1985).*

I. Introduction

Moral philosophers have only quite recently worried over the question of what we are morally obliged to do, or not to do, for the sake of persons who will live after we are dead. Classical moral traditions give us little help with this question. Though ordinary common sense moralities have usually regarded waste as immoral, and have recognized a vague general obligation to leave our camping places as clean as we found them, such popular moral beliefs are not specific about exactly what our duties to future people are, nor about the ground of such obligations — whether for example their basis lies in the rights of our successors to a fair share in what we might squander, to a camping site no dirtier than that enjoyed by their predecessors. We do not find most older moral theorists addressing the questions of what is due to future persons, why it is due, nor how any such moral dues link up with what is due to those persons whose lives overlap with our own.

§1 Seeing into the Future

Several explanations might be offered for this recent emergence of the question of obligations to future persons. The increase in our ability or sense of our ability to foresee the long-term effects of our policies might be thought to explain it. As long as persons could not see how their actions affected later generations, they could not be expected to feel any obligation to bring about good rather than bad effects. Our recently won confidence that we do control the fate of future persons brings with it a moral burden, responsibility for what we knowingly do. As long as our ancestors did not know what they did to us, and could not reasonably be expected to have known it, they cannot be blamed for any ill effects they produced, nor praised for any good effects. We, rightly or wrongly, feel we can estimate the effects of our policies, we think we know just how our great-great-grandchildren's teeth will be set on edge by the sour grapes we eat. . . .

§2 Laws and Consequences

Consequentialist moral theories see the moral status of actions to depend on their good or bad effects. But as long as doing the right thing is equated with doing what one believes God requires, one does not need to know about the long-term consequences of one's actions to discern right and wrong. One can leave it to God to see to it that our doing the right thing does some good to someone or something, at some time or other. The immorality of,

say, willful waste, will be thought to lie not in its causal link with woeful want, but in divine prohibition of wasteful policies. A belief in divine goodwill toward human beings will lead the believer to expect that there is *some* link between the content of the divinely ordained moral law and human welfare, but not a link we need to discern in order to know what is right. Then it would make sense to praise past persons for their great acts, from which we do in fact benefit, without thereby praising them *for* benefiting us. We might praise them because they did what was right or virtuous, and praise God that the consequences of their virtuous action for us are beneficial rather than harmful. For a non-consequentialist moral theory, it is possible that there are duties whose discharge does benefit future generations, yet which are not duties *to* those future generations. They might be the beneficiaries of our obligations, without being either those to whom the obligations are owed, or those for whose sake the obligatory action must be done. "Against thee only have I sinned," said David to God, not thereby denying that his sinful action (arranging the death of his ladylove's husband, [Uriah]) harmed another human, nor even that God prohibits such acts *because* they harm other humans. If our duties are to God and His law, our moral task would not be to fathom God's reasons, but to obey, trusting in the goodness of the will whose word is law. For such a religious non-consequentialist, it might be wrong to squander resources, poison air and water, and the like, not because future generations would thereby suffer (although this consequence of wrongful action is foreseen) but simply because God and His moral law forbids it. Future persons could condemn us for such wrongful action, action which in fact hurt them, but would do so not because it hurt them but because it was wrong, contrary to God's will and so to the moral law.

§3 From Religious Ethics to Secular Ethics

One does not need to equate morality with the revealed content of God's will or God's law in order to be a non-consequentialist in moral theory. The great German philosopher Immanuel Kant (1724–1804) believed that human reason could discern the moral law, and that we need know neither about God's will nor about the actual long-run consequences of individual right and wrong acts in order to recognize this law. Just as it is in the power of human reason, in its scientific employment, to discern regularities or laws which hold good in physical nature, so reason in its practical employment can recognize law — indeed can *make* law to govern human behavior. The moral lawmaker, Kant claimed, was the individual acting as if setting an example all other persons would follow. For us to know what acts to perform, what example to try to set, theoretical predictive reason often has to help practical legislative reason, in order to work out what would be involved if everyone followed a particular example. But once we are satisfied that we can will that everyone follow our example of, say, ceasing to make nuclear weapons, then we have established that policy as morally right, and are not to consider as morally relevant the *actual* consequences of this policy in the real world where others may not and often do not all follow our example. The right thing to do must be seen to have acceptable consequences *were everyone to do likewise*, but may not have good consequences when done only by some. "Let justice be done, though the earth perish," or, in this case, although the just person or just nation perishes.

This complex moral theory of Kant's both gives our power to envisage consequences of various policies an important role to play in moral reasoning, yet does not identify the right action with that which will in the actual state of things have the best consequences. Kant still needs and keeps a divine power in the background of morality, a power who is to see to it that the discrepancy between ideal and real world consequences is somehow compensated for, some day, so that obedience to the moral law does not, *in the end*, prove destructive to those who do what is right or to the world they would will into being. Kant's is a non-consequentialist moral theory where the test of moral rightness is the rational acceptability of hypothetical *universal* conformity to a policy, and of the consequences over time of such conformity. We are to do the act which we can will as universal law in "a system of nature," that is, in an ongoing world with interaction and feedback.

This ethical theory holds out some promise of applicability to the question of our duty to future persons, since any practice like dumping toxic wastes where they will poison soil, air, or water seems forbidden by Kant's test — we cannot conceive of a system of nature in which all humans regularly do this, yet survive as a species. It is not a coherently universalizable practice. Some, such as the contemporary Australian philosopher John Passmore, have seen Kant's ethics as addressing the question of our obligations to future persons, and there is no doubt that Kant's test of moral rightness can easily be applied to condemn many current practices, and also that the very form of his *test* for rightness (Can I will this as a law in a system of nature?) forces us to think about the long-term implications of policies. But, as far as I know, Kant did not himself actually draw out the consequences of his theory for this issue. He did make some claims about our *motivation* — he believed that we cannot help but care to some degree about future persons and the sort of life they will have — but he did not spell out what our duty to such persons is, or even if there are any special duties we owe them. To find out whether we do wrong if we refuse to help our contemporaries when they are in need, Kant's test forces us to consider what our world would be like, over time, if such refusal were the universal rule; so to discern our duty to anybody, we must in a sense think of everybody, future persons included, according to Kant's test. Future persons therefore come into his theory implicitly, but not as ones whose interests give rise to any *special* problems about duties on our part. Future persons themselves, and the foreseeable consequences of our actions for them, come into Kant's theory only indirectly. His theory is usable only by moral agents capable of seeing the long-run implications of policies for whole systems, natural and social, and he believed that we moral agents do in fact care about the future of the human world, but he did not spell out any particular obligations we have or, for that matter, which we fail to have, to future persons.

§4 Modern Moral Theories and the Person-Affecting Principle

Post-Kantian moral theories, both utilitarian and some *rights* theories, have focused attention very strongly on the *effects* of right and wrong actions on the good of human persons, often making this the decisive test of their rightness or wrongness. They see human moral agents, not some supervising God, as responsible for the foreseeable effects of their actions. Modern moral theorists, while agreed on seeing morality as promoting our human good, disagree over what precise effect on human (and perhaps animal) good determines the moral rightness of an action: Utilitarians see the crucial thing to be the effect of an action or policy on people's *happiness*, others emphasize the effect on *interests*, while those who hold a theory of rights (either rights arising from a hypothetical agreement, or so-called natural rights) see the crucial question to be the effect of an action on people as rights holders.

The violation of a right is, of course, a special sort of effect on a person and on his or her good. It cannot be equated with making that person unhappier, or less able to get what she in fact wants. If I don't want to vote, then the violation of my right to vote by the removal of my name from electoral rolls will not hurt me — it may not even be noticed by me. Nevertheless someone else on my behalf might correctly protest the violation of my right, and correctly say that my position is worsened by this inability to do what in fact I have no wish to do. I might even myself protest, and insist on my rights, then never exercise them. Once we see ourselves as right holders, the violation of our rights becomes an injury, even if it makes no *other* difference to our lives. The violation of my rights affects my position among right holders, even if that position is not very important to my particular goals in life. I shall return to this question of the relation between what affects our happiness and what affects our interests and our position among persons in §10. For the moment I want merely to draw attention to the agreement between most utilitarians and most of those who hold a rights theory that the moral wrongness of an act consists in some sort of bad effect it has on people.

The principle which they agree upon (but which religious moralists, or even Kantians, need not accept) has been called the *Person-Affecting Principle*, which says *that for any action to be wrong, it must affect some person or persons (usually other than the agent) for the worse*. This is a minimal requirement of wrongness — the principle does not say that all acts which have any bad effects on others are wrong, but only that, if an action has *no* bad effect on anyone, it cannot be really wrong. . . .

The *Person-Affecting Principle* directs us always to think of the consequences of our actions for other people, when making a moral decision. It is natural, if one finds the principle plausible, to think of consequences for future people as well as for our contemporaries, and to see a moral agent's responsibility as extending to the foreseeable effects of our actions on future and distant as well as present and close persons. . . .

Paradoxically enough, however, that same Person-Affecting Principle which seems to direct us to think about future persons has been invoked by some recent thinkers to reveal a problem in the very idea that future people could possibly be our victims. I turn next to that worry.

II. The Futurity Problem

§5 Our Knowledge of Future People

There are several features of future people, in relation to us, which can make the idea that we have duties to them seem problematic. I shall consider their *unknowability*, their *indeterminacy*, and their *contingency*.

We do not know much about all those children who will be born during the next seven months, although their genetic makeup is now quite fixed and determinate. For people further in the future, not only *do* we not know details about them, those details are not yet fixed, so are unknowable. Such lack of knowledge, especially when due to the not-yet-determinate status of future people, does, I think, rule out our having to them one kind of duty which we can have to our contemporaries. For example, some people now living are accustomed to a particular diet, and *could* not easily adapt to a different one. There would be no point in shipping canned pork and beans off to avert a famine in a Muslim country — the people could not eat it. We know, or can find out, this sort of special need, when we are considering the effects of our policies on our contemporaries, but we cannot know this sort of fact about distant future people. Since they are not yet determinate people, their special requirements are as yet unknowable. *Some* wrongs we can do to our contemporaries, those harmings which depend upon their special needs, we cannot knowingly do to future persons. Their indeterminacy protects us against the charge of doing them that sort of wrong.

But such wrongs, although real, are only one sort of wrong we can do people, and there are plenty of other wrongs which do not depend upon the victims' special needs, but on their common human nature. However little we know about future people, however much about them is not yet fixed, as long as they are human people they can be expected to need air, water, some fruits of the earth to eat. They will be vulnerable to poisons, just as we are, and we can, it seems, affect the availability to them of the unpoisoned air, water, soil, undestroyed naturally self-renewing or self-cleansing basic physical resources, which we as a species need. By the Person-Affecting Principle then, as far as we have seen, there can be wrongs to future persons despite their indeterminacy and our ignorance of their special needs. The principle will not itself tell us how bad the effects of our action must be for future persons to have been wronged, but it allows room for the idea that we really can wrong future persons. So far so good.

There is, however, the third characteristic of future persons to consider, namely their *contingency*. Not merely is their identity now indeterminate, but what will eventually fix it are a host of causal factors including the actions and inactions of their predecessors. It is *this* fact, the *contingency of future people on their predecessors*, which generates what has come to be seen as the worst philosophical "problem of futurity," one which might seem to cancel all duties we may have thought we had to future persons. I turn to that problem.

§6 The Ontological Precariousness of Persons

A thing is ontologically precarious, precarious in its very being, to the extent that its coming into being is dependent on other things. To appreciate just how precarious we all are, or were, we need merely think of the many possible things our parents might have done which would have led to our own nonbeing, to our total absence from the human scene. Not merely do deliberate parental actions of family planning determine which children come to exist, but all sorts of outside factors determining the precise time of conception also play their role — such things as owl hootings or train whistles which wake potential parents in the night. The English philosopher Derek Parfit, who has in the last ten years in a number of influential papers explored this problem thoroughly, asks how many of us could truly claim that we would have existed even if railways had never been invented. A recent electricity blackout in the city of New York was followed nine months later by a significantly increased number of births. As time goes on, the number of descendants of these "blackout babies" will probably become larger and larger, so that factors such as trains and blackouts come to figure in causal ancestry of a larger and larger proportion of the population.

Philosophers have long been aware of this radical contingency of particular existent things on earlier happenings, of the reverberating effects of seemingly trivial events, given a long enough time. In metaphysical discussions of causal determinism, and in theological discussions of divine predestination, the implications of this dependency of future on past realities have often been explored, and moral philosophers have often worried about the implications of this interrelatedness of things for our free will and moral responsibility for what we do or fail to do. Recently the implications for our responsibility for and to future people have been drawn out by Parfit and others.

§7 Wanting the Past to Have Been Different

If anyone's existence would have been prevented by so many thinkable changes in earlier history, it seems to follow that there are severe constraints on seriously judging that it would have been better if some earlier event, no matter how bad it may seem, had not occurred. In particular, one must consider the likelihood that, had it not occurred, one would not have existed at all to do any judging.

I am inclined to judge that the potato famine in Ireland and food shortages in

Scotland in the nineteenth century were bad things, and that it would have been better if those in charge of agricultural policy in Britain had made different decisions which would have averted those hard times. Then I reflect that my great-grandparents left Britain for New Zealand because of those very hard times. Had they not done so, they would not have met one another, married, had the children they did. Had the famine been averted, their great-grandchildren, if any, would have been *other* possible people, and I would not have existed. So do I *sincerely* judge that it would have been better had the past been different, had those persons who, as things actually turned out, did have me as a great-grandchild had a less difficult life, had not been faced with famine? I will sincerely make this judgment only if I can sincerely say that it would have been better, all things considered, that I not have existed. (Alternative interpretations of this judgment are examined below, in §9.) So it is not as easy as one might have thought to judge that it would have been better for the past to have been other than it was. Even to wish that one's own parents had been richer, or more fortunate, or healthier than they were in youth becomes hard, since any change in their lives before the time of one's own conception probably would have brought with it one's own nonexistence.

§8 The No Obligation Argument

Let us now see how this presumed fact, the extreme ontological precariousness of persons (and indeed of all other particular things), and the consequent difficulty of wanting the past to have been different, can be made to yield the conclusion that we have no obligations to future persons. We need to add, to what I shall call the *precariousness* premise (P), a version of the Person-Affecting Principle which I will call the *victim* premise (V), which says that a person has not been wronged by another unless he has been made worse off by the other's act, unless, that is, he is thereby the other's victim. Now we can construct a simple argument from P and V, to give us the conclusion C that nothing which we do can wrong future persons, unless what we do is so bad that future persons wish they had never been born. To spell it out more fully:

V. We do not wrong a person by our current action or policy unless it would have been better for that person had we not acted that way.

P. For any actual future person F, the outcome had we not done what we are doing would (in all likelihood) have been that F not exist at all, rather than that F exist and be better off.

∴ C. Unless it would have been better for F not to exist at all, we are (in all likelihood) not wronging F by what we are doing.

This argument, if it works, works whatever our actions are — however wasteful, depleting, or polluting. As long as future persons are not so affected by our actions that they can make a charge of "wrongful existence" against us, they have no complaint against us, since they cannot claim to have been wronged by what we did. The only wrong, it seems, that we can do future persons is to allow them to exist in an intolerable world. As long as that world is tolerable enough for them not to regret existing, they are not wronged by our world-spoiling activities. No future person will be able to say to us (or to our ghosts), "If you had acted rightly, *I* would have had a better life."

This is a very troubling argument. What troubles most of us about it is that the conclusion seems at odds with our moral intuitions on this matter. For, once the issue has been raised, most of us do feel that we would be wronging our successors by unrestrainedly depleting and polluting the earth even if that did not render their lives intolerable. We may be unclear exactly what we must, in decency, do for the sake of future person . . . , but most of us do feel not only that it is wrong to pollute and deplete, but also that it is "future people," in some sense of that phrase, who are the ones who are wronged if we act wrongly in this regard. The contemporary American political philosopher Thomas Schwartz, when he propounded an early version of our argument above, concluded not that we were free to do what we liked, as far as the consequences for the world future people will live in goes, but rather that *we owe it to one another*, to our *contemporaries* who do happen to care about humanity's future, to restrain our earth-ravaging activities. If Schwartz is right we will have sinned only against our contemporaries, if we poison the wells of the future; we will not have sinned against the persons who suffer the poisoning.

Now although it is good to have our conviction that we are not morally free to pollute the earth endorsed and given some basis, despite the troublesome argument we are examining, I think that we still are apt to feel that Schwartz's proposed basis for our obligations is not the right one. Many of us also care about the future of various precious artworks, or other nonsentient things. If we have a duty to preserve such things, it is a duty to our fellow art lovers, not to the artworks themselves. It seems wrong to put our concern for our successors in the same moral boat as our

concern for the future of anything else which happens at present to have a place in our affections. Surely it must be in some sense for future persons' sakes, not just for our own sakes, that we consider what sort of existence for them our actions entail? If Schwartz is right, then if we could make ourselves or let ourselves cease to feel concerned about the future of our human communities, then we would be rid not only of a sense of obligation not to pollute but also of the obligation itself. If it is only that "those who would like our distant descendants to enjoy a clean commodious well stocked world just may owe it to their like-minded contemporaries to contribute to these goals," then if we all cultivate indifference, cease to care, we can come to owe nothing to anyone in this regard. Can this be right? For whose sake, and for whose good, ought we conserve scarce resources and refrain from putting delayed-action poisons in our common wells—if, that is, we do have a duty to conserve and not to poison? To help us see if it can be said to be for the sake of future persons, despite the troubling argument, we need first to have a closer look at the conclusion C, and the qualification in that conclusion. When would a person judge that it would have been better, for her *own* sake, that she not have been born?

§9 Better For One
Not to Have Been Born

We have already seen in §7 how one can become committed to the judgment that it would have been better if one had not been born. One is committed to this if one seriously judges that some event such as a famine (without whose occurrence one would not have been born) was a bad thing, better averted. But such a judgment (if we ever really do make it) is made from an attempted God's-eye view, so to speak, one that takes into account *all* those who are involved. It is not made from one's own self-concerned standpoint, since one might make it although one's own life was pleasant enough, or was until one starts being obsessed with what went into one's own "prehistory," the human cost of one's own existence. To make the issues clearer, we need to distinguish two "objective" judgments from two subjective judgments. The former are judgments about the comparative value of alternative "world histories," made from no particular person's point of view, while the latter are judgments about a particular life history, made from the point of view of the one whose life it is.

O$_1$ All things considered, the world history (after some chosen fixed point) where F comes to exist is, given the causal chains which produced F, and the nature of F's life, worse than alternative world histories in which F does not exist.

O$_2$ The world history containing F's life is, because of F's own dreadfully intolerable life, *thereby* a worse world history than alternative world histories in which F's existence is prevented.

We could only make this second objective judgment if we (or F) could make one of two more subjective judgments, ones made from F's own point of view:

S$_1$ For F's own sake, or from her own self-concerned point of view, the sooner her life ends the better.

S$_2$ For F's own sake, or from her own self-concerned point of view, it would have been better if her life had never started.

The qualification in C, the conclusion of the No Obligation Argument, seems to refer only to those cases where the judgment O$_2$ could be made, and this in turn requires us to make either S$_1$ or S$_2$. Which of them does O$_2$ presuppose?

I think that S$_2$ is what is needed to support O$_2$. S$_1$ is the judgment made by most suicides, but a person need not be driven to suicide in order to judge S$_2$ and to have a valid claim of wrongful existence against someone. There are powerful forces, religious, instinctive, and altruistic, which may prevent even desperately unhappy people from ending their own lives even when they judge S$_2$. Nor is it true that one need judge S$_2$ in order to judge S$_1$. One's life can *become* intolerable enough to make one judge S$_1$, although long stretches of it were good and one would not judge S$_2$. For one to judge S$_2$, one's life would have had to be continuously intolerable, or some bits so bad that they clearly outweighed the good bits, when weighed not from a momentary but from a "life's-eye" point of view. One does not need to suppose that a suicide's life was as bad as that, bad enough to support S$_2$, in order to understand how suicide can look the best option. But it is just this very strong judgment, S$_2$, which F would need to make to charge her predecessors with wronging her by allowing her to exist at all.

The conclusion, C, of the No Obligation Argument then, presupposes that S$_2$ makes sense, that it is conceivable that a person could be wronged by having been allowed to come into existence at all. Persons who judge S$_2$ are victims of previous events or actions in a sense which is *wider*, or different, than that in which our contemporaries are victims of our assault or neglect. In the latter case, we can say that the victim's *life* is worse than it would have been without the assault or neglect. But the victims of earlier events who are driven to S_2 judgments about their own lives are not complaining that they don't have lives better in this or that respect, they are complaining that they are, and ever were, alive at all, given their life prospects. This means that we must interpret premise V in a fairly wide way, to include this sort of victim, if V is to be even *compatible* with giving any sense to C, the conclusion which is supposed to follow from V and P. The argument itself requires us to recognize that not all victims of policies are victims because their *lives* would have been better in some respect if someone had done something different, rather some people are victims because they are alive — period. This fact will become important in the following sections when I try to diagnose the fault of the No Obligation Argument.

§10 Varieties of Victims,
     Varieties of Ills

So far we have seen that there can be victims of events and policies, those who judge S_2, whose claim is not that their lives would have been better had those events not occurred. Earlier, in §4, we said that one can be affected for good or ill by a policy or action in a variety of ways. One's rights may be violated, even when one might not need to exercise those rights to further the interests one in fact has. Similarly, one's interests can be injured, say by loss of a job opportunity, or a pension scheme, even when one would not have wanted that job and does not yet care about one's old age. Normally what advances one's interests *does* help one get what one wants, and getting what one wants does make one happy, but one's interests can be injured without that affect-

ing one's getting what one wanted, and one's wants can be frustrated, although getting what one wanted would not have made one happy. Misery, frustration, injury to one's interests, violation or denial of rights, all unfavorably affect a person's good but can do so in different ways. The good of a person is complex since persons are and usually see themselves as bearers of rights, possessors of interests, as well as goal-directed and sentient. To act for the sake of some person or group is to act to advance any of these components of their good. The good of persons, seen prospectively, includes more than what will in fact give them happiness, since they may not be aware of some of their interests, so not be unhappy at their non-advancement, and they may neither know nor care about some violations of their rights. One needs not only to be fully self-conscious but also to have what today we call a "raised consciousness" for one's feeling of happiness to reflect the level to which one's rights and interests as well as one's purposes and tastes are respected.

As I am using the term "interests," we have an interest in the obtaining *conditions*, or *states of affairs*, such as our own good health, our prosperity, peace in our time, liberty, where these conditions are favorable for our success in satisfying a whole range of particular desires we have and expect to have in the future. The sort of things a parent or godparent wishes for a child are general goods of this sort, conditions which will enable the child to acquire and cultivate ambitions, desires, and tastes which can in those conditions be satisfied, and give pleasure when satisfied. Although it might occasionally turn out that these conditions are *not* needed or even favorable for the satisfaction of the actual desires the child comes to have, as a general rule the furthering of one's interests *does* increase the extent to which one's desires get satisfied, just as normally getting what one desired does give one the pleasure one expected it would. In acting in the interests of a person, we are trying to increase their *prospects* of satisfying their desires, and so, normally, of being happy with the outcome.

As a person grows from childhood to adulthood, and tastes and concerns become formed, these very general interests, shared with almost all persons, become specified in ways which often limit the number of other persons with whom we share them. An interest in peace in our time will become associated with an interest in the success of the political party whose plan for peace one judges the best one. One will have an interest not only in health but in the maintenance of a specific health insurance scheme, not just in prosperity but in the wise policies of certain banks and corporations, not just in liberty but in the removal of some specific threats to liberty. However specific one's interests become, they usually are still specifications of interests most people have, interests in livelihood, health, peace, in a decent community which provides scope for public participation and for private friendships, for satisfying work and for the enjoyment both of nature and of a rich, varied, and historically conscious cultural tradition.

Among the interests we share with others are interests we have only because we are cooperating with others in some project. Membership in a nation gives us this sort of interest in the nation's affairs, and gives each of us an interest in the protection of our individual roles as citizens and taxpayers. As a member of the taxpaying public my interests are injured by the tax fraud of my fellows as well as by misuse of public funds by officials. Here my interest is the same as that of any other honest taxpayer, an interest in not being ripped off. Yet this interest I share with many others can clash with more private interests I may have, if for example my employer is among those guilty to tax fraud and my job depends on his illgotten "savings." My interest as a member of the taxpaying public and my interest as an employee of this employer may be in conflict with one another. Often we need to refer to the *roles* we play, roles relating us to others and to schemes of cooperation, to specify the variety of our interests, and many of the duties and rights we have, and wrongs done to us, also depend upon these social roles. I have duties as a daughter, family member, department member, teacher, university employee, and citizen, and I have rights as all of these, as well as a member of a particular professional association, health insurance scheme, and so on. Since in most of these roles my rights and interests coincide with those of some others, I will protest any violation of rights, and wrongful injury of interests, even if I foresee that my own goals will not be frustrated by those wrongs. For example I will protest *as* university teacher, if tenure guarantees are broken, even if I am about to retire and so will not be hurt myself.

Let us now try to apply these points about the complexity of a person's good, its inclusion of *interests* to be protected or furthered as well as desires to be satisfied and pleasures to be enjoyed, to the case of future people. Because interests are *always* future-oriented, and because we can know what they are, at least at a general level, without having much if any information about what particular tastes and desires a person has, it seems to me that future persons' *interests* can be determinate even when the persons themselves are not yet determinate, even when the *whole* of what will count as their good is not yet fixed. Of course, in being sure that, whoever they are, they will *have* an interest in clean air, we are also usually assuming that they will *want* to breathe, and be *pained* by inability to do so — some assumptions about their sensitivities and their desires will be included in our claims about their interests. A person whose interests in good health is badly injured will most probably also have frustration and pain, as "ills" which accompany the ill of ill health. We may even feel we know what *particular* desires a future person will have because of grave ill health — for example, in extreme cases the desire to end life. So in concentrating on the *interests* of future people in what follows, I shall not be supposing that in injuring interests we are not usually also frustrating and hurting. I shall, however, be relying on the *possibility* that an injury to a person's interest can (and sometimes should) be averted, although that does *not* bring that person a better life, more satisfaction and less frustration, more pleasure and less pain. Interests are important, and injury to interests is important, *whether or not* averting the injury in fact leads to less frustration and less pain for the one whose interest it is.

Future people, once actual, will come to have specific interests as well as general ones, and will have particular desires and sensitivities, as well as interests, which will need to be taken into account by anyone *then* concerned with their good. We now *cannot* consider their good "all things considered," because all the relevant things are not yet determinate. But we *can* consider some vital dimensions of what will be their good, and do so when we consider those of their interests which are general enough, or, even though specific, predictable enough, to be already fixed. (One specific interest we can be fairly sure that people a few generations

after us will have is an interest in the advancement of knowledge of methods of *detoxifying* all the resources we are currently poisoning. This is not an interest people in the past have needed to have.)

What we now need to consider is whether the fact that our acts help to *determine* both the identity of future persons and some of the specific interests they will have means that *those* acts cannot at the same time damage interests of those persons. The No Obligation Argument seems to allow us to injure only one of the interests a future person might have, a rather complex interest, namely the interest in not existing at all if other vital interests, such as health, are to be very badly served. This is a conditional interest — an interest in not existing unless other unconditional interests can be tolerably well served. The No Obligation Argument in effect claims that unless a future person has *this* exceptional interest injured by us, she is not wronged by us by those policies of ours which "select" her for existence. Is it possible, contrary to what the argument claims, for us to wrong a person by injuring an interest she has even though she comes to *be* a person with that interest only because of the very actions which also injure that interest? Can that person say *both* "If you had acted differently, *my interests* would have been better served," *and* also "Had you acted differently, I would not have been one of those who exist and have such interests"? I shall try to show that such a complaint makes sense.

§11 Selecting Populations by Our Acts

Before looking at future people, let us consider present people, and sketch analogous ways in which our actions can injure their interests, perhaps violate their rights. Take a case such as a teacher who writes a course description. It is surely primarily for the sake of the students who will be in the course that such descriptions are written, with whatever care is taken. Yet *who* precisely they turn out to be depends to some degree on the course description itself, if it is an elective course. The description, and the care taken in writing it, both is for the sake of the students, and also helps to select which students are those for whose sake a course plan is produced. The teacher's actions help to fix the class population. Similar sorts of cases arise with immigration policy — the ways in which a nation encourages or discourages immigrants help to determine who comes, but once in a country an immigrant might complain, "You didn't warn me about the high unemployment. Had you done so, I probably wouldn't have come." (Note that it need *not* be claimed that they regret being there for them to have a complaint.) Have we injured and perhaps wronged the class members who suffer once in the badly described course, the immigrants who come with inadequate advance warning of conditions, even if, once in the class or nation, they do not on balance regret being there?

It is important to see that a version of the No Obligation Argument can be used to give a negative answer here too. To any complainer we can say, "If you wouldn't have been in the relevant population (class member, immigrant) had we done what you say we should have done, then you are not a wronged member of that population. You would not have been a *better-off* class member or immigrant, had we acted as you think we should have, *you* would not have been a member of that population *at all*. So you have no complaint as class member, as immigrant."

Must they then reformulate their complaint, and say that it was the population of those *considering* joining the class or nation, not those actually joining it, whose interests are injured by the poor descriptions and plans? Such wider populations certainly are affected, but it would seem counterintuitive to say that when a teacher designs a course and makes the design known in a course description she is fulfilling a duty only to the wider group of all those who might consider joining, not also to the narrower group who actually join. Any class member (or immigrant) whose complaint is responded to by these moves would, if she had her wits about her, say, "I *as class member* (immigrant) as well as a potential class member have been wronged by the bad advance description. You owe it to all those deciding whether to join, and in particular to those who *do* so decide, to have an adequate plan and to give adequate advance notice of it. Had you done the right thing, I would not have *been* a class member, but you didn't, and I am, and I, like all other members, have been wronged by you."

It seems to me that this response is right. The interests of ours which can be injured include those dependent on the act which does the injury, in this case the act which helped make one a class member. This may sound paradoxical, but the paradox disappears once we are clear about what interests are, and how we can possess them in virtue of roles we fill and come to fill. Sometimes we come to fill a particular role, giving rise to an interest, because of the very act of another person which injures our interest once we are in that role.

Of course the extent of the analogy between this case and the case of future persons is limited. *They* do not *decide* to become actual persons, it is "decided" for them. But we can find, among injuries to present persons, cases on nonvoluntary as well as voluntary membership in some group where the act of determining membership also injures the interests of the members, as members. An annexation of a territory subjects the inhabitants to a new rule, makes them members of a new "population," and may simultaneously make them second-class subjects, a disadvantaged minority. After the second world war, Transylvanians who had been Hungarians became subjects of Rumania, and could complain (as many of them did) that the very act which made them Rumanians also injured their interests as Rumanians. Adopted children sometimes feel that the very fact that they are adopted gives them a lower place in their adoptive parents' affections than those who are the parents' "own" children in the biological sense. The very act which made the adopted children members of their new family, some feel, injured them *as* members of that family. (They may feel this without believing that it would have been better had they never been adopted, without feeling that they are, all things considered, injured by the act of adoption.) Could future persons, as our successors, be injured by us although the injuring act selected them *as* our successors? Well, so far we can say that the fact that they didn't *choose* that status does not rule that out. Nevertheless the fact that our acts determine who will exist, and so do not *shift* them from one "population" into another, but determines their very availability for *any* population, must not be glossed over.

This fact certainly limits the analogy between our relation to future people and our relation to students in our elective courses, to our adopted children, and to members of our annexed territories. We do not by any act literally *select* from a host of already determinate possible people the ones who will become actual, as would-be adoptive parents might survey the row of orphaned babies in a nursery, picking out the one to become their child. If there *are* fully determinate possible people, we cannot distinguish them as such. All we can do is consider similar descriptions of them such as "the next child I shall have," or "my future eldest great-great-grandchild," or "the first future person who may actually formulate a complaint beginning, 'Those Americans who had any say over policy in the 1980s are to blame for. . . .'" Although each of these titles is designed to pick out one and only one person, we have little idea what that person will be like, or what their total good will consist in. To discern injuries to people we know, we consider them, fully determinate people about whose good-all-things-considered we may have opinions, people whose full range of characteristics enables them to fit many descriptions and fill many bills, then we emphasize the role relevant to the injury we discern: "He was injured *as a parent*," or "*as an employee*." With actual people we do not know, we usually know more of the roles and bills they fill than simply the one relevant to the injury, so that although we do not know much about, say, those who are starving in the Sahara, we can say *something* about who it is whose interests in health and nourishment are so injured. With future people, there may be nothing yet fixed and known about them except the general interests we need to consider to try to avoid injuring them. All there is, yet, are those interests, not yet the actual people whose interests they will be, whose good those interests will help comprise. So we should not pretend that our relation to future persons is not significantly different from our relation to already existent persons, nor pretend that making them existent is simply moving them from the "population" of possible people into the more exclusive population of actual people. Any responses we make to the No Obligation Argument should avoid that confusion.

Nevertheless we ought also not forget that any act which injures an actual person's long-term interests is one which looks ahead to the not-yet-fixed *older person* the injured one might become. If I now lose my retirement pension rights, I am injured, even though, as far as I know, the older person of retirement age is not yet fixed in her needs or wants. There are many possible future me's. I may become rich enough not to need any pension, or become a beachcomber and not want one, or I may not live long enough to reach retirement age. All these uncertainties for the future are always there, and my interests lie in being somehow prepared for any of them. My interests are injured if I today lose my pension rights, even if I come into an unexpected inheritance or drop dead tomorrow. We must steer clear, then, not only of blurring the difference between future not-yet-actual people and actual people, but also of exaggerating it, of treating the interests it is wrong to injure as always the interests of people with determinate sets of concerns, wants, tastes. Only the dead are *fully* determinate, and the very finality, fixedness, of the nature of their wants and the character of their lives severely limits the interests they can have.

§12 Past, Present, and Future Persons

Although a past person cannot any longer suffer, nor want anything, some interests and rights of past people can still be protected or neglected. If I tell malicious lies about some dead persons, their interests in having and keeping a good name is injured. I can do things for the sake of past persons, although they neither know nor feel the effects of what I do. Once we are dead, the range of things which it is possible for others to do for our sake, or to do us ill, shrinks. But we may still, for the dead person's sake, protect his reputation, do what he wanted or would have wanted (especially with his estate), and we may even do things like putting flowers on his grave, thinking that to have some link with what pleased or would have pleased him. (If we put flowers on the grave of someone who hated flowers, it certainly is not done for that one's sake.) The very finished fixed character of the past person's life history puts him beyond most of the harms present and future persons can suffer—he cannot be hurt or frustrated, nor has he any longer many of the interests and rights living persons have. He is safe from much but not all ill.

Future persons too seem safe from being harmed by us in certain ways in which we may harm our contemporaries. We cannot deny them their marital rights, nor any contractual rights, nor libel them, nor take an unfairly large share of a good to which they too have *contributors'* rights. (But we *may* take, for ourselves, too large a share of what earlier people "bequeathed" to an indefinite run of future generations, or ruin a "bequest" which could have been enjoyed much longer but for our spoiling activities.) Just as there are many harms and wrongs we *cannot* do past people, so there are many harms and wrongs we *cannot* do future people.

Future people will, whoever they turn out to be, have a good, but only some components of that good are yet fixed.

Must we say the same of the interests which help comprise that good, that they *will be* their interests, but are not yet their interests? We have seen how some interests, like that in not being spoken ill of, last longer than does the person whose interest it is. I have argued that some interests preexist the person whose interests they are. Common predictable human interests, such as the availability of unpoisoned soil as a resource, seem to depend in no way upon that combination of specific interests, concerns, wants, tastes that comprise the concrete *individuality* of persons, which possible people lack, and which future people do not yet have. Whoever becomes actual will have such common interests and we know they will, so I see nothing wrong in saying that those already existent interests are now *theirs*. We do not need to know exactly who "they" are to recognize the reality of their common human interests. Whomever we allow to become actual, those ones have the interests all people have and we can also see what specific form some of those interests will take, since it depends on our policies. Of the interests people claim as their interests, some were predictable before the person's conception or birth, others come into being only because of particular unpredictable facts about them and choices they make. It is the interests which are fixed and predictable in advance which we can say preexist the person of whose good they form a part, and usually it is other less predictable and more specific interests of theirs, such as the success of a particular book they wrote, which last once they are dead. People cast shadows in the form of interests both before them and after them.

We can, then, speak of acting *for the sake of* a person not merely when we act to promote that one's all-things-considered good, as an actual living person, or

act to prevent injuries to their *individual* and perhaps eccentric interests, but also when we protect the general interests they have, *in advance of their existence*, or do things for them *after they are dead*. We can even prevent a person's existence, for that person's sake, when we think that, if she were born, she would judge S_2. The concept of a person's sake is the most flexible and so the best concept for us to use to cover all the ways in which what we do can be *better for* a person. If, contrary to what the No Obligation Argument concluded, there *are* things we can do which are better for future persons, in addition to preventing their coming to exist to judge S_2, then they will be things we do *for their sake*.

§13 The No Obligation Argument Rejected

We can now see what is wrong with the No Obligation Argument. The Victim Premise, V, did not spell out all the ways in which a person can be a victim, and only if some of those ways, especially ways of injuring interests, are neglected or denied does the conclusion C really follow from V and P. To see this we should expand V, mentioning all the ways we have distinguished in which something can be worse or better for a person's sake.

The revised version, V_r, will read

> V_r We do not wrong a person by our action or policy unless it would have been better, for that persons's sake, not to have acted that way because our present actions bring
>
> (1) more suffering than the person would have had, had we acted differently;
>
> or (2) more frustration than the person would have had, had we acted differently;

or (3) greater injury to the person's interests than would have occurred had we acted differently, where such interests include the interest in not existing at all, if other interests are to be very badly injured;

or (4) greater violation of the person's rights than would have occurred had we acted differently.

What do we get when we add the original Precariousness Premise to V_r? I think we need first to add a premise we can derive from the preceding account of the nature and variety of our interests, namely

I   Among the interests of a person which can be injured are interests which are fixed before the identity of those whose interests they are is fixed, and includes interests which a given person comes to possess only because of the very act which injures those interests.

When we add I to P and V_r, I think we can get a revised conclusion, C_r, which is very different from the No Obligation conclusion.

C_r Therefore the wrongs we can do a future person are usually restricted to injuries to interests fixed before the identity of future persons are fixed (and to such frustration and pain as is consequent upon the injury to such interests), and cannot include injury to interests not yet fixed or frustration of wants and concerns not yet fixed or hurts to sensibilities not yet fixed.

C_r is very different from C since it not merely allows the wrong of "wrongful existence," now included as injury of an already fixed conditional interest of all persons, but it also allows those *injuries to other already fixed interests* where the act which does the injury at the same time helps settle who it is whose interest it is.

We have avoided the No Obligation conclusion, C, by allowing the concept of an effect on a person to include "*effect*" *on interests*, including interests which come to be possessed only because of the "affecting" act. Parfit regards such interpretations of the Person-Affecting Principle as a "cheat," and himself avoids the No Obligation conclusion by renouncing the Person-Affecting Principle in favor of a vaguer principle which says, "It is bad if those who live are worse off than those who might have lived," a principle explicitly allowing comparisons between *different* possible people, not just comparisons of the possible fates of people of fixed identity. I think that once we come to see what sort of things interests are, and how indirectly injury to them is linked to worsening of the determinate life history of a person, then it is no "cheat" to allow the Person-Affecting Principle to include effect on interests, including those of the future people whose very existence to possess interests is due to the act which perhaps adversely affects those interests. So although no future person may be able to say to our ghosts, "If you had acted differently and rightly, I would have had a better life," plenty of the future people might well be able to say, "Interests which are, as it turns out, *my* interests, have been injured by what you did, and would have been less injured had you acted differently."

All we have done, so far, is to try to show that there is no good reason to think that the only wrongful injury we can do future people is to inflict "wrongful existence" upon them. We can now admit other injuries to their interests, other things we can, perhaps wrongfully, fail to do *for their sakes*. But which of these other injuries to the interests of future persons *should count as wrongs*? That is a question we have yet to consider, and different moral theories will give different answers. All would agree that our duties to future people are what can in reason be demanded of us for their sake, that wrongs to future people are neglectings of these duties, but there is no agreed way of determining *what* it is reasonable to demand of any of us for others', including our successors', sakes.

MARTI KHEEL

The Liberation of Nature
A Circular Affair

MARTI KHEEL *has been active in the animal-rights movement and is cofounder of Feminists for Animal Rights. She writes about esthetics, ecology, ethics, and feminist thought and is a contributing editor of the journal* Between the Species.

The new understanding of life must be systemic and interconnected. It cannot be linear and hierarchical, for the reality of life on earth is a whole, a circle, an interconnected system in which everything has its part to play and can be respected and accorded dignity.

ELIZABETH D. GRAY

I. Introduction

Over the last ten years feminist thought has shed a radically new light on many fields of inquiry. One of the most recent areas to receive the benefit of such illumination has been that of our society's attitudes toward nature. During this same time period, a voluminous body of literature has emerged in a new field of philosophy called "environmental ethics." The writers in this field (predominantly men) have shown little or no interest in the feminist literature. In the following, I attempt to redress this neglect and to show that feminist thought can, indeed, shed significant light on this important new area of study.

Central to feminist thought has been a critique of Western dualistic thinking. Western dualistic thought sees the world in terms of static polarities — "us and them," "subject and object," "superior and inferior," "mind and body," "animate and inanimate," "reason and emotion," "culture and nature." All such dualities have two characteristics in common: (1) the first half of the duality is always valued more than the other, and (2) the more valued half is always seen as "male" and the less valued half as "female." The Western dualistic world view can be traced back to early Greek philosophy and the Jewish and Christian religions, being reinforced in the 1600s by the increasingly mechanistic world view of modern science. The result of this long history of dualistic thinking has been the ruthless exploitation of women, animals, and all of nature. In place of dualistic thinking feminists have posited a holistic vision of reality in which everything is integrally interconnected and thus part of a larger "whole." Thus, whereas dualistic thought has perceived the world through a "spatial metaphor (up-and-down)," these feminists have seen diversity within a larger whole. The recent findings of quantum physics have reaffirmed this feminist vision. They have verified in the world of matter what many people have experienced in the world of spirit—namely, the oneness of the universe.

Thus, we learn from quantum physics that atoms instead of being hard and indestructible consist, instead, of vast regions of space in which extremely small particles move. At the subatomic level, we are told, matter consists of very abstract entities that have a dual aspect: "Depending on which way the experiments are performed, they appear sometimes as particles, sometimes as waves." The Taoist notion that everything is in flux, and that the only constant is change, turns out to have a solid grounding in the world of matter. Thus, we learn that "subatomic particles do not exist with certainty at definite places, but rather show 'tendencies to exist', and atomic events do not occur with certainty at definite times and in definite ways, but rather show 'tendencies to occur'." Consequently, we can never predict an atomic event with certainty; we can only say how likely it is

to happen. As Capra puts it, "Quantum theory forces us to see the universe not as a collection of physical objects, but rather as a complicated web of relations between the various parts of a unified whole."

II. Hierarchical Thought Within Environmental Ethics

The Dualistic Heritage

By contrast with the holistic vision set forth by both feminists and quantum physicists, the goal of much of the literature in environmental ethics has been the establishment of hierarchies of value for the different parts of nature. It is assumed that hierarchy is necessary to aid us in making moral choices in our interactions with nature. Conflict is taken for granted; it is assumed that one part of nature must always win, while another must always lose. Thus, in a real sense, the field of environmental ethics perpetuates the tradition of dualistic thought.

Holism

The concept of hierarchy finds two major forms of expression in the literature. One form is expressed through the ongoing debate over whether individual beings or the larger concept of "the whole" (or the "biotic community") should be given moral preference. Some "animal liberationists" argue that it is the individual who must be considered over the whole, whereas many "holists" argue that it is the good of the whole that must take precedence. Many holists will protest that theirs is a nonhierarchical paradigm in that everything is viewed as an integral part of an interconnected web. However, holists such as Aldo Leopold and J. Baird Callicott clearly indicate that the interconnected web does, indeed, contain its own system of ranking. Such writers have dispensed with the system of classification that assigns value to a being on the basis of its possession of certain innate characteristics, only to erect a *new* form of hierarchy in which individuals are valued on the basis of their relative contribution to the good of the whole (i.e., the biotic community).

According to Callicott, the "good of the community as a whole, serves as a standard for the assessment of the relative value and relative ordering of its constitutive parts and therefore provides a means of adjudicating the often mutually contradictory demands of the parts considered separately for *equal* consideration." At the top of Callicott's scale are rare and endangered species: "*Specimens* of rare and endangered species, for example, have a *prima facie* claim to preferential consideration from the perspective of the land ethic." At the bottom of Callicott's hierarchy of value are domestic animals: "Environmental ethics sets a very low priority on domestic animals as they very frequently contribute to the erosion of the integrity, stability, and beauty of the biotic communities into which they have been insinuated." Callicott goes so far as to posit a mathematical equation by which the value of an individual being may be gauged: "The preciousness of individual deer, as of any other specimen, is inversely proportional to the population of the species." To eliminate any doubt concerning his views on equality, he adds that "the land ethic manifestly does not accord equal moral worth to each and every member of the biotic community." . . .

Ironically, Callicott's "holism" may be seen to have much in common with utilitarianism. In both systems, the individual is treated, in Kantian terms, as a "means" for the attainment of a greater "end." In the former case, that which is good is judged by the standard of the biotic community, whereas in the latter case, it is gauged by the happiness of the greatest number. Although the content of the hierarchy varies, the structure remains the same. Both systems of thought also share the problem inherent in any scheme that claims the ability to compare the relative value of such abstractions as "happiness" or the "biotic good" — i.e., who should establish such values and how?

Individual Rights

The other form of hierarchical thought within environmental ethics is reflected in the attempt by both "ethical humanists" and "animal liberationists" to establish the relative values of the individual parts of nature. In this endeavor various criteria are proposed such as "sentience," "consciousness," "rationality," "self-determination," "interests," etc. A being that possesses one of these characteristics is said to have "intrinsic value" or the right to "moral consideration," whereas a being without them is said to lack these. A large part of this literature consists of debating which beings possess these characteristics — i.e., arguing whether divisions should occur along the lines of species or whether some overlap may exist. Ironically, although many of these writers feel that they are arguing against notions of hierarchy, the vast majority simply remove one set of hierarchies only to establish another. Thus, many writers on the subject of animal liberation may raise the status of animals to a level that warrants our moral concern only to exclude other parts of nature, such as plants and trees. Thus, Bernard Rollins, who clearly feels that animals merit our ethical consideration, emphatically states that "in and of itself, the physical environment has no interests and life and is, therefore, not a direct object of moral concern."

Some animal liberationists have attempted to expand the notion of rights arguing for the concept of the inherent value of individual beings. Even these writers, however, often fail to overcome the concept of hierarchy. Thus, according to Tom Regan, beings are deserving of rights if they can have a life that is "better or worse for them, independently of whether they are valued by anyone else." But if we were, as Regan suggests, to accord rights or value only to those beings that can have a life that is better or worse for them, our current understanding of the word *life* would exclude from direct moral consideration such parts of nature as streams, mountains, and air.

Regan seems to show some concern over this limitation. In his words, "But limiting the class of beings that have inherent value to the class of living beings seems to be an arbitrary decision and one that does not serve well as a basis for an environmental ethic. . . . if I am right, the development of what can properly be called an environmental ethic requires that we postulate inherent value in nature."

Outside of this important reference, however, Regan has failed to argue for the inherent value of all of nature. What has, perhaps, hindered him from so doing is the belief that this notion necessarily precludes a valuing of the individual parts of nature. The holist camp, by contrast, is convinced that a valuing of the individual for itself will somehow detract from a valuing of the whole. Both schools of thought are trapped within the dualistic mind set. Neither can see that moral worth can exist *both* in the individual parts of nature *and* in the whole of which they are a part. It is reliance on reason as the sole arbiter in our dealings with nature that makes the two schools of thought appear distinct.

But these positions are not polar opposites, nor even part of a "triangular affair" (each position representing one extreme of a triangle, as Callicott argues). If we allow for an element of feeling in our interactions with nature, the positions represented by these camps dissolve into different points on a circle. No point may, thus, be said to be more important than any other. The liberation of nature is, in fact, a circular affair.

A vision of nature that perceives value both in the individual and in the whole of which it is a part is a vision that entails a reclaiming of the term *holism* from those for whom it signifies a new form of hierarchy (namely, a valuing of the whole over the individual). Such a vision asks us to abandon the dualistic way of thinking that sees value as inherently exclusive (i.e., the belief that the value of the whole cannot also be the value of the individual). It invites us to see value not as a commodity to be assigned by isolated rational analysis, but rather as a living dynamic that is constantly in flux. If we can believe the findings of quantum physics, ecology, and the spiritual experiences of many individuals, we can agree with the holists that the nature of reality is, indeed, a web of interconnections, a circle or a "whole." What most holists seem to forget, however, is that the whole consists of individual beings — beings with emotions, feelings, and inclinations — and that these, too, are part of the whole. To rely on rational analysis alone to determine what the good of the whole might be is to ignore the reality of such feelings as well as their expression in particular circumstances.

The concept of holism I am advocating here does not view the "whole" as composed of discrete individual beings connected by static relationships which rational analysis can comprehend and control. Rather, I am proposing a concept of holism that perceives nature (much like the new physics perceives subatomic particles) as comprising individual beings that are part of a *dynamic* web of interconnections in which feelings, emotions, and inclinations (or energy) play an integral role. Just as quantum physics cannot predict atomic events with certainty at exact times and specific places, so too we cannot postulate that one species or one individual is of greater or lesser value than another. The attempt to formulate universal, rational rules of conduct ignores the constantly changing nature of reality. It also neglects the emotional-instinctive or spontaneous component in each particular situation, for in the end, emotion cannot be contained by boundaries and rules; in a single leap it can cross over the boundaries of space, time, and species. It is, I feel, the failure of most writers within environmental ethics to recognize the role of emotion that has perpetuated within the environmental ethics literature the dualistic thinking so characteristic of Western society.

III. Reason Versus Emotion in Environmental Ethics

The Rule of Reason

Most of the literature within the field of environmental ethics may be seen as an attempt to establish rationally both hierarchies of value and universal rules of conduct based on such values. Most such literature presumes that reason alone will tell us which beings are of greatest value and, thus, what rules of conduct should govern our interactions with them. Singer refers to this idea when he states, "Ethics requires us to go beyond 'I' and 'you' to the universal law, the universalizable judgment, the standpoint of the impartial spectator or ideal observer or whatever we choose to call it."

Interestingly, the field of environmental ethics is an outgrowth of two movements that were (and are) highly charged emotionally—i.e., the animal rights and environmental movements. Significantly, the members (mostly women) of the early animal rights movement were often labeled "animal lovers" or "sentimentalists" in an attempt to belittle their concerns. But, as James Turner points out, "animal lovers were not ashamed to admit that their campaign to protect brutes from abuse was more the result of sentiment than of reason."

With the publication of Peter Singer's *Animal Liberation*, the animal liberation movement took a new direction. It was assumed that one of the reasons for the failure of the earlier movement was its appeal to emotion, rather than hard, logical, well-reasoned arguments. The new movement for animal rights (as well as environmental ethics) proudly grounds itself in rationality. As Peter Singer states, "Nowhere in this book, however, do I appeal to the reader's emotions where they cannot be *supported by reason*." Elsewhere Singer elaborates, "Ethics does not demand that we eliminate personal relationships and partial affections, but it does demand that when we act we assess the moral claims of those affected by our actions *independently of our feelings for them*."

The appeal to reason in ethics has a long philosophical tradition. One of its most notable proponents was Kant, who felt that an action was moral only if it was derived from a rationally grounded conception of the right or morally correct course of action. Kant went so far as to maintain that no action that springs from a natural inclination can have moral worth. Although most modern-day philosophers do not elevate reason to quite such heights, most still feel that any appeal to emotion is tantamount to having no argument at all. . . .

The call to reason is also used by other writers as a means of learning our "natural place" within nature. Such writers argue that by understanding our "natural place" within nature we can learn what our moral actions should be. But, one might ask, why should *is* imply *ought*? Why should our natural place within nature dictate what it *should* be? To my knowledge, no philosopher to date has answered this question with a convincing "rational" argument, and I suspect that none will. Pragmatic arguments about how we will destroy all life on Earth unless we find our natural place within nature cannot persuade those who have no regard for life to begin with. Only those who *feel* their connection to all of nature to begin with will take an interest in its continuation. In more ways than one, the liberation of nature is a circular affair.

Dissolving the Dichotomies

What seems to be lacking in much of the literature in environmental ethics (and in ethics in general) is the open admission that we cannot even begin to talk about the issue of ethics unless we admit that we care (or feel something). And it is here that the emphasis of many feminists on personal experience and emotion has much to offer in the way of reformulating our traditional notion of ethics. Although this may appear at first to support the stereotypical divisions of our society which associate men with rationality and women with emotion, the emphasis on feeling and emotion does not imply the exclusion of reason. Rather, a kind of unity of reason and emotion is envisioned by many feminists. . . . Robin Morgan has used the term *unified sensibility* to describe this fusion of feeling and thought. In her words:

> How often have feminists called . . . for the 'peculiar blend of feeling and ratiocination' in our battles against the patriarchal dichotomization of intellect and emotion! It is the insistence on the connections, the demand for synthesis, the refusal to be narrowed into desiring less than everything — that is so much the form of metaphysical poetry and of metaphysical feminism. The unified sensibility.

How, then, are we to attain such a "unified sensibility"? The difficulty lies in conceiving of something as alien to our usual conception of hierarchy and rules as what is proposed. The problem of unifying our own nature is compounded further when we, ourselves, are removed from the rest of nature. Emotion easily divides from reason when we are divorced from the immediate impact of our moral decisions. A possible step, therefore, in striving to fuse these divisions is to experience directly the full impact of our moral decisions. If we *think*, for example, that there is nothing morally wrong with eating meat, we ought, perhaps, to visit a factory farm or slaughter house to see if we still *feel* the same way. If we, ourselves, do not want to witness, let alone participate in, the slaughter of the animals we eat, we ought, perhaps, to question the morality of indirectly paying someone else to do this on our behalf. When we are physically removed from the direct impact of our moral decisions — i.e., when we cannot see, smell, or hear their results — we deprive ourselves of important sensory stimuli which may be important in guiding us in our ethical choices.

Feminists have often emphasized the importance of personal experience in political and other seemingly impersonal matters. Its importance for ethical decisions is equally vital. This is, perhaps, the most practical implication of a feminist ethic: that we must involve ourselves as directly as possible in the *whole* process of our moral decisions. We must make our moral choices a circular affair. . . .

In her book *In a Different Voice*, Carol Gilligan has argued that the emphasis on particularity and feeling is a predominantly female mode of ethical thought. As she puts it,

> The moral imperative that emerges repeatedly in interviews with women is an injunction to care, a responsibility to discern and alleviate the real and recognizable trouble of this world. . . . the reconstruction of the dilemma in its contextual particularity allows the understanding of cause and consequence which engages the compassion and tolerance repeatedly noted to distinguish the moral judgments of women.

Men, on the other hand, she states, develop a sense of morality in which "relationships are subordinated to rules (stage four) and rules to universal principles of justice (stages five and six)." According to Gilligan, "the rights conception of morality that informs [Lawrence] Kohlberg's principled level (stages five and six) is geared to arriving at an objectively fair or just resolution to moral dilemmas upon which all rational persons could agree. . . ."

The problems entailed in implementing a female mode of ethical thought within a patriarchal society are obvious. With men building bigger and better bombs, rapidly depleting our natural resources, and torturing millions of animals in laboratories, one rightly worries what a particular individual's natural inclination might be. As Sara Ebenreck puts it, "If the answer to

how to treat a tree or a field is dependent on what the person 'hears intuitively' from the field or tree, then — as John Kultgen points out — we must be open to the possibility that some people will hear a message which is 'rape us, despoil us, enslave us.'"

It needs to be said in this context that men may respond in different ways to the call to ground our ethics in practical experience. Clearly, men do have a greater propensity toward violence as can be seen by their greater involvement in such violent activities as wars, violent crime, hunting, trapping, etc. Whether this propensity is biological or environmental or a combination of both is still an unanswered question. Whatever else we may conclude from this difference, however, it is difficult to escape the conclusion that in our dealings with nature, men have much to learn from women. Indeed, many men, including Buckminster Fuller, Lionel Tiger, Lyall Watson have concluded that "the only hope may be to turn the world over to women."

Most nonhumans seem instinctively to take only what they need from the environment to survive. If humans ever had such an ability, we seem to have lost it. The further divorced human beings are from this instinct or sensibility that nonhuman animals have, the more we seem to require rationality to act as its substitute. Interestingly, Aldo Leopold suggests that "ethics are possibly a kind of community instinct in-the-making." Perhaps, then, we are fortunate in that the human capacity to destroy life, to ravage the Earth, and to otherwise wreak havoc on the world around us coexists with yet another capacity — namely, the capacity to question our right to do so.

It is only when our instincts have failed us that we turn to such concepts as rights. Thus, it is not surprising that the idea of individual rights and natural law emerged during the civil war in England, a time of great social upheaval. The notion of *rights* can, in fact, be conceived of only within an antagonistic or competitive environment. The concept of competition is inherent in the very definition of rights. As Joel Feinberg states, "To have a right is to have a claim *to* something *against* someone. . . ." The concept of rights is, thus, inherently dualistic. Unfortunately, however, we do live in a dualistic society where competition is a fact of life. The concept of rights in an expanded form to include all of nature may thus be a necessary tactical device within our current society.

Conclusion

Feminist spirituality has shown us how the concept of a patriarchal religion, which views God as a male figure of authority in the sky telling us how we should think or feel, does not speak to the needs of those who feel that their spirituality flows from within. In a similar vein, it may be argued, the concept of ethics as a hierarchical set of rules to be superimposed upon the individual does not address the needs of those people (perhaps, mostly women) who feel that their morality or inclinations toward nature reside within themselves.

For such people, an environmental ethic might be described in the words of Elizabeth Dodson Gray:

> Some day, perhaps, we shall have an identity that can enjoy the earth as friend, provider and home. When that happens, we will know that when the earth hurts, it will hurt us. Then, the environmental ethic will not just be in our heads but in our hearts — in the nerve endings of our sensitivity.

With such a sensitivity we could perhaps, then dispense with the rigid, hierarchical rules of the past. If guidelines were to exist at all, they might simply flow from the desire to minimize human interference with the rest of nature. . . .

How might the field of environmental ethics be changed by a recognition of the importance of feeling and emotion and personal experience in moral decision making? For one thing, writers in environmental ethics might spend less time formulating universal laws and dividing lines and spend more time using reason to show the limitations of its own thought. They might, for instance, show how seemingly "rational" rules and ideas are, in fact, based on distinct feelings. Few of us, for example, would relinquish the idea that we, as humans, are more important than a stone. Yet, by showing that such a thought is based, in fact, on a feeling and that it cannot be justified by rational thought alone, we may be able to detach from our egos long enough to see that we are, indeed, all part of a whole of which no part may rationally be said to be more important than another. Currently, those with power in our society use rationality as a means of enforcing their own morality. If it could also be shown that such rationality is, in fact, derived from particular feelings, we could then begin to genuinely assess those feelings and the morality that flows from them.

Environmental theorists also might begin to talk more openly about their experiences and feelings and their relevance to their ideas and actions. Rather than spending time trying to find a moral dividing line within nature, they might, instead, examine their own internal divisions (such as that between reason and emotion). In order to unite these dualities within themselves they might then attempt as far as possible to experience in practice the full implications of their own moral theories. In a similar vein, an appeal to their readers' emotions and sympathies might be considered more relevant in an argument for moral vegetarianism than an appeal to reason.

Finally, environmental ethics might become more willing to recognize that the most fundamental questions about nature and the universe cannot, in the end, be answered rationally. Such an admission may not leave us with the sense of resolution and control that so many of us seem to hunger for, but it may, on the other hand, bring us closer to a feeling of the wonder of the universe and, perhaps, as a consequence, a greater appreciation of all of life.

<hr/>

JOHN STUART MILL

Against the Glorification of Nature

JOHN STUART MILL (1806–1873) *is best known for his moral and political writings (see his selections in Chapters 7 and 9), particularly* On Liberty *(1859) and* Utilitarianism *(1863).*

HOWEVER offensive the proposition may appear to many religious persons, they should be willing to look in the face the undeniable fact, that the order of nature, in so far as unmodified by man, is such as no being, whose attributes are justice and benevolence, would have made, with the intention that his rational creatures should follow it as an example. If made wholly by such a Being, and not partly by beings of very different qualities, it could only be as a designedly imperfect work, which man, in his limited sphere, is to exercise justice and benevolence in amending. The best persons have always held it to be the essence of religion, that the paramount duty of man upon earth is to amend himself: but all except monkish quietists have annexed to this in their inmost minds (though seldom willing to enunciate the obligation with the same clearness) the additional religious duty of amending the world, and not solely the human part of it but the material; the order of physical nature.

In considering this subject it is necessary to divest ourselves of certain preconceptions which may justly be called natural prejudices, being grounded on feelings which, in themselves natural and inevitable, intrude into matters with which they ought to have no concern. One of these feelings is the astonishment, rising into awe, which is inspired (even independently of all religious sentiment) by any of the greater natural phenomena. A hurricane; a mountain precipice; the desert; the ocean, either agitated or at rest; the solar system, and the great cosmic forces which hold it together; the boundless firmament, and to an educated mind any single star; excite feelings which make all human enterprises and powers appear so insignificant, that to a mind thus occupied it seems insufferable presumption in so puny a creature as man to look critically on things so far above him, or dare to measure himself against the grandeur of the universe. But a little interrogation of our own consciousness will suffice to convince us, that what makes these phenomena so impressive is simply their vastness. The enormous extension in space and time, or the enormous power they exemplify, constitutes their sublimity; a feeling in all cases, more allied to terror than to any moral emotion. And though the vast scale of these phenomena may well excite wonder, and sets at defiance all idea of rivalry, the feeling it inspires is of a totally different character from admiration of excellence. Those in whom awe produces admiration may be æsthetically developed, but they are morally uncultivated. It is one of the endowments of the imaginative part of our mental nature that conceptions of greatness and power, vividly realized, produce a feeling which though in its higher degrees closely bordering on pain, we prefer to most of what are accounted pleasures. But we are quite equally capable of experiencing this feeling towards maleficent power; and we never experience it so strongly towards most of the powers of the universe, as when we have most present to our consciousness a vivid sense of their capacity of inflicting evil. Because these natural powers have what we cannot imitate, enormous might, and overawe us by that one attribute, it would be a great error to infer that their other attributes are such as we ought to emulate, or that we should be justified in using our small powers after the example which Nature sets us with her vast forces. . . .

In sober truth, nearly all things which men are hanged or imprisoned for doing to one another, are nature's every day performances. Killing, the most criminal act recognized by human laws, Nature does once to every being that lives; and in a large proportion of cases, after protracted tortures such as only the greatest monsters whom we read of ever purposely inflicted on their living fellow-creatures. If, by an arbitrary reservation, we refuse to account anything murder but what abridges a certain term supposed to be allotted to human life, nature also does this to all but a small percentage of lives, and does it in all the modes, violent or insidious, in which the worst human beings take the lives of one another. Nature impales men, breaks them as if on the wheel, casts them to be devoured by wild beasts, burns them to death, crushes them with stones like the first christian martyr, starves them with hunger, freezes them with cold, poisons them by the quick or slow venom of her exhalations, and has hundreds of other hideous deaths in reserve, such as the ingenious cruelty of a Nabis or a Domitian never surpassed. All this, Nature does with the most supercilious disregard both of mercy and of justice, emptying her shafts upon the best and noblest indifferently with the meanest and worst; upon those who are engaged in the highest and worthiest enterprises, and often as the direct consequence of the noblest acts; and it might almost be imagined as a punishment for them. She mows down those on whose existence hangs the well-being of a whole people, perhaps the prospects of the human race for generations to come, with as little compunction as those whose death is a relief to themselves, or a blessing to those under their noxious influence.

Such are Nature's dealings with life. Even when she does not intend to kill, she inflicts the same tortures in apparent wantonness. In the clumsy provision which she has made for that perpetual renewal of animal life, rendered necessary by the prompt termination she puts to it in every individual instance, no human being ever comes into the world but another human being is literally stretched on the rack for hours or days, not unfrequently issuing in death. Next to taking life (equal to it according to a high authority) is taking the means by which we live; and Nature does this too on the largest scale and with the most callous indifference. A single hurricane destroys the hopes of a season; a flight of locusts, or any inundation, desolates a district; a trifling chemical change in an edible root, starves a million of people. The waves of the sea, like banditti seize and appropriate the wealth of the rich and the little all of the poor with the same accompaniments of stripping, wounding, and killing as their human antitypes. Everything in short, which the worst men commit either against life or property is perpetrated on a larger scale by natural agents. . . . Even the love of "order" which is thought to be a following of the ways of Nature, is in fact a contradiction of them. All which people are accustomed to deprecate as "disorder" and its consequences, is precisely a counterpart of Nature's ways. Anarchy and the Reign of Terror are overmatched in injustice, ruin, and death, by a hurricane and a pestilence. . . .

The phrases which ascribe perfection to the course of nature can only be considered as the exaggerations of poetic or devotional feeling, not intended to stand the test of a sober examination. No one, either religious or irreligious, believes that the hurtful agencies of nature, considered as a whole, promote good purposes, in any other way than by inciting human rational creatures to rise up and struggle against them. If we believed that those agencies were appointed by a benevolent Providence as the means of accomplishing wise purposes which could not be compassed if they did not exist, then everything done by mankind which tends to chain up these natural agencies or to restrict their mischievous operation, from draining a pestilential marsh down to curing the toothache, or putting up an umbrella, ought to be accounted impious; which assuredly nobody does account them, notwithstanding an undercurrent of sentiment setting in that direction which is occasionally perceptible. On the contrary, the improvements on which the civilized part of mankind most pride themselves, consist in more successfully warding off those natural calamities which if we really believed what most people profess to believe, we should cherish as medicines provided for our earthly state by infinite wisdom. Inasmuch too as each generation greatly surpasses its predecessors in the amount of natural evil which it succeeds in averting, our condition, if the theory were true, ought by this time to have become a terrible manifestation of some tremendous calamity, against which the physical evils we have learnt to overmaster, had previously operated as a preservative. Any one, however, who acted as if he supposed this to be the case, would be more likely, I think, to be confined as a lunatic, than reverenced as a saint. . . .

This brief survey is amply sufficient to prove that the duty of man is the same in respect to his own nature as in respect to the nature of all other things; namely not to follow but to amend it. Some people however who do not attempt to deny that instinct ought to be subordinate to reason, pay deference to nature so far as to maintain that every natural inclination must have some sphere of action granted to it: some opening left for its gratification. . . .

But even if it were true that every one of the elementary impulses of human nature has its good side, and may by a sufficient amount of artificial training be made more useful than hurtful; how little would this amount to, when it must in any case be admitted that without such training all of them, even those which are necessary to our preservation, would fill the world with misery, making human life an exaggerated likeness of the odious scene of violence and tyranny which is exhibited by the rest of the animal kingdom, except in so far as tamed and disciplined by man. There, indeed, those who flatter themselves with the notion of reading the purposes of the Creator in his works, ought in consistency to have seen grounds for inferences from which they have shrunk. If there are any marks at all of special design in creation, one of the things most evidently designed is that a large proportion of all animals should pass their existence in tormenting and devouring other animals. They have been lavishly fitted out with the instruments necessary for that purpose; their strongest instincts impel them to it, and many of them seem to have been constructed incapable of supporting themselves by any other food. If a tenth part of the pains which have been expended in finding benevolent adaptations in all nature, had been employed in collecting evidence to blacken the character of the Creator, what scope for comment would not have been found in the entire existence of the lower animals, divided, with scarcely an exception, into devourers and devoured, and a prey to a thousand ills from which they are denied the faculties necessary for protecting themselves! If we are not obliged to believe the animal creation to be the work of a demon, it is because we need not suppose it to have been made by a Being of infinite power. But if imitation of the Creator's will as revealed in nature, were applied as a rule of action in this case, the most atrocious enormities of the worst men would be more than justified by the apparent intention of Providence that throughout all animated nature the strong should prey upon the weak. . . .

The scheme of Nature regarded in its whole extent, cannot have had, for its sole or even principal object, the good of human or other sentient beings. What good it brings to them, is mostly the result of their own exertions. Whatsoever, in nature, gives indication of beneficent design, proves this beneficence to be armed only with limited power; and the duty of man is to co-operate with the beneficent powers, not by imitating but by perpetually striving to amend the course of nature — and bringing that part of it over which we can exercise control, more nearly into conformity with a high standard of justice and goodness.

12

How Should I Respond to Poverty?

The unprecedented number of homeless people in the United States over the past decade has brought poverty to the attention of the national media. And for many of us, the increased number of individuals asking for money on the street has also brought poverty to our individual attention. Poverty cannot, these days, be seen as the exclusive problem of the Third World and the occasional unfortunate. It is a big problem in all American cities. And every time someone asks you for a quarter on the street, you are confronted with the need to respond. What should you do? Should you give money to anyone you pass who asks for it? Should you refuse to give money to someone whom you expect will use it for alcohol? Should you adopt the habit of giving to established charities in lieu of giving money to people on the streets? Is the need of someone on a street in your city really your problem at all?

When are we required to help other people? Most moral theorists — and most people — believe that we have an obligation to help those who need our help. According to this line of reasoning, if you see a drowning child whom you could easily rescue, you have a moral obligation to attempt the rescue. Philosophers differ in their explanation of why we have this obligation. According to Kant, for instance, we are obliged to help because we could not reasonably live in a world in which people made it a policy to ignore those who need help. According to Mill, we should offer help because this course of action promotes more happiness for more people than does any alternative action. Even before reflecting on the basis for our obligation, most of us share the intuition that never to offer help would be morally offensive.

What, then, is our moral obligation toward poor people? Is it comparable to your obligation to a drowning child whom you are in a position to save? Or is it more similar to your obligation toward a drowning person whom you might save — but only by risking your own life in the process? We can only answer such questions by becoming more specific about what we mean by "helping those in need." Giving a quarter to a street person is not likely to put you in much risk. Becoming a doctor and treating victims of contagious infectious diseases in a poor neighborhood might involve risks. When you think of helping the poor, what strategies do you have in mind?

"Helping those in need" makes little sense as a concept unless we inquire into what it is that impoverished people need. Obviously, they need money. But is money all they need? John D. Jones argues that the psychological needs of those on skid row are necessarily unfulfilled. In fact, he contends that these individuals are victims of what amounts to "social murder." They not only are condemned to monetary impoverishment but are "fundamentally and increasingly impoverished" through "stigmatization, social isolation, poor health, psycho-physical disabilities and addictions" and other social deprivations. Those who are better off stop treating them as fellow persons and treat them instead as "just bums," thus depriving them of social acknowledgement of their human dignity.

Peter Marin agrees with Jones that the attitudes that the rest of us take toward homeless people fundamentally violate their dignity. Our basic desire with respect to homeless people, he argues, is simply to be rid of them. The focus of most of our programs to "help" homeless people aim simply to "rearrange the world cosmetically" to suit our own tastes, as opposed to addressing the needs and desires of the homeless people themselves. Marin urges that our efforts to help homeless people take more account of these people's own understanding of themselves and their world, and that we respect their rights to have aspirations that differ from ours.

Nancy Fraser considers a case in point, the case of impoverished women. She observes that the "feminization of poverty," the tendency for increasing numbers of women to fall below the official poverty line, has not led to the development of programs that actually pertain to women's needs or situations. Moreover, programs actually exacerbate the problems of poor women by ensuring that they assume the position of "dependent" as opposed to that of "rights-bearing beneficiary." Fraser urges the development of programs that address women's needs and that treat women as full adults with rights.

Peter Singer addresses the question of how far we are morally required to go in addressing the needs of poor people. His answer is that we are morally required to do as much as we can without sacrificing anything else "of comparable moral importance." Thus, you ought to give until you reach the point at which further sacrifice would cause more suffering to yourself or your dependents than giving would alleviate. Singer bases his argument on utilitarian grounds. Garrett Hardin also uses utilitarian grounds to counter Singer's view. He contends that, with respect to the poor people of the world, those who are better off are like persons in a lifeboat who can rescue only a limited number from drowning. The alternatives for those better off, as Hardin sees it, are to attempt to do what they can for themselves and posterity or to distribute the goods of the world so thinly that everyone suffers.

The debate between Singer and Hardin raises the question of justice in connection with the distribution of the world's good. Some thinkers question whether wealth can be morally justified in a world in which so many people are impoverished. Andrew Carnegie offers a defense of wealth on the basis of the advantages that competition for wealth provides to society as a whole. Carnegie, however, believes that those who are wealthy have a moral obligation to bestow charity. He thus defends the concept of *noblesse oblige*, the idea that privilege brings with it responsibilities to those who are not so privileged.

Amartya Sen considers the nature of poor people's rights. He observes that property rights have long been considered fundamental in societies with common-law backgrounds, whereas the right not to be hungry has only recently been taken seriously in certain nations. He observes that rights can be understood as instruments to other goals, as constraints, or as goals in their own right. Sen is convinced that the view that rights are themselves goals is the best, but he notes that the right to be free from hunger might be defended both as valuable in itself and as promoting other desirable social goals. However, he concludes that either type of defense depends on our understanding of empirical facts. Thus, our moral thinking about poverty requires that we undertake serious empirical investigations.

Frequently discussions of possible remedies for poverty have considered the basic policy approach that government ought to take. Should government, for instance, be in the business of ensuring the material welfare of its citizens? Some would argue that this is not the proper business of government, and that "welfare governments" are fundamentally harmful to society at large. Many are convinced that the material and spiritual needs of citizens are best met by a government that supports free enterprise and competition. Michael Harrington analyzes the history of American capitalism and reaches different conclusions. In our current situation, as he sees it, free enterprise is not as "free" as many people imagine. Our economy is a planned economy, and it will continue to be so. The question that needs to be addressed is whether the planning will be the province of business or of government. Harrington believes that powerful business leaders currently make major decisions affecting all Americans' lives without sufficient checks and balances. His solution to this problem is greater government control.

JOHN D. JONES
Poverty as a Living Death

JOHN D. JONES *teaches philosophy at Marquette University. His research is primarily in the areas of philosophy, anthropology, and phenomenology.*

II

A.

Human dignity, our worthiness as persons-in-community, is rooted in part in our freedom and understanding and the capacity for self-determination to which they give rise. . . .

This dignity is the basis for how we are to treat ourselves and each other. Further, this worthiness is "inherent"; it is grounded in the fundamental socio-existential structures of our existence. That is, we do not confer dignity on ourselves, either individually or socially; rather, our dignity is to be acknowledged, respected and realized. Human dignity is realized at the level of understanding and action. Both individually and socially we must acknowledge human dignity, explicate what the realization of that dignity involves and, of course, fashion our existence in a way that realizes this dignity. Fundamental to this process is respect and esteem both for self and for others.

The intentional character of human action entails that we cannot fully or meaningfully realize our dignity in action without an acknowledgement and acceptance of that dignity and an understanding of what its realization involves. Such acknowledgement is the basis of respect and esteem. For the purposes of this present paper we must emphasize that, as John Rawls rightly says, self-respect is a fundamental human good. As the awareness that one's life is fundamentally worth living, self-respect is the precondition for the meaningful realization of our dignity.

In light of this, let me in a broad way (which is both provisional and incomplete) characterize poverty as a destructive and degrading phenomenon. Some social scientists define poverty in terms of relative social deprivation. That is, the poor in a given society are those who are significantly deprived of the ability to live a decent and respectable life within their society. However, any society's conception of a decent and respectable life constitutes that society's conception of a life which is fitting and appropriate for its members as a quality human life and, thus, reflects that society's conception of what the realization of human dignity involves. Thus, the poor in society are those who are substantially deprived of being able to realize their human dignity in the context of what their society believes the realization of that involves.

Given that we are fundamentally in the world, as essentially embodied, social and historical, we must emphasize that our freedom, understanding, self-determination, and thus our dignity, are realized in and through a multiplicity of diverse ways: economically, socially, politically, religiously, in work, in leisure, etc. Thus,

we can speak of a variety of social and other deprivations or of ways in which human dignity is frustrated and violated and persons are impoverished: economic destitution, political oppression, degrading work conditions, substandard health care, inadequate housing, etc.

Each of these forms of poverty can be and frequently are profoundly degrading and destructive. Yet, for example, one can be economically destitute, politically oppressed, trapped in degrading work conditions — one can be frustrated in various and fundamental ways from realizing one's dignity in action — and still retain an understanding of one's dignity, a sense of respect and esteem for self and others. Thus, we speak of the dignity of the poor — of the many poor who in the face of brutalizing conditions retain a sense of their human worth and protest against the poverty which envelops them, refusing to be beaten down by it. (The Joad family in Steinbeck's *Grapes of Wrath* is a prime literary example of such poor.) It seems to me that these forms of poverty, as destructive as they might be, do not of themselves constitute poverty in its most destructive form. This poverty — poverty *in extremis* one might say — directly assaults the very reality of the worthiness of persons. As we will show in detail later, such poverty is defined by stigmatization and inferiorization.

This poverty becomes most destructive when the victims of stigmatization accept and internalize that stigmatization and come to regard themselves as worthless. Such persons suffer a radical loss of self-respect and self-esteem; they lose consciousness of their own dignity and of their capacity to live a decent human life. Such poverty does not lie just in being blocked from realizing dignity in action but in the repudiation of the possibility of realizing one's dignity. . . .

B.

Now it seems to me that there are at least four interrelated constituents of meaningful action in everyday existence: a sense of power or self-agency, purposiveness, worth, and efficacy. Power, of course, is required for meaningful action by the very nature of freedom and the self-agency which renders it possible. The everyday exercise of my freedom is meaningful for me only as I have a sense of power and self-agency: I am able to formulate and realize plans of actions; I have the psycho-physical integrity to do so; I am not merely a pawn in the hands of others or the mere product of forces beyond my control. The necessity of worth for meaningful action stems from the fundamental human need for significance: I need my acts and myself to count for something in the eyes of others. Indeed, my self-respect or esteem is never produced simply by me. The development and maintenance of self-respect and esteem is essentially a social process. Children develop self-respect and esteem only because others regard them as worthy; as "brainwashing" techniques show, individuals can maintain such respect over the long haul only if they are acknowledged as worthy by others. Further, in everyday existence self-respect is developed and maintained by and large through accepting and conforming our actions to what is socially regarded as worthy.

Everyday purposiveness stems from the intentional structure of freedom as the everyday exercise of freedom is fundamentally goal oriented. But a sense of purpose in life does not merely arise from formulating plans, in addition those plans must be worthy, generally as socially and self-defined. Finally, efficacy belongs to everyday meaningful action in a two-fold sense. First, it is not enough to formulate plans — I must act and *successfully* realize

those plans. Second, in everyday life we fundamentally strive to transcend the here-and-now of our existence. We strive individually and socially to leave a mark of our lives, something that endures beyond the transience of the here and now.

It seems to me that in everyday existence, we regard the radical frustration and blockage of our drive for transcendence — which occurs, say, in being reduced to a hand-to-mouth existence or condemned to the monotonous repetition of tasks which as soon as completed have to be redone (the plight of Sisyphus) — as stripping our actions and life not only of efficacy, but also of power, purposiveness and worth. . . .

C.

In everyday existence we find ourselves surrounded by others with whom we share a common world for life and action. In the natural attitude my fellow humans are those who, like me, are endowed with intelligence or consciousness and, in principle, experience the world in a way similar to mine. With my fellow humans I take for granted a reciprocity of perspectives. That is, our standpoints are interchangeable: "If I was where he is now I would experience things in the same perspective, distance and reach as the others," and similarly for him were he to occupy my place. Further, our relevance systems are sufficiently congruent to allow for cooperative existence. That is, despite biographical differences between us, our experience of the world, our values, goals and beliefs are sufficiently common to allow for cooperative existence in the world. Now in the everyday attitude, the life-world is understood as potentially accessible to every one who is "willing, fit and able." My fellow humans and I are precisely those whom we take for granted to be fit, willing and able to participate in the life-world, to join in common economic, social, religious and other activities.

Further, as Schultz observes, while the concept "fellow man" can in principle be extended to everyone it can also be restricted in scope. That is, we (my fellow humans and I) can encounter others who do not experience the world as we do, whose relevance systems are radically dispartite from ours and, who therefore are not like "everyone" but are, rather, something else. Accordingly we (my fellow humans and I) can acknowledge that there are different kinds of humans or we can deny that such persons are "normal" and are, therefore, not really fellow humans, or perhaps even human at all. While the first stance (the other as a different kind of person from us) allows for but does not require tolerance of the other; the second stance invites exclusion and marginalization of the other who is viewed as deviant, defective or unworthy.

It is in terms of this second response that we must locate the dynamics of stigmatization and inferiorization. E. Jones gives the following characterization of stigmatization.

> It is the dramatic essence of the stigmatizing process that a label marking the deviant status is applied, and this marking process typically has devastating consequences for emotions, thought and behavior. Many words have been applied to the resulting status of the deviant person. He or she is flawed, blemished, discredited, spoiled or stigmatized. In the classic case, the mark or sign of deviance initiates a drastic inference process that engulfs impressions of the deviant target person and sets up barriers of interaction and intimacy.

Crucial here is the notion of "impression engulfment." The stigmatized condition engulfs or overwhelms the impressions which the marker (the person doing the stigmatizing) has of the stigmatized person. That is, the stigmatized condition dominates the marker's experience of the victim so that it becomes perceived as the dominant trait of the victim's personality. When the process of stigmatization is internalized, when victims stigmatize themselves, then they see themselves as dominated by the marked condition. This means that a stigmatizing condition is not merely a characteristic or attribute of the victim but is taken to define the core of the victim's personality. Thus, it serves as a locus or site within which the victim's life takes on meaning (or, more precisely, loses meaning) both for the victim and for others.

On the basis of the stigmatization, the victim is defined to be deviant, worthless, defective, spoiled, dangerous, etc. and, indeed, so defined at the core of his or her being. So then, stigmatization essentially reifies individuals, for they are viewed as nothing but the bearer of the stigmatized condition (e.g., alcoholic). That is, stigmatizing roles are not simply played out by victims; they engulf and consume the identity of victims. Finally, in extreme form (e.g., with lepers and AIDS victims) stigmatization can involve disaffiliation and banishment from the community of fellow humans.

Now stigmatized persons may not internalize or accept social stigmas. They may form alternate communities with other such persons, constituting a social world for themselves as well as an alternate, legitimating identity which repudiates their stigmatization. However, internalization of stigmas typically has devastating consequences for victims. Viewing themselves as inherently defective, they come to see themselves as deserving of their condition because responsible for it. As Barry Adam argues this establishes the basis for deep seated masochistic behavior and attitudes. In the belief that they are failures and are responsible for that failure such persons through continued failure seek out punishment from those who stigmatize them as well as those who do not. That is, viewing themselves as deserving failure such persons affirm themselves through repeated failure and by the punishment which they receive for their repeated failure.

Stigmatization, as I suggested earlier, engenders the most radical impoverishment of human beings. Marginalized and disaffiliated, victims of stigmatization generally cease to be regarded as fellow humans entitled to participate in the social world. Inferiorized, such persons generally are viewed as incurably and personally responsible for their failure and defectiveness as human beings (i.e., victim blaming). As such they are taken to deserve only punishment, marginalization, abuse or victimization. Denied to be worthy of respect and esteem, the dignity of such persons is fundamentally repudiated both by themselves and society.

III

American skid rows originated during the last century as urban centers for the homeless and unemployed, especially those dislocated by European war, immigration and economic crises. In its heyday the row was, at times, an active, vital area within a city in which persons were helped to regain a more stable and prosperous life. In addition to the homeless, skid row was populated by various agents of social rehabilitation and private charity as well as a variety of colorful transients, such as hoboes, and various political activists and rebels. This situation changed gradually during the mid-years of this

century until the row was populated primarily by a variety of men (and, more recently, women) who settled permanently on the row (or moved from one row to another), unable to function adequately within dominant American society. Such men were frequently old, unemployed, physically and psychologically damaged, disaffiliated and alcoholic.

While it is true that many persons turn to skid row as one of the few if only places that they can find acceptance, Howard Bahr argues that increased acculturation into skid row involves both increased disaffiliation with little or no new establishment of stable, affiliative bonds as well as increased stigmatization (both socially and self-imposed) which marks the skid row resident as increasingly defective and worthless. These processes are frequently exacerbated by alcoholism. In other words, to live on skid row as *skid* row (to be on-the-skids) is to be drawn towards and to allow oneself to be drawn towards chronic, alcoholic dereliction. The fully acculturated member of skid row is the chronic, alcoholic "derelict."

Despite a popular image of skid row residents as gregarious and ready to give "the shirt off their back" to another on skid row, empirical evidence suggests that such persons (especially the alcoholics) show widespread antipathy and lack of trust to one another and that their relationships are stripped of loyalty or responsibility. Further, their socialization onto the row is marked by a hatred of the life there. As Charles Bouge writes:

> . . . the answer to "What do homeless men think of skid row living" is that they hate it. This verdict is shared by controlled and uncontrolled drinkers alike. Moreover these men have so little "we-feeling" that it seems almost a contradiction to speak of skid row society.

Skid row residents, in other words, are not merely disaffiliated from the dominant American society but, with increased acculturation into the row, from one another as well.

Bahr gives a poignant description of the imputed defectiveness that accompanies this disaffiliation:

> The defectiveness of the skid row man stems from his occupying several stigmatized statuses at once. . . . To begin with there is a physical, visible basis for antipathy towards the skid row man. He is defective physically: the scarred face, the toothless mouth, the missing limbs, the strange actions of the psychotic or mental incompetent. . . . Then there are the stigmatizing aspects of his character: the past of drunkenness, arrests and prison and the long periods of institutional living . . . he is old . . . he is deviant . . . he is poor . . . frequently unemployed and has a bad address. Over everything else is the imputed alcoholism, the addiction which makes him a man out of control, perhaps not a man at all.

As Bahr writes elsewhere:

> His defectiveness and powerlessness combine with his other negative characteristics real or imagined and predefine him to involvement in a vicious cycle of negative encounters which serve to bind him to skid row, lower his self-esteem and make a social fact out of what was at first social definition . . . that he is hopeless and unsalvageable.

The dynamics of stigmatization and disaffiliation constitute the social reality of skid row. As individuals tend toward alcoholic dereliction, the conditions of isolation, mutual distrust, self-hatred and powerlessness undermine whatever attempt such persons might make to fashion a social reality that is a stable, viable community. The institutional order imposed on the row by the broader community — especially in the institutions designed for control and rehabilitation — is notorious for its delegitimation of skid row persons and for its failure to positively assist them. There is wide-spread contempt and disgust for skid row residents among the professionals who work with them, the judicial system is a "revolving door," and the institutions for control and rehabilitation form a "loop." That is, the skid row resident is subject to a continuous cycle of arrest, trial, imprisonment, referral to missions, psychiatric units or other rehabilitation agencies only to end up back on the streets in the same or the worse condition than before. Skid row is itself a fundamentally impoverishing social reality. Constituted by stigmatizing, dead-end roles, an institutional order which tends toward indifference or domination and exploitation, as well as dominant ideologies which delegitimate the skid row resident, the row, in the final analysis, ceases to be social world as a domain for meaningful action for the skid row resident completely acculturated to the row.

Locked into the row, the "derelict's" life is played out in essentially stigmatizing, dead-end and reifying roles. Both for society at large and for the "derelict," he or she is nothing but a "bum," a "derelict," a "wino" and, therefore, imputed to be worthless to the core of his or her being. Such acculturation increasingly undermines the possibility of meaningful action as constituted by power, purposiveness, worth and efficacy. The skid row person increasingly suffers a loss of self-worth resulting from social and self-stigmatization and which undermines the possibility of engaging in meaningful action as socially and self-defined. Loss of worth is accompanied by increasing powerlessness. Driven by addictions that appear uncontrollable, often dominated and exploited by the institutional order of the row, subject to continuous vulnerability to and victimization by others, the skid row person's life appears increasingly out of his or her control. Powerlessness and imputed worthlessness engender increasing loss of purpose constituted by failure and passivity. One appears unable either to formulate plans which are worthy of realizing or to realize in a worthy, efficacious manner the plans one might have except in the masochistic affirmation of one's self as a failure. More radically, except for minimal precarious satisfaction of basic physical needs one simply gives up on life, condemned to skid row both by self and society.

To be on-the-skids is to be fundamentally and increasingly impoverished: stigmatization, social isolation, poor health, psycho-physical disabilities and addictions, economic and multiple social deprivations serve to make it increasingly difficult for the person on-the-skids to acknowledge, much less realize, his or her human dignity. We can now express the temporal structure of skid row poverty. In stark contrast to the broader community of fellow humans, of those who are recognized as "fit, willing and able" to participate in the social world and who orient themselves to their past in terms of success, their future in terms of confidence to fashion their lives in a worthy and efficacious manner, and to the present in terms of acknowledged power and self-agency, skid-row poverty is defined by imputed failure, hopelessness and powerlessness. The skid row person's past is dominated by failure — not merely failure at this or that activity, but apparent failure as a human being. For such a person the idealization "I can always do it again" means "I am condemned to repeat past failure" (e.g., recidivism is the dominant

experience of the chronic alcoholic). Thus, the possibility of living in a worthy, efficacious manner becomes inaccessible and hopelessly out of reach. So the present is dominated by powerlessness; believing him or herself to be a failure, the skid row "derelict" acts and appears a failure.

The person who tends toward complete acculturation into skid row inhabits a region of increasing and apparently irrevocable disaffiliation and rejection. Imputed to be unfit, unwilling or unable to dwell in the social world such a person is driven out of the community of fellow humans. Such a person "ceases to be among men" which means, as the ancient Romans understood, that such a person is dead. . . .

The isolation and atomization of skid row is accompanied by a radical undermining of the possibility of concernful dealings with things and people. Past affiliations are infrequent or, more typically, permanently severed; present interrelations become transient and unstable. More often than not the "derelict" finds him or herself powerless, dominated and victimized and, because of his or her imputed worthlessness, cut off from the web of exchange relations — both economic and non-economic — which constitute the fabric of everyday existence. Further, the stigmatizing typifications through which the "derelict" is viewed by others can preclude the possibility of face-to-face encounters with them as fellow human beings. As one social worker observed:

> I began to think that they [Harry and Al] never had an original thought or noble moment. Everything about them — their faces, their bodies, their minds, their souls — was stunted and soiled. They lacked the ability even to *experience* their lives as real.

Economically destitute, the world of

commodities — which in consumeristic, industrialized countries threatens to become coextensive with the world itself — becomes virtually inaccessible. Unemployed, and frequently suffering from multiple physical and mental disabilities, the derelict is prevented from productive, creative work or self-expression. . . .

Thus, skid row poverty engenders the living death of the skid row "derelict." Having come to ruin as totally worthless and solely responsible for this failure, as well as isolated, radically disaffiliated from others and cut off from productive or creative involvement with things, the "derelict" finds that his or her existence is completely defined by the row — he or she is nothing but a "derelict" — and, so apparently hopelessly trapped on the row, condemned to a poverty which will inevitably perdure and which, therefore, appears unsurpassable. The "derelict," as one skid row resident remarked, waits for nothing. Having hit bottom, and thus seemingly irrevocably severed from the possibility of living well, the "derelict" dies only to await what appears the final event — death.

The death of another human being, especially when the death results from human agency, demands moral assessment and response. Given the inherent character of our dignity, the death engendered by skid row poverty, which wrongfully repudiates the dignity of the skid row person, can only be viewed as unjustifiable homicide, caused by a tragic interplay of social murder and suicide. In the face of such a death, one must at the very least, as Dylan Thomas once wrote, "rage, rage against the dying of the light."

PETER MARIN
Helping and Hating the Homeless

PETER MARIN *is a contributing editor of Harper's* Magazine *and has written a book about homelessness.*

THE trouble begins with the word "homeless." It has become such an abstraction, and is applied to so many different kinds of people, with so many different histories and problems, that it is almost meaningless.

Homelessness, in itself, is nothing more than a condition visited upon men and women (and, increasingly, children) as the final stage of a variety of problems about which the word "homelessness" tells us almost nothing. Or, to put it another way, it is a catch basin into which pour all of the people disenfranchised or marginalized or scared off by processes beyond their control, those which lie close to the heart of American life. Here are the groups packed into the single category of "the homeless":

▶ Veterans, mainly from the war in Vietnam. In many American cities, vets make up close to 50 percent of all homeless males.

▶ The mentally ill. In some parts of the

country, roughly a quarter of the homeless would, a couple of decades ago, have been institutionalized.

▶ The physically disabled or chronically ill, who do not receive any benefits or whose benefits do not enable them to afford permanent shelter.

▶ The elderly on fixed incomes whose funds are no longer sufficient for their needs.

▶ Men, women, and whole families pauperized by the loss of a job.

▶ Single parents, usually women, without the resources or skills to establish new lives.

▶ Runaway children, many of whom have been abused.

▶ Alcoholics and those in trouble with drugs (whose troubles often begin with one of the other conditions listed here).

▶ Immigrants, both legal and illegal, who often are not counted among the homeless because they constitute a "problem" in their own right.

▶ Traditional tramps, hobos, and transients, who have taken to the road or the streets for a variety of reasons and who prefer to be there.

You can quickly learn two things about the homeless from this list. First, you can learn that many of the homeless, before they were homeless, were people more or less like ourselves: members of the working or middle class. And you can learn that the world of the homeless has its roots in various policies, events, and ways of life for which some of us are responsible and from which some of us actually prosper.

We decide, as a people, to go to war, we ask our children to kill and to die, and the result, years later, is grown men homeless on the street.

We change, with the best intentions, the laws pertaining to the mentally ill and then, without intention, neglect to provide them with services; and the result, in our streets, drives some of us crazy with rage.

We cut taxes and prune budgets, we modernize industry and shift the balance of trade, and the result of all these actions and errors can be read, sleeping form by sleeping form, on our city streets.

The liberals cannot blame the conservatives. The conservatives cannot blame the liberals. Homelessness is the *sum total* of our dreams, policies, intentions, errors, omissions, cruelties, kindnesses, all of it recorded, in flesh, in the life of the streets.

You can also learn from this list one of the most important things there is to know about the homeless — that they can be roughly divided into two groups: those who have had homelessness forced upon them and want nothing more than to escape it; and those who have at least in part *chosen* it for themselves, and now accept, or in some cases, embrace it.

I understand how dangerous it is to introduce the idea of choice into a discussion of homelessness. It can all too easily be used to justify indifference or brutality toward the homeless, or to argue that they are only getting what they "deserve." And yet it seems to me that it is only by taking choice into account, in all of the intricacies of its various forms and expressions, that one can really understand certain kinds of homelessness.

The fact is, many of the homeless are not only hapless victims but voluntary exiles, "domestic refugees," people who have turned not against life itself but against *us*, our life, American life. Look for a moment at the vets. The price of returning to America was to forget what they had seen or learned in Vietnam, to "put it behind them." But some could not do that, and the stress of trying showed up as alcoholism, broken marriages, drug addiction, crime. And it showed up too as life on the street, which was for some vets a desperate choice made in the name of life — the best they could manage. It was a way of avoiding what might have occurred had they stayed where they were: suicide, or violence done to others.

We must learn to accept that there may indeed be people, and not only vets, who have seen so much of our world, or seen it so clearly, that to live in it becomes impossible. Here, for example, is the story of Alice, a homeless middle-aged woman in Los Angeles, where there are, perhaps, 50,000 homeless people. It was set down a few months ago by one of my students at the University of California, Santa Barbara, where I taught for a semester. I had encouraged them to go find the homeless and listen to their stories. And so, one day, when this student saw Alice foraging in a dumpster outside a McDonald's, he stopped and talked to her:

> She told me she had led a pretty normal life as she grew up and eventually went to college. From there she went on to Chicago to teach school. She was single and lived in a small apartment.
>
> One night, after she got off the train after school, a man began to follow her to her apartment building. When she got to her door she saw a knife and the man hovering behind her. She had no choice but to let him in. The man raped her.
>
> After that, things got steadily worse. She had a nervous breakdown. She went to a mental institution for three months, and when she went back to her apartment she found her belongings gone. The landlord had sold them to cover the rent she hadn't paid.
>
> She had no place to go and no job because the school had terminated her employment. She slipped into depression. She lived with friends until she could muster enough money for a ticket to Los Angeles. She said she no longer wanted to burden her friends, and that if she had to live outside, at least Los Angeles was warmer than Chicago.
>
> It is as if she began back then to take on the mentality of a street person. She resolved herself to homelessness. She's been out West since 1980, without a home or job. She seems happy, with her best friend being her cat. But the scars of memories still haunt her, and she is running from them, or should I say *him*.

This is, in essence, the same story one hears over and over again on the street. You begin with an ordinary life; then an event occurs — traumatic, catastrophic; smaller events follow, each one deepening the original wound; finally, homelessness becomes inevitable, or begins to *seem* inevitable to the person involved — the only way out of an intolerable situation. You are struck continually, hearing these stories, by something seemingly unique in American life, the absolute isolation involved. In what other culture would there be such an absence or failure of support from familial, social, or institutional sources? Even more disturbing is the fact that it is often our supposed sources of support — family, friends, government organizations — that have caused the problem in the first place.

Everything that happened to Alice — the rape, the loss of job and apartment, the breakdown — was part and parcel of a world gone radically wrong, a world, for Alice, no longer to be counted on, no longer worth living in. Her homelessness can be seen as flight, as failure of will or nerve, even, perhaps, as *disease*. But it can also be seen as a mute, furious refusal, a self-imposed exile far less appealing to the rest of us than ordinary life, but *better*, in Alice's terms.

We like to think, in America, that everything is redeemable, that everything broken can be magically made whole again, and that what has been "dirtied" can be cleansed. Recently I saw on television that one of the soaps had introduced the character of a homeless old woman. A woman in her thirties discovers that her long-lost mother has appeared in town, on the streets. After much searching the mother is located and identified and embraced; and then she is scrubbed and dressed in style, restored in a matter of days to her former upper-class habits and role.

A triumph — but one more likely to occur on television than in real life. Yes, many of those on the streets could be transformed, rehabilitated. But there are others whose lives have been irrevocably changed, damaged beyond repair, and who no longer want help, who no longer recognize the *need* for help, and whose experience in our world has made them want only to be left alone. How, for instance, would one restore Alice's life, or reshape it in a way that would satisfy *our* notion of what a life should be? What would it take to return her to the fold? How to erase the four years of homelessness, which have become as familiar to her, and as much a home, as her "normal" life once was? Whatever we think of the way in which she has resolved her difficulties, it constitutes a sad peace made with the world. Intruding ourselves upon it in the name of redemption is by no means as simple a task — or as justifiable a task — as one might think.

It is important to understand too that however disorderly and dirty and unmanageable the world of homeless men and women like Alice appears to us, it is not without its significance, and its rules and rituals. The homeless in our cities mark out for themselves particular neighborhoods, blocks, buildings, doorways. They impose on themselves often obsessively strict routines. They reduce their world to a small area, and thereby protect themselves from a world that might otherwise be too much to bear.

Pavlov, the Russian psychologist, once theorized that the two most fundamental reflexes in all animals, including humans, are those involving freedom and orientation. Grab any animal, he said, and it will immediately struggle to accomplish two things: to break free and to orient itself. And this is what one sees in so many of the homeless. Having been stripped of all other forms of connection, and of most kinds of social identity, they are left only with this: the raw stuff of nature, something encoded in the cells — the desire to be free, the need for familiar space. Perhaps this is why so many of them struggle so vehemently against us when we offer them aid. They are clinging to their freedom and their space, and they do not believe that this is what we, with our programs and our shelters, mean to allow them. . . .

It is important to . . . recognize the immensity of the changes that have occurred in the marginal world in the past twenty years. Whole sections of many cities — the Bowery in New York, the Tenderloin in San Francisco — were once ceded to the transient. In every skid-row area in America you could find what you needed to survive: hash houses, saloons offering free lunches, pawnshops, surplus-clothing stores, and, most important of all, cheap hotels and flophouses and two-bit employment agencies specializing in the kinds of labor (seasonal, shape-up) transients have always done.

It was by no means a wonderful world. But it *was* a world. Its rituals were spelled out in ways most of the participants understood. In hobo jungles up and down the tracks, whatever there was to eat went into a common pot and was divided equally. Late at night, in empties criss-crossing the country, men would speak with a certain anonymous openness, as if the shared condition of transience created among them a kind of civility.

What most people in that world wanted was simply to be left alone. Some of them had been on the road for years, itinerant workers. Others were recuperating from wounds they could never quite explain. There were young men and a few women with nothing better to do, and older men who had no families or had lost their jobs or wives, or for whom the rigor and pressure of life had proved too demanding. The marginal world offered them a respite from the other world, a world grown too much for them.

But things have changed. There began to pour into the marginal world — slowly in the sixties, a bit faster in the seventies, and then faster still in the eighties — more and more people who neither belonged nor knew how to survive there. The sixties brought the counterculture and drugs; the streets filled with young dropouts. Changes in the law loosed upon the streets mentally ill men and women. Inflation took its toll, then recession. Working-class and even middle-class men and women — entire families — began to fall into a world they did not understand.

At the same time the transient world was being inundated by new inhabitants, its landscape, its economy, was shrinking radically. Jobs became harder to find. Modernization had something to do with it; machines took the place of men and women. And the influx of workers from Mexico and points farther south created a class of semipermanent workers who took the place of casual transient labor. More important, perhaps, was the fact that the forgotten parts of many cities began to

attract attention. Downtown areas were redeveloped, reclaimed. The skid-row sections of smaller cities were tuned into "old townes." The old hotels that once catered to transients were upgraded or torn down or became warehouses for welfare families — an arrangement far more profitable to the owners. The price of housing increased; evictions increased. The mentally ill, who once could afford to house themselves in cheap rooms, the alcoholics, who once would drink themselves to sleep at night in their cheap hotels, were out on the street — exposed to the weather and to danger, and also in plain and public view: "problems" to be dealt with.

Nor was it only cheap shelter that disappeared. It was also those "open" spaces that had once been available to those without other shelter. As property rose in value, the nooks and crannies in which the homeless had been able to hide became more visible. Doorways, alleys, abandoned buildings, vacant lots — these "holes" in the cityscape, these gaps in public consciousness, became *real estate*. The homeless, who had been there all the time, were overtaken by economic progress, and they became intruders.

You cannot help thinking, as you watch this process, of what happened in parts of Europe in the eighteenth and nineteenth centuries: the effects of the enclosure laws, which eliminated the "commons" in the countryside and drove the rural poor, now homeless, into the cities. The centuries-old tradition of common access and usage was swept away by the beginnings of industrialism; land became *privatized*, a commodity. At the same time something occurred in the cultural psyche. The world itself, space itself, was subtly altered. It was no longer merely to be lived in; it was now to be owned. What was enclosed was not only the land. It was also *the flesh itself*; it was cut off from, denied access to, the physical world.

And one thinks too, when thinking of the homeless, of the American past, the settlement of the "new" world which occurred at precisely the same time that the commons disappeared. The dream of freedom and equality that brought men and women here had something to do with *space*, as if the wilderness itself conferred upon those arriving here a new beginning: the Eden that had been lost. Once God had sent Christ to redeem men; now he provided a new world. Men discovered, or believed, that this world, and perhaps time itself, had no edge, no limit. Space was a sign of God's magnanimity. It was a kind of grace.

Somehow, it is all this that is folded into the sad shapes of the homeless. In their mute presence one can sense, however faintly, the dreams of a world gone aglimmering, and the presence of our failed hopes. A kind of claim is made, silently, an ethic is proffered, or, if you will, a whole cosmology, one older than our own ideas of privilege and property. It is as if flesh itself were seeking, this one last time, the home in the world it has been denied.

Daily the city eddies around the homeless. The crowds flowing past leave a few feet, a gap. We do not touch the homeless world. Perhaps we cannot touch it. It remains separate even as the city surrounds it.

The homeless, simply because they are homeless, are strangers, alien—and therefore a threat. Their presence, in itself, comes to constitute a kind of violence; it deprives us of our sense of safety. Let me use myself as an example. I know, and respect, many of those now homeless on the streets of Santa Barbara. Twenty years ago, some of them would have been my companions and friends. And yet, these days, if I walk through the park near my home and see strangers bedding down for the night, my first reaction, if not fear, is a sense of annoyance and intrusion, of worry and alarm. I think of my teenage daughter, who often walks through the park, and then of my house, a hundred yards away, and I am tempted—only tempted, but tempted, still—to call the "proper" authorities to have the strangers moved on. Out of sight, out of mind.

Notice: I do not bring them food. I do not offer them shelter or a shower in the morning. I do not even stop to talk. Instead, I think: my daughter, my house, my privacy. What moves me is not the threat of *danger*—nothing as animal as that. Instead there pops up inside of me, neatly in a row, a set of anxieties, ones you might arrange in a dollhouse living room and label: Family of bourgeois fears. The point is this: our response to the homeless is fed by a complex set of cultural attitudes, habits of thought, and fantasies and fears so familiar to us, so common, that they have become a *second* nature and might as well be instinctive, for all the control we have over them. And it is by no means easy to untangle this snarl of responses. What does seem clear is that the homeless embody all that bourgeois culture has for centuries tried to eradicate and destroy.

If you look to the history of Europe you find that homelessness first appears (or is first acknowledged) at the very same moment that bourgeois culture begins to appear. The same processes produced them both: the breakup of feudalism, the rise of commerce and cities, the combined triumphs of capitalism, industrialism, and individualism. The historian Fernand Braudel, in *The Wheels of Commerce*, describes, for instance, the armies of impoverished men and women who began to haunt Europe as far back as the eleventh century. And the makeup of these masses? Essentially the same then as it is now: the unfortunates, the throwaways, the misfits, the deviants. . . .

It is in the nineteenth century, in the Victorian era, that you can find the beginnings of our modern strategies for dealing with the homeless: the notion that they should be controlled and perhaps eliminated through "help." With the Victorians we begin to see the entangling of self-protection with social obligation, the strategy of masking self-interest and the urge to control as *moral duty*. Michel Foucault has spelled this out in his books on madness and punishment: the zeal with which the overseers of early bourgeois culture tried to purge, improve, and purify all of urban civilization — whether through schools and prisons, or, quite literally, with public baths and massive new water and sewage systems. Order, ordure — this is, in essence, the tension at the heart of bourgeois culture, and it was the singular genius of the Victorians to make it the main component of their medical, aesthetic, *and* moral systems. It was not a sense of justice or even empathy which called for charity or new attitudes toward the poor; it was *hygiene*. The very same attitudes appear in nineteenth-century America. Charles Loring Brace, in an essay on homeless and vagrant children written in 1876, described the treatment of delinquents in this way: "Many of their vices drop from them like the old and verminous clothing they left behind. . . . The entire change of circumstances seems to cleanse them of bad habits." Here you have it all: *vices, verminous clothing, cleansing them of bad habits* — the triple association of poverty with vice

with dirt, an equation in which each term comes to stand for all of them.

These attitudes are with us still; that is the point. In our own century the person who has written most revealingly about such things is George Orwell, who tried to analyze his own middle-class attitudes toward the poor. . . .

To put it as bluntly as I can, for many of us the homeless are *shit*. And our policies toward them, our spontaneous sense of disgust and horror, our wish to be rid of them — all of this has hidden in it, close to its heart, our feelings about excrement. Even Marx, that most bourgeois of revolutionaries, described the deviant *lumpen* in *The Eighteenth Brumaire of Louis Bonaparte* as "scum, offal, refuse of all classes." These days, in puritanical Marxist nations, they are called "parasites" — a word, perhaps not incidentally, one also associates with human waste.

What I am getting at here is the *nature* of the desire to help the homeless — what is hidden behind it and why it so often does harm. Every government program, almost every private project, is geared as much to the needs of those giving help as it is to the needs of the homeless. Go to any government agency, or, for that matter, to most private charities, and you will find yourself enmeshed, at once, in a bureaucracy so tangled and oppressive, or confronted with so much moral arrogance and contempt, that you will be driven back out into the streets for relief.

Santa Barbara, where I live, is as good an example as any. There are three main shelters in the city — all of them private. Between them they provide fewer than a hundred beds a night for the homeless. Two of the three shelters are religious in nature: the Rescue Mission and the Salvation Army. In the mission, as in most places in the country, there are elaborate and stringent rules. Beds go first to those who have not been there for two months, and you can stay for only two nights in any two-month period. No shelter is given to those who are not sober. Even if you go to the mission only for a meal, you are required to listen to sermons and participate in prayer, and you are regularly proselytized — sometimes overtly, sometimes subtly. There are obligatory, regimented showers. You go to bed precisely at ten: lights out, no reading, no talking. After the lights go out you will find fifteen men in a room with double-decker bunks. As the night progresses the room grows stuffier and hotter. Men toss, turn, cough, and moan. In the morning you are awakened precisely at five forty-five. Then breakfast. At seven-thirty you are back on the street.

The town's newest shelter was opened almost a year ago by a consortium of local churches. Families and those who are employed have first call on the beds — a policy which excludes the congenitally homeless. Alcohol is not simply forbidden *in* the shelter; those with a history of alcoholism must sign a "contract" pledging to remain sober and chemical-free. Finally, in a paroxysm of therapeutic bullying, the shelter has added a new wrinkle: if you stay more than two days you are required to fill out and then discuss with a social worker a complex form listing what you perceive as your personal failings, goals, and strategies — all of this for men and women who simply want a place to lie down out of the rain!

It is these attitudes, in various forms and permutations, that you find repeated endlessly in America. We are moved either to "redeem" the homeless or to punish them. Perhaps there is nothing consciously hostile about it. Perhaps it is simply that as the machinery of bureaucracy cranks itself up to deal with these problems, attitudes assert themselves automatically. But whatever the case, the fact remains that almost every one of our strategies for helping the homeless is simply an attempt to rearrange the world *cosmetically*, in terms of how it looks and smells to *us*. Compassion is little more than the passion for control.

The central question emerging from all this is, What does a society owe to its members in trouble, and *how* is that debt to be paid? It is a question which must be answered in two parts: first, in relation to the men and women who have been marginalized against their will, and then, in a slightly different way, in relation to those who have chosen (or accept or even prize) their marginality.

As for those who have been marginalized against their wills, I think the general answer is obvious: A society owes its members whatever it takes for them to regain their places in the social order. And when it comes to specific remedies, one need only read backward the various processes which have created homelessness and then figure out where help is likely to do the most good. But the real point here is not the specific remedies required — affordable housing, say — but the basis upon which they must be offered, the necessary underlying ethical notion we seem in this nation unable to grasp that those who are the inevitable casualties of modern industrial capitalism and the free-market system are entitled, *by right*, and by the simple virtue of their participation in that system, to whatever help they need. They are entitled to help to find and hold their places in the society whose social contract they have, in effect, signed and observed.

Look at that for just a moment: the notion of a contract. The majority of homeless Americans have kept, insofar as they could, to the terms of that contract. In any shelter these days you can find men and women who have worked ten, twenty, forty years, and whose lives have nonetheless come to nothing. These are people who cannot afford a place in the world they helped create. And in return? Is it life on the street they have earned? Or the cruel charity we so grudgingly grant them?

But those marginalized against their will are only half the problem. There remains, still, the question of whether we owe anything to those who are voluntarily marginal. What about them: the street people, the rebels, and the recalcitrants, those who have torn up their social contracts or returned them unsigned?

I was in Las Vegas last fall, and I went out to the Rescue Mission at the lower end of town, on the edge of the black ghetto, where I first stayed years ago on my way west. It was twilight, still hot; in the vacant lot next door to the mission 200 men were lining up for super. A warm wind blew along the street lined with small houses and salvage yards, and in the distance I could see the desert's edge and the smudge of low hills in the fading light. There were elderly alcoholics in line, and derelicts, but mainly the men were the same sort I had seen here years ago: youngish, out of work, restless and talkative, the drifters and wanderers for whom the word "wanderlust" was invented.

At supper — long communal tables, thin gruel, stale sweet rolls, ice water — a huge black man in his twenties, fierce and muscular, sat across from me. "I'm from the Coast, man," he said. "Never been away from home before. Ain't sure I like it. Sure don't like *this* place. But I lost my job back home a couple of weeks ago and figured, why wait around for another. I thought I'd come out here, see me something of the world."

After supper, a squat Portuguese man in his mid-thirties, hunkered down against the mission wall, offered me a smoke and told me: "Been sleeping in my car, up the street, for a week. Had my own business back in Omaha. But I got bored, man. Sold everything, got a little dough, came out here. Thought I'd work construction. Let me tell you, this is one tough town."

In a world better than ours, I suppose, men (or women) like this might not exist. Conservatives seem to have no trouble imagining a society so well disciplined and moral that deviance of this kind would disappear. And leftists envision a world so just, so generous, that deviance would vanish along with inequity. But I suspect that there will always be something at work in some men and women to make them restless with the systems others devise for them, and to move them outward toward the edges of the world, where life is always riskier, less organized, and easier going.

Do we owe anything to these men and women, who reject our company and what we offer and yet nonetheless seem to demand *something* from us?

We owe them, I think, at least a place to exist, a way to exist. That may not be a *moral* obligation, in the sense that our obligation to the involuntarily marginal is clearly a moral one, but it is an obligation nevertheless, one you might call an existential obligation.

Of course, it may be that I think we owe these men something because I have liked men like them, and because I want their world to be there always, as a place to hide or rest. But there is more to it than that. I think we as a society need men like these. A society needs its margins as much as it needs art and literature. It needs holes and gaps, *breathing spaces*, let us say, into which men and women can escape and live, when necessary, in ways other wise denied them. Margins guarantee to society a flexibility, an elasticity, and allow it to accommodate itself to the natures and needs of its members. When margins vanish, society becomes too rigid, too oppressive by far, and therefore inimical to life.

It is for such reasons that, in cultures like our own, marginal men and women take on a special significance. They are all we have left to remind us of the narrowness of the received truths we take for granted. "Beyond the pale," they somehow redefine the pale, or remind us, at least, that *something* is still out there, beyond the pale. They preserve, perhaps unconsciously, a dream that would otherwise cease to exist, the dream of having a place in the world, and of being *left alone*.

Quixotic? Infantile? Perhaps. But remember Pavlov and his reflexes coded in the flesh: animal, and therefore as if given by God. What we are talking about here is *freedom*, and with it, perhaps, an echo of the dream men brought, long ago, to wilderness America. I use the word "freedom" gingerly, in relation to lives like these: skewed, crippled, emptied of everything we associate with a full, or realized, freedom. But perhaps this is the condition into which freedom has fallen among us. Art has been "appreciated" out of existence; literature has become an extension of the university, replete with ten-

ure and pensions; and as for politics, the ideologies which ring us round seem too silly or shrill by far to speak for life. What is left, then, is this mute and intransigent independence, this "waste" of life which refuses even interpretation, and which cannot be assimilated to any ideology, and which therefore can be put to no one's use. In its crippled innocence and the perfection of its superfluity it amounts, almost, to a rebellion against history, and that is no small thing.

Let me put it as simply as I can: what we see on the streets of our cities are two dramas, both of which cut to the troubled heart of the culture and demand from us a response we may not be able to make. There is the drama of those struggling to survive by regaining their place in the social order. And there is the drama of those struggling to survive outside of it.

The resolution of both struggles depends on a third drama occurring at the heart of the culture: the tension and contention between the magnanimity we owe to life and the darker tendings of the human psyche: our fear of strangeness, our hatred of deviance, our love of order and control. How we mediate by default or design between those contrary forces will determine not only the destinies of the homeless but also something crucial about the nation, and perhaps — let me say it — about our own souls.

NANCY FRASER

Women, Welfare, and the Politics of Need Interpretation

NANCY FRASER *teaches philosophy, comparative literature, and women's studies at Northwestern University. Since the 1960s, she has been an activist in several oppositional social movements and is the author of* Unruly Practices: Power, Discourse and Gender in Contemporary Social Philosophy *(1989).*

LONG before the emergence of welfare states, governments have defined legally secured arenas of societal action. In so doing, they have at the same time codified corresponding patterns of agency or social roles. Thus, early modern states defined an economic arena and the corresponding role of an economic person capable of entering into contracts. More or less at the same time, they codified the "private sphere" of the household and the role of household head with dependents. Somewhat later, governments were led to secure a sphere of political participation and the corresponding role of citizen with (limited) political rights. In each of these cases, the original and paradigmatic subject of the newly codified social role was male. Only secondarily and much later was it conceded that women, too, could occupy these subject-positions, without however entirely dispelling the association with masculinity.

Matters are different, however, with the contemporary welfare state. When this type of government defined a new arena of activity — call it "the social" — and a new societal role, the welfare client, it included women among its original and paradigmatic subjects. Today, in fact, women have become the principal subjects of the welfare state. On the one hand, they comprise the overwhelming majority both of program recipients and of paid social service workers. On the other hand, they are the wives, mothers and daughters whose unpaid activities and obligations are redefined as the welfare state increasingly oversees forms of caregiving. Since this beneficiary-social worker-caregiver nexus of roles is constitutive of the social-welfare arena, one might even call the latter as feminized terrain.

A brief statistical overview confirms women's greater involvement with and dependence on the U.S. social-welfare system. Consider first women's greater dependence as program clients and beneficiaries. In each of the major "means-tested" programs in the U.S., women and the children for whom they are responsible now comprise the overwhelming majority of clients. For example, more than 81% of households receiving Aid to Families with Dependent Children (AFDC) are headed by women; more than 60% of families receiving food stamps or Medicaid are headed by women; and 70% of all households in publicly owned or subsidized housing are headed by women. High as they are, these figures actually underestimate the representation of women. As Barbara Nelson notes, in the androcentric reporting system, households counted as female-headed by definition contain no healthy adult men. But healthy adult women live in most households counted as male-headed. Such women may directly or indirectly receive benefits going to "male-headed" households, but they are invisible in the statistics, even though they usually do the work of securing and maintaining program eligibility.

Women also predominate in the major U.S. "age-tested" programs. For example, 61.6% of all adult beneficiaries of Social Security are women; and 64% of those covered by Medicare are women. In sum, because women as a group are significantly poorer than men — indeed they now comprise nearly two-thirds of all U.S. adults below the official poverty line — and because women tend to live longer than men, women depend more on the social-welfare system as clients and beneficiaries.

But this is not the whole story. Women also depend more on the social-welfare system as paid human service workers — a category of employment which includes education and health, as well as social work and services administration. In 1980, 70% of the 17.3 million paid jobs in this sector in the U.S. were held by women. This accounts for one-third of U.S. women's total paid employment and a full 80% of all professional jobs held by women. The figures for women of color are even higher than this average, since 37% of their total paid employment and 82.4% of their professional employment is in this sector. It is a distinctive feature of the U.S. social-welfare system, as opposed to, say, the British and Scandinavian systems, that only 3% of these jobs are in the form of direct federal government employment. The rest are in state and local government, in the "private non-profit" sector and in the "private" sector. But the more decentralized and privatized character of the U.S. system

does not make paid welfare workers any less vulnerable in the face of federal program cuts. On the contrary, the level of federal social-welfare spending affects the level of human service employment in *all* sectors. State and local government jobs depend on federal and federally-financed state and local government contracts; and private profit and non-profit jobs depend on federally financed transfer payments to individuals and households for the purchase of services like health care in the market. Thus, reductions in social spending mean the loss of jobs for women. Moreover, as Barbara Ehrenreich and Frances Fox Piven note, this loss is not compensated when spending is shifted to the military, since only 0.5% of the entire female paid workforce is employed in work on military contracts. In fact, one study they cite estimates that with each one billion dollar increase in military spending, 9500 jobs are lost to women.

Finally, women are subjects of and to the social-welfare system in their traditional capacity as unpaid caregivers. It is well known that the sexual division of labor assigns women primary responsibility for the care of those who cannot care for themselves. (I leave aside women's traditional obligations to provide personal services to adult males — husbands, fathers, grown sons, lovers — who can very well care for themselves.) Such responsibility includes child care, of course, but also care for sick and/or elderly relatives, often parents. For example, a 1975 British study cited by Hilary Land found that three times as many elderly people live with married daughters as with married sons, and that those without a close female relative were more likely to be institutionalized, irrespective of degree of infirmity. As unpaid caregivers, then, women are more directly affected than men by the level and character of government social services for children, the sick and the elderly.

As clients, paid human service workers and unpaid caregivers, then, women are the principal subjects of the social-welfare system. It is as if this branch of the state were in effect a "Bureau of Women's Affairs."

Of course, the welfare system does not deal with women on women's terms. On the contrary, it has its own characteristic ways of interpreting women's needs and positioning women as subjects. In order to understand these, we need to examine how gender norms and meanings are reflected in the structure of the U.S. social-welfare system.

This issue is quite complicated. On the one hand, nearly all U.S. social-welfare programs are officially gender neutral. Yet the system as a whole is a dual or two-tiered one; and it has an unmistakable gender subtext. There is one set of programs oriented to *individuals* and tied to participation in the paid workforce, for example, unemployment insurance and Social Security. These programs are designed to supplement and compensate for the primary market in paid labor power. There is a second set of programs oriented to *households* and tied to combined household income, for example, AFDC, food stamps and Medicaid. These programs are designed to compensate for what are considered to be family failures, generally the absence of a male breadwinner.

What integrates the two sets of programs is a common core of assumptions, underlying both, concerning the sexual division of labor, domestic and nondomestic. It is assumed that families do or should contain one primary breadwinner who is male and one unpaid domestic worker (homemaker and mother) who is female. It is further assumed that when a woman undertakes paid work outside the home this is or should be in order to supplement the male breadwinner's wage and so it neither does nor ought override her primary housewifely and maternal responsibilities. It is assumed, in other words, that society is divided into two separate spheres of home and outside work and that these are women's and men's spheres respectively.

These assumptions are increasingly counterfactual. At present, fewer than 15% of U.S. families conform to the normative ideal of a domicile shared by a husband who is the sole breadwinner, a wife who is a full-time homemaker and their offspring.

Nonetheless, the separate spheres norms determine the structure of the social-welfare system. They determine that it contain a primary labor market-related subsystem and a family or household-related subsystem. Moreover, they determine that these subsystems be gender-linked, that the labor market-related system be implicitly "masculine" and the family-related system be implicitly "feminine." Consequently, the normative, ideal-typical recipient of primary labor market-oriented programs is a (white) male, while the normative, ideal-typical client of household-based programs is a female.

This gender subtext of the U.S. welfare system is confirmed when we take a second look at participation figures. Consider again the figures just cited for the "feminine" or family-based programs, which I earlier referred to as "means-tested" programs: more than 81% of households receiving AFDC are female-headed, as are more than 70% of those receiving housing assistance and more than 60% of those receiving Medicaid and food stamps. Now recall that these figures do not compare female vs. male individuals, but rather female vs. male headed-*households*. They therefore confirm four things: 1) these programs have a distinctive administrative identity in that their recipients are not individualized but *familialized*; 2) they serve what are considered to be defective families, overwhelmingly families without a male breadwinner; 3) the ideal-typical (adult) client is female; and 4) she makes her claim for benefits on the basis of her status as an unpaid domestic worker, a homemaker and mother, not as a paid worker based in the labor market.

Now contrast this with the case of a typical labor market-based and thus "masculine" program, namely, unemployment insurance. Here the percentage of female claimants drops to 38%, a figure which contrasts female vs. male *individuals*, as opposed to households. As Diana Pearce notes, this drop reflects at least two different circumstances. First, and most straightforwardly, it reflects women's lower rate of participation in the paid workforce. Second, it reflects the fact that many women wage-workers are not eligible to participate in this program, for example, paid household service workers, part-time workers, pregnant workers and workers in the "irregular economy" such as prostitutes, baby-sitters and home typists. The exclusion of these predominantly female wage-workers testifies to the existence of a gender segmented labor market, divided into "primary" and "secondary" employment. It reflects the more general assumption that women's earnings are "merely supplementary," not on a par with those of the primary (male) breadwinner. Altogether, then, the figures tell us four things about programs like unemployment insurance: 1) they are administered in a way which *individual-*

izes rather than familializes recipients; 2) they are designed to compensate primary labor market effects, such as the temporary displacement of a primary breadwinner; 3) the ideal-typical recipient is male; and 4) he makes his claim on the basis of his identity as a paid worker, not as an unpaid domestic worker or parent.

One final example will round out the picture. The Social Security system of retirement insurance presents the interesting case of a hermaphrodite or androgyne. I shall soon show that this system has a number of characteristics of "masculine" programs in virtue of its link to participation in the paid workforce. However, it is also internally dualized and gendered, and thus stands as a microcosm of the entire dual-benefit welfare system. Consider that, while a majority — 61.6% — of adult beneficiaries are female, only somewhat more than half of these — or 33.3% of all recipients — claim benefits on the basis of their own paid work records. The remaining female recipients claim benefits on the basis of their husbands' records, that is, as wives or unpaid domestic workers. By contrast, virtually no male recipients claim benefits as husbands. On the contrary, they claim benefits as paid workers, a labor market-located as opposed to family-located identity. So the Social Security system is hermaphroditic or androgynous; it is internally divided between family-based, "feminine" benefits, on the one hand, and labor market-based, "masculine" benefits, on the other hand. Thus, it too gets its structure from gender norms and assumptions.

So far, we have established the dualistic structure of the U.S. social-welfare system and the gender subtext of the dualism. Now, we can better tease out the system's implicit norms and tacit assumptions by examining its mode of operation. To see how welfare programs interpret women's needs, we should consider what benefits consist in. To see how programs position women as subjects, we should examine administrative practices. In general, we shall see that the "masculine" and "feminine" subsystems are not only separate but also unequal.

Consider that the "masculine" social-welfare programs are social insurance schemes. They include unemployment insurance, Social Security (retirement insurance), Medicare (age-tested health insurance) and Supplemental Social Security Insurance (disability insurance for those with paid work records). These programs are contributory; wage-workers and their employers pay into trust funds. They are administered on a national basis and benefit levels are uniform across the country. Though bureaucratically organized and administered, they require less, and less demeaning effort on the part of beneficiaries in qualifying and maintaining eligibility than do "feminine" programs. They are far less subject to intrusive controls and in most cases lack the dimension of surveillance. They also tend to require less of beneficiaries in the way of benefit-collection efforts, with the notable exception of unemployment insurance.

In sum, "masculine" social insurance schemes position recipients primarily as *rights-bearers*. The beneficiaries of these programs are in the main not stigmatized. Neither administrative practice nor popular discourse constitutes them as "on the dole." They are constituted rather as receiving what they deserve, what they, in "partnership" with their employers, have already paid in for, what they, therefore, have a *right* to. Moreover, these beneficiaries are also positioned as *purchasing consumers*. They receive cash as opposed to "in kind" benefits and so are positioned as having "the liberty to strike the best bargain they can in purchasing services of their choice on the open market." In sum, these beneficiaries are what C. B. MacPherson calls "possessive individuals." Proprietors of their own persons who have freely contracted to sell their labor-power, they become participants in social insurance schemes and, thence, paying consumers of human services. They therefore qualify as *social citizens* in virtually the fullest sense that term can acquire within the framework of a male-dominated capitalist society.

All this stands in stark contrast to the "feminine" sector of the U.S. social-welfare system. This sector consists in relief programs, such as AFDC, food stamps, Medicaid and public housing assistance. These programs are not contributory, but are financed out of general tax revenues, usually with one-third of the funds coming from the federal government and two-thirds coming from the states. They are not administered nationally but rather by the states. As a result, benefit levels vary dramatically, though they are everywhere inadequate, deliberately pegged below the official poverty line. The relief programs are notorious for the varieties of administrative humiliation they inflict upon clients. They require considerable work in qualifying and maintaining eligibility; and they have a heavy component of surveillance.

These programs do not in any meaningful sense position their subjects as rights-bearers. Far from being considered as having a right to what they receive, recipients are defined as "beneficiaries of governmental largesse" or "clients of public charity." In the androcentric-administrative framework, "welfare mothers" are considered not to work and so are sometimes required, that is to say coerced, to work off their benefits via "workfare." They thus become inmates of what Diana Pearce calls a "workhouse without walls." Indeed, the only sense in which the category of rights is relevant to these clients' situation is the somewhat dubious one according to which they are entitled to treatment governed by the standards of formal-bureaucratic procedural rationality. But if that right is construed as protection from administrative caprice, then even it is widely and routinely disregarded. Moreover, recipients of public relief are generally not positioned as purchasing consumers. A significant portion of their benefits is "in kind" and what cash they get comes already carved up and earmarked for specific, administratively designated purposes. These recipients are therefore essentially *clients*, a subject-position which carries far less power and dignity in capitalist societies than does the alternative position of purchaser. In these societies, to be a client in the sense relevant to relief recipients is to be an abject dependent. Indeed, this sense of the term carries connotations of a fall from autonomy, as when we speak, for example, of "the client-states of empires or superpowers." As clients, then, recipients of relief are *the negatives of possessive individuals*. Largely excluded from the market, both as workers and as consumers, claiming benefits not as individuals but as members of "failed" families, these recipients are effectively denied the trappings of social citizenship as the latter are defined within male-dominated capitalist societies.

Clearly, this system creates a double-bind for women raising children without a male breadwinner. By failing to offer them day care, job training, a job that pays a "family wage" or some combination of these, it constructs them exclusively as mothers. As a consequence, it interprets their needs as maternal needs and their sphere of activity as that of "the family." Now, according to the ideology of separate spheres, this should be an honorific social identity. Yet the system does not honor these women. On the contrary, instead of providing them a guaranteed income equivalent to a family wage as a matter of right, it stigmatizes, humiliates and harasses them. In effect, it decrees that these women must be, yet cannot be, normative mothers.

Moreover, the way in which the U.S. social-welfare system interprets "maternity" and "the family" is race- and culture-specific. The bias is made plain in Carol Stack's study, *All Our Kin*. Stack analyzes domestic arrangements of very poor Black welfare recipients in a midwestern city. Where ideologues see "the disorganization of *the* [sic] black family," she finds complex, highly organized kinship structures. These include kin-based networks of resource pooling and exchange which enable those in direst poverty to survive economically and communally. The networks organize delayed exchanges or "gifts," in Mauss' (1967) sense, of prepared meals, food stamps, cooking, shopping, groceries, furniture, sleeping space, cash (including wages and AFDC allowances), transportation, clothing, child care, even children. They span several physically distinct households and so transcend the principal administrative category which organizes relief programs. It is significant that Stack took great pains to conceal the identities of her subjects, even going so far as to disguise the identity of their city. The reason, though unstated, is obvious: these people would lose their benefits if program administrators learned that they did not utilize them within the confines and boundaries of a "household."

We can summarize the separate and unequal character of the two-tiered, gender-linked, race- and culture-biased U.S. social-welfare system in the following formulae: Participants in the "masculine" subsystem are positioned as *rights-bearing beneficiaries and purchasing consumers of services*. Participants in the "feminine" subsystem, on the other hand, are positioned as *dependent clients*.

PETER SINGER

Famine, Affluence, and Morality

PETER SINGER *teaches philosophy and directs the Center for Human Bioethics at Monash University in Australia. His best-known work is* Animal Liberation *(1975). He has written widely on civil disobedience and medical ethics.*

AS I write this, in November 1971, people are dying in East Bengal from lack of food, shelter, and medical care. The suffering and death that are occurring there now are not inevitable, not unavoidable in any fatalistic sense of the term. Constant poverty, a cyclone, and a civil war have turned at least nine million people into destitute refugees; nevertheless, it is not beyond the capacity of the richer nations to give enough assistance to reduce any further suffering to very small proportions. The decisions and actions of human beings can prevent this kind of suffering. Unfortunately, human beings have not made the necessary decisions. At the individual level, people have, with very few exceptions, not responded to the situation in any significant way. Generally speaking, people have not given large sums to relief funds; they have not written to their parliamentary representatives demanding increased government assistance; they have not demonstrated in the streets, held symbolic fasts, or done anything else directed toward providing the refugees with the means to satisfy their essential needs. At the government level, no government has given the sort of massive aid that would enable the refugees to survive for more than a few days. . . .

What are the moral implications of a situation like this? In what follows, I shall argue that the way people in relatively affluent countries react to a situation like that in Bengal cannot be justified; indeed, the whole way we look at moral issues — our moral conceptual scheme — needs to be altered, and with it, the way of life that has come to be taken for granted in our society. . . .

I begin with the assumption that suffering and death from lack of food, shelter, and medical care are bad. I think most people will agree about this, although one may reach the same view by different routes. I shall not argue for this view. People can hold all sorts of eccentric positions, and perhaps from some of them it would not follow that death by starvation is in itself bad. It is difficult, perhaps impossible, to refute such positions, and so for brevity I will henceforth take this assumption as accepted. Those who disagree need read no further.

My next point is this: if it is in our power to prevent something bad from happening, without thereby sacrificing anything of comparable moral importance, we ought, morally, to do it. By "without sacrificing anything of comparable moral importance" I mean without causing anything else comparably bad to happen, or doing something that is wrong in itself, or failing to promote some moral good, comparable in significance to the bad thing that we can prevent. This principle seems almost as uncontroversial as the last one. It requires us only to prevent what is bad, and not to promote what is good, and it requires this of us only when we can do it without sacrificing anything that is, from the moral point of view, comparably important. I could even, as far as the application of my argument to the Bengal emergency is concerned, qualify the point so as to make it: if it is in our power to prevent something very bad from happening, without thereby sacrificing anything morally significant, we ought, morally, to do it. An application of this principle would be as follows: if I am walking past a shallow pond and see a child drowning in it, I ought to wade in and pull the child out. This will mean getting my clothes muddy, but this is insignificant, while the death of the child would presumably be a very bad thing.

The uncontroversial appearance of the principle just stated is deceptive. If it were acted upon, even in its qualified form, our lives, our society, and our world would be fundamentally changed. For the principle takes, firstly, no account of proximity or distance. It makes no moral difference whether the person I can help is a neighbor's child ten yards from me or a Bengali whose name I shall never know, ten thousand miles away. Secondly, the principle makes no distinction between cases in which I am the only person who could possibly do anything and cases in which I am just one among millions in the same position.

I do not think I need to say much in defense of the refusal to take proximity and distance into account. The fact that a person is physically near to us, so that we have personal contact with him, may make it more likely that we *shall* assist him, but this does not show that we *ought* to help him rather than another who happens to be further away. If we accept any principle of impartiality, universalizability, equality, or whatever, we cannot discriminate against someone merely because he is far away from us (or we are far away from him). . . .

There may be a greater need to defend the second implication of my principle — that the fact that there are millions of other people in the same position, in respect to the Bengali refugees, as I am, does not make the situation significantly different from a situation in which I am the only person who can prevent something very bad from occurring. Again, of course, I admit that there is a psychological difference between the cases; one feels less guilty about doing nothing if one can point to others, similarly placed, who have also done nothing. Yet this can make no real difference to our moral obligations. Should I consider that I am less obliged to pull the drowning child out of the pond if on looking around I see other people, no further away than I am, who have also noticed the child but are doing nothing? One has only to ask this question to see the absurdity of the view that numbers lessen obligation. . . .

The view that numbers do make a difference can be made plausible if stated in this way: if everyone in circumstances like mine gave £5 to the Bengal Relief Fund, there would be enough to provide food, shelter, and medical care for the refugees; there is no reason why I should give more than anyone else in the same circumstances as I am; therefore I have no obligation to give more than £5. Each premise in this argument is true, and the argument looks sound. It may convince us, unless we notice that it is based on a hypothetical premise, although the conclusion is not stated hypothetically. The argument would be sound if the conclusion were: if everyone in circumstances like mine were to give £5, I would have no obligation to give more than £5. If the conclusion were so stated, however, it would be obvious that the argument has no bearing on a situation in which it is not the case that everyone else gives £5. This, of course, is the actual situation. . . .

The outcome of this argument is that our traditional moral categories are upset. The traditional distinction between duty and charity cannot be drawn, or at least, not in the place we normally draw it. Giving money to the Bengal Relief Fund is regarded as an act of charity in our society. The bodies which collect money are known as "charities." These organizations see themselves in this way — if you send them a check, you will be thanked for your "generosity." Because giving money is regarded as an act of charity, it is not thought that there is anything wrong with not giving. The charitable man may be praised, but the man who is not charitable is not condemned. People do not feel in any way ashamed or guilty about spending money on new clothes or a new car instead of giving it to famine relief. (Indeed, the alternative does not occur to them.) This way of looking at the matter cannot be justified. When we buy new clothes not to keep ourselves warm but to look "well-dressed" we are not providing for any important need. We would not be sacrificing anything significant if we were to continue to wear our old clothes, and give the money to famine relief. By doing so, we would be preventing another person from starving. It follows from what I have said earlier that we ought to give money away, rather than spend it on clothes which we do not need to keep us warm. To do so is not charitable, or generous. Nor is it the kind of act which philosophers and theologians have called "supererogatory" — an act which it would be good to do, but not wrong not to do. On the contrary, we ought to give the money away, and it is wrong not to do so. . . .

The conclusion remains: we ought to be preventing as much suffering as we can without sacrificing something else of comparable moral importance. This conclusion is one which we may be reluctant to face. I cannot see, though, why it should be regarded as a criticism of the position for which I have argued, rather than a criticism of our ordinary standards of behavior. Since most people are self-interested to some degree, very few of us are likely to do everything that we ought to do. It would, however, hardly be honest to take this as evidence that it is not the case that we ought to do it.

It may still be thought that my conclusions are so wildly out of line with what everyone else thinks and has always thought that there must be something wrong with the argument somewhere. In order to show that my conclusions, while certainly contrary to contemporary Western moral standards, would not have seemed so extraordinary at other times and in other places, I would like to quote a passage from a writer not normally thought of as a way-out radical, Thomas Aquinas.

> Now, according to the natural order instituted by divine providence, material goods are provided for the satisfaction of human needs. Therefore the division and appropriation of property, which proceeds from human law, must not hinder the satisfaction of man's necessity from such goods. Equally, whatever a man has in superabundance is owed, of natural right, to the poor for their sustenance. So Ambrosius says, and it is also to be found in the *Decretum Gratiani:* "The bread which you withhold belongs to the hungry; the clothing you shut away, to the naked; and the money you bury in the earth is the redemption and freedom of the penniless."

I now want to consider a number of points, more practical than philosophical, which are relevant to the application of the moral conclusion we have reached. These points challenge not the idea that we ought to be doing all we can to prevent starvation, but the idea that giving away a great deal of money is the best means to this end.

It is sometimes said that overseas aid should be a government responsibility, and that therefore one ought not to give to privately run charities. Giving privately, it is said, allows the government and the noncontributing members of society to escape their responsibilities.

This argument seems to assume that the more people there are who give to privately organized famine relief funds, the less likely it is that the government will take over full responsibility for such aid. This assumption is unsupported, and does not strike me as at all plausible. The opposite view — that if no one gives voluntarily, a government will assume that its citizens are uninterested in famine relief and would not wish to be forced into giving aid — seems more plausible. . . .

Another, more serious reason for not giving to famine relief funds is that until there is effective population control, relieving famine merely postpones starvation. If we save the Bengal refugees now, others, perhaps the children of these refugees, will face starvation in a few years' time. In support of this, one may cite the now well-known facts about the population explosion and the relatively limited scope for expanded production.

This point, like the previous one, is an argument against relieving suffering that is happening now, because of a belief about what might happen in the future; it is unlike the previous point in that very good evidence can be adduced in support of this belief about the future. I will not go into the evidence here. I accept that the earth cannot support indefinitely a population rising at the present rate. This certainly poses a problem for anyone who thinks it important to prevent famine. Again, however, one could accept the argument without drawing the conclusion that it absolves one from any obligation to do anything to prevent famine. The conclusion that should be drawn is that the best means of preventing famine, in the long run, is population control. It would then follow from the position reached earlier that one ought to be doing all one can to promote population control (unless one held that all forms of population control were wrong in themselves, or would have significantly bad consequences). . . .

A third point raised by the conclusion reached earlier relates to the question of just how much we all ought to be giving away. One possibility, which has already been mentioned, is that we ought to give until we reach the level of marginal utility — that is, the level at which, by giving more, I would cause as much suffering to myself or my dependents as I would relieve by my gift. This would mean, of course, that one would reduce oneself to very near the material circumstances of a Bengali refugee. It will be recalled that earlier I put forward both a strong and a moderate version of the principle of preventing bad occurrences. The strong version, which required us to prevent bad things from happening unless in doing so we would be sacrificing something of comparable moral significance, does seem to require reducing ourselves to the level of marginal utility. I should also say that the strong version seems to me to be the correct one. I proposed the more moder-ate version — that we should prevent bad occurrences unless, to do so, we had to sacrifice something morally significant — only in order to show that even on this surely undeniable principle a great change in our way of life is required. On the more moderate principle, it may not follow that we ought to reduce ourselves to the level of marginal utility, for one might hold that to reduce oneself and one's family to this level is to cause something significantly bad to happen. Whether this is so I shall not discuss, since, as I have said, I can see no good reason for holding the moderate version of the principle rather than the strong version. Even if we accepted the principle only in its moderate form, however, it should be clear that we would have to give away enough to ensure that the consumer society, dependent as it is on people spending on trivia rather than giving to famine relief, would slow down and perhaps disappear entirely.

GARRETT HARDIN
Lifeboat Ethics

GARRETT HARDIN *is Emeritus Professor of Human Ecology at the University of California at Santa Barbara. He has researched and written extensively on human ecology and evolution.*

ENVIRONMENTALISTS use the metaphor of the earth as a "spaceship" in trying to persuade countries, industries and people to stop wasting and polluting our natural resources. Since we all share life on this planet, they argue, no single person or institution has the right to destroy, waste, or use more than a fair share of its resources.

But does everyone on earth have an equal right to an equal share of its resources? The spaceship metaphor can be dangerous when used by misguided idealists to justify suicidal policies for sharing our resources through uncontrolled immigration and foreign aid. In their enthusiastic but unrealistic generosity, they confuse the ethics of a spaceship with those of a lifeboat.

A true spaceship would have to be under the control of a captain, since no ship could possibly survive if its course were determined by committee. Spaceship Earth certainly has no captain; the United Nations is merely a toothless tiger, with little power to enforce any policy upon its bickering members.

If we divide the world crudely into rich nations and poor nations, two thirds of them are desperately poor, and only one third comparatively rich, with the United States the wealthiest of all. Metaphorically each rich nation can be seen as a lifeboat full of comparatively rich people. In the ocean outside each lifeboat swim the poor of the world, who would like to get in, or at least to share some of the wealth. What should the lifeboat passengers do?

First, we must recognize the limited capacity of any lifeboat. For example, a nation's land has a limited capacity to support a population and as the current energy crisis has shown us, in some ways we have already exceeded the carrying capacity of our land.

Adrift in a Moral Sea

So here we sit, say 50 people in our lifeboat. To be generous, let us assume it has room for 10 more, making a total capacity of 60. Suppose the 50 of us in the lifeboat see 100 others swimming in the water outside, begging for admission to our boat or for handouts. We have several options: we may be tempted to try to live by the Christian ideal of being "our

brother's keeper," or by the Marxist ideal of "to each according to his needs." Since the needs of all in the water are the same, and since they can all be seen as "our brothers," we could take them all into our boat, making a total of 150 in a boat designed for 60. The boat swamps, everyone drowns. Complete justice, complete catastrophe.

Since the boat has an unused excess capacity of 10 more passengers, we could admit just 10 more to it. But which 10 do we let in? How do we choose? Do we pick the best 10, the neediest 10, "first come, first served"? And what do we say to the 90 we exclude? If we do let an extra 10 into our lifeboat, we will have lost our "safety factor," an engineering principle of critical importance. For example, if we don't leave room for excess capacity as a safety factor in our country's agriculture, a new plant disease or a bad change in the weather could have disastrous consequences.

Suppose we decide to preserve our small safety factor and admit no more to the lifeboat. Our survival is then possible, although we shall have to be constantly on guard against boarding parties.

While this last solution clearly offers the only means of our survival, it is morally abhorrent to many people. Some say they feel guilty about their good luck. My reply is simple: "Get out and yield your place to others." This may solve the problem of the guilt-ridden person's conscience, but it does not change the ethics of the lifeboat. The needy person to whom the guilt-ridden person yields his place will not himself feel guilty about his good luck. If he did, he would not climb aboard. The net result of conscience-stricken people giving up their unjustly held seats is the elimination of that sort of conscience from the lifeboat.

This is the basic metaphor within which we must work out our solutions.

Let us now enrich the image, step by step, with substantive additions from the real world, a world that must solve real and pressing problems of overpopulation and hunger.

The harsh ethics of the lifeboat become even harsher when we consider the reproductive differences between the rich nations and the poor nations. The people inside the lifeboats are doubling in numbers every 87 years; those swimming around outside are doubling, on the average, every 35 years, more than twice as fast as the rich. And since the world's resources are dwindling, the difference in prosperity between the rich and the poor can only increase.

As of 1973, the U.S. had a population of 210 million people, who were increasing by 0.8 percent per year. Outside our lifeboat, let us imagine another 210 million people, (say the combined populations of Colombia, Ecuador, Venezuela, Morocco, Pakistan, Thailand and the Philippines) who are increasing at a rate of 3.3 percent per year. Put differently, the doubling time for this aggregate population is 21 years, compared to 87 years for the U.S. . . .

In sharing with "each according to his needs," we must recognize that needs are determined by population size, which is determined by the rate of reproduction, which at present is regarded as a sovereign right of every nation, poor or not. This being so, the philanthropic load created by the sharing ethic of the spaceship can only increase.

The Tragedy of the Commons

The fundamental error of spaceship ethics, and the sharing it requires, is that it leads to what I call "the tragedy of the commons." Under a system of private property, the men who own property recognize their responsibility to care for it,

for if they don't they will eventually suffer. A farmer, for instance, will allow no more cattle in a pasture than its carrying capacity justifies. If he overloads it, erosion sets in, weeds take over, and he loses the use of the pasture.

If a pasture becomes a commons open to all, the right of each to use it may not be matched by a corresponding responsibility to protect it. Asking everyone to use it with discretion will hardly do, for the considerate herdsman who refrains from overloading the commons suffers more than a selfish one who says his needs are greater. If everyone would restrain himself, all would be well; but it takes only one less than everyone to ruin a system of voluntary restraint. In a crowded world of less than perfect human beings, mutual ruin is inevitable if there are no controls. This is the tragedy of the commons.

One of the major tasks of education today should be the creation of such an acute awareness of the dangers of the commons that people will recognize its many varieties. For example, the air and water have become polluted because they are treated as commons. Further growth in the population or per-capita conversion of natural resources into pollutants will only make the problem worse. The same holds true for the fish of the oceans. Fishing fleets have nearly disappeared in many parts of the world, technological improvements in the art of fishing are hastening the day of complete ruin. Only the replacement of the system of the commons with a responsible system of control will save the land, air, water and oceanic fisheries. . . .

Learning the Hard Way

What happens if some organizations or countries budget for accidents and others do not? If each country is solely responsible for its own well-being, poorly managed ones will suffer. But they can learn from experience. They may mend their ways, and learn to budget for infrequent but certain emergencies. For example, the weather varies from year to year, and periodic crop failures are certain. A wise and competent government saves out of the production of the good years in anticipation of bad years to come. Joseph taught this policy to Pharaoh in Egypt more than 2,000 years ago. Yet the great majority of the governments in the world today do not follow such a policy. They lack either the wisdom or the competence, or both. Should those nations that do manage to put something aside be forced to come to the rescue each time an emergency occurs among the poor nations?

"But it isn't their fault!" Some kind-hearted liberals argue. "How can we blame the poor people who are caught in an emergency? Why must they suffer for the sins of their governments?" The concept of blame is simply not relevant here. The real question is, what are the operational consequences of establishing a world food bank? If it is open to every country every time a need develops, slovenly rulers will not be motivated to take Joseph's advice. Someone will always come to their aid. Some countries will deposit food in the world food bank, and others will withdraw it. There will be almost no overlap. As a result of such solutions to food shortage emergencies, the poor countries will not learn to mend their ways, and will suffer progressively greater emergencies as their populations grow.

Population Control
the Crude Way

On the average, poor countries undergo a 2.5 percent increase in population each year; rich countries, about 0.8 percent. Only rich countries have anything in the way of food reserves set aside, and even they do not have as much as they should. Poor countries have none. If poor countries received no food from the outside, the rate of their population growth would be periodically checked by crop failures and famines. But if they can always draw on a world food bank in time of need, their population can continue to grow unchecked, and so will their "need" for aid. In the short run, a world food bank may diminish that need, but in the long run it actually increases the need without limit.

Without some system of worldwide food sharing, the proportion of people in the rich and poor nations might eventually stabilize. The overpopulated poor countries would decrease in numbers, while the rich countries that had room for more people would increase. But with a well-meaning system of sharing, such as a world food bank, the growth differential between the rich and the poor countries will not only persist, it will increase. Because of the higher rate of population growth in the poor countries of the world, 8 percent of today's children are born poor, and only 12 percent rich. Year by year the ratio becomes worse, as the fast-reproducing poor outnumber the slow-reproducing rich.

A world food bank is thus a commons in disguise. People will have more motivation to draw from it than to add to any common store. The less provident and less able will multiply at the expense of the abler and more provident, bringing eventual ruin upon all who share in the commons. Besides, any system of "sharing" that amounts to foreign aid from the rich nations to the poor nations will carry the taint of charity, which will contribute little to the world peace so devoutly desired by those who support the idea of a world food bank. . . .

Overloading the Environment

Every human born constitutes a draft on all aspects of the environment: food, air, water, forests, beaches, wildlife, scenery and solitude. Food can, perhaps, be significantly increased to meet a growing demand. But what about clean beaches, unspoiled forests, and solitude? If we satisfy a growing population's need for food, we necessarily decrease its per capita supply of the other resources needed by men.

India, for example, now has a population of 600 million, which increases by 15 million each year. This population already puts a huge load on a relatively impoverished environment. The country's forests are now only a small fraction of what they were three centuries ago, and floods and erosion continually destroy the insufficient farmland that remains. Every one of the 15 million new lives added to India's population puts an additional burden on the environment, and increases the economic and social costs of crowding. However humanitarian our intent, every Indian life saved through medical or nutritional assistance from abroad diminishes the quality of life for those who remain, and for subsequent generations. If rich countries make it possible, through foreign aid, for 600 million Indians to swell to 1.2 billion in a mere 28 years, as their current growth rate threatens, will future generations of Indians thank us for hastening the destruction of their environment? Will our good intentions be sufficient excuse for the consequences of our actions? . . .

Immigration vs. Food Supply

World food banks *move food to the people*, hastening the exhaustion of the environment of the poor countries. Unrestricted immigration, on the other hand, *moves people to the food*, thus speeding up the destruction of the environment of the rich countries. We can easily understand why poor people should want to make this latter transfer, but why should rich hosts encourage it? . . .

I can hear U.S. liberals asking: "How can you justify slamming the door once you're inside? You say that immigrants should be kept out. But aren't we all immigrants, or the descendants of immigrants? If we insist on staying, must we not admit all others?" Our craving for intellectual order leads us to seek and prefer symmetrical rules and morals: a single rule for me and everybody else; the same rule yesterday, today and tomorrow. Justice, we feel, should not change with time and place.

We Americans of non-Indian ancestry can look upon ourselves as the descendants of thieves who are guilty morally, if not legally, of stealing this land from its Indian owners. Should we then give back the land to the now living American descendants of those Indians? However morally or logically sound this proposal may be, I, for one, am unwilling to live by it and I know no one else who is. Besides, the logical consequence would be absurd. Suppose that, intoxicated with a sense of pure justice, we should decide to turn our land over to the Indians. Since all our other wealth has also been derived from the land, wouldn't we be morally obliged to give that back to the Indians too?

Pure Justice vs. Reality

Clearly, the concept of pure justice produces an infinite regression to absurdity. Centuries ago, wise men invented statutes of limitations to justify the rejection of such pure justice, in the interest of preventing continual disorder. The law zealously defends property rights, but only relatively recent property rights.

Drawing a line after an arbitrary time has elapsed may be unjust, but the alternatives are worse.

We are all the descendants of thieves, and the world's resources are inequitably distributed. But we must begin the journey to tomorrow from the point where we are today. We cannot remake the past. We cannot safely divide the wealth equitably among all peoples so long as people reproduce at different rates. To do so would guarantee that our grandchildren, and everyone else's grandchildren, would have only a ruined world to inhabit.

To be generous with one's own possessions is quite different from being generous with those of posterity. We should call this point to the attention of those who, from a commendable love of justice and equality, would institute a system of the commons, either in the form of a world food bank, or of unrestricted immigration. We must convince them if we wish to save at least some parts of the world from environmental ruin.

Without a true world government to control reproduction and the use of available resources, the sharing ethic of the spaceship is impossible. For the foreseeable future, our survival demands that we govern our actions by the ethics of a lifeboat, harsh though they may be. Posterity will be satisfied with nothing less.

ANDREW CARNEGIE
Wealth

ANDREW CARNEGIE (1835–1919) *was a Scottish-born U.S. businessman and philanthropist. His Pittsburgh-based company, the Carnegie Steel Company, introduced the Bessemer process of making steel to the United States, and was merged with the United States Steel Company at the time of Carnegie's retirement. He is well known for donating hundreds of libraries to towns and schools throughout the U.S. and England, and is the author of a number of books, including* Triumphant Democracy *(1886) and* The Empire of Business *(1902).*

THE problem of our age is the proper administration of wealth, so that the ties of brotherhood may still bind together the rich and poor in harmonious relationship. The conditions of human life have not only been changed, but revolutionized, within the past few hundred years. In former days there was little difference between the dwelling, dress, food, and environment of the chief and those of his retainers. The Indians are today where civilized man then was. When visiting the Sioux, I was led to the wigwam of the chief. It was just like the others in external appearance, and even within the difference was trifling between it and those of the poorest of his braves. The contrast between the palace of the millionaire and the cottage of the laborer with us today measures the change which has come into civilization.

This change, however, is not to be deplored, but welcomed as highly beneficial. It is well, nay essential, for the progress of the race, that the houses of some should be homes for all that is highest and best in literature and art, and for all the refinements of civilization, rather than that none should be so. Much better this great irregularity than universal squalor. Without wealth there can be no Maecetions. When these apprentices rose to be masters, there was little or no change in their mode of life, and they, in turn, educated in the same routine succeeding apprentices. There was, substantially, social equality, and even political equality, for those engaged in industrial pursuits had then little or no political voice in the State.

But the inevitable result of such a mode of manufacture was crude articles at high prices. Today the world obtains commodities of excellent quality at prices which even the generation preceding this would have deemed incredible. In the commercial world similar causes have produced similar results, and the race is benefited thereby. The poor enjoy what the rich could not before afford. What were the luxuries have become the necessaries of life. The laborer has now more comforts than the farmer had a few generations ago. The farmer has more luxuries than the landlord had, and is more richly clad and better housed. The landlord has books and pictures rarer, and appointments more artistic, than the King could then obtain.

The price we pay for this salutary change is, no doubt, great. We assemble thousands of operatives in the factory, in the mine, and in the counting-house, of whom the employer can know little or nothing, and to whom the employer is little better than a myth. All intercourse between them is at an end. Rigid Castes are formed, and, as usual, mutual ignorance breeds mutual distrust. Each Caste is without sympathy for the other, and ready to credit anything disparaging in regard to it. Under the law of competition, the employer of thousands is forced into the strictest economies, among which the rates paid to labor figure prominently, and often there is friction between the employer and the employed, between capital and labor, between rich and poor. Human society loses homogeneity.

The price which society pays for the law of competition, like the price it pays for cheap comforts and luxuries, is also great; but the advantages of this law are also greater still, for it is to this law that we owe our wonderful material development, which brings improved conditions in its train. But, whether the law be benign or not, we must say of it, as we say of the change in the conditions of men to which we have referred: It is here; we cannot evade it; no substitutes for it have been found; and while the law may be sometimes hard for the individual, it is best for the race, because it insures the survival of the fittest in every department. We accept and welcome, therefore, as conditions to which we must accommodate ourselves, great inequality of environment, the concentration of business, industrial and commercial, in the hands of a few, and the law of competition between these, as being not only beneficial, but essential for the future progress of the race. Having accepted these, it follows that there must be great scope for the exercise of special ability in the merchant and in the manufacturer who has to conduct affairs upon a great scale. That this talent for organization and management is rare among men is proved by the fact that it invariably secures for its possessor enormous rewards, no matter where or under what laws or conditions. The experienced in affairs always rate the MAN whose services can be obtained as a partner as not only the first consideration, but such as to render the question of his capital scarcely worth considering, for such men soon create capital; while, without the special talent required, capital soon takes wings. Such men become interested in firms or corporations using millions; and estimating only simple interest to be made upon the capital invested, it is inevitable that their income must exceed their expenditures, and that they must accumulate wealth. Nor is there any middle ground which such men can occupy, because the great manufacturing or commercial concern which does not earn at least interest upon its capital soon becomes bankrupt. It must either go forward or fall behind: to stand still is impossible. It is a condition essential for its successful operation that it should be thus far profitable, and even that, in addition to interest on capital, it should make profit. It is a law, as certain as any of the others named, that men possessed of this peculiar talent for affairs, under the free play of economic forces, must, of necessity, soon be in receipt of more revenue than can be judiciously expended upon themselves, and this law is as beneficial for the race as the others.

Objections to the foundations upon which society is based are not in order, because the condition of the race is better with these than it has been with any others which have been tried. Of the effect of any new substitutes proposed we cannot be sure. The Socialist or Anarchist who seeks to overturn present conditions is to be regarded as attacking the foundation upon which civilization itself rests, for civilization took its start from the day that the capable, industrious workman said to his incompetent and lazy fellow, "If thou dost not sow, thou shalt not reap," and thus ended primitive Communism by separating the drones from the bees. One who studies this subject will soon be brought face to face with the conclusion that upon the sacredness of property civilization itself depends — the right of the laborer to his hundred dollars in the savings bank, and equally the legal right of the millionaire to his millions. To those who propose to substitute Communism for this intense Individualism the answer, therefore, is: The race has tried that. All progress from that barbarous day to the present time has resulted from its displacement. Not evil, but good, has come to the race from the accumulation of wealth by those who have the ability and energy that produce it. But even if we admit for a moment that it might be better for the race to discard its present foundation, Individualism — that it is a nobler ideal that man should labor, not for himself alone, but in and for a brotherhood of his fellows, and share with them all in common, realizing Swedenborg's idea of Heaven, where, as he says, the angels derive their happiness, not from laboring for self, but for each other — even admit all this, and a sufficient answer is, This is not evolution, but revolution. It necessitates the changing of human nature itself — a work of aeons, even if it were good to change it, which we cannot know. It is not practicable in our day or in our age. Even if desirable theoretically, it belongs to another and long-succeeding sociological stratum. Our duty is with what is practicable now; with the next step possible in our day and generation. It is criminal to waste our energies in endeavoring to uproot, when all we can profitably or possibly accomplish is to bend the universal tree of humanity a little in the direction most favorable to the production of good fruit under existing circumstances. We might as well urge the destruction of the highest existing type of man because he failed to reach our ideal as to favor the destruction of Individualism, Private Property, the Law of Accumulation of Wealth, and the Law of Competition; for these are the highest results of human experience, the soil in which society so far has produced the best fruit. Unequally or unjustly, perhaps, as these laws sometimes operate, and imperfect as they appear to the Idealist, they are nevertheless, like the highest type of man, the best and most valuable of all that humanity has yet accomplished.

We start, then, with a condition of affairs under which the best interests of the race are promoted, but which inevitably gives wealth to the few. Thus far, accepting conditions as they exist, the situation can be surveyed and pronounced good. The question then arises — and, if the foregoing be correct, it is the only question with which we have to deal — What is the proper mode of administering wealth after the laws upon which civilization is founded have thrown it into the hands of the few? And it is of this great question that I believe I offer the true solution. It will be understood that *fortunes* are here spoken of, not moderate sums saved by many years of effort, the returns from which are required for the comfortable maintenance and education of families. This is not *wealth*, but only *competence*, which it should be the aim of all to acquire.

. . . Indeed, it is difficult to set bounds to the share of a rich man's estate which should go at his death to the public through the agency of the state, and by all means such taxes should be graduated,

beginning at nothing upon moderate sums to dependents, and increasing rapidly as the amounts swell, until of the millionaire's hoard, as of Shylock's at least

" — The other half
Comes to the privy coffer of the state."

This policy would work powerfully to induce the rich man to attend to the administration of wealth during his life, which is the end that society should always have in view, as being that by far most fruitful for the people. Nor need it be feared that this policy would sap the root of enterprise and render men less anxious to accumulate, for to the class whose ambition it is to leave great fortunes and be talked about after their death, it will attract more attention, and, indeed, be a somewhat nobler ambition to have enormous sums paid over to the state from their fortunes.

There remains, then, only one mode of using great fortunes; but in this we have the true antidote for the temporary unequal distribution of wealth, the reconciliation of the rich and the poor — a reign of harmony — another ideal, differing, indeed, from that of the Communist in requiring only the further evolution of existing conditions, not the total overthrow of our civilization. It is founded upon the present most intense individualism, and the race is prepared to put it in practice by degrees whenever it pleases. Under its sway we shall have an ideal state, in which the surplus wealth of the few will become, in the best sense, the property of the many, because administered for the common good, and this wealth, passing through the hands of the few, can be made a much more potent force for the elevation of our race than if it had been distributed in small sums to the people themselves. Even the poorest can be made to see this, and to agree that great sums gathered by some of their fellow-citizens and spent for public purposes, from which the masses reap the principal benefit, are more valuable to them than if scattered among them through the course of many years in trifling amounts.

The best uses to which surplus wealth can be put have already been indicated. Those who would administer wisely must, indeed, be wise, for one of the serious obstacles to the improvement of our race is indiscriminate charity. It were better for mankind that the millions of the rich were thrown into the sea than so spent as to encourage the slothful, the drunken, the unworthy. Of every thousand dollars spent in so-called charity today, it is probable that $950 is unwisely spent; so spent, indeed, as to produce the very evils which it proposes to mitigate or cure. A well-known writer of philosophic books admitted the other day that he had given a quarter of a dollar to a man who approached him as he was coming to visit the house of his friend. He knew nothing of the habits of this beggar; knew not the use that would be made of this money, although he had every reason to suspect that it would be spent improperly. This man professed to be a disciple of Herbert Spencer; yet the quarter-dollar given that night will probably work more injury than all the money which its thoughtless donor will ever be able to give in true charity will do good. He only gratified his own feelings, saved himself from annoyance — and this was probably one of the most selfish and very worst actions of his life, for in all respects he is most worthy.

In bestowing charity, the main consideration should be to help those who will help themselves; to provide part of the means by which those who desire to improve may do so; to give those who desire to rise the aids by which they may rise; to assist, but rarely or never to do all. Neither the individual nor the race is improved by alms-giving. Those worthy of assistance, except in rare cases, seldom require assistance. The really valuable men of the race never do, except in cases of accident or sudden change. Every one has, of course, cases of individuals brought to his own knowledge where temporary assistance can do genuine good, and these he will not overlook. But the amount which can be wisely given by the individual for individuals is necessarily limited by his lack of knowledge of the circumstance connected with each. He is the only true reformer who is as careful and as anxious not to aid the unworthy as he is to aid the worthy, and perhaps, even more so, for in alms-giving more injury is probably done by rewarding vice then by relieving virtue.

Thus is the problem of Rich and Poor to be solved. The laws of accumulation will be left free; the laws of distribution free. Individualism will continue, but the millionaire will be but a trustee for the poor; intrusted for a season with a great part of the increased wealth of the community, but administrating it for the community far better than it could or would have done for itself. The best minds will thus have reached a stage in the development of the race in which it is clearly seen that there is no mode of disposing of surplus wealth creditable to thoughtful and earnest men into whose hands it flows save by using it year by year for the general good. This day already dawns. But a little while, and although, without incurring the pity of their fellows, men may die sharers in great business enterprises from which their capital cannot be or has not been withdrawn, and is left chiefly at death for public uses, yet the man who dies leaving behind him millions of available wealth, which was his to administer during life, will pass away "unwept, unhonored, and unsung," no matter to what uses he leaves the dross which he cannot take with him. Of such as these the public verdict will then be: "The man who dies thus rich dies disgraced."

Such, in my opinion, is the true Gospel concerning Wealth, obedience to which is destined some day to solve the problems of the Rich and the Poor, and to bring "Peace on earth, among men Good-Will."

AMARTYA SEN

Property and Hunger

AMARTYA SEN *teaches economics at Harvard University. His recent publications include* Commodities and Capabilities *(1985),* The Standard of Living *(1987), and* On Ethics and Economics *(1987). Sen has also conducted research on the role of rationality in social behavior.*

I N an interesting letter to Anna George, the daughter of Henry George Bernard Shaw wrote: "Your father found me a literary dilettante and militant rationalist in religion, and a barren rascal at that. By turning my mind to economics he made a man of me." I am not able to determine what making a man of Bernard Shaw would exactly consist of, but it is clear that the kind of moral and social problems with which Shaw was deeply concerned could not be sensibly pursued without examining their economic aspects. For example, the claims of property rights, which some would defend and some (including Shaw) would dispute, are not just matters of basic moral belief that could not possibly be influenced one way or the other by any empirical arguments. They call for sensitive moral analysis responsive to empirical realities, including economic ones.

Moral claims based on intrinsically valuable rights are often used in political and social arguments. Rights related to ownership have been invoked for ages. But there are also other types of rights which have been seen as "inherent and inalienable," and the American Declaration of Independence refers to "certain unalienable rights," among which are "life, liberty and the pursuit of happiness." The Indian constitution talks even of "the right to an adequate means of livelihood." The "right not to be hungry" has often been invoked in recent discussions on the obligation to help the famished.

Rights: Instruments, Constraints, or Goals?

Rights can be taken to be morally important in three different ways. First, they can be considered to be valuable *in-struments* to achieve other goals. This is the "instrumental view," and is well illustrated by the utilitarian approach to rights. Rights are, in that view, of no intrinsic importance. Violation of rights is not in itself a bad thing, nor fulfillment intrinsically good. But the acceptance of rights promotes, in this view, things that are ultimately important, to wit, utility. Jeremy Bentham rejected "natural rights" as "simple nonsense," and "natural and imprescriptible rights" as "rhetorical nonsense, nonsense upon stilts." But he attached great importance to rights as instruments valuable to the promotion of a good society, and devoted much energy to the attempt to reform appropriately the actual system of rights.

The second view may be called the "constraint view," and it takes the form of seeing rights as *constraints* on what others can or cannot do. In this view rights *are* intrinsically important. However, they don't figure in moral accounting as goals to be generally promoted, but only as constraints that others must obey. As Robert Nozick has put it in a powerful exposition of this "constraint view": "Individuals have rights, and there are things no person or group may do to them (without violating their rights)." Rights "set the constraints within which a social choice is to be made, by excluding certain alternatives, fixing others, and so on."

The third approach is to see fulfillments of rights as goals to be pursued. This "goal view" differs from the instrumental view in regarding rights to be intrinsically important, and it differs from the constraint view in seeing the fulfillment of rights as goals to be generally promoted, rather than taking them as demanding only (and exactly) that we refrain from violating the rights of others. In the "constraint view" there is no duty

to help anyone with his or her rights (merely not to hinder), and also in the "instrumental view" there is no duty, in fact, to help unless the right fulfillment will also promote some other goal such as utility. The "goal view" integrates the valuation of rights — their fulfillment and violation — in overall moral accounting, and yields a wider sphere of influence of rights in morality.

I have argued elsewhere that the goal view has advantages that the other two approaches do not share, in particular, the ability to accommodate integrated moral accounting including inter alia the intrinsic importance of a class of fundamental rights. I shall not repeat that argument here. But there is an interesting question of dual roles of rights in the sense that some rights may be *both* intrinsically important and instrumentally valuable. For example, the right to be free from hunger could — not implausibly — be regarded as being valuable in itself as well as serving as a good instrument to promote other goals such as security, longevity or utility. If so, both the goal view and the instrumental view would have to be simultaneously deployed to get a comprehensive assessment of such a right. This problem of comprehensiveness is a particularly important issue in the context of Henry George's discussion of rights, since he gave many rights significant dual roles.

The instrumental aspect is an inescapable feature of every right, since irrespective of whether a certain right is intrinsically valuable or not, its acceptance will certainly have other consequences as well, and these, too, have to be assessed along with the intrinsic value of rights (if any). A right that is regarded as quite valuable in itself may nevertheless be judged to be morally rejectable if its leads to disastrous consequences. This is a case of the rights playing a *negative* instrumental role. It is, of course, also possible that the instrumental argument will *bolster* the intrinsic claims of a right to be taken seriously. I shall presently argue that such is the case in George's analysis with the right of labor to its produce.

There are two general conclusions to draw, at this stage, from this very preliminary discussion. First, we must distinguish between (1) the intrinsic value of a right, and (2) the overall value of a right taking note inter alia of its intrinsic importance (if any). The acceptance of the intrinsic importance of any right is no guarantee that its overall moral valuation must be favorable. Second, no moral assessment of a right can be independent of its likely consequences. The need for empirical assessment of the effects of accepting any right cannot be escaped. Empirical arguments are quite central to moral philosophy.

Property and Deprivation

The right to hold, use and bequeath property that one has legitimately acquired is often taken to be inherently valuable. In fact, however, many of its defenses seem to be actually of the instrumental type, e.g., arguing that property rights make people more free to choose one kind of a life rather than another. Even the traditional attempt at founding "natural property rights" on the principles of "natural liberty" (with or without John Locke's proviso) has some instrumental features. But even if we do accept that property rights may have some intrinsic value, this does not in any way amount to an overall justification of property rights, since property rights may have consequences which themselves will require assessment. Indeed, the causation of hunger as well as its prevention may materially depend on how property rights are structured. If a set of property rights leads, say, to starvation, as it well might, then the moral approval of these rights would certainly be compromised severely. In general, the need for consequential analysis of property rights is inescapable whether or not such rights are seen as having any intrinsic value.

Consider Henry George's formula of giving "the product to the producer." This is, of course, an ambiguous rule, since the division of the credits for production to different causal influences (e.g., according to "marginal productivities" in neoclassical theory, or according to human efforts in classical labor theory) is inevitably somewhat arbitrary, and full of problems involving internal tensions. But no matter how the ambiguities are resolved, it is clear that this rule would give no part of the socially produced output to one who is unemployed since he or she is producing nothing. Also, a person whose productive contribution happens to be tiny, according to *whichever* procedure of such accounting we use, can expect to get very little based on this so-called "natural law." Thus, hunger and starvation are compatible with this system of rights. George thought that this would not occur, since the economic reforms he proposed (including the abolition of land rights) would eliminate unemployment, and provision for the disabled would be made through the sympathetic support of others. These are empirical matters. If these empirical generalizations do not hold, then the outlined system of rights would yield a serious conflict. The property rights to one's product (however defined) might be of some intrinsic moral importance, but we clearly must also take note of the moral disvalue of human misery (such as suffering due to hunger and nutrition-related diseases). The latter could very plausibly be seen as having more moral force than the former. A positive intrinsic value of the right to one's product can go with an overall negative value, taking everything into account.

I have tried to argue elsewhere — not in the context of disputing these moral theories but in trying to understand the causation of famines in the modern world — that famines are, in fact, best explained in terms of failures of entitlement systems. The entitlements here refer, of course, to legal rights and to practical possibilities, rather than to moral status, but the laws and actual operation of private ownership economies have many features in common with the moral system of entitlements analyzed by Nozick and others.

The entitlement approach to famines need not, of course, be confined to private ownership economies, and entitlement failures of other systems can also be fruitfully studied to examine famines and hunger. In the specific context of private ownership economies, the entitlements are substantially analyzable in terms, respectively, of what may be called "endowments" and "exchange entitlements." A person's endowment refers to what he or she initially owns (including the person's own labor power), and the exchange entitlement mapping tells us what the person can obtain through exchanging what he or she owns, either by production (exchange with nature), or by trade (exchange with others), or a mixture of the two. A person has to starve if neither the endowments, nor what can be obtained through exchange, yields an adequate amount of food.

If starvation and hunger are seen in terms of failures of entitlements, then it becomes immediately clear that the total availability of food in a country is only one of several variables that are relevant. Many famines occur without any decline

in the availability of food. For example, in the Great Bengal famine of 1943, the total food availability in Bengal was not particularly bad (considerably higher than two years earlier when there was no famine), and yet three million people died, in a famine mainly affecting the rural areas, through rather violent shifts in the relative purchasing powers of different groups, hitting the rural laborers the hardest. The Ethiopian famine of 1973 took place in a year of average per capita food availability, but the cultivators and other occupation groups in the province of Wollo had lost their means of subsistence (through loss of crops and a decline of economic activity, related to a local drought) and had no means of commanding food from elsewhere in the country. Indeed, some food moved *out* of Wollo to more prosperous people in other parts of Ethiopia, repeating a pattern of contrary movement of food that was widely observed during the Irish famines of the 1840s (with food moving out of famine-stricken Ireland to prosperous England which had greater power in the battle for entitlements). The Bangladesh famine of 1974 took place in a year of *peak* food availability, but several occupation groups had lost their entitlement to food through loss of employment and other economic changes (including inflationary pressures causing prices to outrun wages). Other examples of famines without significant (or any) decline in food availability can be found, and there is nothing particularly surprising about this fact once it is recognized that the availability of food is only one influence among many on the entitlement of each occupation group. Even when a famine *is* associated with a decline of food availability, the entitlement changes have to be studied to understand the particular nature of the famine, e.g., why one occupation group is hit but not another.

The causation of starvation can be sensibly sought in failures of entitlements of the respective groups.

The causal analysis of famines in terms of entitlements also points to possible public policies of prevention. The main economic strategy would have to take the form of increasing the entitlements of the deprived groups, and in general, of guaranteeing minimum entitlements for everyone, paying particular attention to the vulnerable groups. This can, in the long run, be done in many different ways, involving both economic growth (including growth of food output) and distributional adjustments. Some of these policies may, however, require that the property rights and the corresponding entitlements of the more prosperous groups be violated. The problem, in fact, is particularly acute in the short run, since it may not be possible to engineer rapid economic growth instantly. Then the burden of raising entitlements of the groups in distress would largely have to fall on reducing the entitlements of others more favorably placed. Transfers of income or commodities through various public policies may well be effective in quashing a famine (as the experience of famine relief in different countries has shown), but it may require substantial government intervention in the entitlements of the more prosperous groups.

There is, however, no great moral dilemma in this if property rights are treated as purely *instrumental*. If the goals of relief of hunger and poverty are sufficiently powerful, then it would be just right to violate whatever property rights come in the way, since — in this view — property rights have no intrinsic status. On the other hand, if property rights are taken to be morally inviolable irrespective of their consequences, then it will follow that these policies cannot be morally accept-

able even though they might save thousands, or even millions, from dying. The inflexible moral "constraint" of respecting people's legitimately acquired entitlements would rule out such policies.

In fact this type of problem presents a reductio ad absurdum of the moral validity of constraint-based entitlement systems. However, while the conclusions to be derived from that approach might well be "absurd," the situation postulated is not an imaginary one at all. It is based on studies of actual famines and the role of entitlement failures in the causation of mass starvation. If there is an embarrassment here, it belongs solidly to the consequence-independent way of seeing rights.

I should add that this dilemma does not arise from regarding property rights to be of intrinsic value, which can be criticized on other grounds, but not this one. Even if property rights *are* of intrinsic value, their violation may be justified on grounds of the favorable consequences of that violation. A right, as was mentioned earlier, may be intrinsically valuable and still be justly violated taking everything into account. The "absurdum" does not belong to attaching intrinsic value to property rights, but to regarding these rights as simply acceptable, regardless of their consequences. A moral system that values both property rights and other goals — such as avoiding famines and starvation, or fulfilling people's right not to be hungry — can, on the one hand, give property rights intrinsic importance, and on the other, recommend the violation of property rights when that leads to better overall consequences (*including* the disvalue of rights violation).

The issue here is not the valuing of property rights, but their alleged inviolability. There is no dilemma here either for the purely instrumental view of property rights or for treating the fulfill-ment of property rights as one goal among many, but specifically for consequence-independent assertions of property rights and for the corresponding constraint-based approaches to moral entitlement of ownership.

That property and hunger are closely related cannot possibly come as a great surprise. Hunger is primarily associated with not owning enough food and thus property rights over food are immediately and directly involved. Fights over that property right can be a major part of the reality of a poor country, and any system of moral assessment has to take note of that phenomenon. The tendency to see hunger in purely technocratic terms of food output and availability may help to hide the crucial role of entitlements in the genesis of hunger, but a fuller economic analysis cannot overlook that crucial role. Since property rights over food are de-rived from property rights over other goods and resources (through production and trade), the entire system of rights of acquisition and transfer is implicated in the emergence and survival of hunger and starvation.

The Right Not to Be Hungry

Property rights have been championed for a long time. In contrast, the assertion of "the right not to be hungry" is a com-paratively recent phenomenon. While this right is much invoked in political debates, there is a good deal of skepticism about treating this as truly a right in any sub-stantial way. It is often asserted that this concept of "right not to be hungry" stands essentially for nothing at all ("simple nonsense," as Bentham called "natural rights" in general). That piece of sophis-ticated cynicism reveals not so much a penetrating insight into the practical af-fairs of the world, but a refusal to inves-tigate what people mean when they assert the existence of rights that, for the bulk of humanity, are not in fact guaranteed by the existing institutional arrangements.

The right not to be hungry is not as-serted as a recognition of an institutional right that already exists, as the right to property typically is. The assertion is pri-marily a moral claim as to what should be valued, and what institutional structure we should aim for, and try to guarantee if feasible. It can also be seen in terms of Ronald Dworkin's category of "back-ground rights" — rights that provide a jus-tification for political decisions by society in abstract. This interpretation serves as the basis for a reason to change the exist-ing institutional structure and state policy.

It is broadly in this form that the right to "an adequate means of livelihood" is referred to in the Constitution of India: "The state shall, in particular, direct its policy towards securing . . . that the citi-zens, men and women equally, have the right to an adequate means of livelihood." This does not, of course, offer to each citizen a guaranteed right to an adequate livelihood, but the state is asked to take steps such that this right could become realizable for all.

In fact, this right has often been in-voked in political debates in India. The electoral politics of India does indeed give particular scope for such use of what are seen as background rights. It is, of course, not altogether clear whether the reference to this right in the Indian constitution has in fact materially influenced the political debates. The constitutional statement is often cited, but very likely this issue would have figured in any case in these debates, given the nature of the moral and political concern. But whatever the con-stitutional contribution, it is interesting to ask whether the implicit acceptance of the value of the right to freedom from hunger makes any difference to actual policy.

It can be argued that the general acceptance of the right of freedom from acute hunger as a major goal has played quite a substantial role in preventing famines in India. The last real famine in India was in 1943, and while food availability per head in India has risen only rather slowly (even now the food availability per head is no higher than in many sub-Saharan countries stricken by recurrent famines), the country has not experienced any famine since independence in 1947. The main cause of that success is a policy of public intervention. Whenever a famine has threatened (e.g., in Bihar in 1967–68, in Maharashtra in 1971–73, in West Bengal in 1978–79), a public policy of intervention and relief has offered minimum entitlements to the potential famine victims, and thus have the threatening famines been averted. It can be argued that the quickness of the response of the respective governments (both state and central) reflects a political necessity, given the Indian electoral system and the importance attached by the public to the prevention of starvation. Political pressures from opposition groups and the news media have kept the respective governments on their toes, and the right to be free from acute hunger and starvation has been achieved largely because it has been seen as a valuable right. Thus the recognition of the intrinsic moral importance of this right, which has been widely invoked in public discussions, has served as a powerful political instrument as well.

On the other hand, this process has been far from effective in tackling pervasive and persistent undernourishment in India. There has been no famine in post-independence India, but perhaps a third of India's rural population is perennially undernourished. So long as hunger remains non-acute and starvation deaths are avoided (even though morbidity and mortality rates are enhanced by undernourish-

ment), the need for a policy response is neither much discussed by the news media, nor forcefully demanded even by opposition parties. The elimination of famines coexists with the survival of widespread "regular hunger." The right to "adequate means" of *nourishment* does not at all seem to arouse political concern in a way that the right to "adequate means" to *avoid starvation* does.

The contrast can be due to one of several different reasons. It could, of course, simply be that the ability to avoid undernourishment is not socially accepted as very important. This could be so, though what is socially accepted and what is not is also partly a matter of how clearly the questions are posed. It is, in fact, quite possible that the freedom in question would be regarded as a morally important right if the question were posed in a transparent way, but this does not happen because of the nature of Indian electoral politics and that of news coverage. The issue is certainly not "dramatic" in the way in which starvation deaths and threatening famines are. Continued low-key misery may be too familiar a phenomenon to make it worthwhile for political leaders to get some mileage out of it in practical politics. The news media may also find little profit in emphasizing a non-spectacular phenomenon — the quiet survival of disciplined, non-acute hunger.

If this is indeed the case, then the implications for action of the goal of eliminating hunger, or guaranteeing to all the means for achieving this, may be quite complex. The political case for making the quiet hunger less quiet and more troublesome for governments in power is certainly relevant. Aggressive political journalism might prove to have an instrumental moral value if it were able to go beyond reporting the horrors of visible starvation and to portray the pervasive, non-acute hunger in a more dramatic and telling way. This is obviously not the place to discuss the instrumentalities of practical politics, but the endorsement of the moral right to be free from hunger — both acute and non-acute — would in fact raise pointed questions about the means which might be used to pursue such a goal.

Moral Assessment and Social Relations

. . . If there is one thing that emerges sharply from the discussion I have tried to present in this paper, it is the importance of factual analysis for moral assessment, including moral scrutiny of the acceptability and pursuit of specific rights. This is so even when the right in question is acknowledged to have intrinsic moral value, since valuing a right is not the same thing as accepting it. To affirm acceptability independently of consequences can be peculiarly untenable, as was discussed in analyzing entitlements and hunger. In assessing the claims of property rights, of the right not to be hungry, the examination cannot be confined to issues of basic valuation only, and much of the challenge of assessment lies in the empirical analysis of causes and effects. In the world in which we live — full of hunger as well as wealth — these empirical investigations can be both complex and quite extraordinarily important. The big moral questions are frequently also deeply economic, social, or political.

MICHAEL HARRINGTON
Corporate Collectivism
A System of Social Injustice

MICHAEL HARRINGTON, *chair of the Democratic Socialist Organizing Committee, is also the author of* The Other America *(1981),* Socialism *(1973), and* The Twilight of Capitalism *(1976) and other books. He has taught at Queens College, City University of New York and was chairman of the Socialist Party of the United States from 1968 to 1972.*

I do not believe the United States is a free enterprise society. I think the people who want us to use this term wish to rationalize and defend rather than describe the society. There may have been a free enterprise society for five minutes in Great Britain in the nineteenth century, although personally I doubt it. It certainly has never existed in the United States. Among other things, we fought a war, the Civil War, in which one of the issues was free trade versus protectionism. Protectionism won. The infrastructure of our society, the railroad, was built by federal donations. The United States today does not have a free enterprise society in any kind of Adam Smithian sense of the term. Rather, we have gigantic oligopolies administering prices, shaping tastes, working together with an all-pervasive government which follows corporate priorities. Therefore, I suggest that rather than using the term "free enterprise" to describe our system we get closer to reality and call it "corporate collectivism."

I maintain that corporate collectivism, in its historical thrust and tendency, is not compatible with social justice. Moreover, I am absolutely certain that capitalism — corporate collectivism in its latest phase — is coming to an end. As a socialist, I am not necessarily filled with joy at this prospect because there is more than one end possible to this society. The question before us is not *whether* there is going to be a collectivist society in the future, because that is already decided. The real question is, what kind of collectivist society will there be? When we play around with terms like "free enterprise," we ask the wrong questions and cannot possibly come up with the right answers. . . .

Capitalism: An Historical Perspective

What was the principle of precapitalist society? What was the big gulf between capitalist society and previous societies? In all that went before capitalism, the political, the economic, and the social were one. The individual's economic position in society was not independent of his political and social position. If you were a duke, a slave owner, or a member of a mandarin bureaucracy, there was a seamless whole which defined you politically, economically, and socially. In the Middle Ages, a young serf did not decide to try to become a duke. There was only one institution in the Middle Ages which made that possible — the Catholic Church. But, by and large, it was a society where one's economic, political, and social position was fixed at birth and was part of this whole.

As a result, in these precapitalist societies (what Marx called Oriental despotism, and slave society, as well as feudal society), the ruling class had a very specific way of extracting an economic surplus from the direct producers. Feudal society achieved the surplus through force sanctioned by religion. That is to say, the serf labored free for the lord or gave him rent in kind, or later gave him money, because the lord was his military protector, sanctioned by God, in an order which was accepted from the very start.

Capitalism did a number of absolutely magnificent things in terms of those precapitalist societies. First it separated, or as a system had a tendency to separate, the political, economic, and social orders. Properly speaking, social classes are an invention of capitalism. Before capitalism, there were "estates," caste systems, hereditary systems. Only with the advent of capitalism and its separation of the political, economic, and social systems was there a society that offered individual choice, the possibility of mobility, and an opportunity to rise above the status of one's birth.

Second, capitalism normally did not extract a surplus by naked force. That was a great advance. Capitalism is the system which uses economic means to get the surplus out of the direct producer. That is to say, it is based on a contract. It is absolutely true that the contract is utterly unfair, but it is nevertheless a contract, and that means a rise, so to speak, in civil liberties — a rise in the ethical and personal level of the society. The contract is unfair because, in the capitalist mythology, a free worker with nothing to sell but his labor freely contracts with someone who has enormous wealth and who is able to gain a surplus through that contract. It is an unfair contract, but it is a system that works on the basis of contract and law rather than force. . . .

Third, capitalism discovered the social power of people working together. That, I submit, was its economic invention. . . . What capitalism discovered was not technology; it discovered that allowing people to work together enormously increased their productivity. That was social invention. The discovery of the social nature of work, of people working together rather than in isolation, was the decisive moment in the rise of capitalism and, again, an enormous contribution to humankind.

This brings me to the final point of this brief history: the capitalist system bases itself on a contradiction. It is a system which is increasingly and progressively social capitalism. Capitalism is a socializing system. It first socializes work, with entrepreneurs getting artisans together under a single roof, achieving certain economies of scale. Larger entrepreneurs socialize smaller entrepreneurs. There is a tendency toward concentration, toward monopoly, toward oligopoly, cartels, trusts — larger and larger units. . . .

Capitalism is from the very first moment a world system. It reaches all over the world, destroys ancient cultures, and upsets the international balance. It tries to bring the entire world, every last person, into the same integrated unit. Capitalism is profoundly social and profoundly revolutionary. But at the same time that capitalism becomes more social, at the same time that the technological decisions today of a U.S. Steel or an IBM have more social consequences than most of the decisions of state legislatures, the system remains private in its decision making and its allocation of resources and benefits. And there, I suggest, is the genius of capitalism and the contradiction that will destroy it. Here I am using a paradox defined by Joseph Schumpeter, one of the great conservatives of the modern age, but I think it very much in the spirit of

my good friend, Karl Marx, viz., that capitalism is destroyed by its success, not its failure. Capitalism so successfully socializes that the socialized world which it creates becomes incompatible with the institutional decision-making process in private hands.

Finally, I am perfectly aware that capitalism today is no longer run by individual entrepreneurs making personal decisions. I am perfectly aware that there are huge corporate bureaucracies, technostructures if you want. Of course, corporate bureaucracies tend to view profit maximizing on a much longer time span than a nineteenth century robber baron. But what I am saying is, for example, that the American automobile industry still considers the problem of pollution or the problem of automobile safety from the point of view of making as much money in a sophisticated way as it possibly can. This is in contradiction with the extremely social system which capitalism creates.

So my first point is this. Capitalism is a magnificent, revolutionary, and liberating system which, by its own success, becomes conservative and reactionary. It will bring about its own demise.

Contemporary Capitalism

I call our present system corporate collectivism. Its origins are to be found in three historical periods and the events associated with them. The first period was from about 1880 to 1900, when European and American capitalism went through a crisis which it solved by monopolies, trusts, and by the intervention of the state, the beginning of the state's entrance into the economy. The first move toward corporate collectivism is the end of the entrepreneurial capitalism at the end of the last century.

The second period was World War I, a

tremendous watershed. Here I use the rather classical, conservative, contemporary economist Hicks as my source. Hicks points out that during World War I, the government had to mobilize the war effort. This brought about the discovery of military socialism, the capacity of the state to administer the economy. There had been government intervention into the economy before World War I, particularly social welfare intervention under Bismarck in Germany and Lloyd George in Britain. But in World War I, government actually operated industries. For example, the railroads were run by the United States government. That was, Hicks says, the beginning of an administrative revolution in which the state learned its capacity for economic intervention.

The third period was during the Great Depression of the 1930's, when Keynesianism triumphed in its most conservative variant. In the 1930's, some nations began to understand that the government had to be responsible for the economic management of the macro-economy. . . .

This Keynesian revolution in its democratic variant, particularly in its American variant, was conservative. Many in the United States, including conservatives, think that Keynes was some kind of radical. I suggest they read his life. Keynes was not only a theorist, he was a man who made money for himself and various charitable causes for which he worked as an investment advisor. Keynes was an upper-class aristocratic snob who regarded the workers as a bunch of boobs and who said that he was a Keynesian precisely because he was not a socialist.

Now there are Keynesians who, in my opinion, are much better than Keynes. But American conservatives will have to learn one of these days that the ideology of conservatism in the late twentieth century is Keynesianism or at least conservative

Keynesianism. The point of Keynesianism was that the corporate infrastructure was fundamentally sound and that all the government did, merely by fiscal and monetary policy, was to match the macro-aggregates of supply and demand through public and private investment at a full employment level. But the assumption behind Keynes' policy, and particularly behind the Roosevelt New Deal version of Keynesianism, was that the basic investment decisions are made by corporations and that the government simply creates an environment in which they will be able to carry out that function.

So Keynesianism, I suggest, has this profoundly conservative aspect. It has another aspect — an aspect which makes any government, including a liberal government, a hostage to the corporations. I take a very wise sentence from a contemporary German sociologist, Klaus Hoffa: "The capitalist state is not itself a capitalist." That is to say, the capitalist state is dependent for the success of its policies on the private sector. In this society of supposed equals, some people are more equal than others. When a John Kennedy is elected in 1960 or a Jimmy Carter in 1976, they must assure themselves of the cooperation of the corporate community because that community makes investment decisions, and private investment decisions are the key to full employment.

I therefore suggest that the concept of "trickle down," the concept of the government rewarding the corporate rich more than anyone else, is not a policy of American society. It is *the* policy of American society. The policy is imposed upon this society by the fact that corporations are in charge of the investment process. Therefore, if one considers the Kennedy/Johnson tax cuts, as has Leon Keyserling, who was chairman of the Council of Economic Advisors under

Truman, one finds that the rich received much more than anyone else. Indeed, I would suggest to you that the welfare state does much more for the corporate rich than for anybody else.

For now, I just want to focus on the fact that macroeconomic policy has to be pro-corporate. If we elected a government in the United States composed solely of left-wing trade union leaders, militant civil rights advocates, feminists and reformers, but kept corporations in charge of investment, that government would be nicer to corporations than to workers or minorities or women or to the people in general—not because it sold out but because that is the reality of government in our society. What I am saying is: the political freedom of society is profoundly restricted by the economic and social institutions. So it is that today in Great Britain a Socialist Chancellor of the Exchequer, a former member of the Young Communist League, is presiding over increasing unemployment and holding wages down as a socialist policy. Under the circumstances in Britain, corporate people are more important than working people; people in board rooms are more important than unemployed people. That is built in, I suggest, to this kind of society.

This leads me to a proposition about the kinds of decisions that are made in our society. I am not suggesting that there is a capitalist conspiracy, that there are a bunch of bloated plutocrats in top hats who sit around the table in the morning and say, "Let us now go and see how we can do harm to the weak and the poor in this society." What I am saying is that there is a structure of power that dictates pro-corporate outcomes to democratically elected representatives. . . .

In conclusion, the issue before American society is not whether there will be national economic planning. We already have it. Our problem is that the plan on which we operate today proceeds according to the priorities of a hidden agenda. That hidden agenda, which has a remarkable consistency, is that government shall on all major decisions maximize corporate priorities. I suggest therefore that the issue is whether the plan will become democratic with a small "d," transparent and open, or whether it will remain bureaucratic and secret.

And, in terms of that point, one last unkind word for the American corporation. I believe the American corporation is now becoming decadent. The typical corporate executive, after reading the *Wall Street Journal* editorial in the morning about the glories of free enterprise and the free market system, immediately tries to figure how to get another subsidy from the government. There is a sense—and please understand me clearly, because there are enormous differences between the United States and the Soviet Union—but there is a sense in which executives in the United States are increasingly playing the role that commissars play in the Soviet Union. They act as a bureaucratic elite with a government at their disposal, taking money from the people to fulfill their priorities and their interests and to make their decisions.

My second point, then, is that capitalism, which was such a magnificent and revolutionary system, has by its very socialization now created a corporate collectivist society in which government and the corporations cooperate with the public's money on the basis of corporate priorities. . . .

The Alternatives to Capitalism

What are the alternatives? What would be a perspective for freedom and social justice in the modern world? Now let me state at the outset that I am a socialist, a democratic socialist. That is, I do not regard any of the totalitarian societies which claim to be socialist as being socialist. I think they are bureaucratic collectivisms, not democratic and free collectivisms. But much of what I am going to say does not require that you be a socialist to agree with me. . . .

The principle of the alternative to corporate collectivism, it seems to me, is the democratization of economic and social decision making. This is the fundamental principle that one then wants to follow in absolutely every aspect of the society. Under capitalism, by an (I hope) imperishable conquest of the human spirit, the idea of political freedom came into being, and we are eternally in the debt of the capitalist society for that. But now the concept of freedom and democracy must be applied to areas in which capitalism never applied it. Unless we democratize our increasingly collectivist state, which acts on the basis of a hidden agenda, we will lose freedom. Therefore, I believe that the democratization of economic and social power is the fundamental principle.

Now let me suggest some very specific ways that this can be done. First, there is a very moderate bill to which the Democratic Party platform was formally committed in 1976 and which a good many Democrats are busily running away from as fast as they possibly can. The bill is the Hawkins–Humphrey Full Employment Bill. It is a bill for the most conservative modicum of liberal capitalist planning. It says that the President of the United States every year will make an analysis of all the investment decisions, public and private, that can be anticipated for that year, add up those investment decisions, and discover what level of unemployment will result, given the population, technology,

and so on. If adult unemployment exceeds 3 percent, which in plainer English is about 4 percent total unemployment, then the President is required by law to present to the Congress in an annual message those programs which will make up the shortfall and reduce unemployment to 4 percent or 3 percent adult unemployment. It is a very modest bill. It is viewed in some quarters as being practically the equivalent of Bolshevism. But it would begin to attack the most outrageous and abiding evil in this society today, its high level of unemployment, which is not randomly distributed but particularly discriminates against minorities, youth, and women. . . .

The problem is that many people are now saying we cannot do that, and some of them are liberals. Charles Schultze of the Brookings Institution says, in effect, that American society requires 5 percent unemployment in order to function. He maintains that as soon as we get to 5.5 percent unemployment, the inflationary tendencies become so strong that we must give up our campaign against unemployment in order to fight inflation. This implies that the people composing that reserve army of the unemployed, as Marx would describe it — this reserve army which is disproportionately black, Hispanic, female, and young — will pay for the struggle against inflation.

In conclusion, I suggest three propositions. First, capitalism was a magnificent advance for mankind, but a contradictory advance because it was a system of private socialization. The socialization brought enormous successes, but the private socialization has brought us intolerable contradictions. Second, the contemporary manifestation of the contradictions of private socialization are seen in an American system that is not a free enterprise system but a corporate collectivist system in which government honestly, sincerely, and non-conspiratorially follows corporate priorities because they are natural in this society. Third, the alternative, the way to pursue freedom in the late twentieth century, is to democratize economic and social as well as political institutions.

If we ask: "Shall we have free enterprise or shall we have collectivism?" we have asked a meaningless question, because there is no free enterprise today. There can be no free enterprise given the scale of our technology, given the interdependence of our world. Richard Nixon planned as much as Lyndon Johnson. If Ronald Reagan had been elected President of the United States, he would have planned as much as Lyndon Johnson or anybody else. It is not that people sell out. This is the basic thrust of our society.

Therefore, I think the question, as is often the case, is at least as important as the answer. I would reformulate the question and say the true question before us today in terms of freedom and social justice is: "Will the collectivist economic and social and political structure, which is emerging right now in front of our very eyes, be bureaucratically run by a united front of corporations and government on the basis of a hidden agenda moving toward a post-capitalist bureaucratic collectivist society run by the grandchildren of the executives?" Or is it possible for the collectivism which is emerging here and now to be democratized, to be subjected to the will of the people instead of its dominating the people? It is that second possibility that I am for, that I pose in terms of ethics and freedom and social justice. I am not sure it can prevail. I am not sure it will prevail. The one thing that I am sure of is that it is the only way for freedom to survive in the modern world.

Active euthanasia
passive euthanasia

13

What Are the Proper Ends of Medicine?

Medical ethics is almost as old a field as medicine itself. One of the earliest documents concerning medicine is the Hippocratic oath, a set of ethical standards for the practice of medicine laid down by the Greek physician Hippocrates about 400 B.C. Important as such ethical guidelines were then, they are even more important now. Medicine is much more effective now than it was even a century ago, when there was little that could be done for most illness and injury. Accordingly, we have become far more dependent on the medical establishment to maintain the quality and extend the duration of our lives.

At the same time, medical technology has advanced to a point that the very concepts that have historically framed our moral sensibilities seem in need of drastic redefinition, or abandonment. Even the concept of death has been stretched almost beyond recognition by the wide availability of mechanical means for prolonging cellular activity in the human body. Perhaps a hypothetical example will bring into focus some of the sorts of problems that our culture must face in reaching anything like a clear view of the proper ends of medicine.

Jack O'Conner, age 51, has worked for 32 years as a machinist for a local manufacturing company. Outside of his work, he exercises occasionally, but not with much enthusiasm. He has been married, if not happily, at least to the same person, for 29 years, and has three children: Kathleen, 17, Sean, 19, and Maureen, 22. He and his family are covered by the standard health insurance offered by his company, and they have regular medical checkups which they have generally breezed through without issue. Nevertheless, because his own father died young, he worries about his health, sometimes excessively. He has remarked to his regular physician that if he is dying, he doesn't want to know about it. These remarks have always been an occasion for lighthearted banter between Jack and Dr. Fine. But now Jack has cancer.

Dr. Fine decides to take Jack's expressed wishes seriously; she doesn't know Jack's wife or children and does not feel that she can breach confidentiality by contacting them directly. She knows that Jack will die within six months, and she has seen many cases in which a patient who was informed of his imminent death went into a depression that ruined, literally, the rest of his life. She decides not to tell Jack that he has cancer.

Consequently, three months later when Jack is admitted to the hospital, he is not well-prepared to make important decisions regarding the course of his treatment. He quickly degenerates to a state of severe, unremitting pain, which is treated with heavy doses of narcotic pain-relievers. The medication brings some relief from pain, but the combined effect of the medication and the pain makes it impossible for Jack to discuss coherently his disease or his treatment.

Dr. Fine would like to enroll Jack in an experimental program at one of the other local hospitals. Unfortunately, Jack's medical insurance does not pay for "exotic" treatment. Last year Jack's neighbor, also a machinist, but at a different local plant, became seriously ill and was referred to a specialist in San Francisco. But his insurance covered such referrals, whereas Jack's does not. Consequently, Dr. Fine can do little more than alleviate Jack's increasing pain and the other symptoms of his physical decline.

Within a month, Jack spends his days and nights racked with excruciating pain that is increasingly unresponsive to larger and larger doses of medication. In his few marginally coherent moments, he pleads to be relieved of his pain, and to die in peace. The doctors agreed that if Jack's heart stopped, they would not resuscitate him, and that if he stopped breathing, they would not place him on a mechanical respirator. Nevertheless, his body stubbornly lives on. Jack's wife and children plead with the doctors to give him a lethal injection. But the law, or the doctors' conception of it, and their ethical code, will not permit them either actively to cause his death (even though that is the only thing that would relieve his suffering) or intentionally to fail to treat him as fully as possible so long as he continues breathing and his heart beats. They remark on the possibility of a miracle.

Five weeks later, Jack's body dies. He has spent nine weeks in the hospital, eight of them in intensive care. The hospital bill is nearly $300,000, of which Jack's insurance pays 80%. His family is responsible for the remaining $60,000 which, conveniently, is precisely the amount of the life insurance policy that Jack carefully maintained during the 25 years since he first began paying for it. All of us who participate in health insurance paid the remaining $240,000 of Jack's hospital bill.

Three of the issues that are discussed in the readings in this chapter are illustrated in the case of Jack O'Conner. First, was it permissible for Dr. Fine to withhold from Jack, on his request, the information that he had cancer? If she were right about the quality of his life after her diagnosis, does that justify her decision not to tell him the truth about his illness? This practice has been referred to as a form of **paternalism** in medicine, in which doctors — rightly or wrongly — impinge on the autonomy of patients by withholding important information from them. In his selection, Allen Buchanan argues that withholding the truth from patients is a common practice in medicine, but that the justifications usually given for this practice are insufficient. He concludes that doctors ought to tell their patients the truth about their illnesses. In a rebuttal of Buchanan's position, Donald Vandeveer argues that at least one justification for withholding the truth from patients survives Buchanan's argument: patients have the right to contract with their physicians to have potentially distressing information withheld from them. Such contracts, Buchanan argues, reinforce rather than undermine the autonomy of the patient. If he is right, we are left with at least one area in which physicians are permitted, even obligated, not to tell their patients the truth about their illnesses.

A second issue raised by Jack's case is the cost of medical care. Jack's treatment and care were enormously expensive to him, to his family, and to the rest of us who share the financial burden of his health care through insurance and government health programs. Moreover, if he could have afforded it, Jack could have tried a new sort of treatment that offered more hope of a cure. His neighbor, a person of similar talents and needs, was fortunate enough to have more comprehensive health insurance that paid for such treatment. Should the availability of health care be a matter of how much money a person has, or whom a person works for? Or is health care a basic need that should be guaranteed equally to all? Dan Beauchamp claims that our present health-care system is based on a social ethic of "market-justice" that protects the majority and the most powerful from the burdens of equitable health care. He argues that we need to develop a public-health ethic that would emphasize prevention and collective responsibility rather than autonomy and individual liberty. Loren Lomasky, in his selection, claims to the contrary that we simply could not pay for equity at the level of care that the more privileged of our society currently enjoy. We should, he argues, let individuals — rather than government — make their own choices about health care, based on their ability to pay. In order to protect the poor, Lomasky suggests a system of health-care vouchers to be used in a medical marketplace. He therefore squarely opposes the sort of national health-care system proposed by Beauchamp.

A third issue that Jack's case raises concerns the nature of his death. Jack lived much longer than he wanted to, lost to relentless pain at great financial cost. As an alternative, he could, at a point at which his death was inevitable, simply have requested a lethal injection. Our current laws and codes of medical ethics do not permit this, on the grounds that a doctor may not intentionally bring about the death of a patient. To do so would legally and, it is claimed, morally, constitute murder. In many circumstances, Jack's for example, a doctor is permitted not to treat a patient for whom treatment would only prolong life. This critical distinction between actively causing a person's death and passively, through inaction, allowing a person to die, is a distinction on which a huge amount of legal and moral weight is placed. James Rachels proposes in a crisp selection that it is a distinction without a difference. He agrees that "active euthanasia" and "passive euthanasia" are legally different. But by spelling out for us some of the consequences of trying to hold on to such a distinction, he argues that there is no moral basis to this legal distinction. In her response to Rachels' argument, Bonnie Steinbock claims to the contrary that the distinction between active and passive euthanasia can be supported in cases in which the patient refuses treatment, and in cases in which, like Jack's, the purpose of failing to treat a patient is not the termination of life, but rather the reduction of pain.

The chapter ends with two articles that deal not so much with particular questions but rather with the structure of concepts that leads us to think about these questions as we do. Virginia Warren argues that the very framing of issues often reveals "sexist ethics." For example, she sees the focus on paternalism in medicine as an instance of a preoccupation with issues of authority and power — characteristically masculine approaches. She then explores what an alternative medical ethics might look like if it were created in response to central themes in feminist philosophy. The novel result is suggestive of quite different approaches to moral problems in the conduct of medicine.

Finally, Daniel Callahan's article questions our prevailing concept of the aim of medical practice. He argues, in response to costs of medical care that we cannot possibly pay, that we must adopt a view of medical care that is not focused exclusively on the goal of curing illness. His startling proposal is that we employ age as a specific criterion in the allocation of medical treatment. His proposal has been nearly unspeakable in current political circles, but his thoughtful and sensitive defense of it challenges our received thinking both about equity in the allocation of resources and about the ends of medicine.

ALLEN BUCHANAN

Medical Paternalism

ALLEN BUCHANAN *is a philosopher who is interested in medical ethics. He was a member of the President's Commission for the Study of Ethical Problems in Medicine, Bio-Medicine and Behavior. He has taught at the University of Minnesota and at the University of Arizona.*

Benefits not to tell.

I

There is evidence to show that among physicians in this country the medical paternalist model is a dominant way of conceiving the physician-patient relationship. I contend that the practice of withholding the truth from the patient or his family, a particular form of medical paternalism, is not adequately supported by the arguments advanced to justify it. Beyond the issue of telling patients the truth is the distinction between "ordinary" and "extraordinary" therapeutic measures, a distinction which, I argue, both expresses and helps to perpetuate the dominance of the medical paternalist model.

There are two main types of arguments against paternalism. First are the arguments that rely upon a theory of moral rights rooted in a conception of personal autonomy. These arguments are more theoretically interesting and perhaps in the end they are the strongest arguments against paternalism. Second are the arguments that meet the paternalist on his own ground and then attempt to cut it from beneath him by showing that his arguments are defective. I shall concentrate on the second type of antipaternalist argument because I wish my arguments to have some practical effect, and I believe that this goal can best be achieved if they are directed against paternalist justifications which are actually employed by the practitioners of medical paternalism. . . .

II

Paternalism is usually characterized as interference with a person's liberty of action, where the alleged justification of the interference is that it is for the good of the person whose liberty of action is thus restricted. To focus exclusively on interference with liberty of *action* however, is to construe paternalism too narrowly. If a government lies to the public or withholds information from it, and if the alleged justification of its policy is that it benefits the public itself, the policy may properly be called paternalistic.

On the one hand, there may be a direct connection between such a policy and actual interference with the citizen's freedom to act. In order to withhold information from the public, agents of the government may physically interfere with the freedom of the press to gather, print, or distribute the news. Or government officials may misinform the public in order to restrict its freedom to perform specific acts. The police, for example, may erect signs bearing the words "Detour: Maintenance Work Ahead" to route unsuspecting motorists around the wreckage of a truck carrying nerve gas. On the other hand, the connection between withholding of information and actual interference with freedom of action may be indirect at best. To interfere with the public's freedom of information the government need not actually interfere with anyone's freedom to act—it may simply not divulge certain information. Withholding information may preclude an *informed* decision, and it may interfere with attempts to reach an informed decision, without thereby interfering with a person's freedom to decide and to act on his decision. Even if I am deprived of information which I must have if I am to make an informed decision, I may still be free to decide and to act.

Granted the complexity of the relations between information and action, it seems plausible to expand the usual characterization of paternalism as follows: paternalism is interference with a person's freedom of action or freedom of information, or the deliberate dissemination of misinformation, where the alleged justification of interfering or misinforming is that it is for the good of the person who is interfered with or misinformed. The notion of freedom of information is, of course, unsatisfyingly vague, but the political examples sketched above along with the medical examples to follow will make it clearer. We can now turn to a brief consideration of evidence for the claim that medical paternalism is a widespread phenomenon in our society.

III

The evidence for medical paternalism is both direct and indirect. The direct evidence consists of the findings of surveys which systematically report physicians' practices concerning truth-telling and decision-making and of articles and discussions in which physicians and others acknowledge or defend paternalistic medical practices. The indirect evidence is more subtle. One source of indirect evidence for the pervasiveness of medical paternalist attitudes is the language we use to describe physician-patient interactions. Let us now consider some of the direct evidence.

Though there are many ways of classifying cases of medical paternalism, two distinctions are especially important. We can distinguish between the cases in which the patient is legally competent and those in which the patient is legally incompetent; and between those cases in which the intended beneficiary of paternalism is the patient himself and those in which the intended beneficiary is the patient's guardian or one or more members of the patient's family. The first distinction classifies cases according to the *legal status of the patient*, the second according to the *object of paternalism*.

A striking revelation of medical paternalism in dealings with legally competent adults is found in Donald Oken's essay, "What to Tell Cancer Patients: A Study of Medical Attitudes." The chief conclusion of this study of internists, surgeons, and generalists is that ". . . there is a strong and general tendency to withhold" from the patient the information that he has cancer. Almost 90 percent of the total group surveyed reported that their usual policy is not to tell the patient that he has cancer. Oken also notes that "no one reported a policy of informing every patient." Further, Oken reports that some physicians falsified diagnoses.

> Some physicians avoid even the slightest suggestion of neoplasia and quite specifically substitute another diagnosis. Almost everyone reported resorting to such falsification on at least a few occasions, most notably when the patient was in a far-advanced stage of illness at the time he was seen.

The physicians' justifications for withholding or falsifying diagnostic information were uniformly paternalistic. They assumed that if they told the patient he had cancer they would be depriving him of all hope and that the loss of hope would result in suicidal depression or at least in a serious worsening of the patient's condition. . . .

There is also considerable evidence of medical paternalism in the treatment of legally incompetent individuals through the withholding of information from the patients or their guardians or both.

The law maintains that it is the parents who are primarily responsible for decisions concerning the welfare of their minor children. Nonetheless, physicians sometimes assume primary or even total responsibility for the most awesome and morally perplexing decisions affecting the welfare of the child.

The inescapable need to make such decisions arises daily in neonate intensive care units. . . . A. Shaw notes that some physicians undertake the responsibility for making decisions about life and death for defective newborns in order to relieve parents of the trauma and guilt of making a decision. He cites the following comment as an example of this position.

> At the end it is usually the doctor who has to decide the issue. It is . . . cruel to ask the parents whether they want their child to live or die. . . .

The growing literature on life or death decisions for defective neonates reveals more complex paternalistic practices. Some physicians routinely exclude parents from significant participation in decision-making either by not informing the parents that certain choices can or must be made, or by describing the child's condition and the therapeutic options in such a skeletal way as to preclude genuinely informed consent.

A case cited by Shaw is a clear example of a physician withholding from parents the information that there was a choice to be made.

> Baby A was referred to me at 22 hours of age with a diagnosis of esophageal atresia and tracheo-esophageal fistula. The infant, the firstborn of a professional couple in their early thirties had obvious signs of mongolism, about which they were fully informed by the referring physician. After explaining the nature of the surgery to the distraught father, I offered him the operative consent. His pen hesitated briefly above the form and then as he signed, he muttered, "I have no choice, do I?" He didn't seem to expect an answer and I gave him none. The esophageal anomaly was corrected in routine fashion, and the infant was discharged to a state institution for the retarded without ever being seen again by either parent. . . .

Not every case in which a physician circumvents or overrides parental decision-making is a case of paternalism toward the parents. In ignoring the parents' primary legal responsibility for the child, the physician may not be attempting to shield the parents from the burdens of responsibility — he may simply be attempting to protect what he perceives to be the interests of the child.

These examples are presented, not as conclusive evidence for the claim that paternalist practices of the sorts discussed above are widespread, but as illustrations of the practical relevance of the justifications for medical paternalism, which I shall now articulate and criticize.

IV

In spite of the apparent pervasiveness of paternalistic practices in medicine, no systematic justification of them is available for scrutiny. Nonetheless, there appear to be at least three main arguments which advocates of paternalism could and sometimes do advance in justification of withholding information or misinforming the patient or his family. Since withholding information seems to be more commonly practiced and advocated than outright falsification, I shall consider the three arguments only as justifications of the former rather than the latter. Each of these arguments is sufficiently general to apply to each of the types of cases distinguished above. For convenience we can label these three arguments (A) the Prevention of Harm Argument, (B) the Contractual Version of the Prevention of Harm Argument, and (C) the Argument from the Inability to Understand.

The Prevention of Harm Argument is disarmingly simply. It may be outlined as follows.

> 1. The physician's duty — to which he is bound by the Oath of Hippocrates — is to prevent or at least to minimize harm to his patient.
> 2. Giving the patient information X will do great harm to him.
> 3. (Therefore) It is permissible for the physician to withhold information X from the patient.

Several things should be noted about this argument. First of all, the conclusion is much weaker than one would expect, granted the first premise. The first premise states that it is the physician's *duty* to prevent or minimize harm to the patient, not just that it is *permissible* for him to do so. However, since the weaker conclusion — that withholding information is permissible — seems more intuitively plausible than the stronger one, I shall concentrate on it.

Second, the argument as it stands is invalid. For the claims that (1) the physician's duty (or right) is to prevent or minimize harm and that (2) giving information X will do the patient great harm, it does not follow that (3) it is permissible for the physician to withhold information X from the patient. At least one other premise is needed: (2′) giving information X will do greater harm to the patient on balance than withholding the information will.

The addition of (2′) is no quibble. Once (2′) is made explicit we begin to see the tremendous weight which this paternalist argument places on the physician's power of judgment. He must not only determine that giving the information will do harm or even that it will do great harm. He must also make a complex comparative judgment. He must judge that withholding the information will result in less harm on balance than divulging it. Yet neither the physicians interviewed by Oken nor those discussed by Shaw even mention this comparative judgment in their justifications of withholding information. They simply state that telling the truth will result in great harm to the patient or his family. No mention was made of the need to compare this expected harm with harm which might result from withholding the information, and no recognition of the difficulties involved in such a comparison was reported. . . .

In order to justify withholding the diagnosis of terminal cancer from the patient the physician must not only determine that informing the patient would do great harm but that the harm would be greater on balance than whatever harm may result from withholding information. Since the notion of "great harm" here is vague unless a context for comparison is supplied, we can concentrate on the physician's evidence for the judgment that the harm of informing is greater on balance than the harm of withholding. Oken's study showed that the evidential basis for such comparative judgments was remarkably slender.

> It was the exception when a physician could report known examples of the unfavorable consequences of an approach which differed from his own. It was more common to get reports of instances in which different approaches had turned out satisfactorily. Most of the instances in which unhappy results were reported to follow a differing policy turned out to be vague accounts from which no reliable inference could be drawn.

Oken then goes on to focus on the nature of the anticipated harm.

> It has been repeatedly asserted that disclosure is followed by fear and despondency which may progress into overt depressive illness or culminate in suicide. This was the opinion of the physicians in the present study. Quite representative was the surgeon who stated, "I would be afraid to tell and have the patient in a room with a window." When it comes to actually documenting the prevalence of such untoward reactions, it becomes difficult to find reliable evidence. Instances of depression and profound upsets came quickly to mind when the subject was raised, but no one could report more than a case or two, or a handful at most. . . . The same doctors could remember many instances in which the patient was told and seemed to do well. . . .

Consider the case of a person with terminal cancer. To eliminate the complication of interpersonal net harm comparisons, let us suppose that this person has no relatives and is himself legally competent. Suppose that the physician withholds informa-

tion of the diagnosis because he believes that knowledge of the truth would be more harmful than withholding the truth. . . . Even if we view this judgment of comparative harm as a purely clinical judgment — more specifically a clinical psychiatric judgment — it is difficult to see how the physician could be in a position to make it. But it is crucial to note that the notions of harm and benefit appropriate to these deliberations are not exclusively clinical notions, whether psychiatric or otherwise. In taking it upon himself to determine what will be most beneficial or least harmful to this patient the physician is not simply making ill-founded medical judgments which someday might be confirmed by psychiatric research. He is making *moral* evaluations of the most basic and problematic kind.

The physician must determine whether it will be better for the patient to live his remaining days in the knowledge that his days are few or to live in ignorance of his fate. But again, this is a gross simplification: it assumes that the physician's attempt to deceive the patient will be successful. E. Kübler-Ross claims that in many, if not most, cases the terminally ill patient will guess or learn his fate whether the physician withholds the diagnosis from him or not. Possible harm resulting from the patient's loss of confidence in the physician or from a state of uncertainty over his prospects must be taken into account.

Let us set aside this important complication and try to appreciate what sorts of factors would have to be taken into account in a well-founded judgment that the remainder of a person's life would be better for that person if he did not know that he had a terminal illness than if he did.

Such a judgment would have to be founded on a profound knowledge of the most intimate details of the patient's life history, his characteristic ways of coping with personal crises, his personal and vocational commitments and aspirations, his feelings of obligation toward others, and his attitude toward the completeness or incompleteness of his experience. In a society in which the personal physician was an intimate friend who shared the experience of families under his care, it would be somewhat more plausible to claim that the physician might possess such knowledge. Under the present conditions of highly impersonal specialist medical practice it is quite a different matter.

Yet even if the physician could claim such intimate personal knowledge, this would not suffice. For he must not only predict, but also *evaluate*. On the basis of an intimate knowledge of the patient as a person, he must determine which outcome would be *best* for that person. It is crucial to emphasize that the question which the physician must pose and answer is whether ignorance or knowledge will make possible a life that is better *for the patient himself*. The physician must be careful not to confuse this question with the question of whether ignorance or knowledge would make for a better life for the physician if the physician were terminally ill. Nor must he confuse it with the question of whether the patient's life would be a *better life* — a life more valuable to others or to society — if it ended in ignorance rather than in truth. The question, rather, is whether it would be better *for the patient himself* to know or not to know his fate.

To judge that a certain ending of a life would be best for the person whose life it is, is to view that life as a unified process of development and to conclude that that ending is a fitting completion for that process. To view a human life as a unified process of development, however, is to view it selectively. Certain events or patterns of conduct are singled out as especially significant or valuable. To ascertain the best completion of a person's life for that person, then, is to make the most fundamental judgments about the value of that person's activities, aspirations, and experiences.

It might be replied that we do make such value judgments when we decide to end the physiologic life of a permanently comatose individual. In such cases we do make value judgments, but they are not judgments of this sort. On the contrary, we believe that since this individual's experience has ended, his life-process is already completed.

When the decision to withhold information of impending death is understood for what it is, it is difficult to see how anyone could presume to make it. My conjecture is that physicians are tempted to make these decisions in part because of a failure to reflect upon the disparity between two quite different kinds of judgments about what will harm or benefit the patient. Judgments of the first sort fall within the physician's competence as a highly trained medical expert. There is nothing in the physician's training which qualifies him to make judgments of the second sort — to evaluate another human being's life as a whole. Further, once the complexity of these judgments is appreciated and once their evaluative character is understood, it is implausible to hold that the physician is in a better position to make them than the patient or his family. The failure to ask what sorts of harm/ benefit judgments may properly be made by the physician in his capacity as a physician is a fundamental feature of medical paternalism.

There is a more sophisticated version of the attempt to justify withholding of information in order to minimize harm to the patient or his family. This is the

Contract Version of the Prevention of Harm Argument. The idea is that the physician-patient relationship is contractual and that the terms of this contract are such that the patient authorizes the physician to minimize harm to the patient (or his family) by whatever means he, the physician, deems necessary. Thus if the physician believes that the best way to minimize harm to the patient is to withhold information from him, he may do so without thereby wronging the patient. To wrong the patient the physician would either have to do something he was not authorized to do or fail to do something it was his duty to do and which was in his power to do. But in withholding information from the patient he is doing just what he is authorized to do. So he does the patient no wrong.

First of all, it should be noted that this version is vulnerable to the same objections just raised against the non-contractual Argument from the Prevention of Harm. The most serious of these is that in the cases of paternalism under discussion it is very doubtful that the physician will or even could possess the psychiatric and moral knowledge required for a well-founded judgment about what will be least harmful to the patient. In addition, the Contract Version is vulnerable to other objections. Consider the claim that the patient-physician relationship is a contract in which the patient authorizes the physician to prevent or minimize harm by whatever means the physician deems necessary, including the withholding of information. This claim could be interpreted in either of two ways: as a descriptive generalization about the way physicians and patients actually understand their relationship or as a normative claim about the way the physician-patient relationship should be viewed or may be viewed.

As a descriptive generalization it is certainly implausible — there are many people who do not believe they have authorized their physician to withhold the truth from them, and the legal doctrine of informed consent supports their view. Let us suppose for a moment that some people do view their relationship to their physician as including such an authorization and that there is nothing morally wrong with such a contract so long as both parties entered into it voluntarily and in full knowledge of the terms of the agreement.

Surely the fact that some people are willing to authorize physicians to withhold information from them would not justify the physician in acting toward other patients as if they had done so. The physician can only justify withholding information from a particular patient if this sort of contract was entered into freely and in full knowledge *by this* patient.

What, then, is the physician to do? Surely he cannot simply assume that all of his patients have authorized him to withhold the truth if he deems it necessary. Yet if in each case he inquires as to whether the patient wishes to make such an authorization, he will defeat the purpose of the authorization by undermining the patient's trust.

There is, however, a more serious difficulty. Even the more extreme advocates of medical paternalism must agree that there are some limits on the contractual relationship between physician and patient. Hence the obligations of each party are conditional upon the other party's observing the limits of the contract. The law, the medical profession, and the general public generally recognize that there are such limits. For example, the patient may refuse to undergo a certain treatment, he may seek a second opinion, or he may terminate the relationship altogether. Moreover, it is acknowledged that to decide to do any of these things the patient may — indeed perhaps must — rely on his own judgment. If he is conscientious he will make such decisions on consideration of whether the physician is doing a reasonable job of rendering the services for which he was hired.

There are general constraints on how those services may be rendered. If the treatment is unreasonably slow, if the physician's technique is patently sloppy, or if he employs legally questionable methods, the patient may rightly conclude that the physician has not lived up to the implicit terms of the agreement and terminate the relationship. There are also more special constraints on the contract stemming from the special nature of the problem which led the patient to seek the physician's services in the first place. If you go to a physician for treatment of a skin condition, but he ignores that problem and sets about trying to convince you to have cosmetic nose surgery, you may rightly terminate the relationship. These general and special constraints are limits on the agreement from the patient's point of view.

Now once it is admitted that there are any such terms — that the contract does have some limits and that the patient has the right to terminate the relationship if these limits are not observed by the physician — it must also be admitted that the patient must be in a position to discover *whether* those limits are being observed. But if the patient were to authorize the physician to withhold information, he might deprive himself of information which is relevant to determining whether the physician has observed the limits of the agreement.

I am not concerned to argue that authorizing a physician to withhold information is logically incompatible with the contract being conditional. My point, rather, is that to make such an authorization would show either that (a) one did

not view the contract as being conditional or that (b) one did not take seriously the possibility that the conditions of the contract might be violated or that (c) one simply did not care whether the conditions were violated. Since it is unreasonable to expect a patient to make an unconditional contract or to ignore the possibility that conditions of the contract will be violated, and since one typically does care whether these conditions are observed, it is unreasonable to authorize the physician to withhold information when he sees fit. The Contract Version of the Argument from the Prevention of Harm, then, does not appear to be much of an improvement over its simpler predecessor.

There is one paternalist argument in favor of withholding of information which remains to be considered. This may be called the Argument from the Inability to Understand. The main premise is that the physician is justified in withholding information when the patient or his family is unable to understand the information. This argument is often used to justify paternalistic policies toward parents of defective infants in neonate intensive care units. The idea is that either their lack of intelligence or their excited emotional condition prevents parents from giving informed consent because they are incapable of being adequately informed. In such cases, it is said, "the doctrine of informed consent does not apply."

This argument is also vulnerable to several objections. First, it too relies upon dubious and extremely broad psychological generalizations — in this case psychological generalizations about the cognitive powers of parents of defective neonates.

Second, and more importantly, it ignores the crucial question of the character of the institutional context in which parents find themselves. To the extent that paternalist attitudes shape medical institutions, this bleak estimate of the parental capacity for comprehension and rational decision tends to be a self-fulfilling prophecy. In an institution in which parents routinely sign operation permits without even having seen their newborn infants and without having the nature of the therapeutic options clearly explained to them, parents may indeed be incapable of understanding the little that they are told.

Third, it is a mistake to maintain that the legal duty to seek informed consent applies only where the physician can succeed in adequately informing parents. The doctor does not and cannot have a duty to make sure that all the information he conveys is understood by those to whom he conveys it. His duty is to make a reasonable effort to be understood.

Fourth, it is important to ask exactly why it is so important not to tell parents information which they allegedly will not understand. If the reason is that a parental decision based on inadequate understanding will be a decision that is harmful to the *infant*, then the Argument from the Inability to Understand is not an argument for paternalism toward *parents*. So if this argument is to provide a justification for withholding information from parents for *their* benefit then the claim must be that their failure to understand will somehow be harmful to *them*. But why should this be so? If the idea is that the parents will not only fail to understand but become distressed because they realize that they do not understand, then the Argument from the Inability to Understand turns out not to be a new argument at all. Instead, it is just a restatement of the Argument from the Prevention of Harm examined above — and is vulnerable to the same objections. I conclude that none of the three justifications examined provide adequate support for the paternalist practices under consideration. If adequate justification is

to be found, the advocate of medical paternalism must marshal more powerful arguments.

V

So far I have examined several specific medical paternalistic practices and criticized some general arguments offered in their behalf. Medical paternalism, however, goes much deeper than the specific practices themselves. For this reason I have spoken of "the medical paternalist model," emphasizing that what is at issue is a paradigm, a way of conceiving the physician-patient relationship. Indirect evidence for the pervasiveness of this model is to be found in the very words we used to describe physicians, patients, and their interactions. Simply by way of illustration, I will now examine one widely used distinction which expresses and helps perpetuate the paternalist model: the distinction between "ordinary" and "extraordinary" therapeutic measures.

Many physicians, theologians, ethicists, and judges have relied on this distinction since Pius XII employed it in an address on "The Prolongation of Life" in 1958. In reply to questions concerning conditions under which physicians may discontinue or refrain from initiating the use of artificial respiration devices, Pius first noted that physicians are duty-bound "to take the necessary treatment for the preservation of life and health." He then distinguished between "ordinary" and "extraordinary" means.

> But normally one is held to use only ordinary means — according to circumstances of persons, places, times, and culture — means that do not involve any grave burden for oneself or another.

Though he is not entirely explicit about this, Pius assumes that it is the right of the physician to determine what will count as "ordinary" or "extraordinary" means in any particular case.

In the context of the issue of when a highly trained specialist is to employ sophisticated life-support equipment, it is natural to assume that the distinction between "ordinary" and "extraordinary" means is a distinction between higher and lower degrees of technological sophistication. The Pope's unargued assumption that the medical specialist is to determine what counts as "ordinary" or "extraordinary" reinforces a technological interpretation of the distinction. After all, if the distinction is a technological one, then it is natural to assume that it is the physician who should determine its application since it is he who possesses the requisite technical expertise. In my discussions with physicians, nurses, and hospital administrators I have observed that they tend to treat the distinction as a technological one and then to argue that since it is a technological distinction the physician is the one who should determine in any particular case whether a procedure would involve "ordinary" or "extraordinary" means.

Notice, however, that even though Pius introduced the distinction in the context of the proper use of sophisticated technical devices and even though he assumed that it was to be applied by those who possess the technical skills to use such equipment, it is quite clear that the distinction he explicitly introduced is not itself a technological distinction. Recall that he defines "ordinary" means as those which "do not involve any grave burden for oneself or another." "Extraordinary" means, then, would be those which do involve a grave burden for oneself or for another.

If what counts as "extraordinary" measures depended only upon what would constitute a "grave burden" to the patient himself, it might be easier to preserve the illusion that the decision is an exercise of medical expertise. But once the evaluation of burdens is extended to the patient's family it becomes obvious that the judgment that a certain therapy would be "extraordinary" is not a technological or even a clinical, but rather a *moral* decision. And it is a moral decision regardless of whether the evaluation is made from the perspective of the patient's own values and preferences or from that of the physician.

Even if one is to evaluate only the burdens for the patient himself, however, it is implausible to maintain that the application of the distinction is an exercise of technological or clinical judgment. For as soon as we ask what would result in "grave burdens" for the patient, we are immediately confronted with the task of making moral distinctions and moral evaluations concerning the quality of the patient's life and his interests as a person.

When pressed for an explanation of how physicians actually apply the distinction between "ordinary" and "extraordinary" therapeutic measures, the director of a neonate intensive care unit explained to me that what counts as "ordinary" or "extraordinary" differs in "different contexts." Surgical correction of a congenital gastrointestinal blockage in the case of an otherwise normal infant would be considered an "ordinary" measure. But the same operation on an infant with Down's syndrome would be considered extraordinary.

I am not concerned here to criticize the moral decision to refrain from aggressive surgical treatment of infants with Down's syndrome. My purpose in citing this example is simply to point out that this decision *is* a moral decision and that the use of the distinction between "ordinary" and "extraordinary" measures does nothing to help one make the decision. The use of the distinction does accomplish something though: it obscures the fact that the decision *is* a moral decision. Even worse, it is likely to lead one to mistake a very controversial moral decision for a "value-free" technological or clinical decision. More importantly, to even suggest that a complex moral judgment is a clinical or technological judgment is to prejudice the issue of *who* has the right to decide whether life-sustaining measures are to be initiated or continued. Once controversial moral decisions are misperceived as clinical or technological decisions it becomes much easier for the medical paternalist to use the three arguments examined above to justify the withholding of information. For once it is conceded that his medical expertise gives the physician the right to make certain decisions, he can then argue that he may withhold information where this is necessary for the effective exercise of this right. By disguising complex moral judgments as medical judgments, then, the "ordinary/extraordinary" distinction reinforces medical paternalism.

VI

In this paper I have attempted to articulate and challenge some basic features of the medical paternalist model of the physician-patient relationship. I have also given an indication of the powerful influence this model exerts on medical practice and on ways of talking and thinking about medical treatment.

There are now signs that medical paternalism is beginning to be challenged from within the medical profession itself. This I believe, is all to the good. So far, however, challenges have been fragmentary and unsystematic. If they are to be theoretically and practically fruitful they must be grounded in a systematic understanding of what medical paternalism is and in a critical examination of justifications for medical paternalist practices. The present paper is an attempt to begin the task of such a systematic critique.

DONALD VANDEVEER

The Contractual Argument for Withholding Medical Information

DONALD VANDEVEER *teaches philosophy at North Carolina State University. He has undertaken research in political philosophy, ethics, and medical ethics and has published widely in these areas.*

PATERNALISTIC grounds for justifying presumptively wrongful treatment of competent adults are widely looked upon as suspect. Allen Buchanan, in an instructive and generally careful essay, has shown that the presence of paternalistic attitudes and paternalistic treatment is not uncommon in physicians' dealings with their patients. In particular he contends that "the practice of withholding the truth from the patient or his family, a particular form of medical paternalism, is not adequately supported by the arguments advanced to justify it." Buchanan distinguishes two types of arguments which may be advanced against paternalism. The first sort would appeal to a theory of moral rights and would seek (I presume, although Buchanan does not say so explicitly) to show that instances of medical paternalism unjustifiably infringe one or more rights of the patient. Assuming the absence of an adequate defense of a full-blown theory of moral rights Buchanan prefers to advance an alternative critique. He seeks to show that "paternalist justifications which are actually employed by the practitioners of medical paternalism" are inadequate. Contrary to Buchanan's claims I shall show that (1) his attack on one attempt to justify the physician's withholding of information in a restricted range of cases is wrongheaded and that there is in fact a strong presumption that it is permissible and (2) the physician's withholding information in these cases is not appropriately described as "medical paternalism."

I

Buchanan observes that paternalism is usually characterized as "interference with a person's liberty of action, where the alleged justification of the interference is that it is for the good of the person whose liberty is thus restricted." Regarding the focus on liberty of *action* as too narrow, he prefers to include the withholding of information under similar conditions as also an instance of paternalistic interference. The characterization of paternalism is thus revised to include "interference with a person's freedom of action or freedom of information, or the deliberate dissemination of misinformation." I shall not object here to this extension of the more usual characterization.

After instructively documenting a tendency among physicians to attempt to justify withholding, or even falsifying, diagnostic information from their patients, Buchanan attempts to show the inadequacy of three arguments advanced to defend such practices. My focus will be solely on what he labels "the Contractual Version of Prevention of Harm Argument." It is worth quoting here his formulation of what I shall henceforth refer to as the Contractual Argument:

> The idea is that the physician-patient relationship is contractual and that the terms of this contract are such that the patient authorizes the physician to minimize harm to the patient (or his family) by whatever means he, the physician, deems necessary. Thus if the physician believes that the best way to minimize harm to the patient is to withhold information from him, he may do so without thereby wronging the patient. To wrong the patient the physician would either have to do something he was not authorized to do or fail to do something it was his duty to do and which was in his power to do. But in withholding information from the patient he is doing just what he is authorized to do. So he does the patient no wrong.

Buchanan raises a series of objections against this argument. The first is one that may be brought against the claim that the physician may and ought to treat the patient in whatever way will be "least harmful" even in cases where there is no contractual agreement as described above. So a physician may legitimately withhold diagnostic information if he deems it the least harmful course of action. Buchanan objects that "it is very doubtful that the physician will or even could possess the psychiatric and moral knowledge required for a well-founded judgment about what will be least harmful for the patient." Elsewhere he emphasizes that a physician's judgments about certain matters are problematic — for example, when the judgment is made that a patient is likely to become fearful and develop a despondency which may progress into depressive illness (or culminate in suicide) if certain information is revealed to him (say he has terminal cancer). Such judgments, in Buchanan's view, involve *psychiatric generalizations* made typically on the basis of scanty evidence. He claims, further, that *even* if a physician is in a position to reliably predict, he may simply be assuming that suicide "is not a rational choice" for the patient. Buchanan is correct, I believe, in judging that the physician who decides to withhold information on such grounds must make difficult empirical judgments and also difficult evaluative judgments about which alternative will be "least harmful" on balance for the patient. Several points, however, seriously weaken Buchanan's first objection to the Contractual Argument. Buchanan's reservations, if correct, serve only as a counsel of caution to the conscientious physician who wants to do what is least harmful to the patient. They do not show that it is impossible for a physician to arrive at a reasonable judgment that withholding information will be least harmful to the patient. Second, a physician may be in no more difficult position to make this judgment than the patient himself. Physicians are more likely, on average, than patients to have had training in psychiatric or psychological theory relevant to predicting the consequences of revealing disturbing information to patients. Further, they are more likely to have observed the effects of doing so in a wide variety of cases than laypersons. More significant, perhaps, is the point that as the Contract Argument is

described, the patient has authorized the physician to minimize harm to the patient by *whatever means the physician deems necessary*. The contract is not and could not plausibly be one where the physician is authorized to act only on *correct* judgments. It must be an authorization for the physician to act only on the basis of what *he believes to be* a well-founded judgment. If the physician does so, he does not violate the terms of the contract *even if*, as it turns out, his judgment is not well-founded. That such judgments are difficult to make or that a physician may have failed to make one would not, thereby, show that he has done a wrong to his patient. An unwise judgment is not necessarily an unconscientious, negligent, or reckless one.

A second objection proposed by Buchanan is that not all patients understand their relationship with their physician to be one where they have authorized him (or her) to withhold information when deemed necessary to minimize harm. So the physician, it is implied, cannot assume the existence of such a contract with a particular patient unless it is clear that *this* patient has contracted freely and with full knowledge that he has done so. These points are surely correct. It should be clear, however, that neither supposition undermines the Contractual Argument for it purports to justify withholding information *only* when there *is* a contractual authorization to do so. Again, we can only advise caution for physicians who may be tempted to assume authorization when there is inadequate reason to make such an assumption. Buchanan's claims may also be taken to urge patients to make explicit agreements with physicians so that there are no false or unfounded assumptions about the reciprocal rights and duties of the contracting parties. Since such matters are often not well defined, the point is well taken. Once more, it does not strike a blow against the Contractual Argument.

Buchanan presses his point further by claiming that if the physician inquires in each case whether the patient wishes to authorize the withholding of certain information "he will defeat the purpose of the authorization by undermining the patient's trust." If correct this claim shows, not that the Contractual Argument is unsound, but that such contracting is not likely to occur or that there is a reason to avoid forming such contracts. Hence, claims that such a contract was agreed upon ought to be viewed skeptically. The claim that such inquiries do or would undermine the patient's trust is itself, I think, a dubious empirical generalization although I cannot disprove it. A patient asked by his physician if he wishes to have possibly disturbing diagnostic information withheld from him when the physician may judge its revelation harmful to him would be inclined to judge that his physician is conscientious and principled, that he is a person unwilling to treat a patient in a presumptively wrong manner in the absence of his express consent to such a policy. Such an inquiry would tend to confirm a patient's hope that his physician respects the patient's right to decide how he shall be treated and will not treat him in a suspect way just because the physician judges it to be "for the patient's own good." That is, the inquiry would support the claim that the physician was *not* a member of the fraternity of paternalists.

Buchanan claims, however, that there is yet "a more serious difficulty." He states that even extreme advocates of medical paternalism must agree that there must be some limits on the contractual relationship between patient and physician. In particular, the patient needs to be able to determine whether the physician is observing the limitations imposed by the contractual relationship. If the patient authorizes the physician to withhold information he may deprive himself of the information necessary to determine *whether or not* those limits are being observed. In Buchanan's view such an authorization would show that "(a) one did not view the contract as being conditional or that (b) one did not take seriously the possibility that the conditions of the contract might be violated or that (c) one simply did not care whether the conditions were violated." Thus, it is concluded that it is unreasonable to authorize the physician to withhold information when he sees fit. There are difficulties with this line of thought. Surely, it cannot be maintained that the patient should do nothing which would make it impossible or difficult to determine whether contractual limits are being observed. If so, the patient would never submit to anesthesia which would, after all, impair his ability to oversee a surgeon's procedure. More importantly it is possible that a patient might authorize the withholding of information and yet the conditions mentioned in (a), (b), and (c) are not true of the patient. For example, I might want certain information revealed to me and other information not revealed. Recognizing the benefits frequently associated with the "placebo effect" I may reasonably prefer not to be told when a placebo has been prescribed as part of my treatment. Also, I may recognize my penchant for undue anxiety and worry over the fact that certain of my symptoms are suggestive but not conclusive evidence of the presence of some dreaded disease. Hence, I may choose to remain ignorant of such matters until the physician is certain of its presence. Further, if my affairs are in order, I may even prefer to live out my last days falsely hopeful of recovery even when the physician is certain that I have terminal cancer. These preferences for ignorance with regard to a certain range of information may be made clear to the physician in a contract. With regard to certain matters I may authorize the physician to use his best judgment about whether it will be least harmful to disclose or to withhold information. Ignorance is not always bliss, but an individual may prefer ignorance under certain conditions. The nature of the contract made would obviously depend on one's preferences and one's degree of trust and confidence in the judgment in one's physician.

Thus, whether or not the physician wrongfully withholds information will depend on the nature of the contract. It may authorize and require disclosure of certain information *and also* authorize and require the withholding of other information. An interesting result shows up here. If I contract *not* to be informed of terminal cancer should I have it and the physician later decides that my *not* being informed of this fact is more harmful to me on balance than my being informed and he thus informs me his *disclosure* would be *paternalistic interference* with my chosen course, with my freedom to choose what information I shall receive. Hence, it is misleading to focus solely on the cases of withholding information or giving misinformation proceeding from paternalistic motives as actions requiring justification. Disclosing information may also be a paternalistic act and, possibly, an unjustifiable form of paternalism.

Buchanan maintains that "it is unreasonable to authorize the physician to withhold information when he sees fit." If he means "whenever, without qualification," I certainly agree. I have tried to show how it may be reasonable to authorize withholding information on certain matters. Hence, withholding information need not be paternalistic interference, and, indeed, disclosure may be. That depends on the nature of the contract, whether its authorizations are reasonable or not.

II

In view of the preceding remarks my second basic point can be defended more briefly. It is that in a certain range of cases where the physician withholds information from the patient, we do not have a case of medical paternalism. Hence, a justification for doing so is not a justification of medical paternalism.

As noted earlier, since Buchanan regards the (partial) characterization of paternalism as interference with "freedom of action" as too narrow, he expands the characterization to include "freedom of information, or the deliberate dissemination of misinformation." For reasons mentioned "freedom of information" may be understood to mean "freedom to be provided with information" or "freedom to not be subjected to information." Whether the disclosure of information or its being withheld is an *interference* depends on whether what the physician does violates the terms of the contract which, if well-made, will express the patient's preference for ignorance or disclosure, or some combination thereof. Hence, what the patient prefers and consents to is a crucial determinant in deciding whether a physician *interferes* with the patient, and, therefore, whether the physician *paternalistically interferes* with the patient. If a patient contracts to authorize his physician to withhold information under certain conditions, then the physician's doing so *under those conditions* is not a case of interference and, hence, not paternalistic interference. It is rather a case of compliance with the terms of the contract and not appropriately adduced as an instance of "medical paternalism." The withholding of information in such a case may even be an act the physician reluctantly agrees to but, in order to respect his *patient's* judgment about what is "for his (the patient's) own good," he complies with such a wish. So the withholding of information need not be paternalistic at all and, if it is justified, may be justified because it is the honoring of a contractual agreement, a respecting of the patient's autonomy rather than an overriding or disregarding of it.

If my arguments succeed, they are of course compatible with the overly neglected fact that medical paternalism is not uncommon and that purported justifications of it bear critical attention. If such paternalism is suspect, as I believe, it is important to identify ways of minimizing or avoiding it. In fact the making of explicit contracts with adequate checks on compliance by both parties seems just such a way of doing so. Whether any particular physician-patient relationship involves a contract of this more or less ideal sort is an empirical question about which I have avoided generalizing. A purported justification of a particular withholding of information may fail in its appeal to contractual authorization to do so simply because there has been no such contractual authorization. The remedy for practices lacking such authorization may be an increased turn toward the making of such contracts. The Contractual Argument, then, proffers not a justification of paternalistic interference, but rather a non-paternalistic justification of treating patients in ways that, abstractly considered, would be judged presumptively wrong. As such it is not vulnerable to the sorts of objections which may be brought against purported justifications of genuinely paternalistic treatment of patients.

DAN E. BEAUCHAMP
Public Health as Social Justice

DAN E. BEAUCHAMP *writes on medical policy. He teaches at the University of North Carolina in Chapel Hill.*

ANTHONY Downs has observed that our most intractable public problems have two significant characteristics. First, they occur to a relative minority of our population (even though that minority may number millions of people). Second, they result in significant part from arrangements that are providing substantial benefits or advantages to a majority or to a powerful minority of citizens. Thus solving or minimizing these problems requires painful losses, the restructuring of society and the acceptance of new burdens by the most powerful and the most numerous on behalf of the least powerful or the least numerous. As Downs notes, this bleak reality has resulted in recent years in cycles of public attention to such problems as poverty, racial discrimination, poor housing, unemployment or the abandonment of the aged; however, this attention and interest rapidly wane when it becomes clear that solving these problems requires painful costs that the dominant interests in society are unwilling to pay. Our public ethics do not seem to fit our public problems.

It is not sufficiently appreciated that these same bleak realities plague attempts to protect the public's health. Automobile-related injury and death; tobacco, alcohol and other drug damage; the perils of the workplace; environmental pollution; the inequitable and ineffective distribution of medical care services; the hazards of biomedicine—all of these threats inflict death and disability on a minority of our society at any given time. Further, minimizing or even significantly reducing the death and disability from these perils entails that the majority or powerful minorities accept new burdens or relinquish existing privileges that they presently enjoy. Typically, these new burdens or restrictions involve more stringent controls over these and other hazards of the world.

This somber reality suggests that our fundamental attention in public health policy and prevention should not be directed toward a search for new technology, but rather toward breaking existing ethical and political barriers to minimizing death and disability. This is not to say that technology will never again help avoid painful social and political adjustments. Nonetheless, only the technological Pollyannas will ignore the mounting evidence that the critical barriers to protecting the public against death and disability are not the barriers to technological progress—indeed the evidence is that it is often technology itself that is our own worst enemy. The critical barrier to dramatic reductions in death and disability is a social ethic that unfairly protects the most numerous or the most powerful from the burdens of prevention.

This is the issue of justice. In the broadest sense, justice means that each person in society ought to receive his due and that the burdens and benefits of society should be fairly and equitably distributed. But what criteria should be followed in allocating burdens and benefits: Merit, equality or need? What end or goal in life should receive our highest priority: Life, liberty or the pursuit of happiness? The answer to these questions can be found in our prevailing theories or models of justice. These models of justice, roughly speaking, form the foundation of our politics and public policy in general, and our health policy (including our prevention policy) specifically. Here I am speaking of politics not as partisan politics but rather the more ancient and venerable meaning of the political as the search for the common good and the just society.

These models of justice furnish a symbolic framework or blueprint with which to think about and react to the problems of the public, providing the basic rules to classify and categorize problems of society as to whether they necessitate public and collective protection, or whether individual responsibility should prevail. These models function as a sort of map or guide to the common world of members of society, making visible some conditions in society as public issues and concerns, and hiding, obscuring or concealing other conditions that might otherwise emerge as public issues or problems were a different map or model of justice in hand.

In the case of health, these models of justice form the basis for thinking about and reacting to the problems of disability and premature death in society. Thus, if public health policy requires that the majority or a powerful minority accept their fair share of the burdens of protecting a relative minority threatened with death or disability, we need to ask if our prevailing model of justice contemplates and legitimates such sacrifices.

Market-Justice

The dominant model of justice in the American experience has been market-justice. Under the norms of market-justice people are entitled only to those valued ends such as status, income, happiness, etc., that they have acquired by fair rules of entitlement, e.g., by their own individual efforts, actions or abilities. Market-justice emphasizes individual responsibility, minimal collective action and freedom from collective obligations except to respect other persons's fundamental rights.

While we have as a society compromised pure market-justice in many ways to protect the public's health, we are far from recognizing the principle that death and disability are collective problems and that all persons are entitled to health protection. Society does not recognize a general obligation to protect the individual against disease and injury. While society does prohibit individuals from causing direct harm to others, and has in many instances regulated clear public health hazards, the norm of market-justice is still dominant and the primary duty to avert disease and injury still rests with the individual. The individual is ultimately alone in his or her struggle against death.

Barriers to Protection

This individual isolation creates a powerful barrier to the goal of protecting all human life by magnifying the power of death, granting to death an almost supernatural reality. Death has throughout history presented a basic problem to humankind, but even in an advanced society with enormous biomedical technology, the individualism of market-justice tends to retain and exaggerate pessimistic and fatalistic attitudes toward death and injury. This fatalism leads to a sense of powerlessness, to the acceptance of risk as an essential element of life, to resignation in the face of calamity, and to a weakening of collective impulses to confront the problems of premature death and disability.

Perhaps the most direct way in which market-justice undermines our resolve to preserve and protect human life lies in the primary freedom this ethic extends to all individuals and groups to act with minimal obligations to protect the common good. Despite the fact that this rule of self-interest predictably fails to protect adequately the safety of our workplaces, our modes of transportation, the physical environment, the commodities we consume, or the equitable and effective distribution of medical care, these failures have resulted so far in only half-hearted attempts at regulation and control. This response is explained in large part by the powerful sway market-justice holds over our imagination, granting fundamental freedom to all individuals to be left alone — even if the "individuals" in question are giant producer groups with enormous capacities to create great public harm through sheer inadvertence. Efforts for truly effective controls over these perils must constantly struggle against a prevailing ethical paradigm that defines as threats to fundamental freedoms attempts to assure that all groups — even powerful producer groups — accept their fair share of the burdens of prevention.

Market-justice is also the source of another major barrier to public health measures to minimize death and disability — the category of voluntary behavior. Market-justice forces a basic distinction between the harm caused by a factory polluting the atmosphere and the harm caused by the cigarette or alcohol industries, because in the latter case those that are harmed are perceived as engaged in "voluntary" behavior. It is the radical individualism inherent in the market model that encourages attention to the individual's behavior and inattention to the social preconditions of that behavior. In the case of smoking, these preconditions include a powerful cigarette industry and accompanying social and cultural forces encouraging the practice of smoking. These social forces include norms sanctioning smoking as well as all forms of media, advertising, literature, movies, folklore, etc. Since the smoker is free in some ultimate sense to not smoke, the norms of market-justice force the conclusion that the individual voluntarily "chooses" to smoke; and we are prevented from taking strong collective action against the powerful structures encouraging this so-called voluntary behavior. . . .

The prestige of medical care encouraged by market-justice prevents large-scale research to determine whether, in fact, our medical care technology actually brings about the result desired — a significant reduction in the damage and losses suffered from disease and injury. The model conceals questions about our pervasive use of drugs, our intense specialization, and our seemingly boundless commitment to biomedical technology. Instead, the market model of justice encourages us to see problems as due primarily to the failure of individual doctors and the quality of their care, rather than to recognize the possibility of failure from the structure of medical care itself. Consequently, we seek to remedy problems by trying to change individual doctors through appeals to their ethical sensibilities, or by reshaping their education, or by creating new financial incentives. . . .

Public Health Measures

I have saved for last an important class of health policies — public health measures to protect the environment, the workplace, or the commodities we purchase and consume. Are these not signs that the American society is willing to accept collective action in the face of clear public health hazards?

I do not wish to minimize the importance of these advances to protect the public in many domains. But these separate reforms, taken alone, should be cautiously received. This is because each reform effort is perceived as an isolated exception to the norm of market-justice; the norm itself still stands. Consequently, the predictable career of such measures is to see enthusiasm for enforcement peak and wane. These public health measures are clear signs of hope. But as long as these actions are seen as merely minor exceptions to the rule of individual responsibility, the goals of public health will remain beyond our reach. What is required is for the public to see that protecting the public's health takes us beyond the norms of market-justice categorically, and necessitates a completely new health ethic.

I return to my original point: Market-justice is the primary roadblock to dramatic reductions in preventable injury and death. More than this, market-justice is a pervasive ideology protecting the most powerful or the most numerous from the burdens of collective action. If this be true, the central goal of public health should be ethical in nature: The challenging of market-justice as fatally deficient in protecting the health of the public. Further, public health should advocate a "counter-ethic" for protecting the public's health, one articulated in a different tradition of justice and one designed to give the highest priority to minimizing death and disability and to the protection of all human life against the hazards of this world. . . .

Ideally . . . the public health ethic is not simply an alternative to the market ethic for health — it is a fundamental critique of that ethic as it unjustly protects powerful interests from the burdens of prevention and as that ethic serves to legitimate a mindless and extravagant faith in the efficacy of medical care. In other words, the public health ethic is a *counter-ethic* to market-justice and the ethics of individualism as these are applied to the health problems of the public.

This view of public health is admittedly not widely accepted. Indeed, in recent times the mission of public health has been viewed by many as limited to that minority of health problems that cannot be solved by the market provision of medical care services and that necessitate organized community action. It is interesting to speculate why many in the public health profession have come to accept this narrow view of public health—a view that is obviously influenced and shaped by the market model as it attempts to limit the burdens placed on powerful groups.

Nonetheless, the broader view of public health set out here is logically and ethically justified if one accepts the vision of public health as being the protection of all human life. The central task of public health, then, is to complete its unfinished revolution: The elaboration of a health ethic adequate to protect and preserve all human life. This new ethic has several key implications which are referred to here as "principles": 1) Controlling the hazards of this world, 2) to prevent death and disability, 3) through organized collective action, 4) shared equally by all except where unequal burdens result in increased protection of everyone's health and especially potential victims of death and disability.

These ethical principles are not new to public health. To the contrary, making the ethical foundations of public health visible only serves to highlight the social justice influences as work behind pre-existing principles.

Controlling the Hazards

A key principle of the public health ethic is the focus on the identification and control of the hazards of this world rather than a focus on the behavioral defects of those individuals damaged by these hazards. . . .

Public health should—at least ideally—be suspicious of behavioral paradigms for viewing public health problems since they tend to "blame the victim" and unfairly protect majorities and powerful interests from the burdens of prevention. It is clear that behavioral models of public health problems are rooted in the tradition of market-justice, where the emphasis is upon individual ability and capacity, and individual success and failure. . . .

Prevention

Like the other principles of public health, prevention is a logical consequence of the ethical goal of minimizing the numbers of persons suffering death and disability. The only know way to minimize these adverse events is to prevent the occurrence of damaging exchanges or exposures in the first place, or to seek to minimize damage when exposures cannot be controlled.

Prevention, then, is that set of priority rules for restructuring existing market rules in order to maximally protect the public. These rules seek to create policies and obligations to replace the norm of market-justice, where the latter permits specific conditions, commodities, services, products, activities or practices to pose a direct threat or hazard to the health and safety of members of the public, or where the market norm fails to allocate effectively and equitably those services (such as medical care) that are necessary to attend to disease at hand.

Thus, the familiar public health options:

1.   Creating rules to minimize exposure of the public to hazards (kinetic, chemical, ionizing, biological, etc.) so as to reduce the rates of hazardous exchanges.

2.   Creating rules to strengthen the public against damage in the event damaging exchanges occur anyway, where such techniques (fluoridation, seat-belts, immunization) are feasible.

3.   Creating rules to organize treatment resources in the community so as to minimize damage that does occur since we can rarely prevent all damage.

Collective Action

Another principle of the public health ethic is that the control of hazards cannot be achieved through voluntary mechanisms but must be undertaken by governmental or non-governmental agencies through planned, organized and collective action that is obligatory or non-voluntary in nature. This is for two reasons.

The first is because market or voluntary action is typically inadequate for providing what are called public goods. Public goods are those public policies (national defense, police and fire protection, or the protection of all persons against preventable death and disability) that are universal in their impacts and effects, affecting everyone equally. These kinds of goods cannot easily be withheld from those individuals in the community who choose not to support these services (this is typically called the "free rider" problem). Also, individual holdouts might plausibly reason that their small contribution might not prevent the public good from being offered.

The second reason why self-regarding individuals might refuse to voluntarily pay the costs of such public goods as public health policies is because these policies frequently require burdens that self-interest or self-protection might see as too stringent. For example, the minimization of rates of alcoholism in a community clearly seems to require norms or controls over the substance of alcohol that limit the use of this substance to levels that are far below what would be safe for individual drinkers.

With these temptations for individual noncompliance, justice demands assurance that all persons share equally the costs of collective action through obligatory and sanctioned social and public policy.

Fair-Sharing of the Burdens

A final principle of the public health ethic is that all persons are equally responsible for sharing the burdens — as well as the benefits — of protection against death and disability, except where unequal burdens result in greater protection for every person and especially potential victims of death and disability. In practice this means that policies to control the hazards of a given substance, service or commodity fall unequally (but still fairly) on those involved in the production, provision or consumption of the service, commodity or substance. The clear implication of this principle is that the automotive industry, the tobacco industry, the coal industry and the medical care industry — to mention only a few key groups — have an unequal responsibility to bear the costs of reducing death and disability since their actions have far greater impact than those of individual citizens.

Doing Justice:
Building a New Public Health

I have attempted to show the broad implications of a public health commitment to protect and preserve human life, setting out tentatively the logical consequences of that commitment in the form of some general principles. We need however, to go beyond these broad principles and ask more specifically: What implications does this model have for doing public health and the public health profession?

The central implication of the view set out here is that doing public health should not be narrowly conceived as an instrumental or technical activity. Public health should be a way of doing justice, a way of asserting the value and priority of all human life. The primary aim of all public health activity should be the elaboration and adoption of a new ethical model or paradigm for protecting the public's health. This new ethical paradigm will necessitate a heightened consciousness of the manifold forces threatening human life, and will require thinking about and reacting to the problems of disability and premature death as primarily collective problems of the entire society.

These new definitions would reveal the collective and structural aspects of what are termed voluntary risks, challenging attempts to narrowly and persuasively limit public attention to the behavior of the smoker or the drinker, and exposing pervasive myths that "blame the victim." These collective definitions and descriptions would focus attention on the industry behind these activities, asking whether powerful producer groups and supporting cultural and social norms are not primary factors encouraging individuals to accept unreasonable risks to life and limb, and whether these groups or norms constitute aggressive collective structures threatening human life.

A case in point: Under the present definition of the situation, alcoholism is mostly defined in individual terms, mainly in terms of the attributes of those persons who are "unable" to control their drinking. But I have shown elsewhere that this argument is both conceptually and empirically erroneous. Alcohol problems

are collective problems that require more adequate controls over this important hazard.

This is not to say that there are no important issues of liberty and freedom in these areas. It is rather to say that viewing the use of, for example, alcohol or cigarettes by millions of American adults as "voluntary" behavior, and somehow fundamentally different from other public health hazards, impoverishes the public health approach, tending . . . to divorce the behavior of the individual from its social base.

In building these collective redefinitions of health problems, however, public health must take care to do more than merely shed light on specific public health problems. The central problems remain the injustice of a market ethic that unfairly protects majorities and powerful interests from their fair share of the burdens of prevention, and of convincing the public that the task of protecting the public's health lies categorically beyond the norms of market-justice. This means that the function of each different redefinition of a specific problem must be to raise the common and recurrent issue of justice by exposing the aggressive and powerful structures implicated in all instances of preventable death and disability, and further to point to the necessity for collective measures to confront and resist these structures.

I also believe that the realism inherent in the public health ethic dictates that the foundation of all public health policy should be primarily (but not exclusively) national in locus. I simply disagree with the current tendency, rooted in misguided pluralism and market metaphors, to build from the bottom up. This current drift will, in my opinion, simply provide the medical care industry and its acolytes (to cite only one powerful group) with the tools necessary to further elaborate and extend its hegemony. Confronting organizations, interests, ideologies and alliances that are national and even international in scope with such limited resources seems hopelessly sentimental. We must always remember that the forces opposed to full protection of the public's health are fundamental and powerful, deeply rooted in our national character. We are unlikely to successfully oppose these forces with appeals or strategies more appropriate for an earlier and more provincial time.

Finally, the public health movement must cease being defensive about the wisdom or the necessity of collective action. One of the most interesting aspects of market-justice — and particularly its ideological thrusts — is that it makes collective or governmental activity seem unwise if not dangerous. Such rhetoric predictably ignores the influence of private power over the health and safety of every individual. Public health need not be oblivious to the very real concerns about a proliferating bureaucracy in the emergent welfare state. In point of fact, however, the preventive thrust of public health transcends the notion of the welfare or service state and its most recent variant, the human services society. Much as the ideals of service and welfare are improvements over the simple working of market-justice, the service society frequently functions to spread the costs of public problems among the entire public while permitting the interests, industries, or professions who might remedy or prevent many of these problems to operate with expanding power and autonomy.

Conclusion

The central thesis of this article is that public health is ultimately and essentially an ethical enterprise committed to the notion that all persons are entitled to protection against the hazards of this world and to the minimization of death and disability in society. I have tried to make the implications of this ethical vision manifest, especially as the public health ethic challenges and confronts the norms of market-justice.

I do not see these goals of public health as hopelessly unrealistic nor destructive of fundamental liberties. Public health may be an "alien ethic in a strange land." Yet, if anything, the public health ethic is more faithful to the traditions of Judeao-Christian ethics than is market-justice.

The image of public health that I have drawn here does raise legitimate questions about what it is to be a professional, and legitimate questions about reasonable limits to restrictions on human liberty. These questions must be addressed more thoroughly than I have done here. Nonetheless, we must never pass over the chaos of preventable disease and disability in our society by simply celebrating the benefits of our prosperity and abundance, or our technological advances. What are these benefits worth if they have been purchased at the price of human lives?

LOREN E. LOMASKY

Medical Progress and National Health Care

LOREN E. LOMASKY *is a professor of philosophy at the University of Minnesota at Duluth. His interests are in the fields of ethics and social philosophy and he has done research in natural-rights theory and in the ethical basis of health-care allocation.*

AN individual's access to medical care should not be determined exclusively by his ability to pay the going price. From this starting point, alternatives beckon. One is the traditional system of health-care delivery within which eleemosynary [nonprofit] and religious institutions are prominent in providing medical services to those unable to pay. Before the emergence of modern medicine the poor could not expect treatment equivalent to that received by the rich, but this was a general disability of poverty, not specifically a problem of medical access. Indeed, in an era when health care had little positive correlation with health outcomes and hospitals were chiefly places where one went to die, inequities in the provision of medical services were among the least of the burdens borne by the poor.

Medical Progress and the "Right" to Health Care

The ability of medicine to produce favorable results has increased exponentially in this century. At the same time, for understandable reasons, dissatisfaction with the traditional model has also increased. It is criticized as being too haphazard and arbitrary. More fundamentally, it is argued that medical care is a good to which individuals have a right, and that it ought to be distributed impartially in line with the criterion: to each according to his need. Medical care is not simply one consumer good among others; because it bears so directly on life itself as well as the ability to lead a good life, medical care cannot be left to the vagaries of the market.

But this argument is met with a counterargument that also emphasizes the role of rights. Medical services are, after all, not endowments provided cost-free by a bountiful nature. Rather, they are made available in finite quantities by individuals who must expend effort to produce them. The state can enforce equity in the delivery of these services only by coercing service providers, taxpayers and would-be recipients. State-controlled health care is thus founded on widespread rights violations.

When right contends with right, the heroic seek victory, the wary hunt for accommodation. It is wariness that will be pursued here.

A Right to What?

It should be obvious that no claim of the form, "persons have a right to X" can be addressed without determining what kind of entity X is. Unless one is clear about what type of good health care is, resulting appraisals of its value and proper apportionment are hobbled. It will be suggested below that arguments for the provision of national health care pay insufficient attention to the changed and changing nature of health care. . . .

The first large-scale campaign for universal health insurance in the United States dates back to World War I. At that time Americans were far less wealthy than they are now. Paradoxically, however, they were better equipped to provide genuinely full and equal access to health services. Medicine's power to intervene effectively in crises was then extremely limited. Patients recovered in short order or died, in either case removing themselves from the need for ongoing attention. Chronic diseases, especially those associated with aging, were predominantly dealt with outside of medical contexts. In consequence, little extra benefit could be accorded the richest patients beyond what was available to those of more modest means.

In the last quarter of the twentieth century, however, there exist numerous high technology procedures that can be provided to only a fraction of those who could benefit from them. Computerized axial tomography, organ transplants, and coronary arteriograms are but three conspicuous therapeutic measures whose use is limited by financial or biological factors. It is incumbent upon those who demand that medical care of the highest quality be universally provided as a matter of right to explain how this can be done. And if it cannot, which would they dispense with: equity or the lives that could be saved by selective use of expensive technology? (I shall return later to this dilemma.)

The preceding remarks suggest that there is a wide gulf between medical care being an important human *interest* or *need* and its being a *right*. Interests admit of a wide range of degree and can be freely traded off, one for another. Needs are interests that possess a high degree of urgency, but carry no explicit entitlement to the goods or services of other people. Rights, though, are demands that others *must* comply with; where compliance is impossible or unwarranted, no right exists.

The Welfare Case for a National Health Program

Even if health care in all its dimensions cannot, strictly speaking, be made out to be a human right, proponents of a national health program can argue that it is a good that ought to be provided to all irrespective of the ability to pay. Economic impoverishment would no longer follow in the wake of major illness. Government would be able to address directly the problem of ever rising costs instead of trying to influence at arm's length the fragmented health care industry. Finally, a more rational allocation of scarce medical resources to those who are most in need of them would be achieved. The de facto rationing of services by the market would be replaced by explicit consideration of how most equitably to optimize benefits for a given level of expenditure.

Major medical treatments *are* enormously expensive; for many persons the expense occasioned by an illness is its most persistent burden. We are all roughly equal in our vulnerability to debilitating disease or accident. Therefore, everyone would receive benefit from a national health plan that removed the threat of impoverishment as a consequence of medical disability. But this end can be achieved equally well by less sweeping measures. The risk of large economic loss can easily be guarded against by insurance. Its characteristic function is to protect against infrequent, unpredictable events which, when aggregated over a large population, are statistically regular.

Medical insurance is readily available

in a variety of forms from private insurance companies. Like fire, automobile, and life insurance, it offers a means for persons to pool economic risks that are too great to hazard on an individual basis. Health maintenance organizations (HMOs) represent another and growing means by which prepayment allows individuals to spread risks. (In addition, HMOs offer service providers added inducement to economize on hospital stays and questionable surgical intervention, thus moderating overall medical expenditures.) The special problems of the poor can be met by cash grants or by healthcare vouchers exchangeable for prepaid services. Given the availability of these sharply focused means for dealing with unpredictable expense, the threat of major economic loss cannot provide a sound justification for a national health program.

Ever-rising total health care expenditure creates a different dilemma, one that is also far more unyielding. As long as the demand for medical services (especially those embracing high technology) keeps growing, continuous cost increases largely represent an efficient response to consumers' preferences. Of course, these preferences can be questioned. Critics of prevailing practices have frequently argued that a more rational allocation of resources would redirect funds away from costly acute intervention procedures to preventive medicine and health education. However, even if this shift in emphasis could be carried out, benefits might prove to be less than anticipated. Annual physical checkups have long been advocated as worthwhile prophylaxis. Although they clearly impose substantial burdens on health care delivery systems, there is little evidence demonstrating significant health gains. . . .

Education to alter unhealthy lifestyles would undoubtedly have a momentous positive impact — if we know how to provide it. Wide dissemination of the relevant information may accomplish little: there is probably not a smoker in the country unaware of cigarettes' deleterious effects or a motorcyclist uninformed about the dangers of riding helmetless. In a free society there are limits to how much good one can do for another who is not very interested.

Governmental control typically features politically motivated decisions and cozy relationships between an industry and its regulators that work against economic efficiency. In addition, there are good reasons to believe that a national health program would be even *more susceptible* to escalating costs than most federal ventures. First, to be workable it would need the support of health professionals. It is therefore unlikely that they will be pressured to accept lower fees in order to realize monetary savings. Witness the boon to physicians' incomes provided by Medicare. Second, few citizens clamor for the purchase of another battleship, and even highly subsidized train fares move few people out of automobiles and airplanes. But health care is a commodity that most people desire. To lower or eliminate out-of-pocket expenses for it will predictably increase demand and thus further burden the public purse. Costs may be shared more evenly, but they will not be small.

The only way a nationalized program can realistically hope to keep costs in line is to enforce strict schedules of permissible treatments for all illnesses. These would be established on the basis of empirical studies detailing cost-effectiveness — assuming that political pressures to act otherwise are avoided. Therapeutic measures failing to come up to the stipulated benefit-per-dollar level would simply be disallowed. In effect, the goal of moderating overall costs would be subsumed under that of equitable rationing. So, if the case for a national health program can be made at all, it is on the grounds of enforcing the equal provision of health services based solely on need.

Equality and Health Care

The case for equality in the delivery of health-care services may be presented as simply one specification of the general brief for economic equality. But then it is subject to all the standard criticisms that beset rigid egalitarianism. If equality of condition is to be enforced, the liberty to pursue projects that generate differential rewards must be restricted. Substitutes must be found for the motivating force provided by the desire to better one's estate and the fear of seeing it diminished. The intuition that some merit more than others in return for greater effort or services rendered must be set aside. In short, the single-minded pursuit of equality is exceedingly costly in terms of other values surrendered, other goods forgone.

An alternative defense focuses on the special nature of health. The value of experiencing grand opera, vintage Chablis, a Yankee-Red Sox doubleheader or a trek up a mountain will vary greatly from individual to individual. Differences in talents and preferences will render ludicrous any program intent on providing these goods in equal measure to the entire populace. It is clearly preferable to allow individuals to pursue them as they will. But health is different. Whatever else one wants, good health is not only wanted but needed. Failure in securing it jeopardizes all other attainments. Moreover, its absence is rarely an indication of culpability; it is bad luck. Coordinated activity of men in civil society cannot abolish luck but it can ameliorate the stark randomness of its effects. The case for treating health care as a public good, subsidized by the common treasure, is that to do so is the most effective way we have of counteracting the vagaries of nature and providing each person with the preconditions for living a satisfying life. . . .

Being the sole possessors of a right to exercise coercion, governments are obliged to undertake the functions of protection, apprehension, and punishment that citizens are prohibited from carrying out on an individual basis. There exists no similar necessity that states monopolize the provision of health services. Health may indeed be a primary human good, but whether it is distributed centrally or by independent contractors is irrelevant to the continued existence of a political order. That is not to deny that states have obligations to their citizenry respecting health care delivery. A state acts unjustly if it forbids crucial health services to some or all persons or if it promotes economic inequalities that deprive disadvantaged social classes of adequate medical care. It should be noted though that unjust health policies may appear either in states with comprehensive national health care or those without it. In either, services may be discriminatorily distributed, subverted for political ends, irrationally regulated, or irresponsive to consumer demand. The desirability of national health care cannot be deduced from a pure philosophical theory of justice; rather, its desirability hinges on whether, in the actual world, it promises to promote a fair and efficient allocation of resources. . . .

Collective vs. Private Choice: Some Examples

A foretaste of the difficulties that would regularly confront a nationalized health program is provided by the debate over Medicaid funded abortion. Each year the nation is treated to a ritualized congressional confrontation that changes no minds, produces no consensus, yet paralyzes essential legislative operations throughout its duration. Few can believe that this public fanning of already polarized attitudes is worthwhile; yet there seems to be no way to avoid it so long as the provision of specific medical services to the poor remains an item for legislative decision. The right of women to procure abortions may have been conclusively established by judicial action, but a democracy must also recognize the right of individual citizens to participate in processes determining how their tax monies will be spent. Either the public treasure will release funds to pay for abortion or it will not; room for compromise is narrowly constricted.

Entirely removing abortion related issues from the public agenda may be neither feasible nor desirable. But this especially futile contest is the direct product of choosing to meet the health needs of the poor through a centrally funded and regulated program. If Medicaid and related welfare measures were replaced by a negative income tax or some other device guaranteeing all persons a minimally adequate income, recipients would be free to purchase those goods and services of greatest personal urgency. Poor persons, if they so chose, could avail themselves of abortions on the same basis as other members of the population. A less sweeping alteration of current welfare programs would be to provide health care vouchers. In either case, we would be spared a situation in which others decide for the poor what specific services they can or cannot have. Perhaps these proposed alternatives are defective on other grounds, but they do point up the advantages of leaving medical questions that touch on basic values up to individual discretion.

By means of amniocentesis, dozens of hereditary fetal traits can presently be detected. They range from its sex to the presence of debilitating diseases such as Tay-Sachs or mongolism. Occasionally the procedure is useful for diagnosing a condition that can be treated in utero, but it is also employed to procure information on which the decision whether or not to abort will be based. Will a national health program routinely provide amniocentesis when abortion is intended if results are negative? Or will it attempt somehow to keep to a middle course, allowing procedures leading to the abortion of severely incapacitated fetuses but not, say, those of the parentally disfavored sex? Alternatively, a cost-conscious program could require as a condition of coverage that women at risk undergo amniocentesis and abortion when a live birth will entail huge medical costs. These hypothetical policies are not of equal likelihood, but any one of them would engender pitched battles whose outcome would certainly leave large sections of the population dissatisfied. Pollyannas may expect the passage of time to ease these problems. Just the reverse will be the case: as techniques of genetic screening and engineering become more sophisticated, moral quandaries will ineluctably multiply. Sometimes polarization is the inescapable consequence of forging a national policy, but in this case divisiveness can be minimized by leaving decisions in the hands of private citizens.

The other end of human existence has also been profoundly affected by advances in medical capabilities. The hospital has replaced the home as the usual place to die, and it is increasingly the case that the exact time of death is a matter for choice. Biological function can be preserved in so attenuated a state that physicians have been forced to move toward a redefinition of "death" in order to avoid the ghoulish indefinite preservation of living corpses. But most ethical dilemmas surrounding death and dying are untouched by semantic legerdemain. Unless one supposes that each advance in the power to sustain life creates a corresponding imperative for its universal employment — and also creates the funds to pay for them — there is no simple answer to the question of when to extend life and when to terminate it. Here I shall sidestep substantive matters to raise instead a procedural issue: to what extent is it desirable that government intrude upon deliberations at the edge of life?

It is unrealistic to deny that the state does have some legitimate interests. Inevitably it must confront practices that raise the specter of homicide. The law must also establish standards concerning informed consent and the contractual obligations obtaining between patient and physician. But beyond staking out legal terrain within which concerned parties can take their bearings, government may move in either of two opposed directions: it can issue detailed regulations pertaining to the application of lifesaving technology or, within broad guidelines, it can return decision-making prerogatives to individual patients, their families and physicians. For two major reasons, the latter course is to be preferred whenever possible.

First, individual discretion promotes autonomy. Persons differ in their judgments concerning the conditions under which life is no longer worth living. They will also vary in their willingness to forgo other possible satisfactions for the sake of securing incremental health gains. A liberal society is one that values the ability of individuals to direct their own lives. One significant way in which this value can be pursued is to allow people to determine for themselves what course their medical treatments will take. A recent expression of this policy is the granting of legal status to "living wills," documents that spell out conditions under which the signator desires that heroic medical procedures be terminated. The gradual development of hospice programs also provides enhanced opportunities for terminally ill patients to take charge of their own destinies. Instead of being shunted aside as medicine's embarrassing failure, the hospice patient is encouraged to accept the fact of his upcoming death and to influence the conditions under which he will depart from life. As technology continually enlarges the scope for intervention into the process of dying, further methods will be required to ensure that the party most directly affected is able to play a significant role.

Second, an active governmental role in mandating standards for care poses the same danger of political disruption that has already been experienced in the case of publicly funded abortion. All citizens have a fundamental stake in how they and their loved ones will die. Decisions in this sphere do not come easily under the best of circumstances. But burdens will be exacerbated if matters of personal decision are transformed into public policy questions. Regulation is, in essence, inflexible. If national standards are to be formulated that adjudicate among basic and deeply felt values, diverse groups will want to see their own attitudes enshrined in law. A zero-sum game will develop in which one side's gain is another's loss, and so each will attempt to use the political machinery for its own ends.

If the state assumes full responsibility for the provision of health services, it will be unable to avoid dictating standards for the utilization of life sustaining services. Extraordinary means for staving off death are inordinately costly both in monetary terms and in demands placed upon highly trained personnel. If the ability of patients to pay is entirely removed as a factor influencing their use, there will be an increased call for their employment. To remain solvent, a national health program will have to contain some formula for determining when the cost of procuring and employing expensive technology are justified by realizable benefits. If such a formula is not to be subverted from within, little room for exceptions can be permitted. Whatever structure emerges is sure to leave many health professionals and consumers dissatisfied. They will be informed that their own personal discretion must give way to considerations of the public good — as defined by a distant bureaucracy. . . .

Deciding when treatment shall cease involves ethical questions of considerable magnitude. A yet more vexing range of dilemmas surround triage: the selection of some for treatment when not all can be saved. If resources are indispensable to a group of persons at peril but too limited to accommodate all, to save one life is to sacrifice another. Our moral principles are severely strained by circumstances that require the balancing of one innocent life against another. Such choices, however, promise to intrude upon us increasingly.

Two classic examples of triage are the dangerously overloaded lifeboat and the harried medic patching up the wounded on a battlefield. Whatever is done, some salvageable lives will be forfeited. The dreadfulness of these choices, though, is somewhat softened by the urgency of a crisis: action must be immediate and there is little luxury for reflective deliberation. If called upon to justify his actions, an agent could plead that he was reacting instinctively to the needs of the moment.

Contemporary medical technology is responsible for triage situations of a rather different character. A mechanism is devised that is effective against some previously untreatable condition. Unfortunately, only a small percentage of those afflicted can receive treatment. Who shall be allowed to live? Here decision-makers are dealing with a series of events predictable well in advance. Not enmeshed in a precipitously developing crisis, they are privileged to assume the role of detached administrator. There is, however, a price to be paid for this relative ease: whatever standards are developed and employed are subject to close scrutiny. Those disfavored in the selection process are perfectly entitled to ask why. Persuasive answers will not be easily forthcoming. . . .

Should triage decisions be left to numerous private groups acting independently, or should responsibility be assumed by a national health care delivery board? The latter would, I believe, be a profoundly unsatisfactory state of affairs. The least of its drawbacks is that treatment decisions would be thrust into the arena of public choice where diverse groups would lobby intensively for special consideration. It requires little imagination to foresee the young, those with dependents, military veterans, persons holding responsible positions, and others all claiming to merit a preferred status. A policy of random selection might appease these contending forces, but it also might appear to each of them as unjustly slighting legitimate merit. The trouble arises precisely because no process of choice presents itself as clearly superior; whichever method is imposed will be open to objections rendering it unstable.

Consider a further complication: wealthy individuals may not be content to leave their survival to the vagaries of a national health care system. Suppose they choose to go outside of the system to procure lifesaving technology; how will authorities respond? If the rich are allowed carte blanche, the egalitarianism of national health care is compromised in a context where the stakes are no less than life and death. If outside access is forbidden by law, the situation is even more anomalous. Persons who are entitled to spend their money for utterly frivolous purposes will be precluded from using it to remain alive. No compensating gain for the poor would be realized — unless a surrender to envy is counted as a gain. . . .

Triage is never unproblematic, but on what basis could a creature of the state adopt *any* principle of selection? Whoever is excluded can justifiably complain that he is thereby being disadvantaged by the very institution whose special duty is to extend equal protection to all persons. The essential point is not that government will do a poorer job of allocating lifesaving technology than would non-governmental units — although, given the nature of the political pressures to which it is subject, it very well might — but that *this is a singularly inappropriate area for any governmental choice*, no matter how conscientiously it is made. Neutrality among all citizens is a political ideal that is easily subverted and, once breached, difficult to restore. I suggest that this ideal is well worth preserving, and that to establish a precedent of forcing the state to determine that some named individuals shall live and others die is to do that ideal possibly irreparable damage. When such decisions have to be made, it is far better that they be carried out by non-public boards not constrained by obligations of equal protection to an entire citizenry. Flexibility is enhanced, and the implications of unsavory choices are localized.

One objection to this argument is that government can and should avoid the necessity of triage by providing resources sufficient to accommodate all patients. Indeed, precisely this intent motivated the passage of the 1972 legislation providing dialysis treatment to all end-stage renal disease sufferers in need of it. Could not a well-funded national health-care program act similarly in all other cases?

The answer is no. There are some shortages that not even unlimited finances can eliminate. The number of persons who can be benefited by organ transplants already exceeds the available supply. As further advances in immunosuppression and surgical technique are realized, the disparity will grow. Transplantable hearts cannot be produced by governmental edict. Further, there is always a gap between the time the procedure is experimentally introduced and its widespread implementation.

In the real world, finances are not unlimited. Money used to counter one life-threatening syndrome is unavailable for others. For example, the huge infusion of Medicare funds for kidney disease sufferers could have been devoted to the comparably expensive treatment of hemophiliacs. That it was not may be due only to the greater muscle of the kidney disease lobby. Even if sufficient funds to eliminate all triage situations could be raised, it does not follow that to do so is advisable. A commitment to treat every salvagable patient will shortchange other legitimate health goals as well as competing goods in other spheres. An ironic result of nationalized health care might be that to avoid the undoubted evil of governmental triage, grotesque misallocations of resources will ensue. Is it really desirable that education, housing and general economic advancement be penalized so that a 110-year-old patient can receive his third kidney transplant and second artificial heart?

National Health Care and Non-Standard Options

The terms with which a debate is pursued can become frozen while the underlying real dimensions continue to change. This has been the fate of the case for national health care. Its desirability cannot be assessed in a vacuum, as the nature of the commodity health care evolves so too do reasons for and against its provision by the state. The most revolutionary development in medical practice since national health care was initially broached is the increasing prominence of *non-standard options*. By "non-standard option" I mean a medical service possessing the following three features: (1) Each occasion on which it is delivered entails great expense; (2) It has little effect on mortality or morbidity configurations for the population as a whole; (3) Individuals who receive the service are substantially benefited or perceive themselves to be substantially benefited.

Proliferation of non-standard options bedevils egalitarianism in health care delivery. A system that undertook to fulfill all requests on the basis of demonstrated need at no charge to recipients would soon be bankrupt. If non-standard options were excluded from the system but could be secured privately, major inequalities in health-care delivery would thereby be reintroduced. Finally, if non-standard options that cannot be offered to all are forbidden to all, government is placed in the uncomfortable position of abridging the liberty of citizens to preserve health and life.

Health-care delivery has often been cited as an area in which the case for equality is especially convincing, even self-evident. In an important paper, Bernard Williams has maintained that, "leaving aside preventive medicine, the proper ground of distribution of medical care is ill health: this is a necessary truth." I have argued that it is not a necessary truth but rather a seductive falsehood based on an obsolete model of medical care. It does indeed seem intolerable that anyone should die or continue to suffer from disease when, for a relatively small expenditure, his plight can be alleviated. Even on

coldly economic grounds, it is irrational not to invest a sum that will be returned many times over in a life of increased productivity. But non-standard options do not fit this model. Their opportunity costs are extremely high, they rarely provide restoration to full health, and the need for them continually outstrips the available supply.

Suggestions for a Medical Marketplace

I have been arguing that national health care is an idea whose time has come — and gone. That should not be interpreted as a brief for the status quo. Ongoing expansion of the medical role argues against imposing uniformity in the delivery of health services. It is not enough, however, to reject national health care; positive steps should be taken to enable consumers to choose for themselves the goods and services they most want. This requires a genuine marketplace: a sector in which alternative products are offered and where those who receive a good are the ones who pay for it. I conclude with five brief suggestions concerning how diversity and consumer sovereignty can be enhanced.

First, there are better and worse means by which society can respond to the health needs of the poor. Routing all medical care through a monolithic national health service has already been amply criticized. Somewhat preferable would be the provision of a suitably defined "minimum decent standard" of health care. One drawback of this proposal is that not all will agree on what counts as minimally decent. The acrimonious debate over Medicaid funded abortion is a case in point. Also, the poor will still be precluded from acting on their own preferences. Therefore, I suggest instead a cash grant or voucher program enabling the poor to purchase their own medical services on a prepaid basis. How generous this program should be is a crucial question that cannot be explored in this paper.

Second, influential health-care spokespersons should avoid making extravagant claims heralding the accomplishments of highpowered medicine. Such statements lead to unrealistic expectations on the part of consumers and consequent pressure upon the health care system to deliver more than it is capable of providing. Newly developed technology provides genuine health gains, but its effect on mortality and morbidity are inconsequential compared to the dramatic gains realized between the 1930s and 1950s. Predictions are hazardous, but we very probably have reached a point of drastically diminishing returns on the health care dollar. Pessimism concerning future health gains need not follow: health care is not the same as health. There are a great number of steps individuals can take to live longer and healthier lives: avoid smoking, eat breakfasts, get and stay married (especially significant for males), sleep at least seven hours each night, consume alcohol in moderation. These "life-style" patterns are free of cost, undeliverable by professionals, but wonderfully responsive to individual choice. Because what individuals can do for themselves far exceeds what can be done for them, we ought to begin to emphasize the former.

Third, there is need to expand the variety of health-insurance policies and other prepaid packages. Not everyone needs or desires the same level of coverage. I see no reason to suppose that consumers are generally unable to choose rationally how much of their resources to devote to health goods. Nor is there any evidence that welfare gains are realized if central planning boards are vested with the responsibility for such choices. Some persons are very sensitive to increased probabilities of an extended life span; they ought to have the opportunity to purchase expensive policies that include coverage for a wide range of non-standard options. Those who place a premium on present consumption should be free to devote only a minimal amount of income to health care coverage. Both will thus be able to maximize expected utility while assuming responsibility for their own choices. A not incidental benefit is that triage dilemmas will be minimized; or rather, *individuals will be making such decisions for themselves* through genuine market arrangements. The prospective demand for some item of expensive lifesaving technology will tend to create its own supply.

Fourth, consumers of medical services will never reclaim control of their health care programs until what Charles Fried characterizes as "a guild system as tight and self-protective as any we know" is broken. Physicians make virtually all medical decisions and are loath to relinquish any of this power either to public agencies or to consumers. Even the choice of a primary care physician is usually made blind because organized medicine has traditionally execrated advertising or any other means which would afford consumers the basis for making a cost-conscious selection. Physicians' domination of health-care delivery is made possible by a legal structure that grants them unparalleled powers to control entry into the profession, set fees, and regulate their own practice. The results are remarkably high incomes and an almost total immunity from normal market forces. Numerous steps could be undertaken to transform this cartel into competitive purveyors of service to an informed clientele: eliminating all bans on advertising, easing the formation of HMOs and other alternatives to fee-for-service medicine, eliminating or drastically abridging entry restricting requirements, allowing patients and pharmacists more say in the selection of prescription drugs, and enabling other health professionals to provide services that do not require a physician's expertise.

Fifth, what ought to be done to hold down the nation's spiraling medical bill? Nothing. To be more precise, external bureaucratic regulation is the wrong prescription for the ills of our health care delivery system. If, as I have suggested above, consumers are afforded the opportunity to make informed purchases in a genuine medical marketplace, they will be able to determine what percentage of their income is devoted to health care. Is 5% of GNP too little, 15% too much? I suggest that there is no a priori answer to these questions. Health care is one among many services persons can choose for themselves in whatever quantity they desire — if they are given the chance to do so.

JAMES RACHELS
Active and Passive Euthanasia

JAMES RACHELS *is a professor of philosophy at the University of Alabama in Birmingham who has written extensively on ethical issues. This selection is taken from his influential book,* The End of Life.

THE distinction between active and passive euthanasia is thought to be crucial for medical ethics. The idea is that it is permissible, at least in some cases, to withhold treatment and allow a patient to die, but it is never permissible to take any direct action designed to kill the patient. This doctrine seems to be accepted by most doctors, and it is endorsed in a statement adopted by the House of Delegates of the American Medical Association on December 4, 1973:

> The intentional termination of the life of one human being by another — mercy killing — is contrary to that for which the medical profession stands and is contrary to the policy of the American Medical Association.
>
> The cessation of the employment of extraordinary means to prolong the life of the body when there is irrefutable evidence that biological death is imminent is the decision of the patient and/or his immediate family. The advice and judgment of the physician should be freely available to the patient and/or his immediate family.

However, a strong case can be made against this doctrine. In what follows I will set out some of the relevant arguments and urge doctors to reconsider their views on this matter.

To begin with a familiar type of situation, a patient who is dying of incurable cancer of the throat is in terrible pain, which can no longer be satisfactorily alleviated. He is certain to die within a few days, even if present treatment is continued, but he does not want to go on living for those days since the pain is unbearable. So he asks the doctor for an end to it, and his family joins in the request.

Suppose the doctor agrees to withhold

treatment, as the conventional doctrine says he may. The justification for his doing so is that the patient is in terrible agony, and since he is going to die anyway, it would be wrong to prolong his suffering needlessly. But now notice this. If one simply withholds treatment, it may take the patient longer to die, and so he may suffer more than he would if more direct action were taken and a lethal injection given. This fact provides strong reason for thinking that, once the initial decision not to prolong his agony has been made, active euthanasia is actually preferable to passive euthanasia, rather than the reverse. To say otherwise is to endorse the option that leads to more suffering rather than less, and is contrary to the humanitarian impulse that prompts the decision not to prolong his life in the first place.

Part of my point is that the process of being "allowed to die" can be relatively slow and painful, whereas being given a lethal injection is relatively quick and painless. Let me give a different sort of example. In the United States about one in 600 babies is born with Down's syndrome. Most of these babies are otherwise healthy — that is, with only the usual pediatric care, they will proceed to an otherwise normal infancy. Some, however, are born with congenital defects such as intestinal obstructions that require operations if they are to live. Sometimes, the parents and the doctor will decide not to operate, and let the infant die. Anthony Shaw describes what happens then:

> When surgery is denied [the doctor] must try to keep the infant from suffering while natural forces sap the baby's life away. As a surgeon whose natural inclination is to use the scalpel to fight off death, standing by and watching a salvageable baby die is the most emotionally exhausting experience I know.

It is easy at a conference, in a theoretical discussion to decide that such infants should be allowed to die. It is altogether different to stand by in the nursery and watch as dehydration and infection wither a tiny being over hours and days. This is a terrible ordeal for me and the hospital staff — much more so than for the parents who never set foot in the nursery.

I can understand why some people are opposed to all euthanasia, and insist that such infants must be allowed to live. I think I can also understand why other people favor destroying these babies quickly and painlessly. But why should anyone favor letting "dehydration and infection wither a tiny being over hours and days"? The doctrine that says that a baby may be allowed to dehydrate and wither, but may not be given an injection that would end its life without suffering, seems so patently cruel as to require no further refutation. The strong language is not intended to offend, but only to put the point in the clearest possible way.

My second argument is that the conventional doctrine leads to decisions concerning life and death made on irrelevant grounds.

Consider again the case of the infants with Down's syndrome who need operations for congenital defects unrelated to the syndrome to live. Sometimes, there is no operation, and the baby dies, but when there is no such defect, the baby lives on. Now, an operation such as that to remove an intestinal obstruction is not prohibitively difficult. The reason why such operations are not performed in these cases is, clearly, that the child has Down's syndrome and the parents and the doctor judge that because of that fact it is better for the child to die.

But notice that this situation is absurd, no matter what view one takes of the lives and potentials of such babies. If the life of such an infant is worth preserving what does it matter if it needs a simple operation? Or, if one thinks it better that such a baby should not live on, what difference does it make that it happens to have an unobstructed intestinal tract? In either case, the matter of life and death is being decided on irrelevant grounds. It is the Down's syndrome, and not the intestines, that is the issue. The matter should be decided, if at all, on the basis, and not be allowed to depend on that essentially irrelevant question of whether the intestinal tract is blocked.

What makes this situation possible, of course, is the idea that when there is an intestinal blockage, one can "let the baby die," but when there is no such defect there is nothing that can be done, for one must not "kill" it. The fact that this idea leads to such results as deciding life or death on irrelevant grounds is another good reason why the doctrine would be rejected.

One reason why so many people think that there is an important moral difference between active and passive euthanasia is that they think killing someone is morally worse than letting someone die. But is it? Is killing, in itself, worse than letting die? To investigate this issue, two cases may be considered that are exactly alike except that one involves killing whereas the other involves letting someone die. Then, it can be asked whether this difference makes any difference to the moral assessments. It is important that the cases be exactly alike, except for this one difference, since otherwise one cannot be confident that it is this difference and not some other that accounts for any variation in the assessments of the two cases. So, let us consider this pair of cases:

In the first, Smith stands to gain a large inheritance if anything should happen to his six-year-old cousin. One evening while the child is taking his bath, Smith sneaks into the bathroom and drowns the child, and then arranges things so that it will look like an accident.

In the second, Jones also stands to gain if anything should happen to his six-year-old cousin. Like Smith, Jones sneaks in planning to drown the child in his bath. However, just as he enters the bathroom Jones sees the child slip and hit his head, and fall face down in the water. Jones is delighted; he stands by, ready to push the child's head back under if it is necessary, but it is not necessary. With only a little thrashing about, the child drowns all by himself, "accidentally," as Jones watches and does nothing.

Now Smith killed the child, whereas Jones "merely" let the child die. That is the only difference between them. Did either man behave better, from a moral point of view? If the difference between killing and letting die were in itself a morally important matter, one should say that Jones's behavior was less reprehensible then Smith's. But does one really want to say that? I think not. In the first place, both men acted from the same motive, personal gain, and both had exactly the same end in view when they acted. It may be inferred from Smith's conduct that he is a bad man, although that judgment may be withdrawn or modified if certain further facts are learned about him—for example, that he is mentally deranged. But would not the very same thing be inferred about Jones from his conduct? And would not the same further considerations also be relevant to any modification of this judgment? Moreover, suppose Jones pleaded, in his own defense, "After all, I didn't do anything except just stand there and watch the child drown. I didn't kill him; I only let him die." Again, if letting die were in itself less bad than killing, this defense should have at least some weight. But it does not. Such a "defense" can only be regarded as a grotesque perversion of moral reasoning. Morally speaking, it is no defense at all.

Now, it may be pointed out, quite properly, that the cases of euthanasia with which doctors are concerned are not like this at all. They do not involve personal gain or the destruction of normal healthy children. Doctors are concerned only with cases in which the patient's life is of no further use to him, or in which the patient's life has become or will soon become a terrible burden. However, the point is the same in these cases: the bare difference between killing and letting die does not, in itself, make a moral difference. If a doctor lets a patient die, for humane reasons, he is in the same moral position as if he had given the patient a lethal injection for humane reasons. If his decision was wrong — if, for example, the patient's illness was in fact curable — the decision would be equally regrettable no matter which method was used to carry it out. And if the doctor's decision was the right one, the method used is not in itself important.

The AMA policy statement isolates the crucial issue very well; the crucial issue is "the intentional termination of the life of one human being by another." But after identifying this issue, and forbidding "mercy killing," the statement goes on to deny that the cessation of treatment is the intentional termination of a life. This is where the mistake comes in, for what is the cessation of treatment, in these circumstances, if it is not "the intentional termination of the life of one human being by another"? Of course it is exactly that, and if it were not, there would be no point to it.

Many people will find this judgment hard to accept. One reason, I think, is that it is very easy to conflate the question of whether killing is, in itself, worse than letting die, with the very different question of whether most actual cases of killing are more reprehensible than most actual cases of letting die. Most actual cases of killing are clearly terrible (think, for example, of all the murders reported in the newspapers), and one hears of such cases every day. On the other hand, one hardly ever hears of a case of letting die, except for the actions of doctors who are motivated by humanitarian reasons. So one learns to think of killing in a much worse light than of letting die. But this does not mean that there is something about killing that makes it in itself worse than letting die, for it is not the bare difference between killing and letting die that makes the difference in these cases. Rather, the other factors — the murderer's motive of personal gain, for example, contrasted with the doctor's humanitarian motivation — account for different reactions to the different cases.

I have argued that killing is not in itself any worse than letting die; if my contention is right, it follows that active euthanasia is not any worse than passive euthanasia. What arguments can be given on the other side? The most common, I believe, is the following:

> The important difference between active and passive euthanasia is that, in passive euthanasia, the doctor does not do anything to bring about the patient's death. The doctor does nothing, and the patient dies of whatever ills already afflict him. In active euthanasia, however, the doctor does something to bring about the patient's death: he kills him. The doctor who gives the patient with cancer a lethal injection has himself caused his patient's death; whereas if he merely ceases treatment, the cancer is the cause of the death.

A number of points need to be made here. The first is that it is not exactly correct to say that in passive euthanasia the doctor does nothing, for he does do one thing that is very important: he lets the patient die. "Letting someone die" is certainly different, in some respects, from other types of action — mainly in that it is a kind of action that one may perform by way of not performing certain other actions. For example, one may let a patient die by way of not giving medication, just as one may insult someone by way of not shaking his hand. But for any purpose of moral assessment, it is a type of action nonetheless. The decision to let a patient die is subject to moral appraisal in the same way that a decision to kill him would be subject to moral appraisal: it may be assessed as wise or unwise, compassionate or sadistic, right or wrong. If a doctor deliberately let a patient die who was suffering from a routinely curable illness, the doctor would certainly be to blame if he had needlessly killed the patient. Charges against him would be appropriate. If so, it would be no defense at all for him to insist that he didn't "do anything." He would have done something very serious indeed, for he let his patient die.

Fixing the cause of death may be very important from a legal point of view, for it may determine whether criminal charges are brought against the doctor. But I do not think that this notion can be used to show a moral difference between active and passive euthanasia. The reason why it is considered bad to be the cause of someone's death is that death is regarded as a great evil — and so it is. However, if it has been decided that euthanasia — even passive euthanasia — is desirable in a given case, it has also been decided that in this instance death is no greater an evil than the patient's continued existence. And if this is true, the usual reason for not wanting to be the cause of someone's death simply does not apply.

Finally, doctors may think that all of this is only of academic interest — the sort of thing that philosophers may worry about but that has no practical bearing on their own work. After all, doctors must be concerned about the legal consequences of what they do, and active euthanasia is clearly forbidden by the law. But even so, doctors should also be concerned with the fact that the law is forcing upon them a moral doctrine that may be indefensible, and has a considerable effect on their practices. Of course, most doctors are not now in the position of being coerced in this matter, for they do not regard themselves as merely going along with what the law requires. Rather, in statements such as the AMA policy statement that I have quoted they are endorsing this doctrine as a central point of medical ethics. In that statement, active euthanasia is condemned not merely as illegal but as "contrary to that for which the medical profession stands," whereas passive euthanasia is approved. However, the preceding considerations suggest that there is really no moral difference between the two, considered in themselves (there may be important moral differences in some cases in their *consequences*, but, as I pointed out, these differences may make active euthanasia, and not passive euthanasia, the morally preferable option). So, whereas doctors may have to discriminate between active and passive euthanasia to satisfy the law, they should not do any more than that. In particular, they should not give the distinction any added authority and weight by writing it into official statements of medical ethics.

No breathing
No heart
No brain

BONNIE STEINBOCK

The Intentional Termination of Life

BONNIE STEINBOCK *teaches philosophy at the State University of New York at Albany. She is the author of* Killing and Letting Die *(1980).*

ACCORDING to James Rachels and Michael Tooley, a common mistake in medical ethics is the belief that there is a moral difference between active and passive euthanasia. This is a mistake, they argue, because the rationale underlying the distinction between active and passive euthanasia is the idea that there is a significant moral difference between intentionally killing and intentionally letting die. "This idea," Tooley says, "is admittedly very common. But I believe that it can be shown to reflect either confused thinking, or a moral point of view unrelated to the interests of individuals." Whether the belief that there is a significant moral difference (between intentionally killing and intentionally letting die) is mistaken is not my concern here. For it is far from clear that this distinction *is* the basis of the doctrine of the American Medical Association which Rachels attacks. And if the killing/letting die distinction is not the basis of the AMA doctrine, then arguments showing that the distinction has no moral force do not, in themselves, reveal in the doctrine's adherents either "confused thinking" or "a moral point of view unrelated to the interests of individuals". Indeed, as we examine the AMA doctrine, I think it will become clear that it appeals to and makes use of a number of overlapping distinctions, which may have moral significance in particular cases, such as the distinction between intending and foreseeing, or between ordinary and extraordinary care. Let us then turn to the statement, from the House of Delegates of the American Medical Association, which Rachels cites:

> The intentional termination of the life of one human being by another — mercy-killing — is contrary to that for which the medical profession stands and is contrary to the policy of the American Medical Association.
>
> The cessation of the employment of extraordinary means to prolong the life of the body when there is irrefutable evidence that biological death is imminent is the decision of the patient and/or his immediate family. The advice and judgment of the physician should be freely available to the patient and/or his immediate family.

Rachels attacks this statement because he believes that it contains a moral distinction between active and passive euthanasia. . . .

I intend to show that the AMA statement does not imply support of the active/passive euthanasia distinction. In forbidding the intentional termination of life, the statement rejects both active and passive euthanasia. It does allow for ". . . the cessation of the employment of extraordinary means . . ." to prolong life. The mistake Rachels and Tooley make is in identifying the cessation of life-prolonging treatment with passive euthanasia or intentionally letting die. If it were right to equate the two, then the AMA statement would be self-contradictory, for it would begin by condemning, and end by allowing the intentional termination of life. But if the cessation of life-prolonging treatment is not always or necessarily passive euthanasia, then there is no confusion and no contradiction.

Why does Rachels think that the cessation of life-prolonging treatment is the intentional termination of life? He says:

> The AMA policy statement isolates the crucial issue very well; the crucial issue is "the intentional termination of the life of one human being by another". But after identifying this issue, and forbidding "mercy-killing", the statement goes on to deny that the cessation of treatment is the intentional termination of a life. This is where the mistake comes in, for what is the cessation of treatment, in these circumstances, if it is not "the intentional termination of the life of one human being of another"? Of course it is exactly that, and if it were not, there would be no point to it.

However, there *can* be a point (to the cessation of life-prolonging treatment) other than an endeavor to bring about the patient's death, and so the blanket identification of cessation of treatment with the intentional termination of a life is inaccurate. There are at least two situations in which the termination of life-prolonging treatment cannot be identified with the intentional termination of the life of one human being by another.

The first situation concerns the patient's right to refuse treatment. Both Tooley and Rachels give the example of a patient dying of an incurable disease, accompanied by unrelievable pain, who wants to end the treatment which cannot cure him but can only prolong his miserable existence. Why, they ask, may a doctor accede to the patient's request to stop treatment, but not provide a patient in a similar situation with a lethal dose? The answer lies in the patient's right to refuse

treatment. In general, a competent adult has the right to refuse treatment, even where such treatment is necessary to prolong life. Indeed, the right to refuse treatment has been upheld even when the patient's reason for refusing treatment is generally agreed to be inadequate. This right can be overridden (if, for example, the patient has dependent children) but, in general, no one may legally compel you to undergo treatment to which you have not consented. "Historically, surgical intrusion has always been considered a technical battery upon the person and one to be excused or justified by consent of the patient or justified by necessity created by the circumstances of the moment. . . ."

At this point, it might be objected that if one has the right to refuse life-prolonging treatment, then consistency demands that one have the right to decide to end his life and to obtain help in doing so. The idea is that the right to refuse treatment somehow implies a right to voluntary euthanasia, and we need to see why someone might think this. The right to refuse treatment has been considered by legal writers as an example of the right to privacy or, better, the right to bodily self-determination. You have the right to decide what happens to your own body, and the right to refuse treatment in an instance of that more general right. But if you have the right to determine what happens to your body, then should you not have the right to choose to end your life, and even a right to get help in doing so?

However, it is important to see that the right to refuse treatment is not the same as, nor does it entail, a right to voluntary euthanasia, even if both can be derived from the right to bodily self-determination. The right to refuse treatment is not itself a "right to die"; that one may choose to exercise this right even at the risk of death or even *in order to die*, is irrelevant.

The purpose of the right to refuse medical treatment is not to give persons a right to decide whether to live or die, but to protect them from the unwanted interferences of others. Perhaps we ought to interpret the right to bodily self-determination more broadly so as to include a right to die: but this would be a substantial extension of our present understanding of the right to bodily self-determination, and not a consequence of it. Should we recognize a right to voluntary euthanasia, we would have to agree that people have the right not merely to be left alone, but also the right to be killed. I leave to one side that substantive moral issue. My claim is simply that there can be a reason for terminating life-prolonging treatment other than "to bring about the patient's death".

The second case in which termination of treatment cannot be identified with intentional termination of life is where continued treatment has little chance of improving the patient's condition and brings greater discomfort than relief.

The question here is what treatment is appropriate to the particular case. A cancer specialist describes it in this way:

> My general rule is to administer therapy as long as a patient responds well and has the potential for a reasonably good quality of life. But when all feasible therapies have been administered and a patient shows signs of rapid deterioration, the continuation of therapy can cause more discomfort than the cancer. From that time I recommend surgery, radiotherapy, or chemotherapy only as a means of relieving pain. But if a patient's condition should once again stabilize after the withdrawal of active therapy and if it should appear that he could still gain some good time, I would immediately reinstitute active therapy. The decision to cease anticancer treatment is never irrevocable, and often the desire to live will push a patient to try for another remission, or even a few more days of life.

The decision here to cease anticancer treatment cannot be construed as a decision that the patient die, or as the intentional termination of life. It is a decision to provide the most appropriate treatment for that patient at that time. Rachels suggests that the point of the cessation of treatment is the intentional termination of life. But here the point of discontinuing treatment is not to bring about the patient's death but to avoid treatment that will cause more discomfort than the cancer and has little hope of benefiting the patient. Treatment that meets this description is often called "extraordinary". The concept is flexible, and what might be considered "extraordinary" in one situation might be ordinary in another. The use of a respirator to sustain a patient through a severe bout of respiratory disease would be considered ordinary; its use to sustain the life of a severely brain damaged person in an irreversible coma would be considered extraordinary.

Contrasted with extraordinary treatment is ordinary treatment, the care a doctor would normally be expected to provide. Failure to provide ordinary care constitutes neglect, and can even be construed as the intentional infliction of harm, where there is a legal obligation to provide care. The importance of the ordinary/extraordinary care distinction lies partly in its connection to the doctor's intention. The withholding of extraordinary care should be seen as a decision not to inflict painful treatment on a patient without reasonable hope of success. The withholding of ordinary care, by contrast, must be seen as neglect. Thus, one doctor says, "We have to draw a distinction between ordinary and extraordinary means. We never withdraw what's needed to make a baby comfortable, we would never withdraw the care a parent would provide. We never kill a baby. . . . But we may decide certain heroic intervention is not worthwhile."

We should keep in mind the ordinary/extraordinary care distinction when considering an example given by both Tooley and Rachels to show the irrationality of the active/passive distinction with regard to infanticide. The example is this: a child is born with Down's syndrome and also has an intestinal obstruction which requires corrective surgery. If the surgery is not performed, the infant will starve to death, since it cannot take food orally. This may take days or even weeks, as dehydration and infection set in. Commenting on this situation, Rachels says:

> I can understand why some people are opposed to all euthanasia, and insist that such infants must be allowed to live. I think I can also understand why other people favor destroying these babies quickly and painlessly. But why should anyone favor letting "dehydration and infection wither a tiny being over hours and days"? The doctrine that says that a baby may be allowed to dehydrate and wither, but may not be given an injection that would end its life without suffering, seems so patently cruel as to require no further refutation.

Such a doctrine perhaps does not need further refutation; but this is not the AMA doctrine. For the AMA statement criticized by Rachels allows only for the cessation of extraordinary means to prolong life when death is imminent. Neither of these conditions is satisfied in this example. Death is not imminent in this situation, any more than it would be if a normal child had an attack of appendicitis. Neither the corrective surgery to remove the intestinal obstruction, nor the

intravenous feeding required to keep the infant alive until such surgery is performed, can be regarded as extraordinary means, for neither is particularly expensive, nor does either place an overwhelming burden on the patient or others. (The continued existence of the child might be thought to place an overwhelming burden on its parents, but that has nothing to do with the characterization of the means to prolong its life as extraordinary. If it had, then *feeding* a severely defective child who required a great deal of care could be regarded as extraordinary.) The chances of success if the operation is undertaken are quite good, though there is always a risk in operating on infants. Though the Down's syndrome will not be alleviated, the child will proceed to an otherwise normal infancy.

It cannot be argued that the treatment is withheld for the infant's sake, unless one is prepared to argue that all mentally retarded babies are better off dead. This is particularly implausible in the case of Down's syndrome babies who generally do not suffer and are capable of giving and receiving love, of learning and playing, to varying degrees.

In a film on this subject entitled, "Who Should Survive?", a doctor defended a decision not to operate, saying that since the parents did not consent to the operation, the doctors' hands were tied. As we have seen, surgical intrusion requires consent, and in the case of infants, consent would normally come from the parents. But, as their legal guardians, parents are required to provide medical care for their children, and failure to do so can constitute criminal neglect or even homicide. In general, courts have been understandably reluctant to recognize a parental right to terminate life-prolonging treatment. Although prosecution is unlikely, physicians who comply with invalid instructions from the parents and permit the infant's death could be liable for aiding and abetting, failure to report child neglect, or even homicide. So it is not true that, in this situation, doctors are legally bound to do as the parents wish.

To sum up, I think that Rachels is right to regard the decision not to operate in the Down's syndrome example as the intentional termination of life. But there is no reason to believe that either the law or the AMA would regard it otherwise. Certainly the decision to withhold treatment is not justified by the AMA statement. That such infants have been allowed to die cannot be denied; but this, I think, is the result of doctors misunderstanding the law and the AMA position.

Withholding treatment in this case is the intentional termination of life because the infant is deliberately allowed to die; that is the point of not operating. But there are other cases in which that is not the point. If the point is to avoid inflicting painful treatment on a patient with little or no reasonable hope of success, this is not the intentional termination of life. The permissibility of such withholding of treatment, then would have no implications for the permissibility of euthanasia, active or passive. . . .

Someone might say: Even if the withholding of treatment is not the intentional termination of life, does that make a difference, morally speaking? If life-prolonging treatment may be withheld, for the sake of the child, may not an easy death be provided, for the sake of the child, as well? The unoperated child with spina bifida may take months or even years to die. Distressed by the spectacle of children "lying around, waiting to die", one doctor has written, "It is time that society and medicine stopped perpetuating the fiction that withholding treatment is ethically different from terminating a life. It is time that society began to discuss mechanisms by which we can alleviate the pain and suffering for those individuals whom we cannot help."

I do not deny that there may be cases in which death is in the best interests of the patient. In such cases, a quick and painless death may be the best thing. However, I do not think that, once active or vigorous treatment is stopped, a quick death is always preferable to a lingering one. We must be cautious about attributing to defective children *our* distress at seeing them linger. Waiting for them to die may be tough on parents, doctors and nurses — it isn't necessarily tough on the child. The decision not to operate need not mean a decision to neglect, and it may be possible to make the remaining months of the child's life comfortable, pleasant and filled with love. If this alternative is possible, surely it is more decent and humane than killing the child. In such a situation, withholding treatment, foreseeing the child's death, is not ethically equivalent to killing the child, and we cannot move from the permissibility of the former to that of the latter. I am worried that there will be a tendency to do precisely that if active euthanasia is regarded as morally equivalent to the withholding of life-prolonging treatment.

VIRGINIA L. WARREN
Feminist Directions in Medical Ethics

VIRGINIA L. WARREN *teaches philosophy at Chapman College in California. She writes on ethics and feminist philosophy.*

WE might as well admit it. Medical ethics has grown a bit stale. Hot new topics continue to arise — such as whether to withhold artificial food and fluids from patients, or to "harvest" organs for transplant from fetuses and anencephalic newborns. But calling on the same list of Basic Moral Principles does not produce the thrill it once did, though the issues are as significant and heart-breaking as ever. My aim here is to see whether feminism can suggest some new directions for medical ethics, and for philosophical ethics generally.

I shall begin with two disclaimers. First, I am *not* claiming that a feminist medical ethics must develop in any particular ways, only that certain paths are suggested by feminism. Second, I am *not* claiming that these possibilities could *only* have come from a feminist perspective. These directions may, for example, reinforce some ideas from Marxism or from the holistic health movement. I have no desire to plant a flag on the moon and claim, "Feminists got here first." I do hope, however, that the speculations emerging from the cross-fertilization of medical ethics and feminism will bear fruit.

"Sexist Ethics"

Before pondering what a feminist medical ethics might look like, however, muse about what a *Sexist Ethics* might be like.

My aim is neither to condemn philosophic ethics through caricature, nor to search for sexist villains. The sexism — of which I, too, am guilty — is mostly unintended. Rather, I want to spur the imagination. What would academic moral philosophy be like if it were sexist? Let us begin with *substance* — with what questions and solutions are discussed. Later we will consider *process*: how moral debates are conducted. And, should the resulting picture fit real life, let us recognize it.

First, a Sexist Ethics would use a male perspective to frame moral questions and to shape solutions. Magicians know to keep the audience's attention away from the action. But moral philosophers may be magicians who have tricked even themselves by concentrating on the topic at hand, without asking which topic most deserves study or what will result from approaching this topic this way. In a Sexist Ethics, moral questions would often involve competitions for power, status or authority. For example, the autonomy-paternalism debate in medical ethics concerns who has the moral authority to make the final decision: patient or physician. And solutions to moral problems would often downplay or ignore the interests of women (and children). For example, when medical costs are contained by sending hospital patients home "quicker and sicker," family members — usually females — must nurse them at home. This unpaid labor — by mothers, wives, daughters, and daughters-in-law — needs to be given more weight. Even now, women's work is often "invisible."

Second, a Sexist Ethics would never appear sexist. It would be clothed in a cloak of neutrality because favoring some group or position would be unthinkable. The dominant trend in philosophical ethics has been to regard people as best able to decide what is moral when least tied to place and time, when least connected through ties of partiality to family and community. Ideal moral decision-makers are viewed as common denominators — e.g., rational egos (Kant) or calculators of utility — who are more likely to adopt the proper universal perspective when the veneer of particularity is stripped away.

Two distortions may result from this approach to ethics. First, although some moral agents may adopt a common denominator moral perspective without feeling that anything of value is lost, others may feel the loss intensely. The reason for this loss is that persons whose unique experiences have been largely omitted from the dominant culture — e.g., women, Blacks, gay males and lesbians — may find the stripping away of particularity from the moral observer to be anathema to self. By subtracting those features that shed light on their experience and life, such individuals may become, at least in part, invisible to themselves.

A second distortion may arise because adopting a universal perspective toward moral situations tends to (although it does not need to) reveal generic persons and relationships whose psychological subtleties have been washed away. Specifically, the fact that human beings are gendered is likely to be deemed irrelevant to moral deliberation. It is too bad if the stereotypic woman — with all her reproductive organs, emotions, and kinship ties to particular others — does not fit the category of Plain Wrap Human Being. Of course, men are also gendered. Sexist Ethics would not take sufficient account of males *qua* males, any more than it does of females *qua* females. Ironically, distortion may be the likely result of our trying so hard not to distort.

Third, a Sexist Ethics would frame the ethical debate so that women would be kept on the defensive. Women would spend much time for little gain. A Sexist Ethics would seduce women to work within its framework by offering hope for improvement — but only if they did not rock the patriarchal boat too vigorously. "Strive for *equality* with men," it would say, "and all will be well. There is no need for more fundamental change." Such a domesticated ethics would, for example, allow women and men to compete equally for the positions of nurse and physician, without questioning the roles themselves, which were founded on an unequal power relationship between females and males.

Women might be kept on the defensive in another way: topics chosen for moral debate might have the unintended effect of fanning the flames of sexism. In moral philosophy in the past fifteen years, the two most commonly discussed topics concerning women have been abortion and preferential hiring. In both cases, women's interests and rights are pitted against the interests and rights of "innocent" others: fetuses, and young (white) male applicants to law or medical school who are not principally responsible for the worst sexist practices.

The central place of preferential hiring in the "contemporary moral issues" literature is particularly instructive. Women (and minorities) studying preferential hiring are made to feel how many expectations of males (and whites) they are crushing, and how much hostile backlash awaits, if they push too hard to be let into the club. With sexism (and racism) so prevalent, it borders on the scandalous that so much philosophical energy is focused on preferential hiring. For, while this issue clearly merits attention, it directly affects a relatively small percentage of job-holders for brief periods, mainly in decisions about hiring and promotion. I say this even though I know that believing that one has been, or might be, passed over for a desired job may profoundly affect one's self-conception and self-worth; hence, the *indirect* effects of a policy of preference may extend far beyond the period of hiring.

My point is threefold. First, enough moral philosophers have focused so narrowly on preferential hiring and on whether white males are wronged by it that the full burden on women (and minorities) of sexist (and racist) practices tends to get insufficient attention. . . . Second, the preferential hiring debate is inflammatory because a zero-sum, us-against-them attitude is presupposed, and often goes unchallenged. Alternative, non-zero-sum approaches to ending discrimination and to securing women's (and minorities') rightful interests usually go unexplored. Third, even if the preferential hiring debate (framed now in terms of justice and utility) were resolved one way or the other, that would not help people of different genders (and races) to *relate* to each other better on the job: to respect each other, and to overcome suspicion and hostility. . . .

In addition to substantive questions about the rightness of actions, *how* philosophical ethics is done — the process — is important. First, the theories and arguments of Sexist Ethics would be used as weapons in a competitive power struggle. Participants in the ethical debate would have an ulterior purpose. Over and above seeking the truth about what is morally

right, they would want to win the debate, including to look good at someone else's expense. Second, the "star" system would be part of the Sexist Ethics game. In academia, a huge disparity exists between ability and productivity (as judged on a fair merit system), on the one hand, and reputation, on the other. Would-be "stars" aim at advancing their reputations, and at gaining prestige and the power and perquisites which accompany prestige. Thus, over and above any substantive differences between sexist and feminist ethics, we must attend to how the philosophical "ethics game" is played in discussions, at conferences, and in print.

In my view, contemporary philosophical ethics — including medical ethics — has all of the features described under "Sexist Ethics" to *some* degree, even though the intention to be sexist is usually absent. The degree varies dramatically with the topic, the author or speaker, and the occasion. Imagining how philosophical ethics might become increasingly less sexist is the challenge.

Feminist Medical Ethics: What Is Studied

Which questions moral philosophers choose to study — and choose not to study — is itself a moral issue, yet one that is hardly ever raised. In this section I will sketch some changes — suggested by feminism — in the questions addressed in medical ethics.

Feminists could add the perspectives of women of different races, classes, sexual preferences, etc., to questions and solutions already discussed in the literature of medical ethics. For example, more weight would be given in cost-cutting debates to the effects on families — especially on female caretakers — of patients released from hospitals earlier.

In addition, feminists could include women's perspectives — along with the perspectives of males *qua* males, and the interests of children — by *posing new questions*. Carol Gilligan interviewed women who were considering abortion, and listened to how they framed moral questions and to which moral values they appealed. We, too, need to listen. I will discuss four categories of new questions: (1) inequalities, (2) sexist occupational roles, (3) personal issues, and (4) relationship issues that do not involve deciding the winner of power struggles.

(1) *Inequalities*. The treatment of women patients, women physicians, and people in traditionally female occupations such as nursing or social work should be examined. After exposing any unequal treatment of women in health care, solutions could be sought. An example of unequal treatment of female patients is the policy in many *in vitro* fertilization programs of excluding all women who are not married heterosexuals; that is, only women who want to raise a child with a husband need apply. When this policy is criticized, one response is to point out the scarcity of places in IVF programs — with no attempt to defend this particular allocation of scarce resources. The issue is deflected, but not taken seriously; and male privilege is protected, but not justified.

(2) *Sexist occupational roles*. Historically, the roles of physician and nurse were designed for males and females, respectively. Tasks were assigned based on what was appropriate masculine and feminine behavior, with nurses expected to defer to physicians. So far, the basic question in nursing ethics has been what hospital nurses should do when their moral views clash with those of physicians, who have more institutional and legal power.

Moreover, physicians' training is largely theoretical and technological, and they have final decision-making authority for patient treatment. The role of nurse has always included nurturing patients' psyches (and although much knowledge and skill is required to perform nurturing tasks well, that is often overlooked and labeled "intuition"); and nurses' decision-making authority is subordinated to "doctor's orders." This division of labor in health care — based on which gender the role was designed for — remains, even though an increasing number of physicians are now female. (Male nurses remain a rarity.)

A second type of new question would go further, examining sexism in occupational roles. We need to stop segregating nurturing from theory — whether in health care (the work of nurses and social workers from that of physicians) or in academia (undergraduate teaching from research). Giving females and males equal opportunity to enter occupations in which nurturing and theory are pulled apart does not solve the problem. The answer is not to have fifty percent of nurses be caring, responsive males, while fifty percent of physicians are oriented toward technology and research and professionally distant — but are female. Nor is the answer to have RNs imitate the higher paid, higher status, traditionally male occupations; for then the caring tasks would be delegated to others (e.g., to licensed vocational nurses). Nurturing needs to be valued more highly, including monetarily, and integrated with technical and theoretical expertise, particularly in medicine. (Nursing is already attempting such integration.) We need to redefine the roles and relationships of all members of the "health care team," making roles more androgynous.

(3) *Personal issues*. . . . Philosophical ethics routinely ignores the little — and not so little — domestic problems of life,

which I call *"housekeeping issues."* These "personal" issues contrast with the *"crisis issues"* (e.g., abortion or withdrawal of life-support) that are the bread and butter of contemporary moral philosophy. Perhaps an analogue to the feminist slogan, "The personal is political," is needed: "The personal is professional." That is, what is "merely" personal may profoundly affect how one acts on and off the job, and thus should play a significant role in professional ethics.

An example of an important housekeeping issue is how to help people *use* such valuable legislation (in California and some other states) as the Durable Power of Attorney for Health Care. Should one become incompetent, a Durable Power specifies what medical treatment one does and does not want, and invests a designated person (e.g., spouse, friend) with the legal authority to make one's other medical decisions. While bioethicists have discussed moral reasons for and against passing such legislation (a crisis issue), they rarely address problems of implementation (housekeeping issues). Nor do physicians raise the possibility of signing such a document with patients very often. When physicians do think of it, they may fear that even raising the issue with terminal patients will cause despair and hasten death. Often it is thought of too late: when patients are already comatose, or weakened by illness and confused by drugs. Nor do we help families learn how to discuss such grave matters openly and "before need" (the phrase used in cemetery commercials). If most laypeople are unaware that such legislation exists, they cannot raise the issue of signing a Durable Power with physicians. And few physicians are raising it with them. (Nurses sometimes do, but risk being criticized for encroaching on the physician's prerogative.)

These two categories of moral issues — crisis and housekeeping issues — contrast in several ways.

First, with crisis issues, moral decisions are more or less final. A moral problem arises; one decides; one moves on and feels a sense of progress. With housekeeping issues, however, *the problematic situation is ongoing, rather than resolved once and for all*; and decisions need to be made continually. Job stress, for example, can be contained but not eliminated.

Second, the significance of crisis issues immediately catches our attention. We take pride in facing a difficult challenge. By contrast, housekeeping issues *seem trivial*. Even if we handle these problems well, we feel we have not accomplished much, and others are unlikely to laud our efforts. For example, we discuss crisis issues related to AIDS, such as whether AIDS antibody testing should be mandatory in some cases. But few are discussing housekeeping issues, e.g., how sexually active persons can raise the question of AIDS exposure and protection with prospective sexual partners, while trying to respect privacy and avoid manipulation. Even if housekeeping issues were trivial when considered one at a time, their collective impact on individuals and institutions would be anything but trivial.

Third, crisis issues usually involve a narrow range of alternative actions. By contrast, housekeeping issues commonly *require us to reassess large parts of our lives*: our character traits, how we think about ourselves, and how we relate to others. Their impact is thus felt long after a particular crisis is past. . . .

For example, informed consent is standardly interpreted as a crisis issue: "Was an autonomous and informed consent obtained from the patient before this treatment, or did the physician withhold relevant information or pressure the patient?" Compare this to informed consent interpreted as a housekeeping issue: "How should we foster the conditions which make informed consent more likely?" The whole physician-patient relationship is thereby called into question: How much time should physicians spend with patients, and on whose terms — when it is convenient for the doctor or when the patient is well-rested and psychologically prepared? How involved should physicians be with patients' value choices and anguish? Should the relationship between physicians and nurses be changed so that they can work together more effectively to encourage patient autonomy?

Fourth, crisis issues are more readily handled using such standard moral principles as justice, autonomy, beneficence and non-maleficence, and utility. *Applying these principles to housekeeping issues helps only up to a point.* These principles do not deal satisfactorily with psychological subtleties, especially with the intricacies of longer-term relationships. For example, autonomy and beneficence will offer only rudimentary guidance to a health professional deciding whether and how to approach a specific patient about signing a Durable Power of Attorney. Utilitarians, it is true, hold that the Utility Principle always applies. Yet, reducing character traits and relationships to how much happiness and unhappiness they can be expected to produce seems to me to drain them of much of their significance.

Overall, what are we to make of these housekeeping issues, which refer to one's everyday life and to on-going relationships, and which are routinely overlooked? On a given topic, should housekeeping issues replace crisis issues? Not necessarily. I view it as an open question whether, for a given area, both crisis and housekeeping issues need to be discussed, or whether one of these sets of issues is sufficient. What matters is that we neither ignore important questions, nor distort the moral debate by asking questions in the wrong way — for we sometimes turn housekeeping issues into crisis issues just so they will be resolved.

(4) *Relationship issues that do not involve deciding who wins various power struggles.* The main relationship questions in medical ethics now involve competitions for power, status or authority. Who should have the moral authority to make the final decision: the patient or the physician (in the autonomy-paternalism debate), the physician or the nurse (in nursing ethics)? Relationships are incorrectly assumed to be fine when there is no overt struggle for power.

Moral philosophers should consider ways of resolving power conflicts other than declaring a winner. For example, a strategy of "preventive ethics" could be adopted. Instead of asking who should be "King of the Hill" — physician or patient — ask how the conflict might be prevented in the future. Changes might be needed in medical education or in the social organization of hospitals.

On a larger scale, I believe that the feminist goal of eliminating conflicts over power can be permanently attained only by solving this problem: How can people be helped to develop a sense of self and of self-worth (identity) that is not based on putting down or controlling someone else (power over others)? This question is important because simply trying to eliminate one form of discrimination — against women, gays and lesbians, the disabled — and then another will never have an end. We will be playing musical chairs: there will always be an odd person out. To eliminate discrimination across the board, a radical strategy is needed: educating people to value themselves in a way that does not depend on branding anyone else inferior.

In addition to preventing or eliminating power struggles, other questions about relationships might be asked by a feminist medical ethics. Relationship ethics should discuss openness, responsiveness and caring. For example, how personally involved with patients should health care professionals be in different situations? In order to encourage more sensitivity to their patients and co-workers, how should health care professionals — including physicians — be trained, and what should their working conditions be?

Some issues in medical ethics have been much debated but, in those discussions, crucial questions about relationships have been downplayed or ignored. For example, in the philosophical literature, abortion is often interpreted as a power struggle. Whose rights are more important: the fetus's right to life, if it has one, or the mother's right to autonomously guide her life? What is usually left out of the abortion debate is a network of issues surrounding the parent- (especially mother-) child relationship.

I have been amazed by the casualness with which many opponents of abortion offer adoption as an alternative. Nor have moral philosophers considered the following question in any depth: If a pregnant woman has decided not to abort, when is it morally permissible for her to give up the newborn for adoption? Whenever she wants to? Is adoption permissible only if the baby would be better off being raised by someone else — and, then, only if the mother is unwed? (Can you imagine telling your parents or in-laws that you and your partner have decided to give up their grandchild for adoption? Or telling an older child that its sibling-to-be will be given up for adoption?) Is it permissible for a woman to conceive *in order* that the child be adopted — if everyone, including the child and the adoptive parents, benefit? If it is, then surrogate motherhood (money issues aside) would have a more solid moral foundation. My point is that, regarding abortion and adoption (as well as child custody disputes during divorce), we need to get to the heart of matters of the heart: relationships between parents and children, between life partners, between siblings, between grandparents and grandchildren. At present, we have not identified what the important relationship issues are, nor do we know how to weigh these values against such standard ones as rights, autonomy, and beneficence/utility.

One way to move health care relationships away from the issue of power struggles is to downplay the traditional view of the physician as authority, and to emphasize their role as *educators*. In most fields, teaching non-experts has traditionally been viewed as a female task. Not surprisingly, patient education is often delegated to the predominantly female occupations of nursing and social work.

Observe what happens when informed consent is viewed in terms of an educational model, with the physician as teacher, instead of a medical model, in which treating disease is paramount. Using the medical model, many physicians relate to patients based on whether the interaction will promote patient health. Thus, information is given to patients only if it will not harm the patient's medical condition. For example, a physician might ponder, "Will these facts depress the patient, thereby lowering her immune response?" Moreover, using the medical model, when a patient fails to understand the risks and benefits of alternative treatments, the first explanation is probably psychiatric: the patient is in denial, unable to accept disturbing facts. Maybe, maybe not. Of course people sometimes refuse to hear frightening facts. But, as a teacher, I know how hard it is to communicate even when the subject is emotionally bland, as in logic. Teachers need to repeat, to connect with *this* student's experience, and to get feedback from students so that inaccuracies can be corrected. Teaching skills are hard-won — requiring practice, experimentation, and sensitivity to audience. The medical model downplays the difficulties of teaching well, tends to attribute failures of communication to patients, and lets physicians who are poor teachers off the hook.

In sum, there are many ways to add the perspectives of women to the questions asked in medical ethics. Existing questions can be rethought. And new questions can be posed: about inequality, occupational roles, "housekeeping issues," and relationship issues other than power struggles.

Feminist Medical Ethics: How Ethics Is Debated

Over and above which questions are studied, how discussions in moral philosophy are conducted is crucial. I will briefly discuss three feminist themes which suggest directions for how academic medical ethics might be done: (1) diversity, (2) relationships, and (3) basing theory on ordinary experience.

(1) The first theme is *diversity*. Women (and other groups) have had their perspectives and interests minimized or omitted from textbooks and theories. After devising theories that take account of women's experiences, feminist theorists are often ambivalent about establishing these ideas as the paradigm for all humanity. (For ex-

ample, Gilligan is still working out to what degree the "justice perspective" and the "care perspective" in ethics are both needed, and to what degree they compete.) And rightfully so: feminists know that "one size fits all" usually does not. We need fully to explore the degree to which philosophical ethics should accommodate multiplicity. . . .

We need to explore not only new questions, but also alternative moral principles or values. Those we have now (except in virtue ethics) are best suited to handling conflicts over power and authority. I believe that autonomy, in particular, needs to be reconceived. In medical ethics, the principle of autonomy is most frequently used to fend off others' attempts to make one's decisions. But it may prove wanting as a positive conception of human agency at its noblest. Alternative conceptions might include self-expression (as opposed to self-mastery) or effortlessness (that is, not needing to "make laws for oneself"). More radically, we should question whether the aim is to find one, rather small, set of moral principles or values for everyone (all races, genders, cultures, etc.) at all times in their lives. Some feminists have questioned universalizability or have otherwise tried to find room in moral theory for caring for particular others. Universalizability may indeed be compatible with caring for particular persons. Still, we may seek a tolerable, even desirable, amount of diversity in ethics — both in the normative principles themselves and in the solutions they yield when applied to specific situations — that will not lead to chaos.

(2) A second feminist theme is *relationships*. Accordingly, a feminist approach might examine *how* people in academia relate to each other when discussing ethics.

First, the social interaction occurring

during academic debates (written or oral) about ethics should itself be morally evaluated. Did people treat each other with respect? Was good will fostered among the participants? Motives are important. Sometimes, people simply serve as sounding boards for each other as they try to discover what the right response to a morally complex issue is. However, the absence of ulterior motives in ethics discussions is, I suspect, at least as rare in academia as in the rest of life — that is, rare indeed. When participants in moral dialogues have ulterior purposes co-existing with (and sometimes overshadowing) the desire to seek the truth about right and wrong, they are playing a "game": *The Ethics Game*.

In academia, the Ethics Game is sometimes played to one-up the opposition. The goals include proving oneself right (about what is morally right) *and* proving the "opposition" wrong. Moral theories and arguments are used as weapons. Philosophical reputations are at stake: who can poke holes in the opponent's position and defend an alternative position against all objections — for all to see? Winning may take precedence over truth. Most women and some men feel demeaned by playing this game; they feel sullied when they win, foolish when they lose.

When we think of ulterior motives — anything besides simply seeking the truth about right and wrong — we usually think of bad motives, especially of manipulating others in ways that harm their interests. However, playing the Ethics Game need not be bad; both the intentions and the results may be good. For example, during classroom ethics discussions, teachers often desire (an ulterior motive) that students will learn to express their ideas more confidently in public and increase their self-esteem. Here the Ethics Game is played to encourage trust and re-

spect among participants, instead of scoring points at others' expense. Feminists could explore the moral merits of different variations of the Ethics Game. . . .

(3) A third feminist theme is that *theory should be constructed from one's life experience*, that life precedes theory. In the 1960s and 70s, small consciousness-raising groups were pivotal in spreading the feminist spirit. Accepted ideas in politics, morality, science, and everyday living had to be reexamined; and the bedrock of this critique and exploration was to be each woman's experience. It was thought that feminist theory should *not* come down from on high by "experts" and famous authors, even if they were feminists.

The belief that feminist theory should be grounded on the experiences of ordinary women is not a naive philosophical claim. Feminists know that our experience is shaped, even constructed, by our system of (patriarchal and other) beliefs. Rather, it is a political commitment which accomplishes two things. First, one learns to trust one's own judgment, listening to oneself and to other ordinary folk, even if all the books say otherwise. (Not until I taught my first Philosophy of Women course did I realize that *my* conception of God was based on my mother — not on my father, as Freud had said.) Second, the authority of established experts — and one's relationship to them — is challenged. If knowledge is power, "life precedes theory" is social revolution.

This social revolution could be extended to academic ethics. Moral philosophy would not be assumed mainly to trickle down from the experts to students. . . . Despite the fact that we philosophers champion "critical thinking," our students are expected, to a great degree, to accept their teachers' framework, methods, and basic assumptions — which form the criteria for doing good philosophy.

(How many times did I force students, when they offered moral reasons, to "identify the relevant moral principle" from a short list, before I realized how many of their reasons simply did not fit, unless mutilated?) I have no desire to expel the philosophical baby with the bathwater, but maybe, all along, we have been discarding only part of the water after each bath. It may be time for moral philosophers to question not only the power relationship between physicians and patients, but that between themselves and those they would instruct; and that between themselves and the philosophers (from Plato to Rawls) they turn to for guidance.

Coda

I have described some directions which a medical ethics inspired by the insights of feminism might take. Two overall points will, I believe, prove useful in rethinking philosophical ethics, particularly medical ethics. First, *moral philosophers should decide which moral issues merit attention*. Neglect is not always benign. And raising certain questions — especially in the absence of a wider context — may deeply influence people's beliefs and attitudes. Second, *we need to consider how philosophical moral debates should be conducted*, including how ulterior motives influence us. What we select — and neglect — to study as well as the "games" we play may be sending a message as loud as the words we do speak on ethics. These two points are instances of the claim that *doing philosophy — including moral philosophy — is a part of life, and so may be evaluated morally*.

DANIEL CALLAHAN
Aging and the Ends of Medicine

DANIEL CALLAHAN *received his Ph.D. from Harvard and is Director of the Hastings Center for Bioethics. A philosopher by training, he has written extensively on bio-medical ethics and abortion.*

IN October of 1986, Dr. Thomas Starzl of the Presbyterian-University Hospital in Pittsburgh successfully transplanted a liver into a 76-year-old woman. The typical cost of such an operation is over $200,000. He thereby accelerated the extension to the elderly of the most expensive and most demanding form of high-technology medicine. Not long after that, Congress brought organ transplantation under Medicare coverage, thus guaranteeing an even greater extension of this form of life-saving care to older age groups.

This is, on the face of it, the kind of medical progress we have long grown to hail, a triumph of medical technology and a new-found benefit to be provided by an established entitlement program. But now an oddity. At the same time those events were taking place, a parallel government campaign for cost containment was under way, with a special targeting of health care to the aged under the Medicare program.

It was not hard to understand why. In 1980, the 11% of the population over age 65 consumed some 29% of the total American health care expenditures of $219.4 billion. By 1986, the percentage of consumption by the elderly had increased to 31% and total expenditures to $450 billion. Medicare costs are projected to rise from $75 billion in 1986 to $114 billion in the year 2000, and in real not inflated dollars.

There is every incentive for politicians, for those who care for the aged, and for those of us on the way to becoming old to avert our eyes from figures of that kind. We have tried as a society to see if we can simply muddle our way through. That, however, is no longer sufficient. The time has come, I am convinced, for a full and open reconsideration of our future direction. We can not for much longer continue on our present course. Even if we could find a way to radically increase the proportion of our health care dollar going to the elderly, it is not clear that that would be a good social investment. . . .

Three major concerns have . . . surfaced over the past few years. They are symptoms that a new era has arrived. The first is that an increasingly large share of health care is going to the elderly in comparison with benefits for children. The federal government, for instance, spends six times as much on health care for those over 65 as for those under 18. . . .

The second concern is that the elderly dying consume a disproportionate share of health care costs. . . .

The third concern is summed up in an observation by Jerome L. Avorn, M.D., of the Harvard Medical School:

> With the exception of the birth-control pill, each of the medical-technology interventions developed since the 1950s has its most widespread impact on people who are past their fifties — the further past their fifties, the greater the impact.

Many of these interventions were not intended for the elderly. Kidney dialysis, for example, was originally developed for those between the age of 15 and 45. Now some 30% of its recipients are over 65.

These three concerns have not gone unchallenged. They have, on the contrary, been strongly resisted, as has the more general assertion that some form of rationing of health care for the elderly might become necessary. To the charge that the elderly receive a disproportionate share of resources, the response has been that what helps the elderly helps every other age group. It both relieves the young of the burden of care for elderly parents they would otherwise have to bear and, since they too will eventually become old, promises them similar care when they come to need it. There is no guarantee, moreover, that any cutback in health care for the elderly would result in a transfer of the savings directly to the young. Our system is not that rational or that organized. And why, others ask, should we contemplate restricting care for the elderly when we wastefully spend hundreds of millions of dollars on an inflated defense budget?

The charge that the elderly dying receive a large share of funds hardly proves that it is an unjust or unreasonable amount. They are, after all, the most in need. As some important studies have shown, moreover, it is exceedingly difficult to know that someone is dying; the most expensive patients, it turns out, are those who are expected to live but who actually die. That most new technologies benefit the old more than the young is perfectly sensible: most of the killer diseases of the young have now been conquered.

These are reasonable responses. It would no doubt be possible to ignore the symptoms that the raising of such concerns represents, and to put off for at least a few more years any full confrontation with the overpowering tide of elderly now on the way. There is little incentive for politicians to think about, much less talk about, limits of any kind on health care for the aged; it is a politically hazardous topic. Perhaps also, as Dean Guido Calabresi of the Yale Law School and his colleague Philip Bobbitt observed in their thoughtful 1978 book *Tragic Choices*, when we are forced to make painful allocation choices, "Evasion, disguise, temporizing . . . [and] averting our eyes enables us to save some lives even when we will not save all."

Yet however slight the incentives to take on this highly troubling issue, I believe it is inevitable that we must. Already rationing of health care under Medicare is a fact of life, though rarely labeled as such. The requirement that Medicare recipients pay the first $500 of the costs of hospital care, that there is a cutoff of reimbursement of care beyond 60 days, and a failure to cover long-term care, are nothing other than allocation and cost-saving devices. As sensitive as it is to the votes of the elderly, the Reagan administration only grudgingly agreed to support catastrophic health care costs of the elderly (a benefit that will not, in any event, help many of the aged). It is bound to be far more resistant to long-term care coverage, as will any administration.

But there are other reasons than economics to think about health care for the elderly. The coming economic crisis provides a much-needed opportunity to ask some deeper questions. Just what is it that we want medicine to do for us as we age? Earlier cultures believed that aging should be accepted, and that it should be in part a time of preparation for death. Our culture seems increasingly to reject that view, preferring instead, it often seems, to think of aging as hardly more than another disease, to be fought and rejected. Which view is correct? To ask that question is only to note that disturbing puzzles about the ends of medicine and the ends of aging lie behind the more immediate financing worries. Without some kind of answer to them, there is no hope of finding a reasonable, and possibly even a humane, solution to the growing problem of health care for the elderly.

Let me put my own view directly. The future goal of medicine in the care of the aged should be that of improving the quality of their life, not in seeking ways to extend that life. In its longstanding ambition to forestall death, medicine has in the care of the aged reached its last frontier. That is hardly because death is absent elsewhere — children and young adults obviously still die of maladies that are open to potential cure — but because the largest number of deaths (some 70%) now occur among those over the age of 65, with the highest proportion in those over 85. If death is ever to be humbled, that is where the essentially endless work remains to be done. But however tempting that challenge, medicine should now restrain its ambition at that frontier. To do otherwise will, I believe, be to court harm to the needs of other age groups and to the old themselves.

Yet to ask medicine to restrain itself in the face of aging and death is to ask more than it, or the public that sustains it, is likely to find agreeable. Only a fresh understanding of the ends and meaning of aging, encompassing two conditions, are likely to make that a plausible stance. The first is that we — both young and old — need to understand that it is possible to live out a meaningful old-age that is limited in time, one that does not require a compulsive effort to turn to medicine for more life to make it bearable. The second condition is that, as a culture, we need a more supportive context for aging and death, one that cherishes and respects the elderly while at the same time recognizing that their primary orientation should be to the young and the generations to come, not to their own age group. It will be no less necessary to recognize that in the passing of the generations lies the constant reinvigoration of biological life.

Neither of these conditions will be easy to realize. Our culture has, for one thing, worked hard to redefine old age as a time of liberation, not decline. The terms "modern maturity" or "prime time" have, after all, come to connote a time of travel, new ventures in education and self-discovery, the ever-accessible tennis court or golf course, and delightfully periodic but gratefully brief visits from well-behaved grandchildren.

This is, to be sure, an idealized picture. Its attraction lies not in its literal truth but as a widely-accepted utopian reference point. It projects the vision of an old age to which more and more believe they can aspire and which its proponents think an affluent country can afford if it so chooses. That it requires a medicine that is singleminded in its aggressiveness against the infirmities of old age is of a piece with its hopes. But as we have come to discover, the costs of that kind of war are prohibitive. No matter how much is spent the ultimate problem will still remain: people age and die. Worse still, by pretending that old age can be turned into a kind of endless middle age, we rob it of meaning and significance for the elderly themselves. It is a way of saying that old age can be acceptable only to the extent that it can mimic the vitality of the younger years.

There is a plausible alternative: that of a fresh vision of what it means to live a decently long and adequate life, what might be called a natural life span. Earlier generations accepted the idea that there was a natural life span — the biblical norm of three score years and ten captures that notion (even though, in fact, that was a much longer life span than was then typically the case). It is an idea well worth reconsidering, and would provide us with a meaningful and realizable goal. Modern medicine and biology have done much, however, to wean us away from that kind of thinking. They have insinuated the belief that the average life span is not a natural fact at all, but instead one that is strictly dependent upon the state of medical knowledge and skill. And there is much to that belief as a statistical fact: the average life expectancy continues to increase, with no end in sight.

But that is not what I think we ought to mean by a natural life span. We need a notion of a full life that is based on some deeper understanding of human need and sensible possibility, not the latest state of medical technology or medical possibility. We should instead think of a natural life span as the achievement of a life long enough to accomplish for the most part those opportunities that life typically affords people and which we ordinarily take to be the prime benefits of enjoying a life at all — that of loving and living, of raising a family, of finding and carrying out work that is satisfying, of reading and thinking, and of cherishing our friends and families.

If we envisioned a natural life span that way, then we could begin to intensify the devising of ways to get people to that stage of life, and to work to make certain they do so in good health and social dignity. People will differ on what they might count as a natural life span; determining its appropriate range for social policy purposes would need extended thought and debate. My own view is that it can now be achieved by the late 70s or early 80s.

That many of the elderly discover new interests and new facets of themselves late in life — my mother took up painting in her seventies and was selling her paintings up until her death at 86 — does not mean that we should necessarily encourage a kind of medicine that would make that the norm. Nor does it mean that we should base social and welfare policy on possibilities of that kind. A more reasonable approach is to ask how medicine can help most people live out a decently long life, and how that life can be enhanced along the way.

A longer life does not guarantee a better life — there is no inherent connection between the two. No matter how long medicine enabled people to live, death at any time — at age 90, or 100, or 110 — would frustrate some possibility, some as-yet-unrealized goal. There is sadness in that realization, but not tragedy. An easily preventable death of a young child is an outrage. The death from an incurable disease of someone in the prime of young adulthood is a tragedy. But death at an old age, after a long and full life, is simply sad, a part of life itself.

As it confronts aging, medicine should have as its specific goal that of averting premature death, understood as death prior to a natural life span, and the relief of suffering thereafter. It should pursue those goals in order that the elderly can finish out their years with as little needless pain as possible, and with as much vigor as can be generated in contributing to the welfare of younger age groups and to the community of which they are a part. Above all, the elderly need to have a sense of the meaning and significance of their stage in life, one that is not dependent for its human value on economic productivity or physical vigor.

What would a medicine oriented toward the relief of suffering rather than the deliberate extension of life be like? We do not yet have a clear and ready answer to that question, so long-standing, central, and persistent has been the struggle against death as part of the self-conception of medicine. But the Hospice movement is providing us with much helpful evidence. It knows how to distinguish between the relief of suffering and the extension of life. A greater control by the elderly over their dying — and particularly a more readily respected and enforceable right to deny aggressive life-extending treatment — is a long-sought, minimally necessary goal.

What does this have to do with the rising cost of health care for the elderly? Everything. The indefinite extension of life combined with a never-satisfied improvement in the health of the elderly is a recipe for monomania and limitless spending. It fails to put health in its proper place as only one among many human goods. It fails to accept aging and death as part of the human condition. It fails to present to younger generations a model of wise stewardship.

How might we devise a plan to limit health care for the aged under public entitlement programs that is fair, humane, and sensitive to their special requirements and dignity? Let me suggest three principles to undergird a quest for limits. First, government has a duty, based on our collective social obligations to each other, to help people live out a natural life span, but not actively to help medically extend life beyond that point. Second, government is obliged to develop under its research subsidies, and pay for, under its entitlement programs, only that kind and degree of life-extending technology necessary for medicine to achieve and serve the end of a natural life span. The question is not whether a technology is available that can save the life of someone who has lived out a natural life span, but whether there is an obligation for society to provide them with that technology. I think not. Third, beyond the point of natural life span, government should provide only the means necessary for the relief of suffering, not life-extending technology. By proposing that we use age as a specific criterion for the limitation of life-extending health care, I am challenging one of the most revered norms of contemporary geriatrics: that medical need and not age should be the standard of care. Yet the use of age as a principle for the allocation of resources can be perfectly valid, both a necessary and legitimate basis for providing health care to the elderly. There is not likely to be any better or less arbitrary criterion for the limiting of resources in the face of the open-ended possibilities of medical advancement in therapy for the aged.

Medical "need," in particular, can no longer work as an allocation principle. It is too elastic a concept, too much function of the state of medical art. A person of 100 dying from congestive heart failure "needs" a heart transplant no less than someone who is 30. Are we to treat both needs as equal? That is not economically feasible or, I would argue, a sensible way to allocate scarce resources. But it would be required by a strict need-based standard.

Age is also a legitimate basis for allo-

cation because it is a meaningful and universal category. It can be understood at the level of common sense. It is concrete enough to be employed for policy purposes. It can also, most importantly, be of value to the aged themselves if combined with an ideal of old age that focuses on its quality rather than its indefinite extension. . . .

The elderly will not be served by a belief that only a lack of resources, or better financing mechanisms, or political power, stand between them and the limitations of their bodies. The good of younger age groups will not be served by inspiring in them a desire to live to an old age that will simply extend the vitality of youth indefinitely, as if old age is nothing but a sign that medicine has failed in its mission. The future of our society will not be served by allowing expenditures on health care for the elderly endlessly and uncontrollably to escalate, fueled by a false altruism that thinks anything less is to deny the elderly their dignity. Nor will it be served by that pervasive kind of self-serving that urges the young to support such a crusade because they will eventually benefit from it also.

We require instead an understanding of the process of aging and death that looks to our obligation to the young and to the future, that recognizes the necessity of limits and the acceptance of decline and death, and that values the old for their age and not for their continuing youthful vitality. In the name of accepting the elderly and repudiating discrimination against them, we have mainly succeeded in pretending that, with enough will and money, the unpleasant part of old age can be abolished. In the name of medical progress we have carried out a relentless war against death and decline, failing to ask in any probing way if that will give us a better society for all age groups.

The proper question is not whether we are succeeding in giving a longer life to the aged. It is whether we are making of old age a decent and honorable time of life. Neither a longer lifetime nor more life-extending technology are the way to that goal. The elderly themselves ask for greater financial security, for as much self-determination and independence as possible, for a decent quality of life and not just more life, and for a respected place in society.

The best way to achieve those goals is not simply to say more money and better programs are needed, however much they have their important place. We would do better to begin with a sense of limits, of the meaning of the human life cycle, and of the necessary coming and going of the generations. From that kind of a starting point, we could devise a new understanding of old age.

COPYRIGHTS AND ACKNOWLEDGMENTS

Chapter 5

Chapter 6

Chapter 7

Chapter 8

Chapter 9

Chapter 10

Chapter 11

Chapter 12

Chapter 13